D0202477

ILLINOIS PRAIRIE DPL
A65500 928833

THE
ABC-CLIO
COMPANION TO

The Native American Rights Movement

A Native American woman paints "Indian America Land" on a building on Alcatraz Island in 1969. College students occupied the abandoned federal prison site in October of that year, an event that marked a new and continuing effort for Native Americans to claim their rights and to celebrate their cultural identity.

THE
ABC-CLIO
COMPANION TO

The Native American Rights Movement

Mark Grossman

ABC-CLIO

Library of Congress Cataloging-in-Publication Data

Grossman, Mark.
The ABC-CLIO companion to the Native American Rights movement / Mark Grossman.
p. cm. — (ABC-CLIO companions to key issues in American history and life)
Includes bibliographical reference and index.
1. Indians of North America—Legal status, laws, etc.—United States—Cases—Digests. 2. Indians of North America—Civil rights—United States—Cases—Digests. 3. Indians of North America—United States—Biography. 4. Indians of North America—Legal status, laws, etc.—United States—Dictionaries.
I. Title. II. Series.
KF8203.36.G76 1996 342.72'0872—dc21 96-36782

ISBN 0-87436-822-7 (alk. paper)

02 01 00 99 98 97 96 95 10 9 8 7 6 5 4 3 2 1

ABC-CLIO, Inc.
130 Cremona Drive, P.O. Box 1911
Santa Barbara, California 93116-1911

This book is printed on acid-free paper ∞.
Manufactured in the United States of America

This book is dedicated to my parents, Larry and Lois, who have stood by me during the greatest of times and the worst of them, and whose confidence in me has never diminished; and to the memory of my cousin, Irving Earl "Dave" Davidson (1920-1989), who served this nation with honor and courage, here and overseas, and is beloved by those who knew him.

ABC-CLIO Companions to Key Issues in American History and Life

The ABC-CLIO Companion to the American Labor Movement
Paul F. Taylor

The ABC-CLIO Companion to American Reconstruction, 1862–1877
William L. Richter

The ABC-CLIO Companion to the American Peace Movement
Christine A. Lunardini

The ABC-CLIO Companion to the Civil Rights Movement
Mark Grossman

The ABC-CLIO Companion to the Environmental Movement
Mark Grossman

The ABC-CLIO Companion to the Media in America
Daniel Webster Hollis III

The ABC-CLIO Companion to the Native American Rights Movement
Mark Grossman

The ABC-CLIO Companion to Transportation in America
William L. Richter

The ABC-CLIO Companion to Women in the Workplace
Dorothy Schneider and Carl J. Schneider

The ABC-CLIO Companion to Women's Progress in America
Elizabeth Frost-Knappman

Contents

Preface

You may bury my body in Sussex grass,
You may bury my tongue at Campmedy,
I shall not be there.
I shall rise and pass,
Bury My Heart at Wounded Knee.

These words, from Stephen Vincent Benet's haunting poem, "American Names," may reflect more poignantly the perspective of American Indians today than ever before. "Like the miner's canary, the Indian marks the shifts from fresh air to poison gas in our political atmosphere; and our treatment of Indians, even more than our treatment of other minorities, reflects the rise and fall in our democratic faith," Indian activist Felix S. Cohen wrote in 1953. Chief Justice John Marshall, writing in the landmark Supreme Court case Cherokee Nation v. Georgia, explained, "The condition of the Indians in relation to the United States is perhaps unlike that of any other two people in existence—the relation of the Indians to the United States is marked by peculiar and cardinal distinctions which exist no where else."

In 1492, there were probably several million native people in what was to become the United States; by 1890, that number had declined to 250,000, the result of disease, social and economic dislocation, and a relationship with Euroamerican invaders that looks, from a modern perspective, remarkably like genocide. Today's Indians are only just beginning to redefine themselves not as marginalized survivors of a holocaust but as heirs to an extraordinary cultural tradition and full and deserving participants in American society.

The social movement for American Indian rights has depended both on Indian activists and on whites—reformers, jurists, legislators, and others. The cross-cultural nature of the movement is reflected in this book, which covers not just Indians and Indian case law, but whites who shaped Indian policy, fought for—and often against—Indian rights, dedicated their lives as missionaries, or recorded Indian languages and culture. This book also stresses the legal foundation of Indian rights, especially as it has been structured by Congress and the courts. Our society is rarely anarchic; the destruction of Indian cultures through American history has nearly always been given the substance and authority of colonial and later state and national government. The editors of *Felix S. Cohen's Handbook of Federal Indian Law* wrote in 1982, "Law dominates Indian life in a way not duplicated in other segments of American society. The federal Congress, which early in the Nation's history was found to possess extensive power over Indians, has enacted over four thousand treaties and statutes dealing with Native Americans. Regulations and guidelines implementing these laws are even more numerous. The tribes' own laws, and some state statutes dealing with Indians, add to the complexity. There are thousands of reported judicial decisions in Indian law. Litigation has dealt extensively with Indian rights to valuable resources such as land, minerals, wildlife, and water. Self-government in Indian country, a right that has always been central to the Indian people, has continuously been challenged in court by state officials, private interests, and others who argue that separate Indian governments should not persevere."

I would like to thank the following individuals and institutions, without whose assistance this work could not have been completed: the staff of the library of the U.S. Interior Department in Washington, D.C., for the use of their collection on American Indians; the staff of the James R. Dickinson Library at the University of Nevada, Las Vegas; the staff of the Clark County (Nevada) Law Library, who tolerated my insufferable scurrying about for obscure law cases; the staff of the Manuscript Division, Newspaper Reading Room, Law Library, and Main Reading Room of the Library of Congress, for their work in finding books, microfilms, and manuscript collections; the staff of the National Archives; the staff of the Washington, D.C., office of Senator Ben Nighthorse Campbell for their help in getting me an appointment on short notice to interview the senator, and to Senator Campbell for giving me a little of his time to discuss his life and his views; the staff of the Maricopa County Library, Phoenix, Arizona; the staff of the Civic Center and Mustang Libraries, Scottsdale, Arizona; the staff of the Manuscript Reading Room of the New York Public Library; Dina M. Young, Assistant Archivist at the Missouri Historical Society, St. Louis, for her help in accessing the Bogy Family papers; Robert W. Lyle, Curator of the Peabody Room at the District of Columbia Library, Georgetown Branch, in Washington, D.C., for his help in accessing the Charles E. Mix File; Tacie Campbell, Curator of the Mississippi River Museum at the Dubuque County Historical Society, Dubuque, Iowa, for her assistance in locating the Dennis Nelson Cooley interview in their collections; Harold L. Miller of the State Historical Society of Wisconsin at Madison; the staff of the Salem Public Library, Salem, Massachusetts; the staff—especially the interlibrary loan department—of the Phoenix Public Library, Phoenix, Arizona; Katherine G. Wilkins, staff librarian at the Amistad Research Center at Tulane University, New Orleans, Louisiana, for her help in getting a copy of the work on the life of Edward Parmelee Smith and accessing Smith's papers at that institution; Mary Rea Eubanks, head of Adult and Children Services, Benton (Illinois) Public Library, for her wonderful help in finding information on Daniel M. Browning; the staff of the Hayden, Noble, and Law libraries, Arizona State University, Tempe, Arizona; Dennis Bigler of the Harry S Truman Library in Independence, Missouri, for his aid in accessing the papers of Dr. John Ralph Nichols and Philleo Nash, as well as pertinent office files of President Truman; Anna Estep of the Elizabethton-Carter County Public Library, Elizabethton, Tennessee; the staff of the Broward County Main Library, Ft. Lauderdale, Florida, for tolerating me and my persistent scavenging through their collections; the staff of the Kansas State Historical Society, Topeka; Karen Grady, Acting State Registrar, and the hardworking people in her office at the Bureau of Vital Records and Health Statistics, Department of Health and Human Services, Concord, New Hampshire; Janet Fisher and the rest of the staff of the state library at the Arizona State Capitol, Phoenix, Arizona; Frances Desmond, Assistant Division Director of Research, and all the staff at the Arizona State Law Library, Phoenix; the Interlibrary Loan departments of the William D. McIntyre Library at the University of Wisconsin, Eau Claire, and the Carol Grotnes Belk Library at Appalachian State University in Boone, North Carolina; the wonderful folks in the Public Information Office of the Supreme Court of the United States in Washington, D.C.; and, finally, my cousin, Aubrey Grossman, who instilled in me a better sense of equal rights for the American Indian people.

Mark Grossman
27 April 1996

THE
ABC-CLIO
COMPANION TO

The Native American Rights Movement

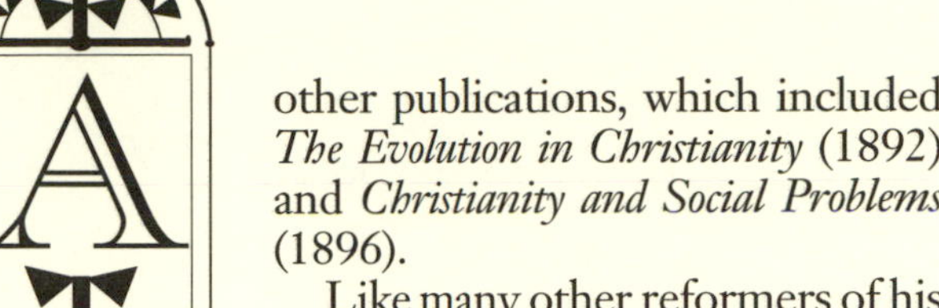

Abbott, Lyman (1835–1922)
The Reverend Lyman Abbott was an American Congregationalist minister who worked to reform Indian laws and to change attitudes of whites toward Indians. He was born in Roxbury, Massachusetts, on 18 December 1835, the son of Jacob Abbott, a minister and teacher (while at the Portland Academy in Hallowell, Maine, Jacob Abbott taught Henry Wadsworth Longfellow), and Harriet (née Vaughan) Abbott. Lyman was descended from one George Abbot, who migrated from Yorkshire about 1640 and settled in Massachusetts. It was Lyman's father Jacob, the third in his line to have that first name, who added the extra *t* to his surname. Jacob, himself a writer as his son would become, authored many religious and educational texts for young people, including *The Young Christian, or a Familiar Illustration of the Principles of Christian Duty* (1832) and *The Teacher, or Moral Influences Employed in the Instruction and Government of the Young* (1833). For Lyman Abbott, graduation from the University of New York with a degree in law and subsequent private law practice with two of his brothers did not bring him the inner peace he desired. After studying theology under his uncle, John S. C. Abbot, he entered the ministry in 1860. He held several pastorates, particularly in Terre Haute, Indiana, served as the editor of such popular magazines as the *Illustrated Christian Weekly*, and authored the "Literary Record" column in *Harper's Magazine*. Lyman's literary efforts helped to popularize his liberal theology, which he also spelled out in his sermons and speeches. In 1876, he joined the Reverend Henry Ward Beecher (a fellow reformer and a member of philanthropist Peter Cooper's U.S. Indian Commission) in editing the *Christian Union* (called the *Outlook* after 1893); he succeeded Beecher in 1888 as pastor of the Plymouth Congregational Church in Brooklyn, New York, and went on to write the *Life of Henry Ward Beecher*. Abbott's convictions and ideas on church doctrine and the evolution of society were asserted with great intensity in his many other publications, which included *The Evolution in Christianity* (1892) and *Christianity and Social Problems* (1896).

Like many other reformers of his day, Abbott became interested in the plight of minorities, particularly the American Indian. Abbott's biographer, Ira V. Brown, explains, "The Indian question, of perennial concern to Abbott, received much attention in the *Christian Union* and the *Outlook*. Although the editor never visited a reservation and never met more than a dozen Indians during his entire life, he played an important part in the movement which led to the Dawes Severalty Act of 1887. His journal, indeed, was one of the first to advocate the abandonment of the tribal system. As early as 1879, when the first severalty proposals were introduced in Congress, it declared that the red men should be assimilated and given citizenship. To reserve land for 'barbarism' was patently wrong." On 22 January 1879, Lyman Abbott wrote in the *Union*, "Sooner or later the entire territory of the nation will be given to civilization, and the sooner the better." At the third meeting of the Lake Mohonk conference in 1885, Abbott addressed the attendees: "I declare my conviction then that the reservation system is hopelessly wrong; that it cannot be amended or modified; that it can only be uprooted, root, trunk, branch and leaf, and a new system put in its place. We evangelical ministers believe in immediate repentance. I hold to immediate repentance as a national duty. Cease to do evil, cease instantly, abruptly, immediately. I hold that the reservation barriers should be cast down and the land given to the Indians in severalty; that every Indian should be protected in his right to his home, and in his right to free intercourse and free trade, whether the rest of the tribe wish him so protected or not; that these are his individual, personal rights, which no tribe has the right to take from him, and no nation the right to sanction the robbery of." Abbott died on 22 October 1922.

See also Lake Mohonk Conferences of the Friends of the Indian.

References Bridgman, Howard Allen, "Abbott, Lyman." In Dumas Malone et al., eds., *Dictionary of American Biography*, vol. 1 (1988); Brown, Ira V., *Lyman Abbott, Christian Evolutionist: A Study in Religious Liberalism* (1970); *National Cyclopedia of American Biography*, vol. 1 (1977); *Proceedings of the Third Annual Meeting of the Lake Mohonk Conference* (1885).

Acculturation

Defined as "the processes of change in artifacts, customs, and beliefs that result from the contact of societies with different traditions," acculturation was the policy of the United States to have Native Americans conform with the ways of American society. Historian Paul Stuart writes that after the Civil War, "Acculturation, or the 'civilization' of the Indians, while a stated goal, did not receive organizational expression in terms of the allocation of funds or personnel to the task. By the end of the century, however, Indian civilization was both a stated goal and one which received organizational expression. Land allotment, education, and citizenship were the mechanisms for integrating Indians into American life. By 1900, the Indian Office had acquired a mission around which the organization had unified and become coherent." Acculturation as a firm objective of the government was ended when the Indian Reorganization Act of 1934 allowed Indians once again to practice the tenets of their tribal ways.

Reference Stuart, Paul, *The Indian Office: Growth and Development of an American Institution, 1865–1900* (1979).

Administration for Native Americans

This division of the Department of the Health and Human Services "promote[s] social and economic self-sufficiency for American Indians, Alaska Natives, Native Hawaiians, and Native American Pacific Islanders (American Samoa Natives, indigenous peoples of Guam, and Natives of the Commonwealth of the Northern Marianas Islands and the Republic of Palau). The agency's activities include the provision of financial assistance grants, technical assistance and training, research, demonstrations, and pilot projects."

Reference Utter, Jack, *American Indians: Answers to Today's Questions* (1993).

Akin v. United States

See Colorado River Water Conservation District v. United States.

Alaska Native Claims Settlement Act (P.L. 92–203)

In this federal action of 18 December 1971 (codified at 85 Stat. 688 and 43 U.S.C. 1601 et seq.), Congress found that "there is an immediate need for a fair and just settlement of all claims by Natives and Native groups of Alaska, based on aboriginal land claims; the settlement should be accomplished rapidly, with certainty, in conformity with the real economic and social needs of Natives, without litigation, with maximum participation by Natives in decisions affecting their rights and property, without establishing any permanent racially defined institutions, rights, privileges, or obligations, without creating a reservation system or lengthy wardship or trusteeship, and without adding to the categories of property and institutions enjoying special tax privileges or to the legislation establishing special relationships between the United States and the State of Alaska." The act extinguished further Alaska Native title to lands in Alaska, ordered an enrollment of all Alaska Natives to be conducted within the two years after the passage of the act, established an "Alaska Native Fund" of some $462,500,000 to be appropriated to the Alaska Natives over a period of 11 fiscal years, and separated the state of Alaska into 12 regional "corporations" of Alaska Natives who share a "common heritage." In 1988, Congress, frustrated by the lack of progress in implementing these reforms, passed the Alaska Native Claims Settlement Act Amendments of 1987.

See also Alaska Native Claims Settlement Act Amendments of 1987.

Reference *United States Code Congressional and Administrative News*, 92d Congress, 1st Session, vol. 1 (1971).

Traditionally dressed Sioux Chief Yellow Robe, right, greets his son Chauncey, a recent graduate of the Indian School in Carlisle, Pennsylvania, upon his return to Rosebud, South Dakota, in 1896. Chauncey's clothing and the education he received reflect the federal government's aggressive policy of acculturation, a policy that survived until 1934.

Alaska Native Claims Settlement Act Amendments of 1987 (P.L. 100–241)

Codified at 101 Stat. 1788, this federal action of 3 February 1988 was enacted in response to a congressional finding that the Alaska Native Claims Settlement Act of 1971 was not working. In this legislation, Congress found that "(1) the Alaska Native Claims Settlement Act was enacted in 1971 to achieve a fair and just settlement of all aboriginal land and hunting and fishing claims by Natives and Native groups of Alaska with maximum participation by Natives in decisions affecting their rights and property; (2) the settlement enables Natives to participate in the subsequent expansion of Alaska's economy, encouraged efforts to address serious health and welfare problems in Native villages, and sparked a resurgence of interest in the cultural heritage of the Native people of Alaska; (3) despite these achievements and Congress' desire that the settlement be accomplished rapidly without litigation and in conformity with the real economic and social needs of Natives, the complexity of the land conveyance process and frequent and costly litigation have delayed implementation of the settlement and diminished its value." The amendments allowed shareholders of stock in each Native Corporation to decide "when restrictions on alienation of stock issued as part of the settlement should be terminated, and whether Natives born after December 18, 1971, should participate in the settlement."

Reference *United States Code Congressional and Administrative News*, 100th Congress, 1st Session, vol. 2 (1987).

Alberty v. United States **(162 U.S. 499 [1896])**

Could a freedman, a former slave, be considered a Cherokee Indian when the Cherokees promised to free their slaves and provide them with "all the rights of native Cherokees"? This was the issue in this Supreme Court case. Alberty, a black man (Alberty was his owner's name; he also went by the name of Burns, his natural father), was formerly a slave of the Cherokee Indians of Arkansas. Both sides in this case agreed that Alberty was the son of a Choctaw Indian, Burns, and a black woman who was Burns's slave. About 1880 (the indictment reads 15 May 1879, but Justice Henry Brown of the Supreme Court found evidence to his satisfaction that that date was inaccurate), Alberty murdered one Phil Duncan, a Cherokee Indian, on the Cherokee Reservation in Indian Territory. Indicted, convicted, and sentenced to death, Alberty appealed to the Supreme Court on the grounds that because he was an Indian, the U.S. courts did not have jurisdiction over his case. By the ninth article of the Treaty of 1866 (14 Stat. 799, at 801), the Cherokees had abolished slavery and agreed "that all freedmen who have been liberated by voluntary act of their former owners or by law, as well as free colored persons who were in the country at the commencement of the Rebellion and are now residents therein or who may return within six months, shall have all the rights of native Cherokees." In his opinion, holding for a unanimous court on 20 April 1896, Justice Brown explained, "While this article of the treaty gave him the rights of a native Cherokee, it did not, standing alone, make him an Indian...or absolve him from responsibility to the criminal laws of the United States." Justice Brown also held that Duncan, who was also the son of a Choctaw Indian and his slave, was also not an Indian, and Alberty's appeal was therefore moot. He added, "For the purposes of jurisdiction, then, Alberty must be treated as a member of the Cherokee Nation, but not as an Indian; and Duncan as a colored citizen of the United States." Although finding against him as to his citizenship, the court struck down Alberty's conviction because of errors in his prosecution and remanded the case back for a new trial.

Alcatraz, Occupation of

Its Spanish name is *La Isla de los Alcatraces*—Island of the Pelicans—and for 30 years, from 1933 to 1963, it served as the most impregnable bastion of its kind. A federal prison situated on this small and desolate island in San Francisco Bay held such notorious criminals as Al Capone, "Machine Gun" Kelly, and bank robbers Frank Lee Morris and Clarence and John Anglin; the escape of the last three in 1962 precipitated the closing of the prison.

On 14 November 1969, 14 Native American college students sailed to the island and occupied it for several hours until the Coast Guard convinced the Indians to leave. A week later, on 21 November, another group of 89 Indians, calling themselves the "Indians of All Tribes" (IAT) and led by Mohawk activist Richard Oakes, again occupied the island and claimed it on behalf of all Native Americans, asserting that under the Treaty of Fort Laramie of 1868 (15 Stat. 649), all unused federal land should revert back to the Indians. The occupiers, mocking the "sale" of Manhattan Island to European colonists in 1626, then offered the government $24 in beads and cloth. They also offered to open a "Bureau of Caucasian Affairs" to aid whites in becoming "civilized."

Oakes biographer Cynthia R. Kasee writes, "IAT intended to use the landing to get media attention for Indian issues, with the call for an Indian center to be built on the island.…In the early days of the occupation, Oakes was the acknowledged leader of IAT. His compatriot, Santee Sioux John Trudell, became the official spokesperson for the media, and so Oakes remained a shadowy figure to many reporters." The members of IAT then released the Alcatraz Proclamation, which laid out their reasons for taking over the island and what they intended to do with it if allowed to remain. Yet the government did not intend for them to stay. Water and electricity were cut off in the spring of 1970, leading to a fire that destroyed the warden's home, the lighthouse, and the infirmary. On 11 June 1971, federal agents raided the island and

Richard Oakes, left, Earl Livermore, center, and Al Miller, right, at an Alcatraz press conference in December 1969, followed the lead of Native American college students and members of the National Indian Youth Council by joining their occupation of the abandoned federal penitentiary site in October 1969. Oakes and others used the event to publicize grievances against the government; the occupation lasted until June 1971.

removed the activists, bringing the occupation to an end. (The 20 September 1972 murder of Oakes incited the leaders of the American Indian Movement to action. He is considered the leading martyr in the Native American rights cause.) Today Alcatraz is part of the Golden Gate National Recreation Area.

See also Alcatraz Proclamation.

References Hurtado, Albert L. and Peter Iverson, eds., *Major Problems in American Indian History: Documents and Essays* (1994); Kasee, Cynthia R., "Richard Oakes." In Sharon Malinowski, ed., *Notable Native Americans* (1995).

Alcatraz Proclamation

This was the statement of the Native Americans who occupied Alcatraz Island in 1969. Despite its sardonic tone, the declaration plainly puts forth the grievances being addressed by the Indians of All Tribes:

A Proclamation from the Indians of All Tribes, Alcatraz Island, 1969

To the Great White Father and All *His* People—We, the native Americans, reclaim the land known as Alcatraz Island in the name of all American Indians by right of discovery.

We wish to be fair and honorable in our dealings with the Caucasian inhabitants of this land, and hereby offer the following treaty:

We will purchase said Alcatraz Island for twenty-four dollars (24) in glass beads and red cloth, a precedent set by the white man's purchase of a similar island about 300 years ago. We know that $24 in trade goods for these 16 acres is more than was paid when Manhattan Island was sold, but we know that land values have risen over the years. Our offer of $1.24 an acre is greater than the 47 cents an acre the white men are now paying the California Indians for their land.

We will give to the inhabitants of this island a portion of the land for their own to be held in trust...by the bureau of Caucasian Affairs to hold in perpetuity—for as long as the sun shall rise and the rivers go down to the sea. We will further guide the inhabitants in the proper way of living. We will offer them our religion, our education, our life-ways, in order to help them achieve our level of civilization and thus raise them and all their white brothers up from their savage and unhappy state. We offer this treaty in good faith and wish to be fair and honorable in our dealings with all white men.

We feel that this so-called Alcatraz Island is more than suitable for an Indian reservation, as determined by the white man's own standards. By this we mean that this place most resembles Indians reservations in that:

1. It is isolated from modern facilities, and without adequate means of transportation.
2. It has no fresh running water.
3. It has inadequate sanitation facilities.
4. There are no oil or mineral rights.
5. There is no industry and so unemployment is very great.
6. There are no health care facilities.
7. The soil is rocky and non-productive, and the land does not support game.
8. There are no educational facilities.
9. The population has always exceeded the land base.
10. The population has always been held as prisoners and kept dependent upon others.

Further, it would be fitting and symbolic that ships from all over the world, entering the Golden Gate, would first see Indian land, and thus be reminded of the true history of this nation. This tiny island would be a symbol of the great lands once ruled by free and noble Indians.

What use will we make of this land?

Since the San Francisco Indian Center burned down, there is no place for Indians to assemble and carry on tribal life here in the white man's city. Therefore, we plan to develop on this island several Indian institutions:

1. A Center for Native American Studies which will educate them to the skills

and knowledge relevant to improve the lives and spirits of Indian peoples....

2. An American Indian Spiritual Center which will practice our ancient tribal religious and sacred healing ceremonies....
3. An Indian Center of Ecology which will train and support our young people in scientific research and practice to restore our lands and waters to their pure and natural state....
4. A Great Indian Training School will be developed to teach our people how to make a living in the world, improve our standard of living, and to end hunger and unemployment among all our people....

Some of the present buildings will be taken over to develop an American Indian Museum which will depict our native food & other cultural contributions we have given to the world. Another part of the museum will present some of the things the white man has given to the Indians in return for the land and life he took: disease, alcohol, poverty and cultural decimation (As symbolized by old tin cans, barbed wire, rubber tires, plastic containers, etc.)....

In the name of all Indians, therefore, we re-claim this island for our Indian nations....

See also Alcatraz, Occupation of.

Reference Hurtado, Albert L. and Peter Iverson, eds., *Major Problems in American Indian History: Documents and Essays* (1994).

Alcohol on Reservations

Under the provisions of an act of Congress of 30 January 1897 (29 Stat. 506), "An Act to prohibit the sale of intoxicating drinks to Indians, providing penalties therefore, and for other purposes....any person who shall sell, give away, dispose of, exchange, or barter any malt, spirituous, or vinous liquor, including beer, ale, and wine, or any ardent or other intoxicating liquor of any kind whatsoever, or any essence, extract, bitters, preparation, compound, composition, or any article whatsoever, under any name, label, or brand, which produces intoxication," was in violation of the act and liable for fines up to $100 for the first offense.

Alcoholism and the selling of alcohol on Indian reservations have been longstanding and seemingly endemic problems destructive both of culture and economy. For American Indians and Alaska Natives ages 25 to 44, alcoholism has made chronic liver disease and cirrhosis leading causes of death. Alcoholism rates among these two groups are 630 percent greater than those of the general American population. To combat this problem, Congress has instituted many acts to stop the flow of liquor into Indian country. The Indian Health Service (IHS), the arm of the Department of Health and Human Services that oversees reservation health care, is today the main government agency dealing with reservation alcoholism.

Under federal legislation, the area where alcohol could be sold was restricted by the definition of "Indian country," particularly by treaties and by acts of Congress. Justice Samuel Freeman Miller reasoned in *Bates v. Clark* (1877), "It follows from this that all the country described by the Act of 1834 [the Trade and Intercourse Act of 1834] as Indian country remains Indian country so long as the Indians retain their original title to the soil, and ceases to be Indian country whenever they lose that title, in the absence of any different provision or by Act of Congress." Attorney A. E. Crane, in his arguments for petitioner John Butler in the Supreme Court case of *In re Heff*, wrote, "The leading case on this subject is *United States v. Holliday*, 3 Wall. 407, 18 L. Ed. 182, where the act of Congress of February 13, 1862 (12 Stat. at 339), which made it a penal offense for any person to sell spirituous liquors to any Indian under the charge of any Indian superintendent or Indian agent appointed by the United States, was held to be constitutional."

See also Indian Country—Definition; Indian Health Service.

References *Bates v. Clark*, 95 U.S. 207 (1877) at 208; *In re Heff*, 197 U.S. 488 (1905) at 497; Indian Health Service, *Regional Differences in Indian Health 1994* (1994); Indian Health Service, *Trends in Indian Health 1994* (1994).

Alcohol in Indian Country Cases, U.S. Supreme Court

See Bates v. Clark; Clairmont v. United States; Dick v. United States; Ex parte Charley Webb; Hallowell v. United States; In re Heff; Johnson et al. v. Gearlds et al.; Perrin v. United States; Pronovost v. United States; United States v. Lariviere; United States v. Mazurie; United States v. Sandoval; United States v. Sutton et al.

Allotment Policy

Allotment, the apportioning out of Indian reservation lands to individuals, became official government policy with the passage of the General Allotment Act (Dawes Act) of 1887. According to Curtis E. Jackson and Marcia J. Galli, between 1887 and 1934, the Indians lost more than 87 million acres of land through allotment. Their figures run thus:

Type of Loss	Acres lost
Surplus reservation land sold	22,694,658
Allotted land sold or alienated	23,225,472
Ceded reservation land	38,229,109
Miscellaneous losses	3,474,456
Total	87,623,675

The final report of the American Indian Policy Review Commission stated, "By the end of the 19th century, Federal policy flowing from the Dawes Act…dictated that the solution to the 'Indian problem' required that Indian reservations be broken up, that the communal holdings of the Indians be individualized into allotments in severalty."

See also Assimilation and Allotment Era.

References *American Indian Policy Review Commission, Final Report*, vol. 1 (1977); Jackson, Curtis E., and Marcia J. Galli, *A History of the Bureau of Indian Affairs and Its Activities among Indians* (1977).

Allotment Era

See Assimilation and Allotment Era.

American Association on Indian Affairs

See Collier, John.

American Fur Company v. United States (2 Peters [27 U.S.] 358 [1829])

Known by its official name, *Sundry Goods, Wares and Merchandise, The American Fur Company, Claimants, Plaintiffs in Error, v. The United States, Defendants in Error*, this litigation rested on the issues of whether a defendant carried "ardent spirits" into Indian country and whether his goods could be confiscated by the U.S. government. On 24 September 1824, William H. Wallace, a trader with a license from the government to trade with the Indians, traveled to the Tippecanoe River in Indiana with goods from his company, the American Fur Company. An Indian agent at Fort Wayne, John Tipton, suspected that Wallace was carrying liquor and when he crossed out of Indian country and back into the United States; Tipton searched the goods, found the liquor (described as "seven kegs of whiskey and one keg of shrub" and confiscated the liquor. In the District Court of the United States for the District of Ohio, where a district attorney filed a suit against Wallace, the defendant was tried and found guilty of violating the law against introducing intoxicating liquors into the Indian country. Wallace and his company appealed to the U.S. Supreme Court. Justice Bushrod Washington held for the court in remanding the case back to the lower court for retrial. Justice Washington explained that the issue of where Tipton confiscated the goods was of key importance because if the place was not within Indian territory, Wallace should not have to surrender his merchandise.

American Indian Association

See Society of American Indians.

American Indian Aid Association

This organization existed for a few short years in the 1870s as one of the first non-Indian groups to fight for Indian rights. Formed just five years after New York philanthropist Peter Cooper established the U.S. Indian Commission, a private rights group, the American Indian Aid Association worked hand in hand with them. Its most notable attempt at reform was to issue, under the name of member John Beeson (a British reformer), a petition for tolerance and patience following the killing by Modoc Indians in northern California of General Edward Richard Sprigg Canby in 1873 and the attempted murder of Oregon Indian agent Alfred B. Meacham. Beeson argued that the Modocs had been driven by years of attacks by soldiers and settlers to strike at the Canby party, which had come to negotiate a peace treaty with the tribe. Historian Armand S. LaPotin speculates that the organization dissolved after the end of the trials of the Modocs in 1874.

Reference LaPotin, Armand S., "American Indian Aid Association." In Armand S. LaPotin, ed., *Native American Voluntary Organizations* (1987).

American Indian Anti-Defamation Council
See Means, Russell Charles.

American Indian Chicago Conference
This convention of concerned Indian activists took place in Chicago from 13 to 20 June 1961. According to writer Virgil J. Vogel, "Independently of [predominantly white Indian rights] organizations, a nationwide Indian conference was convened at the University of Chicago...Technical arrangements were handled by a committee headed by Sol Tax, but the conference itself was restricted to Indians, whites being permitted as silent observers at some of the open sessions. Seven hundred Indians from sixty-four tribes took part and produced a 'Declaration of Indian Purpose.'"

Among the Indian activists who attended the conference were Herbert Blatchford (Navajo), Vivian One Feather (Navajo), Mel Thom (Paiute), Clyde Warrior (Ponca), and Shirley Hill Witt (Mohawk). In their statement which indicated the direction the Native American rights movement would take, excerpts of which appear below, the AICC spoke to the issues that concerned Indians the most, including the right of self-government, government assistance to formulate programs, and the cessation of the termination policy then being established by Congress.

...It is a universal desire among all Indians that their treaties and trust-protected lands remain intact and beyond the reach of predatory men.

This is not special pleading, although Indians have been told often enough by members of Congress and the courts that the United States has the plenary power to wipe out our treaties at will. Governments, when powerful enough, can act in this arbitrary and immoral manner.

Still we insist that we are not pleading for special treatment at the hands of the American people. When we ask that our treaties be respected, we are mindful of the opinion of Chief Justice John Marshall on the nature of the treaty obligations between the United States and the Indian tribes.

Marshall said that a treaty "...is a compact between two nations or communities, having the right of self-government. Is it essential that each party possess the same attributes of sovereignty to give force to a treaty? This will not be pretended, for on this ground, very few valid treaties could be formed. The only requisite is, that each of the contracting parties shall possess the right of self-government, and the power to perform the stipulations of the treaty."

And he said, "We have made treaties with [the Indians]; and are those treaties to be disregarded on our part, because they were entered to with an uncivilized people? Does this lessen the obligation of such treaties? By entering into them have we not admitted the power of this people to bind themselves, and to impose obligations on us?"

The right of self-government, a right which the Indians possessed before the coming of the white man, has never been extinguished; indeed, it has been repeatedly sustained by the courts of the United States. Our leaders made binding agreements—ceding lands as requested by the United States; keeping the peace; harboring no enemies of the nation. And the people stood with the leaders in accepting those obligations.

A treaty, in the minds of our people, is an eternal word. Events often make it seem expedient to depart from the pledged word, but we are conscious that the first departure creates a logic for the second departure, until there is nothing left of the word.

We recognize that our view of these matters differs at times from the prevailing legal view regarding due process.

When our lands are taken for a declared public purpose, scattering our people and threatening our continued existence, it grieves us to be told that a money payment is the equivalent of all the things we surrender. Our forefathers could be generous when the continent was theirs. They could cast away whole empires for a handful of trinkets for their children. But in our day, each remaining acre is a promise that we will still be here tomorrow. Were we paid a thousand times the market value of our lost holdings, still the payment would not suffice. Money never mothered the Indian people, as the land has mothered them, nor have any people become more closely attached to the land, religiously and traditionally....

To complete our Declaration, we point out that in the beginning the people of the New World, called Indians by accident of geography, were possessed of a continent and a way of life. In the course of many lifetimes, our people had adjusted to every climate and condition from the Arctic to the torrid zones. In their livelihood and family relationships, their ceremonial observances, they reflected the diversity of the physical world they occupied.

The conditions in which Indians live today reflect a world in which every basic aspect of life has been transformed. Even the physical world is no longer the controlling factor in determining where and under what conditions men may live. In region after region, Indian groups found their means of existence either totally destroyed or materially modified. Newly introduced diseases swept away or reduced regional populations. These changes were followed by major shifts in the internal life of the tribe and family.

The time came when the Indian people were no longer the master of their situation. Their life ways survived subject to the will of a dominant sovereign power. This is said, not in a spirit of complaint; we understand that in the lives of all nations of people, there are times of plenty and times of famine. But we do speak out in a plea for understanding.

When we go before the American people, as we do in this Declaration, and ask for material assistance in developing our resources and developing our opportunities, we pose a moral problem which cannot be left unanswered. For the problem we raise affects the standing which our nation sustains before world opinion.

Our situation cannot be relieved by appropriated funds alone, though it is equally obvious that without capital investment and funded services, solutions will be delayed. Nor will the passage of time lessen the complexities which beset a people moving toward new meaning and purpose.

The answers we seek are not commodities to be purchased, neither are they evolved automatically through the passing of time.

The effort to place social adjustment on a money-time interval scale which has characterized Indian administration, has resulted in unwanted pressure and frustration.

When Indians speak of the continent they yielded, they are not referring only to the loss of some millions of acres in real estate. They have in mind that the land supported a universe of things they knew, valued, and loved.

With that continent gone, except for the few poor parcels they still retain, the basis of life is precariously held, but they mean to hold the scraps and parcels as earnestly as any small nation or ethnic group was ever determined to hold to identity and survival.

What we ask of America is not charity, not paternalism, even when benevolent. We ask only that the nature of our situation be recognized and made the basis of policy and action.

In short, the Indians ask for assistance, technical and financial, for the time needed, however long that might be, to regain in the

America of the space age some measure of the adjustment they enjoyed as the original possessors of their native land.

Following the close of the conference, those in attendance moved to the University of New Mexico in Gallup, where a month later they helped to found the National Indian Youth Council. On 15 August 1962, the activists who participated in the conference presented the report of the group to President John F. Kennedy, symbolically taking the results of a pan-Indian meeting to the steps of the White House.

See also National Indian Youth Council.

References Hurtado, Albert L. and Peter Iverson, eds., *Major Problems in American Indian History: Documents and Essays* (1994); Vogel, Virgil J., *This Country Was Ours: A Documentary History of the American Indian* (1972).

American Indian Federation

This Indian rights organization, composed entirely of Native Americans, was founded in 1934 and dissolved in the mid-1940s. Leadership of the group was vested in such activists as Joseph Bruner (Creek), Alice Lee Jemison (Seneca), Thomas Sloan (Omaha), and Jacob C. Morgan (Navajo), later chairman of his tribe.

Founded in 1934 by Bruner, it was, as historian Laurence M. Hauptman writes, "a loose, umbrella-like federation composed of many strands of Indian thinking: the Indian National Confederacy of Oklahoma, which included members of the Five Civilized Tribes; the Mission Indian Federation of California; the Intertribal Committee for the Fundamental Advancement of the American Indian, based in Buffalo and Detroit and largely dominated by Iroquois Indians; and the Black Hills Treaty Council, composed of a substantial number of Sioux Indians opposed to the BIA." Through the pages of its two official journals, *The American Indian* and *The First American*, the AIF preached a rhetoric of hatred for the BIA within an anti–New Deal message. The central goal for Bruner and the organization was to end the BIA's influence over Indian affairs. Many of Bruner's followers saw the imposition of the Indian Reorganization Act (1934) as the means for the government to strengthen its hold on Indian life. Joining forces with such groups as the Daughters of the American Revolution and the Silver Shirts of America, a quasi-fascist organization, the AIF was a major force in the fight to end the New Deal, and its influence caused the Interior Department in 1938 to begin a spying campaign against the AIF's members and its tactics. The outspokenness of Alice Jemison and the connection of AIF member Elwood Towner to neo-Nazis caused a decline in the group's membership. By the early 1940s it was a shell of its former self, and it ceased operations soon after.

See also Jemison, Alice Mae Lee.

Reference Hauptman, Laurence M., "American Indian Federation (1934)." In Armand S. LaPotin, ed., *Native American Voluntary Organizations* (1987).

American Indian Movement

Judith Harlan writes, "In the 1970s the American Indian Movement and other Indian civil rights organizations brought Indian people into public consciousness again. With demonstrations and sit-ins, including the occupation of Alcatraz Island in California and the town of Wounded Knee in the Pine Ridge Reservation in South Dakota, Native Americans forced the rest of the country to notice their plight: poverty and lack of opportunity."

The story of the American Indian Movement begins with four Native American activists—Dennis Banks, Clyde Bellecourt, Eddie Benton-Bonai, and George Mitchell—establishing the first AIM chapter in Minneapolis in 1968 with the help of an older Indian woman named Pat Ballanger, who has been called the "Mother of the American Indian Movement." Historian Rex Weyler relates, "This was the time of the anti-war movement and the Black Power movement, and signs of Red Power had begun to appear beside Black Power slogans across the country. But soon the Red Power graffiti changed to AIM. The movement caught on quickly. AIM was decidedly different, however, from

Members of the American Indian Movement (AIM) beat a drum in support of their cause during the 1973 occupation of Wounded Knee in the Pine Ridge Indian Reservation, South Dakota. AIM's flag is displayed behind the group.

the black movement, the anti–Vietnam War protests, or the San Francisco, Woodstock hippie generation. AIM was an indigenous, land-based spiritual movement, a call to Indian people to return to their sacred traditions and, at the same time, to stand firm against the tide of what they call European influence and dominance." Modeled on the African American civil rights organizations, AIM sought, starting in 1973, to advance the Native American rights movement. In that year, Vernon Bellecourt, Clyde's brother and himself an AIM activist of some note, wrote:

For the past several years, the struggle for full civil rights for minority groups has been a central issue in American society. The sit-ins, freedom rides, and court battles waged by the blacks are well-known—but equally significant—is the growing concern and increasing activity among Indians to gain equal and fair treatment for their people. Thus, the American Indian Movement (AIM) was formed in July of 1968. It was first known as the Concerned Indian American Coalition. Many Indians who attended the first meeting felt that very little, if anything, was being done to give Indians the opportunity to help themselves. The Coalition had originally hoped to generate unification among Indian groups; however, this ideal has changed somewhat; it now reads—to unify Indian people. This change of direction was taken because other Indian groups have been merchandise of the Indian people for years. The American Indian Movement was formed with the idea of doing effective work among the Indian people. Most, although not all, Indian groups treat Indians as though they are children and cannot manage their own affairs. This is what we call Paternalism. Many of the Indian organizations are run by white groups or individuals. The American Indian Movement is Indian and thinks Indian. We do welcome and solicit advice from "well meaning whites and blacks"; however, we make the decisions and determine the course of action.

Other less well-known groups conducted demonstrations—such as fish-ins and the "occupation" of Alcatraz Island in 1964 and 1969, including the invasion of Wounded Knee on the Pine Ridge Reservation in South Dakota to protest the strong-armed tactics of Dick Wilson, president of the Oglala Nation, and the Trail of Broken Treaties to declare their opposition to government policy toward the Indians. In 1973, in a secret F.B.I. memo, the Denver office wrote to headquarters in Washington, D.C., "During the past two years AIM has participated in confrontations and takeovers of buildings as a result of issues affecting American Indians...AIM members provided the primary leadership for the confrontation between Indians and local authorities at Custer, South Dakota, which resulted in the burning of the Court House and Chamber of Commerce buildings." The attack at Wounded Knee was the first such use of government power to forcibly stop a demonstration by minority activists. Following the end of the siege there, AIM released what it called its "three-point program"; these were:

Point 1. A Senate Treaty Commission should examine the 371 treaties the U.S. has made (and broken) with Indians. All treaty rights should be enforced.

The land rights involved here for reservations are very large. The 1972 "Trail" [of Broken Treaties] proposal called, at a minimum, for restoration to Indian control of at least 110 million acres of land. Presently, the federal government holds "in trust" about 40 million tribal acres (much of it used for mineral, park, and other interests), with an additional 10 million acres held "in trust" for individual tribal members. Much of this land is leased out, advantageously to white interests. On Pine Ridge Reservation (South Dakota), Indian range land is leased for 80 cents an acre; this land is exactly like land owned by whites, which brings $15 an acre.

One response to the efforts to enforce the rights of this treaty (re. the 1868

Sioux/U.S. treaty) has been a government "offer" to settle a 50–year-old claim based on it. The U.S. National Indian Claims Commission finds about $102 million (or $2,000 per person for about 60,000 Sioux) a fair settlement for 7.5 million acres of land—including the Homestake Mine, largest gold producing mine in the Western Hemisphere, and the sacred Paha Sapa—the beautiful Black Hills. However, old habits of cheating Indians die hard. By the time the U.S. government finished taking deductions for "money spent on the Sioux," only about $4 million is left. We don't want little bits of cash; we want a land base which is ours by right and could support meaningful lives...

We need a Treaty Commission, and it should get to work quickly. The sort of litigation which goes on forever is all too familiar...From Washington to New York, there have been many such incidents and cases; it should not be necessary for Indians to go to court to win rights they (supposedly) already have by treaty.

Point 2. Repeal the Indian Reorganization Act of 1934 (Wheeler-Howard Act); it has been a major weapon used in robbing Indians of their land, settling white-controlled governments on many reservations, and establishing tribal constitutions which offer no real protection against sale and wholesale lease-out of tribal lands.

Point 3. Remove the Bureau of Indian Affairs from the Department of the Interior, restructure it as an independent agency, controlled by and accountable to, Indian people; audit the BIA records and make reparations for the many crooked land deals; cancel BIA-sanctioned non-Indian leasing of Indian land.

The BIA should never have been located in the Department of the Interior. (Maybe that's better than its original location—the Department of War—but not much.) The Department of the Interior serves oil, mineral, lands trusts, transportation, shipping, wood forestry, and energy interests; these usually conflict with Indian rights.

The BIA has a long history of corruption and mismanagement of our affairs. A tough, independent audit of BIA books and land rent records should be supported by all. Forced land sales and lease rentals arranged by the BIA should be examined, with returns and reparations made.

Pine Ridge data show part of the reason why this needs to be done. As of 1969, the federal government was spending, through BIA, about $8,040 a year per family, to "help the Oglala Sioux out of poverty." But median family income from all sources (employment, land rental, and federal) was only $1,910 per family—supporting many children and old people. Where did the rest of it go? The fact that there was about one well-paid bureaucrat per family gives part of the answer; kickbacks and corruption give the other part. All Indians would benefit if this inept and corrupt agency were accountable to us...

This Three Point Program provides a strategy for a nationally coordinated attack on powerful financial and political interests, which have used the U.S. government to take advantage of Native Americans for more than a century. It will require strong commitment and wide support to win against these interests. Indian rights of sovereignty, self-government, and a decent means of living in accordance with traditions and beliefs will not come easily. Without massive public pressure, the government will simply continue its present treatment of Indians, a continuing shame to all, and a continuing profit source to a few.

In the last two decades, AIM has not been as effective as it once was. While AIM activists Russell Means and Dennis Banks have remained at the forefront of the fight for Native American rights, the organization as a whole has lost some of its high national profile.

See also Alcatraz, Occupation of; Banks, Dennis J.; Means, Russell Charles; Peltier, Leonard; Trail of Broken Treaties; Wounded Knee (1973).

References "American Indian Movement," memo from Denver to Washington, D.C., 20 March 1973, American Indian Movement Papers,

F.B.I. file 100–462483, vol. 6; Bellecourt, Vernon, "Overview [of American Indian Movement]," American Indian Movement Papers, F.B.I. file 100–462483, vol. 12; Council on Interracial Books for Children, ed., *Chronicles of American Indian Protest* (1971); Harlan, Judith, *American Indians Today: Issues and Conflicts* (1987); Moses, Lester George, "American Indian Movement." In Armand S. LaPotin, ed., *Native American Voluntary Organizations* (1987); Weyler, Rex, *Blood of the Land: The Government and Corporate War against the American Indian Movement* (1982).

American Indian Policy Review Commission

This commission was established by the act of Congress of 2 January 1975 (88 Stat. 1910); the chairman was Senator James G. Abourezk (D-South Dakota), and the members included Congressman Lloyd Meeks (R-Washington), commission vice chairman, Senator Lee Metcalf (D-Montana), Senator Mark Hatfield (R-Oregon), Congressman Sidney R. Yates (D-Illinois), Congressman Sam Steiger (R-Arizona, who served on the commission during the 94th Congress), Congressman Don Young (R-Alaska, who replaced Steiger on the commission), John Borbridge (Tlingit-Haida), Louis Rook Bruce (Mohawk/Oglala Sioux, who served from 1969 to 1973 as commissioner of Indian Affairs under Richard Nixon), Ada Deer (Menominee, who would later serve as commissioner of Indian Affairs under Bill Clinton), Adolph Dial (Lumbee), and Jake Whitecrow (Quapaw-Seneca-Cayuga).

Committee member Meeks wrote in 1976, "'Congress declares that it is timely and essential to conduct a comprehensive review of the historical and legal developments underlying the Indians' unique relationship with the Federal Government in order to determine the nature and scope of necessary revisions in the formulation of policies and programs for the benefit of the Indians.' With these profound words, the American Indian Policy Review Commission was born in the Ninety-Third Congress. All of us in the field of Indian affairs in Congress have realized for some time that an organized study must be initiated and plausible legislation must be enacted to bring order and aid to the chaotic world of Indian affairs. This power enables Congress to legislate, clarify, define, and create policy." He added, "Congress is now in the position to assess the role of history in Indian affairs, to view it own responsibility, and to be aware of the possible consequences of suggested legislative change. Through the American Indian Policy Review Commission it is hoped that a thorough study can be made and that new legislation can be recommended to a waiting Congress." The commission submitted its final report in 1977 in two volumes (with 11 accompanying reports on various subjects, including Indian health [report 6] and alcoholism [report 11]).

References *American Indian Policy Review Commission, Final Report* (1977); Meeds, Lloyd, "The Indian Policy Review Commission." *Law & Contemporary Problems* 40.

American Indian Religious Freedom Act (92 Stat. 469)

Now codified at 42 U.S.C. 1996, this federal action of 11 August 1978 was enacted to safeguard the traditional religious practices and religions of Native Americans. The act, as codified, reads:

Henceforth it shall be the policy of the United States to protect and preserve for American Indians their inherent right of freedom to believe, express, and exercise the traditional religions of the American Indian, Eskimo, Aleut, and Native Hawaiians, including but not limited to access to sites, use and possession of sacred objects, and the freedom to worship through ceremonials and traditional rites.

Sec. 2. The President shall direct the various Federal departments, agencies, and other instrumentalities responsible for administering relevant laws and evaluate their policies and procedures in consultation with native traditional religious leaders in order to determine appropriate changes necessary to protect and preserve Native American religious cultural rights and practices. Twelve months after approval of this [act], the President shall report back to the Congress the results of his evaluation, including any changes which were made in administrative policies and procedures, and any recommendations he may have for legislative action.

In 1988, the U.S. Supreme Court held in *Oregon v. Smith* and *Oregon v. Black* that the American Indian Religious Freedom Act did not recognize the right of Indians to use peyote in religious ceremonies without regard for state laws against the use of illegal drugs. In response, Congress enacted the American Indian Religious Freedom Amendments of 1994 (108 Stat. 3125), which established that "notwithstanding any other provision of law, the use, possession, or transportation of peyote by an Indian for bona fide traditional ceremonial purposes in connection with the practice of a traditional Indian religion is lawful, and shall not be prohibited by the United States or any State. No Indian shall be penalized or discriminated against on the basis of such use, possession or transportation, including, but not limited to, denial of otherwise applicable benefits under public assistance programs."

See also *Oregon v. Smith* and *Oregon v. Black* ("*Oregon I*" and "*Oregon II*").

Andrus, Secretary of the Interior et al. v. Glover Construction Company (446 U.S. 608 [1980])

This Supreme Court case, decided in 1980, held that the Buy Indian Act of 1908, enacted to protect the hiring of Indian labor and the purchase of Indian products, was superseded by Title III of the Federal Property and Administrative Services Act (FPASA) of 1949 (63 Stat. 393), which requires nondiscriminatory bids be entered into for work in Indian service contracts. The Bureau of Indian Affairs invited bids from three Indian-owned companies to repair a road to be used by Indian bureau personnel. After one of the companies owned by Indians was awarded the contract, a non-Indian company, the Glover Construction Company of Oklahoma, filed suit in the U.S. District Court for the Eastern District of Oklahoma, claiming that under Title III of the FPASA, the Department of the Interior had to advertise for such bids publicly, not just among Indian-owned companies. Secretary of the Interior Cecil Dale Andrus defended his decision by citing the Buy Indian Act, which allows the secretary to purchase "the products of Indian industry...in open market." The district court held that the contract violated the FPASA, and voided it, and at the same time enjoined the secretary from circumventing the FPASA to invite bids for the road in question as well as all future road work. On appeal, the U.S. Court of Appeals for the Tenth Circuit affirmed. The U.S. Supreme Court granted certiorari; Justice Potter Stewart held for a unanimous court on 27 May 1980 that the Bureau of Indian Affairs must comply with Title III of the FPASA and advertise publicly among all companies for contract bids for agency work. Justice Stewart explained,

It is fairly debatable, we think, simply as a matter of language, whether a road constructed or repaired by an Indian-owned enterprise is a "product of Indian industry" within the meaning of the Buy Indian Act. But even if that Act could in isolation be construed to embrace road construction or repair, the petitioners' argument must still be rejected because of another provision of Title II of the FPASA expressly related to contracts of the sort at issue here. Title 41 U.S.C. 252 (subsection e) states that section 252 "shall not be construed to...permit any contract for the construction or repair of...roads...to be negotiated without advertising..., unless...negotiation of such contract is authorized by the provisions of paragraphs (1), (2), (3), (10), (11), (12), or (14) of subsection (c) of this section." Not contained in this list of exceptions is paragraph (c)(15). From this omission only one inference can be drawn: Congress meant to bar the negotiation of road construction and repair projects under the authority of laws like the Buy Indian Act.

Andrus, Secretary of the Interior et al. v. Weeks

See Delaware Tribal Business Committee v. Weeks.

Antoine et ux. v. Washington (420 U.S. 194 [1975])

In this Supreme Court case, decided in 1975, the court held that once Congress ratifies an agreement with a tribe of Indians, the provisions of that agreement, including hunting and fishing rights, must be protected for those Indians. Appellant Alexander J. Antoine was an enrolled member of the Confederated Tribes of the Colville Indian Reservation (which includes the tribes of the Colville, Columbia, San Poil, Okanogan, Nez Percé, Lake, Spokane, and Coeur d'Alene), located in Washington State. (Appellant's wife, not mentioned, but considered a party in this case, was a Canadian Indian and could not be brought under the jurisdiction of American courts.) An agreement (treaties had been prohibited in 1871) with the Colville Confederated Tribes of 9 May 1891 established that "the right to hunt and fish in common with all other persons on lands not allotted to said Indians shall not be taken away or in anywise abridged." Antoine was convicted of hunting deer on the reservation in violation of state law, and he appealed to the Supreme Court of Washington; that court, agreeing that his defense of agreement rights was properly excluded, affirmed. The U.S. Supreme Court granted certiorari. Justice William Brennan, expressing the views of six members of the court (Justice William O. Douglas concurred, but gave a differing reason, and justices William H. Rehnquist and Potter Stewart dissented) that the 1891 agreement gave the Indians a right of hunting and fishing that could not be abrogated by state law. Justice Brennan wrote, "I agree with the Court that conservation measures, applicable to all, are available to the State, but discrimination against Indians by conservation measures is not permissible. In any case, no conservation interest has been tendered here."

Apes (also Apess), William (Pequot) (1798–1839)

Early Native American writer and chronicler of his people, William Apes has today been nearly forgotten by Native American historians. Born on 31 January 1798 in Colrain, Massachusetts, he was the son of William and Candace Apes. There is no certain record of when he began using the alternate spelling *Apess;* historian Barry O'Connell, who has collected Apes's writings, documents that in a debt action in the Barnstable, Massachusetts, Court of Common Pleas in September 1836, he entered his name as "Apess." Up until that time, it seems that he used the name "Apes" with all regularity; his works, including *A Son of the Forest: The Experience of William Apes, a Native of the Forest, Comprising a Notice of the Pequot Tribe of Indians* (1829) and *The Experiences of Five Christian Indians of the Pequot Tribe; or, An Indian's Looking-Glass for the White Man* (1833), were published under the name Apes. However, the 1837 edition of *Experiences* lists the author as "William Apess," with no explanation given as to the differential in names. According to biographer Arnold Krupat, "His grandfather, says Apess, was a white man who married the granddaughter of King Philip, or Metacomet, a Pequot leader, and the loser, in 1637, of what has been called the first deliberately genocidal war conducted by the English in North America." Little is known of Apes's early life; what few details exist were detailed by Indian writer A. LaVonne Brown Ruoff, as well as historian Kim McQuaid in his article "William Apes, Pequot: An Indian Reformer in the Jackson Era," which appeared in 1977. As a member of the Pequot ("destroyers of men") tribe, which by 1740 numbered about 250, Apes considered himself to be of a dying race. Ruoff notes, "In his autobiographies, he gives a moving account of the abuse he suffered as a child at the hands of his alcoholic grandparents. (He used the experience to introduce an attack on Indian alcoholism, a problem for which he held whites responsible.) After a severe beating, Apes was taken in by a white family and bound out from age five to a series of masters, a common practice in dealing with orphans and foster children." "Until 1818, Apes had survived a broken family, difficult apprenticeships, war, liquor, and poverty," McQuaid writes. Apes himself wrote that he was treated as "a degraded African slave."

After converting to Methodism, and serving in the American army during the War of 1812 as an infantryman, Apes settled down and began to write his autobiography, which was published at the height of the removal debate in Washington, D.C. *A Son of the Forest*, while the first autobiography published by a Native American, was not the first publication; that honor belongs to Samson Occom (Mohegan), who issued a sermon in 1771. Apes's *The Increase of the Kingdom of Christ* appeared in 1831, and *The Experiences of Five Christian Indians of the Pequot Tribe* came out two years later. In 1835, Apes wrote in his *Indian Nullification of the Unconstitutional laws of Massachusetts, relative to the Marshpee Tribe; or, the pretended riot explained*, "If, in the course of this little volume, I have been obliged to use language that seems harsh, I beg my readers to remember that it was in defence of the character of the people under my spiritual charge and of my own. The Marshpees have been reviled and misrepresented in the public prints, as much more indolent, ignorant, and degraded that they really are, and it was necessary, for their future welfare, as it depends in no small degree upon the good opinion of their white brethren, to state the real truth of the case, which could not be done in gentle terms. The causes which have retarded our improvement could not be explained without naming the individuals who have been the willing instruments to enforce them."

In his final years, details on Apes's life become hazy. His *Eulogy on King Philip, as Pronounced at the Odeon, in Federal Street, Boston*, delivered in 1836, became so popular that it was issued as a small pamphlet. Historian Ruoff opines, "Originally delivered as a series of lectures in Boston, this book traces white abuse of New England Indians in the seventeenth and eighteenth centuries. After the publication of this book, Apes disappeared from public view." According to Arnold Krupat, "Only recently have obituaries in the *New York Sun* and the *New York Observer* been found recording his death, as the result of alcoholism, in New York, in the spring of 1839."

References Apes, William, "The Experience of Five Christian Indians of the Pequot Tribe." In Arnold Krupat, ed., *Native American Autobiography: An Anthology* (1994); Apes, William, *Indian Nullification of the Unconstitutional Laws of Massachusetts, relative to the Marshpee Tribe; or, the Pretended Riot Explained* (1835); Apes, William, *A Son of the Forest: The Experience of William Apes, A Native of the Forest* (1831); McQuaid, Kim, "William Apes, Pequot: An Indian Reformer in the Jacksonian Era." *New England Quarterly* 50 (4); O'Connell, Barry, ed., *On Our Own Ground: The Complete Writings of William Apess, a Pequot* (1992); Ruoff, A. LaVonne Brown, *American Indian Literatures: An Introduction, Bibliographic Review, and Selected Bibliography* (1990); Ruoff, A. LaVonne Brown, "On Literature in English: American Indian Authors, 1774–1899." In Andrew Wiget, ed., *Critical Essays on Native American Literature* (1985); Sutherland, Ernest, "Apes, William." In Dumas Malone et al., eds., *Dictionary of American Biography*, vol. 1.

Archaeological Resources Protection Act of 1979 (93 Stat. 721)

Enacted on 31 October 1979 "to protect archaeological resources on public lands and Indian lands," this federal action was enacted "to secure, for the present and future benefit of the American people, the protection of archaeological resources and sites which are on public lands and Indian lands, and to foster increased cooperation and exchange of information between governmental authorities, the professional archaeological community, and private individuals having collections of archaeological resources and data which were obtained before the date of the enactment of this Act." The term *archaeological resource* was defined as "any material remains of past human life or activities which are of archaeological interest..."; these may include, but are not limited to, "pottery, basketry, bottles, weapons, weapon projectiles, tools, structures or portions of structures, pit houses, rock paintings, rock carvings, intaglios, graves, human skeletal remains, or any portion or piece of any of the foregoing items." The act established a fine of up to $10,000 for violating any of the archaeological resources listed in the act.

See also Native American Graves Protection and Repatriation Act.

Arenas v. United States (322 U.S. 419 [1944])

Allotment patents promised to American Indians must be delivered, the Supreme Court held in this case, according to government legislation, and cannot be avoided by the secretary of the interior. Lee Arenas, a Mission Indian, sued the U.S. government after his tribe, the Agua Caliente or Palm Springs Band of California, was promised allotments from the government under section 4 of the Mission Indian Act of 1891 (26 Stat. 712). The allotments were not made. In 1917, Secretary of the Interior Franklin K. Lane asked Congress to pass further legislation to allow him to allot the lands to the Mission Indians as part of the General Allotment Act of 1887 and its amendment act of 25 June 1910. Congress ratified Lane's proposal, enacting the act of 2 March 1917 (39 Stat. 969, 976). Lane then approved an agent, Henry E. Wadsworth, to allot the lands in severalty by drawing up rolls of Indians. Wadsworth found that many of the Mission Indians did not want their reservation split into allotments and refused to have their names added to the roll. Wadsworth went ahead, allotted these dissenting Indians allotments as he saw fit, and submitted his report to Secretary of the Interior Albert Bacon Fall. Secretary Fall disapproved of awarding allotments to Indians who did not want them and refused to honor the schedule. Wadsworth submitted a second schedule in 1927, but that too was refused. No further action was taken. Arenas, among others, wanted his allotment, and pressed the government for it. The government refused to honor the allotment plan until the entire reservation could be allotted, and Arenas sued in district court for his patent. Both the district court and the Circuit Court of Appeals for the Ninth Circuit dismissed his suit, and Arenas appealed to the U.S. Supreme Court for relief.

Arguments were heard on 6 and 7 March 1944 and the court handed down its decision on 22 May of the same year. Speaking for a unanimous court, Justice Robert H. Jackson held that the government could not avoid awarding Arenas his allotment as promised under the General Allotment Act of 1887 and the subsequent legislation of 25 June 1910 and 2 March 1917. Justice Jackson found that Secretary of the Interior Harold Ickes was against the allotment arrangement as it stood and was willing to fight it in court. In his opinion, Justice Jackson wrote, "The Government brief says, 'Meanwhile, opposition to the making of allotments in severalty developed among the members of the Palm Springs band of Indians, and as a result administrative action on the 1927 schedule was further delayed. During this period the conclusion was reached in the Department that in fairness to the band as a whole and from the standpoint of their best interests the lands scheduled for allotment should be held in a tribal status and dealt with as a tribal asset.' It says further, 'The Secretary has determined that it would be inequitable and detrimental to the Palm Springs band of Indians as a whole to approve any allotments on their reservation.' Again, 'The Secretary should not be compelled to carry through a plan of allotment in severalty which in his judgment will operate contrary to the best interests of the Palm Springs band of Indians, but he should be permitted to stay his hand and seek a time which would be more in the interests of that band.'" Justice Jackson then explained why, under the three federal acts, Ickes, or any other sitting secretary of the interior, had to allot the lands to Indians who did want them.

Arizona v. San Carlos Apache Tribe of Arizona (463 U.S. 545, 103 S.Ct. 3201 [1983])

See *Montana et al. v. Northern Cheyenne Tribe of the Northern Cheyenne Indian Reservation et al.*

Ash Sheep Company v. United States (252 U.S. 159, 64 L.Ed. 510, 40 S.Ct. 241 [1920])

In this landmark case, the Supreme Court held that "Lands within that part of the Crow Indian Reservation in Montana as to which the Indians released their possessory right to the United States by an agreement ratified and amended by the Act of 27 April 1904, which contains many provisions intended to secure to the Indians the fullest possible value for what are referred to in the grant as 'their lands,' and to make use of the proceeds for their benefit, are Indian lands within the meaning of U.S. Rev. Stat. 2117, forbidding the pasturing of cattle upon lands belonging to any Indian or Indian tribe without the consent of such tribe." This was actually two cases: in the first, the Ash Sheep Company was suing the United States to force an end to an enjoinment placed on it by the U.S. Court of Appeals for the Ninth Circuit; in the second, the Ash Sheep Company was suing the United States to recover a penalty imposed on it by the District Court for the District of Montana for trespass on what the United States claimed as the Crow Indian reservation in Montana. According to the case notes, "The company [Ash Sheep] admits that it pastured 5,000 sheep on the described lands without the consent of the Crow tribe of Indians or of the United States, but denies that they were 'Indian lands,' and contends that they were 'public lands' upon which it was lawful for it to pasture stock." According to the act of Congress of 27 April 1904 (22 Stat 352), entitled "An Act to Ratify and Amend an Agreement with the Indians of the Crow Reservation of Montana, and Making Appropriations to Carry the Same into Effect," the Crows "ceded, granted, and relinquished" to the United States all of their "right, title, and interest" in certain lands belonging to the reservation. The company argued that this implied that the United States, not the Crows, owned the land, making it public lands, and not Indian territory.

Justice John Hessin Clarke delivered the court's opinion as to the two questions. As to the first, Clarke held that the enjoinment must stand because the land was still, by law, considered "Indian lands." He explained, "Taking all of the provisions of the agreement together, we cannot doubt that while the Indians by the agreement released their possessory right to the government, the owner of the fee, so that, as their trustee, it could make perfect title to purchasers, nevertheless, until sales should be made, any benefits which might be derived from the use of the lands would belong to the beneficiaries, and not to the trustee, and that they did not become 'public lands' in the sense of being subject to sale or other disposition, under the General Land Laws." As to the second point, the penalty for trespass, Clarke upheld the lower court's imposition of the penalty. He noted, "The company contends that the judgment should be reversed for the reason that Rev. Stat. 2117 imposes the penalty prescribed only for ranging and feeding on the lands of an Indian tribe without permission 'any stock of horses, mules, or cattle,' and that 'sheep' are not within its terms. If this were a recent statute, and if we were giving it a first interpretation, we might hesitate to say that by the use of the word 'cattle' Congress intended to include 'sheep.' But the statute is an old one, which has been interpreted in published reports of the courts for almost fifty years, and in an opinion by the Attorney General of the United States, rendered in 1884, as fairly comprehending 'sheep' within the meaning of the word 'cattle' as used in it."

Assimilation

Defined as "the process by which one group of people of a special and distinct culture is absorbed into the culture of another group," the official U.S. government policy of assimilation of American Indians lasted from 1871 until 1928, or from the end of the "treaty-making" period until the publication of the Meriam Report, which called for an end to the allotment policy and the restoration of reservations and Indian rights. From the 1830s until the 1870s, tribal government as a whole was on the decline; there was a mass removal of whole nations of Indians from their ancestral homes to reservations in virtually uninhabited, agriculturally unstable areas, primarily in the American West. Assimilation became the official policy of the government at the same time that Jim Crow laws came to the South and Progressivism became established as a political force. It was a time of white supremacy and the downgrading of other cultures. James S. Olson and Raymond Wilson, two noted Indian historians, write, "During the Progressive period, the older faith in the possibilities of rapid assimilation of Native Americans weakened somewhat, raising doubts in the minds of some reformers. Francis Ellington Leupp, commissioner of Indian Affairs under President Theodore Roosevelt between 1905 and 1909, wondered about the new racial theories and their meaning for assimilation policies."

In his annual report for 1905, Leupp penned, "If nature has set a different physical stamp upon different races of men it is fair to assume that the variation of types extends below the surface and is manifested in mental and moral traits as well.…What good end shall we serve by trying to blot out these distinctions…? Nothing is gained by trying to undo nature's work and do it over, but grand results are possible, if we simply turn her forces into the best channels."

References Olson, James S. and Raymond Wilson, *Native Americans in the Twentieth Century* (1984); U.S. Congress, House of Representatives, *Annual Report of the Commissioner of Indian Affairs for the Year 1905*, House Document No. 5, 59th Congress, 1st Session (serials 4959 and 4960).

Assimilation and Allotment Era

Historians regard this period of American government policy toward the Indians as ranging from 1871 to 1928, ending the two concurrent periods usually known as the Formative or Treaty Era (1789–1871) and the Removal Era (1830–1871). Historian Paul Stuart comments simply, "Whether described as an 'assault on Indian tribalism,' a 'movement for Indian assimilation,' or simply as 'Americanizing the American Indian,' the new system envisioned the integration of American Indians into the mainstream of white American life."

Allotment of Indian lands started early in the nation's history, perhaps during the early seventeenth century. It became official government policy with the passage of the General Allotment Act (Dawes Act) of 1887, in which Indians were not only expected to conform to the norms of white society but to assimilate into it. Missionaries from various religious denominations sought to acclimate American Indians with education and a demonization of tribal ways. Indian historians Vine Deloria, Jr., and Clifford M. Lytle write, "As a consequence of the allotment policy, Indian landholdings were reduced from 138 million acres in 1887 to 48 million in 1934. Of this 48 million acres, nearly 20 million were desert or semiarid and virtually useless for any kind of annual farming ventures." In addition, the Dawes Act "gave the Secretary of the Interior almost dictatorial powers over the use of allotments since, if the local agent disagreed with the use to which the lands were being put, he would intervene and lease the land to whomsoever he pleased."

The allotment era ended with the publication of the Meriam Report and the subsequent passage of the Indian Reorganization Act (Wheeler-Howard Act) in 1934 and its companion legislation, the Oklahoma Indian Welfare Act, in 1936.

See also Acculturation; Allotment Policy; Assimilation; Formative or Treaty Era; Removal Policy, U.S.; Reorganization and Reform Era; Self-Determination; Termination Policy.

References Deloria, Vine, Jr., and Clifford M. Lytle, *American Indians, American Justice* (1983); Stuart, Paul, *The Indian Office: Growth and Development of an American Institution, 1865–1900* (1979).

Association on American Indian Affairs (AAIA)

Founded in 1922, this organization has 15,000 Indian and non-Indian members, with its headquarters in New York City. Originally formed as the American Indian

Defense Association (AIDA) in 1923 by activist John Collier (who served as commissioner of Indian Affairs, 1933–1945), it merged with reformer Oliver La Farge's National Association on Indian Affairs in 1937 to become the AAIA. According to author Jack Utter, "The AAIA works to perpetuate the well-being of Native people through efforts that (1) help sustain cultures and languages, (2) protect sovereign, constitutional, legal, religious, and human rights, (3) protect natural resources, and (4) improve health, education, and economic and community development."

See also Collier, John.

Reference Utter, Jack, *American Indians: Answers to Today's Questions* (1993).

Atkins, John DeWitt Clinton (1824–1908)

The twenty-second commissioner of Indian Affairs, John D. C. Atkins oversaw the Indian Office during the most productive period in its history, including the expansion of Indian education programs and the passage of the General Allotment Act of 1887. Little is known of his life; he was born on 4 June 1824, near Manly's Chapel, Tennessee, attended East Tennessee University, and graduated in 1846. He studied the law and was enlisted into the Tennessee bar, but there is no evidence that he ever practiced the law. After a period of farming, he won election to the lower house of the Tennessee state legislature, and six years later to a seat in the state senate. In 1857, he was elected to the U.S. House of Representatives. A secessionist, he enlisted as a general in the Confederate army, but there is no record of his service. Instead, he later took a seat representing his home state in the Confederate Congress. Eight years after the end of the Civil War, he was elected again to the U.S. House of Representatives, where he served (1873–1885) until chosen to head the Indian Office, at one point serving as chairman of the Appropriations Committee.

When President Grover Cleveland chose Atkins, as well as Atkins's superior, Secretary of the Interior Lucius Quintus Cincinnatus Lamar, he was naming the first southerners to hold executive branch positions since the end of the Civil War. Atkins would ultimately serve from March 1885 to June 1888. In those three years, he argued that the Five Civilized Tribes of Oklahoma be "absorbed" into white society as soon as possible, maintained that English be mandatory in Indian schools, requested additional appropriations for the expansion of Indian educational facilities, and directed the first policy directives under the General Allotment Act of 1887. Atkins's annual report as Indian commissioner for 1886, the second of his three reports, directed his shining comments on his administration to Secretary of the Interior Lucius Quintus Cincinnatus Lamar. "It is with pleasure that you, and through you Congress and the American people, are invited to mark the unmistakable evidences of progress made by many of the tribes within the last twelve months," Atkins wrote. "These evidences are apparent from several standpoints. The excellent temper, subordination, and general tranquillity which, with two or three exceptions, have everywhere prevailed among the Red Men under the charge of the Indian Bureau are of themselves a most auspicious omen of progress. The active inquiry among many of the tribes for further knowledge of the arts of agriculture; the growing desire to take lands in severalty; the urgent demand for agricultural implements with modern improvements; the largely increased acreage which the Indians have put to tillage, exceeding that of any preceding year; the unprecedented increase in the number of Indian children who have been enrolled in the schools—these and many other facts fully establish the claim that during the past year the Indian race has taken a firmer step and a grander stride in the great march toward civilization than ever before in the same length of time." In his discourse for 1887, Atkins composed, "My third annual report, which is hereby submitted, gives substantial evidence of continued progress on the part of the Indians toward civilization. This is gratifying to every American patriot and to the humanitarian of any clime or country. The progress shows itself all along the line, in increased knowledge and experience as to the arts of agriculture, in enlarged facilities for stock-growing, in better buildings and better home appointments, and in the adoption of the dress and customs of the white man. Even higher evidence of progress is given in the largely increased attendance of pupils at school, which has been greater during the past year than during any proceeding year, and in the still more gratifying fact, admitted by all intelligent and close observers of Indians, that the parents desire that their children shall avail themselves of the generous opportunities for education afforded by the Government, and by kind-hearted Christian missionaries who unselfishly devote time, labor, and money to the education of Indian youth." However, he added, in discussing the ramifications of the General Allotment Act, "There is danger that the advocates of land in severalty will expect from the measure too immediate and pronounced success. Character, habits, and antecedents can not be changed by an enactment…Thus the real work yet remains to be done and can be accomplished only by persistent personal effort. In fact, the allotment act instead of being the consummation of the labors of missionaries, philanthropists, and Government agents, is rather an introduction and invitation to effort on their part, which by the fact of this new legislation may be hopeful and should be energetic."

On 14 June 1888, Atkins resigned as Indian commissioner to seek a U.S. Senate seat, but when he failed to gain the Democratic nomination, he returned to his farm. The *New York Times*, in its 27 September 1888 edition, wrote of John H. Oberly and the man he replaced, Atkins: "The latter resigned some time ago in order to devote himself to the task of defeating Senator Isham G. Harris in the race for a seat in the Senate from Tennessee." In 1898, he moved to Paris, Tennessee, where he died on 2 June 1908, two days shy of his eighty-sixth birthday.

See also Bureau of Indian Affairs.

References "Mr. Oberly Transferred." *New York Times* (27 September 1888); "Pearson and His Office." *New York Times* (20 March 1885); Prucha, Francis Paul, ed., *Documents of United States Indian Policy* (1990); Thompson, Gregory C., "John D. C. Atkins." In Robert M. Kvasnicka and Herman J. Viola, eds., *The Commissioners of Indian Affairs, 1824–1977* (1979); U.S. Congress, House of Representatives, *Annual Report of the Commissioner of Indian Affairs for the Year 1886*, House Executive Document No. 1, 49th Congress, 1st Session (serial 2467); U.S. Congress, House of Representatives, *Annual Report of the Commissioner of Indian Affairs for the Year 1887*, House Executive Document No. 1, 50th Congress, 1st Session (serial 2542).

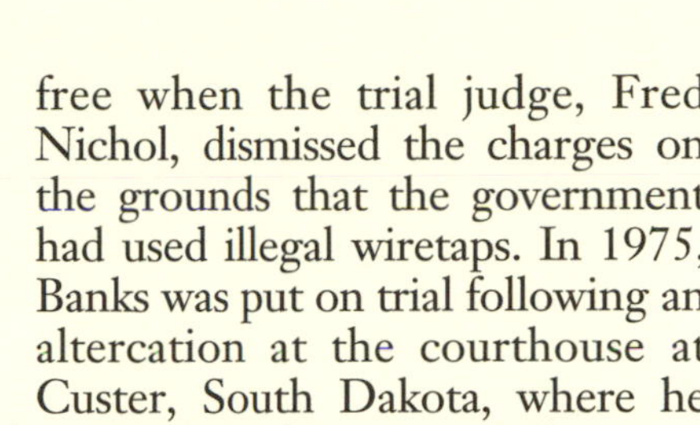

Banks, Dennis J. (Anishinabe Ojibwa) (1930–)
One of the best-known Indian activists of the late twentieth century, Dennis Banks, whose Indian name is *Nowa-cumig*, was a cofounder of the American Indian Movement. He was born on 12 April 1930 (some sources gave the date as 1937) on the Leech Lake Reservation in northern Minnesota. He was taken from his home when only five years old and sent to the Pipestone Indian School, a Bureau of Indian Affairs boarding institution. In 1953, after going to other BIA schools, he enlisted in the U.S. Air Force and served in Korea and Japan. After his return home he became a drifter and spent some time in prison for check forgery and burglary. When he was released in 1968, he became associated with several activists, including George Mitchell, Russell Means, and Clyde and Vernon Bellecourt, all of whom despised the government's treatment of their people and desired radical action to change the situation. While in Minneapolis, the men founded the Concerned Indian American Coalition (CIAC), but they soon changed the name because it contained the letters *CIA*. Now the group was called the American Indian Movement. One of Banks's first activities was to join a group of organized Indians to occupy Alcatraz Island in November 1969; later, he helped to organize the Trail of Broken Treaties, which led to the seizure of the Bureau of Indian Affairs office in Washington, D.C. Yet his most enduring action was as a member of the party that occupied a church and trading post at Wounded Knee, on the Pine Ridge Reservation in Nebraska, in 1973. Peter Matthiessen, in his *In The Spirit of Crazy Horse*, writes of him, "A handsome man with an intense, brooding expression, Banks was quickly established as the most thoughtful and articulate leader in the new Movement."

With the end of the crisis, Banks and fellow AIM member Means stood trial for their part in the Wounded Knee occupation; defended by radical attorneys William Kunstler and Mark Lane, the men were set free when the trial judge, Fred Nichol, dismissed the charges on the grounds that the government had used illegal wiretaps. In 1975, Banks was put on trial following an altercation at the courthouse at Custer, South Dakota, where he and other AIM members protested a manslaughter charge against a white man accused of killing an Indian activist, Wesley Bad Heart Bull. After Banks accused South Dakota assistant attorney general William Janklow of sexual misconduct, Janklow targeted Banks for prosecution; found guilty, Banks fled the jurisdiction to avoid going to prison. For several years he hid in California and that state's governor, Jerry Brown, refused to extradite him. During this time, Banks taught at Deganawidah-Quetzalcoatl University, a minority college at Davis, California. When Brown left office, Banks fled to the Onondaga Reservation in New York. In 1984, he finally surrendered and served one year of a three-year sentence. Having battled alcohol when he was younger, he became an alcoholism counselor, an anti-drug use advocate, and promoter of increased employment on reservations. Continuing to advance Native American rights, he established the Sacred Run program in 1991 to reinvigorate traditional foot races among Indian peoples. His autobiography, *Sacred Soul*, was published in 1988.

See also American Indian Movement; Means, Russell Charles; Wounded Knee (1973).

References Matthiessen, Peter, *In the Spirit of Crazy Horse* (1991); Rosenberg, Ruth, "Dennis J. Banks." In Sharon Malinowski, ed., *Notable Native Americans* (1995); Wilson, Raymond, "Dennis Banks." In David DeLeon, ed., *Leaders from the 1960s: A Biographical Sourcebook of American Activism* (1994).

Baraga, Father Frederic (1797–1868)
A Catholic missionary who published the first works for Indians in the Ojibwa, or Chippewa, language, the name of Frederic Baraga lives on in the remembrance of his missionary work among the Indians of the

American Indian Movement leader Dennis J. Banks waits at the Pine Ridge Indian Reservation in March 1973 to negotiate with federal government officials during the American Indian Movement's occupation of Wounded Knee.

Great Lakes region. He was born on 29 June 1797 at the castle called Malavas, near Döbernig, Austria, the son of Johann Nepomuc Baraga and Maria Katharin Josefa (née Jencic) Baraga, both of Slovenian (Balkan) heritage. Educated by a private tutor and at a gymnasium (then the name for a semi-private school of higher learning) in Laibach, he enrolled at the University of Vienna, which bestowed upon him a law degree in 1821. At that time, he entered the church, and studied at the seminary at Laibach. For seven years after being ordained in 1823, he served several parishes in his native land. In 1830, the Leopoldine Society, a group which offered missionaries tours of foreign lands, was established, and Baraga volunteered to be sent to the United States to live among the American Indians. He first settled among the Ottawa people near Arbe Croche (now Harbor Springs, Michigan), but within five years he came across the Chippewas of Michigan and Wisconsin, and it was here that he found his life's calling. In 1843, he founded the L'Anse Mission at L'Anse at the foot of Keweenaw Bay, and ten years later was made bishop and vicar-apostolic of Upper Michigan. Beginning in 1850, he composed two works on the Ojibwa dialect: *Practical and Theoretical Grammar of the Otchipewe Language* (1850), and *Dictionary of the Otchipewe Language* (1853). His other works appeared in 1900 under the title *Life and Letters of Rt. Rev. Frederic Baraga, First Bishop of Marquette.* Baraga moved his bishopric to Marquette, Michigan (now Wisconsin) in 1865 and built a cathedral there. Two and half years later, on 19 January 1868, he died and was buried on the grounds of the cathedral. He had given the last 30 years of his life to the Indians and for his work steps have recently been taken by the Catholic Church toward his canonization.

References Kerby, William Joseph, "Baraga, Frederic." In Dumas Malone et al., eds., *Dictionary of American Biography* (1930–88); Waldman, Carl, *Who Was Who in Native American History: Indians and Non-Indians from Early Contacts through 1900 (1990).*

Barker v. Harvey (181 U.S. 481 [1901])

Officially titled *Allejandro Barker, Baleriana Barker, Angela Barker et al., Plaintiffs in Error, v. J. Downey Harvey, Administrator of the Estate of John G. Downey, Deceased, and the Merchants' Exchange Bank of San Francisco,* this Supreme Court case dealt with the narrow matter of whether Mission Indians, owning title to lands ceded by Mexico to the United States, could claim those same lands as theirs after the lands have been claimed by another. A companion case, *Jesus Quevas, Sometimes Called Jesus Cuevo et al., Plaintiffs in Error, v. J. Downey Harvey, Administrator of the Estate of John G. Downey, Deceased,* was heard by the court at the same time. The plaintiffs, Mission Indians who claimed lands in California as their native land, sued the estate of John G. Harvey, who had been awarded the title of the lands by the state of California after statehood. The California Supreme Court decided for the estate of Harvey; the plaintiffs sued to the U.S. Supreme Court. The case was argued before the high court on 20 and 21 March 1901, and decided on 13 May of that same year. Writing for the eight-member court (Justice Edward Douglass White did not participate), Justice David Josiah Brewer held that the Indians had no title to the land. He wrote that "Mission Indians claiming a right of permanent occupancy of land in California under a Mexican grant are within the provisions of the act of Congress of 3 March 1851, requiring every person claiming lands in California by virtue of any right or title derived from Spanish or Mexican government to present the same to commissioners, and their failure to do so within the two years limited for that purpose by [section] 13 [of the 1851 act] constitutes an abandonment of their rights."

Bates v. Clark (95 U.S. 207 [1877])

Another in the long line of cases dealing with issue of the sale of intoxicating liquors in Indian country, *Bates* upheld that the definition of such country must be strictly determined. W.N. Belmont Clark owned, with an unnamed plaintiff, a mercantile business on the James River in the Dakota Territory. Captain John C. Bates, and an unnamed lieutenant who was just below Bates in rank, entered Clark's place of business, charged him with selling intoxicating liquors in Indian country, and seized a lot of whiskey. Clark and his partner sued to get the lot of whiskey returned. After it was, Clark continued his lawsuit to recover damages. The Supreme Court for the Dakota Territory found for Clark, and Bates sued to the U.S. Supreme Court. General John B. Sanborn, who had served as a member of the Indian Peace Commission ten years before this case came before the Supreme Court, served as counsel for defendants in error Clark et al. The case was submitted to the court on 15 November, and a decision was handed down on 3 December of that same year. Justice Samuel Freeman Miller, writing for a unanimous court, held that because the area where Clark had his business was not legally considered Indian country, as the Indians had extinguished title to it, Bates had no authority to seize the whiskey and was thus liable for damages. As Justice Miller opined, "It follows from this that all the country described by the Act of 1834 [the Trade and Intercourse Act of 1834] as Indian country remains Indian country so long as the Indians retain their original title to the soil, and ceases to be Indian country whenever they lose that title, in the absence of any different provision or by Act of Congress. The plaintiffs below [Clark et al.] violated no law in having the whiskey for sale at the place where it was seized; and the 20th section of the Act of 1834, as amended by the Act of 1864, conferred no authority whatever on the defendants to seize the property." In 1913 and 1914, the U.S. Supreme Court handed down three decisions which clarified its ruling in *Bates*. These cases were *Donnelly v. United States*, *United States v. Sandoval*, and *United States v. Pelican*.

See also *Donnelly v. United States; United States v. Sandoval.*

Beecher v. Wetherby et al. (95 U.S. 523 [1877])

Officially titled *Fanny Beecher, Executrix of Laban S. Beecher, Deceased, Plaintiff in Error, v. David Wetherby et al.*, the Supreme Court used this case to hold that the only right Indians had to their native lands was the right of occupancy, and that the government had the right to sell those lands at any time. Fanny Beecher served as the executrix of the estate of Laban S. Beecher in this case. (It may be assumed that Laban was Fanny's husband, but the case does not address the relationship.) David Wetherby received a patent in 1870 from the state of Wisconsin for some land that had belonged to the Menominee Indians in Wisconsin but had been given to the state by the government. Two years later, the federal government sold Laban Beecher a patent for the same plot of land that Wetherby had been sold. In 1873, Wetherby cut and sold two million feet of pine logs from the land and pocketed $25,000. Beecher sued him to recover the funds, claiming that only the federal government could sell former Indian lands. The Circuit Court for the Eastern District of Wisconsin found for Wetherby. Fanny Beecher, acting on behalf of the estate of Laban Beecher, sued to the U.S. Supreme Court. The Court heard arguments in the case on 7 November 1877 and handed down a decision a mere 12 days later, on 19 November. Speaking for a unanimous court, Justice Stephen Johnson Field held for defendant Wetherby. "The right which the Indians held was only that of occupancy," explained Justice Field. "The fee was in the United States, subject to that right, and could be transferred by them whenever they chose. The grantee, it is true, would only take the naked fee, and could not disturb the occupancy of the Indians; that occupancy could only be interfered with or determined by the United States. It is to be presumed that in this matter the United States would be governed by such considerations of justice as would control a Christian people in their treatment of an ignorant and dependent race. Be that as it may, the propriety or justice of their action towards the Indians with respect to their lands is a question of governmental policy, and is not a matter open to discussion in a controversy between third parties, neither of whom derives title from the Indians. The right of the United States to dispose of the fee of lands occupied by them has always been recognized by this court from the formulation of the government…It follows that the plaintiff acquired no title by his patents, to the land in question and, of course, no property in the timber cut from it. Judgment affirmed."

Bennett, Robert LaFollette (Oneida) (1912–)

In 1966, Robert L. Bennett became the first Native American to be named commissioner of Indian Affairs since Ely S. Parker served in that position from 1869 to 1871. A lawyer and administrator of some note, he was born on the Oneida Reservation near Green Bay, Wisconsin, on 16 November 1912, on the farm owned by his father, a Pennsylvania Dutch farmer; his mother was a full-blooded Oneida who named her son after the powerful Wisconsin politician Robert LaFollette. Although he spent his early years on the Oneida Reservation, he never learned to speak the language of his people. "I have known the pangs of trying to live in two worlds, understanding one with my heart, the other with my head," he said in a 1967 interview soon after becoming commissioner. He attended public and parochial schools before enrolling at the Haskell Institute, an Indian school in Lawrence, Kansas, from which he earned an associate's degree in business administration in 1931. He worked as a clerk during the Depression for the Bureau of Indian Affairs office in Washington, D.C., and on the Navajo Reservation in Arizona and the Ute Reservation in Colorado. When he returned to Washington, he worked nights at the Southeastern School of Law to get his law degree, which he earned in 1941. After serving as an administrative assistant on the Navajo Reservation from 1941 to 1943, he joined the Marines, where he served with distinction.

For the next twenty years, Bennett worked in a series of positions with the Bureau of Indian Affairs, including superintendent of the Southern Ute and Ute Mountain Reservations in Colorado, and area director for the Juneau (Alaska) area Office. For his lifetime of work with his people, in 1962 he was awarded the Indian Achievement Award, and in 1966 the Outstanding American Indian Citizen Award. In that latter year, he was chosen to succeed anthropologist Philleo Nash as only the second Native American commissioner of Indian Affairs. On 27 April 1966, President Lyndon B. Johnson administered the oath of office to Bennett, while stating, "The time has come to put the first Americans first on our agenda…to begin work on the most comprehensive program for the advancement of the Indians that the Government of the United States has ever considered. I want it to be sound, realistic, progressive, venturesome, and farsighted…If you fulfill this charge, you will have the full power of the institution of the Presidency of the United States behind you." Bennett served at the height of the so-called "Red Power" movement, when Indians expressed an appreciation and reverence for their culture. In his first annual report, that for 1966 Bennett wrote, "When I accepted the post of Commissioner of Indian Affairs, I expressed faith and confidence in the Indian people, their abilities and capabilities, and my firm belief that great things can be accomplished if tribal and Federal officials pool their best thinking." He added, "There is a new social and political interest stirring among Indians. I believe it is a positive sign that they are determined to take their place in our society as fully participating Americans—without loss of all the values they have so long and vigilantly guarded. And I am certain that in the years ahead the Indian heritage of this country will come to be regarded as a national treasure. It should not be otherwise."

Ruth Rosenberg writes, "Bennett helped set up a coalition of all the federal groups who could render services to the Indian people, enlisted the Vice President

[Hubert H. Humphrey] in a National Council of Indian Opportunity, and sent messages to Congress. He worked to transfer self-governance to the tribes and fought Termination. Simultaneously he engaged in campaigns to preserve tribal culture and to convince the public of the competence of Native peoples to manage their own affairs as well as to prove themselves capable citizens." In his 1968 report, Bennett penned, "The Commissioner of Indian Affairs has espoused greater Indian involvement in decision-making and program execution and emphasized the concept that the reality facing young Indian people in Indian areas is: they must learn to live in two worlds so as not to become the victims of either or both."

Bennett served from 1966 until replaced by Louis Rooks Bruce, Jr. (Oglala Sioux/Mohawk) in August 1969. After leaving office, he helped found the American Indian Athletic Hall of Fame and served as director of the American Indian Law Center in Albuquerque, New Mexico, where he now resides.

See also Bureau of Indian Affairs.

References Ellis, Richard N., "Robert L. Bennett." In Robert M. Kvasnicka and Herman J. Viola, eds., *The Commissioners of Indian Affairs, 1824–1977* (1979); *Indian Affairs, 1966: A Progress Report from the Commissioner of Indian Affairs* (1968); *Indian Affairs, 1968: A Progress Report from the Commissioner of Indian Affairs* (1968); Rosenberg, Ruth, "Robert LaFollette Bennett." In Sharon Malinowski, ed., *Notable Native Americans* (1995).

Blackfeather v. United States (190 U.S. 368 [1903])

This Supreme Court case was settled on the narrow issue of whether the Court of Claims, sitting in judgment of Indian claims on their lands, could set an amount of compensation to a single Indian tribe. Johnson Blackfeather, principal chief of the Shawnee tribe, was unhappy that the Court of Claims refused to set a amount for reimbursement over lands and other articles that the tribe claimed were taken by the U.S. government. Blackfeather then sued the government for $530,945.14. The Court of Claims requested that the U.S. Supreme Court review the case and decided whether it had the appropriate jurisdiction to hear the Shawnee claims to hand out monetary awards. The Supreme Court heard the case on 28 April 1903 and handed down a decision on 1 June of the same year. Writing for a unanimous court, Justice Rufus Wheeler Peckham held that under two federal acts that allowed the Court of Claims to hear cases involving the Shawnees, Congress made no provision for that tribunal to hand out monetary awards.

See also *United States v. Blackfeather.*

Bland, Thomas Augustus (1830–1906?)

White Indian reformer, and founder of the National Indian Defense Association and cofounder of its national organ, the *Council Fire,* Thomas Bland remains little known even among those in the Indian reform movement. According to his autobiography, a 1906 privately printed work entitled *Pioneers of Progress,* as well as a recent biography of reformer Alfred Meacham, Bland was born in 1830 in Orange County, Indiana, to parents who belonged to a radical North Carolina Quaker community. His only education seems to have been eight years in a log cabin school and the study of medicine, from which he earned his medical degree. He served as a surgeon in the Union Army during the Civil War. In the years after the war Bland and his wife Cora founded a series of farming journals, including *The Northwestern* and *The Home Visitor.* In addition, he published the first of many works, *Farming as a Profession* (1870). He was also involved in the Greenback party, which ran candidates for president in 1892, 1896, and 1904, and the People's (Populist) party movement, which ran third-party candidates for president in 1872 and 1884. After being involved in Indian reform for many years, his last work, *Pioneers of Progress,* reflected his love of 32 "pioneers" of reform, including William Lloyd Garrison, Peter Cooper, Horace Greeley, Alfred Meacham, and, in many ways, Bland himself.

After Meacham was attacked and nearly fatally wounded in an attack by Modoc Indians in northern California in 1873, he met Bland, who took care of him and returned him to a semblance of good health. In 1877 he and Meacham founded the *Council Fire* (although the first issue bears the date of January 1878), which became in its time one of the leading journals of the white-led Indian reform movement. Among those asked to contribute to the publications were abolitionist Wendell Phillips, Samuel F. Tappan, and Bland himself. When Meacham succumbed to his wounds in 1882, Bland and his wife took control of the magazine, even subsidizing its costs. Three years later, Bland was instrumental in the establishment of the National Indian Defense Association (NIDA), which became, with the Women's National Indian Association and the Indian Rights Association, one of the most influential Native American reform organizations of the late nineteenth century. Historian Jo Behrens, in her study of the group, writes, "Another influential NIDA founder was Thomas A. Bland, editor of the *Council Fire*, a monthly journal that had waged war against Indian Office abuses since its initial publication by Alfred B. Meacham in 1878. Like most Americans, Bland had no quarrel with the methods used to incorporate foreign minorities into America's political process. Immigrants received voting privileges and could advance their standard of living to the extent their personal work ethic allowed, whether they chose an urban or rural area as their home. In Bland's view, however, America's Indians could not be absorbed in the same manner. This 'exceptional minority' who could not vote had to be acquainted gradually with Anglo-American concepts, especially that of private landownership, before they could be expected to become successful, capitalistic farmers."

Little is known of Bland's work outside NIDA; among his published works are *The Life of Alfred B. Meacham* (1883), *A Brief History of the Late Military Invasion of the Home of the Sioux* (1891), and *A History of the Sioux Agreement: Some Facts Which Should Not Be Forgotten* (1888).

See also Meacham, Alfred Benjamin; National Indian Defense Association.

References Behrens, Jo Lea Wetherilt, "In Defense of 'Poor Lo': National Indian Defense Association and *Council Fire's* Advocacy for Sioux Land Rights." *South Dakota History* 24 (3–4); Bland, Thomas Augustus, *Pioneers of Progress* (1906); Fritz, Henry E., *The Movement for Indian Assimilation, 1860–1890* (1963); Phinney, Edward Sterl, *Alfred B. Meacham: Promoter of Indian Reform* (Ph.D. dissertation, University of Oregon at Salem, 1963).

***Blanset v. Cardin* (256 U.S. 319 [1921])** Considered the leading case involving Indian heirship administration, *Blanset* upheld the right of the secretary of the interior to approve a will of an Indian women which conflicted with the laws of the state that her reservation was located in. The case is officially titled *Blanset v. Cardin, as Guardian of Daylight, a Minor, et al.* Appellant Blanset, a white man, was married to Fannie Crawfish Blanset, a member of the Quapaw tribe. In her will, she conveyed an allotment and all trust funds that the United States may hold in her name to defendants, who were her children and grandchildren from an earlier marriage. The assistant commissioner of Indian Affairs and the assistant secretary of the interior, as per law, approved the will and filed it in the office of the secretary of the interior. Congress, in a series of laws, made it clear that the secretary of the interior must approve all Indian wills; however, an Oklahoma statute voids such wills when a wife wills away more than three-fourths of her estate. Accordingly, if the will were followed, Blanset would get $5; if voided, he was eligible to inherit some $40,000 in allotments. Blanset sued in the District Court for the Eastern District of Oklahoma, which dismissed the suit; the U.S. Circuit Court for the Eighth Circuit upheld that ruling. Blanset appealed to the U.S. Supreme Court. After the case was argued on 20 April 1921, Justice Joseph McKenna held for a unanimous court on 16 May of that same year that such state laws were superseded by the will of Congress, and that Blanset had no standing. Justice McKenna wrote emphatically, "Our conclusion is the same as that of the Court of Appeals, 'that it was the intention of Congress that this class of Indians should have the right to dispose of property by will under this act of Congress, free from restrictions on the part of the state as to the portions to be conveyed...provided such wills are in accordance with the regulations and meet the approval of the Secretary of the Interior.'"

Board of Indian Commissioners
See United States Board of Indian Commissioners.

***Board of County Commissioners et al. v. Seber et al.* (318 U.S. 705, 87 L.Ed. 1094, 63 S.Ct. 920 [1943])**
In this Supreme Court case, the court found that "lands purchased with restricted funds derived from an oil and gas lease of restricted allotted lands of a Creek Indian" are held to be "immune from tax by Oklahoma." Prior to 1931, the secretary of the interior purchased for Wosey John Deere, a full-blooded member of the Creek Nation of Oklahoma, three tracts of land, utilizing funds from an oil and gas lease of her restricted allotment. Under the act of Congress of 20 June 1936 (49 Stat. 1542), as amended by the act of 19 May 1937 (50 Stat. 188), Indians with allotted lands subject to restrictions against alienation without the approval of the secretary of the interior were to be exempt from state taxes for the year 1937 and for years before that. Prior to the enactment of the 1936 act, these lands were subject to state taxes. In 1937, Deere conveyed her land, with the approval of the secretary of the interior, to respondents Seber et al. Respondents paid the state taxes on the land under protest, and in 1940 filed an action in the federal district court for the return of the taxes for 1936, 1937, 1938, and part of 1939, and to have the lands declared as homestead lands free of taxes until 1956. The district court held for Seber, the U.S. Court of Appeals for the Tenth Circuit affirmed, and the U.S. Supreme Court granted certiorari. After arguments were heard on 3 and 4 March 1943, Justice Frank Murphy delivered the court's unanimous opinion on 19 April 1943 in holding that the two pieces of legislation were constitutional and that the taxes must be returned to respondents. Justice Murphy noted:

The Acts of 1936 and 1937 are constitutional. From almost the beginning, the existence of federal power to regulate and protect the Indians and their property against interference even by a state has been recognized.... This power is not expressly granted in so many words by the Constitution, except with respect to regulating commerce with the Indian tribes, but its existence cannot be doubted. In the exercise of the war and treaty powers, the United States overcame the Indians and took possession of their lands, sometimes by force, leaving them an uneducated, helpless and dependent people, needing protection against the selfishness of others and their own improvidence. Of necessity, the United States assumed the duty of furnishing that protection, and with it the authority to do all that was required to perform that obligation and to prepare the Indians to take their place as independent, qualified members of the modern body politic.

Bogy, Lewis Vital (1813–1877)
The fourteenth commissioner of Indian Affairs, later a U.S. senator from his home state of Missouri, Lewis Vital Bogy served about four months as Indian commissioner and engraved but little imprint on that post. He was born Vital Bogy in Sainte Genevieve, Missouri Territory, approximately 40 miles south of St. Louis along the Mississippi River, on 9 April 1813, the son and one of 11 children (of whom 5 survived to adulthood) of Joseph Bogy and Marie (née Sainte Gemme Beauvais) Bogy. Of Joseph Bogy (1786–1842), the son of Charles Baugis, a French emigré, biographer William E. Unrau writes, "Joseph Bogy served as a secretary to Intendant Juan Ventura Morales during the Spanish occupation of Louisiana, and following the American purchase of this vast area from France in 1803, moved from Kankaskia [Illinois] to Sainte Genevieve, where he soon emerged

as a commanding figure in local political and economic affairs. It was here also that he married Marie Beauvais," of French-Canadian background. According to family genealogies, Vital Bogy added a new first name while in his youth. "'Lewis was a name he took from Dr. Lewis F. Linn with whom he read law thinking that going into the English speaking world and possibly among people who had no knowledge of the French language, they would pronounce the name as in English." Bogy attended a local rural school before entering a Catholic school in Perryville, Missouri. After an illness which left him bedridden for eighteen months, he took up the study of Latin and the law. He interrupted his studies in 1832 to enlist as a private in the American army to fight in the Black Hawk War, an Indian engagement. Afterwards, he read the law in several offices of esteemed attorneys, and attended the law school at Transylvania University in Lexington, Kentucky, from which he earned a degree in 1835.

In the 1840s and 1850s, Bogy served as an alderman in St. Louis and in the lower house of the Missouri legislature. With the onset of the Civil War, he took the side of the Confederacy, and refused at the end of the war to take the loyalty oath to the United States. In 1862 he was defeated for a seat in Congress by Francis Preston Blair, Jr., scion of a popular Missouri family and himself a Lincoln Republican (he later became a Democrat and was his party's vice presidential candidate in 1868). Bogy made himself more unpopular among the people of his state when he loudly spoke out against the Radical Republicans and their program to grant blacks the right to vote, and called for the establishment of a national committee to support President Andrew Johnson's veto of the Freedman's Bill. When Orville Hickman Browning was named secretary of the interior in 1866, Johnson needed a man who was sympathetic to his agenda to fill the post of Commissioner of Indian Affairs, left empty when Lincoln appointee Dennis Nelson Cooley resigned. On 8 October 1866, Johnson informed Bogy that he was appointing him to the position. Congressional opponents of Bogy, however, soon held up confirmation, and Bogy served as a recess appointment. In his short time on the job, Bogy insisted that the Indian Bureau be removed to the War Department; the release of the report of the special Senate committee under the leadership of Senator James R. Doolittle in January 1867, which recommended that Indian affairs remain in the Department of the Interior, made Bogy more unpopular on Capitol Hill. Indian historian Robert M. Utley writes, "Both Secretary of the Interior Orville H. Browning and Commissioner of Indian Affairs Lewis V. Bogy favored sending out peace emissaries to restore harmonious relations and gather data to support a comprehensive program for assembling all western tribes on reservations. On this and other issues the army and the Indian Bureau feuded openly during the winter of 1866–67. Much of the contention centered on whether licensed traders should be allowed to sell arms and ammunition to peaceful Indians. Secretary Browning and Commissioner Bogy contended that they were necessary for hunting purposes. The army, aware that the Indians had got along fairly well with bows and arrows for generations, vigorously condemned such sales." After the army banned the arms sales, adds Utley, "Both Browning and Bogy regarded this prohibition as the chief cause of Indian hostility and the army's intervention not only uncalled for but unlawful. Bogy complained that his greatest burden was 'the constant interference on the part of the military with all Indian affairs.'" On 12 March 1867, the Senate refused to confirm Bogy, and while he fought with the Republicans, calling the refutation a political move, he was soon removed from the office when Nathaniel Green Taylor was confirmed on 29 March. Unrepentant, on 12 July 1867, Bogy wrote to Acting Secretary of the Interior W.T. Otto concerning information that the U.S. Senate requested about Indian depredations and hostilities on the frontier. In his letter, Bogy wrote, "In my judgment, the Indians can only be saved from extinction by consolidating them as rapidly as it can be peacefully done, on large reservations, from which all whites except government employees shall be excluded, and educating them intellectually and morally, and training them in the arts of civilization, so as to render them at the earliest practicable moment self-supporting, and at the proper time to clothe them with the rights and immunities of citizenship."

Bogy returned to St. Louis, where he remained influential in local politics there. In 1870 he briefly flirted with Horace Greeley's Liberal Republican movement, but soon returned to the Democratic party. Three years later, he won the U.S. Senate seat held ironically by Francis P. Blair, Jr., but Bogy's time in the Senate was without distinction, and he died in office in the fifth year of his term on 20 September 1877 at the age of 64.

See also Bureau of Indian Affairs.

References "History of Joseph Bogy's Family." Bogy Family Papers, Box 1, Genealogy Folder, Missouri Historical Society, St. Louis; *Letter of the Secretary of the Interior [W. T. Otto], Communicating, in Compliance with a Resolution of the Senate of the 8th Instant, Information Touching the Origins and Progress of Indian Hostilities on the Frontier*, Senate Executive Document No. 13, 40th Congress, 1st Session, 1867; Stevens, Walter B., *St. Louis: History of the Fourth City, 1763–1909* (1909); Unrau, William E., "Lewis Vital Bogy." In Robert M. Kvasnicka and Herman J. Viola, eds., *The Commissioners of Indian Affairs, 1824–1977* (1979); Utley, Robert M., *Frontier Regulars: The United States Army and the Indian, 1866–1891* (1973).

Boldt Decision

***See** United States v. Washington.*

Bonney, Mary Lucinda

See Rambaut, Mary Lucinda Bonney.

Bonnin, Gertrude Simmons (Yankton Sioux) (1876–1938)

Her Indian name was Zitkala-Sa ("Red Bird"); she was a Yankton writer and educator, as well as a noted activist in the early twentieth century. Yet little is known of Gertrude Simmons Bonnin's early life. She was probably born on 22 February 1876 at the Yankton Sioux Agency in South Dakota. According to historian Gail J. Hardy, she was born "to Ellen Tate'Iyohinwin Simmons ["Reaches for the Wind"], a full-blood Sioux. Details regarding her father are sketchy, but it is possible that he was a white man named Felker who deserted Ellen before Gertrude's birth. Her mother named the child Simmons after her second husband, John Haysting Simmons; Gertrude took the name *Zitkala-Sa* later. Her mother had two other children: David Simmons, almost ten years older than Gertrude, and Peter St. Pierre, by her first marriage, about three years older." Mary E. Young, another Simmons biographer, adds that while Gertrude represented herself as the granddaughter of Sitting Bull, "tribal census rolls indicate that her mother was older than Sitting Bull." Ellen Simmons's hatred of whites increased, sources report, after Gertrude's abusive father left the family home.

Gertrude describes her childhood in her superb autobiography, *American Indian Stories* (1921). She was taken from her mother at age eight by Quakers and sent to their missionary school, White's Manual Labor Institute in Wabash, Indiana, which her older brother David had earlier attended. She left after just three years and went to the Santee Normal Training School in Nebraska, but later returned to White's to earn her diploma. Against her mother's wishes, Gertrude then attended graduate school at Earlham College in Richmond, Indiana. She later taught at the Carlisle Indian School, a missionary school for Indians in Pennsylvania. Her musical talent (which allowed her to travel with Carlisle students to the Paris Exposition of 1900 as a violin soloist) gave way to literary skill, which she demonstrated in two short articles, "Impressions of an Indian Childhood" and "Indian Teacher Among Indians," both of which appeared in *The Atlantic Monthly* magazine in January and March 1900, respectively, under the name Zitkala-Sa. Finally, her first published work, *Old Indian Legends*, which was illustrated by Indian artist Angel de Cora, was printed in 1901. On

Activist, writer, and suffragist Gertrude Simmons Bonnin, a Yankton Nakota, attends the February 1921 National Women's Party convention in Washington, D.C.

her return to the Yankton reservation in 1901, Gertrude met Raymond Talesfase Bonnin, a Nakota Sioux who worked for the Indian Bureau. They were married the following year and had one child, a son named Raymond Ohiya *(Winner* in the Nakota dialect) Bonnin.

The Bonnins moved to the Uintah and Ouray Reservation in Utah, where Gertrude worked as a clerk and teacher. In 1911, one of her close friends, Dr. Carlos Montezuma, was one of the founding members of the Society of American Indians, the first pan-Indian rights organization. Gertrude Bonnin's close relationship with Montezuma led her to be named as the society's secretary in 1916. From her home in Washington, D.C. (Raymond Bonnin was a U.S. Army captain during World War I), she served as editor of the society's periodical, *American Indian Magazine.* She was also instrumental in persuading the General Federation of Women's Clubs to establish an Indian Welfare Committee and she worked for the creation of the Meriam Commission, which released a report in 1928 criticizing the government's handling of Indian affairs. She traveled to Indian reservations asking them to support the Indian Citizenship Act of 1924 and helped found the National Council of American Indians in 1926. Her exposé of fraud by Oklahoma state courts led her to coauthor *Oklahoma's Poor Rich Indians: An Orgy of Graft and Exploitation* with Charles H. Fabens and Matthew K. Sniffen, which was published by the Indian Rights Association in 1924. She was also an outspoken advocate on behalf of Indian health programs. In testimony before Congress in 1927, Bonnin said, "As president of the National Council of American Indians, I have the honor to ask that [Utah] Senator [William Henry] King's resolution be adopted, and that a committee be appointed there under to investigate Indian affairs generally, with respect to their health, living conditions, education, property, and care of the poor and indigent Indians."

In the last decade of her life, Gertrude Bonnin worked to elect Franklin D. Roosevelt for president in 1932, but soon thereafter became sharply critical of the so-called "Indian New Deal" of Commissioner of Indian Affairs John Collier because of her changing thinking about assimilation. Suffering from renal failure, she died at her home in Washington, D.C., on 26 January 1938, just a month short of her sixty-second birthday, and was buried in Arlington National Cemetery.

See also Montezuma, Carlos; Society of American Indians.

References Bonnin, Gertrude Simmons, *American Indian Stories* (1921); Bonnin, Gertrude Simmons, *Old Indian Legends* (1901); Fenichell, Lois F., "Bonnin, Gertrude Simmons." In Alden Whitman, ed., *American Reformers: An H. W. Wilson Biographical Dictionary* (1985); Fisher, Alice Poindexter, *The Transformation of Tradition: A Study of Zitkala Sa and Mourning Dove, Two Traditional American Indian Writers* (Ph.D. dissertation, City University of New York, 1979); Hardy, Gail J., *American Women Civil Rights Activists: Biobibliographies of 68 Leaders, 1825–1992* (1993); "Mrs. Bonnin, Sitting Bull Kin, Is Dead at 62." *Washington Post,* 27 January 1938; U.S. Congress, Senate, *Survey of Conditions of the Indians in the United States: Hearing before a Subcommittee of the Committee on Indian Affairs Pursuant to S. Res. 341, a Resolution Providing for a General Survey of the Conditions of the Indians in the United States, and for Other Purposes* (1927); Welburn, Ron, "Bonnin, Gertrude Simmons." In Sharon Malinowski, ed., *Notable Native Americans* (1995); Welch, Deborah Sue, *Zitkala-Sa: An American Indian Leader, 1876–1938* (Ph.D. dissertation, University of Wyoming, 1985); Young, Mary E., "Bonnin, Gertrude Simmons." In Edward T. James, ed., *Notable American Women, 1607–1950: A Biographical Dictionary* (1971).

Bowen et al. v. Roy et al. (476 U.S. 693, 90 L.Ed. 2d 735, 106 S.Ct. 2147 [1986])

The use of Indians' social security numbers by the government to administer food stamps and other benefits does not violate Indians' right to the free exercise of religion, the Supreme Court found in this 1986 decision. Stephen J. Roy, an Abenaki Indian, and Karen Miller were recipients of food stamps and AFDC (Aid to Families with Dependent Children) in the state of Pennsylvania. The two protested when their daughter, Little Bird of the Snow, was notified that she would be forced to get a social security number in order to receive benefits as well. When Roy and Miller refused to have a number assigned to their daughter, claiming that such an act would "rob their daughter of her spirit," the state cut off benefits to the daughter and sought to reduce the family's overall benefits. Roy and Miller then sued Otis Bowen, the secretary of health and human services, as well as the secretary of the Pennsylvania Department of Public Welfare and the secretary of agriculture. In trial in the District Court for the Middle District of Pennsylvania, Roy was forced to admit that he and his wife, as well as their older daughter, Renee, had social security numbers, but that his daughter's spirit would be robbed even by obtaining a number. During the trial, the government admitted that it had already assigned a number in the name of Little Bird of the Snow Roy and claimed that the issue was moot. At this point, Roy claimed that the *use* of the number as well would harm his daughter, and continued his litigation. The district court refused Roy and Miller relief as to their daughter's case (they wanted damages for her), but enjoined the state from cutting off other benefits and from using Little Bird of the Snow's social security number. On direct appeal to the U.S. Supreme Court, the court vacated the judgment and returned the case for further hearings. Expressing the opinion of eight of the justices, some of whom concurred in part and some of whom dissented in part (Justice Byron White was the only justice to entirely dissent), Chief Justice Warren Burger allowed for the use of the social security number on the grounds that to receive benefits such utilization was required by statutory authority, and held that the use of social security numbers did not violate the appellants' free exercise of religion as guaranteed by the U.S. Constitution. Justice Harry Blackmun concurred as to the first part of the decision, but dissented as to whether the rest of the decision should be vacated as well as to damages. Chief Justice Burger explained,

The statutory requirement that applicants provide a Social Security number is wholly neutral in religious terms and uniformly applicable. There is no claim that there is any attempt by Congress to discriminate invidiously or any covert suppression of particular religious beliefs. The administrative requirement does not create any danger of censorship or place a direct condition or burden on the dissemination of religious views. It does not intrude on the organization of a religious institution or school. It may indeed confront some applicants for benefits with choices, but in no sense does it affirmatively compel applicants, by threat of sanctions, to refrain from religiously motivated conduct or to engage in conduct that they find objectionable for religious reasons. Rather, it is appellees who seek benefits from the Government and who assert that, because of certain religious beliefs, they should be excused from compliance with a condition that is binding on all other persons who seek the same benefits from the Government.

Bowling v. United States (233 U.S. 528 [1914])

"The guardianship of the Federal government over an Indian does not cease when an allotment is made and the allottee becomes a citizen of the United States," states the headnote of this Supreme Court case. Officially titled *George F. Bowling and Miami Investment Company, Appellants, v. United States*, it deals with whether a deceased Indian's heirs could convey an allotment. The heirs of Pe-te-lon-o-zah, also known as William Wea, a member of the confederated Wea, Peoria, Kaskaskia and Piankeshaw tribes of Oklahoma, conveyed Wea's allotment after his death, and after several deals it wound up in the hands of George F. Bowling and his enterprise, the Miami Investment Company. The U.S. government sued Bowling for the return of the allotment, claiming that the patent in the land, issued in 1890, was to be held in trust for Wea and his heirs for 25 years. Bowling argued that Wea's heirs did not sell the land directly to him, so he had not broken the law. The District Court for the Eastern District of Oklahoma set aside the conveyance to Bowling, and on appeal the U.S. Circuit Court for the Eighth Circuit upheld the lower court's decision. Bowling appealed to the U.S. Supreme Court. Submitted to the court on 17 April 1914, the case was decided on 4 May of that same year. Justice Charles Evans Hughes spoke for a unanimous court in holding that the United States had the authority to demand the return of a conveyance within the trust period established for an Indian's allotment. As Hughes pointedly stated, "The conveyance by Wea's heirs came directly within the statutory prohibition, and the later conveyance under which the appellants claim must fall with it. Affirmed."

Brader v. James (246 U.S. 88, 62 L.Ed. 591, 38 S.Ct. 121 [1918])

The question of whether the child of an Indian allottee could legally convey her land to another without the approval of the secretary of the interior was at issue in this case. Cerena Wallace, a full-blooded Choctaw Indian, died on 27 October 1905, leaving her allotment to her daughter, Rachel James, also a full-blood Choctaw. In 1907, James and her husband sold the allotment to J.H. Brader without the approval of the secretary of the interior. She then sued Brader for the return of the land, basing her suit on the fact that the secretary of the interior had to approve such sales. The district court agreed with James, and the Supreme Court of Oklahoma affirmed. The U.S. Supreme Court agreed to hear the case, and arguments were heard on 7 and 8 January 1918. Justice William Rufus Day held for a unanimous court on 4 March 1918 that the act of Congress of 26 April 1906 (34 Stat. 137) prohibited Indians from conveying land which they had inherited without the approval of the secretary of the interior. In discussing an earlier court's actions in such cases as *United States v. First National Bank* and *United States v. Waller*, Justice Day wrote, "Those decisions do not place limitations upon the right of Congress to deal with a tribal Indian whose relation of ward to the government still continues, and concerning whom Congress has not evidenced its intention to release its authority."

Brendale v. Confederated Tribes and Bands of the Yakima Indian Nation et al. (492 U.S. 408 [1989])

Decided together with *Wilkinson v. Confederated Tribes and Bands of the Yakima Indian Nation* and *County of Yakima et al. v. Confederated Tribes and Bands of the Yakima Indian Nation*, this Supreme Court case dealt with the issue of whether an Indian tribe can zone fee lands owned by nonmembers on its reservation. The Yakima Indian Nation reservation, mostly located inside Yakima County, Washington, has roughly 80 percent of the reservation held in trust by the United States, with the additional 20 percent owned by Indians and non-Indians. The reservation is divided into a "closed area," where the general public cannot go, and an "open area," which has fewer restrictions. Petitioners Philip Brendale, a mixed-blood Indian but not a member of the Yakima Nation, and Stanley Wilkinson, a non-Indian, owned land in the closed and open areas respectively. In 1982, Brendale, who had received his 160-acre tract as part of an allotment given to his aunt (herself a member of the Yakima Nation), went to the Yakima County government for permission to build on the land. The zoning, while it did meet with county regulations, conflicted with the tribe's, and an Environmental Impact Statement (EIS) was ordered. Wilkinson intended to divide his 40–acre plot into areas for homes; after the county government held that an EIS was not necessary, the Yakima Nation filed suit against both Brendale and Wilkinson to stop them from using their land. The district court held that the tribe had jurisdiction over Brendale's property but did not over Wilkinson's. On appeal, the U.S. Court of Appeals for the Ninth Circuit affirmed the lower court's ruling as to Brendale but reversed as to Wilkinson, holding that the tribe had the ultimate zoning authority. On appeal, the U.S. Supreme Court granted certiorari.

After arguments were heard on 10 January 1989, the court handed down its decision in all three cases (which included a challenge to the county's zoning authority from the tribe in which the county sided with Wilkinson but not Brendale) on 29 June of that same year. Several of the justices concurred with the court's result in one case but dissented in another. As to *Wilkinson*, Chief Justice William Rehnquist, and Justices Byron White, Antonin Scalia, Anthony Kennedy, John Paul Stevens, and Sandra Day O'Connor all held against the Yakima tribe (with justices Harry Blackmun, William Brennan and Thurgood Marshall dissenting); in *Brendale*, justices Stevens, O'Connor, Blackmun, Brennan, and Marshall all sided with the tribe (Chief Justice Rehnquist, and justices White, Scalia and Kennedy dissenting); and, as to *Yakima County*, Chief Justice Rehnquist, and justices White, Scalia, Kennedy, Stevens, and O'Connor all held for the county. The majority in *Wilkinson* held that "The Tribe [does not] derive authority from its inherent sovereignty to impose its zoning ordinance on petitioners' lands. Such sovereignty generally extends only to what is necessary to protect tribal self-government or to control internal relations, and is divested to the extent it is inconsistent with a tribe's dependent status—i.e., to the extent it involves the tribe's external relations with nonmembers—unless there has been an express congressional delegation of power to the contrary." The *Brendale* majority, in upholding the right of the tribe to regulate the zoning of Brendale's land, wrote, "The Tribe has the power to zone the Brendale property, which is in the reservation's closed area. Although the presence of logging operations, the construction of Bureau of Indian Affairs roads, and the transfer of ownership of a relatively insignificant amount of land in that area unquestionably have diminished the Tribe's power to exclude non-Indians from the area, this does not justify the conclusion that the Tribe has surrendered its historic right to regulate land use there. To the contrary, by maintaining the power to exclude nonmembers from entering all but a small portion of that area, the Tribe has preserved the power to define the area's essential character and has, in fact, exercised that power through its zoning ordinance."

British-American Oil Producing Company v. Board of Equalization of the State of Montana et al. (299 U.S. 159, 81 L.Ed. 95, 57 S.Ct. 132 [1936])

The question of whether Congress gave its explicit permission for state taxes to be instituted on the production of oil and gas under a lease on allotted Indian lands was at issue in this Supreme Court case. The state of Montana's Board of Equalization sought to impose a gross production tax and a net proceeds tax on the British-American Oil Producing Company, doing business on the Blackfeet Reservation in Montana. Under the act of Congress of 29 May 1924 (25 U.S.C. 398), the Congress established that "unallotted land on Indian reservations" be subject for leasing for the production of mining and oil resources upon the approval of the secretary of the interior, "provided, that the production of oil and gas and other minerals on such lands may be taxed by the State in which said lands are located in all respects the same as production on unrestricted lands." A district court held for the state, and the Supreme Court of Montana affirmed. On certiorari, the U.S. Supreme Court agreed to hear the case. Justice Willis Van Devanter spoke for a unanimous court (Justice Harlan Fiske Stone did not participate) on 7 December 1936 in holding that because Congress had created the Blackfeet Reservation (it was not established by an executive order, as were other reservations) and had passed the 30 June 1919 act that allowed "that the lands containing such materials may be leased under such rules and regulations and upon such terms and conditions as the Secretary of the Interior may prescribe," such regulations may include the taxation of the production of mineral resources. Justice Van Devanter noted, "We conclude that the lease was given under the special provision of the Act of June 30, 1919, taken in connection with the general provisions. The Act of May 29, 1924, is one of the general provisions, and in it Congress assents to taxation by the State of production of oil and gas through a lease given under its provisions." A rehearing of the case was denied on 4 January 1937 (299 U.S. 624, 57 S.Ct. 314).

Brophy, William Aloysius (1903–1962)

A transitional figure in the formulation of national Indian policy, William A. Brophy was sick for most of his term as the thirty-fourth commissioner of Indian Affairs and was replaced by William Zimmerman, Jr. Brophy was born in New York City on 7 February 1903. After attending public schools in New York and Chicago, he worked a series of jobs as a clerk in New York with the Norwegian-American shipping Line, then in Chicago as the Western Freight Manager for the line. In 1927, he left that company and went to New Mexico, where he entered the University of New Mexico. In 1931, he received a law degree from the University of Colorado. After being allowed to enter the bar in New Mexico, he took up a law practice in Albuquerque with the firm of Hanna & Wilson (later Hanna, Wilson, and Brophy), a partnership which dealt with the problems of the Pueblo Indians of New Mexico. From 1932 to 1933, Brophy was the assistant city attorney for that city, and after 1934 he served as the special U.S. attorney for the Pueblo Indians. In that capacity he argued two cases before the U.S. Supreme Court: *United States v. Santa Fe Railroad Company* (1941), and *Toledo v. Pueblo de Jemez* (1954).

In 1942, the secretary of the interior, Harold L. Ickes, requested the services of Brophy in Washington to help the Department of the Interior on Puerto Rican matters. Although he returned to Albuquerque, he was again asked by Secretary Ickes in 1943 to head the Puerto Rican section of the department's Division of Territories and Island Possessions. Less than a year and a half later, President Truman nominated Brophy to be the commissioner of Indian Affairs to replace John Collier. In his confirmation hearings, Brophy concurred that he would be comfortable with following congressional policymaking, and that a program of assimilation was the correct path. On 6 March 1945, the Senate approved Brophy as the thirty-fourth commissioner.

Brophy's stint as Indian commissioner was brief; he was the first of President Harry S Truman's three Indian commissioners (the others being John R. Nichols and Dillon S. Myer, both of whom had more of an impact on the office). Kenneth R. Philp writes, "After 1945, Secretary of the Interior Oscar L. Chapman, Indian Commissioner William A. Brophy...and other members of the Truman administration followed an assimilationist Indian policy mandated by Congress. There was bipartisan support in Congress for equal Indian citizenship, the abolition of the federal trust over Indian property, increased state responsibility for Indians to replace New Deal statism under the IRA [Indian Reorganization Act], and the rapid economic development of [the] western United States." Brophy oversaw the enactment of the landmark Indian Claims Commission Act (passed 13 August 1946) and the reorganization of the Bureau of Indian Affairs into five geographical districts (Billings, Minneapolis, Oklahoma City, Phoenix, and Portland). In his annual report for 1947, Brophy wrote, "The Bureau of Indian Affairs is charged with the responsibility of so administering the resources held in trust by the United States for Indian tribes and individuals that, through the development of these resources for effective use by the Indians, it may remove itself as trustee and withdraw the public services which it now provides for the Indian population."

Brophy was ill most of his term, and his duties were carried out by Assistant Commissioner William Zimmerman, Jr., who essentially oversaw day-to-day affairs. Zimmerman signed the 1948 annual report, in which he blasted the government's widespread program of issuing patents-in-fee to the Indians. "Having in mind the Indian record of increasing use of the land and its resources, it is disheartening to report that the demand for fee patents and the removal of restrictions against alienation has been greater during the past year than at any time in the past 15 years," he penned. "The present policy with respect to Indian-owned lands originated in the 1920s, following a brief period of forcing fee patents upon Indians, even when Indians expressed objection. The results of forced patenting were disastrous, in terms of land losses and subsequent impoverishment. This fact was pointed out in the Meriam Report, which found that 'a relatively small proportion of the Indians who have been declared competent to manage their own affairs have retained possession of their property.'" He added, "Unless the Nation is prepared to pauperize the Indian people, discretion must continue to be exercised in issuing patents-in-fee, and that discretion to be effective must be lodged in a responsible official."

In his letter of resignation, dated 31 December 1947, Brophy wrote to President Harry S Truman, "It is with deep regret that I am compelled to inform you that my health will not permit me to carry on fully the vigorous work that must be done by the Commissioner of Indian Affairs if the Indians are to be protected in their treaty, civil and property rights. I ask you, therefore, to relieve me of my duties." He added, "It has been gratifying and a great inspiration to me that in the midst of momentous world events you have not dismissed the Indian's problems as unimportant, but, on the other hand, have given them a large share of your attention." President Truman answered Brophy, "On March thirtieth Secretary [of the Interior Julius] Krug transmitted a letter of resignation as Commissioner of Indian Affairs which you submitted for health reasons. In the meantime, I am advised that you have improved to an extent that you now feel able to undertake employment that would be less taxing on your physical energies than the Commissionership, and that the Secretary proposes to assign you to a field position where your experience will be valuable. I would be reluctant to accept your resignation under other conditions since your administration of the Office of Indian Affairs has been marked by a spirit of humanity and a genuine interest in the progress of the Indians." At the end of the letter, the president added, "We need to make much further progress in our efforts to bring all the Indians to full participation in our national life, and I am glad that we shall still have available your advice and counsel."

In 1953, Congress enacted House Concurrent Resolution 108, which began the process of terminating the federal jurisdiction over Indian tribes. In response to this legislation, the Commission on the Rights, Liberties, and Responsibilities of the American Indian was created in 1957. O. Meredith Wilson, president of the University of Oregon (and later of the University of Minnesota) served as chairman, while Brophy was the executive director. The report notes that "in addition to serving as director of research, he also did research of striking insight and power himself, writing the chapter on tribal governments (Chapter Two), and the section on water rights in Chapter Seven." And although he resigned from the Commission in 1957 to become "the Indians' special legal consultant on Indian policy," Brophy did not live to see the report's completion. After a lifetime of ill health, he died on 24 March 1962. He was replaced on the commission by his wife, Dr. Sophie D. Aberle, and the commission's final report, *The Indian: America's Unfinished Business*, was released in 1966.

See also Bureau of Indian Affairs.

References "Annual Report of the Commissioner of the Bureau of Indian Affairs." *Annual Report of the Secretary of the Interior for 1947*, quoted in Rennard Strickland, ed., *Felix Cohen's Handbook of Federal Indian Law* (1982); *Annual Report of the Secretary of the Interior for 1948* (1948); Brophy to Harry S Truman, 31 December 1947, Harry S Truman Library, Independence, Missouri; Brophy, William A. and Sophie D. Aberle, *The Indian: America's Unfinished Business. Report of the Commission on the Rights, Liberties, and Responsibilities of the American Indian* (1966); Philp, Kenneth R., "Indian Policy." In Richard S. Kirkendall, ed., *The Harry S. Truman Encyclopedia* (1989); "[Resume of] William

A. Brophy," undated document, Papers of William A. Brophy, Harry S Truman Library, Independence, Missouri.

Brown, Orlando (1801–1867)

The fifth commissioner of Indian Affairs, Orlando Brown seemed to be unprepared for his office, and resigned less than a year after taking the position. A noted newspaper editor who served as secretary of state of Kentucky, Brown's short reign left him unknown outside of his native state. He was born in Frankfort, Kentucky, on 26 September 1801, the son of John Brown, who had been Kentucky's first representative in Congress. Orlando Brown attended Princeton College (now Princeton University), from which he received a bachelor's degree in 1820, and Transylvania University in Lexington, Kentucky, where he studied law. In 1833, he became the editor of the *Frankfort Commonwealth*, where he wrote antinullification and antisecessionist editorials. A supporter of Kentucky's eminent politician John J. Crittenden (whose so-called Crittenden Compromise tried to head off the Civil War just before it broke out), Brown became secretary of state in Crittenden's administration when the latter became governor of Kentucky. The election of Whig Zachary Taylor to the presidency in 1848 opened the door to Whigs to be placed in office; to placate Crittenden, Brown was handed the plum position of commissioner of Indian Affairs. He took office on 30 June 1849.

As commissioner, Brown released a single annual report of the Bureau of Indian Affairs; however, that report was one of the Bureau's lengthiest of its early years, encompassing nearly 240 pages (the 1862 report of Commissioner William Palmer Dole ran a lengthier 407 pages.) In the discourse, Brown discussed among other subjects how deeply the U.S. government should become involved in Indian-on-Indian warfare, as well as the refusal of the new state of Texas to recognize any of the rights of the Indians within its borders. Because Brown served during the second decade of the so-called "Removal era," he was forced to deal with many aspects of that policy. In an answer to a petition from Representative Robert Ward Johnson of Arkansas, chairman of the House Committee on Indian Affairs, Brown responded, "In reply of your letter of the 13th instant, re-enclosing certain petitions of citizens of Rapids Parish, Louisiana, in relation to Biloxi and Choctaw Indians in their vicinity by which they complain that they are annoyed, I have the honor to inform you that the Biloxies are a clan of the Choctaws, whose proper residence, it is believed, is in Mississippi or Alabama, but who with other Choctaws, are in the habit of roaming about—sometimes going to the Gulf shore to fish, and at others, to different sections of the country and being employed by the planters in picking cotton and in other light labor. Their being so employed is one of the obstacles in the way of affecting their emigration to the country of their brethren west of the Mississippi. The Department [of the Interior] has no idea that those complained of belong to that portion of the Choctaws that have been removed, though they are in a portion of Louisiana that is west of the Mississippi. If they do, the report of the emigrating agent who has been written to will disclose the fact, and measures will be taken to compel their adieu to their own country. If they do not, they are citizens of the States, and the general government has no right to interfere with them, though the agent has been instructed to effect their removal if they can be persuaded to go."

Brown had replaced the more popular William Medill, whose work to end alcoholism among Indians was lauded. Brown received scathing criticism in the press. By early 1850, after less than a year on the job, Brown had resigned himself to leaving office. He sent a letter of resignation to Taylor on 22 May 1850 with an intention to step down on 1 July. Taylor replaced him with the affable Luke Lea, but the president's death just days after Lea's appointment left the government, and particularly the Indian office, in shambles. Brown returned to Kentucky, where during the Civil War he again edited the *Frankfort Commonwealth*, where he showed support of the Union and Abraham Lincoln. Brown died on 26 July 1867, having been forgotten for his single year as Indian commissioner.

See also Bureau of Indian Affairs.

References Commissioner Orlando Brown to Representative Robert Ward Johnson, 15 February 1850, Records of the House of Representatives, RG 233, Committee on Indian Affairs, file HR 31A-D8.4, "Various Subjects"; Trennert, Robert A., "Orlando Brown." In Robert M. Kvasnicka and Herman J. Viola, eds., *The Commissioners of Indian Affairs, 1824–1977* (1979); U.S. Congress, House of Representatives, *Annual Report of the Commissioner of Indian Affairs for the Year 1849*, House Executive Document No. 5, 31st Congress, 1st Session (serial 550).

Browning, Daniel M. (1846–03)

Biographer William T. Hagan writes of Browning, the twenty-sixth commissioner of Indian Affairs, "He left no permanent mark on the Indian Office." A judge and attorney in Illinois, Browning was appointed to the Indian Office as a partisan bone thrown to him by a grateful Grover Cleveland, for whom Browning had campaigned in Illinois. Little is known of Browning's life. He was born in Benton, Illinois, in the southern part of Illinois, on 11 October 1846, the son of William R. and Lydia Browning. William Browning was the son of John Browning, the first Baptist preacher in Franklin County, Illinois; four years after his son William was born in 1810, John settled on Browning Hill in Benton, and his encampment became known as the Spring Settlement. William Browning was a county judge and merchant. Daniel Browning attended local schools, and was awarded a law degree from the State University of Indiana in 1866, and was admitted to the Illinois state bar when he was 20 years old. A prominent Mason, he was elected as a county judge before serving as a circuit judge on the First Judicial Circuit. He was also a devoted worker for the Democratic party, and the election of Grover Cleveland for his second nonconsecutive term in 1892 (he had been elected in 1884, but defeated in 1888) gave Vice President Adlai E. Stevenson of Illinois a chance to name someone from his state to high office; Browning was that man, and while he was originally slated to be the commissioner of the General Land Office, he settled for the Indian Office.

Serving from 18 April 1893 until 3 May 1897, he had little chance to change national Indian policy. He began his 1893 annual report, "I entered upon the discharge of duties of this Office April 18 last. For four weeks of the time since then I have been engaged in New York City making contracts for the purchase of goods and supplies for the Indian Service, and I have had not time as yet to visit Indian reservations and to inspect personally the workings of the agencies and schools." In his 1894 annual report, Browning did not attempt to discuss policy: "The sixty-third annual report of the Indian Bureau, herewith submitted, aims only to give a resume of noteworthy events which have occurred in the Indian service during the year and of the work for Indian civilization which has been in progress. No attempt is made to theorize upon the Indian question or to point out a way by which to 'solve the Indian problem.' It is a plain recital of facts, accompanied by the report of the superintendent of Indian schools and reports of agents and school superintendents, tables giving educational, agricultural, industrial, and financial statistics of general interest, with other information required by law to be embodied in this report." In the 1896 report, Browning stated, "With no outbreak or disturbance during the year, the progress of Indians generally in education and civilization has been uninterrupted and substantial. The main effort now is, and for many years must be, to put the Indian upon his allotment, get him to support himself there, protect him from encroachment and injustice, and educate and train his children in books and industries." On 30 September 1896, Browning was asked in a letter whether parents of Indian children had the right to decide where their children could attend school. His answer to the writer, later called "the

Browning Ruling," was: "It is your duty first to build up and maintain the government day schools, as indicated in your letter, and the Indian parents have no right to designate which school their children shall attend." The ruling was revoked by President William McKinley in 1901 and, by order within the bureau, by Commissioner William A. Jones on 17 January 1902.

With the election of Republican William McKinley in 1896, Browning's days in the Indian Office were numbered. He resigned on 3 May 1897 just as his replacement, William Arthur Jones, was being sworn in. The former commissioner returned to his true vocation, the law, taking up practice in East Saint Louis, Illinois, where he died on 13 January 1903. He was buried in the Masonic and Oldfellow Cemetery in Benton.

See also Bureau of Indian Affairs.

References "Browning Ruling." Letter discussed in *Quick Bear v. Leupp et al.* (210 U.S. 50 [1908]), at 81; Hagan, William T., "Daniel M. Browning." In Robert M. Kvasnicka and Herman J. Viola, eds., *The Commissioners of Indian Affairs, 1824–1977 (1979); History of Gallatin, Saline, Hamilton, Franklin and Williamson Counties, Illinois, From the Earliest Time to the Present; Together with Sundry and Interesting Biographical Sketches, Notes, Reminiscences, Etc., Etc., Illustrated* (1887); U.S. Congress, House of Representatives, *Annual Report of the Commissioner of Indian Affairs for the Year 1893*, House Executive Document No. 1, 53d Congress, 2d Session (serial 3210); U.S. Congress, House of Representatives, *Annual Report of the Commissioner of Indian Affairs for the Year 1894*, House Executive Document No. 1, 53d Congress, 3d Session (serial 3306); U.S. Congress, House of Representatives, *Annual Report of the Commissioner of Indian Affairs for the Year 1896*, House Document No. 5, 54th Congress, 2d Session (serial 3489).

Bruce, Louis Rooks, Jr. (Mohawk/Oglala Sioux) (1906–1989)

Bruce served as Indian commissioner during the siege of Wounded Knee and the Trail of Broken Treaties. During his years in office, he tried to help his people as much as he did in private life. He was born on the Oglala Sioux Reservation at Pine Ridge, in South Dakota, on 30 December 1906, the son of Louis Bruce, Sr., a dentist of the Mohawk Nation, and Nellie (née Rooks) Bruce, an Oglala Sioux. Before becoming a dentist, Louis Sr. was a professional baseball player whose father had been a Mohawk chief. After his son's birth, he became a minister and took his family to the Onondaga Reservation near Syracuse, New York, to minister to the Indians there. Louis Jr. was educated on reservation schools and in a white seminary, then attended and graduated from Syracuse University in 1930 with a degree in psychology.

Having worked in a series of jobs to put himself through college, during the Depression Bruce established a program to allow Indian children to attend summer camps to teach them Indian culture. He also was the owner of a large dairy in New York and one of the founders of the National Congress of American Indians. For advising President Roosevelt, Truman, and Eisenhower on Indian affairs, Bruce was awarded the Freedom Award in 1949 by Eisenhower. He also served on the President's Advisory Committee on American Indian Affairs. This lifetime of work led President Richard M. Nixon to name Bruce as the thirty-fifth commissioner of Indian Affairs on 8 August 1969. Bruce wrote in 1976, "When President Nixon appointed me commissioner of the Bureau of Indian Affairs in August 1969, I immediately set about the monumental task of acquainting myself with as much as possible of the written material about American Indians that is available in the libraries and archives of Washington, D.C., and New York. I confess I did not even finish all of the annual reports of my predecessors in the Office of the Commissioner of Indian Affairs. Nor was I able to get through so much as a small percentage of the massive collection of historical and social documents that make up the extant body of American Indian history." He added, "Soon after I assumed the position of commissioner, I announced, with President Nixon's approval, a realignment of the top positions in the BIA central office and appointed a new executive staff composed of fifteen Indians and Alaskan natives. This marked a milestone in BIA history. Today more Indians than ever are holding key BIA management positions and working to implement the self-determination policy of this administration. Indian direction of Indian Affairs has become the cornerstone for policy making in the Nixon administration."

Nixon's message to Congress in November 1970 on Indian affairs was a blueprint for Bruce to follow. Yet because he had worked largely behind the scenes, he was not considered a major Indian activist and was called an "Uncle Tomahawk" on his appointment. Yet two years later, writes Joseph H. Case, "he was widely respected; one militant Indian leader, who had denounced his appointment, called him 'the greatest Indians commissioner since John Collier.'" Key to his program was transforming the Bureau of Indian Affairs from an institution of authority over Indians to one of assistance in the improvement of their lives. Awarded with the Indian Council Fire Achievement Award, he explained, "The way to Indian progress is involvement…I want to see Indians buying cars from Indians on reservations, buying food from Indian stores, driving on Indian-planned and Indian-built roads, talking on Indian-owned telephone systems, and living in an Indian-managed community." Bruce was unfortunate to be the head of the BIA when the Trail of Broken Treaties caravan came to Washington, D.C., and occupied the offices of the bureau for six days. Bruce and several of his top aides, blamed for the crisis, lost their jobs on 20 January 1973. The commissioner's position was not filled until Morris Thompson was named to the post in December 1972.

From 1976 to 1977 Bruce served as a member of the American Indian Policy Review Commission, a committee of lawmakers and Indians established to review government policy toward the Indians. Little is known of his final years. He died on 20 May 1989.

See also *Morton, Secretary of the Interior, v. C. R. Mancari et al. and Amerind v. C. R. Mancari et al.*; Trail of Broken Treaties.

References Bruce, Louis Rooks, "The Bureau of Indian Affairs, 1972." In Jane F. Smith and Robert M. Kvasnicka, eds., *Indian-White Relations: A Persistent Paradox* (1976); Cash, Joseph H., "Louis Rooks Bruce." In Robert M. Kvasnicka and Herman J. Viola, eds., *The Commissioners of Indian Affairs, 1824–1977* (1979); Tower, Christopher B., "Louis R. Bruce, Jr." In Sharon Malinowski, ed., *Notable Native Americans* (1995).

Bryan v. Itasca County (426 U.S. 373 [1976])

The issue of whether a state could levy personal property taxes against Indians living on reservations with such federal assent as Public Law 280 (codified at 28 U.S.C. 1360) was in question in this Supreme Court case. Russell Bryan was an enrolled member of the Minnesota Chippewa Tribe. When the county of Itasca levied a personal property tax on his mobile home, he sued in the District Court of Itasca County for relief from the tax. The District Court and, on appeal, the Minnesota Supreme Court, upheld the tax. Bryan sued to the U.S. Supreme Court. After arguments were heard on 20 April 1976, Justice William Brennan delivered the unanimous opinion of the court in striking down the tax in the absence of any federal consent to levy such a tax on Indians. Justice Brennan explained, "The…Congress that enacted Public Law 280 also enacted several termination Acts—legislation which is cogent proof that Congress knew well how to express its intent directly when that intent was to subject reservation Indians to the full sweep of state laws and state taxation. *Board of County Commissioners v. Seber*, 318 U.S. 705, [at] 713, 87 L.Ed. 1094, 63 S.Ct. 920 (1943); *Goudy v. Meath*, 203 U.S. 146, [at] 149, 51 L.Ed. 130, 27 S.Ct. 48 (1906). These termination enactments provide expressly for subjecting distributed property 'and any income derived therefrom by the individual, corporation, or other legal entity…to the same taxes, State and Federal, as in the case of non-Indians.' 25 U.S.C. 564j, 749, 898, and provide that 'all statutes of the United States which affect Indians because of their status as Indians shall no longer be applicable to the members of the tribe, and the laws of the several States shall apply to the tribe and its members in the same manner as they apply to other citizens or persons within their jurisdiction.' 25 U.S.C. 564q, 757, 899; 25 U.S.C.

726. These contemporaneous termination Acts are in pari materia with Public Law 280." He added, "If Congress in enacting Public Law 280 had intended to confer upon the States general civil regulatory powers, including taxation, over reservation Indians, it would have expressly said so."

Bureau of Indian Affairs

The oldest bureau in the federal government, established as the Office of Indian Affairs in 1824 under the tutelage of Thomas L. McKenney, one of the nineteenth century's greatest Indian reformers, the Bureau of Indian Affairs (BIA) is one of the largest divisions of the Department of the Interior. Its main mission, as authors Arlene Hirschfelder and Martha Kreipe de Montaño write, "is to protect Native Americans and their land and resources and to turn federal programs that benefit Indians over to the administration of the tribes. Since 1972, hiring, training, and promotions in BIA have been governed by Indian preference. Each president since Richard Nixon has reaffirmed the government-to-government relationship."

Official seal of the Bureau of Indian Affairs

From the earliest times of the nation, white people have had to deal with the Indian tribes which inhabited this land before they did. With the establishment of the United States, this relationship became one of a trust and ward. First the framers of the Articles of Confederation, and later the Constitution, foresaw the need for a governmental program to deal with the Native Americans. At first, the secretary of war (starting with Henry Knox in 1786) was in charge of Indian affairs; in 1806, the Office of the Superintendent of Indian Trade was created. In 1824, Secretary of War John C. Calhoun established the Office of Indian Affairs in the Department of War, with former Superintendent of Indian Trade Thomas L. McKenney as the first head. It was not until 1832 that Congress gave the office statutory authority, and gave its chief the title of commissioner of Indian Affairs. The first man in this now more official position was Elbert Herring, who served from 1831 until 1836. Perhaps the most important of these early commissioners was Thomas Hartley Crawford, of whom historian Theodore Taylor opines, "Crawford had the longest tenure of any Indian commissioner during the Jacksonian era and made an indelible imprint on the office during his seven years as its head. The Pennsylvanian was a patient, careful, consistent, and devoted public servant. Although he served four chief executives—Van Buren, William Henry Harrison, John Tyler, and James K. Polk—his exceptionally long tenure was not the result of being apolitical." William Medill, 1845–49, was the last commissioner in the War office, while Orlando Brown, 1849–50, was the first in the Interior Department.

Possibly the most influential Indian commissioner of the nineteenth century was George Washington Manypenny (served 1853–57), who oversaw the greatest era of treaty-making with the Indian tribes. Manypenny later served on the commission that exacted the exile of the Lakota Sioux from the Black Hills of South Dakota. William Palmer Dole (served 1861–65) oversaw the Indian bureau during the Civil War, while Ely Samuel Parker (served 1869–71) was the first Native American to occupy the post. The tenure of Hiram Price (1881–85) saw the establishment of the oldest Native American rights organization, the Indian Rights Association (1882).

During the administration of John DeWitt Clinton Atkins, 1885–88, the General Allotment Act, or Dawes Act, was enacted, making way for the largest allotment scheme of Indian land in history. Two of the last three commissioners of the nineteenth century, Thomas Jefferson Morgan (served 1889–93) and William Arthur Jones (served 1897–1905) oversaw an expansion of Indian education.

The first decades of the twentieth century saw such Indian reformers as Francis Ellington Leupp (served 1905–09), Robert Grosvenor Valentine (served 1909–12), and Charles James Rhoads (served 1921–29) head the Indian office, at the same time delivering speeches before the annual Mohonk conference held in New York and working with the Board of Indian Commissioners and other reform organizations. Under Rhoads, the Indian Citizenship Act (1924) was enacted, and the landmark Meriam Report, condemning incompetence in the way the nation conducted Indian affairs and calling for a massive change in that program, was prepared. However, Rhoads was replaced by John Collier, who oversaw perhaps the greatest period of Indian reform measures to come out of Congress. Collier, a worker with the Indian Defense Association (IDA) before his rise to Indian Commissioner, pushed for such action as the Indian Reorganization Act (Wheeler-Howard Act, 1934), Johnson-O'Malley Act (1934), and Indian Arts and Crafts Act (1935), which drastically changed the way Indians were dealt with by the federal government. Collier served from 1933 to 1945, longer than any other Indian commissioner. His successors, including educator John Ralph Nichols (1949–50) and anthropologist Philleo Nash (1961–66), did not leave much of an imprint on the office or its policies but did preside over the important era of termination of federal tribes from federal jurisdiction, and that of self-determination, in which Indian tribes would control their own affairs. In 1966, President Lyndon Johnson named Robert LaFollette Bennett (Oneida) as the second Native American to become commissioner. Bennett's ascension to the position made Nash the last non-Indian to hold the post. Bennett was succeeded most ably by Louis Rooks Bruce (Sioux-Mohawk), Morris Thompson (Tanana), and Benjamin Reifel (Sioux). The last official commissioner of Indian Affairs was William E. Hallett (Chippewa), who served under Jimmy Carter from 1979 until 1981, when the power of the bureau was officially vested in the assistant secretary of the interior for Indian Affairs. Among the leading secretaries who have served in this post since the abolition of the commissioner's position include Forrest Gerard (Blackfeet) (who served at one time as a legislative assistant in the office of Senator Henry Jackson of Washington), Kenneth Smith (Wasco), Ross Owen Swimmer (Cherokee), Ed Brown (Pascua Yaqui), and Ada Elizabeth Deer (Menominee).

Over the years, there has been much criticism of the bureau for ineptitude and fraud. The "Indian Ring" investigations of the late nineteenth century led to the resignation of Commissioner Ezra Ayres Hayt (served 1877–80), but the investigations did little to curb the excesses of Indian agents in the field. The Society of American Indians, an early twentieth-century pan-Indian rights group, harshly denounced the bureau and demanded its abolition, but its recommendations were ignored. In 1987, in an eight-part series entitled "Fraud in Indian Country: A Billion-dollar Betrayal," the *Arizona Republic* editorialized, "Despite scores of billions of dollars spent to improve Indian lives during the past century, Washington has succeeded primarily in building the most intractable and convoluted bureaucracy in the federal government. Many Washington lawmakers and federal employees say the bureau of Indian Affairs has earned the dubious reputation of being the worst-managed agency in the whole U.S. government."

According to the *U.S. Government Manual, 1993–94*, "The principal objectives of the bureau are to encourage and assist

Indian and Alaska Native people to manage their own affairs under the trust relationship to the Federal Government; to facilitate, with maximum involvement of Indian and Alaska Native people, full development of their human and natural resource potential; to mobilize all public and private aids to the advancement of Indian and Alaska Native people for use by them; and to promote self-determination by utilizing the skill and capabilities of Indian and Alaska Native people in the direction and management of programs for their benefit." The bureau has area offices in Aberdeen, South Dakota; Billings, Montana; Juneau, Alaska; Minneapolis, Minnesota; Portland, Oregon; Sacramento, California; Phoenix, Arizona; Albuquerque, New Mexico; Anadarko and Muskogee, Oklahoma; the Navajo office in Window Rock, Arizona; and an eastern office in Arlington, Virginia.

References "Fraud in Indian Country: A Billion-Dollar Betrayal." *Arizona Republic*, 4 October 1987, A1; Hirschfelder, Arlene, and Martha Kreipe de Montaño, *The Native American Almanac: A Portrait of Native America Today* (1993); Taylor, Theodore W., *American Indian Policy* (1983); *U.S. Government Manual, 1993–94* (1994).

Burke, Charles Henry (1861–1944)

His service as commissioner of Indian Affairs lasted eight years, during the Harding and Coolidge administrations, but Charles Henry Burke's stint in that position remains relatively unstudied by historians of the government's Indian policy. He was born on a farm near Batavia, in Genesee County, New York, on 1 April 1861. In 1882, Burke left his family and moved west to Dakota Territory, settling on a homestead in Beadle County but moving to Hughes County the following year. During this time, he studied the law and in 1886 he was admitted to the territorial bar. He then moved to the capital, Pierre, where he would make his home. Twice elected to the South Dakota state legislature (1895, 1897), in 1898 Burke was elected to the U.S. House of Representatives and went to Washington for the first of four terms (1899–1907). In 1906, in an attempt to amend section 6 of the General Allotment Act (also known as the Dawes Act) of 1887, Burke introduced what would be titled the Burke Act, which extended the probationary period under which Indians would be unable to sell their allotments, thus protecting them from unscrupulous land speculators. Burke was defeated for renomination in 1906, but two years later ran for his old seat and won, serving three additional terms (1909–1915). In the sixty-first Congress (1909–11), he was chairman of the House Committee on Indian Affairs; in the sixty-third (1913–15) he was minority whip. He was nominated for the U.S. Senate in 1914 but was defeated, and he resumed his business activities.

With the election of Warren G. Harding to the presidency in 1920, Burke desired a post in the Interior Department, but instead Harding named him as commissioner of Indian Affairs on 1 April 1921, and he took office on 7 May. In his eight years in the post, Burke apparently played such a small role in Harding's administration that Francis Russell, Harding's biographer, did not even mention Burke or the work of the Bureau of Indian Affairs in his *The Shadow of Blooming Grove: Warren G. Harding and His Times* (1968). For his annual report for the year 1925, Burke wrote as to health of the Indians, "It is indeed gratifying to report that our health campaign for the conquest of diseases among the Indians has achieved a fair degree of success, notwithstanding the difficulties under which it has been carried on. Statistics will show that the Indian is not a dying race, but a race which is gradually gaining in number and responding to the impulse imparted by education and changing environment." In his 1926 treatise, he detailed how the Indian Medical Service (now the Indian Health Service) was reorganized into four districts. "Each district will be under the immediate supervision of a medical director whose functions will be to make inspections of the various Indian activities with respect to the school, hospital, sanatorium, and health features; to study and report upon standardized methods of procedure and facilities, including personnel; to coordinate medical and sanitary activities by means of conferences; to investigate and adjust controversies; to report on matters affecting the Indian medical service and its public health policies; to promote cordial relations with State and local sanitary authorities and other public health organizations, and to maintain and office in such district which shall serve as a general center for Indian medical service activities."

During his time in office, Burke had to deal with sniping from John Collier, executive secretary of the American Indian Defense Association (and later commissioner of Indian Affairs himself) and an investigation into the case of Jackson Barnett, an Indian who, it was claimed, Burke was allowing to give away all of his trust funds, some $1.1 million, to his white wife and others. Burke also got into trouble with Senator William Bliss Pine of Oklahoma when he accused the senator of trying to "destroy [him] because James Hepburn, a certain Oklahoma politician, was not appointed superintendent of the Five Civilized Tribes." The subsequent investigation by the Senate Committee on Indian Affairs found no evidence for Burke's charges. The *Indian Leader*, the journal of the Haskell Institute, a government training school for Indians in Lawrence, Kansas, editorialized in 1928, "It seems a proper time to bring to the attention...some of the more important accomplishments of the Indian Service during the administration of Commissioner Burke. For more than seven years he has served as commissioner of Indian Affairs and notwithstanding the fact that during that time the Service has been greatly handicapped because of inadequate funds much has been done for the advancement of the Indians and the improvement of the Indian Service."

From 1923 until 1929, Burke was repeatedly investigated in the Barnett case. Even though Burke had been cleared in early 1929, he resigned his office on 9 March of that same year. The *New York Times* reported on his tenure, "His eight stormy years as Commissioner ended in 1929 with his resignation after a House committee exonerated him on charges of corruption." His administration was under continuous fire from Congress, whose investigations into the Barnett case lasted from 1923 until his resignation. In 1931, in what would be his final government work, Burke was appointed commissioner to the International Colonial Exposition, then being held in Paris. He spent his final years in the real estate and loan business both in Pierre and Washington, D.C., where he also spoke out in the interest of Indians. Burke died at his home in Washington on 7 April 1944; his body was returned to Pierre for burial.

See also Bureau of Indian Affairs.

References "Accomplishments of Indian Bureau under Commissioner Burke's Guidance." *Indian Leader* 32 (14); *Biographical Directory of the United States Congress, 1774–1989*, Senate Document 100–34, 100th Congress, Second Session (1989); "C. H. Burke, Ex-Head of Indian Affairs," *New York Times*, 8 April 1944, 13; Department of the Interior, *Report of the Commissioner of Indian Affairs to the Secretary of the Interior, 1925;* Department of the Interior, *Report of the Commissioner of Indian Affairs to the Secretary of the Interior, 1926;* "Director of Indian Affairs Says Pine Seeks to Ruin Him," *Washington Star*, 7 January 1929, 1; "Sen. Pine Flayed by U.S. Indian Chief," *The News*, 7 January 1929, 2; U.S. Congress, Senate, *Survey of Conditions of Indians of the United States*, Senate Report 1490, 70th Congress, 2d Session, 1929.

Burke Act (34 Stat. 182)

In 1906, Congressman Charles Henry Burke of South Dakota introduced a bill, later named the Burke Act, which effectively rewrote section 6 of the General Allotment Act of 1887. As historian Lawrence C. Kelly wrote, "[The Burke Act] was designed to provide additional protection for Indians during the twenty-five year probationary period during which their land allotments were held in trust by the federal government. Specifically, it provided that citizenship be withheld from Indian allottees until the expiration of the trust period; that as wards of the federal government, Indian allottees should be subject to federal rather than state controls during the probationary period; and that the trust period be extended beyond twenty-five years if the allottee was judged incompetent to handle his own affairs. In recognition of the fact that some Indians were competent to handle their property before the expiration of the probationary period, the act also provided that Indian allottees could be given title to their allotments, made citizens, and subjected to state laws before the twenty-five years had elapsed." However, adds Marshall Dwight Moody in his history of the Board of Indian Commissioners, "In 1906 the Burke Act further complicated matters by giving the Secretary of the Interior wide discretionary powers to judge and declare an Indian competent and release him from the restrictions imposed by the Dawes Act. The Board of Indian Commissioners saw great danger in this act and disapproved it strongly but was powerless to combat it successfully. For a time great care was used in issuing patents but a few years later the Department became overtly liberal in releasing the Indians from restrictions with the inevitable result that the allotment policy concluded in virtual failure and is now regarded as having been a serious mistake." The text of the act reads:

Be it enacted...That section six of an Act approved February eighth, eighteen hundred and eighty-seven, entitled "An Act to provide for the allotment of lands in severalty to Indians on the various reservations, and to extend the protection of the laws of the United States and the Territories over the Indians, and for other purposes," be amended to read as follows:

Sec. 6. That at the expiration of the trust period and when the lands have been conveyed to the Indians by patent in fee, as provided in section five of this Act, then each and every allottee shall have the benefit of and be subject to the laws, both civil and criminal, of the State or Territory in which they may reside; and no Territory shall pass or enforce any law denying any such Indian within its jurisdiction the equal protection of the law. And every Indian born within the territorial limits of the United States to whom allotments shall have been made and who has received a patent in fee simple under the provisions of this Act, or under any law or treaty, and every Indian born within the territorial limits of the United States who has voluntarily taken up within said limits his residence, separate and apart from any tribe of Indians therein, and has adopted the habits of civilized life, is hereby declared to be a citizen of the United States, and is entitled to all the rights, privileges, and immunities of such citizens, whether said Indian has been or not, by birth or otherwise, a member of any tribe of Indians within the territorial limits of the United States without in any manner impairing or otherwise affecting the right of any such Indian to tribal or other property: Provided, That the Secretary of the Interior may, in his discretion, and he is hereby authorized, whenever he shall be satisfied that any Indian allottee is competent and capable of managing his or her affairs at any time to cause to be issued to such allottee a patent in fee simple, and thereafter all restrictions as to sale, incumbrance, or taxation of said land shall be removed and said land shall not be liable to the satisfaction of any debt contracted to prior to the issuing of such patent: Provided further, That until the issuance of fee-simple patents all allottees to whom trust patents shall hereafter be issued shall be subject to the exclusive jurisdiction of the United States: And provided further, That the provisions of this Act shall not extend to any Indians in the Indian Territory.

That hereafter when an allotment of land is made to any Indian, and any such Indian dies before the expiration of the trust period, said allotment shall be cancelled and the land shall revert to the United States, and the Secretary of the Interior shall ascertain the legal heirs of such Indian, and shall cause to be issued to said heirs and in their names, a patent in fee simple for said land, or he may cause the land to be sold as provided by law and issue a patent therefor to the purchaser or purchasers, and pay the net proceeds to the heirs, or their legal representatives, of such deceased Indian. The action of the Secretary of the Interior in determining the legal heirs of any deceased Indian, as provided herein, shall in respects be conclusive and final.

See also Burke, Charles Henry.

References Kelly, Lawrence C., "Charles Henry Burke." In Robert M. Kvasnicka and Herman J. Viola, eds., *The Commissioners of Indian Affairs, 1824–1977* (1979); Moody, Marshall Dwight, *A History of the Board of Indian Commissioners and Its Relationship to the Administration of Indian Affairs, 1869–1900* (Master's thesis, American University, 1951).

Buttz, Executor, v. Northern Pacific Railroad Company (119 U.S. 55 [1886])

The right of a preemptor to seize land not yet extinguished of its Indian title, land set aside for the construction of a railroad, was at issue in this Supreme Court case. When the act of Congress of 2 July 1864 (13 Stat. 365), titled "An act granting lands to aid in the construction of a railroad and telegraph line from Lake Superior to Puget Sound, on the Pacific Coast, by the northern route," was enacted, the government had not yet convinced the Sisseton and Wahpeton bands of Dakota, or Sioux, to relinquish the land to the United States. In an 1867 treaty, (15 Stat. 505), these bands ceded to the United States the right to "construct wagon roads, railroads, mail stations, telegraph lines, and such other public improvements as the interest of the government may require." However, the bands did not renounce their rights to the land to the government until May of 1873. Peronto, the original defendant in this litigation, settled on the land in question on 5 October 1871. He later claimed that under the Preemption Act of 4 September 1841 (5 Stat. 453), which allowed "settlers to locate a piece of unsurveyed land and stake a claim to it at $1.25 an acre," he had settled on the land and built a house. A district court ruled for the right of the railway company to own the land, and the Supreme Court of the Territory of Dakota affirmed. The U.S. Supreme Court granted certiorari but, before the case could be heard, Peronto died, leaving Buttz, the executor of his estate, to carry on with the litigation. Justice Stephen Johnson Field held for a unanimous court on 15 November 1886 that Peronto's claim to the land was invalid. He wrote, "The right of the company, freed from an incumbrance of the Indian title, immediately attached to the alternate sections, a portion of which constitutes the premises in controversy. The defendant could not initiate any pre-emptive right to the land so long as the Indian title remained unextinguished. The act of Congress excludes lands in that condition from pre-emption."

Buy Indian Act (35 Stat. 71)

This simple federal legislation of 30 April 1908 was enacted to protect the employment of Indian labor and the purchase of products of Indian industry. Now codified at 25 U.S.C. 47, the act reads: "So far as may be practicable Indian labor shall be employed [in the creation of Indian products], and purchases of the products of Indian industry may be made in open market in the discretion of the Secretary of the Interior."

See also *Andrus, Secretary of the Interior et al. v. Glover Construction Company.*

***California et al. v. Cabazon Band of Mission Indians et al.* (480 U.S. 202, 94 L.Ed. 2d 244, 107 S.Ct. 1083 [1987])**
The issue of the application of state and local laws to gambling on reservations was involved in this Supreme Court case. The Cabazon and Morongo Bands of Indians live inside separate reservations in Riverside County, California. Pursuant to an ordinance approved by the secretary of the interior, the two bands started gambling operations on their respective reservations. The tribes sued in federal district court to enjoin the state of California, joined by Riverside County, from enforcing its gambling laws. The court granted a summary judgment as to the federal-state jurisdictional question and issued a permanent restraint on the state and county enforcement of the regulations. The U.S. Court of Appeals for the Ninth Circuit affirmed, holding that state jurisdiction was lacking over the reservations in both Public Law 280 and the Organized Crime Control Act (OCCA, 18 U.S.C. 1955), which governs state jurisdiction over federal matters regarding gambling. On appeal from the state of California, the U.S. Supreme Court granted certiorari. The case was argued before the court on 9 December 1986, with a decision being handed down on 25 February 1987. In a 6–3 decision (justices John Paul Stevens, Sandra Day O'Connor, and Antonin Scalia dissenting), Justice Byron White upheld the appeals court's judgment and struck down the state statute regarding gambling. Justice White explained, "The sole interest asserted by the State to justify the imposition of its bingo laws on the Tribes is in preventing the infiltration of the tribal games by organized crime. To the extent that the State seeks to prevent any and all bingo games from being played on tribal lands while permitting regulated, off-reservation games, this asserted interest is irrelevant and the state and county laws are pre-empted. Even to the extent that the State and county seek to regulate short of prohibition, the laws are pre-empted. The state insists that the high stakes offered at tribal games are attractive to organized crime, whereas the controlled games authorized under California law are not. This is surely a legitimate concern, but we are unconvinced that it is sufficient to escape the pre-emptive force of federal and tribal interests apparent in this case. California does not allege any present criminal involvement in the Cabazon and Morongo enterprises, and the Ninth Circuit discerned none. An official of the Department of Justice has expressed some concern about tribal bingo operations, but far from any action being taken evidencing this concern—and surely the Federal Government has the authority to forbid Indian gambling enterprises—the prevailing federal policy continues to support these tribal enterprises, including those of the Tribes involved in this case."

***California State Board of Equalization et al. v. Chemehuevi Indian Tribe* (474 U.S. 9, 88 L.Ed. 2d 9, 106 S.Ct. 289 [1985])**
In this important taxation case decided in 1985, the U.S. Supreme Court held that the states could require Indian tribes to collect taxes on cigarettes sold to non-Indians. After the California State Board of Equalization demanded that the Chemehuevi Indian Tribe collect taxes on cigarettes that tribal smoke shops sold to non-Indians, the Chemehuevis sued in the U.S. District Court for the Northern District of California to enjoin the levying of such a tax. At the same time, the board countersued to recover past taxes that had not been paid. The district court ruled that the counterclaim was barred because of the tribe's sovereign immunity, but held that the tribe had to collect the taxes on sales to non-Indians. The U.S. Court of Appeals for the Ninth Circuit affirmed as to the first determination, but reversed on the second, claiming that because the tribe was not a "taxable entity," the state law did not properly impose liability on the ultimate purchaser of the cigarettes.

The U.S. Supreme Court granted certiorari and, in a rare move, decided the case without hearing oral arguments or asking for a submission of briefs. In a *per curiam* opinion (without an acknowledged author) expressing the views of Chief Justice Warren Burger and justices Byron White, Lewis Powell, William H. Rehnquist, and Sandra Day O'Connor, the court held on 4 November 1985 that the state's statutory scheme was aimed at non-Indians. In an opinion somewhat like its 1980 holding in *Washington v. Confederated Tribes of the Colville Indian Reservation*, which struck down state sales taxes on cigarettes sold on reservations as they applied to Indians, the justices in the majority held that since the tax is based on products sold by a nontaxable entity, it is fair to require that entity to collect the tax for the state. A rehearing was denied in the case (474 U.S. 1077, 88 L.Ed. 2d 810, 106 S.Ct. 839).

Campbell, Ben Nighthorse (Northern Cheyenne) (1933–)

The second Native American elected to the U.S. Senate, Ben Nighthorse Campbell of Colorado stunned the political world when he switched from the Democratic Party to the Republican Party in 1995. He was born in Auburn, California, on 13 April 1933, the son of Albert Campbell, who was of Apache, Pueblo, and Northern Cheyenne descent, and Mary Vierra, a Portuguese immigrant. He most likely is a descendant of Reuben Black Horse, who fought Custer at the Little Big Horn in 1876, and his great-grandmother was at Sand Creek in 1864 when a massacre by army troops occurred there. In an interview with the author in his Washington, D.C., office in June 1995, Senator Campbell spoke out on several issues relating to Native Americans and the obstacles they face, but particularly on his childhood. "In those days things were so bad on the reservation that a lot of people left, changed their names, tried to change their identities, and ended up telling their children when they came along, 'don't even talk about it.'" "We were told just, kind of, 'keep your mouth shut,' you're not an Indian, you're just Americans." Campbell dropped out of high school in his junior year to join the U.S. Air Force, in which he served until 1953. During his military service he spent a year as a military policeman in Korea, where he learned judo. In 1953 he was honorably discharged with the rank of airman second class. Having earned his high school equivalency degree while in the Air Force, he was able to enroll at San Jose City College and put himself through college by utilizing the G.I. Bill and working as a teamster. He graduated in 1957 with a bachelor's degree in physical education and fine arts. During his college days he continued his interest in judo: he was captain of the collegiate team and advanced to the rank of fourth-degree black belt. He then enrolled in the judo program at Meiji University in Tokyo, Japan. He was a three-time U.S. champion, and went on to win a gold medal at the 1963 Pan American games in São Paulo, Brazil, and captained the 1964 Olympic judo team in Tokyo. After his return to the United States, Campbell became a teacher. Failing to be named captain of the 1972 Olympic judo team, Campbell switched to the raising and breeding of horses. However, his main business was the designing and creation of Indian jewelry, named Nighthorse Jewelry Designs. His business was so successful that he was featured in the April 1979 issue of *Arizona Highways*.

In 1982, Campbell became interested in Colorado politics (he had moved to the state in 1969), and ran for a seat in the Colorado House of Representatives. His time there was marked notably by his effort to get the site of the Sand Creek Massacre designated as a memorial. In 1986, he won a seat in the U.S. House of Representatives, representing Colorado's Third Congressional District, by defeating an incumbent Republican. He was reelected in 1988 and 1990 with more than 70 percent of the vote. In 1991, he introduced a bill in the House that changed the named of the Custer National Battlefield Monument to the Little Bighorn National Battle Field Monument, and sponsored the Colorado Indian Water Rights Set-

Ben Nighthorse Campbell, far right, with fellow members of the 1964 U.S. Olympic judo team, left to right, George Harris, Jim Bregman, Coach Yoshiro Uchida, and Paul Maruyama. Campbell, a Northern Cheyenne, was elected to the U.S. Senate by Coloradans in 1993.

tlement Act, which secured drinking water rights for the Ute Indians of Colorado, and the authorization of construction of the Museum of the American Indian in Washington, D.C.

When Senator Timothy Wirth of Colorado did not seek reelection, Campbell stepped forward and, giving up a safe House seat, sought the open position and won it with 55 percent of the vote against a veteran Republican state senator. In the Senate, he worked to bring greater attention to the problems surrounding Fetal Alcohol Syndrome (FAS), supported the National Rifle Association, and worked to defeat plans by the Clinton Administration to raise grazing and mining fees in the western United States. A writer for the European magazine *The Economist* wrote that Campbell "could easily have been a magazine cover-man." The author of *Championship Judo: Drill Training* (1974), Campbell dramatically switched from the Democratic Party to the Republican Party in January 1995.

See also Curtis, Charles Brent; Sand Creek Massacre.

References Champagne, Duane, ed., *The Native North American Almanac:* A Reference Work on Native North Americans in the United States and Canada (1994); Viola, Herman J., *An American Warrior: Ben Nighthorse Campbell* (1993); Winsell, Keith A., "Ben Nighthorse Campbell." In Sharon Malinowski, ed., *Notable Native Americans.*

Carpenter v. Shaw (280 U.S. 363, 74 L.Ed. 478, 50 S.Ct. 121 [1930])

Tax deferments established by the federal government on Indians must be "liberally construed," and as such cannot stand, according to the Supreme Court decision. Under section 29 of the act of Congress of 28 June 1898 (30 Stat. 495), Congress established that "all the lands allotted [to the Choctaw and Chickasaw Indians of Oklahoma] shall be non-taxable while the title remains in the original allottees, but not to exceed 21 years from date of patent." The patents were finalized with these Indians in

1908. In 1928, the Congress repealed the tax provisions of the act, enabling the state of Oklahoma to levy taxes on oil and gas found on the reservations. Anticipating the repeal, the state of Oklahoma taxed the Indians starting in 1926. Plaintiffs T. L. Carpenter and Lillie V. Carpenter paid the 1926 and 1927 taxes under protest. They then sued A. S. J. Shaw, state auditor of the state of Oklahoma, to have the taxes returned. The Supreme Court of the State of Oklahoma upheld the taxes. The Carpenters sued to the U.S. Supreme Court. The Supreme Court heard the arguments in *Carpenter* on 5 December 1929 and handed down its decision on 6 January 1930. Speaking for a unanimous court, Justice Harlan Fiske Stone held that tax laws imposed on Indians must be construed strictly, and as such, the 1928 law was void. As he wrote, "Whatever the meaning of the present exemption clause at the time of its adoption must be taken to be its effect now, since it may not be narrowed by any subsequently declared intention of Congress."

Catlin, George (1796–1872)

George Catlin is considered one of the greatest artists to capture the Indian way of life before it vanished on the prairies. Born on 26 July 1796, in Wilkes-Barre, Pennsylvania, the fifth of 14 children of Putnum and Polly (née Sutton) Catlin, George Catlin began his artistic life at an early age. After a common education and the studying of the law, he opened a practice about 1820 but began to see that his real calling was painting. In his first years in the field he painted political portraits, including images of Governor DeWitt Clinton of New York and, later, after he had resided in Washington, D.C., former First Lady Dolly Madison. While on a visit to Philadelphia he saw a delegation of Indians, and he became determined, as he wrote later, "to use my art and so much of the labors of my future life as might be required in rescuing from oblivion the looks and customs of the vanishing races of native man in America." He then spent the years 1829 to 1838 traveling across the wilds of the nation documenting some 600 Indians in natural poses, wearing native attire, and in their natural surroundings. At one point in his life Catlin remarked about the Indians, "I love a people who have always made me welcome to the best they had...who are honest without laws, who have no jails and no poor-house...who never take the name of God in vain...who worship God without a Bible...who are free from religious animosities...who have never raised a hand against me, or stolen my property...who have never fought a battle with white men except on their own ground...and oh! how I love a people who don't live for the love of money." In a letter to an unknown correspondent written on 4 January 1849, Catlin wrote, "I take the liberty to transmit herewith, a Catalogue of my North Am[erican] Indian Collection, to which are appended numerous extracts from the leading journals of England, France, and our own country relative to its interest and value; and to which I beg to solicit your attention. I also enclose a copy of my memorials to the Congress, and their

Artist George Catlin, 1796–1872

two reports thereon; and I confidently believe that in my present prayer to that body (and the last that I can possibly make) I shall have your aid in securing to our country, where they do peculiarly belong, the memorials of a Race of human beings who are so rapidly passing away, and for the collection and preservation of whose history I have applied all the hard earnings and best energies of my life."

Catlin did spend the rest of his life trying to get the government to purchase his collection of paintings (called by historians the "Catlin Gallery") so that they might have a proper home, petitioning Congress several times to appropriate the funds, but to no avail. He then took the paintings overseas and exhibited them in England, where amazed Europeans got their first up-close views of American Indians. The editors of the National Cyclopedia of American Biography write, "In 1842 he was invited to lecture in London at the Royal Institution, and took this opportunity to prepare a matter which he had had long under consideration, that of establishing a museum of mankind which would contain and perpetuate the appearance, history and manners of all the declining races." In the years before his death, Catlin wrote many books, including *Letters and Notes on the Manners, Customs, and Condition of the North American Indians* (1841); *Catlin's North American Indian Portfolio: Hunting, Rocky Mountains and Prairies of America* (1845); *Catlin's Notes of Eight Years' Travel and Residence in Europe* (1848); and *Last Rambles amongst the Indians of the Rocky Mountains and the Andes* (1867).

In 1852, Catlin, facing bankruptcy, sold his collection to a wealthy American, Joseph Harrison, which left the artist 56 years old, nearly penniless, and losing his hearing. He spent the last twenty years of his life "recreating" many of his works from memory and finding new subjects to paint. He died poor and alone (his wife and three children had died from pneumonia in Europe) in an tenement in Jersey City, New Jersey, on 23 December 1872. Among his last words were, "What will happen to my Gallery?" Seven years after Catlin's death, the heirs of Joseph Harrison donated the Catlin Gallery to the Smithsonian Institution.

References "Catlin, George." *National Cyclopedia of American Biography* (1898–1977); Catlin letter, 4 January 1849, George Catlin Miscellaneous Manuscripts, New-York Historical Society; Grossman, Mark, *The ABC-CLIO Companion to the Environmental Movement* (1994); Haberly, Lloyd, *Pursuit of the Horizon: A Life of George Catlin, Painter and Recorder of the American Indian* (1948); McCracken, Harold, *George Catlin and the Old Frontier* (1959); Tolman, R. P., "Catlin, George." In Dumas Malone et al., eds., *Dictionary of American Biography* (1930–88).

Central Machinery Company v. Arizona State Tax Commission (448 U.S. 160, 65 L.Ed. 2d 684, 100 S.Ct. 2592 [1980])

In this Supreme Court decision, it was held that federal law preempted a state's taxation scheme involving the sale of machinery on an Indian reservation. The Central Machinery Company, chartered as an Arizona corporation, sold several tractors to the Gila River Indian Tribe with the prior approval of the Bureau of Indian Affairs, even though the company had no permanent place of business on an Indian reservation and was not licensed under the so-called "Indian Trader Statutes" (25 U.S.C. 261–264). The Arizona State Tax Commission applied a general tax on corporations doing business in the state, which the company paid under protest. The company asked the state for a refund. The company's request was denied, and it instituted proceedings in state court. The Superior Court for Maricopa County, in Phoenix, ordered the state to refund the tax, but the Supreme Court of Arizona reversed, holding that the company's failure to obtain a license as an "Indian trader" made the application of the tax a state matter not subject to federal law. On appeal, the U.S. Supreme Court agreed to hear the company's arguments. After the controversy was heard by the court on 14 January 1980, Justice Thurgood Marshall spoke for a 5–4 court (justices Potter Stewart, Lewis Powell, William H. Rehnquist, and John Paul Stevens dissenting) in holding that federal law preempted the state tax.

Justice Marshall used the precedent of *Warren Trading Post Company v. Arizona Tax Commission* (1965). "It is important to recognize the limits inherent in the principles of federal pre-emption on which the Warren Trading Post decision rests," he explained. "Those limits make necessary in every case such as this a careful inquiry into pertinent federal, tribal, and state interests, without which a rational accommodation of those interests is not possible. Had such an inquiry been made in this case, I am convinced the Court could not have concluded that Arizona's exercise of the sovereign power to tax its non-Indian citizens had been pre-empted by federal law." In a separate and stinging dissent, Justice Powell rationalized that such a seller of products to Indians must undergo a stricter standard of scrutiny, as established by federal law, and since the company did not follow this set of rules, it was liable to be taxed.

***See also** Warren Trading Post Company v. Arizona State Tax Commission.*

Cherokee Indians, Removal of—Congressional and Governmental Debate

Perhaps the greatest controversy to come before the U.S. Congress apart from the slavery issue was that involving the removal of Indian tribes from their native lands in the eastern United States to new reservations in Oklahoma. The most important of these removals was that of the Cherokees in the 1830s, which resulted in the Trail of Tears.

The debate before Congress on the Removal Bill was raucous and barely restrained among the members debating this important issue. Senator Theodore Frelinghuysen of New Jersey was one of the strongest speakers in opposition to removal. His remarks before the Senate, which occurred on 7 and 9 April 1830, took up a total of six hours. His most eloquent commentary addressed the right he felt that Indians had to their lands:

...God, in his providence, planted these tribes on this Western continent, so far as we know, before Great Britain herself had a political existence. I believe, sir, it is not now seriously denied that the Indians are men, endowed with kindred faculties and powers with ourselves; that they have a place in human sympathy, and are justly entitled to a share in the common bounties of a benignant Providence. And, with this conceded, I ask in what code of the law of nations, or by what process of abstract deduction, their rights have been extinguished? Where is the decree or ordinance that has stripped these early and first lords of the soil? Sir, no record of such measure can be found. And I might triumphantly rest the hopes of these feeble fragments of once great nations upon this impregnable foundation. However mere human policy, or the law of power, or the tyrant's pleas of expediency, may have found it convenient at any or in all times to recede from the unchangeable principles of eternal justice, no argument can shake the political maxim, that, where the Indian always has been, he enjoys an absolute right still to be, in the free exercise of his modes of thought, government and conduct.

Representative Edward Everett, later known as one of the nation's greatest orators (he delivered the speech which proceeded Abraham Lincoln's at Gettysburg in 1863), said,

...Sir, if Georgia will recede, she will do more for the Union, and more for herself, than if she would add to her domain the lands of all the Indians, though they were paved with gold. The evil, Sir, is enormous; the inevitable suffering incalculable. Do not stain the fair fame of the country; it has been justly said, it is in the keeping of Congress, on this subject. It is more wrapped up in this policy, in the estimation of the civilized world, than in all your other doings. Its elements are plain, and tangible, and few. Nations of dependent Indians, against their will, under color of law, are driven from their homes into the wilderness. You cannot explain it; you cannot reason it away. The subtleties which satisfy you will not satisfy the severe judgement of enlightened Europe. Our friends will view this measure with sorrow, and our enemies alone with joy. And we ourselves, Sir, when the interests and passions of the day are past, shall look back upon it, I fear, with self-reproach, and a regret as bitter as unavailing.

In his seventh annual message to Congress in 1835, President Andrew Jackson wrote,

The plan of removing the aboriginal people who yet remain within the settled portions of the United States to the country west of the Mississippi River approaches its consummation. It was adopted on the most mature consideration of the condition of this race, and ought to be persisted in till the object is accomplished, and prosecuted with as much vigor as a just regard to their circumstances will permit, and as fast as their consent can be obtained. All preceding experiments for the improvement of the Indians have failed. It seems now to be an established fact that they can not live in contact with a civilized community and prosper. Ages of fruitless endeavors have at length brought us a knowledge of this principle of intercommunication with them. The past we can not recall, but the future we can provide for. Independently of the treaty stipulations into which we have entered with the various tribes for the usufructuary rights they have ceded to us, no one can doubt the moral duty of the Government of the United States to protect and if possible to preserve and perpetuate the scattered remnants of this race which are left within our borders. In the discharge of this duty an extensive region in the West has been assigned for their permanent residence. It has been divided into districts and allotted among them. Many have already removed and others are preparing to go, and with the exception of two small bands living in Ohio and Indiana, not exceeding 1,500 persons, and of the Cherokees, all the tribes on the east side of the Mississippi, and extending from Lake Michigan to Florida, have entered into engagements which will lead to their transplantation.

The plan for their removal and reestablishment is founded upon the knowledge we have gained of their character and habits, and has been dictated by a spirit of enlarged liberality. A territory exceeding in extent that relinquished has been granted to each tribe. Of it climate, fertility, and capacity to support an Indian population the representations are highly favorable. To these districts the Indians are removed at the expense of the United States, and with certain supplies of clothing, arms, ammunition, and other indispensable articles; they are also furnished gratuitously with provisions for the period of a year after their arrival at their new homes. In that time, from the nature of the country and of the products raised by them, they can subsist themselves by agricultural labor, if they choose to resort to that mode of life; if they do not they are upon the skirts of the great prairies, where countless herds of buffalo roam, and a short time suffices to adapt their own habits to the changes which a change of the animals destined for their food may require. Ample arrangements have also been made for the support of schools; in some instances council houses and churches are to be erected, dwellings constructed for the chiefs, and mills for common use. Funds have been set apart for the maintenance of the poor; the most necessary mechanical arts have been introduced, and blacksmiths, gunsmiths, wheelwrights, millwrights, etc., are supported among them. Steel and iron, and sometimes salt, are purchased for them, and plows and other farming utensils, domestic animals, looms, spinning wheels, cards, etc., are presented to them. And besides these beneficial arrangements, annuities are in all cases paid, amounting in some instances to more than $30 for each individual of the tribe, and in all cases sufficiently great, if justly divided and prudently expended, to enable them, in addition to their own exertions, to live comfortably. And as a stimulus for exertion, it is now provided by law that 'in all cases of the appointment of interpreters or other persons employed for the benefit of the Indians a preference shall be given to persons of Indian descent, if such can be found who are properly qualified for the discharge of duties.

Another leading voice against Jackson's policy was Thomas L. McKenney, head of the Office of Indian Affairs in the Indian Department since 1824. After he requested an audience with the president, he delivered to Jackson a stinging rebuke of the Removal policy and its intended consequences. In August 1830, shortly after the meeting, McKenney was dismissed from government service. In 1854, five years before his death, he wrote of the episode in the third edition of his *Sketches of Travels Among the Northern and Southern Indians:*

The fifth article of the treaty of Washington, of the 27th of February, 1819, between John C. Calhoun, on the part of the United States, and a delegation of chiefs and head men from the Cherokee nation, duly authorized and empowered by said nation, contains this provision: "And all white people who *have* intruded, or may *hereafter* intrude, on the lands reserved for the Cherokees, *shall be removed by the United States*, and proceeded against, according to the provisions of the act passed thirtieth of March, eighteen hundred and two, entitled an act to regulate trade and intercourse with the Indian tribes, and to preserve peace of the frontiers."

The solemn compacts with the Indians, guaranteeing them "protection," were treated as things obsolete, or regarded as mockeries. In the face, and in violations of the provisions of the one, and of the enactments of the other, surveyors were permitted to penetrate the Indian territory, roam over it, lay it off into counties, and to proceed, in all things, for its settlement, as though no Indians occupied it, and no laws existed, demanding the interference of the government to prevent it! In vain did the Indians implore the government to protect them; in vain did they call the attention of the Executive to the provisions of treaties, and to the pledges of the law. It was when these outrages first began to show themselves, and thinking President Jackson could not be aware of their existence, that I called on him, and referred to them, and also to the provisions of laws and treaties that guarantied [*sic*] to the Indians a freedom from such trespasses. His answer was, "*Sir, the sovereignty of the States must be preserved,*" concluding with a termination so solemn, and the whole being in a manner so emphatic, as to satisfy me that he had concluded to permit Georgia, and the other States in which the Indians were included, to take their own way in their plans, to harass, persecute, and force out their Indian population." After receiving a letter stating that he was no longer needed at the Indian Office, McKenney added, "Returning to Washington, I inquired of him [Dr. Randolph of the War Department] what the grounds of my dismissal were. 'Why, sir,' was his reply, 'everybody knows your qualifications for the place, but General Jackson has been long satisfied that you are not in harmony with him, and in his views in regard to the Indians.' And thus closed my connexion [*sic*] with the government."

See also Indian Removal Act; Jackson, Andrew—Message on Indian Removal.

References "Address of Senator Theodore Frelinghuysen, 7 April 1830" and "Address of Representative Edward Everett." In Evarts, Jeremiah, ed., *Speeches on the Passage of the Bill for Removal of the Indians Delivered in the Congress of the United States, April and May 1830* (1830); McKenney, Thomas L., *Memoirs, Official and Personal; with Sketches of Travels among the Northern and Southern Indians; Embracing a War Excursion and Descriptions of Scenes along the Western Borders* (1854); "President Jackson's Seventh Annual Message, 7 December 1835." In James Richardson, ed., *A Compilation of the Messages and Papers of the Presidents, 1789–1914*, vol. 3, (1897–1917).

Cherokee Intermarriage Cases (203 U.S. 76 [1906])

This series of four cases, heard before the U.S. Supreme Court in 1906, dealt with the issue of the intermarriages between whites and Cherokee Indians that took place before 1875, when a Cherokee council law denied whites in such marriages rights as Indian citizens, and whether whites in such marriages had the right to share in allotments of land to the Indians. The cases, *Daniel Red Bird et al., Citizens of the Cherokee Nation by Blood, Appellants, v. United States; Cherokee Nation, Appellant, v. United States; Francis B. Fite et al., Intermarried White Persons, Claiming to be Entitled to Citizenship in the Cherokee Nation, Appellants, v. United States*, and *Persons Claiming Rights in the Cherokee Nation by Intermarriage, Appellants, v. United States*, dealt with whether such whites married to Cherokees were entitled to a portion of more than 4 million acres of land allotted to the Cherokees by the U.S. government in 1903. Under a law passed by the Cherokees on 1 November 1875, persons married to Cherokees at that time "acquired no rights of soil or interest in the vested funds of the [Cherokee] Nation." When the government tried to allot the lands in 1903, the Cherokees claimed that their tribe did not recognize intermarriage, and that those whites who were married to Cherokees, even before 1875, were not considered part of the tribe. The government sided with the Cherokees. In a Court of Claims review, the court held that while those whites who were married prior to the 1875 law were considered Cherokees, they had "acquired no rights and have no interest or share in any funds belonging to the Cherokee Nation except where such funds were derived from lease, sale or otherwise from the lands of the Cherokee Nation." The appellants sued to the U.S. Supreme Court for relief.

The Supreme Court heard arguments in the related cases on 19 and 20 February 1906, and handed down a decision on 5 November of that same year. Speaking for a unanimous court, Chief Justice Melville Weston Fuller held that under Cherokee law, the whites were not full Cherokee citizens, and thus could not share in the allotments. "We are dealing with the right of enrollment so as to entitle the persons enrolled to participate in the distribution of the lands and vested funds of the Cherokee Nation, and not with question arising in respect of improvements on the public domain," Fuller wrote in his decision. "As to improvements, they seem to have been treated as those of a tenant who had made them under an agreement that they should remain his. Any citizen of the Nation could use the public domain, and it is not asserted that the intermarried whites failed to obtain their share of such use, but because they have enjoyed that benefit, free from tax or burden, is no reason for giving them a share in the lands and vested funds, which has never been granted to them, and for which they have never paid."

Cherokee Nation et al. v. Hitchcock (187 U.S. 294, 47 L.Ed. 183, 23 S.Ct. 115 [1902])

In this Supreme Court case, the Cherokee Nation sued Secretary of the Interior Ethan A. Hitchcock, asserting that "the Cherokee Nation and its citizens possessed the exclusive right to the use, control, and occupancy of its tribal lands," and that "the Secretary of the Interior, without having lawful authority to do so, was assuming the power to, and was about to, pass favorably upon applications for leases, and was about to grant leases of lands belonging to said nation for the purpose of mining for oil, gas, coal, and other minerals." Section 13 of the act of Congress of 28 June 1898 (30 Stat. 495), known as the Curtis Act, reads, "the Secretary of the Interior is hereby authorized and directed from time to time to provide rules and regulations in regard to the leasing of oil, coal, asphalt, and other materials in said territory, and all such leases shall be made by the Secretary of the Interior; and any lease for any such materials otherwise made shall be absolutely void." Hitchcock granted a lease to the Cherokee Oil & Gas Company, an Arkansas corporation, to begin drilling for oil and gas on the Cherokee Nation reservation. The Cherokee Nation, claiming that "irreparable injury would be caused and wrong and oppression result," sued in the supreme court of District of Columbia to enjoin the issuance of the leases. The court refused to enjoin, or stop, the secretary, and that decision was affirmed by the Court of Appeals for the District of Columbia. Justice Edward Douglass White spoke for a unanimous court in holding that Hitchcock did have the power under the Curtis Act to grant the leases without the consent of the Cherokee Nation. Justice White explained, "There is no question involved in this case as to the taking of property; the authority which it is proposed to exercise, by virtue of the act of 1898, was related merely to the control and development of the tribal property, which still remains subject to the administrative control of the government, even though the members of the tribe have been invested with the status of citizenship under recent legislation." He added, "We are not concerned in this case with the question whether the act of June 28, 1898, and the proposed action thereunder, which is complained of, is or is not wise, and calculated to operate beneficially to the interests of the Cherokees. The power existing in Congress to administer upon and guard the tribal property, and the power being political and administrative in its nature, the manner of its exercise within the province of the legislative branch to determine, and is not one for the courts."

Cherokee Nation v. Georgia (5 Peters [30 U.S.] 1 [1831])

Cherokee Nation v. Georgia was among the most important cases to come before the Supreme Court in its first half century. Together with *Worcester v. Georgia*, which involved many of the same issues and was decided the following year, *Cherokee Nation* established the legal underpinnings for the relationship between government and Indian nations. Supreme Court historian Robert Shnayerson writes, "The Court suffered a collision with prevailing public opinion during Andrew Jackson's first term, when frontier values dominated national politics and the President saw no reason to put judicial interpretations of the Constitution ahead of his own. The Court's clash with Jacksonian Democracy arose from Georgia's harsh treatment of the Cherokee Indians living on their own lands within that state. Jackson, an old Indian fighter, had a low opinion of Indians, as did most white men of the day, and he openly approved of the state's actions. Americans then considered it humane to 'remove' Indians from the path of western settlement (the alternative being slaughter). Jackson himself insisted that 'this unhappy race' be fairly paid for leaving their native grounds and that the government should finance their resettlement on distant lands not yet covered by white Americans. Most tribes submitted; some resorted to armed resistance, but to no avail. The Cherokees of Georgia made an ingenious attempt to retain their lands, however, by adopting white customs. They began farming, created a written language, drafted a constitution, and established a 'nation' in northwestern Georgia. Georgians found this galling, and the state refused to recognize another state within its borders."

In 1823, President James Monroe tried to persuade the Cherokees of Georgia to remove to the western United States when Georgia told him it would not comply with federal laws dealing with the tribe. The Cherokee leaders answered; in an appeal written to the president in 1823, they wrote, "Sir, to these remarks [asking them to remove west] we beg leave to observe and to remind you that the Cherokee are not foreigners but original inhabitants of America, and that they now inhabit and stand on the soil of their own territory and that the limits of this territory are defined by the treaties which they have made with the government of the United States, and that the states by which they are now surrounded have been created out of land which was once theirs, and that they cannot recognize the sovereignty of any state within the limits of their territory."

The Supreme Court had first held in *Fletcher v. Peck* (1810) that the states held a fee simple interest in the title to Indian lands within their borders. In the 1820s, the

Cherokees and other tribes refused to cede any more land to the states, simultaneously forming democratic institutions, such as the establishment of constitutions, tribal bylaws, and such. According to Professor John R. Wunder, "To meet this diplomatic and domestic dilemma, Georgia adopted laws that placed Cherokee lands within organized Georgia counties. Georgia law was to be enforced in these counties, and Cherokee law was to be rendered void. Other legal restrictions on Indian rights were also passed. The laws were not enforced at first while Georgians were waiting to see how the new administration in Washington would react. They were not disappointed. President Jackson made it clear that Cherokees and other Indian nations had only two choices: move to western lands to be set aside for them or live under state law. The Cherokees did not plan to let this matter end. They petitioned Congress to protect their rights. They traveled throughout the Northeast encouraging memorials on their behalf. And they hired a respected Washington, D.C., attorney, William Wirt, to begin planning for a Supreme Court challenge. This law went further than previous removal laws because it lessened the requirement of native American permission before removals could be ordered." Faced with a necessary challenge to the state law, Wirt appealed directly to the U.S. Supreme Court.

On 5 March 1831, the court held its hearing into the case. Representatives for the state of Georgia refused to attend, declaring that the court had no jurisdiction over the matter. The Supreme Court at that time was composed of some of the most brilliant jurists ever to sit on the bench. As chief justice, John Marshall had already served 28 years on the court. Next to him were Joseph Story, William Johnson, and the new justices, Smith Thompson, Henry Baldwin, and John McLean. Justice Gabriel Duval did not participate. In his appeal to the court, Wirt tried to demonstrate that the court's opinion in *Johnson and Graham's Lessee v. McIntosh* (8 Wheaton [21 U.S.] 543 [1823]), which held that the Indians had a right to occupancy of their lands and could only sell them to the United States, displayed a unique federal-Indian relationship with which the states could not interfere. He begged, "If we have a government at all, there is no difficulty in [enforcing Supreme Court decrees]. In pronouncing your decree you will have declared the law; and it is part of the sworn duty of the President of the United States to 'take care that the laws be faithfully executed.' It is not for him, nor for the state [of Georgia] to sit in appeal on your decision.... If he refuses to perform his duty, the Constitution has provided a remedy...." He added, "The legislation of Georgia proposes to annihilate them, as its very end and aim.... If those laws be fully executed, there will be no Cherokee boundary, no Cherokee nation, no Cherokee lands, no Cherokee treaties.... They will all be swept out of existence together, leaving nothing but the monuments in our history of the enormous injustice that has been practised towards a friendly nation."

On 19 March, just two weeks after arguments were heard, Chief Justice Marshall read the court's majority opinion. In an extraordinary development, Justice Thompson, supported by Justice Story, dissented (throughout the Marshall years, few dissents were ever registered). In his opinion, the chief justice expressed his sympathy for the Cherokees, but held that the court lacked jurisdiction because the Indian nations were not "foreign nations," a prerequisite for the court to intervene. As to this issue, he wrote, "The Court has bestowed its best attention on this question, and, after mature deliberation, the majority is of the opinion than an Indian tribe or nation within the United States is not a foreign state in the sense of the constitution, and cannot maintain an action in the Courts of the United States." He added,

A serious additional objection exists to the jurisdiction of the Court. Is the matter of the bill the proper subject for judiciary inquiry and decision? It seeks to restrain a state from the forcible exercise of legislative power over a neighbouring people, asserting their independence; their right to which the state denies. On several of the matters alleged in the bill, for example on the laws making it criminal to exercise the usual powers of self government in their own country by the Cherokee nation, this Court cannot interpose; at least in the form in which those matters are presented. The part of the bill which respects the land occupied by the Indians, and prays the aid of the Court to protect their possession, may be more doubtful. The mere question of right might perhaps be decided by this Court in a proper case with proper parties. But the Court is asked to do more than decide on the title. The bill requires us to control the legislature of Georgia, and to restrain the exertion of its physical force. The propriety of such an interposition by the Court may be well questioned. It savours too much of the exercise of political power to be within the proper province of the judicial department. But the opinion on the point respecting parties makes it unnecessary to decide this question. If it be true that the Cherokee nation have rights, this is not the tribunal in which those rights are to be asserted. If it is true that wrongs have been inflicted, and that still greater are to be apprehended, this is not the tribunal which can redress the past to prevent the future.

In his dissent, Justice Thompson explained,

In the opinion by the Court, the merits of the controversy between the state of Georgia and the Cherokee Indians have not been taken into consideration. The denial of the application for an injunction has been placed solely on the ground of want of jurisdiction in this Court to grant the relief prayed for. It became, therefore, unnecessary to inquire into the merits of the case. But thinking as I do, that the Court has jurisdiction of the case, and may grant relief, at least in part; it may become necessary for me, in the course of my opinion, to glance at the merits of the controversy; which I shall, however, do very briefly, as it is important so far as relates to the present application....If they are entitled to other than judicial relief, it cannot be admitted that in a government like ours, redress is not to be had in some of its departments; and the responsibility for its denial must rest upon those who have the power to grant it. But believing as I do, that relief to some extent falls properly under judicial cognizance, I shall proceed to the examination of the case under the following heads. 1. Is the Cherokee nation of Indians a competent party to sue in this Court? 2. Is a sufficient case made out in the bill, to warrant this court in granting any relief? 3. Is an injunction the fit and appropriate relief?... Whether the Cherokee Indians are to be considered a foreign state or not, is a point on which we cannot expect to discover much light from the law of nations. We must derive this knowledge chiefly from the practice of our own government, and the light in which the nation has been viewed and treated by it. The numerous tribes of Indians, and among others the Cherokee nation, occupied many parts of this country long before the discovery by Europeans, is abundantly established by history; and it is not denied but that the Cherokee nation occupied the territory now claimed by them long before that period....That they are entitled to such occupancy, so long as they quietly and peaceably remain upon the land, cannot be questioned. The circumstance of their original occupancy is here referred to, merely for the purpose of showing, that if these Indian communities were then as they certainly were, nations, they must have been foreign nations, to all the world; not having any connexion [*sic*], or alliance of any description, with any other power on earth. And if the Cherokees were then a foreign nation; when or how have they lost that character, and ceased to be a distinct people, and become incorporated with any other community? . . . It is the political relation in which one government or country stands to another, which constitutes it foreign to the other. The Cherokee territory being within the chartered limits of Georgia, does not affect the question.

The following year, in *Worcester v. Georgia*, Marshall adopted Thompson's arguments and held that the Indians were a "foreign state" separate from the states of the nation and that their dealings could only be with the federal government. Indian historian Reid Peyton Chambers mentions this case as the first leading to the "Trust Doctrine" enunciated by the U.S. Supreme Court through a number of cases. This "Trust Doctrine," according to Chambers, "has been variously described as 'resembling' a guardianship, as a guardian-ward relationship, as a fiduciary, or as a trust responsibility."

See also *Worcester v. Georgia*.

References Chambers, Reid Peyton, "Judicial Enforcement of the Federal Trust Responsibility to Indians." *Stanford Law Review* 27; "Cherokee Proclamation of Their Rights, 1823." In R. S. Cotterill, *The Southern Indians* (1954); Christianson, Stephen G., "Cherokee Nation v. Georgia: 1831." In Edward W. Knappman, ed., *Great American Trials* (1994); Kittrie, Nicholas N., and Eldon D. Wedlock, Jr., eds., *The Tree of Liberty: A Documentary History of Rebellion and Political Crime in America* (1986); "Notes on *The Cherokee Nation of Indians v. The State of Georgia,*" Smith Thompson Papers, Box 1, Library of Congress; Shnayerson, Robert, *An Illustrated History of the Supreme Court of the United States* (1986); U.S. Supreme Court, "Minutes of the Supreme Court of the United States (January 12, 1829–August 7, 1837)," *Papers of the U.S. Supreme Court*, Microfilm Publication No. 215, roll 2; White, G. Edward, *The Marshall Court and Cultural Change, 1815–1835* (1991); Wunder, John R., "The Cherokee Cases (Cherokee Nation v. Georgia and Worcester v. Georgia)." In John W. Johnson, ed., *Historic U.S. Court Cases, 1690–1990: An Encyclopedia* (1992).

Cherokee Nation v. Journeycake (155 U.S. 196 [1894])

In this case, the U.S. Supreme Court decided the narrow issue of whether an Indian tribe incorporated into another tribe could sue that tribe for proceeds from land sold to the government. In 1866, the Delaware Indians were removed from their native lands in Delaware to the Cherokee Nation in Kansas. They paid the Cherokees for a strip of land and received money from the federal government in return for the tribe's land back east. In 1867, the Cherokees made them part of the Cherokee Nation, incorporating them into that tribe part and parcel. In 1890, the Cherokees ceded certain lands to the government that had belonged to their tribe before the Delawares had been removed there. The sums received by the Cherokees were deemed to be for that tribe only, and not for the Delawares. Charles Journeycake, principal chief of the Delawares, took the issue to the Court of Claims, which at that time heard Indian complaints. The Court of Claims held that the sums had to be shared with the Delawares. The Cherokee Nation, joined by the United States as appellants, appealed to the U.S. Supreme Court.

Argued before the court on 18 October 1894, the case was decided on 19 November. Writing for a unanimous court, Justice David Josiah Brewer held that the Delawares, as "adopted" citizens of the Cherokee Nation, must share in the funds from the land sale. A companion case, *United States v. Blackfeather*, was decided at the same time. Ten years after this case was decided, the Delaware Indians sued the Cherokee Nation again (*Delaware Indians, Residing in the Cherokee Nation et al. v. Cherokee Nation* [193 U.S. 127 (1904)]), a decision in which the court held that the Cherokees must submit to the Court of Claims to determine the contractual rights pertaining to the lands and funds of their nation.

See also *United States v. Blackfeather*.

Cherokee Nation v. Southern Kansas Railway Company (135 U.S. 641 [1890])

In this Supreme Court case, the high court held that Congress had the power of eminent domain under which it could seize lands, even from Indians, with the intent to provide adequate compensation, in this case an amount established by three commissioners chosen by Congress. By an act of 4 July 1884 entitled "An act to grant the right of way through the Indian Territory to the Southern Kansas Railway Company, and for other purposes," Congress exercised its power of eminent domain, which allows it to take private lands, in this case Indian lands, in return for fair compensation. As part of the act, Congress provided for the appointment of three commissioners to set a fair price for the land. According to the act, if the Indians dissented from the price arrived at, they could appeal to a circuit court. After judging that 35.5 miles were needed for the main line of the railroad, and 112.54 miles for the branch line, and establishing a price of $93 a mile for the main line and $36 a mile for the branch, the commissioners arrived at the sum of $7,358.94. Meeting in council on 17 December 1886, the Cherokee Indian leadership dissented from the judgment and asked for a trial de novo to reflect on the facts in the case. The litigation was heard in the Circuit Court of the Western District of Arkansas. The circuit court dismissed the Indians' suit as having no merit; the U.S. Supreme Court offered to hear the case. The Indians appealed on the grounds that the government had no right to take lands that belonged to an Indian tribe because such entities were considered sovereign nations. On 19 May 1890, Justice John Marshall Harlan delivered the unanimous opinion of the court. He found that under the theory of eminent domain, the United States had a right to take land from the Indians in exchange for a fair value on such land. But, as Harlan explained, "the court below [the circuit court] ought not…to have dismissed the plaintiff out of court without making some provision, by appropriate orders, for the protection of its rights as against the railway company. Congress gave the Cherokee Nation, if dissatisfied with the allowances provided for in the above act, the right, within 90 days after the making of the award and notice of the same, 'to appeal by original petition to the courts,' and have a trial of the case de novo." Harlan then sent the case back to the circuit court and demanded it hear the Indians' appeal.

The Cherokee Tobacco Case (11 Wallace [78 U.S.] 616 [1871])

Officially titled *Two Hundred and Seven Half Pound Papers of Smoking Tobacco, etc. Elias C. Boudinot et al., Claimants, Plaintiffs in Error, v. United States*, this Supreme Court decision, dubbed "The Cherokee Tobacco Case" by constitutional scholars, dealt with the narrow issue of whether tobacco grown and sold on an Indian reservation was liable to be taxed by the federal government as prescribed by Congress. Elias C. Boudinot and his partner, Stand Watie, a Cherokee who had fought with the Confederacy during the Civil War, attempted to sell 207 half-pound papers of tobacco that they had grown on their farms that were undoubtedly on the Cherokee Nation lands in Oklahoma. The U.S. government, citing "An Act Imposing Taxes on Distilled Spirit, and for Other Purposes" of 20 July 1868, claimed that the two men owed taxes on the tobacco and confiscated the leaves. Boudinot and Watie sued to have the goods returned to them. The District Court for the Western District of Arkansas found for the government; Boudinot and Watie appealed to the U.S. Supreme Court.

The Supreme Court heard the arguments in the case on 11 April 1871 and handed down a decision on 1 May of that same year. Justice Noah Haynes Swayne spoke for the court (Justice Joseph Bradley dissented and Justice Stephen Johnson Field did not participate) when he held that section 107 of the act of 20 July 1868 "was intended to apply and does apply to the country of the Cherokee Nation." In his dissent, Justice Bradley wrote, "In my judgment it was not the intention of Congress to extend the internal revenue law to the Indian country. That territory is an exempt jurisdiction. Whilst the United States has not relinquished its power to make such regulations as it may deem necessary in relation to that territory, and whilst Congress has occasionally passed laws affecting it, yet by repeated treaties the government has, in effect, stipulated that in all ordinary cases the Indian populations shall be autonomies, invested with the power to make and execute all laws for their domestic government. Such being the case, all laws of a general character passed by Congress will be considered as not applying to the Indian territory, unless expressly mentioned."

Reference Colbert, Thomas Burnell, "The Death Knell of the Nations (Boudinot v. United States)." In Johnson, John W., ed., *Historic U.S. Court Cases, 1690–1990: An Encyclopedia* (1992).

Childers v. Beaver et al. (270 U.S. 555 [1926])

In this Supreme Court decision, the court held that a federal enactment sanctioned the inheritance of an allotted tract without state inheritance taxes being levied against the transaction. See-sah Quapaw, a full-blood Quapaw Indian, died on 4 March 1920, leaving behind certain allotted lands which, under the act of Congress of 2 March 1895 (28 Stat. 876, at 907), were declared to be inalienable for a period of 25 years. Upon See-sah Quapaw's death, the secretary of the interior, acting under the order of the act of Congress of 25 June 1910 (36 Stat. 855), proclaimed her only heirs to be her husband, John Beaver, and her brother, Benjamin Quapaw, and conveyed the allotments to them. At this point Charles C. Childers, the state auditor of Oklahoma, stepped in to levy inheritance taxes against the allotments. Beaver and Benjamin Quapaw sued in the District Court for the Eastern District of Oklahoma to stop the tax from being imposed. The court held for Beaver and Quapaw, and Childers appealed to the U.S. Supreme Court. Justice James McReynolds spoke for a unanimous court on 12 April 1926 in refusing Childers's attempts to collect the inheritance tax. Justice McReynolds explained, "It must be accepted as established that during the trust or restrictive period Congress has power to control lands within a state which have been duly allotted to Indians by the United States and thereafter conveyed through trust or restrictive patents. This is essential to the proper discharge of their duty to a dependent people, and the means or instrumentalities utilized therein cannot be subjected to taxation by the state without the consent of the federal government."

Chippewa Indians of Minnesota v. United States (307 U.S. 1 [1939])

In this Supreme Court case, the court held on the narrow grounds that an act of Congress did not necessarily create a trust, and that the Chippewa had no standing to ask Congress to reimburse a fund created for the tribe. The act of 14 January 1889 (25 Stat. 642) allowed the Chippewa to cede the rights to the timber of their native lands if the U.S. government would sell the timber, collect the proceeds, and hold the monies in trust for a term of fifty years, when all the Chippewa alive at that time would receive the assets. Over the years, Congress took monies from the fund to reimburse the Treasury for benefits given to Chippewa, as well as other expenditures not related in the act. As such, the Chippewa charged, the U.S. government was guilty of a diversion and must make good the missing funds. The Court of Claims, sitting in judgment, held that the 1889 act did not establish a trust, so the U.S. government could use the money as it wished. The Chippewa appealed to the U.S. Supreme Court. The court heard the case on 30 March 1939 and decided the case on 17 April. Writing for a unanimous court, Justice Owen Roberts held that the 1889 act did not establish a trust and that Congress could use the money for the advancement of the Indians. "It is not contended that the expenditures made from the fund, or reimbursed from it, were not for the benefit of the Indians or were not such as properly might be made for their education and civilization, the purposes stated in the Act of 1889," Roberts wrote. "We hold that the Act did not tie the hands of Congress so that it could not depart from the plan envisaged therein, in the use of the tribal property for the benefit of its Indian wards."

See also *Chippewa Indians of Minnesota v. United States, Red Lake Band of Chippewa Indians of Minnesota (Interveners).*

*Chippewa Indians of Minnesota v. United States (*Red Lake Band of Chippewa Indians of Minnesota, Interveners) (301 U.S. 358, 81 L.Ed. 1156, 57 S.Ct. 826 [1937])

The narrow matter decided in this Supreme Court case was whether the illegal diminishment of a reservation affected a certain tribe of Indians or all of the Indians of that nation. The Chippewa Indians of Minnesota sued the U.S. government for what it claimed was the illegal taking of 663,421 acres of land it had ceded to the government in trust and which had been sold without its consent. The United States countered that the land had belonged to the Red Lake Band of Chippewa Indians of Minnesota and, in a strange twist, the Red Lake Band intervened in the case to side with the United States. The Chippewa, claiming that the members of the Chippewa nation "were members of the great Chippewa family," continued its suit. The Court of Claims rendered a judgment against the Chippewa and, under a special act of Congress, were allowed to appeal directly to the U.S. Supreme Court. Arguments in the case were heard on 2 February 1937.

Justice Willis Van Devanter delivered the court's unanimous opinion upholding the Court of Claims' decision. Justice Van Devanter explained, "Complaint is made of the action of the court in regarding the Indian title to the lands in the Red Lake Reservation prior to and at the time of the cession as material. Plainly the complaint is without merit. Whether the title was in the Red Lake band's alone or in all of the Minnesota bands has a material bearing on the construction and effect of the cession, and also on the question of who, after the cession, had the title to the lands reserved." He added, "It is insisted that even though the Indian title was in the Red Lake bands, Congress, in section 1 of the act of 1889 [14 January 1889 (25 Stat. 642), which provided for the cession and allotment of the Chippewa lands] declared that as to the Red Lake Reservation the cession should be sufficient if made by 'two-thirds of the male adults of all the Chippewa Indians in Minnesota,' and thereby enabled the Chippewa as a whole to cede that reservation, even over the objection of the Red Lake bands. To this we do not agree. Our decision, while recognizing that the government has power to control and manage the property and affairs of its Indian wards in good faith for their welfare, shows that this power is subject to constitutional limitations and does not enable the government to give the lands of one tribe or band to another, or to deal with them as its own."

***See also** Chippewa Indians of Minnesota v. United States.*

Choate v. Trapp (224 U.S. 665 [1912])

Under a provision of the Curtis Act (30 Stat. 497, at 505), enacted 28 June 1898, Congress allowed that allotments held by the original allottee were to remain untaxable. In this case, officially titled *George W. Choate et al., Plaintiffs in Error, v. M. F. Trapp, Secretary of the State Board of Equalization et al.*, the U.S. Supreme Court held that "where the property of a citizen of the United States is exempted from taxation for a consideration, he cannot be deprived of that exemption by subsequent legislation without his consent, and it is immaterial whether the citizen be an Indian or not." Under the Curtis Act, Congress provided that "all the lands allotted be nontaxable while the title remains in the original allottee, but not to exceed twenty-one years from the date of patent...." Under a subsequent act of 27 May 1908 (35 Stat. 312), Congress removed all restrictions from such allotted lands and provided that lands removed from restrictions be liable to taxation. George Choate and eight thousand members of the Choctaw and Cherokee Nations of Oklahoma sued M. F. Trapp, secretary of the Oklahoma State Board of Equalization, among others, to enjoin the state officials from taxing their original allotments in 1908. A superior court found for Trapp and the Supreme Court of Oklahoma upheld the judgment. Choate and the other plaintiffs sued to the U.S. Supreme Court.

Arguments in the case were held on 23 February 1912 and the case was decided on

13 May of that same year. Writing for a unanimous court, Justice Joseph Rucker Lamar held that the second federal action allowing for the taxation of the allotments was unconstitutional. As Lamar opined, "There was no intimation that the power of wardship [by Congress over the Indians] conferred authority on Congress to lessen any of the rights of property which had been vested in the individual Indian by prior laws or contracts. Such rights are protected from repeal by the provisions of the Fifth Amendment. The constitution of the state of Oklahoma itself expressly recognizes that the exemption here granted must be protected until it is lawfully destroyed. We have seen that it was a vested property right which could not be abrogated by statute. The decree refusing to enjoin the assessment on the exempt lands of the plaintiffs must therefore be reversed." Two other cases relavant to this issue were decided at the same time: *English v. Richardson* and *Gleason et al. v. Wood et al.*

See also Curtis Act; *English v. Richardson; Gleason et al. v. Wood et al.; Jones v. Meehan.*

The Choctaw Nation and the Chickasaw Nation v. the State of Oklahoma et al. (397 U.S. 620, 25 L. Ed. 2d 615, 90 S.Ct. 1328 [1970])

The narrow question decided in this Supreme Court case was whether an Indian nation received title to the bed of a river which in some places constituted part of an Indian nation and in others as the boundary between the Indian reservation and the state. By the Treaty of Dancing Rabbit Creek (7 Stat. 333) of 27 September 1830, and the Treaty of New Echota (7 Stat. 478) of 29 December 1835, the United States took the lands of two Indian nations, the Chickasaw (in the former treaty) and the Cherokees (in the latter), and moved them to what is now Oklahoma, promising the Indians that they would not be forced to remove from these new homes. In the new lands, portions of the Arkansas River came entirely within the apportioned reservations, and in other areas the river formed the border between the reservations and the state of Oklahoma. It was these border regions on the Arkansas that form the basis of this controversy. In 1966, the Cherokee Nation sued in the U.S. District Court for the Eastern District of Oklahoma, seeking to recover from the state proceeds from oil and mineral resources the state had taken from the river bed in the areas where the reservations bordered the river. The Choctaw and Chickasaw nations were asked to join the suit, which sought to recover the profits and enjoin any further taking of the resources. The district court held that the granting of the land rights gave the Indians no title to the river bed. On appeal, the U.S. Court of Appeals for the Tenth Circuit affirmed. The U.S. Supreme Court granted certiorari. Justice Thurgood Marshall expressed the views of four members of the court on 27 April 1970 (Justice William O. Douglas concurred in a separate opinion, Chief Justice Warren Burger and justices Byron White and Hugo Black dissented, and Justice John Marshall Harlan did not participate) when he struck down the court of appeals decision. The court held that the two treaties gave the Indians rights to the river where it was inside the reservation, as well as rights to the river bordering the reservation. As Justice Marshall explained, "Together, petitioners were granted fee simple title to a vast tract of land through which the Arkansas River winds it course. The natural inference from these grants is that all the land within their metes and bounds was conveyed, including the banks and bed of rivers. To the extent that the documents speak of the question, they are consistent with and tend to confirm this natural reading. Certainly there was no express exclusion of the bed of the Arkansas River by the United States as there was to other land within the grants." A rehearing in the matter was denied (398 U.S. 945, 26 L.Ed. 2d 285, 90 S.Ct. 1834 [1970]).

Choctaw Nation v. United States (119 U.S. 1, 30 L. Ed. 306, 7 S.Ct. 75 [1886])

The matter settled in this Supreme Court decision was the amount of the award bestowed on the Choctaw Nation for damages by the U.S. government. By a treaty of 1855, the U.S. Senate awarded the Choctaws $500,000 for certain lands that were taken from the tribe. In 1861, $250,000 was disbursed, but the remainder of the award was never paid and in 1882 the Senate asked the Court of Claims, then with jurisdiction over Indian claims, to adjudicate a proper sum. The court, after deducting expenses and other costs, refused to abide by the Senate's original award of $500,000 and instead arrived at an amount of $658,120.32; deducting the 1861 payment of $250,000, the court awarded the Choctaws $408,120.32. The U.S. government disagreed and sued to the U.S. Supreme Court. In a separate motion, the Choctaws felt the amount was too low and they, too, appealed to the Supreme Court. The two cases were argued before the court on 19–21 October 1886 and a decision was handed down on 15 November of that year.

Justice Stanley Matthews spoke for the 8–1 decision (Chief Justice Morrison Remick Waite dissented) in throwing out the Court of Claims award and awarding a much larger sum to the Indians than even the Court of Claims awarded. In the end, Matthews found that "the final result is that the Choctaw Nation is entitled to a judgment against the United States for the following sums: First, $2,981,247.30, subject to the deduction of $250,000 paid under the act of 1861; second, for unpaid annuities, $59,449.32; third, for lands taken in fixing the boundary between the State of Arkansas and the Choctaw Nation, $68,102." The final total was $2,858,798.60. Chief Justice Waite disagreed, arguing that "all that remains, then, is to ascertain what is legally due from the United States on account of the national and individual claims not included in that settlement; and upon this I am entirely satisfied with what was done by the Court of Claims. I think the judgment should be affirmed."

See also *United States v. Choctaw Nation and Chickasaw Nation.*

Choctaw, Oklahoma, & Gulf Railway Company v. Harrison (235 U.S. 292, 59 L.Ed. 234, 35 S.Ct. 27 [1914])

Can a state tax the proceeds of a federal instrumentality, a railway company acting under a federal grant, on an Indian reservation? That was the issue in this Supreme Court case. The Choctaw, Oklahoma, & Gulf Railway Company was granted by the federal government the power to lease and operate coal mines, which it did on the Choctaw and Chickasaw Indian reservations in Oklahoma. The railroad sought in court to enjoin John A. Harrison, the sheriff of Pittsburg County, Oklahoma, from collecting a tax levied by the state on the gross sale of coal dug in the mines. The District Court for the Eastern District of Oklahoma refused to enjoin Harrison, forcing the railway company to appeal to the U.S. Supreme Court, which handed down its decision on 30 November 1914. Justice James McReynolds spoke for a unanimous court in reversing the lower court's ruling and holding that because the railway was considered an instrumentality of the federal government, the state could not legally tax it. Justice McReynolds argued that under the Atoka Agreement embodied in the Curtis Act, the lease of coal mines and the sale of the coal that was mined was an exclusive right of the federal government, not the state.

See also Curtis Act.

Civilization Fund Act (3 Stat. 516)

This federal action of 3 March 1819 was enacted to "encourage the activities of benevolent societies in providing schools for the Indians." The act provided a fund to establish and maintain such schools. The act reads:

Be it enacted..., That for the purpose of providing against the further decline and final extinction of the Indian tribes, adjoining the frontier settlements of the United States, and for introducing among them the habits and arts of civilization, the President of the United States shall be, and he is hereby authorized, in every case where he shall judge improvement in the habits and condition of such Indians practicable, and that the means of instruction can be introduced with their own consent, to employ capable persons of good and moral character, to instruct them in the mode of agriculture suited to their situation; and for teaching their children in reading, writing, and arithmetic, and performing such other duties as may be enjoined, according to such instructions and rules as the President may give and prescribe for the regulation of their conduct, in the discharge of their duties.

Sec. 2. And be it further enacted, That the annual sum of ten thousand dollars be, and the same is hereby appropriated, for the purpose of carrying into effect the provisions of this act; and account of the expenditure of the money, and proceedings in execution of the foregoing provisions, shall be laid annually before Congress.

Reference Prucha, Francis Paul, ed., *Documents of United States Indian Policy* (1990).

Clairmont v. United States (225 U.S. 551 [1912])

In this noted U.S. Supreme Court case, the court held that once Congress granted a right of way from Indian land, that land was no longer part of a reservation, and thus not subject to laws such as those prohibiting the sale of alcohol. Henry Clairmont, a Flathead Indian, was returning to his home on the Flathead reservation in Montana on a train of the Northern Pacific Railway. The train stopped at a point that had once been part of the Flathead reservation; the land had been ceded to the government by an act of 30 January 1882; the railway had been granted a right of way to the land in 1864. An Interior Department official boarded the train, discovered a pint of whiskey on Clairmont's person, and arrested him for introducing liquor into "Indian country," as prohibited by the act of 30 January 1897 (29 Stat. 506). A grand jury indicted Clairmont and after a trial he was found guilty. Clairmont appealed to the District Court of the United States for the District of Montana, which asked the U.S. Supreme Court to examine the conviction. The court granted certiorari; the case was submitted on 1 May 1912 and a decision was handed down on 10 June of that same year.

Writing for a unanimous court, Justice Charles Evans Hughes held that because the Flatheads had ceded the land to the government, and because the land was used to give the railroad a right of way, that land was no longer considered "Indian country" as defined in the law, and thus Clairmont was not guilty of introducing liquor into Indian country. As Hughes wrote,

> In the present case there was no provision, either in the treaty with the Indians, or by an act of Congress, which limited the effect of the surrender of the Indian title. . . . The Indian title or right of occupation was extinguished, with reservation; and the relinquished strip came under the jurisdiction of the then territory, and later under that of the state of Montana. It was not "unappropriated public land," or land "owned or held by any Indian or Indian tribe." To repeat, the plaintiff in error was not charged with "attempting to introduce" the liquor into Indian country, but with the actual introduction. If having the liquor in his possession on the train on this right of way did not constitute such introduction, is immaterial, so far as the charge is concerned, whether or not he intended to take it elsewhere. Nor is it important that the plaintiff in error is an Indian. The statute makes it an offense for "any person" to introduce liquor into Indian country. Our conclusion must be that the right of way had been completely withdrawn from the reservation by the surrender of the Indian title, and that in accordance with the repeated rulings of this court, it was not Indian country. The district court, therefore, had no jurisdiction of the offense charged, and the judgment must be reversed.

See also *Ex parte Webb.*

Cohen, Felix Solomon (1907–1953)

Cohen was responsible for the enactment of the Indian Reorganization Act (IRA) of 1934 and for tireless efforts inside the federal government to improve the lot of the American Indian; Felix Cohen was, without doubt, one of the great Indian civil rights advocates who ever lived, as well as a noted attorney and writer. Born the son of Morris Raphael Cohen, a Russian Jew who was a professor of mathematics and philosophy at the City College of New York, and Mary (née Ryshpan) Cohen, a former schoolteacher, on 3 July 1907 in New York City, Felix Cohen went to elementary school in Yonkers at age eight, graduated when he was 12, and spent four years at the Townsend Harris High School in college courses. Subsequently he spent three years at the City College of New York, from which he received his bachelor's degree *magna cum laude* when he 19. He was the editor of the college paper, *The Campus*. Although his career is not intertwined with his father's, they both contributed to a book published by Felix Cohen after his father's death, *Readings in Jurisprudence and Legal Philosophy* (1951). Felix Cohen received his doctorate from Harvard University in 1929 and his law degree from Columbia just two years later.

Cohen entered private law practice in 1932. The following year, when Harold L. Ickes became secretary of the interior, he brought on board Professor Nathan Margold to be the department's solicitor. Margold then asked Cohen to join interior to spend one year helping to draft fundamental laws to change the government's Indian policy. Cohen's first draft, officially named the Wheeler-Howard Act after its congressional sponsors, became known as the Indian Reorganization Act of 1934. Cohen's single year in Washington ultimately became 15 years, during which time Cohen established the blueprint for future government Indian policy, including helping to create the Indian Claims Commission Act of 1946. In the first years of the 1940s, he argued two important cases on behalf of Indians before the U.S. Supreme Court: *United States v. Santa Fe Railroad* (314 U.S. 339 [1942]) and *Tulee v. State of Washington* (315 U.S. 681 [1942]). In 1942 he published his landmark *Handbook of Federal Indian Law*, now entitled *Felix S. Cohen's Handbook of Federal Indian Law* and edited by Rennard Strickland. It was, and remains to this day, the leading authority on Indian law. The introduction to the most recent edition states, "The *Handbook* has its genesis in a forty-six volume collection of federal laws and treaties compiled primarily by Cohen and his lifetime colleague and friend, Theodore H. Haas. In 1939 Cohen was appointed special assistant to the attorney general to direct an 'Indian Law Survey.' After intensive work by some forty-seven staff members and contributors, the *Handbook* was published in 1942 under the auspices of the Department of the Interior.... Cohen was the Blackstone of American Indian law. He brought organization and conceptual clarity to the field. Although the 1942 work was prefaced with the disclaimer that 'this handbook does not purport to be a cyclopedia,' it was in fact a thorough and comprehensive treatise that attended to virtually every nook and cranny of the field. The 1942 *Handbook* was also blessed with a philosophical breadth that only a scholar of Cohen's background and vision could provide." Cohen also produced a number of articles on American Indians, including "Anthropology and the Problems of Indian Administration" *(Southwestern Social Science Quarterly* 43 [2]), "Indian Rights and the Federal Courts" *(Minnesota Law Review* 1940), "The Spanish Origin of Indian Rights in the Law of the United States" *(Georgetown Law Journal* 1942), "Original Indian Title" *(Minnesota Law Review* 1947), and "The Erosion of Indian Rights, 1950–53: A Case Study in Bureaucracy" *(Yale Law Journal* February 1953). Many of these papers were collected by his widow, Lucy Kramer Cohen, in *The Legal Conscience: Selected Papers of Felix S. Cohen* (1960).

In 1948, Cohen resigned from his government position and reentered private practice. Biographer Robert E. Bieder wrote of him, "Although his defense of Indian rights and his work in Indian affairs absorbed much of his energies, Cohen also wrote on legal philosophy, especially on the working of American democracy.... Throughout his career Cohen strongly supported civil rights and freedom from discrimination for all minorities, believing that 'oppression against a racial minority is more terrible than most other forms of oppression, because there is no escape from one's race.'" Dedicated to eradicating economic discrimination, he proved an active proponent of the Fair Employment Practices Commission, which he had helped to create. He also labored for legislation allowing Indians to receive Social Security benefits."

On 19 October 1953, Cohen died suddenly, apparently of a heart attack; he was only 46 years old. John Collier said of him in eulogy, "Not only was he an important factor in formulating the Indian Reorganization Act, but through the ensuing years, for fifteen years, he was a leading factor in construing the Act, in implementing it through the Solicitor's opinions and legal constructions. And he exercised a severely disciplinary control, if you will, over tendencies of the Indian Bureau to deviate from the spirit of the Act." He added, "In losing him, I say, as I said before, the Indians, the tribes, their white friends, the cause of the Indians, have suffered an irreparable, mournful loss."

See also Collier, John; Indian Reorganization Act; Myer, Dillon Seymour.

References Bieder, Robert E., "Cohen, Felix Solomon." In Dumas Malone et al., eds., *Dictionary of American Biography* (1930–88); "Felix Cohen Dead; Aided U.S. Indians." *New York Times*, 20 October 1953, 29; Kelly, William H. ed., *Indian Affairs and the Indian Reorganization Act: The Twenty Year Record* (1954); Moran, Gerard R., "Felix S. Cohen." In "A Jurisprudential Symposium in Memory of Felix S. Cohen." *Rutgers Law Review* 9 (2); Strickland, Rennard, ed., *Felix S. Cohen's Handbook of Federal Indian Law* (1982).

Collier, John (1884–1968)

The jacket of the 1962 edition of John Collier's 1949 work, *On the Gleaming Way: Navajos, Eastern Pueblos, Zuñis, Hopis, Apaches, and Their Land; and Their Meanings to the World* contains the following inscription: "Probably no American of this century has had so deep an interest in Indians as John Collier, so close an association with them, or so profound a knowledge of their ways." His administration as commissioner of Indian Affairs from 1933 until 1945, the height of the New Deal, years in which much government legislation in favor of Indians was passed, was only a part of his lifelong service devoted to the rights of Native Americans. Collier was born in Atlanta, Georgia, on 4 May 1884, the son of Charles Allen Collier, the mayor of Atlanta and a wealthy merchant and attorney, and Susie (née Rawson) Collier. He attended local schools, Columbia University (1902–05), and the Collège de France in Paris. In 1905, he was named executive secretary of the Associated Charities of Atlanta, where he tried new ways to aid the poor, but resigned soon after when he conflicted with the board of directors over policy. In 1908, he became the civic secretary of the People's Institute in New York City, where he worked with immigrants on the Lower East Side of Manhattan. As well, he helped to organize the National Board of Review of Motion Pictures and served as its secretary, 1910–14. He also worked for the National Training School for Community Centers and to establish the Child Health Organization in Atlanta. In 1919, he moved to California and for the next four years he studied the Indians of the southwestern United States, particularly the Taos Pueblo Indians of New Mexico. In 1922, after being named as the agent for the Indian Welfare Committee of the General Federation of Women's Clubs, he lobbied Congress and assembled a number of popular artists of the time, including Nicholas Vachel Lindsay, to defeat the Bursum Bill, which would have sold many of the lands of Taos Pueblo. This work made him nationally prominent and gave him the impetus to further Indian reform. In 1923, he formed and became the executive secretary of the American Indian Defense Association (AIDA).

Collier's work was not unopposed. On 19 October 1924, Herbert Welsh, president of the Indian Rights Association, wrote that "through the extremely skillful propaganda conducted by John Collier, the able and many-sided executive secretary of the American Indian Defense Association, there has been effected in recent years a revival of ancient pagan ideas of obsolete communal Indian management, which if it is not promptly stopped threatens to upset the most fundamental principle of American free life and intellectual progress among the considerable proportion of Christian progressive Indians." As secretary of the AIDA, Collier wrote a scathing response to Welsh's letter on 16 November 1924. Biographer Kenneth Philp writes, "During the 1920s Collier was a brilliant propagandist for Indian causes. Beginning in 1925, he employed articles in *American Indian Life* and other AIDA publications to discredit land allotment, to criticize the government for failing to protect Indian water rights and provide necessary social services, and chastise the Indian Bureau for banning certain tribal dances. In 1927 he worked for the passage of the Indian Oil Act, which guaranteed Indian royalties from subsurface minerals on executive-order reservations."

In 1933, the election of Franklin D. Roosevelt to the presidency led newly installed Secretary of the Interior Harold L. Ickes to ask Collier to fill the commissioner of Indian Affairs position and put into play some of the proposals he had been advocating for the better part of a decade. Working hand in hand with Felix S. Cohen, a New York attorney, the Indian office produced legislation such as the Indian Reorganization Act of 1934, the Johnson-O'Malley Act of 1934, the Oklahoma Indian Welfare Act of 1936, the Indian Arts and Crafts Board Act, and the act that established the Indian Civilian Conservation Corps. According to New Deal historian Peter Wright, "As commissioner, Collier was officially responsible for 'the Indians of the United States, their education, lands, moneys, schools, and general welfare.…' At the time he took over the BIA, it was a highly centralized, inefficient, and bureaucratic adjunct of the Interior Department. The BIA had been insulated from modern developments in medicine, anthropology, education, sociology, and psychology, and 'it continued to exist and work not even in the nineteenth but the eighteenth century.' The Indian Service became a 'callous, hardened, and solidified system,' unresponsive to the needs of its wards in the enforcement of policy."

John Collier

Collier organized the Institute for Ethnic Affairs in Washington, D.C., and then campaigned for self-government and economic self-sufficiency for Native Americans and native peoples of the South Pacific. He also taught sociology at the City College of New York. In 1956, he moved to Taos, where he spent the rest of his life, composed articles on Indian life and wrote his memoirs, *From Every Zenith: A Memoir and Some Essays on Life and Thought* (1963). Collier died in Taos on 8 May 1968, four days after his eighty-fourth birthday. Philp writes, "Collier's death ended a remarkable career—a career which demonstrated the strengths and weaknesses of twentieth century social reform in the United States. Characteristic of many American reformers, Collier believed that society would advance to higher levels of progress through creative planning and the revitalization of group living. This evolutionary, positivist world view was the dynamic behind Collier's successful efforts to promote social justice. But it also caused him to believe erroneously that he could create a cooperative commonwealth by combining the attributes of preindustrial ethnic cultures with the requirements of a capitalist civilization."

See also Bureau of Indian Affairs; Indian Arts and Crafts Board Act; Indian Reorganization Act; Johnson-O'Malley Act; Oklahoma Indian Welfare Act.

References Collier, John, *On the Gleaming Way: Navajos, Eastern Pueblos, Zuñis, Apaches, and Their Land; and Their Meanings to the World* (1962); Collier, letter to the editor, *New York Times*, 16 November 1924; "John Collier, Ex-Commissioner of Indian Affairs, Is Dead at 84." *New York Times*, 9 May 1968, 47; Downes, Randolph C., "A Crusade for Indian Reform, 1922–1934." *Mississippi Valley Historical Review* 32 (2); Kelly, Lawrence, "Indian Policy." In Otis L. Graham, Jr., and Meghan Robinson Wander, eds., *Franklin D. Roosevelt, His Life and Times: An Encyclopedic View* (1985); Long, Anton V., *Senator Bursum and the Pueblo Indians Lands Act of 1924* (Master's thesis, University of New Mexico, 1949); Philp, Kenneth R., "Collier, John." In Dumas Malone et al., eds., *Dictionary of American Biography* (1930–88); Philp, Kenneth, "John Collier." In Robert M. Kvasnicka and Herman J. Viola, eds., *The Commissioners of Indian Affairs, 1824–1977* (1979); Philp, Kenneth, *John Collier's Crusade for Indian Reform, 1920–1954* (1977); Strickland, Rennard, ed., *Felix Cohen's Handbook of Federal Indian Law* (1982); Welsh, letter to the editor, *New York Times*, 19 October 1924; Wright, Peter M., "John Collier and the Oklahoma Indian Welfare Act of 1936." *Chronicles of Oklahoma* 50 (3).

Colorado River Water Conservation District v. United States (424 U.S. 800 [1976])

In this U.S. Supreme Court case (which also involved the case of *Mary Akin v. United States)*, the court held on the narrow issue of whether the federal courts could intervene in matters involving Indian water rights. According to the case notes, "The United States, as trustee for certain Indian tribes and as owner of various non-Indian government claims, brought an action in the U.S. District Court for the District of Colorado to obtain a determination of its rights in certain waters and tributaries located in Colorado Water Division No. 7." Under the McCarran Amendment (also known as the McCarran Water Rights Suit Act, 66 Stat. 560, codified at 43 U.S.C. 666), the federal government was given the right to join as a defendant in any lawsuit that involved (1) the adjudication of rights to the use of water of a river system or other source, and (2) where it appears that the United States is the owner, or is about to become the owner, of such water rights, making the government a "necessary party" to any such lawsuit. However, several of the plaintiffs moved in federal court to dismiss the charges as to federal action, claiming that under the McCarran Amendment, the government must defer to state courts. The federal district court agreed, dismissing the lawsuit; however, on appeal, the U.S. Court of Appeals for the Tenth Circuit reversed, holding that under 28 U.S.C. 1345, the federal courts had jurisdiction in all civil actions set forth by the United States "[e]xcept as otherwise provided by an Act of Congress." On appeal the U.S. Supreme Court granted certiorari, and arguments were heard on 14 January 1976. On 24 March of that same year, Justice William Brennan delivered the 6–3 decision of the court (justices Potter Stewart, Harry Blackmun, and John Paul Stevens dissenting) that the McCarran Amendment did not defer such civil proceedings from state court to federal court and so struck down the appeals court action. The three dissenters argued that because the issues involved in the case were those "of federal law," the federal courts were the best place to hear them out.

Commission on Organization of the Executive Branch of the Government

See Hoover Commission Report.

Commission to the Five Civilized Tribes in the Indian Territory

Also known as the Dawes Commission after its chairman, Senator Henry L. Dawes of Massachusetts, who authored the General Allotment Act of 1887, this delegation of several leading politicians was sent in 1893 to the Five Civilized Tribes (which had been excluded from the General Allotment Act) to offer the individual Indians citizenship so as to break up the reservations into allotments. The commission was established by section 16 of the Appropriations Act of 1893 (27 Stat. 645–46), which reads in part:

Sec. 16. The President shall nominate and, by and with the advice and consent of the Senate, shall appoint three commissioners to enter into negotiations with the Cherokee Nation, the Choctaw Nation, the Chickasaw Nation, the Muscogee (or Creek) Nation, and the Seminole Nation, for the purpose of the extinguishment of the national or tribal title to any lands within that Territory now held by any and all of such nations or tribes, either by cession of the same or some part thereof to the United States, or by the allotment and division of the same in severalty among the Indians of such nations or tribes, respectively, as may be entitled to the same, or by such other method as may be agreed upon between the several nations and tribes aforesaid, or each of them, with the United States, with a view to such an adjustment, upon the basis of justice and equity, as may, with the consent of such nations or tribes of Indians, so far as may be necessary, be requisite and suitable to enable the ultimate creation of a State or States of the Union which shall embrace the lands within said Indian Territory.

In their first report to the Congress, 20 November 1894, the commissioners wrote, "Justice has been utterly perverted in the hands of those who have thus laid hold of the forms of its administration in this Territory and who have inflicted irreparable wrongs and outrages upon a helpless people for their own gain." In a progress report released on 3 October 1898, the council informed the Congress that the Indians were resisting allotment and that the Congress should use all of its powers to get them to submit. Such legislation was introduced by Representative Charles Curtis of Kansas and with its passage the allotment of the lands of the Five Civilized Tribes was mandated by law. In 1899, the Supreme Court heard the case of *Stephens v. Cherokee Nation*, in which it examined the constitutionality of the Curtis Act and the legality of the decisions of the Dawes Commission. The decision in *Stephens* allowed the court to uphold Congress' unlimited power to enact such legislation as the Curtis Act and to create such councils as the Dawes Commission. The commission also worked closely with the Senate Select Committee (1887–1909) and Senate Committee (1909–1921) on the Five Civilized Tribes of Indians, which was chaired by such men as Henry Teller (1893–95) and Benjamin Tillman (1905–13).

See also Curtis Act; *Stephens v. Cherokee Nation.*

Reference U.S. Congress, Senate, *Report of the Dawes Commission*, Senate Miscellaneous Document No. 24, 53d Congress, 3d Session (serial 3281).

Committee of One Hundred

This commission was created by Secretary of the Interior Hubert Work (who served under President Warren G. Harding) to "advise with him concerning the interests of the American Indian." The commission included such Indian activists as Charles A. Eastman (Santee) and Arthur C. Parker (Seneca), and non-Indians such as John J. Pershing, William Jennings Bryan, Bernard Baruch, and activists John Collier (later F.D.R.'s Commissioner of Indian Affairs) and Matthew K. Sniffen of the Indian Rights Association. The commissioners met in Washington from 12 to 13 December 1923, and Arthur C. Parker was named committee chairman. The commission report, submitted on 7 January 1924, detailed recommendations in several areas, including the early ending of government "activities" in Indian life, education, health and sanitation, and the disposition of pueblo lands. Committee member Joseph E. Otis wrote in his letter of submission to Secretary Work, "There is more to do than merely discharge a sentimental obligation.

Mr. Edward E. Ayer, recognized as a practical student of Indian affairs and for many years a member of the Indian Commission [the U.S. Board of Indian Commissioners], has pointed out in an interview that in spite of 400 years of debauchery at the hands of the white man, the American Indian retains his racial trait of honesty toward and confidence in his fellow man. No nation can ask a finer quality than this for its people, and it would be a policy of enlightened selfishness to salvage this quarter of a million of human near-wreckage and thus enrich our citizenship. In doing this it is quite possible that we shall best meet our obligation." He added, "Until the Indian question is settled right, disposed of for all time, it is obvious that the need for constant exercise of substantial authority renders the situation inevitably one for the U.S. Government to handle. If the Government is to pursue a constructive policy toward a definite end, it is essential in a popular government that there should exist a real public sentiment with reference to the matter, not an emotional reaction of vague and perhaps unfortunate direction, but a keen appreciation both of the magnitude of the problem and of some of the concrete difficulties and objectives."

While much of the committee's report did not see action, some of the reforms demanded in its pages were enacted by Congress or by member John Collier when he became head of the Indian Office less than 10 years later.

Reference U.S. Congress, House of Representatives, *The Indian Problem: Resolution of the Committee of One Hundred Appointed by the Secretary of the Interior and a Review of the Indian Problem*, House Document No. 149, 68th Congress, 1st Session (1924) (serial 8273).

Confederated Bands of Ute Indians v. United States (330 U.S. 169, 91 L.Ed. 823, 67 S.Ct. 650 [1947])

In this Supreme Court decision, the court held that when certain lands were given to an Indian tribe outside of a reservation, and later returned to the public domain, the Indians were not deserving of compensation for the taking of those lands. The treaty of 2 March 1868 (15 Stat. 619) established the Ute Reservation in Colorado. By an executive order of 22 November 1875, signed by President Ulysses S. Grant, the Ute reservation was extended to incorporate some land not included in the original treaty. In 1879, a detachment of American troops was attacked near the Ute reservation; several soldiers were killed in the so-called Meeker massacre. To punish the Utes, who were believed to be responsible, Congress passed the act of 15 June 1880 (21 Stat. 199), which extinguished their title to the Ute reservation and forced their removal from Colorado. In 1909, Congress awarded the Utes payment for the lands of the reservation only. Under the act of Congress of 28 June 1938 (52 Stat. 1209), the Court of Claims was conferred with the jurisdiction to hear, determine, and render final claims on matters dealing with Indian treaties. The Utes sued to the Court of Claims for compensation for the lands given them by the executive order but for which no compensation had been made by the government after the extinguishment of the reservation. The Court of Claims dismissed the suit; the plaintiffs—the Confederated Bands of Ute Indians—appealed to the U.S. Supreme Court. Justice Hugo Black spoke for a divided court (justices Frank Murphy, Felix Frankfurter, and William O. Douglas dissented) when he upheld the Court of Claims judgment. Justice Black explained, "The 1880 act, we believe, did not enlarge upon the limited purpose of the Executive Order. To compensate the Indians for lands, not intended to be conveyed by the 1868 treaty, the Executive Order, nor the 1880 act, would be to pay them for lands which neither they nor their ancestors ever owned and to which they had no claim in equity or justice, so far as the transactions here at issue are concerned. No rule of construction justifies such a result. Affirmed."

Reference Kappler, Charles, *Indian Affairs, Laws and Treaties* (1904).

Congress' Plenary Power over Indian Affairs

The U.S. Supreme Court long held that Congress has a plenary, or unrestricted, power over Indian affairs, a doctrine only recently overturned. In *Lone Wolf v. Hitchcock* (1903), the Supreme Court held that this power included the right to abrogate treaties with the Indians. Justice Edward Douglass White explained in that case, "Plenary authority over the tribal relations of the Indians has been exercised by Congress from the beginning, and the power has always been deemed a political one, not subject to be controlled by the judicial department of the government. Until the year 1871 the policy was pursued of dealing with the Indian tribes by means of treaties, and, of course, a moral obligation rested upon Congress to act in good faith in performing the stipulations entered into on its behalf. But, as with treaties made with foreign nations, the legislative power might pass laws in conflict with treaties made with the Indians. The power exists to abrogate the provisions of an Indian treaty, though presumably such power will be exercised only when circumstances arise which will not only justify the government in disregarding the stipulations of the treaty, but may demand, in the interest of the country and the Indians themselves, that it should do so. When, therefore, treaties were entered into between the United States and a tribe of Indians it was never doubted that the power to abrogate existed in Congress, and that in a contingency such power might be availed of from considerations of governmental policy, particularly if consistent with perfect good faith towards the Indians."

In 1980, the *Lone Wolf* doctrine was overturned by the Supreme Court in *United States v. Sioux Nation of Indians*, effectively limiting the Congress' plenary power.

See also *Cherokee Nation v. Hitchcock; Cherokee Nation v. Southern Kansas Railroad Company; Ex parte Wilson; In re Heff; Lone Wolf v. Hitchcock; Santa Clara Pueblo v. Martinez; Stephens v. Cherokee Nation; Thomas v. Gay; United States v. Rickert; United States v. Rogers; United States v. Sioux Nation of Indians.*

Condition of the Indian Tribes

See Doolittle Commission.

Conley v. Ballinger et al. (216 U.S. 84, 54 L.Ed. 393, 30 S.Ct. 224 [1910])

Are the former members of an Indian tribe no longer in existence able to keep the United States from destroying an Indian burial ground? This was the question involved in this Supreme Court case, decided in 1910. The plaintiff, Lyda B. Conley, was identified in the opinion as a "descendant of the Wyandotte Indians dealt with in the treaty of 31 January 1855" (10 Stat. 1159). By article 2 of that treaty, the Wyandottes ceded their land to the United States "except...the portion now enclosed and used as a public burying ground shall be permanently reserved and appropriated for that purpose." However, by an act of Congress of 21 June 1906 (34 Stat. 325, at 348), the secretary of the interior was authorized to remove the Indian remains from the burial ground and sell the land. Conley, claiming that her constitutional rights were about to be violated, sued Secretary of the Interior James R. Garfield and as well as Horace B. Durant, Thomas G. Walker, and William A. Simpson, commissioners appointed by Garfield to sell the land. In 1909, Garfield left office, and the new secretary of the interior, Richard A. Ballinger, was substituted as the defendant in his place. Conley's suit to the Circuit Court of the United States for the District of Kansas was dismissed for want of jurisdiction, allowing Conley to appeal to the U.S. Supreme Court. Justice Oliver Wendell Holmes delivered the court's unanimous opinion on 31 January 1910 (only two weeks after arguments were heard on 14 January) in holding for Ballinger and the right to disturb the cemetery. Justice Holmes, in remanding the case back to the lower court to be dismissed without costs being passed onto the plaintiff, explained, "There is no question as to the complete legislative power of the United States over the land of the Wyandottes while it remained in their occupation before their quitclaim to the United States.

Lone Wolf v. Hitchcock, 187 U.S. 553, [at] 565, 47 L.Ed. 299, [at] 306, 23 S.Ct. 216. When they made that grant they excepted this parcel. Therefore it remained, as the whole of the land had been before, in the ownership of the United States, subject to the recognized use of the Wyandottes. But the right of the Wyandottes was in them only as a tribe or nation. The right excepted was a right of the tribe. The United States maintained and protected the Indians use or occupation against others, but was bound itself only by honor, not by law."

*Conners v. United States (*180 U.S. 271 [1901])

In this case, the U.S. Supreme Court held on the narrow issue of whether the U.S. government was responsible for Indian depredations caused by Indians "in amity" [harmony] with the government. When Northern Cheyenne and Arapahoe Indians were removed from their ancestral home on the Red Cloud reservation in Nebraska to Fort Reno in Indian Territory (now Oklahoma) in 1877, several independent bands of Cheyennes, led by such chiefs as Dull Knife, Little Wolf, Wild Hog, and Old Crow, went along, with the proviso that if they did not like the new home they could return to the Red Cloud reservation upon application. After a period of time at Fort Reno, these independent bands expressed their dissatisfaction, and applied to be removed back to Nebraska. This was refused to them as they were not a majority of the Cheyennes. In 1878, these independent Indians fled Fort Reno. A chase ensued, and at that time while the military was battling the Indians, appellant Milton C. Conners, Jr., suffered losses of livestock that he claimed were killed by the marauding bands. He sued the U.S. government in the Court of Claims, asserting that because the Cheyennes were "in amity" with the government, it was responsible for the depredations committed by the Cheyennes. The Court of Claims held for the government, and Conners appealed to the U.S. Supreme Court.

The case was argued before the Court on 17 December 1900, and a decision was handed down on 11 February 1901 (in addition to another amity case, *Montoya v. United States*). Writing for a unanimous court, Justice Henry Brown sustained the Court of Claims decision on the grounds that as independent bands, the Cheyennes who committed the depredations were not "in amity" with the government, and thus the government was not at fault for the atrocities. In dismissing Conners' appeal, Justice Brown explained, "While the ghastly facts of this case, which are set forth with much greater detail in the opinion of the Court of Claims, appeal strongly to the generosity of Congress to compensate those who have suffered by the inconsiderate and hasty action of the troops in driving these Indians into hostility, they afford no ground whatever for a judgment against the tribes to which these Indians originally belonged, but from which they separated and carried on independent operations. In fact, it would be highly unjust to add to their manifest sufferings the payment of these damages from their annuities, or from other funds standing to their credit. Nor does the claim make a case against the United States under the act vesting jurisdiction in the Court of Claims."

See also *Montoya v. United States.*

Converse, Harriet Arnot Maxwell Clarke (1836–1903)

For most of her life she advocated rights for Native Americans and studied their customs and culture, earning from the Indians the title "The Great White Mother." Yet few historians remember Harriet Converse. She was born Harriet Arnot Maxwell on 11 January 1836 in Elmira, New York, the youngest of seven children of Thomas Maxwell, a politician and an attorney of Scottish heritage, and his second wife Marie Maxwell (née Purdy). Guy Maxwell, Thomas's father, had been an Indian agent whose concern for Native Americans led him, as well as his son, to be adopted by the Senecas. After her mother's death, Harriet was raised by relatives in Ohio, where she met and married George B. Clarke, a wealthy land owner. When Clarke and Harriet's father (who was vice president of the Erie Railroad and a former Congressman) died about the same time, she was a widow who inherited a large amount of money. In 1861 she met and married Frank Buchanan Converse, a musician who had lived with the Indians in the west and was an accomplished showman. For the next five years, the two toured Europe so that Converse could write a book on instruments that he loved, and Harriet wrote several articles in Old Scottish under the pseudonyms "Salome" and "Musidora." The two then moved to New York City, where Harriet opened their house to visiting Indians. She was a personal friend of the poet John Greenleaf Whittier.

In 1881, Harriet Converse met Ely S. Parker (Seneca), who had been an aide to General Ulysses S. Grant during the Civil War and who had served as Grant's commissioner of Indian Affairs from 1869 to 1871. Parker convinced Converse that the study and understanding of Indian culture was essential for its continued preservation. She began a tour of Indian reservations, principally in New York, and started collecting and preserving Indian cultural objects, particularly masks. For her lifetime of work in preserving such objects, and for her work in defeating bills to end tribal life and resort to allotments, she was adopted into the Seneca clan in 1885, and in 1891 given the honorary name Yi-ie-Wa-Noh ("She Who Watches Over Us" or "Ambassador"). In 1892, because she was held "in such high esteem and affection" among the peoples of the Six Nations, she was made an honorary chief of the Senecas, the only white woman in the history of the Americas ever to receive this honor. In addition, she published such works as *The Ho-de-no-sau-nee: The Confederacy of the Iroquois: A Poem* (1884), *The Iroquois Silver Brooches" (1902), and Myths and Legends of the New York State Iroquois* (1908).

In 1897, the *New York Times* reported, "The Indian is very popular at the American Museum of Natural History. When he arrives in town he is introduced to the sculptors' studio on the top floor of the building, and if he proves to be a fair type of his family or tribe he is at once engaged to pose. A mask is taken of his face to facilitate matters, and he lends his presence for a short time. When he leaves, his counterpart in plaster is set up in the glass cases below, where primitive American art is exhibited. Kasper Mayer, a young Bavarian sculptor, a pupil of J.Q.A. Ward, has been engaged on this work for more than a year. He returned from the Indian reservation of New York State last week, whither he journeyed with Mrs. Harriet Maxwell Converse, honorary chief of the Iroquois, who went along to introduce him and to vouch for him. He brought home with him several barrels of masks representing the various tribes of the Iroquois nation."

Harriet Converse died of kidney failure brought on by nephritis (more commonly called Bright's disease) on 18 November 1903, just two months after the death of her husband; she was 67. Upon her death, Harriet Converse was mourned by many Indians who showed up for her funeral. The *New York Times* reported, "The chapel was crowded with curious people, but seats had been reserved for the Indians, known to be coming, and for the white friends of the dead woman...Shortly before the services began, the Indians from the New York State reservation came to the city on the Erie Railway. They were escorted to the undertaking establishment by Policeman Keough of the West Twenty-third Street Police Station, and ushered unto the mourners' room at the rear of the chapel. They were men and women of the Senecas, Onondagas, Cayugas, and Mohawks. Fifteen delegates had been selected at the conference of the Six Nations on the announcement of the death of Mrs. Converse." She was buried in Woodlawn Cemetery in Elmira.

References Fenichell, Lois F., "Converse, Harriet Arnot Maxwell." In Aden Whitman, ed., *American Reformers: An H. W. Wilson Biographical Dictionary* (1985); Fenton, William N., "Converse, Harriet Maxwell." In Edward T. James, ed., *Notable American Women, 1607–1950: A Biographical Dictionary* (1971); Hardy, Gail J., *American Women*

Civil Rights Activists: Biobibliographies of 68 Leaders, 1825–1992 (1993); "Indians as Models in Art." *New York Times Illustrated Magazine*, 12 September 1897, 7; "Mrs. H. M. Converse Dead." *New York Times*, 20 November 1903, 16; "Indians Mourn at Mrs. Converse's Bier." *New York Times*, 23 November 1903, 12.

Cooley, Dennis Nelson (1825–1892)

Brought in to fill the position of Indian commissioner shortly after the Sand Creek massacre, Dennis N. Cooley was a political intimate of newly installed Secretary of the Interior James Harlan, former Senator and critic of the army's handling of the Sand Creek affair. The thirteenth commissioner, Cooley was born on his father's farm near Lisbon, New Hampshire, on 7 November 1825, the son and one of ten children of Benjamin Cooley, a farmer, and Polly (née Taylor) Cooley. He was descended from Benjamin Cooley of St. Albans, Hertfordshire, "a skilled weaver of linen and wools." Benjamin Cooley, whose father Aaron fought in the Revolutionary War, died when his son Dennis was but two years old. In transmitting his experiences to his own son, Harlan Ward Cooley, many years later, Dennis Cooley explained that "it was my mother's father, Timothy Taylor, who was my instructor, guide, philosopher and friend and I learned much of political affairs, American history and local tradition from him." Dennis Cooley worked on his family's farm, "leaving time for attendance at the district school for only about three months in winter and summer school for eight or ten weeks in summer." He attended Newbury Academy in Newbury, Vermont, was awarded a teacher's certificate, and taught at the academy for several years. Visiting his sister in Wisconsin impressed upon him that a his life was to be in the West. Although he went to work in a law office in Woodstock, Vermont, his interest in antislavery agitation led him to move in 1854 to Dubuque, Iowa, which eventually became his permanent home. That year he was admitted to the Iowa bar, and he opened a practice in Dubuque. Bronchitis forced him to avoid service during the Civil War, but work on Lincoln's 1864 reelection campaign (in which he became close friends with James Harlan of Iowa) led to an appointment as commissioner for the District of South Carolina, to preside over tax matters and land title controversies in the wake of the end of the war. With Lincoln's assassination, Cooley declined an offer to be Judge Advocate of the U.S. Navy, but instead accepted the post of commissioner of Indian Affairs.

Cooley had been the Indian commissioner for only three months when he submitted the first of his two annual reports. Of this treatise, historian Henry E. Fritz writes, Cooley supposed the Department [of the Interior] would not be startled by the novelty of his suggestion that the agents and traders were often in collusion. He also called attention to circumstances which engendered fraud, stating that an innumerable list of applicants for the office of agent was not proof that the salary of $1,500 was adequate to procure high-class personnel; it was rather, he said, an indication of outside income. No other explanation of why agents scurried to Washington upon a change of administration will do. The abuses were legion: agency buildings erected and sold to the government for several times their cost, Texas cattle furnished at prices of Northern beef, shorts substituted for flour, and transportation accounts falsified.

Biographer Gary L. Roberts writes, "In August 1865, Cooley chaired a commission appointed to treat [negotiate] with the southern Indians. The commissioners were carefully instructed, and Cooley was told, 'The President is willing to grant them peace; but wants land for other Indians, and a civil government for the whole Territory'...The commission met with representatives of the tribes at Fort Smith, Arkansas, in September. It was Cooley's first real encounter with Indian leaders, and his inexperience showed. He manifested a complete ignorance of and lack of respect for Indian customs, rights, or opinions. He appeared highhanded and arrogant, making demands the Indians were unprepared to meet. He ignored entirely the written legal structure of the Cherokees, modeled after the U.S. Constitution, and virtually deposed John Ross. Cooley soon discovered that the Indians were quite capable of defending their interests. While most of them accepted Cooley's demands, they insisted on carrying the proposals back to their councils. The commission acquiesced, and Cooley was able to report a successful meeting." He met with the Indian leaders again in the summer of 1866, and, having educated himself to properly deal with the Indians, found himself given by the Cherokee and Chickasaw delegations a silver-headed cane, a treasured memento which his family kept.

In November 1866, Cooley resigned as Indian commissioner, because, according to him, "President Johnson had swung around." He added, "Our relations, however, were always pleasant and I considered him a smart businessman and a patriot." Cooley's second annual report was submitted in November 1866, soon after he had resigned as commissioner. In the latter report, Cooley provided the Congress a compendium of his recommendations for the improvement of the Indian service:

Early attention needed to certain treaties pending in the Senate.

Provisions should be made for treaty arrangements with remaining bands of Santee Sioux in northeastern Dakota.

Arrangements, by legislation or otherwise, for settlement of Wyandott[e] difficulties.

Laws needed for punishment of crimes in the Indian country.

Revision of system of trade and licenses.

Appropriation of a fund for rescuing and restoring captives to their homes.

Appropriation of a fund for securing memorials of Indians.

Revision of laws relating to depredations.

Appropriation for surveys of allotments to Indians.

Legislation to prevent taxation of Indian lands.

Reorganization of clerical force of Indian Office.

Reorganization of superintendencies and agencies.

Increase of salaries of commissioner and officers.

Special appropriations for education in several superintendencies.

Provisions for a treaty with the Coast Range Indians in Oregon.

Increased appropriations in several superintendencies, as Arizona, Nevada, Utah, New Mexico, &c.

In the years he lived after leaving the Indian Office, Cooley served as a lawyer in Washington, and handled before the Court of Claims a large number of petitions by citizens of South Carolina that the government had illegally taken their land after the end of the Civil War. He served as a state senator in Iowa from 1874 to 1878, and narrowly lost the Republican nomination for the U.S. Senate to William B. Allison. He was also offered consulships to Moscow and Spezia, Italy, but refused both. In 1882, he suffered a stroke which slowed his activities. On 13 November 1892, while visiting his daughter in New York City, Cooley suffered a second stroke that proved fatal.

See also Bureau of Indian Affairs.

References Altrocchi, Julia Cooley, *A Brief Biography of the Honorable Dennis Nelson Cooley* (manuscript in the possession of the Mississippi River Museum, Dubuque County Historical Society, Dubuque, Iowa); Fritz, Henry E., *The Movement for Indian Assimilation, 1860–1890* (1963); Roberts, Gary L., "Dennis Nelson Cooley." In Robert M. Kvasnicka and Herman J. Viola, eds., *The Commissioners of Indian Affairs, 1824–1977* (1979); U.S. Congress, House of Representatives, *Annual Report of the Commissioner of Indian Affairs for the Year 1866*, House Executive Document No. 1, 39th Congress, 1st Session (serial 1284).

Copway, George (Ojibway) (1818–1869?)

Although not born in the United States, George Copway, also known as *Kahgegwagebow* ("He Who Stands Forever" or "Stands Fast") did spend much of his life in the United States, but his career as an early

Indian missionary and writer remains only poorly known. He was born in the fall of 1818 at Rice Lake, near the mouth of the Trent River in Ontario, now Canada (then British North America), the son of an Ojibway chief. In 1828, a group of missionaries, led by one Peter Jones, established a mission at Rice Lake and converted some of the Indians, particularly Copway's parents, to Christianity. By this conversion, Copway's father was renamed John Copway, and his son became George Copway. George attended the mission school established by Jones, and his teacher, the Reverend James Evans, an English Wesleyan missionary, later invented the syllabus for the Cree Indians. When he was 16, George Copway, along with his uncle and cousin and another man from his tribe, were selected by Peter Jones to go to the United States to work as interpreters for the American Methodist Church in the Lake Superior region. He soon advanced from interpreter to teacher. For several years he traveled across what is now the American Midwest to teach among the Indians. According to biographer Lisa Wroble, "He traveled to the La Pointe Mission on Madeline Island, and while there helped the Reverend Sherman Hall translate the Gospel of St. Luke and the Acts of the Apostles into Ojibway."

After he attended Ebenezer Academy near Jackson, Illinois, from 1838 to 1839, Copway journeyed to the eastern coast of the United States, spending time in Boston and New York and making the acquaintance of such noted writers as James Fenimore Cooper and Henry Wadsworth Longfellow. The latter may have used Copway as the model for his poem *The Song of Hiawatha* (1855). After 1850, he went into the business of journalism in New York. During this time he began to write on his experiences. His works include *The Life, History, and Travels, of Kah-ge-ga-gah-bowh (George Copway), a Young Indian Chief of the Ojebwa Nation, a Convert to the Christian Faith, and a Missionary to his People for Twelve Years* (1847); *Organization of a New Indian Territory, East of the Missouri River. Arguments and Reasons Submitted to the Honorable Members of the Senate and House of Representatives of the 31st Congress of the United States, by the Indian chief Kah-ge-ga-gah-bouh, or Geo. Copway* (1850); and *The Traditional History and Characteristic Sketches of the Ojibway Nation* (1850).

Many sources claim that George Copway died near Pontiac, Michigan, in 1863. Other sources claim that he lived past the end of the Civil War, and that after working as a doctor and faith healer, he died on 17 January 1869, just days after being converted to the Roman Catholic faith.

References Genzmer, George Harvey, "Copway, George." In Dumas Malone et al., eds., *Dictionary of American Biography* (1930–88); Waldman, Carl, *Who Was Who in Native American History: Indians and Non-Indians from Early Contacts through 1900* (1990); Wroble, Lisa A., "George Copway." In Sharon Malinowski, ed., *Notable Native Americans* (1995).

Cotton Petroleum Corp. v. New Mexico (490 U.S. 163 [1989])

Justice John Paul Stevens asked the parties in this case before the case was heard before the Supreme Court: "Does the Commerce Clause [of the U.S. Constitution] require that an Indian tribe be treated as a State for purposes of determining whether a state tax on nontribal activities conducted on an Indian reservation must be apportioned to account for taxes imposed on those same activities by the Indian tribe?" He declared, "This case is a sequel to *Merrion v. Jicarilla Apache Tribe*, 455 U.S. 130, 71 L.Ed. 2d 21, 102 S.Ct. 894 (1982), in which we held that the Jicarilla Apache Tribe has the power to impose a severance tax on the production of oil and gas by non-Indian lessees of wells located on the Tribe's reservation." In *Cotton*, the court had to decide if a further tax by the state on such non-Indian lessees was to be considered double taxation. The Cotton Petroleum Corporation was a lessee of oil and gas wells on the Jicarilla Apache Tribe's reservation in northwestern New Mexico under the Indian Mineral Leasing Act of 1938. In 1969, the tribe received the permission of the secretary of the interior to levy taxes against non-Indian users of its natural resources. In addition to the taxes imposed on it by the tribe, the company had to endure further taxes levied by the state of New Mexico. In 1982, the company paid the state taxes under protest, and then filed a lawsuit in the District Court for Santa Fe County, charging that the state taxes were a violation of Indian Commerce, Interstate Commerce, Due Process, and Supremacy Clauses of the U.S. Constitution. The tribe filed an *amicus curiae* ("friend of the court") brief, claiming that if the state tax was upheld, it could jeopardize the tribe's ability to raise funds. The district court, however, upheld the state tax as legal and not overlapping. On appeal, the New Mexico Court of Appeals affirmed, claiming that the state tax did not offend the Commerce Clause of the Constitution. The New Mexico Supreme Court at first granted a writ of certiorari, then quashed it. The U.S. Supreme Court then granted certiorari, and heard arguments in the case on 30 November 1988. In a 6–3 decision (justices Harry Blackmun, William Brennan, and Thurgood Marshall dissenting), the court held that an Indian tribe was not a "state" as defined by the Commerce Clause, and as such the state of New Mexico could impose separate taxes. Writing for the majority, Justice John Paul Stevens explained, "In our order noting probable jurisdiction we invited the parties to address the question whether the Tribe should be treated as a State for the purpose of determining whether New Mexico's taxes must be apportioned. All of the Indian tribes that have filed *amicus curiae* briefs addressing this question—including the Jicarilla Apache Tribe—have uniformly taken the position that Indian tribes are not States within the meaning of the Commerce Clause. This position is supported by the text of the Clause itself. Article I, section 8, clause 3, provides the 'Congress shall have the Power...To regulate Commerce with foreign Nations, and among the several States, and with the Indian Tribes.' Thus, the Commerce Clause draws a clear distinction between 'States' and 'Indian Tribes.' As Chief Justice Marshall observed in *Cherokee Nation v. Georgia*, 5 Peters 1, 18, 8 L.Ed. 25 (1831): 'The objects to which the power of regulating commerce might be directed, are divided into three distinct classes—foreign nations, the several states, and Indian Tribes. When forming this article, the convention declared them as entirely distinct.' In fact, the language of the Clause no more admits of treating Indian Tribes as States than of treating foreign nations as States." He added, "Accordingly, we have no occasion to modify our comment on this question in the Bracker case [*White Mountain Apache Tribe v. Bracker*, 1980]: 'Tribal reservations are not States, and the differences in the form and nature of their sovereignty make it treacherous to import to one notions of pre-emption that are properly applied to the other.'"

See also *Kerr-McGee Corporation v. Navajo Tribe of Indians et al.; Merrion et al. v. Jicarilla Apache Tribe.*

Council Fire

See Bland, Thomas Augustus; Meacham, Alfred Benjamin; National Indian Defense Association.

County of Oneida, New York et al. v. Oneida Indian Nation of New York State et al. (470 U.S. 226, 84 L.Ed. 2d 169, 105 S.Ct. 1245 [1985])

The combined cases of *County of Oneida, New York et al., v. Oneida Indian Nation of New York State et al.* and *New York v. Oneida Indian Nation of New York State et al.*, the second time the issues in this case came before the Supreme Court, presented the court with the question of whether three distinct tribes of Oneida Indians could bring suit for "the occupation and use of tribal land allegedly conveyed unlawfully" to the state of New York. In 1795, the Oneida Indians ceded some 100,000 acres to the state of New York. In 1970, the three clans of Oneidas (the Oneida Nation of New York, the Oneida Indian Nation of Wisconsin, and the Oneida of the Thames Band

Council) sued in U.S. District Court for the Northern District of New York, seeking damages for the occupation and use of the land, claiming that under section 8 of the Trade and Intercourse Act of 1793, "no purchase or grant of lands, or of any title or claim thereto, from any Indians or nation or tribe of Indians, within the bounds of the United States, shall be of any validity in law or equity, unless the same be made by treaty or convention entered into pursuant to the constitution...[and] in the presence, and with the approbation of the commissioner or commissioners of the United States" appointed to oversee such matters. The district court dismissed the claim, holding that there was no basis for action under federal law. The U.S. Court of Appeals for the Second Circuit affirmed, but the U.S. Supreme Court reversed (414 U.S. 661), remanding the case back to the district court. That court then found the counties of Oneida and Madison liable for wrongful possession, awarded damages to the Oneida, and held that the State of New York must repay the counties for the damages. The Court of Appeals for the Second Circuit upheld the judgment as to liability and indemnification, but remanded the case back to district court as to the amount of damages. On certiorari, the Supreme Court, on 4 March 1985, affirmed as to liability, but reversed as to indemnification. Holding for a divided court, Justice Lewis F. Powell (justices William Brennan and Thurgood Marshall concurred as to liability but dissented as to indemnification, in which point they were joined by Chief Justice Warren Burger and justices Byron White and William H. Rehnquist; Justice John Paul Stevens filed a separate concurring opinion on point one but a dissenting one on point two) explained that "The decisions of this Court emphasize 'Congress' unique obligation toward the Indians.' *Morton v. Mancari*, 417 U.S. 535, [at] 55, 41 L.Ed. 2d 290, 94 S.Ct. 2474 (1974). The Solicitor General [Edwin S. Kneedler], in an *amicus curiae* brief for the United States, urged the Court to affirm [the decision] of the Court of Appeals. The Solicitor General recognized, as we do, the potential consequences of affirmance. He observed, however, that 'Congress has enacted legislation to extinguish Indian title and claims related thereto in other eastern States...and it could be expected to do the same in New York should the occasion arise. We agree that this litigation makes abundantly clear the necessity for congressional action. One would have thought that claims dating back for more than a century and a half would have been barred long ago. As our opinion indicates, however, neither petitioners nor we have found any applicable statute of limitations or other relevant legal basis for holding that the Oneidas' claims are barred or otherwise have been satisfied."

See also *Oneida Indian Nation of New York State et al. v. County of Oneida, New York;* Trade and Intercourse Act of 1793.

Crawford, Thomas Hartley (1786–1863)

The third commissioner of Indian Affairs, serving from 1838 until 1845, Thomas H. Crawford, who was also known as T. Hartley Crawford, was born in Chambersburg, Pennsylvania, on 14 November 1786, the son of Edward and Catherine Crawford. He graduated from Princeton College (now Princeton University) in 1804, then read the law for three years before opening his own office in Chambersburg. He was elected to Congress as a Jacksonian Democrat in 1828, and marked his service by supporting passage of the Removal Bill in 1830. After serving two short terms (he left in 1833), Crawford served briefly in the Pennsylvania legislature.

Crawford's support for Jackson led the president to name him to a commission to investigate frauds perpetrated against Creek Indians by white speculators in Alabama. This service, as well as his loyalty on the Removal Bill, made him a prime candidate for the post of commissioner of Indian Affairs in 1838. Historian Theodore W. Taylor pens, "Van Buren appointed...Crawford to succeed [Cary Allen] Harris. Crawford was an 'old and warm friend' of Andrew

Jackson who happened to be out of political office at the time. The Pennsylvanian, fifty-two years of age when he became commissioner, was a Princeton graduate, lawyer, former U.S. congressman, and former state legislator. Crawford had defied public opinion in 1830 when he supported Jackson's Removal Bill in the House of Representatives. Later, in 1836, Jackson appointed him to investigate frauds in the purchases of Creek allotments, and his report was a condemnation of the speculation and fraud committed against the Indians. Crawford was the only commissioner during the Jacksonian era who had some prior experience in actually dealing with the Indians, but Henry R. Schoolcraft, an enlightened Indian agent and a good Jacksonian Democrat, feared that [Crawford] was 'personally unacquainted with the character of the Indians, and the geography of the western country, and not likely, therefore, to be very ready or practical in the administrative duties of the office.' Crawford's nomination, however, met Jackson's wholehearted approval. Old Hickory wrote from the Hermitage that 'Mr. Crawford is a man of talents, and with his late duties, must have become familiar with the Indian character and I have no doubt [he] will fill the office to which you have assigned him well—he is honest, & faithful to the constitution.'"

On 1 March 1841, Crawford wrote to Major Joshua Pilcher in arguing for the removal of the Sac, Fox, and Winnebago from the Iowa Territory (after they had already been removed from Illinois and Wisconsin), "The citizens of the Territory have a right to expect that its growth will not long be retarded by the occupancy of so large and valuable a tract within its limits by a people...whose wild and savage character renders them dangerous neighbors."

Indian historian Robert A. Trennert, Jr., writes, "In the 1840s a strong wave of reformism, inspired in part by the reform spirit of the Jacksonian age, swept Indian administrators. Attempts were made to bring education to the tribes behind the barrier and settle them down to an agricultural life. During the early part of the decade, Commissioner Crawford devoted a great deal of energy to promoting manual-labor schools among the transplanted tribes. He saw such schools as being 'not only deserving of favor,' but 'indispensable to the civilization of the Indians.' The government also actively encouraged religious societies to enter the Indian country and help bring civilization to the Indians. By 1842 some fifty-two schools, mostly operated by missionaries, were in existence with an enrollment of over 2,000 pupils."

Thomas H. Crawford served as Indian commissioner from 1838 until 1845. A friend of President James K. Polk, Crawford was discharged from the Indian office in exchange for a federal justiceship, given to him in the days of political patronage. The *Daily National Intelligencer* of Washington, D.C., explained that in his last years Crawford was "infirm in body, but still vigorous in mind, striving with manly fortitude to resist the encroachments of disease and age, and to infuse the vigor of his clear intelligence into the duties of his high office." He died in Washington, D.C., on 27 January 1863 at the age of 76.

References Thomas H. Crawford to Major Joshua Pilcher, 1 March 1841, Indian Office Letter Book, 30: 146–47 (1841), RG 75, National Archives, quoted in Christopher Vecsey and Robert W. Venables, eds., *American Indian Environments: Ecological Issues in Native American History* (1980); *Daily National Intelligencer*, 28 January 1863, 3; Satz, Ronald N., "Thomas Hartley Crawford." In Robert M. Kvasnicka and Herman J. Viola, eds., *The Commissioners of Indian Affairs, 1824–1977* (1979); Taylor, Theodore W., *American Indian Policy* (1983); Trennert, Robert A., Jr., *Alternative to Extinction: Federal Indian Policy and the Beginnings of the Reservation System, 1846–1851* (1975).

Creek Nation v. United States (318 U.S. 629 [1943])

Combined with the joint case of *Seminole Nation v. United States*, this action, which was heard before the U.S. Supreme Court, dealt with the Indians' grants of railroad rights-of-way through their reservations and whether these grants were abused. By the treaties of 1866 with the Seminoles (14 Stat. 755) and the Creeks (14 Stat. 785), these two Indian nations granted the U.S.

government the right to authorize railroads a right-of-way through their reservations and simultaneously conferred on the railroads the right to purchase strips of land three miles in width for use in railroad operations. Section 16 of the act of Congress of 28 February 1902 (32 Stat. 48) allowed for these railroads to pay a fixed sum per mile to the secretary of the interior for the future benefit of the Indians. In 1924, Congress passed two pieces of legislation allowing the Court of Claims to adjudicate any lawsuit involving "any treaty or agreement between the United States" and Indian tribes. Both the Creek and Seminole nations sued the U.S. government in 1926 under the 1924 acts, seeking damages by claiming that the railroads had not complied with the terms of the treaties by taking possession of pieces of land and using them to charge rents, instead of for railroad operations, and that the mileage charge was not paid. The Court of Claims ruled against the tribes and the U.S. Supreme Court agreed to hear their arguments. Justice Hugo Black held for a 6–2 court (justices Frank Murphy and Felix Frankfurter dissented and Justice Wiley Rutledge did not participate) upholding the Court of Claims decision. Justice Black wrote, "We are asked here to impose a liability on the government to these Indians for wrongs allegedly committed against the Indians by others. Appreciating the desire of Congress to recognize the 'full obligation of this nation to protect the interests of a dependent people,' *Tulee v. State of Washington*, 315 U.S. 681, [at] 685, 62 S.Ct. 862, [at] 864, 86 L.Ed. 1115, we are unable to find in the words of the treaties of statutes upon which this action rests any such prodigal assumption by the government of other people's liabilities as that for which the petitioners contend here. Affirmed."

Crews et al. v. Burcham et al. (1 Black [67 U.S.] 352 [1862])

Officially titled *Jonathan Crews, Lycurgus Sherman, Mason G. Sherman, and David G. Rose, Appellants, v. Henry L. Burcham et al.*, this Supreme Court case dealt with the issue of whether an Indian treaty allowed for Indians to convey their land "to heirs and devisees or assigns of such a deceased Indian." By a treaty with the Pottawatomi of Illinois of 27 October 1832, the tribe ceded all of its lands in Illinois and other states to the United States in trust, with patents to be issued to the individual members of the tribe. One such individual was Francis Besion. On 4 February 1833, he conveyed the interest in his patent to William Armstrong. Besion died in 1843, before his patent could be issued. The heirs of Besion, including Crews, took possession of the tract of land as his heirs. Henry Burcham, an heir to Armstrong, claimed that he owned the land. Crews and his fellow plaintiffs sued in the Circuit Court of the United States for the Northern District of Illinois to dismiss Burcham's title to the land. The court held that Besion had the right to convey his title; Crews and the others then appealed to the U.S. Supreme Court. Justice Samuel Nelson delivered the court's opinion on 3 February 1862 when he ruled that Burcham's hold on the land was legal. Justice Nelson explained, "The main and controlling questions involved in this case were before this court in the case of *Doe v. Wilson*, 23 How[ard] 457, which arose under a reservation in this Treaty in behalf of the chief, Pet-chi-co. It was there held, that the reservation created an equitable interest to the land to be selected under the Treaty; that it was the subject of sale and conveyance; that Pet-chi-co was competent to convey it; and that his deed, upon the selection of the land and the issue of the patent, operated to vest the title in his grantee."

See also *Doe ex dem. Mann v. Wilson.*

Curtis, Charles Brent (Kaw) (1860–1936)

Famed editor Oswald Garrison Villard wrote that Charles Curtis was "the apotheosis of mediocrity." Yet his place in history is secure: Curtis, a Native American, was a U.S. senator from Kansas and, from 1929 until 1933, vice president of the United

States, the first Indian to hold these positions. He was also the key sponsor of the Curtis Act of 1898, which bears his name. He was born on the Kaw Reservation in Morris County, Kansas, on 25 January 1860, the only son and one of two children of Oren A. ("Jack") Curtis, an ardent abolitionist, and Ellen Pappan, who was part Kaw Indian. Ellen Pappan was the daughter of Nom-pa-wa-rah, known as "White Plume," a Kaw chief who took as his wife Wy-he-see, the daughter of an Osage chief. According to the *New York Times*, which covered Curtis's two campaigns for the vice presidency (in 1928 and 1932), "His grandmother was Princess Julie, daughter of the chieftain White Plume, and granddaughter of Pawhuska, chief of the Osage tribe. She married Louis Granville, a French trader, and the daughter of their union was the Senator's mother. William *[sic]* Curtis, the father of Charles, seems to have played little part in the upbringing of the son after his wife's death, which occurred when the child was three years old." At that time, Charles was sent to live on the Kaw Reservation, first with his paternal grandmother, Permelia Hubbard Curtis, then with his maternal grandmother, Julie Gonville Pappan.

Charles Curtis was educated in both the public and mission schools of the reservation, spending much of his time learning to be a jockey. In 1881, after studying the law, he was admitted to the Kansas state bar. After a short time involved in his own practice, he was elected to a series of local offices, including county attorney of Shawnee County, Kansas, in which post he served from 1885 to 1889. In 1892, he was elected to a seat in the U.S. House of Representatives representing Kansas' fourth congressional district. William E. Unrau, one of Curtis's biographers, writes, "From 1892 until January 1907, when the Kansas legislature selected him to fill out the term of Senator Joseph R. Burton, who had resigned after he lost his appeal on a conviction for having accepted a bribe...Curtis represented Kansas from the Fourth and First districts in Congress. Although a 'standpat' Republican, he nevertheless displayed remarkable dexterity in weathering the storms of populism and progressivism in Kansas." During this time, Indian affairs was one of his leading concerns. Historian Berlin B. Chapman wrote in 1947, "An examination of the Kaw papers in the [National] archives in Washington showed that Curtis had been a man of peculiar importance among the Kaws. From his paramount influence among them came the policy and plan by which the reservation was broken up. His influence at Washington during the dissolution may be judged from the fact that he was chairman of the house committee on expenditures in the Interior Department, a member of the committee on Indian affairs, and chairman of the subcommittee having charge of Indian territory legislation." In 1898, Curtis authored the act that bears his name, which allotted the lands of the Indians of Kansas, among others, in an attempt to save the Kaws and Osages from tribal destruction. He was also one of the earliest supporters of women's suffrage, and helped push what became the Twenty-First Amendment through the Senate. He served as Republican party whip, and in 1924, he became majority leader. That year, he authored the legislation which became the Indian Citizenship Act. He was, someone said of him, an ultraconservative for whom the "Trinity" was the Republican Party, the high protective tariff, and the Grand Army of the Republic. He was, however, what one fellow legislator called "a square shooter." Senator George Norris, upon Curtis's death, said in tribute to the man he had differed with philosophically, "I would sooner take the word of Curtis than the sworn oath of a good many other men in the Capitol. I have never known Curtis to fail his word."

In 1928, Curtis sought the presidency, but came up short behind Harding's secretary of commerce, Herbert Hoover. Once an avowed enemy of Hoover, Curtis accepted the number two place on the Republican ticket, which went on to win that November against Governor Alfred E. Smith of New York. The vice presidency seemed to change Curtis. Where he had once been in charge of writing legislation and speaking on the Senate floor, as vice president he could only sit and moderate the activities of the Senate. Always called "Charley" by his friends, he snapped at one of them while presiding over the Senate, "Where do you get that 'Charley' stuff? Don't you know I am Vice President now?"

The onset of the Great Depression and Hoover's inability to deal with its devastating effects upon the American populace led to the disastrous Republican campaign of 1932, in which a renominated Hoover and Curtis went down to defeat against Franklin D. Roosevelt. Curtis retired to private life, serving as an attorney in the District of Columbia. On 8 February 1936, a maid found him dead in his bed. He was 76. Journalist and newspaperman William Allen White wrote in 1946 of the first time he had met Curtis, "His politics were always personal. Issues never bothered him. He was a handsome fellow, five feet ten, straight as his Kaw Indian grandfather must have been, with an olive skin that looked like old ivory, a silky, flowing, handlebar mustache, dark shoe-button eyes, beady, and in those days always gay, a mop of crow's-wing hair, a gentle ingratiating voice, and what a smile!...[He] was headed for political glory when I saw him."

See also Curtis Act.

References Chapman, Berlin B., "Charles Curtis and the Kaw Reservation," *Kansas Historical Quarterly* 40 (4); Connelley, William Elsey, "The Ancestry of Hon. Charles Curtis." Charles Curtis Papers, Box 1, Kansas State Historical Society, Topeka; "Curtis in Boyhood with Indian Tribe." *New York Times*, 16 June 1928, 5; "Curtis' Career Embraced Nearly 40 Years in High Office in Nation's Capitol." *New York Times*, 9 February 1936, 32; Seitz, Don Carlos, *From Kaw Teepee to Capitol: The Life Story of Charles Curtis, Indian, Who Has Risen to High Estate* (1928); Unrau, William E., *Mixed-Bloods and Tribal Dissolution: Charles Curtis and the Quest for Indian Identity* (1989); White, William Allen, *The Autobiography of William Allen White* (1946).

Curtis, Edward Sheriff (1868–1952)

Edward Curtis is considered perhaps the finest photographer of Indians who ever lived, a man whose multivolume work, *The North American Indian: Being a Series of Volumes Picturing and Describing the Indians of the United States and Alaska*, is regarded as a composition without peer. Yet Curtis remains an obscure figure. Born near Whitewater, Wisconsin, on 19 February 1868, Edward Sheriff Curtis was the second of four children of Johnson and Ella (née Sheriff) Curtis. At an early age Edward became fascinated with photography. The family moved to Sydney, Washington, in 1887 and Curtis became interested in the Indians of the Puget Sound area. To support his family after the death of his father, he began to photograph the Indians and sell the portraits to local dealers. In 1892 he opened his own studio, and four years later won a bronze medal from the Photographer's Association of America for his images. A chance meeting in 1898 led to Curtis's discovery. While climbing on Mt. Rainier he came across a party of lost climbers that included George Bird Grinnell, editor of *Field and Stream* magazine and a devotee of American Indians, and Clinton Hart Merriam, chief of the U.S. Biological Survey. The following year, Merriam invited Curtis to join the Harriman Expedition to Alaska, which was being financed by wealthy railroad magnate Edward Henry Harriman. Joining the mission were Grinnell, Merriam, William Healey Dall, and Grove Karl Gilbert of the U.S. Geological Survey, Frederick S. Dellenbaugh, who had gone with John Wesley Powell down the Colorado River in 1871, and Frederick V. Colville of the U.S. Department of Agriculture. On the journey, Curtis produced more than 5,000 pictures of Alaska natives and their surroundings. Grinnell also introduced Curtis to the Piegan and Blackfoot tribes of the Plains and Curtis set out to document their lives. He spent most of the rest of his life capturing the image of the Native American: he felt that that Indian culture was dying and he felt a responsibility to preserve it in the only way he saw possible.

A friend of Theodore Roosevelt (he had photographed his daughter Alice's wedding at the White House), Curtis was backed in 1906 by financier J. P. Morgan to publish a multivolume set of his Indian pictures. For the next five years, Morgan pumped $75,000 into the project. Starting in 1907, and lasting until 1930, twenty full volumes in his series, *The North American Indian*, were published, to be sold at $3,000 a set. (Only five hundred sets were published, and can found only in major libraries.) The title page reported that the collection was "a Series of Volumes Picturing and Describing the Indians of the United States and Alaska, written, illustrated and published by Edward S. Curtis, edited by Frederick Webb Hodge, foreword by Theodore Roosevelt, field research conducted under the patronage of J. Pierpont Morgan, in twenty volumes." In the foreword, Roosevelt wrote, "In Mr. Curtis we have both an artist and a trained observer, whose pictures are pictures, not merely photographs; whose work has far more accuracy, because it is truthful."

In addition to the volumes of *The North American Indian*, Curtis also wrote *Indian Days of Long Ago* (1914) and filmed *In the Land of the Head Hunters* (1915). He also worked as a still photographer for Cecil B. DeMille during the filming of the epic *The Ten Commandments*. Curtis died on 19 October 1952 in Los Angeles, California, at the age of 84. Jean-Anthony Du Lac said of him, "Edward S. Curtis, like all great artists, succeeded in making his process invisible. So complete was his mastery of craft and so sensitive his perceptions, so secure was he in his technique and so trusting in his subjects, that the viewer—as many have noted—feels able to enter into the very lives of the people he portrayed." Curtis was the subject of a 1975 documentary, *Shadow Catcher*.

References Du Lac, Jean-Anthony, "The Photographer and His Equipment." In Florence Curtis Graybill and Victor Boeson, *Edward Sheriff Curtis: Visions of a Vanishing Race* (1976); Mason, Jerry, ed., *International Center of Photography Encyclopedia of Photography* (1984); Thrapp, Dan L., *Encyclopedia of Frontier Biography* (1990); Waldman, Carl, *Who Was Who in Native American History: Indians and Non-Indians From Early Contacts through 1900* (1990); Weinberger, Caspar, Jr., "Classic Images of Dying Nations Enjoy a Rebirth," *Smithsonian*, 6 (1); Weinberger, Caspar, Jr., "Curtis, Edward Sheriff." In Dumas Malone et al., eds., *Dictionary of American Biography* (1930–88).

Curtis Act (30 Stat. 495)

This federal legislation, enacted on 28 June 1898, was sponsored in the U.S. House of Representatives by Republican representative Charles Curtis of Kansas, who later served in the U.S. Senate and became the thirty-first vice president of the United States. It was officially titled "An Act for the protection of the people of the Indian Territory, and for other purposes." It included what is known as the Atoka Agreement, which reads, "It is further agreed that the Choctaw orphan lands in the State of Mississippi, yet unsold, shall be taken by the United States at one dollar and twenty-five cents ($1.25) per acre, and the proceeds placed to the credit of the Choctaw orphan fund in the Treasury of the United States, the number of acres to be determined by the General Land Office." The agreement also included a proviso that allowed for the sale of coal on Indian lands, and for profits from such sales to be set aside for the education of Indian children. As Justice Joseph Rucker Lamar wrote in the U.S. Supreme Court case *Choate v. Trapp*, "These two acts [the Curtis Act and a subsequent act of July 1902 (32 Stat. 657)], containing what is known as the Atoka Agreement, provided that Indian laws and courts should at once be abolished; that there should be an enrollment of all the members of the tribes; and that the members of the two tribes [the Cherokee and Choctaw] should become citizens of the United States." Curtis biographer Marvin Ewy explains, "[The Curtis Act was] designed to protect the Indians. It allowed the Indians of Indian Territory the right to incorporate towns and elect their own town officials, and it provided that the land and money of the Five Civilized Nations be allotted in severalty. For 97,000 Indians this was the act which wound up their communal affairs." However, according to Indian historian Francis Paul Prucha, "With the Curtis Act, Congress accomplished by legislation what the Dawes Commission had been unable to do by negotiation—effectively destroy the tribal governments in the Indian Territory.

This long and detailed act provided for establishment and regulation of townsites, for management of leases of mineral rights, and for other technical matters." He continues, "[The act] authorized the Dawes Commission to draw up rolls and allot the lands to Indians on the rolls, prohibited aggrandizement of lands, and abolished the tribal courts."

See also *Cherokee Nation et al. v. Hitchcock; Choctaw, Oklahoma, & Gulf Railway Company v. Harrison;* Curtis, Charles Brent; *Stephens v. Cherokee Nation.*

References Ewy, Marvin, *Charles Curtis of Kansas: Vice President of the United States, 1929–1933* (1961); Prucha, Francis Paul, ed., *Documents of United States Indian Policy* (1990).

Cushing, Frank Hamilton (1857–1900)

Noted for his anthropological studies of Native Americans, Frank Cushing was also an accomplished and distinguished ethnologist. He was born the son of Dr. Thomas Cushing and his wife Sarah (née Crittenden) Cushing near the shores of Lake Erie in Northeast Township, Erie County, Pennsylvania, on 22 July 1857. He was a seventh-generation descendant of Cossyns de Limesi, who emigrated from Bingham, Norfolk County, England, to Massachusetts in 1636. He is also a distant cousin of William Cushing, a chief justice of the U.S. Supreme Court, as well as a fourth cousin to Howard Bass Cushing, who was killed in the Indian Wars in 1871 in Arizona, and Alonzo Hersford Cushing, a hero (and casualty) of Pickett's Charge at the Battle of Gettysburg. Biographer Ray Brandes writes, "In his youth, Cushing grew to love the outdoors, particularly the backwoods near Shelby, New York, which were rich in Indian fortifications and burial grounds. He became an avid collector of minerals, fossils, and arrowheads, trained himself in the art of stone-chipping and basket weaving, and developed an interest in archaeology." He submitted an article to the Smithsonian Institution in 1874 on his findings in Orleans County, New York, which was published that year in the Smithsonian's *Annual Report.* Although he enrolled in Cornell University to study with naturalist Charles Hartt, he was soon called to Washington by Smithsonian director Spencer Fullerton Baird to help Dr. Charles Rau to organize and classify the Indian artifacts in the museum's collections for display at the Centennial Exposition in Philadelphia in 1876.

Cushing was not formally hired by the Smithsonian for three years, but in 1879, when a field position opened, he was again called to Washington, this time by Bureau of American Ethnology director John Wesley Powell. Powell sent the young Cushing to the Southwest under the direction of anthropologist James Stevenson and his wife Matilda to make "as careful a study as circumstances will permit of the Pueblo Ruins and caves of that district." In his review of a reprint of Cushing's *Zuñi Breadstuff,* which appeared as articles in the magazine *Milstone* in 1884 and 1885, Jesse Green, an authority on Cushing, wrote, "In 1879, the year of Cushing's arrival at Zuñi Pueblo, the conquest of the Indians was nearly complete and the new Americans had begun to indulge an interest in the waning culture of the old. The Bureau of American Ethnology had just been established, and the 'collecting party' to which the twenty-two-year-old Cushing was assigned was one of its first expeditions. The expectation was that he would spend three months finding out all there was to know, camping the while with his colleagues in tents outside the pueblo. One of his first professional field experiences, however, was frustration at how little he could learn as an outsider, and he soon abandoned the tents of his colleagues and to the consternation of everyone, including the Zuñis, moved in with the Indians, establishing himself, without invitation, in a room belonging to the governor, or head chief. 'How long will it be before you go back to Washington?' asked the governor, upon discovering his guest. As it turned out, Cushing remained for four and a half years, became proficient in the language, and winning his way partly through a combination of charm, luck, and stubbornness, and partly by being pulled along by the Indians' own determination to convert and absorb him so far into the life of the pueblo that he not only was formally initiated into the tribe but became a member of the tribal council and of the priesthood."

His works on the Zuñi became famous for their clarity and objectivity. "The A-shi-wi, or Zuñis, suppose the sun, moon, and stars, the sky, earth and sea, in all their phenomena and elements; and all inanimate objects, as well as plants, animals, and men, to belong to one great system of all-conscious and interrelated life, in which the degrees of relationship seem to be determined largely, if not wholly, by the degrees of resemblance," Cushing wrote in his *Zuñi Fetiches*, published in 1883 as part of the Second Annual Report of the Bureau of Ethnology. His other works include "My Adventures in Zuñi" (which appeared in *Century* magazine in 1882 and 1883), "Outlines of Zuñi Creation Myths" (Thirteenth Annual Report of the Bureau of Ethnology, 1892–93), and "Contributions to Hopi History" *(American Anthropologist*, April-June 1907). Always sickly, he was recuperating in a Washington, D.C., hospital on 10 April 1900 when he choked on a fishbone and died. He was just 42 years old. Curtis M. Hinsley, in his history of the Bureau of American Ethnology, writes of the almost mystical Cushing, "The Indian cultures of the region apparently focused unusual attachment and possessiveness, and under the exposure of public popularity anthropology in the Southwest became heavily infused with personal style. Frank Hamilton Cushing certainly had style. Cushing was the precocious young genius of Bureau ethnology, and Powell doted paternally on this chronically ill, eccentric, and uncontrollable spirit. Cushing remains enigmatic. Matilda Stevenson considered him a fool and a charlatan. Powell and [J. W.] McGee called him a genius for his ability to enter into savage thought, while [Franz] Boas stated that Cushing's genius 'was his greatest enemy' and suggested that all his work would have to be done over. Alfred Kroeber valued Mrs. Stevenson's sobriety above Cushing's flamboyance and judged their work accordingly. On the other hand, Claude Lévi-Strauss has seen in Cushing a brilliant, intuitive precursor of structuralism. Cushing remains a live issue even today."

References Brandes, Raymond Stewart, "A Dedication to the Memory of Frank Hamilton Cushing, 1857–1900." *Arizona and the West* 4 (3); Brandes, Raymond Stewart, *Frank Hamilton Cushing: Pioneer Americanist* (Ph.D. dissertation, University of Arizona, 1965); *Cushing, Frank Hamilton, Zuñi Fetiches,* Second Annual Report of the Bureau of Ethnology (1883); Green, Jesse D., "Frank Hamilton Cushing: The Man Who Became an Indian." *New York Review of Books* 22 (9); Hinsley, Curtis M., Jr., *The Smithsonian and the American Indian: Making a Moral Anthropology in Victorian America* (1981);Thrapp, Dan L., *Encyclopedia of Frontier Biography* (1990).

Dances with Wolves

This landmark 1990 motion picture was the first to be filmed among the Lakota Sioux tribe of South Dakota, and to use the Lakota Sioux language as part of the dialogue, the first time a major motion picture made use of an Indian tongue. Director and leading actor Kevin Costner writes, "The language spoken by the Sioux people in the film is Lakota, one of several Sioux dialects. This native language was nearly lost in the government's attempt to assimilate the tribes. Few people speak it today, but community colleges on the reservations have recently begun teaching it to younger people again. The producers were fortunate in having the assistance of Doris Leader Charge, an instructor of Lakota language and culture at Sinte Glaska College on the Rosebud Reservation. Doris translated the screenplay dialogue and served as coach and technical advisor during the shooting, conducting a three-week 'crash course' for the principal actors." Film critic Leonard Maltin wrote of the picture, "[It is an] altogether extraordinary film (all the more so for being Costner's directing debut)...simply and eloquently told, with every element falling into place (on breathtaking South Dakota locations)." Based on the book by Michael Blake, the picture starred Costner as Lieutenant Dunbar, Mary McDonnell as Stands with a Fist, Graham Greene as Kicking Bird, Rodney A. Grant as Wind in His Hair, Floyd "Red Crow" Westerman as Ten Bears, and Doris Leader Charge as Ten Bears' wife, Pretty Shield. It was awarded the 1990 Academy Award for Best Picture, Director (Costner), Screenplay (Blake, adapted from his novel), Original Score (John Barry), Cinematography (Dean Semler), Editing (Neil Travis), and Sound Recording.

Reference Costner, Kevin, et al., *Dances with Wolves: The Illustrated Story of the Epic Film* (1990); Maltin, Leonard, *Leonard Maltin's Movie and Video Guide: 1996 Edition* (1995).

Left to right, language coach Doris Leader Charge, and actors Mary McDonnell and Graham Greene gather at the 1990 Washington, D.C., premiere of Dances with Wolves, *a benefit for the Smithsonian Institution's National Museum for the Native American.*

Dawes Allotment Act
See General Allotment Act.

Dawes Commission
See Commission to the Five Civilized Tribes in the Indian Territory.

Dawes, Henry Laurens (1816–1903)
He was perhaps the most influential person in Congress in changing federal government policy toward American Indians in the nineteenth century. The years he served in the U.S. Senate, where he was chairman of the Senate Committee on Indian Affairs from 1881 to 1893, are considered by some historians to be the most important years in that century for the passage of federal legislation dealing with Native Americans. Henry Laurens Dawes, whose name unofficially graces the enactment that opened Indian land to allotment, was born on 30 October 1816 in Cummington, Hampshire County, Massachusetts, the eldest of three sons of Mitchell Dawes, a farmer, and Mercy (née Burgess) Dawes. The *Boston Evening Transcript,* in its obituary of the senator, editorialized, "in spite of unfavorable surroundings he managed to fit himself for Yale College, paying his own way through most of his course, and graduating in 1889." He taught school and wrote editorials for two local papers, the Greenfield *Gazette and Courier* and the North Adams *Transcript,* then opened a law practice in North Adams after being admitted to the state bar in 1842.

Dawes entered the political arena in 1840, when he "spoke for William Henry Harrison" for president, and by 1848 was ready to run for office. That year, he was elected to the first of three terms (1848, 1849, 1852) in the Massachusetts state house; he also served a single term (1850) in the state senate. From 1853 to 1857 he served as the U.S. attorney for the Western District of Massachusetts. In 1857, he was elected to the thirty-fifth Congress from the Berkshire District of Massachusetts and he served in the House of Representatives until 1875, when he was elected to the U.S. Senate.

Biographer Claude M. Fuess writes, "His most enduring work...was accomplished as chairman of the Committee on Indian Affairs. A faithful and intelligent friend of the red men, he did his utmost to make their lot a happy one, and Edward Everett Hale said of him, 'While he held the reins, nobody talked of dishonor in our dealings with the Indians.'" From the early 1880s until its ultimate passage in 1887, the General Allotment Act, also known unofficially as the Dawes Allotment Act, was his consuming passion; it resulted in the allotment in severalty of more than 23 million acres of land to the Indians. Section 16 of the act of Congress of 3 March 1893 established the Commission to the Five Civilized Tribes in the Indian Territory, and when Dawes was made chairman of the commission just a year after he retired from the Senate, it became better known as the Dawes Commission. On 22 November 1893, Commissioner of Indian Affairs Daniel M. Browning wrote to Dawes, "I transmit herewith your commission from the President, as one of the commissioners to negotiate with the Cherokee Nation, &c., under Section 16, Act approved March 3, 1893, 27 Stats. [*sic*] 645....It is my wish that the commission meet here on Monday, the 4th day of December next, for consultation and instructions in regard to their duties. You will, therefore, before leaving your home take the official oath under this appointment and be careful to take receipts for any traveling expenses you may necessarily incur in coming to Washington." The other members of the commission were Meredith H. Kidd and Archibald L. McKennon. Their 1894 report was the basis for the dissolution of the tribal governments of the Five Civilized Tribes and the allotment of their lands in severalty.

In the last decade of his life, Dawes returned to his native Massachusetts, where he became known as "the Sage of Pittsfield." He died there on 5 February 1903 at the age of 86.

See also Allotment Policy; Commission to the Five Civilized Tribes in the Indian Territory; General Allotment Act.

References Daniel M. Browning to Dawes, 22 November 1893, Box 51, Folder 3, "Indian Affairs, 1893," Henry Laurens Dawes Papers; "Ex-Senator Dawes Dead." *Boston Evening Transcript*, 5 February 1903, 1; Fuess, Claude M., "Henry Laurens Dawes." In Dumas Malone et al., eds., *Dictionary of American Biography* (1930–88); "Thirty-six Years in Congress: Henry Laurens Dawes, 1816–1903: Tributes from the *Boston Herald*, 6 March 1893, and the *Springfield Republican*, 13 March 1893," Box 36, Folder 3, Henry Laurens Dawes Papers, Library of Congress.

DeCoteau v. The District County Court for the Tenth Judicial District (420 U.S. 425 [1975])

The joint cases of *Cheryl Spider DeCoteau, Natural Mother and Next Friend of Robert Lee Feather and Herbert John Spider, etc., Petitioner, v. The District Court for the Tenth Judicial District* and *Don R. Erickson, Warden, Petitioner, v. John Lee Feather et al.* dealt with whether Indians living on former reservation land that was sold after allotment came under state or tribal jurisdiction. According to the case notes, "An 1867 treaty (15 Stat. 505) between the United States and Sisseton and Wahpeton bands of Sioux Indians created the Lake Traverse Indian Reservation in what is now South Dakota." Under the act of Congress of 3 March 1891 (26 Stat. 1035), each member of the reservation was allotted 160 acres of land and any unallotted lands were sold to the United States, which opened the tracts for settlement by non-Indians. The issues in this case started on such former Indian lands. Cheryl Spider DeCoteau's two children were removed from her home by the District County Court for the Tenth Judicial District of South Dakota and placed in a non-Indian foster home; DeCoteau sued for a writ of habeas corpus in the Circuit Court of Roberts County, South Dakota, claiming that the district court lacked jurisdiction over Indian affairs. The circuit court denied DeCoteau relief; on appeal, the Supreme Court of South Dakota affirmed. In the second action, John Lee Feather and other members of the tribe who were serving jail sentences claimed that the state lacked jurisdiction over them. The U.S. District Court for the District of South Dakota denied the petitions, but on appeal the U.S. Court of Appeals for the Eight Circuit held that the 1891 act did not terminate the reservation, and therefore the state courts did not have jurisdiction. In both cases, the U.S. Supreme Court granted certiorari. Arguments in both cases were held on 16 December 1974.

On 3 March 1975, the court handed down its decision. The question the court faced was: Was this area of land not distinctly owned by Indians considered Indian country? Did it meet the definition of Indian country as codified at 18 U.S.C. 1151? In an opinion by Justice Potter Stewart, representing six members of the court (justices William O. Douglas, William Brennan, and Thurgood Marshall dissenting in both cases), the court upheld the judgment in the DeCoteau matter and reversed the court of appeals as to *Erickson v. Feather*. Justice Stewart explained,

In Mattz [Mattz v. Arnett, 412 U.S. 481, 1973], the Court held that an 1892 act of Congress [Act of 17 June 1892, 27 Stat. 52] did not terminate the Klamath River Indian Reservation in northern California. That Act declared the reservation lands "subject to settlement, entry, and purchase" under the homestead laws of the United States, empowered the Secretary of the Interior to allot tracts to tribal members, and provided that any proceeds of lands sales to settlers should be placed in a fund for the tribe's benefit. The 1891 statute could be considered a termination provision only if continued reservation status were inconsistent with the mere opening of lands to settlement, and such is not the case. But the 1891 Act before us is a very different instrument. It is not a unilateral action by Congress but the ratification of a previously negotiated agreement, to which a tribal majority consented. The 1891 Act does not merely open lands to settlement; it also appropriates and vests in the tribe a sum certain—$2.50 per acre—in payment for the express cession and relinquishment of "all" of the tribe's "claim, right, title and interest" in the unallotted lands. The statute in Mattz by contrast, benefited the tribe only indirectly, by establishing a fund dependent on uncertain future sales of its lands to settlers. Furthermore, the circumstances surrounding federal action in Mattz mitigated persuasively against a finding of termination. That action represented a clear retreat from previous congressional attempts to vacate the Klamath River Reservation in express terms; and the Department of the Interior had consistently regarded the Klamath River Reservation as a continuing one, despite the 1892 legislation. In the present case, by contrast, the surrounding circumstances are fully consistent with an intent to terminate the reservation, and inconsistent with any other purpose.

See also Indian Country—Definition.

Menominee Ada Elizabeth Deer, sixth assistant secretary for Indian Affairs, Department of the Interior. Deer is the first woman to head the Bureau of Indian Affairs.

Deer, Ada Elizabeth (Menominee) (1935–)

An Indian rights activist, noted for her fight in overturning the Menominee Termination Act of 1954, which abolished federal control over Menominee tribal affairs, Ada Deer was named as the sixth assistant secretary for Indian Affairs in the Interior Department, the first woman to head the Bureau of Indian Affairs. Born on 7 August 1935 in Keshena, Wisconsin, a village on the Menominee Reservation in that state, she was the eldest of nine children (four of whom died in infancy) of Joseph Deer, a nearly full-blooded Menominee, and Constance Stockton (née Wood) Deer, a white BIA nurse from Philadelphia. As Deer sat before the Senate Committee on Indian Affairs in the hearings on her appointment to head the BIA, she described the conditions she grew up in, living in a log cabin near Wisconsin's Wolf River. "While all the statistics said we were poor, I never felt poor in spirit. My mother…was the single greatest influence on my life. She instilled in me rich values which have shaped my lifetime commitment to service." Attending Indian schools and public schools in Milwaukee, Deer enrolled at the University of Wisconsin at Madison on a scholarship and received her bachelor's degree in social work in 1957. Four years later, she was awarded a master's degree in social work from Columbia University, the first Native American to achieve that degree.

While studying at Columbia, Deer was also employed as a social worker in New York City. After her graduation, she became the community service coordinator for the BIA in Minneapolis. Unhappy with that position, she worked in a series of jobs that stressed Indian pride and advancement, including the post of director of Wisconsin's Program for Recognizing Individual Determination through Education (PRIDE). Yet her most important work at this time was the formation of the grassroots organization called Determination of Rights and Unity for Menominee Shareholders (DRUMS), established to end white development of Menominee land and reverse the termination of the tribe, which had occurred in 1954. Although this tribe (their name means "People of the Wild Rice") had signed away much of its land in the controversial Wolf River Treaty of 1854, it resisted allotment in 1887 and kept the 25,000–acre reservation that it received under the treaty. With the passage of the Menominee Termination Act on 18 June 1954, all federal services to the reservation ended. To raise revenue, tribal leaders sold some of the reservation land, a policy Deer and her supporters set out to end. In a speech delivered in 1974, she said of the situation,

Th[e] thing that galvanized us into action was the fact that our board of directors got into a partnership with land developers. Land developers are not only a problem to the Indians but to every single person in this country, because we don't have enough land that's beautiful that we can preserve for everyone. I think that every one of us ought to be concerned about this.…To increase the tax base, we had some fast-talking developers come up there. We have an area of over 80 natural lakes; they created an artificial lake. They channeled some of these; it's an ecological disaster. The lakes are continually changing. They're pumping water from one to another. The shoreline trees have been destroyed in many areas. We've got motor boats, snowmobiles, pollution, terrible situations. Two thousand lots were slotted for sale and we started demonstrating. We demonstrated, we marched, we started to use the press, we formed a grass roots group called DRUMS, "Determination of Rights and Unity for Menominee Shareholders." This is a real grass roots group, because there were several of us that got together in 1970 and decided that no matter what we felt, it was important to fight for our land and people.…Restoration has three points: (1) putting our land assets into trust, (2) making us eligible for federal services, such as education and health services, and (3) giving us federal recognition as a tribe.

In order to advance this agenda, Deer served for a time in Washington, D.C., as a lobbyist for the National Committee to Save the Menominee People and Forest. Publicity over the destruction that termination was bringing on the Indians resulted in the passage of the Menominee Restoration Act in 1973.

In the years after this legislative victory, Deer worked behind the scenes to advance the Native American rights movement's agenda. She served as chairman of the Menominee tribe and for a time headed the Menominee Restoration Committee. From 1979 to 1981 she was a liaison for the Native American Rights Fund and a senior lecturer at the School of Social Work at the University of Wisconsin at Madison, where she taught until 1993. She made a failed run for Congress in 1992 and in 1993 was appointed as the sixth assistant secretary for Indian Affairs in the Interior Department, the post that has overseen the Bureau of Indian Affairs since the position of commissioner of Indian Affairs was abolished in 1977.

Her primary strategy for the BIA was to implement Public Law 93–638, the Indian Self-Determination Act, which gives greater autonomy to tribal leaders and councils, and the transference of BIA functions in Washington to regional offices closer to the reservations. According to the editors of *Current Biography Yearbook 1994*, "In addition, Deer is pushing for what she has called 'a holistic approach' to economic development on Indian reservations, one that would foster diverse, culturally appropriate, and environmentally benign business ventures." As of this writing, she continues as assistant secretary for Indian Affairs.

See also Bureau of Indian Affairs.

References "Deer, Ada E." In Judith Graham, ed., *Current Biography Yearbook 1994* (1994); Hardy, Gail J., *American Women Civil Rights Activists: Biobibliographies of 68 Leaders, 1825–1992* (1993); Hurtado, Albert L. and Peter Iverson, eds., *Major Problems in American Indian History: Documents and Essays* (1994); Wong, Hertha D., "Deer, Ada." In Gretchen M. Bataille, ed., *Native American Women: A Biographical Dictionary* (1993); Worthington, Roger, "Woman Picked to Lead Indian Bureau." *Chicago Tribune*, 20 May 1993, 24.

***Delaware Indians v. Cherokee Nation* (193 U.S. 127, 48 L.Ed. 646, 24 S.Ct. 342 [1904])**
***See** Cherokee Nation v. Journeycake.*

***Delaware Tribal Business Commission v. Weeks* (430 U.S. 73, 51 L.Ed. 2d 173, 97 S.Ct. 911 [1977])**
Combined with the cases of *Absentee Delaware Tribe of Oklahoma Business Committee et al. v. Weeks* and *Andrus, Secretary of the Interior et al. v. Weeks*, this Supreme Court action dealt with the issue of claims arising from the extinguishment of Indian title. According to the case notes,

> Approximately 100 years after the United States had breached an 1854 treaty with the Delaware Indians by privately selling certain reservation tribal trust lands, rather than selling them at public auction as required under the treaty, claims arising out of the breach were brought before the Indian Claims Commission by two federally recognized Indian tribes—(1) the "Cherokee Delawares," the descendants of Delawares who moved from Missouri to a reservation in Kansas, and then, as a result of an 1866 treaty, to lands in Oklahoma, and (2) the "Absentee Delawares," the descendants of Delawares who never moved to the Kansas reservation, but migrated to Oklahoma and settled with the Wichita and Caddo Indians.

In 1969, after hearings as to what claims these two tribes had, the Indian Claims Commission awarded them $1,385,617.81, and including interest, concluded with a figure of $9,168,171.13. By an act of Congress of 26 December 1969 (83 Stat. 447, at 453), the Congress appropriated this sum. A further act, Public Law 92–456 (86 Stat. 762), authorized the secretary of the interior to disburse these funds. It was at this time that plaintiff Wanda June Weeks stepped forward representing the "Kansas Delawares"—a portion of the tribe that moved to Kansas, like the "Cherokee Delawares," but remained in Kansas instead of removing to Oklahoma. Weeks et al. filed an action against Secretary of the Interior Cecil Andrus to enjoin him from disbursing the funds and at the same time filed an action against the two tribes from accepting what Weeks considered were funds properly belonging, in part, to the Kansas Delawares. The U.S. District Court for the Western District of Oklahoma found that the failure of the "Kansas Delawares" to receive a portion of the funds was a denial of the due process clause of the U.S. Constitution. On a direct appeal, the U.S. Supreme Court granted certiorari and heard arguments on 10 November 1976. On 23 February 1977, Justice William Brennan delivered the 8–1 decision (Justice John Paul Stevens dissenting) in holding that because the "Kansas Delawares" signed an 1866 treaty extinguishing their title to the land and entering into citizenship, they were not to be part of the settlement. Justice Brennan added, "Our conclusion that the exclusion of the Kansas Delawares from distribution under Public Law 92–456 does not offend the Due Process Clause of the Fifth Amendment of course does not preclude Congress from revising the distribution scheme to include the Kansas Delawares. The distribution authorized by Public Law 92–456 has not yet occurred, and Congress has the power to revise its original allocation." Justice Harry Blackmun and Chief Justice Warren Burger concurred in the court's majority opinion, but argued that "Congress must have a large measure of flexibility in allocating Indian awards."

Reference Haught, Steven, "Due Process: Delaware Tribal Business Committee v. Weeks. The Participation of Kansas Delawares in Tribal Awards." *American Indian Law Review* 5(2).

Deloria, Vine Victor, Jr. (Standing Rock Sioux) (1933–)
A prolific writer on Indian history and civil rights, himself a Standing Rock Sioux, Vine Deloria is one of the most important Indian authors today. He was born on 26 March 1933 in Martin, South Dakota, a small town on the border of the Pine Ridge Reservation, the son of Episcopal minister Vine Deloria, Sr., and his wife Barbara (née Eastman) Deloria. Descended from a French fur

Historian Vine Victor Deloria, Jr., teaches a class at the University of Colorado, Boulder, in February 1992.

trader named Des Lauriers who married into the Sioux tribe, Deloria's grandfather, Philip, who was one of the first Indian converts to the Episcopal Church and later became a noted Episcopal priest, anglicized the family name to Deloria. Their work as missionaries took them to the religious heart and soul of Indian reservations. Vine, Jr., was educated at the reservation school. He says of his childhood, "In those days, the reservation was isolated and unsettled. One could easily get lost in the wild back country as roads turned into cowpaths without so much as a backward glance." Among his degrees are a bachelor's degree in general science from Iowa State University, a master's degree in theology from Augustana Lutheran Seminary in Rock Island, Illinois, and a juris doctor degree from the University of Colorado.

After graduating from Augustana, he joined the staff of the United Scholarship Service, a church group in Denver, Colorado, where he was placed in charge of establishing a program for the education of Indian students in preparatory programs. Soon disgusted by the paternalism that he felt pervaded the organization, he left, and served as executive director of the National Congress of American Indians (NCAI) from 1964 to 1967. His election to this position is generally regarded as having come with the support of Robert Warrior, a leader in the National Indian Youth Council (NIYC). Clifford M. Lytle, Jr., writes, "When the older tribal leader discovered that the younger Indians had in effect engineered a major political coup in Deloria's election, they withheld funds from the NCAI, hoping to force Deloria's resignation and the appointment of an older Indian leader more in tune with their views. Deloria's response was simply to announce that he was filing bankruptcy for the organization, a very unexpected move that brought the reluctant tribal leaders into line and gave Deloria tremendous influence with both Indian youth and longtime organizational dissidents." When he found that Indians needed capable attorneys to pursue their agenda in the courts, he resigned as head of the NCAI and went to law school at the University of Colorado, and earned his aforementioned Juris Doctor degree in 1970.

In 1969, Deloria wrote *Custer Died for Your Sins: An Indian Manifesto*, an exposé of the government's treatment of its native citizens. J. A. Phillips, writing a review of the work, explained, "If this book is indicative of Deloria's methods, he's more interested in results than in being tactful. Nauseated by the traditional Indian image, he asserts the worth if not the dignity of the redman and blasts the political, social, and religious forces that perpetuate the Little Big Horn and wigwam stereotyping of his people." The work was published at the height of the American Indian Movement's drive for recognition of Indian rights, as was his second publication, *We Talk, You Listen: New Tribes, New Turf* (1970), which, according to biographer Karen P. Zimmerman, "addressed the issue of tribalism and advocated a return to tribal social organization in order to save society." His other works include *Of Utmost Good Faith* (1971), *God is Red: A Native View of Religion* (1973), *Behind the Trail of Broken Treaties* (1974), *The Indian Affair* (1974), and *The Metaphysics of Modern Existence* (1979). In his capacity as a teacher, he has served as professor of American Indian Studies at the University of Arizona at Tucson.

References "Deloria, Vine Victor, Jr." In Clare D. Kinsman, ed., *Contemporary Authors: A Bio-Bibliographical Guide to Current Authors and Their Works* (1962–1995); Lytle, Clifford M., Jr., "Vine Deloria, Jr." In David DeLeon, ed., *Leaders from the 1960s: A Biographical Sourcebook of American Activism* (1994); Moritz, Charles, ed., *Current Biography 1974* (1974); Warrior, Robert Allen, *Tribal Secrets: Recovering American Indian Intellectual Traditions* (1995); Zimmerman, Karen P., "Vine Deloria Jr." In Sharon Malinowski, ed., *Notable Native Americans* (1995).

Deming Investment Company v. United States (224 U.S. 471 [1912])

This 1912 Supreme Court case dealt with the narrow issue of whether members of an Indian tribe, not full blood Indians, could sell surplus allotted land before it was allotted to individuals. The Deming Mortgage Company of Oklahoma City, Oklahoma, attempted to sell mortgages on surplus allotted land on the Seminole Indian reservation in Oklahoma. The U.S. government sued to enjoin, or stop, the company from selling the mortgages. The Circuit Court for the Eastern District of Oklahoma refused to authorize an end to the mortgages, but the U.S. Court of Appeals for the Eighth Circuit overturned the decision. The Deming Investment Company appealed to the U.S. Supreme Court. Arguments were held before the court on 12 and 13 October 1911, and a decision was handed down on 29 April 1912. Justice Charles Evan Hughes delivered the unanimous decision of the court: he held that lands conveyed by freedmen Seminoles could be sold for mortgage; those by minor allottees or adult allottees conveyed before 21 April 1904, the date a federal act removed restrictions on adult allottees, were off limits. Hughes thus sustained the action as to lands conveyed by adults, which in this case constituted a majority of the lands conveyed to Deming. The Justice ordered the case to be remanded to the lower court for consideration based on the high court's decision.

The Supreme Court decided three other cases dealing with this issue in 1912: *Goat v. United States; Heckman v. United States; Mullen v. United States.*

Denver, James William (1817–1892)

The eighth commissioner of the Bureau of Indian Affairs, James W. Denver was the fifth governor of the Kansas Territory (1858); the Colorado state capital is named in his honor. Of Irish and Scottish ancestry, Denver was born in Winchester, in Frederick County, Virginia, on 23 October 1817, one of eleven children (three of which died in infancy) of Patrick and Jane (née Campbell) Denver. Denver's biographer, George C. Barns, traced Denver's family back to the Domesday Book (compiled by William the Conqueror in the eleventh century of citizenry and property in medieval England), when the family name was either Danefella or Danefela. James W. Denver's grandfather, Patrick Denver, escaped northern Ireland in 1799 after rebelling against the English crown, and came to

James W. Denver, Bureau of Indian Affairs commissioner

America, where he died in 1831. With him during his escape was his son Patrick, father of the subject of this biography. Jane Campbell Denver, according to Barns, was of Scottish descent.

About 1831, the Denvers moved from Virginia to Wilmington, Ohio, where James Denver was educated in surveying and engineering in the local schools. With this education in hand, he went to Missouri to survey the public lands, but his failure to obtain a contract to survey forced him to teach for a year. In 1842 he returned to Ohio; two years later was awarded a law degree from the Cincinnati Law School, and he began a practice in the town of Xenia while at the same time editing a small Democratic newspaper, *The Thomas Jefferson.* Prior to March 1847, he removed to Platte City, Missouri. In 1847 Denver was commissioned a captain in a company of Missouri volunteers brought together to fight in the Mexican War with the 12th Missouri Infantry. He fought with General Winfield Scott at the battles of Puebla and Mexico City. After the war, he founded and served as the president of the National Association of Mexican War Veterans. He returned to Missouri, where he restarted his law practice and edited *The Platte Argus*, a Democratic journal.

After only two short years in Missouri, Denver moved once again, this time to the growing territory of California, where gold was luring thousands of seekers. Opening a small business in the capital, Sacramento, Denver was elected to the California State Senate, where he was noted for his duel, after a long series of accusatory letters, with Edward Gilbert, editor of the *Daily Alta California* newspaper. Denver's murder of Gilbert on 2 August 1852 did not result in any charges; in fact, it did not diminish Denver's developing political career. The following year Governor John Bigler named Denver as secretary of state, and in 1854 he was elected to the U.S. House of Representatives, where he served in the thirty-fourth Congress, particularly as chairman of the special committee on the Pacific Railroad. In 1856, he did not run for reelection; instead, on 17 April 1857, President James Buchanan named him as commissioner of Indian Affairs, to replace the highly successful George W. Manypenny. In his short stint as commissioner, Denver visited Kansas Territory and Nebraska to negotiate treaties with the Pawnees and other tribes. Seeing him as a stabilizing influence in the sea of turmoil that was the Kansas Territory at that time, Buchanan, on 24 February 1858, appointed Denver to the position of Kansas Territorial Governor. Denver may or may not have resigned as Indian commissioner; he did sign the 1857 annual report of the Bureau of Indian Affairs, and his replacement, Major Charles E. Mix, is considered by historians to have been a temporary stand in. States historian Donald Chaput, "In most of the reports, correspondence, and statements of the commissioner issued during Denver's administration it is impossible to separate Mix from Denver."

Denver accepted the governorship with the intention in mind that the duty would be temporary. He had good reason to be apprehensive as to his new assignment: Kansas was in the midst, aside from its problems with the Indians, of full-scale civil war between advocates of slavery and abolitionists. The Kansas-Nebraska Act of 1854, the Supreme Court's decision in *Dred Scott v. Sanford* and the passage of the proslavery Lecompton Constitution, the two latter events occurring in 1857, had made the settlement of the slavery question all the more important in the fractured territory. Historians Thomas A. McMullin and David Walker write, "Seeking to establish a calm, impartial administration, Denver knew that free staters formed the majority of the territory's residents. He warned Buchanan that angry Republicans planned to assassinate anyone who attempted to hold office under the proslavery Lecompton Constitution, and that most Kansas preferred to begin the constitutional process over again. Buchanan, however, refused to disregard the Lecompton document, and submitted it to Congress on 2 February 1858. Denver also battled with territorial lawmakers over their attempt to move the capital of Kansas from Lecompton to Minneola, an undeveloped townsite in which thirty-five of fifty-two legislators had made investments. After his veto of the bill was overridden, he refused to leave or transfer any records. The U.S. Attorney General finally declared the move to be unconstitutional. During his brief term Denver authorized the establishment of a government and appointed officials for Arapahoe County. Located over three hundred miles west of any other county, that region included the Pike's Peak and Cherry Creek gold sites." When miners from Arapahoe County moved to Colorado Territory (Arapahoe County was later made a part of the state of Colorado), they named their new territorial capital (originally called St. Charles) after the former Kansas governor.

On 10 October 1858, exhausted from his work and disgusted with the White House reaction to his attempts at reconciliation, Denver resigned as governor and returned to Washington to once again work as Indian commissioner. His position with the president, however, was damaged, and Denver only served from 9 November 1858 until 12 March 1859, when he formally resigned the office. In that short time, he made little imprint on national Indian policy. On 18 January 1859, Denver wrote to Representative Alexander H. Stephens of Georgia (who would later serve as the only vice president of the Confederacy) on his thoughts regarding Indians in the newly proposed Colorado Territory. Denver penned, "Of the Indians found in the proposed territory, I believe none of them have settled in permanent habitations, but are purely nomadic in their habits. Their numbers are not known with any degree of certainty, but they consist of various tribes known as Comanches, Kinneys, Arapahoes, Cheyennes, Emus, Sioux, Shoshones or Snakes, and Utahs. My opinion is that the proper course for the government to pursue towards the Indians would be to assign them to a small reservation, furnish them with an instructor and the means of cultivating the soil, and then require them to support themselves. If they have settled habitations[,] give them the lands they occupy, but in no instance to give them money annuities or other presents, except such as necessary to carry on their farming or agricultural operations. Everyone must admit that the system heretofore pursued towards the Indians has proved a most lamentable failure. Taking them as a mass they are not as well off today as they were half a century ago, notwithstanding [that] more than fifty millions of dollars have been expended by the government in efforts to civilize, to say nothing about the expenditures...of other parties. Instead of civilizing, it has converted much of the larger portion of them into paupers, who rely on the small sum of money paid to each once or twice a year for subsistence, and which generally draws around them some of the very worst of the whites. Naturally disinclined to labor they rely on the government for support, and thus we have gone year after year building into a vast pauper establishment without conferring any corresponding benefit. Our presents attract the cupidity of the whites, and the Indian having got rid of his share, sits down and listlessly ekes out a miserable existence until the next payment is made, when the same thing is done over again. Then there seems to be no likelihood of a termination of this pauper system but with the extinction of the whole race. Some change is necessary in order to stay their downward course, and in my opinion the first step to be taken is to teach them to labor. This can only be done by making their subsistence depend on their own exertions. I know of no reason why the government should be required to support the Indians in idleness, while the whites are competent to labor for a livelihood."

Denver lived 33 years after leaving the Indian office. His most important work in this period came when he served as a brigadier general with the Union army during the Civil War. He was highly criticized in this role; Adjutant General William C. Kibbe of California wrote to Secretary of War Simon Cameron on 6 September 1861, "Many of the officers who have been mustered into the service openly declare that if General Denver assumed the command over them that they will at once resign; that they have no confidence in his loyalty, but on the contrary they believe him to be at least a sympathizer with the rebel cause and opposed to the war, and also that he is totally unfitted in point of military skill or experience to command a brigade." He cited an article in the *Columbia* (Missouri) *Weekly Times*, 29 August 1861, which read, "General Denver, an aspirant for the U.S. Senatorship on the [Stephen A.] Douglas ticket, who a short time ago wrote a letter in California on favor of the forcible suppression of the rebellion, now writes from Ohio, according to a letter to his brother which the *Marysville Express* publishes, bewailing the war, calling Lincoln a usurper of power, the Congress venal [dishonest] and subservient, and free government in danger of being converted into a military despotism. There's another nice Douglas Democrat for you!" Denver ultimately served until March 1863, when he retired to Washington, D.C., to practice law. Later, he established a practice at his old home in Wilmington, Ohio. He ran unsuccessfully for a seat in Congress from Ohio in 1870, but in 1884 he was mentioned quite highly as a possible Presidential candidate of the Democratic party. Denver died while on a trip to the nation's capital on 9 August 1892, and his body was returned to Wilmington for burial.

See also Bureau of Indian Affairs; Mix, Charles E.

References Barns, George C., *Denver, the Man, The Life, Letters and Public Papers of the Lawyer, Soldier, and Statesman* (1949); Chaput, Donald, "James W. Denver." In Robert M. Kvasnicka and Herman J. Viola, eds., *The Commissioners of Indian Affairs, 1824–1977* (1979); James W. Denver to Alexander H. Stephens, 18 January 1859, Office of Indian Affairs, Letters Sent, RG 75; McMullin, Thomas A. and David Walker, *Biographical Directory of American Territorial Governors* (1984).

Department of Game v. Puyallup Tribe (414 U.S. 44 [1973])

See *Puyallup Tribe v. The Department of Game of the State of Washington et al.*

Department of Taxation and Finance of New York et al. v. Milhelm Attea & Bros., Inc., etc. et al. (512 U.S.—, 129 L.Ed. 2d 52, 114 S.Ct.—[1994])

This Supreme Court case was decided in the line of cases which upheld the court's 1991 decision in *Oklahoma Tax Commission v. Citizen Band Potawatomi Indian Tribe of Oklahoma*, where it was held that Indian reservation stores selling cigarettes to non-Indians must collect the tax for states. In this case, however, to make sure that the tax was being collected, the New York state Department of Taxation and Finance required record keeping, while at the same time limiting the number of cigarettes that could be sold on Indian reservations. Before the state regulations could go into effect, a cigarette wholesaler who sold to Indian reservations with the approval of the Bureau of Indian Affairs sued in the Supreme Court of New York of Albany County, alleging that the regulations were a violation of the Indian Trader Statutes (15 U.S.C. 261 et seq.), which gave the sole authority over this area to the commissioner of Indian Affairs (now the assistant secretary of the interior for Indian affairs). The state supreme court issued an injunction against the regulations but the Supreme Court of New York Appellate Division reversed. The Court of Appeals of New York then reversed that court. The State Department then appealed to the U.S. Supreme Court. Justice John Paul Stevens, reflecting the views of a unanimous court in reversing the New York Court of Appeals, held on 13 June 1994 that the state regulations were not pre-empted by the Indian Trader Statutes, that Indian traders were not "wholly immune" from state regulation over the affairs of non-Indians on reservations, that the effect of the state regulations to collect taxes on non-Indians "outweighed" the effect of such regulations on commerce on the reservations, and that these regulations did not "unnecessarily intrud[e] on core tribal interests." In a lengthy opinion, Justice Stevens explained, "In *Potawatomi*, we held that sovereign immunity barred the State of Oklahoma's suit against a Tribe to recover cigarette taxes owed for sales to non-Indians at a convenience store owned by the Tribe. In response to the state's protest that the Tribe's immunity from suit made the State's recognized authority to tax cigarette sales to non-Indians a 'right without any remedy,'...we explained that alternative remedies existed for state tax collectors, such as damage actions against individual tribal officers or agreements with the tribes. We added that 'States may of course collect the sales tax from cigarette wholesalers, either by seizing unstamped cigarettes off the reservation...or by assessing wholesalers who supplied unstamped cigarettes to the tribal stores." He added, "This is another case in which we must 'reconcile the plenary power of the States over residents within their borders with the semi-autonomous status of Indians living on tribal reservations.'"

See also *Oklahoma Tax Commission v. Citizen Band Potawatomi Indian Tribe of Oklahoma.*

Dick v. United States (208 U.S. 340 [1908])

This case was another in the line of cases involving the issue of the definition of Indian country, whether it still existed with or without the extinguishment of title, and whether it was constitutional to outlaw the introduction of intoxicating beverages into Indian country. George Dick, the plaintiff in error, was arrested and convicted of selling whiskey on the Nez Percé reservation in Idaho. Dick appealed his conviction on the grounds that the laws of Congress outlawing the introduction of intoxicating beverages into Indian country were made void when the reservation was subjected to allotment under the General Allotment Act of 1887, and the Indians came under the laws of Idaho. The District Court of the United States for the District of Idaho upheld the conviction (Dick was sentenced to a year and ten days in a penitentiary and fined $100), and the plaintiff appealed to the U.S. Supreme Court. The case was submitted on 3 December 1907, and Justice John Marshall Harlan delivered the unanimous opinion of the court on 24 February 1908. Harlan, in upholding the conviction, explained,

Section 2139 [of the Revised Statutes], as amended and re-enacted in 1892, makes it an offense against the United States for anyone to introduce intoxicating liquors into the "Indian country," and the offense charged against Dick was the introduction by him of whisky [*sic*] into that country on the 15th day of March 1905. The transaction out of which the present prosecution arose occurred, as we have seen, within the village of Culdesac, a municipal organization existing under and by virtue of the laws of Idaho, and the parties involved in it were Dick and Te-We-Talkt, who were at that time Indian allottees in severalty and holders of trust patents, and therefore, according to the decision in *Re Heff*, 197 U.S. 488, 49 L.Ed. 848, 25 Sup. Ct. Rep. 506, citizens of the United States. If this case depended alone upon the Federal liquor statute forbidding the introduction of intoxicating drinks into the Indian country, we should feel obliged to adjudge that the trial court erred in not directing a verdict for the defendant; for that statute, when enacted, did not intend by the words "Indian country" to embrace any body of territory in which, at the time, the Indian title had been extinguished, and over which and over the inhabitants of which (as was the case of Culdesac) the jurisdiction of the state, for all purposes of government, was full and complete. Bates v. Clark, 95 U.S. 204, 24 L.Ed. 471; Ex parte Crow Dog (Ex parte Kang-Gi-Shun-Ca), 109 U.S. 556, 561, 27 L.Ed. 1030, 1032, 3 Sup. Ct. Rep. 396. But this case does not depend upon the construction of the Federal liquor statute, considered alone. That statute must be interpreted in connection with the agreement of 1893 between the United States and the Nez Percé Indians. By that agreement, as we have seen, the United States stipulated that the lands ceded by the Nez Percé Indians, and those retained as well as those allotted to the Indians (which embraced all the lands in the original reservation) should be subject for the limited period of twenty-five years, to all federal laws prohibiting the introduction of intoxicants into the Indian country.

Dickson v. Luck Land Company (242 U.S. 371, 61 L.Ed. 371, 37 S.Ct. 167 [1917])

An Indian must attain the age of majority to be able to receive his patent for his allotment, and thus to be able to properly convey it, the Supreme Court found in this 1917 case. A mixed-blood Chippewa Indian of the White Earth Indian Reservation in Minnesota, who remained unidentified, received his allotment with a restriction on conveyance for a period of 25 years. In 1907, the Congress enacted a law (34 Stat. 1015) which patented all lands to Indian allottees once they had reached their majority. The mixed-blood in question sold his land to F.A. Dickson before he reached age 18, and then sold it again to the Land Luck Company after he reached that age. A local Minnesota district court held that the sale to Dickson was illegal, and sided with the Land Luck Company; the Supreme Court of Minnesota affirmed the judgment. The U.S. Supreme Court granted certiorari, and the case was submitted on 6 December 1916. Justice Willis Van Devanter held for a unanimous court on 8 January 1917 (in an opinion that runs less than two pages) in affirming the district court's holding as to the illegality of the conveyance of the allotment to Dickson. Justice Van Devanter explained, "It would seem that the situation was one in which all questions pertaining to the disposal of the lands naturally would fall within the scope and operation of the state. And that Congress so intended is shown by the Act of May 8, 1906, 34 Stat. 182, which provides that when an Indian allottee is given a patent in fee for his allotment he 'shall have the benefit of and be subject to all the laws, both civil and criminal, of the state.' Among the laws to which the allottee became subject, and to the benefit of which he became entitled, under this enactment, were those governing the transfer of real property, fixing the age of majority, and declaring the disability of minors. Affirmed."

See also *United States v. Waller et al.*

Dodge, Henry Chee (Mixed Navajo) (1857? or 1860?-1947)

His Indian name was *Hastiin Adits'aii*, which translates into "Man Who Interprets" or "One Who Hears and Understands"; the name Chee is interpreted as "Red Boy." Yet Henry Chee Dodge, who was more commonly known as Chee Dodge, should rank among the leaders of those who tried to improve the lot of the American Indian people. He was born between 1857 and 1860 in Fort Defiance, Arizona, the son of a Navajo-Jemez mother, Bisnayanchi. Although there was speculation that his father was a Mexican smith named Aneas or Anaya, there is, according to historian Carl Waldman, evidence that Dodge was the illegitimate son of Indian agent Henry Lafayette Dodge (known as "Red Shirt"; 1810–1856), and was born after his father had died. Aneas or Anaya became his surrogate father, but he too died when Henry was an infant. Bisnayanchi died during Kit Carson's foray into Navajo country in 1864, leaving young Henry in the care of an old man and his granddaughter, who carried the orphaned child on the Long Walk when the Navajos were forced onto settlements in New Mexico. Chee Dodge was raised for a time by his mother's sister, but they left him and he was forced to live with an Indian girl and her grandfather; the family later adopted him. He remained with this family through the four years of the Navajo captivity, 1864–68, and their return to the Navajo nation.

About 1872, after eight years with his adopted family, he was found by his mother's sister, who had married a white man, Perry Williams, and who desired to get the young man an education. After going to a Presbyterian school, Chee was given a job as a clerk by Williams at Fort Defiance. At the same time that he was learning business techniques that he would later utilize, he was also becoming proficient in English, and when he was 20 he was named as the official interpreter to the whites for the Navajo nation. He then went into business for himself, opening with a white man, Stephen Aldrich, the Round Rock Trading Post in New Mexico. After his first marriage collapsed, he married the daughter of the girl who had saved him when he was four. Of the children of this marriage, his son Tom became chairman of the Navajo nation in 1932, and his daughter Annie Dodge Wauneka was awarded the Presidential Medal of Freedom by President John F. Kennedy in 1963 for her work to improve Indian health.

In 1923, after nearly 60 years without a tribal government, the Navajos were asked to form a tribal council by the Bureau of Indian Affairs so it could properly sell oil leases on the Navajo reservation. At the first meeting on 7 July 1923 at Toadlena, New Mexico, Dodge was elected as the council's first chairman. Biographer Mary Shepardson writes, "He had experience as an interpreter, a headman, and a businessman. Above all, he possessed oratorical ability, a traditionally appreciated qualification for leadership." Working with New Mexico Territorial Governor Herbert J. Hagerman, the council approved several leases. Catherine Clay pens, "The council represented all nine of the Navajo districts with 12 delegates and 12 alternate members. They approved Hagerman's position, giving him the authorization to sign all oil and mineral leases in exchange for a federal promise to obtain more land for the Navajos." Dodge, an opponent of assimilation, fought for the right of the council to spend the royalties from the oil sales to purchase more land. His influence helped Congress to enact the Indian Oil Act of 1927, in which states that took a percentage of the royalties from such sales must use those funds for projects that benefit Indians. Although he stepped down from the council in 1928 (he was elected again in 1942 and served until his death), Dodge may have been the most influential Indian activist of his time. When the Bureau of Indian Affairs called upon Navajos to reduce its sheep stocks to prevent erosion, Dodge publicly accused Indian Commissioner John Collier of trying to starve the Indians.

Dodge was elected to the tribal council in 1942, and reelected to 1946. But before completing the second term, he died of pneumonia in Ganado, Arizona, on 7 January 1947, when he was in his late eighties or early nineties. Biographer David Brugge writes, "While Dodge was influential in the development of the values of modern Navajo society, he was not a proponent of radical change, nor could he have effected such change had he desired to do so."

References Brugge, David M., "Henry Chee Dodge: From the Long Walk to Self-Determination." In Lester George Moses and Raymond Wilson, eds., *Indian Lives: Essays on Nineteenth- and Twentieth-Century Native American Leaders* (1985); Clay, Catherine A., "Henry Chee Dodge." In Sharon Malinowski, ed., *Notable Native Americans* (1995); Malone, Dumas, et al., eds., *Dictionary of American Biography* (1930–88); Shepardson, Mary, "Development of Navajo Tribal Government." In Alfonso Ortiz, ed., *Handbook of North American Indians*, vol. 10 (1983); Waldman, Carl, *Who Was Who in Native American History: Indians and Non-Indians from Early Contacts through 1900* (1990).

Dodge, William Earl (1805–1883)

See United States Board of Indian Commissioners; United States Indian Commission.

Doe ex dem. Mann v. Wilson (23 Howard [64 U.S.] 457 [1860])

In the case of *John Doe, ex dem. Curtis Mann and Dolphus Hannah, Plaintiffs in Error, v. William Wilson,* decided by the U.S. Supreme Court in 1860, the court held that an Indian holding an "interest" in lands belonging to an Indian reservation whose tribal rights to the land are about to be extinguished may convey the title to his land to whites who wish to purchase it, even if that land had yet to be surveyed and a patent distributed. Under the treaty with the Potawatomie of 27 October 1832, that Indian nation agreed to cede all of its land in the states of Indiana and Illinois, as well as land that was then the Michigan Territory, to the U.S. government. The government agreed to establish reservations for some of the Indians who wished to live in a community, while providing land patents for those who desired to live individually. Pet-chi-co, a Potawatomie chief, was granted his individual patent, and in 1833, shortly before he died, he sold it to two white men, Alexis Coquillard and David H. Colerick, both of Indiana. By 1860, these two men had passed the patent down to one William Wilson, the defendant in this case. In 1855, descendants of Pet-chi-co sold this same patent to a group of men, including John Doe, (an unidentified party), Curtis Mann, and Dolphus Hannah. These men then sued Wilson in the Circuit Court of the United States for the District of Indiana to recover the patent to the land, claiming than since Pet-chi-co died before the land was surveyed (a prerequisite before a patent could be issued), his conveyance of the land was void. The circuit court held for Wilson and the plaintiffs appealed to the U.S. Supreme Court for relief. Arguments were heard on 1 May 1860, with Justice John Catron holding for a unanimous court just three days later that Pet-chi-co's conveyance was legal. Justice Catron explained, "Although the government alone can purchase lands from an Indian Nation, it does not follow that when the rights of the Nation are extinguished, an individual of the Nation who takes [the land] as private owner cannot sell his interest. The Indian title is property, and alienable [able to be sold], unless the treaty had prohibited its sale. So far from this being the case in the instance before us, it is manifest [apparent] that sales of the reserved sections [of the Indian reservation] were contemplated, as the lands ceded were forthwith to be surveyed, sold, and inhabited by a white population, among whom the Indians could not remain. We hold that Pet-chi-co was a tenant in common with the United States, and could sell his reserved interest; and that when the United States selected the lands reserved to him, and made partition (of which the patent is conclusive evidence), his grantees took the interest he would have taken if living."

For a similar case, one which referred to *Doe*, see *Crews et al. v. Burcham et al.*

Dole, William Palmer (1811–1889)

The twelfth commissioner of Indian Affairs, William Palmer Dole served during the Lincoln and Andrew Johnson administrations and was the chief administrator of governmental policy toward the Indians during the Civil War. Little is known of his life, as he left few tangible traces for historians to follow. Born on 3 December 1811 (The obituary of Dole in the *Indiana Sentinel* [Indianapolis] for 3 October 1889 states that he was born in 1810) in Danville, Vermont, the eldest son of Enoch and Harriet (née Dexter) Dole. (The *Bedford* [New Hampshire] *Messenger*, a church publication, mentioned in its 29 August 1883 edition that William was Enoch's eldest son.) What is known of his parents is that they moved soon after their son's birth to a home in Bedford, then to Ohio about 1818, and finally to Indiana about 1831, settling in or near Terre Haute. It was Indiana with which Dole would be identified for the rest of his life. The details of his education are unknown; he did spend much of his young adulthood in various business enterprises, including working as a pork packer and dry goods wholesaler. Only a few of Dole's letters are extant, and these mainly concern his boating trade from 1836 until

1843. As historian Donald Carmony wrote, "Most of the letters were penned by Dole while floating downstream or from various market points along the lower Mississippi. They reveal much about the obstructions to and hazards from flatboat navigation, offer interesting vignettes of life aboard flatboats, afford glimpses of the difficulties, disappointments, and delays often involved in disposing of produce; and indicate the personal inconveniences and concerns arising from weeks away from home and business."

In 1838, when only 28, Dole was elected to a seat in the lower house of the Indiana General Assembly, and in 1844 to the state Senate. Sometime during the 1850s, Dole moved his dry goods business over the river from Indiana to Paris, Illinois, where he went into a partnership with one William Kile. Although he had been a Whig in the legislature, Dole soon moved over to the growing Republican party, and in 1860 he was a delegate to the Republican Convention in Chicago that nominated Abraham Lincoln for president. With Lincoln's election, the new President turned to Dole, an ardent supporter during the campaign, to fill the role of commissioner of Indian Affairs in the new administration.

Dole served as Indian commissioner for the length of the entire Civil War, and as such he spent a considerable amount of time discussing the effect of the war on the Indian tribes. He also reflected on continued governmental policy and its impact on the Indians; in his 1862 annual report, he discussed, "Another year has but served to strengthen my conviction that the policy, recently adopted, of confining the Indians to reservations, and, from time, as they are gradually taught and become accustomed to the idea of individual property, allotting to them lands to be held in severalty, is the best method yet devised for their reclamation and advancement in civilization. The successful working of this policy is not, however, unattended with difficulties and embarrassments, arising chiefly from the contact of the red and white races. This is especially the case in relation to Indians whose reservations are located within the limits of States." The following year, 1863, his treatise described the condition of the Indian tribes located in the southern Confederate states, which had remained loyal to the Union:

The reports of the superintendent, the agents, and employe[e]s of this superintendency, to be found among the accompanying papers, possess an unusual degree of interest. A careful perusal of these reports, and those made during the existence of the present rebellion, will, I think, demonstrate that no portion of our people have suffered greater calamities, have met with more overwhelming disasters, or have more heroically battled for the common interests of the country, than have the loyal Indians within its limits. Possessing one of the most beautiful, fertile, and desirable portions of our country, and almost completely removed from the baneful effects so often attendant upon close proximity to white settlements, many of them were, prior to the rebellion, in the quiet enjoyment of most of the comforts and conveniences of civilized life; the various tribes were at peace with each other, and the whole people were presenting unmistakable evidences of improvement, thrift, and prosperity. During the vicissitudes of the war they have been visited by its direst calamities. They have been robbed, plundered and murdered, their homes burned, their fields laid waste, their property seized and destroyed; they have been compelled to flee from their country, and from a condition of plenty and independence they have been reduced to the most abject poverty, suffering, and distress.

Because Dole was a close friend of President Lincoln's, he carried on the affairs of the Indian Bureau with the president's complete confidence. Historian Gary E. Moulton writes, "Chief John Ross and Dole developed substantial areas of accord and became close friends. They concurred particularly on the coercive nature of Cherokee defection to the Confederacy, and on support for the Federal refugee Cherokees driven from their homes during the Civil War to bleak confinement in Kansas and Missouri. This basic unity seemed a good omen for the difficult reconstruction period which lay ahead, but Lincoln was assassinated and the understanding and agreement which Ross had reached with Dole did not carry over into President Andrew Johnson's administration. In fact, the newly appointed commissioner of Indian Affairs, Dennis N. Cooley, questioned the loyalty of the Cherokees and the integrity of Ross and nearly a year elapsed after Cooley took office before the Cherokees signed a somewhat disappointing reconstruction treaty with the United States."

The Sand Creek massacre led to Dole's leaving the Indian bureau. In the wake of the carnage an outraged Congress demanded the heads of Indian agents, politicians, and military men connected in any way to the massacre. As the administrator of government policy, Dole's head was first on the chopping block. Although the president promised to try to save his friend's career, after Lincoln's assassination the new president, Andrew Johnson, ceremoniously dumped Dole in favor of his own, scandal-free, candidate, Dennis Nelson Cooley. Dole resigned on 6 July 1865, and left office 5 days later when Cooley took over. He lived in Washington, D.C., for the remainder of his life, even though the Doolittle Report of 1867 was harshly critical of his administration. He died in Washington on 30 September 1889, and was buried in Edgar Cemetery in Paris, Illinois.

See also Bureau of Indian Affairs.

References *Bedford Messenger*, 1 (8); Carmony, Donald F., ed., "William P. Dole: Wabash Valley Merchant and Flatboatman." *Indiana Magazine of History* 67 (4); Kelsey, Harry, "William P. Dole." In Robert M. Kvasnicka and Herman J. Viola, eds., *The Commissioners of Indian Affairs, 1824–1977* (1979); Moulton, Gary E., "Chief John Ross and William P. Dole: A Case Study of Lincoln's Indian Policy." In LeRoy H. Fischer, *The Civil War Era in Indian Territory (1974); U.S. Congress, House of Representatives, Annual Report of the Commissioner of Indian Affairs for the Year 1862*, House Executive Document No. 1, 37th Congress, 3d Session (serial 1157), 1862; U.S. Congress, House of Representatives, *Annual Report of the Commissioner of Indian Affairs for the Year 1863*, House Executive Document No. 1, 38th Congress, 1st Session (serial 1182).

Donnelly v. United States (228 U.S. 213 [1913])

The definition of "Indian country" was a key element in this important Supreme Court decision. The essential question in the case was whether the government's powers were extended when a president, through an executive order, expanded an Indian reservation to include lands that previously had not been native to the reservation. James Donnelly, a white man, was indicted and convicted of killing a Chickasaw Indian on the Hoopa Valley reservation in Humboldt County, California. The prosecution admitted that Donnelly committed the crime on a river bed that was actually a part of the so-called Extension of the Hoopa Valley reservation, land added to the original reservation by an executive order of 23 June 1876, signed by President Ulysses S. Grant. This "extension" had not been, before the order was signed, a part of the native lands of the reservation. Donnelly appealed his conviction, on the grounds that the "extension" could not legally be considered Indian country, to the Circuit Court of the United States for the Northern District of California, which upheld it. Donnelly then appealed to the U.S. Supreme Court.

The court heard arguments in the case on 18 December 1912, and handed down a decision on 7 April 1913. Holding for a badly divided 6–3 court, Justice Mahlon Pitney spoke for the majority in upholding Donnelly's conviction. In dissent, Justice Oliver Wendell Holmes (who was joined by justices Horace Harmon Lurton and Charles Evans Hughes) decried on a separate issue that Donnelly was refused the right to introduce a deathbed confession made by another Indian named Dick, who claimed that he had committed the murder. The dissenters felt that the confession should have been introduced in court, while Pitney labeled it as "hearsay" and ruled that it was properly precluded.

Doolittle Commission

Established under the leadership of Senator James Rood Doolittle of Wisconsin, this special joint committee of the two houses of Congress was sanctioned by an act of Congress of 3 March 1865, "directing an inquiry into the condition of the Indian tribes and their treatment by the civil and military authorities of the United States." The final report of the commission, entitled *Condition of the Indian Tribes*, was issued in 1867 and is considered one of the major documents of American Indian study. Included as members of the commission were General John B. Sanborn; General William S. Harney; Colonel Christopher ("Kit") Carson; Colonel William W. Bent (who was married to a Cheyenne woman); Judge James Steele; Thomas Murphy, who was the superintendent of Indian affairs in St. Louis, Missouri; and Jesse H. Leavenworth, Indian agent for the southern plains.

Reproduced below are excerpts of the text of the commission's findings, which gave reasons for the declining numbers of American Indians at the time and "made recommendations for ameliorating the conditions."

First. The Indians everywhere, with the exception of the tribes within the Indian Territory, are rapidly decreasing in numbers from various causes; By disease; by intemperance; by wars, among themselves and with the whites; by the steady and resistless emigration of white men into the territories of the west, which, confining the Indians to still narrower limits, destroys that game which, in their normal state, constitutes their principal means of subsistence; and by the irrepressible conflict between a superior and an inferior race when brought in presence of each other. Upon this subject all the testimony agrees....

Second. The committee are of the opinion that in a large majority of cases Indian wars are to be traced to the aggressions of lawless white men, always to be found upon the frontier, or boundary line between savage and civilized life. Such is the statement of the most experienced officers of the army, and of all those who have been long conversant [familiar] with Indian affairs....

From whatever cause wars may be brought on, either between different Indian tribes or between the Indians and the whites, they are very destructive, not only of the lives of the warriors engaged in it, but of the women and children also, often becoming a war of extermination. Such is the rule of savage warfare, and it is difficult if not impossible to restrain white men, especially white men upon the frontiers, from adopting the same mode of warfare against the Indians. The indiscriminate slaughter of men, women, and children has frequently occurred in the history of Indian wars. But the fact which gives such terrible force to the condemnation of the wholesale massacre of Arrapahoes [*sic*] and Cheyennes, by the Colorado troops under Colonel Chivington, neat Fort Lyon, was, that those Indians were there encamped under the direction of our own officers, and believed themselves to be under the protection of our flag...To the honor of the government it may be said that a just atonement for this violation of its faith was sought to be made in the late treaty with these tribes.

Third. Another potent cause of their decay is to be found in the loss of their hunting grounds and in the destruction of that game upon which the Indian subsists. This cause, always powerful, has of late greatly increased. Until the white settlements crossed the Mississippi, the Indians could still find hunting grounds without limit and game, especially the buffalo, in great abundance upon the western plains.

But the discovery of gold and silver in California, and in all the mountain territories, poured a flood of hardy and adventurous miners across these plains, and into the valleys and gorges of the mountains from the east....

Fourth. The question whether the Indian bureau should be placed under the War Department or retained in the Department of the Interior is one of considerable importance, and both sides have very warm advocates. Military men generally, unite in recommending that change to be made, while civilians, teachers, missionaries, agents and superintendents, and those not in the regular army generally oppose it. The arguments and objections urged by each are not without force....

Fifth. In our Indian system, beyond all doubt, there are evils, growing out of the nature of the case itself, which can never be remedied until the Indian race is civilized or shall entirely disappear.

The committee are satisfied that these evils are sometimes greatly aggravated not so much by the system adopted by the government in dealing with the Indian tribes, as by the abuses of that system.

As the best means of correcting those abuses and ameliorating those evils, the committee recommend[s] the subdivision of the Territories and States wherein the Indian tribes remain into five inspection districts, and the appointment of five boards of inspection; and they earnestly recommend the passage of Senate bill 188, now pending before the House. That bill was unanimously recommended by the joint special committee, and also recommended by the committees of both Houses upon Indian Affairs. It is the most certainly efficient mode of preventing these abuses which they have been able to devise....

References Chaput, Donald, "Generals, Indian Agents, Politicians: The Doolittle Survey of 1865." *Western Historical Quarterly* 3 (1972); Kelsey, Harry, "The Doolittle Report of 1867: Its Preparation and Shortcomings." *Arizona and the West* 17 (Summer 1975); Prucha, Francis Paul, ed., *Documents of United States Indian Policy* (1990); U.S. Congress, Senate, *Condition of the Indian Tribes: Report of the Joint Special Committee, Appointed under Joint Resolution of March 3, 1865, with an Appendix* [The Doolittle Commission Report], Senate Report No. 156, 39th Congress, 2d Session (serial 1279), 1867.

Draper v. United States (164 U.S. 240 [1896])

In this Supreme Court decision, decided in 1896, the court held that even though a state's enabling act (an action which allows it to join the Union) requires federal jurisdiction for crimes committed on Indian reservations, that state still has jurisdiction over crimes committed in that territory by non-Indians. Pleasant Draper, a black man, was tried, convicted, and sentenced to death in the circuit court of Montana, a federal court, for the murder of an unnamed man (who was also black) on the Crow Reservation in Montana. Draper asked for a dismissal of the conviction on the grounds that the circuit court did not have the jurisdiction to try him. The state contended that federal jurisdiction was proper: the Enabling Act of 1864 (13 Stat. 5) required that "Indian lands shall remain under the absolute jurisdiction and control of the Congress of the United States." The U.S. Supreme Court agreed to hear the issues in this case, and the action was submitted on 23 October 1896. Five weeks later, on 30 November, Justice Edward Douglass White delivered the court's unanimous opinion in striking down Draper's federal conviction and remanding the case back to a state court for retrial. Comparing the case to the landmark decision in *United States v. McBratney* (104 U.S. 621 [1882]), which originally held that non-Indians accused of committing a murder against another non-Indian on an Indian reservation must be tried by a state court, Justice White reasoned, "Our conclusion is that the circuit court of the United States for the district of Montana had no jurisdiction of the indictment, but, 'according to the practice heretofore adopted in like cases, should deliver up the prisoner to the authorities of the state of Montana to be dealt with according to law.'"

See also *United States v. McBratney.*

Duro v. Reina et al. (495 U.S. 676 [1990])

In this case, officially titled *Albert Duro, Petitioner, v. Edward Reina, Chief of Police, Salt River Department of Public Safety, Salt River Pima-Maricopa Indian Community et al.*, the U.S. Supreme Court found that an Indian tribal court did not have the authority to assert criminal jurisdiction over a nonmember Indian who had allegedly killed another nonmember Indian on a tribe's reservation. Albert Duro, a member of the

Torres-Martinez Band of Cahuilla Mission Indians of California, lived and worked on the reservation of the Salt River Pima-Maricopa Indians near Phoenix, Arizona. On 15 June 1984, Duro allegedly killed a 14-year old boy who was a member of the Gila River band of Indians, another Arizona tribe. A warrant was sworn for Duro on the grounds that the murder violated the Indian Major Crimes Act (23 Stat. 362) of 3 March 1885, which allowed for the federal prosecution of Indians who committed crimes against other Indians in Indian country. The U.S. Attorney in the matter asked for the indictment to be dismissed without prejudice, and Duro was handed over to Salt River Pima-Maricopa tribal authorities and tried in that tribe's Indian Community Court. Because tribal law covered only misdemeanors and other minor crimes, Duro was charged with the illegal firing of a gun on a reservation. Duro asked that the indictment on the gun charge be dismissed for lack of jurisdiction; when the tribal court refused, he sued for a writ of habeas corpus to the U.S. District Court for the District of Arizona. The District Court granted the writ, holding that because Duro was not a member of the Salt River Pima-Maricopa community, his prosecution by that tribe was a violation of his equal protection rights bestowed under the Indian Civil Rights Act (25 U.S.C. 1302 et seq.). On appeal, the U.S. Court of Appeals for the Ninth Circuit in San Francisco reversed, claiming that Indian tribes had an inviolate jurisdiction over minor crimes involving Indians on reservations. Duro appealed to the U.S. Supreme Court. The court heard arguments in the case on 29 November 1989, and handed down a decision on 29 May 1990. Writing for the court in a 7–2 decision (justices William Brennan and Thurgood Marshall dissented) that held that the tribe lacked jurisdiction to try Duro, Justice Anthony Kennedy explained, "If the present jurisdictional scheme proves insufficient to meet the practical needs of reservation law enforcement, then the proper body to address the problem is Congress, which has the ultimate authority over Indian affairs. We cannot, however, accept these arguments of policy as a basis for finding tribal jurisdiction that is inconsistent with precedent, history, and the equal treatment of Native American citizens. The judgment of the Court of Appeals is hereby reversed." In his dissent, Justice Brennan wrote, "The Court today holds that an Indian tribal court has no power to exercise criminal jurisdiction over a defendant who is an Indian but not a tribal member. The Court concedes that Indian tribes never expressly relinquished such power. Instead, the Court maintains that tribes implicitly surrendered the power to enforce their criminal laws against non-member Indians when the tribes became dependent on the Federal Government. Because I do not share such a parsimonious view of the sovereignty retained by Indian tribes, I respectfully dissent."

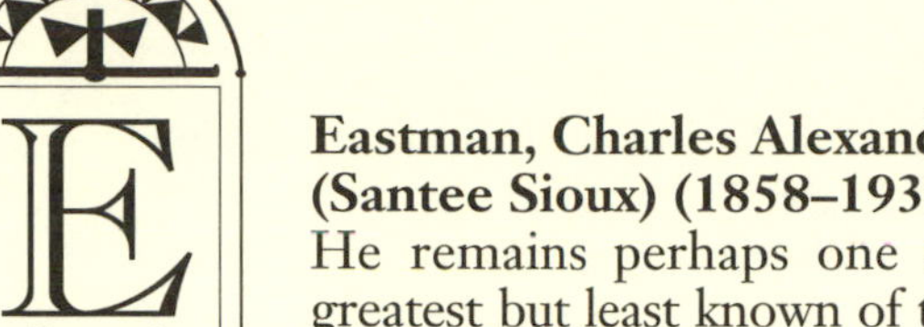

Eastern Band of Cherokee Indians v. The United States and the Cherokee Nation (commonly called Cherokee Nation West) (117 U.S. 880 [1886])

The split of the Cherokee Indians caused by the removal of most of that tribe west to Oklahoma was the issue in this Supreme Court case, in which the court held that those Indians who had stayed behind were not to be considered part of the Cherokee Nation. The Eastern Band of Cherokees, comprised of Cherokees who had fled into the hills of North Carolina rather than be forced to walk the Trail of Tears to exile in Oklahoma, sued to have a stake in annuity funds paid to the Cherokee Nation by the U.S. government. The Court of Claims ruled that because they were separated from the Cherokee Nation, these eastern Cherokees had no stake in these annuities. The Eastern Band, challenging both the United States and the Cherokee Nation in Oklahoma, appealed for relief from the U.S. Supreme Court. The case was argued on 4, 5, and 6 January 1886, and decided by a unanimous vote on 1 March 1886. Justice Stephen Johnson Field delivered the court's opinion. He held that eastern Cherokees "dissolved their connection with their nation" when they fled to North Carolina, and as such they had to reapply for citizenship in the tribe to share in the annuities. As Justice Field wrote, "If Indians in that State or in any other State east of the Mississippi wish to enjoy the benefits of the common property of the Cherokee Nation, in whatever form it may exist, they must, as held by the Court of Claims, comply with the constitution and laws of the Cherokee Nation and be readmitted to citizenship as there provided. They cannot live out of its Territory, evade the obligations and burdens of citizenship, and at the same time enjoy the benefits of the funds and common property of the Nation."

Eastman, Charles Alexander (Santee Sioux) (1858–1939)

He remains perhaps one of the greatest but least known of the Indian reformers, a noted physician who treated his own people and worked tirelessly for the recognition of their accomplishments. Indian writer Hazel Hertzberg said of him, "[He] was probably the most famous Indian of his day; a physician who wrote popular books on Indian life, a reformer active in many causes of the time." He was born in 1858 on the Santee Sioux reservation in Minnesota. His father, a full-blood Sioux, was rumored killed in the Sioux Uprising of 1862, and his mother, Mary Nancy Eastman, a mixed-blood Sioux who was the daughter of noted white artist Seth Eastman (1808–1875) and Stand Like a Spirit, known as Lucy, the daughter of Chief Cloudman of the Lakota of South Dakota. After Eastman and Lucy were married, they had one child, known as Mary Nancy Eastman. Mary died shortly after her son's birth, and Charles, who was named Ohiyesa, was raised by his paternal

Charles Alexander Eastman, physician and activist, 1858–1939

grandmother and uncle in Ontario. When he was 15 his father returned as the converted Jacob Eastman, and took his son to Flandreau, North Dakota, where the young Sioux was named Charles Alexander Eastman and sent to a mission school. He attended "several institutions of higher learning" before he graduated with a bachelor's degree from Dartmouth College in 1887 and a medical degree from the Boston University School of Medicine in 1890. He married Elaine Goodale, a white Indian reformer who with her husband called for the assimilation of the Indian into American society.

As the government physician for the Pine Ridge Agency in South Dakota, Eastman was on the scene to give aid and comfort to the injured and dying after the massacre at Wounded Knee in 1890, and the experience made him a critical advocate for the rights of Native Americans. He found that reliving the days of his youth, when he grew up on the reservation, confirmed values that he felt Indians could take pride in. The synthesis of this idea came to fruition in his 1902 work, *Indian Boyhood.* In the foreword for the book, Eastman wrote, "The North American Indian was the highest type of pagan and uncivilized man. He possessed not only a superb physique but a remarkable mind. But the Indian no longer exists as a natural and free man. Those remnants which now dwell upon the reservations present only a sort of tableau—a fictitious copy of the past." In the next two decades, he composed *Red Hunters and Animal People* (1904), a book of Indian legends; *Old Indian Days* (1907); *Wigwam Evenings: Sioux Folktales Retold* (1909) (written with his wife Elaine Goodale); *The Soul of the Indian* (1911); *Indian Scout Talks: A Guide for Boy Scouts and Campfire Girls* (1914); *The Indian Today: The Past and Future of the First American* (1915); *From the Deep Woods to Civilization: Chapters in the Autobiography of an Indian* (1916), his autobiography; and *Indian Heroes and Chieftains* (1918). He may have been the most prolific Native American writer ever.

On 3 April 1911, Eastman, along with other Native American activists, met at Ohio State University in Columbus, Ohio, where they formed the American Indian Association, later the Society for American Indians, the first pan-Indian rights group. Eastman's part in the formation of the organization was key, but he became disenfranchised from it because of his stands against the Bureau of Indian Affairs (BIA) and his assimilationist attitude. In 1912, according to Eastman biographer Raymond Wilson, "Eastman learned that he was among the leading candidates considered to become commissioner of Indian Affairs. Although he had frequently advocated abolition of the Indian Bureau, the chances of that happening were remote. If he could become commissioner, perhaps many of his ideas as well as other constructive programs on how to improve conditions among Indians could be implemented. Eastman's major support for the office came from Professor Warren K. Moorehead, a member of the Board of Indian Commissioners and a teacher at Phillips Academy in Andover, Massachusetts. In their correspondence on this matter, Eastman appeared anxious to obtain the appointment. He secured letters of recommendation from influential friends, and several eastern newspapers gave him their endorsements." In the end, however, the post went to Cato Sells, a banker and Democratic politician from Texas.

In the last two decades of his life, Eastman stressed Indian health and improved educational standards for Indian children. In 1918 he joined with activist Gertrude Bonnin to support a bill in Congress outlawing the use of peyote on Indian reservations. Although he was a member of the Committee of One Hundred, which released its final report on Indian matters in 1924, little is known of his participation. After he divorced his wife, Eastman retreated from public life. He died in 1939, forgotten by all but historians.

References "Charles Alexander Eastman's *Indian Boyhood:* Romance, Nostalgia, and Social Darwinism." In David H. Brumble III, *American Indian Autobiography* (1988); Eastman, Charles Alexander, *Indian Boyhood* (1933); Hertzberg, Hazel W., *The Search for an American Identity: Modern Pan-Indian Movements* (1971); Hughes, Thomas, *Indian Chiefs* *of Southern Minnesota, Containing Sketches of the Prominent Chieftains of the Dakota and Winnebago Tribes from 1825 to 1865* (1969); Wilson, Raymond, "Dr. Charles A. Eastman, Early Twentieth-Century Reformer." *Journal of the West* 23 (3); Wilson, Raymond, *Dr. Charles Alexander Eastman (Ohiyesa), Santee Sioux* (Ph.D. dissertation, University of New Mexico at Albuquerque, 1977).

Egan v. McDonald (246 U.S 227, 62 L.Ed. 680, 38 S.Ct. 223 [1918])

The heirs of adult Indian allottees could convey their allotment with the approval of the secretary of the interior because Congress permitted such sales to proceed—so held the Supreme Court in this case decided in 1918. George W. Egan agreed to purchase from Charles S. McDonald a parcel of land in South Dakota, and gave McDonald $1,000 to secure the amount arrived at. The land, an Indian allotment, had originally belonged to Weasel, a Crow Creek Sioux, who, upon his death in 1908, conveyed the allotment to his heirs, Plays and two other unidentified Indians, who sold the allotment to one R. J. Huston with the consent of the secretary of the interior. Under the act of Congress of 2 March 1889 (25 Stat. 888, at 891), Weasel and his heirs must wait 25 years after the issuance of the patent before they could convey the land; however, by section 7 of the act of 27 May 1902 (32 Stat. 275), Congress removed the restriction on alienation (sale) with the approval of the secretary of the interior if the sale involved adult heirs only. Huston sold the allotment to McDonald in 1910. McDonald gave Egan the title and, when Egan decided that the title was worthless, he demanded his money back; he claimed that the heirs of Weasel had no power to sell their allotment, and as such the sale was void. A district court disagreed, and that judgment was upheld by the Supreme Court of South Dakota. Egan sued to the U.S. Supreme Court. Justice Louis Brandeis delivered the opinion of a unanimous court in siding with McDonald and holding that the federal statute removing the restriction on adult heirs was constitutional.

Elk v. Wilkins (112 U.S. 94, 28 L.Ed. 643, 5 S.Ct. 41 [1884])

Elk was perhaps the leading landmark case that involved whether the Fifteenth Amendment was applicable to Indians and that resulted in the implementation of the allotment policy in 1887. Decided in 1884, *Elk* held that Indians were not U.S. citizens, fully deserving of all privileges of citizenship, but citizens of Indian nations separate from the United States. John Elk was an Indian who was born on the reservation but left at some point to live among whites. More than a year later, he attempted to vote in Omaha, Nebraska, but was denied. He then sued Charles Wilkins, the registrar of the fifth ward in Omaha, for the right to vote, in the Circuit Court of the District of Nebraska, which ruled against him. Elk then appealed to the U.S. Supreme Court. He was defended before the high Court by attorneys Andrew J. Poppleton and John L. Webster, who had taken on the landmark *Standing Bear* case, which held that "Indians are persons within the meaning of the law" in 1879.

It was Justice Horace Gray who delivered the court's opinion on 3 November 1884, with Justices William Woods and John Marshall Harlan dissenting. (Justice Harlan is better noted for his dissent 12 years later in *Plessy v. Ferguson*, in which the court upheld racial segregation as constitutional, but his dissent in *Elk* is just as important.) In a lengthy opinion Justice Gray explained,

> The plaintiff, in support of his action, relies on the first clause of the first section of the Fourteenth Article of Amendment of the Constitution of the United States, by which "all persons born or naturalized in the United States, and subject to the jurisdiction thereof, are citizens of the United States and of the State wherein they reside"; and on the Fifteenth Article of Amendment, which provides that "the right of the citizens of the United States to vote shall not be denied or abridged by the United States or by any State on account of race, color, or previous condition of servitude...." The petition, while it does not show of what Indian tribe the plaintiff was a member, yet, by the

allegations that he "is an Indian, and was born within the United States," and that "he had severed his tribal relation to the Indian tribes," clearly implies that he was born a member of one of the Indian tribes within the limits of the United States, which still exists and is recognized as a tribe by the government of the United States. Though the plaintiff alleges that he "had fully and completely surrendered himself to the jurisdiction of the United States," he does not allege that the United States accepted his surrender, or that he has ever been naturalized, or taxed, or in any way recognized or treated as a citizen, by the State of the United States. Nor is it contended by his counsel that there is any statute or treaty that makes him a citizen. The question then is, whether an Indian, born a member of one of the Indian tribes within the United States, is, merely by reason of his birth within the United States, and of his afterwards voluntarily separating himself from his tribe and taking up his residence among white citizens, a citizen of the United States, within the meaning of the first section of the Fourteenth Amendment of the Constitution...Indians born within the territorial limits of the United States, members of, and owing immediate allegiance to, one of the Indian tribes (an alien, though dependent, power), although in a geographical sense born in the United States, are no more "born in the United States and subject to the jurisdiction thereof," within the meaning of the first section of the Fourteenth Amendment, than the children of subjects of any foreign government born within the domain of that government, or the children born within the United States, of ambassadors or other public ministers of foreign nations. This view is confirmed by the second section of the Fourteenth Amendment, which provides that "representatives shall be apportioned among the several States according to their respective numbers, counting the whole number of persons in each State, excluding Indians not taxed." Slavery having been abolished, and the persons formerly held as slaves made citizens, this clause fixing the apportionment of representatives has abrogated so much of the corresponding clause of the original Constitution as counted only three-fifths of such persons. But Indians not taxed are still excluded from the count, for the reason that they are not citizens. Their absolute exclusion from the basis of representation, in which all other persons are now included, is wholly inconsistent with their being considered citizens...The plaintiff, not being a citizen of the United States under the Fourteenth Amendment of the Constitution, has been deprived of no right secured by the Fifteenth Amendment, and cannot maintain this action.

In his dissent, Justice Harlan angrily dismissed the majority's finding. "Mr. Justice Woods and myself feel constrained to express our dissent from the interpretation which our brethren give to that clause of the fourteenth amendment which provides that 'all persons born or naturalized in the United States, and subject to the jurisdiction thereof, are citizens of the United States and of the state wherein they reside.'" After rearguing the facts in the case, he added, "If he did not acquire national citizenship on abandoning his tribe and becoming, by residence in one of the states, subject to the complete jurisdiction of the United States, then the [F]ourteenth [A]mendment has wholly failed to accomplish, in respect of the Indian race, what, we think, was intended by it; and there is still in this country a despised and rejected class of persons with no nationality whatever, who, born in our country, owing no allegiance to any foreign power, and subject, as residents of the states, to all the burdens of government, are yet not members of any political community, nor entitled to any of the rights, privileges, and immunities of citizens of the United States."

Reference Konvitz, Milton R., *Civil Rights in Immigration* (1977).

Emmons, Glenn Leonidas (1895–1982)

In 1952, many Native Americans were fearful that the retention of a Democrat in the

White House would mean a continuation of the Dillon Myer administration of the Bureau of Indian Affairs. In fact, Dan Madrano of the National Congress of American Indians, at the time the largest organization composed of Native Americans, approached the Republican Party prior to its 1952 convention to promise to have the Indians select a new commissioner if General Eisenhower was elected President. The Republicans included a plank in their party platform promising at the least to "consult and confer" with the Indians on the selection. With Eisenhower's election, the leading candidate was New Mexico Governor Edwin Mechem's representative on the Governors' Interstate Indian Council (GIIC), Alva Adams Simpson, who won the support of the NCAI. A second candidate, who seemed to have less of a chance than Simpson, was Gallup, New Mexico, banker Glenn Emmons. After inauguration, Eisenhower sent Phoenix attorney Orme Lewis to visit with the Indian tribes to get their opinions; yet even though most endorsed Simpson, Eisenhower went with Emmons, who he felt had more business experience, and submitted his nomination to the U.S. Senate. Who was this businessman from New Mexico who rose from obscurity to commissioner of Indian Affairs, with responsibility for the nation's Indian tribes? Leonidas Glenn Emmons was born in Atmore, Alabama, on 15 August 1895, the youngest of four sons of John D. Emmons, a former member of the Florida State legislature and businessman, and Martha Jane (née Huggins) Emmons. According to an interview done with Emmons in 1976, he discovered that he had been named after a local black boy and, in the South where racial animosity was still the norm, was so embarrassed that he changed the order of his name. In 1905, the Emmons family transferred to Albuquerque, New Mexico, because Martha Jane Emmons, whose health was precarious from malaria, wanted to move to the desert Southwest for the climate. Glenn Emmons attended local Albuquerque schools, but also worked as a fireman in the Zuni Mountains for the American Lumber Company. He attended the University of New Mexico, but left in 1917 to enlist in the United State Air Service. After the war, he settled in Gallup, New Mexico, to enter the banking business. He remained there for the next quarter century, and by 1953 he was president of the First State Bank of Gallup.

Emmons's nomination for Indian commissioner came at a time when the policy of termination was at its height. Started by Emmons's predecessor, Dillon S. Myer, whose unpopularity among the Indians was intense, the termination of the Indian tribes from federal recognition and programs needed a thorough examination to see if its effects were what those who drafted it foresaw. President Eisenhower then decided to send Emmons on a tour of the Indian reservations to see and hear for himself what effect termination was having and alter the BIA program accordingly. On 2 September 1953, Eisenhower wrote to Emmons,

> This administration, as you know, has pledged itself to consult with the Indian people of this country and to give them every opportunity for a full expression of their desires, suggestions, hopes and aspirations. In order to fulfill this pledge, I am asking you, as my personal representative, to go into the home territory of the Indians during the next several months and meet with each of the major tribal groups of the country. Please emphasize to the Indian people our sincere desire for the benefit of their views. While we cannot anticipate that there will always be agreement between the Indians and their government as a result of these conferences, it is essential for us to learn first-hand their thoughts, needs and aspirations. Only with such knowledge can we move forward with a warm and realistic understanding in shaping policies and programs for the future administration of Indian affairs.

His visit to 150 reservations (in which Emmons was said to have been quite disturbed at the living conditions of the Indians) left the Indian commissioner no choice but to announce that he was concentrating his energies into three main areas: improved education, Indian health, and expanded economic opportunity. Under Emmons, the BIA initiated the Navajo Education Emergency Program (NEEP), which called for the rapid construction of schools on the Navajo reservations. On 3 March 1954, the Navajo Tribal Council unanimously endorsed NEEP and granted Commissioner Emmons the power to implement the program as fast as possible. Later, the council objected to a provision of the action, which initiated border-town dormitories to assimilate Indian children into American society at a quickened pace. Emmons supported the passage of Public Law 568, enacted 5 August 1954, which transferred the Indian Health Service from the BIA to the U.S. Public Health Service in what was then the Department of Health, Education, and Welfare. Further, he initiated a program of "positive programming" to increase economic opportunities on reservations. In a speech to the Governors' Interstate Indian Council, Sheridan, Wyoming, 6 August 1956, Emmons said,

> Let me emphasize, however, that I am talking about opportunity for the Indian people and not about anything compulsive or coercive. I recognize, of course, that the Indian people are by no means all of one mind about the kind of life they want to lead. A substantial number of them, particularly in the younger generations and among the veterans of military service, have made it quite clear that they want to take their place in the non-Indian society of the Nation and made their way without discrimination and without special favors. Others, at the opposite extreme, prefer to go on living in the old tribal way, following the customs and religion of their ancestors, and having no more than necessary to do with what we call modern American life. Still others stand somewhere in between. They are the people—and I suspect they constitute a majority of the whole Indian population—who want a kind of mixture of the two cultures. They like many aspects of modern American life and want to enjoy its benefits and its fruits the same as the rest of us. Yet, for wholly understandable reasons, they also want to preserve their tribal affiliations and maintain their heritage as Indian people.

Emmons was unable to stop the bills on termination that came out of the Congress, but he tried to minimize their effects. When Indian tribes blasted Washington for the policy, their anger was not laid at the feet of the commissioner. In March 1957, former commissioner William A. Brophy sat as a member of the Commission on the Rights, Liberties, and Responsibilities of the American Indians, a private group, to investigate the effect of termination on the reservations and what the government could do to alleviate its consequences. Released in 1966 after Emmons had departed the BIA, the report was critical of the whole termination policy, which by then was in full reverse. It was not until 1973, when President Nixon signed the Menominee Restoration Act, that the policy was put to rest.

Glenn Emmons served as Indian commissioner until 7 January 1961, when he resigned to make way for President-elect John Kennedy's nominee, who turned out to be anthropologist Philleo Nash. After living in Washington, Emmons and his wife moved to Albuquerque, where he remained active in many civic causes. In 1977, he was given the Zimmerman Award by the University of New Mexico for his services to the state and the nation. He was also awarded an honorary law degree that same year from that institution. He died in 1982.

References Boender, Debra R., *Glenn Emmons of Gallup* (Master's thesis, University of New Mexico, 1976); Burt, Larry, *Tribalism in Crisis: Federal Indian Policy, 1953–1961* (1982); Department of the Interior Information Service, "Address by Glenn L. Emmons, Commissioner of Indian Affairs, Before the Governors' Interstate Indian Council, Sheridan, Wyoming, August 6, 1956"; Eisenhower to Emmons, letter quoted in William H. Kelly, ed., *Indian Affairs and the Indian Reorganization Act: The Twenty Year Record* (1954); Emerson, Gloria J., "Navajo Education." In Alfonso Ortiz, ed. *Handbook of North American Indians*, vol. 10 (1983); "Emmons Criticizes Kennedy Approach to Indian

Problem." *Albuquerque Journal*, 1 August 1961, 1; Fixico, Donald L., *Termination and Relocation Federal Indian Policy, 1945–1960* (1986); Ourada, Patricia K., "Glenn L. Emmons." In Robert M. Kvasnicka and Herman J. Viola, eds., *The Commissioners of Indian Affairs, 1824–1977* (1979).

English v. Richardson (224 U.S. 680 [1912])

This was the second companion case to *Choate v. Trapp* (the other was *Gleason et al. v. Wood et al.)*, the landmark 1912 case in which the Supreme Court held taxation of allotted Indians lands to be beyond the scope of states. Justice Joseph Rucker Lamar (who wrote the court's opinions in *Choate* and *Gleason*) delivered the opinion in *English*, which is less than half a page long. In it, Justice Lamar wrote, "The plaintiff [Bessie Brown En-glish] holds a patent dated December 12, 1902. It was issued to her as a member of the Creek Nation when the tribal lands were divided in pursuance of the same general policy as that discussed in *Choate v. Trapp*, just decided. There were, however, a few differences. The tax exemption covered only the homestead of 40 acres, and there was a restriction on alienability for twenty-one years. The patent, instead of being 'framed in conformity with the agreement,' as in the case of the Choctaws and Chickasaws, bore on its face a provision that the land should be nontaxable; the language of the agreement incorporated in the act of Congress being that 'each citizen shall select from his allotment 40 acres of land…as a homestead, which shall be and remain nontaxable, inalienable, and free from any encumbrance whatever for twenty-one years from the date of the deed therefor, and a separate deed shall be issued to each allottee for his homestead, in which this condition shall appear.' (32 Stat. at 503)." He ended, "These differences are not material. The right of the plaintiff to the exemption granted by Congress is protected by the Constitution on principles stated and applied in *Choate v. Trapp*. The judgment dismissing her complaint is therefore reversed, and the case remanded for proceedings not inconsistent with that opinion."

See also *Choate v. Trapp; Gleason et al. v. Wood et al.*

Ewert v. Bluejacket et al. (259 U.S. 129, 66 L.Ed. 858, 42 S.Ct. 442 [1922])

This series of cases, which includes *Bluejacket v. Ewert*, delineated the perimeter beyond which government employees working "in Indian affairs" could be excluded from "hav[ing] any interest in trade with the Indians." The Trade and Intercourse Act of 1834 (4 Stat. 729, at 738) maintained that "no person employed in the Indian department shall have any interest or concern in any trade with the Indians." Paul A. Ewert, appointed a special assistant to the attorney general to prosecute suits relating to Quapaw Indians, was sent to Miami, Oklahoma, and opened an office there in December 1908. At that same time, he purchased (with the approval of the secretary of the interior) an allotment belonging to Charles Bluejacket, a full-blood Quapaw. When Bluejacket died, his widow, Carrie Bluejacket, demanded that the land be returned. She sued in district court, which ruled that because Ewert was not employed in the Bureau of Indian Affairs, 4 Stat. 738 did not apply to him. The U.S. Court of Appeals for the Eighth Circuit reversed as to minor heirs of Bluejacket, but held that the land conveyance was approved by the secretary of the interior and was so allowed. The U.S. Supreme Court agreed to hear the case, and arguments were heard on 17 March 1922 (Paul Ewert defended his own interests before the high court). Justice John Hessin Clarke held for a unanimous court on 15 May 1922 that the sale to Ewert was void, affirming as to the minor heirs and reversing as to the adult heirs. Clarke states simply, "We fully agree with the Circuit Court of Appeals that Ewert was employed in Indian affairs, within the meaning and intendment of the act, when he purchased the land." A joint case, in which Ewert was also sued for purchasing an Indian allotment, appeared in *Kendall v. Ewert*.

See also *Kendall v. Ewert.*

Ex parte Crow Dog (also known as *Ex parte Kan-gi-Shun-ca*) (109 U.S. 556 [1883])

Crow Dog is one of the landmark Indian cases of the Supreme Court and particularly significant in its implications for Indian law. In the case, Kan-gi-Shun-ca, otherwise known as Crow Dog, a Brulé Sioux, was indicted, tried, convicted, and sentenced to death for the murder of another Brulé Sioux, Sin-ta-ge-lae-Scka, otherwise known as Spotted Tail. The editors of *Felix S. Cohen's Handbook of Federal Indian Law* write, "The case excited nationwide interest in the 1880s. Tribal law required that Crow Dog support Spotted Tail's dependent relatives, but he was not to be further punished. His attorney [A.J. Plowman] petitioned the Supreme Court claiming that his client was not amenable to the criminal laws of the United States or of the Dakota Territory, but was governed in his relations with the reservation Indians solely by tribal law, and therefore, was responsible only to tribal authorities." Argued before the court on 26 November 1883, the case was decided unanimously on 17 December of the same year. Holding that Crow Dog be granted a writ of habeas corpus which would release him from custody, Justice Stanley Matthews ruled that because there was no federal legislation dealing with the matter, Crow Dog's case was beyond the jurisdiction of state and federal courts and thus must be handled strictly by tribal authorities. Justice Matthews explained, "The pledge to secure to these people, with whom the United States was contracting as a distinct political body, an orderly government, by appropriate legislation thereafter to be framed and enacted, necessarily implies, having regard to all the circumstances attending the transaction, that among the arts of civilized life, which it was the very purpose of all these arrangements to introduce and naturalize among them, was the highest and best of all, that of self-government, the regulation by themselves of their own domestic affairs, the maintenance of order and peace among their own members by the administration of their own laws and customs." Outraged that the court allowed Crow Dog to walk free, Congress enacted the Indian Major Crimes Act in response to this decision. That legislation was upheld in 1886 in *United States v. Kagama, alias Pactah Billy*.

See also Indian Major Crimes Act; *United States v. Kagama, alias Pactah Billy*.

References Hyde, George E., *Spotted Tail's Folk: A History of the Brule Sioux* (1961); Seagle, William, "The Murder of Spotted Tail." *Indian Historian* 3 (4); Strickland, Rennard, ed., *Felix Cohen's Handbook of Federal Indian Law* (1982).

Ex parte Gon-shay-ee (130 U.S. 343, 32 L.Ed. 973, 9 S.Ct. 542 [1889])

Did the Indian Major Crimes Act of 1885 allow for the prosecution of an Indian accused of murder in a district court of a territory that also prosecuted trials involving the United States? That was the question at issue involving Gon-shay-ee, an Apache Indian, accused of murdering a white man, one William Deal, in or near Phoenix, Arizona, on 29 May 1888. Justice Samuel Freeman Miller wrote in the opinion of this case, "The controversy in this case seems to turn upon the question [of] whether the offense for which Gon-shay-ee was tried was an offense against the United States, and was of that character which ought to have been tried by the court sitting to try such cases, or whether it was an offense against the laws of the territory, and should have been tried under those laws and by the court sitting to administer justice under them." Section nine of the Indian Major Crimes Act (IMCA) of 3 March 1885 (23 Stat. 362, at 385) reads: "That immediately upon and after the date of the passage of this act all Indians committing against the person or property of another Indian or other person any of the following crimes, namely, murder, manslaughter, rape, assault with intent to kill, arson, burglary, and larceny, within any territory of the United States, and either within or without an Indian reservation, shall be subject therefor to the laws of such territory relating to said crimes, and shall be tried therefor in the same courts and in the same manner, and shall be subject to the same penalties, as are all other persons charged with the commission of said crimes, respectively." Gon-shay-ee was brought to trial in district court in Phoenix, the same court where trials involving the United States were held. As per the Indian Major Crimes Act, Gon-shay-ee was tried under territorial law, convicted, and sentenced to death. Gon-shay-ee then appealed to the U.S. Supreme Court to grant him a writ of habeas corpus, to be tried by a court representing the territory only. Justice Miller noted that "It is very clear from these transcripts of the proceedings in the court below that on this trial it proceeded and considered itself as acting as a court for the trial of offenses arising under the constitution and laws of the United States, and as administering them with the same powers as those vested in the circuit and district courts of the United States generally." Justice Miller's opinion, reflecting the thoughts of a unanimous court, was delivered on 15 April 1889, and it granted Gon-shay-ee the writ he had been requesting.

Reference "Case of Gon-shay-ee, As-ke-say-la-ha, As-Con-qui-Say, and Be-Cho-on-Doth," case no. 49, court dockets of the Arizona Supreme Court, RG 92, Department of Library, Archives and Public Records, Arizona State Capitol, Phoenix.

Ex parte Mayfield (141 U.S. 107 [1891])

In this Supreme Court case, the issue of whether an Indian involved in an adulterous affair with a non-Indian could be prosecuted under the Indian Major Crimes Act (23 Stat. 362). Petitioner John Mayfield, a quarter-blooded Cherokee Indian, and an acknowledged member of the Cherokee Nation, was indicted in the District Court of the United States for the Western District of Arkansas, tried, and convicted of carrying on an adulterous affair with one Mollie Phillips, a white woman, while his wife, also a white woman, was still alive. Mayfield was convicted under an act of Congress of 3 March 1887, which was an amendment to the Indian Major Crimes Act and added adultery as a prosecutable offense. Upon an application for a writ of habeas corpus freeing him from further prosecution, the U.S. Supreme Court granted Mayfield certiorari; submission of the writ occurred on 27 April 1891. Justice Henry Brown spoke for the court when it handed down its decision on 25 May 1891 granting Mayfield his writ of habeas corpus and dismissing the conviction against him. Brown found that the act of 3 March 1887 was unconstitutional in that it allowed Congress to intrude judicially into areas that Brown and his fellow justices felt were subject only to the jurisdiction of the Indian courts, if they desired to make adultery a crime. Justice Brown wrote, "The policy of Congress has evidently been to vest in the inhabitants of the Indian country such power of self-government as was thought to be consistent with the safety of the white population with which they may have come in contact, and to encourage them as far as possible in raising themselves to our standard of civilization. We are bound to recognize and respect such policy and to construe the Acts of the legislative authority in consonance therewith. The general object of these Statutes is to vest in the courts of the nation jurisdiction of all controversies between Indians, or where a member of the nation is the only party to the proceeding, and to reserve to the courts of the United States jurisdiction of all actions to which its own citizens are parties on either side. It is needless to say that the fact, if it be a fact, that the laws of the Cherokees make no provision for the punishment of the crime of adultery, would not extend to the courts of the United States a power to punish this crime that did not otherwise exist. As Mayfield was a member of the Cherokee Nation by adoption, if not by nativity, and was the sole party to these proceedings, we think it clear that under the treaties and Acts of Congress he is amenable only to the courts of the [Cherokee] nation, and that his petition should be granted." This case was subsequently upheld in *United States v. Quiver*, a case involving two Indians in an adulterous relationship.

Ex parte Webb **(225 U.S. 663 [1912])**
This was another case involving the issue of the introduction of intoxicating liquors into Indian country. Charley Webb and Otis Tittle, both white men, received a shipment of 17 gallons of intoxicating liquors which was shipped by train, a train which passed through Indian territory. When the men picked up their shipment, they were arrested. Webb and Tittle claimed that because the Indian country was not part of a state, the Congress had no right to enact laws involving alcohol on the reservations, and thus local courts, and not federal court, should try them. After a federal grand jury indicted the two men, they appealed for an application of a writ of habeas corpus, asking for the bench warrant calling for their arrest to be dismissed. The U.S. Supreme Court granted certiorari on the matter. The case was argued before the court on 13 May 1912, and a decision was handed down on 10 June of that same year.

Writing for a unanimous court, Justice Mahlon Pitney held that Congress had the right to enact laws regarding a prohibition of the introduction of intoxicating liquors into Indian territory, and that such crimes were of a federal nature. In dismissing the application for a writ of habeas corpus, Pitney acknowledged Congress' "constitutional power…to regulate commerce with the Indian tribes" as his basis for holding as he did. The case was remanded for trial.

Ex parte Wilson **(140 U.S. 298 [1891])**
This 1891 Supreme Court case hinged on whether a murder committed by an non-Indian upon another non-Indian on an Indian reservation should be adjudicated in a territorial court or in a federal court. Jefferson Wilson, identified as "a citizen of the United States, of African descent," was accused of murdering William Fleming, "another negro," on the White Mountain Indian Reservation in Arizona, in the Second Judicial District of that state. Wilson was taken to the court in Gila County, seat of the Second Judicial District at that time, tried, found guilty by a federal jury, and sentenced to death. Wilson appealed his sentence directly to the U.S. Supreme Court, claiming that because his crime was committed in Indian country, he should have been tried by a territorial jury, and asking that his sentence be set aside. Further, he argued that since the White Mountain Reservation did not exist when Arizona was granted territorial status, the reservation could not be considered as Indian country. The Supreme Court granted certiorari (the right to hear the case), and allowed the case to be submitted on 27 April 1891. The court's decision was handed down on 25 May 1891; Justice David Josiah Brewer held for a unanimous court in refusing Wilson's application to dismiss his sentence. "His [Wilson's] proposition is, that 'Congress by Act approved March 3, 1885 (23 Stat. 385), conferred upon the Territory and her courts full jurisdiction of the offense when committed on an Indian reservation by an Indian. *Ex parte Gon-shay-ee*, 130 U.S. 343," Brewer explained. "This offense had heretofore, when committed in such place by others than an Indian, been cognizable [understood] by the courts of the United States under sec. 2145, Rev[ised] Stat[utes]. The petitioner believes that the United States, by yielding up a part of her jurisdiction over the offense of murder when committed on an Indian reservation, lost all; that is, that her jurisdiction of the offense in the particular place must be 'sole and exclusive,' or will not exist at all; that it cannot be that there shall be one law and one mode of trial for a murder in a particular place if committed by an Indian, and another law and mode of trial for the identical offense in the same place committed by a white man or a negro. We are unable to yield our assent to this argument. The question is one of statutory construction. The jurisdiction of the United States over these reservations, and the power of Congress to provide for the punishment of all offenses committed therein, by whomsoever committed them, are not open questions. *United States v. Kagama*, 118 U.S. 375. And this power being a general one, Congress may provide for the punishment of one class of offenses in one

court, and another class in a different court…Section 2145 extends to the Indian country the general laws of the United States, as to the punishment of crimes committed in any place within the sole and exclusive jurisdiction of the United States, except as to crimes the punishment of which is otherwise expressly provided for. This Indian reservation is a part of the Indian country within the meaning of that section."

See also *Bates v. Clark; Dick v. United States; Donnelly v. United States; Ex parte Gon-shay-ee;* Indian Country—Definition.

Executive Order 12401 of 14 January 1983

See Presidential Commission on Indian Reservation Economies.

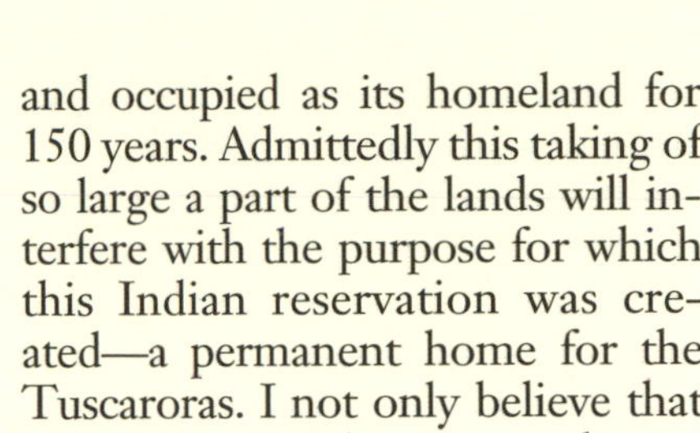

Federal Power Commission v. Tuscarora Indian Nation (362 U.S. 99, 4 L.Ed. 2d 584, 80 S.Ct. 543 [1960])
Combined with the case of *Power Authority of the State of New York v. Tuscarora Indian Nation*, this Supreme Court case dealt with the issue of whether lands held by an Indian nation in fee simple could be taken by the government with just compensation. The Power Authority of the State of New York, armed with a license issued it by the Federal Power Commission (FPC), took lands held in fee simple by the Tuscarora Indian Nation of New York for a water storage reservoir to be built next to a hydroelectric project on the Niagara River, and offered the Indians fair compensation for the land. The Court of Appeals for the District of Columbia ordered that the commission hold new hearings as to whether the lands were considered "Indian country"; the commission then held the hearings and decided to not to issue the license because the storage facility would "interfere" with the purposes for the reservation's creation. The Court of Appeals then overruled the commission, allowing for the issuance of the license with the exception that the Indian lands could not be included in the equation. The U.S. Supreme Court, granting certiorari, decided to hear the issues in the matter. After hearing arguments by the parties on 7 December 1959, the high court reversed the court of appeals judgment relating to the Indian lands issue on 7 March 1960. In an opinion expressing the will of five members of the court (Chief Justice Earl Warren and justices Hugo Black and William O. Douglas dissented), Justice Charles E. Whittaker held that under the Federal Power Act (41 Stat. 1063, as amended at 16 U.S.C. 791a-828c), Congress only outlawed the taking of lands "owned by the United States," considered by the court to define reservations. The dissenters were adamant. Justice Black wrote, "The Court holds that the Federal Power Act authorizes the taking of 22 percent (1,383 acres) of the single tract which the Tuscarora Indian Nation has owned and occupied as its homeland for 150 years. Admittedly this taking of so large a part of the lands will interfere with the purpose for which this Indian reservation was created—a permanent home for the Tuscaroras. I not only believe that the Federal Power Act does not authorize this taking, but that the Act positively prohibits it."

Federal Trust Cases, U.S. Supreme Court
***See** Cherokee Nation v. Georgia; Lone Wolf v. Hitchcock; United States v. Kagama, alias Pactah Billy; Worcester v. Georgia.*

Federal Trust Responsibility or Relationship, Doctrine of
In 1977, the American Indian Policy Review Commission examined the federal trust responsibility and its impact on federal-Indian relations. As the commission explained in its final report, "The concept of the trust relationship of the United States is one which is not well understood and is the subject of frequent debate regarding both its source and its scope. We have already noted that the trust relationship is one of the two [the other being the concept of sovereignty] most important concepts underlying Federal-Indian law. This responsibility originates first from the treaties negotiated with Indian tribes in which the United States acquired vast areas of land in exchange for its solemn commitment to protect the people and property of the tribes from encroachment by U.S. citizens. Secondly, from statutory enactment dating from the Continental Congress to the present, regulating transactions between U.S. citizens and Indian people. A third major source of this responsibility arises from a course of dealing in which the United States in the latter half of the nineteenth century assumed dominion and control over the people and property of Indian tribes, imposing a vast array of regulatory authority over Indians and their property. When the

United States assumed this authority over Indian people, it accepted the accompanying responsibility to Indian people."

See also *Cherokee Nation v. Georgia; Lone Wolf v. Hitchcock; United States v. Kagama, alias Pactah Billy; Worcester v. Georgia.*

Reference *American Indian Policy Review Commission, Final Report: Submitted to Congress May 17, 1977* (1977).

Fellows v. Blacksmith (19 Howard [60 U.S.] 366 [1857])

Officially titled *Joseph Fellows, Survivor of Robert Kendle, Plaintiff in Error, v. Susan Blacksmith and Ely S. Parker, Administrators of John Blacksmith, Deceased,* this early U.S. Supreme Court case held that only the government, and not individuals, had the power to remove Indians from their ancestral lands. According to the case notes, "The suit in the [New York state] Supreme Court was an action of trespass...brought by the intestate John Blacksmith, against the defendants, Joseph Fellows and Robert Kendle, for entering, with force and arms, into the close [enclosure] of the plaintiff, commonly known as the Indian saw-mill and yard, at the Town of Pembroke, County of Genesee, and then and there having expelled and dispossessed the said plaintiff." The defendants claimed that the area in question was considered part of the Seneca reservation, and as such, the two individuals had no right to remove them. The New York State Court of Appeals held for Susan Blacksmith and Ely Samuel Parker, who later served as Ulysses S. Grant's commissioner of Indian Affairs, the first Native American to hold that post. Plaintiffs in error Fellows and Kendle (the latter had died before the action was heard) sued for relief to the New York state Supreme Court, which asked the U.S. Supreme Court to hear the appeal. Arguments were heard on 19 January 1857, and a decision was handed down on 5 March of that same year.

Speaking for a unanimous court, Justice Samuel Nelson held that only the government had the right to remove Indians from the native lands, and that individuals not affiliated with the government could not do so. He explained that "They [the Indians] cannot be expelled from their homes by the irregular force and violence of individuals." Justice Nelson later wrote in his opinion in *The New York Indians,* "We have already given the answer which we think satisfactory to this ground in support of the judgment below. Until the Indians have sold their lands, and removed from them in pursuance of the treaty stipulations, they are to be regarded as still in their ancient possessions, and are in under their original rights, and entitled to the undisturbed enjoyment of them. This was the effect of the decision in the case of *Fellows v. Blacksmith.*"

See also The Kansas Indians; The New York Indians; Parker, Ely Samuel.

References *The New York Indians,* 5 Wallace [72 U.S.] 761 (1867).

First Moon v. White Tail (270 U.S. 243 [1926])

The U.S. Supreme Court found in this case that the secretary of the interior had the sole determination in deciding which Indians were heirs to deceased Indians allottees. Under the Act of 25 June 1910, the Congress established that if an Indian allottee of land died before his or her patent is issued, the secretary of the interior had the sole power to determine the allottee's heirs and present them with the patent for the deceased Indian's allotment. Little Soldier, a Ponca Indian, was issued an allotment for land in 1919, but died before he could be issued a patent. The secretary of the interior, Walter Lowrie Fisher, decided that Starling White Tail, another Ponca, was Little Soldier's heir. Henrietta First Moon then sued Starling White Tail in a local district court, with the U.S. government as co-defendant. She claimed that under the Act of 21 December 1911, in which Congress conferred upon district courts jurisdiction of "all actions, suits or proceedings involving the right of any person of Indian blood to an allotment of land under any act of treaty," she had the right to appeal Fisher's decision in the local courts. The District Court for the Western District of

Oklahoma dismissed First Moon's suit, and she appealed to the U.S. Supreme Court.

Arguments were heard in the case on 29 January 1926, and a decision was handed down on 1 March of that same year. Justice James Clarke McReynolds held for a unanimous court that Congress' granting of the power to determine heirs to allotments with the Act of 25 June 1910 was constitutional, and that the subsequent Act of 21 December 1911 did not invalidate the secretary's power. In dismissing Henrietta First Moon's suit, McReynolds found that the district court had decided correctly. We think that it was without jurisdiction since the matter had been entrusted to the exclusive cognizance of the Secretary of the Interior." This case differed from the court's earlier decision in *Lane v. United States ex rel. Mickadiet.*

See also *Lane v. United States ex rel. Mickadiet.*

Fisher v. The District Court of the Sixteenth Judicial District of Montana, In and For the County of Rosebud (In the Matter of the Adoption of Ivan Firecrow, etc.) (424 U.S. 382, 47 L.Ed. 2d 106, 96 S.Ct. 943 [1976])

The Supreme Court held in this 1976 case that "the jurisdiction of [a] tribal court was exclusive" to settle matters of Indian adoptions. Petitioner Alva Fisher is a member of the Northern Cheyenne Tribe of Montana. In 1969, after she divorced her husband, the Tribal Court of the tribe found that her son, Ivan Firecrow, was neglected, and removed the boy from Fisher's custody. In 1974, after several further hearings, that same tribal court allowed Fisher to have temporary custody. Meanwhile, Josephine Runsabove and her husband, both members of the Northern Cheyenne tribe, initiated proceedings in the District Court of the Sixteenth Judicial District of Montana, In and For the County of Rosebud, Montana, to adopt Ivan. Petitioner Fisher moved to have the proceedings dismissed for lack of jurisdiction, claiming that matters regarding Indian adoptions were for the tribal court to decide. The Appellate Court of the Northern Cheyenne Tribe issued an opinion that the tribal court had complete jurisdiction, and dismissed the action. The Supreme Court of Montana, after hearing the Runsaboves' appeal, held that the district court did have jurisdiction and that such a rejection of the state courts of this administration would deny the respondents the right to equal protection. Fisher appealed to the U.S. Supreme Court. The court handed down a unanimous decision *per curiam* (without an acknowledged author), which held that in the matter of adoptions, the tribal court had complete jurisdiction. The opinion addresses this matter as follows: "No federal statute sanctions this interference with tribal self-government. Montana has not been granted, nor has it assumed, civil jurisdiction over the Northern Cheyennes Indian Reservation, either under the Act of August 15, 1953 [Public Law 280], 67 Stat. 588, or under Title IV of the Civil Rights Act of 1968 [known as the Indian Civil Rights Act], 82 Stat. 78." A request for a rehearing was denied (425 U.S. 926, 47 L.Ed. 2d772, 96 S.Ct. 1524).

Fish-In

The Indian version of the civil rights movement's "sit-in," in which young blacks sat inside facilities (diners, bus stations, and the like) from which they were prohibited because of the color of their skin, fish-ins were demonstrations by young Indian activists to prove that they had a right, established by treaties, to fish as they wanted to, unobstructed by the state. They were sponsored, starting in March 1964, by activists of the National Indian Youth Council (NIYC), an activist group composed mainly of college students. The confrontation led to police, attempting to arrest hundreds of protesters, to withdraw when the Quillayute River in Washington State became clogged with Native Americans asserting fishing rights reserved by treaty. The NIYC continued the fight for fishing rights until the decision by Judge George H. Boldt in 1974 confirmed these rights.

See also *United States v. Washington.*

Native Americans stage a fish-in using nets on the Nisqually River in Washington State in 1966. Fishing and hunting rights on Indian lands have long been a contentious issue. The 1974 Supreme Court ruling in United States v. Washington upheld Indian rights granted in treaties over state laws governing hunting and fishing on Indian lands.

Fleming et al. v. McCurtain et al. (215 U.S. 56 [1909])

Indians not included on rolls of membership in Indian nations, rolls that had been approved by the secretary of the interior, were not allowed to reopen the rolls to include themselves so as to share in the allotment of Indian lands, the Supreme Court held in this 1909 case. J.E. Fleming (the opinion did not say if he was an Indian or not) sued on behalf of 13,000 "persons of Choctaw and Chickasaw Indian blood and descent" who had been left off the membership rolls put together to establish who was eligible to receive allotments of those nations. Fleming sued the secretary of the interior, Richard A. Ballinger (for some reason his name is not mentioned in the opinion), as well as Green McCurtain, the chief of the Choctaws, and Douglas B. Johnson, governor of the Chickasaws, to include them in the rolls which had already been closed. The District Court for the Eastern District of Oklahoma dismissed Fleming's suit, and the U.S. Supreme Court granted certiorari (the right to hear the case); arguments were held on 21 and 22 October 1909. Justice Oliver Wendell Holmes spoke for a unanimous court less than three weeks later, on 8 November, in upholding the secretary of the interior's right to keep the rolls closed and proceed with the allotment to those already on those rolls. Justice Holmes explained, "They [the plaintiffs] do not allege that they are citizens [of the respective Indian nations]...They disclose that their names are not upon the rolls, and that the decision of the Secretary of the Interior has been against them, and they show no reason for our not accepting the rolls and decision as final."

Fletcher, Alice Cunningham (1838–1923)

Historian Nancy Oestreich Lurie wrote in 1966, "When Alice Cunningham Fletcher set out from Boston over eighty years ago to study the Omaha Indians, she was to initiate a career which would win her a secure place among those pioneer anthropologists whose works are still widely respected and consulted." Considered a leading ethnologist on Indian culture, she was born in Havana, Cuba, on 15 March 1838, the daughter of Thomas Gilman Fletcher and his wife Lucinda Adeline (née Jenks) Fletcher, both of whom were on vacation for Thomas Fletcher's health when their daughter was born. Thomas Fletcher, a promising attorney and the descendant of one Robert Fletcher who came to America in 1630, was suffering from consumption (now called tuberculosis) and died on 7 November 1839, leaving his second wife, Lucinda, to care for their daughter and two sons from a previous marriage, one of whom died as a youngster. After the family returned to New York City, Alice received a common school education in the city schools. According to biographer Joan Mark, she attended the Brooklyn Female Academy (later renamed Packer Collegiate Institute). After a journey to Europe, she returned to the United States and began her lengthy career as a member of Sorosis, a pioneer women's rights group in New York, and by 1873 she was its secretary. She was a member of the women's congress which met that year and founded the Association for the Advancement of Women.

Soon after, she began an interest in American Indian ethnology after being influenced by Professor Frederic Ward Putnam of the Peabody Museum of American Archaeology at Harvard University. By 1878, she was deeply involved in field work in Florida and Massachusetts collecting samples of Indian culture. That year she met and befriended Susan La Flesche, known as "Bright Eyes," and soon "adopted" as her son Susan's half-brother Francis, who in his own right became a leading Indian ethnologist. As biographer Walter Hough wrote on the occasion of her death, "Miss Fletcher was instrumental in securing land in severalty for the Omaha Indians and was appointed a special agent to carry out the work of allotment, in April 1883. She completed this in June 1884, and between July 1887 and April 1889 performed a similar service for the Winnebago. Immediately afterward she was given charge of allotment among the Nez Perc and this absorbed her attention until 1893. Her work among these many Indian tribes led her to file many reports and articles, most of which appear in the records of the Smithsonian Institution. On 23 February 1885, the Senate passed a resolution calling for a report to be prepared discussing Indian education in the United States. The task of devising the report fell on Fletcher because of her vast well of experience with the Indians, and she spent the next three years putting it together. She began the 1888 treatise, *Indian Education and Civilization*, "Whence come the American Indians? This question still engages the attention of scientific scholars. Archaeological research reveals the fact of the high antiquity of man upon this continent, making it equal to, if not exceeding, that already accorded to man in Europe. The remains of habitations are plentiful and varied; they indicate movements of peoples over our country, one group displacing another; but whence the first impulse started remains unsolved." As a result of her work, appropriations for Indian education increased from $20,000 in 1877 to $1 million in 1900. In addressing the Women's Council in Washington, D.C., on 24 February 1891, Fletcher explained in a discourse entitled *Our Duty toward Dependent Races*,

The Indian holds toward us different historic relations from those of the negro, but our ignorance of him is equally profound. We have learned to fear the red man. And our fears, often well founded, have so distorted our vision that it is hard to get a sight of the man as he really is. We have fought him with guns, with whisky [*sic*], with disease. We have fought to get him out of the way, regardless of the moral consequences to ourselves. He has fought us, and he has bred evil among us by turning loose the lightly leased savage elements in our nature: our greed, our hatred, our contempt. The

Anthropologist Alice Cunningham Fletcher, seated center, at the Omaha Reservation, Walthill, Nebraska, in 1883–1884

conduct of the white man among the Indians, and the conduct of those same men here in the East, shows by contrasts how slight is the hold our race-civilization has over our primitive savagery, how strong is atavism among us. I do not care to dwell upon this picture of our race. It is too true that we are not yet civilized; one day we may be, but the rear of our column straggles far behind, and often reverts to types that outherald in cruelty those whom we call barbarian. Happily, the better element among is now strong enough to prevail, and Christian sentiment finds cordial reinforcement from those in authority. The present Commissioner of Indian Affairs [Thomas Jefferson Morgan] is whole-hearted in his efforts to set the Indian upon his land in severalty, to provide him with educational facilities, to open the way for his self-support and entrance into the rights of citizenship. The landed wealth of the Indian has been his bane; this is now being turned as rapidly as may be to serve him in his future efforts to maintain himself amid a new and difficult future. It is a cause of gratulation that so fearless, tireless conscientious an officer as General Morgan is at the head of Indian affairs. Let the public uphold him in his work, and he will soon make the 'Indian problem' a thing of the past.

Alice Fletcher devoted her life to her work among the Indians, writing and collecting information on their rich culture. Some of her more famous works include *Sun Dance of the Ogallala Sioux* (1883), *The White Buffalo Festival of Uncpapas* (1884), *Phonetic Alphabet of the Winnebago Indians* (1890), *A Study of Omaha Indian Music* (1893), which she wrote with Francis La Flesche, and "Tribal Life among the Omahas" (1896). She was the first anthropologist who truly understood the American Indian, although her work for the allotment of lands in severalty, found to have been a disaster for the Indian people, does leave a blemish on her career. She died in Washington, D.C., on 6 April 1923 after suffering a stroke. Walter Hough's eulogy states: "She placed the Indian on a higher plane than that to which less critical observers assigned him. Her collection of data was expedited by the simplicity of her dealings with the Indians and her entire sympathy with them. She was a friend among friends, and all her inquiries were answered freely and with confidence as one of the family. Such conditions are not often granted to anthropological investigators and for this reason much information on various lines of Indian life is irreparably lost; the essence of the matter, one would say, is not appreciated and is thought to be non-existent. As an interpreter of the Indian Miss Fletcher ranks among the highest."

References Fletcher, Alice C., *Indian Education and Civilization: A Report Prepared in Answer to Senate Resolution of February 23, 1885*, Report of the Bureau of Education, Senate Executive Document No. 95, 48th Congress, 2d Session, 1888; Fletcher, Alice Cunningham, "Our Duty toward Dependent Races." *The Christian Union*, undated fragment in the Henry L. Dawes Papers, Box 55, Folder 6, "Indian Affairs, Printed Matter," Library of Congress; Hough, Walter, "Alice Cunningham Fletcher." *American Anthropologist* 25 (2); Lurie, Nancy Oestreich, "The Lady from Boston and the Omaha Indians," *American West* 3 (4); Mark, Joan,

"Fletcher, Alice Cunningham." In Alden Whitman, ed., *American Reformers: An H. W. Wilson Biographical Dictionary* (1985); Mark, Joan, *A Stranger in Her Native Land: Alice Fletcher and the American Indians* (1988); Wilkins, Thurman, "Fletcher, Alice Cunningham." In Edward T. James, ed., *Notable American Women, 1607–1950: A Biographical Dictionary* (1971).

Formative or Treaty Era

This first era of U.S. government policy towards the Indian tribes lasted from about 1789 to 1871, overlapping the so-called Removal Era. It was a period during which Congress dealt with the Indian nations through treaties, statutes, and laws. Indian historian Ronald N. Satz pens, "Between 1789 and 1829 the U.S. government managed to avoid confronting some of the most vexing and embarrassing legal, political, and moral problems of Indian-white relations. The executive department claimed the exclusive right to treat with the Indians, and Indian affairs were managed by War Department personnel in Washington and in the field. Anxious to placate settlers and speculators whose ever increasing demands for Indian land could not be ignored, government officials used force, bribery, deception, and threats, among other things, to convince Indian leaders to sign land cession treaties. By acknowledging tribal sovereignty to ratify formal purchases of land, the government found a convenient means of justifying its dispossession of the Indians." At the height of the era, Indian affairs were transferred to the Bureau of Indian Affairs, placed in the Department of the Interior in 1849. Noted Supreme Court cases during this period include *Cherokee Nation v. Georgia*, *Worcester v. Georgia*, and *United States v. Ritchie*.

In 1869, Commissioner of Indian Affairs Ely S. Parker wrote in the Annual Report of the Bureau of Indian Affairs, "A treaty involves the idea of compact between two or more sovereign powers, each possessing sufficient authority and force to compel a compliance with the obligations incurred. The Indian tribes of the United States are not sovereign nations, capable of making treaties, as none of them have an organized government of such inherent strength as would secure a faithful obedience of its people in the observance of compacts of this character. They are held to be wards of the government, and the only title the law concedes to them to the lands they occupy is a mere possessory one." The formative era ended with Congress banning the further signing of treaties with the Indians, policy enumerated in the Appropriations Act of 3 March 1871 (16 Stat. 544, at 566).

See also Allotment Policy; Assimiliation and Allotment Era; *Cherokee Nation v. Georgia;* Manypenny, George Washington; Parker, Ely Samuel; Removal Policy; Self-Determination; Termination; Termination Era; *United States v. Ritchie; Worcester v. Georgia.*

References Hayden, Joseph R., *The Senate and Treaties, 1789–1817: The Development of the Treaty-Making Functions of the U.S. Senate during Their Formative Period* (1920); Prucha, Francis Paul, *American Indian Policy in the Formative Years: The Indian Trade and Intercourse Acts, 1790–1834* (1962); Satz, Ronald N., *American Indian Policy in the Jacksonian Era* (1975); Strickland, Rennard, ed., *Felix Cohen's Handbook of Federal Indian Law* (1982); U.S. Congress, House of Representatives, *Annual Report of the Commissioner of Indian Affairs for the Year 1869*, House Executive Document No. 1, 41st Congress, 2d Session (serial 1414).

Frost v. Wenie (157 U.S. 46 [1895])

This Supreme Court case dealt with the narrow issue of whether the government, having taken Indian lands for use for a military fort, is obligated to return those lands once finished with them, or if they can be given to settlers as public land. By an act of Congress of 15 December 1880, the Fort Dodge military reservation in Kansas was declared not to be needed any longer, and proclaimed the former Osage Indian lands as public lands for settlement. Daniel M. Frost, the appellant in this case, took title to some of the lands, and soon after built a house on this property. Frederick T.M. Wenie (whom the opinion does not identify as being an Osage Indian or not) claimed title of the lands as part of the Osage reservation, and demanded that Frost relinquish title. Frost refused, even though two secretaries of the interior, through official decisions of the Interior Department, backed up

Wenie's claim. Frost sued to the Circuit Court of the United States for the District of Kansas to enjoin Wenie from taking title to the land; the court refused, and Frost sued for relief to the U.S. Supreme Court.

The court heard arguments in the case on 24 January 1895, and handed down a decision on 4 March of that same year. Writing for a unanimous court, Justice John Marshall Harlan held that the 1880 law unconstitutionally overrode the treaty with the Osages that had originally secured the land for the military reservation, in effect invalidating Frost's title and returning the interest in the lands to Wenie.

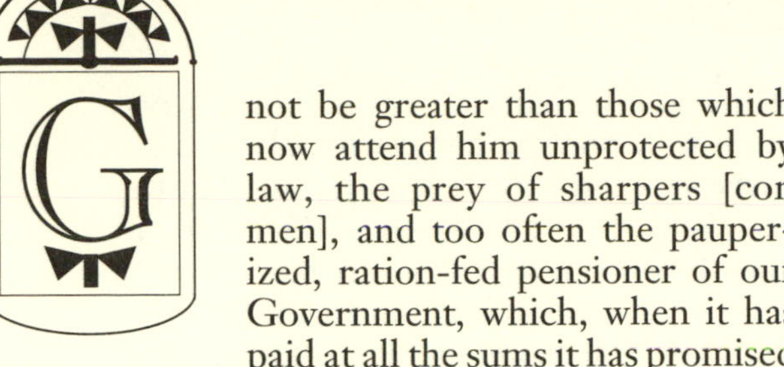

Gates, Merrill Edwards (1848–1922)

Indian historian Francis Paul Prucha writes of Merrill Gates, "No man was more closely identified with the humanitarian Indian reformers at the end of the nineteenth century than Merrill E. Gates. He was a highly respected educator, serving as president of Rutgers College and then as president of Amherst College." He added, "Gates was a man of deep religious feeling, and his work for Indian welfare was an expression of the obligation he acknowledged to help those fellowmen who were less fortunate than he." He was a member of the Board of Indian Commissioners from 1884, when he was appointed by President Chester A. Arthur, until his death in 1922, and chairman of the board from 1890 to 1899.

At the seventeenth meeting of the Board of Indian Commissioners, Gates spoke out on his view of the ultimate goal of reformers presently working for the Indians.

For what ought we hope as the future of the Indian? What should the Indian become? To this there is one answer—and but one. He should become an intelligent citizen of the United States. There is no other "manifest destiny" for any man or any body of men on our domain. To this we stand committed by all the logic of two thousand years of Teutonic and Anglo-Saxon history, since Arminius with his sturdy followers made a stand for liberty against the legions of Rome. Foremost champions of that peculiarly Anglo-Saxon idea, that supports a strong central government, moves as a whole, yet protects carefully the local and individual freedom of all the parts, we are, as a matter of course, to seek to fit the Indians among us as we do all other men for the responsibilities of citizenship. And by the stupendous precedent of eight millions of freedmen made citizens in a day, we have committed ourselves to the theory that the way to fit men for citizenship is to make them citizens. The dangers that would beset Indian voters solicited by the demagogue would not be greater than those which now attend him unprotected by law, the prey of sharpers [con men], and too often the pauperized, ration-fed pensioner of our Government, which, when it has paid at all the sums it has promised to pay to Indians, has paid them in such a way as to undermine what manhood and self-respect the Indian had. For one, I would willingly see the Indians run the risk of being flattered a little by candidates for Congress. None of their tribes are destitute of shrewd men who would watch the interests of the race.

Has our Government in its dealings with the Indians hitherto adopted a course of legislation and administration, well adapted to build up their manhood and make them intelligent, self-supporting citizens? They are the wards of the Government. Is not a guardian's first duty so to educate and care for his wards as to make them able to care for themselves? It looks like intended fraud if a guardian persists in such management of his wards and such use of their funds intrusted to him as in the light of experience clearly unfits them and will always keep them unfit for the management of their own affairs and their own property.

The author of *International Arbitration* (1897), Gates died at his home in Washington, D.C., on 11 August 1922, at the age of 74.

See also United States Board of Indian Commissioners.

References Gates, Merrill, "Land and Law as Agents in Educating Indians." In U.S. Congress, House of Representatives, *Annual Report of the Commissioner of Indian Affairs for the Year 1885,* House Executive Document No. 1, 49th Congress, 1st Session (serial 2379); "Gates, Merrill Edwards." In *Who Was Who in America, 1897–1942* (1981); Prucha, Francis Paul, ed., *Americanizing the American Indians: Writings by the "Friends of the Indians," 1880–1890* (1973).

General Allotment Act (24 Stat. 388)

Considered the most important piece of federal legislation dealing with Indian land rights, this act, also called the Dawes

Allotment Act and the Dawes Severalty Act after its principal congressional sponsor, Senator Henry Dawes of Massachusetts, was enacted on 8 February 1887. Its provisions Swere not extended to the members of the Five Civilized Tribes, located in Oklahoma, who demanded to be excluded; the Curtis Act in 1898 extended allotment to them. The act was also amended as to requirements regarding alienation of lands and the extension of the trust period with the enactment of the Burke Act in 1906. In 1934, the trust period was extended indefinitely, as per section 2 of the Indian Reorganization Act (Wheeler-Howard Act) of 1934. The General Allotment Act reads:

An Act to provide for the allotment of lands in severalty to Indians on the various reservations, and to extend the protection of the laws of the United States and the Territories over the Indians, and for other purposes.

Be it enacted by the Senate and House of Representatives of the United States in Congress assembled,

1. That in all cases where any tribe or band of Indians has been, or shall hereafter be, located upon any reservation created for their use, either by treaty stipulation or by virtue of an act of Congress or executive order setting apart the same for their use, the President of the United States be, and he hereby is, authorized, whenever in his opinion any reservation or any part thereof of such Indians is advantageous for agricultural and grazing purposes, to cause said reservation, or any part thereof, to be surveyed, or resurveyed if necessary, and to allot the lands in said reservation in severalty to any Indian located thereon in quantities as follows:

   To each head of family, one-quarter of a section;
   To each person over eighteen years of age, one-eighth of a section;
   To each orphan child under eighteen years of age, one-eighth of a section; and

   To each other single person under eighteen years now living, or who may be born prior to the date of the order of the President directing an allotment of the lands embraced in any reservation, one-sixteenth of a section: Provided, That in case there is not sufficient land on any of the said reservations to allot lands to each individual of the classes above named in quantities as above provided, the lands embraced in such reservation or reservations shall be allotted to each individual of each of said classes pro rata in accordance with the provisions of this act: And provided further, That where the treaty or act of Congress setting apart such reservation provides for the allotment of lands in severalty in quantities in excess of those herein provided, the President, in making allotments upon such reservation, shall allot the lands to each individual Indian belonging thereon in quantity as specified in such treaty or act: And provided further, That when the lands allotted are only valuable for grazing purposes, an additional allotment of such grazing lands, in quantities as above provided, shall be made to each individual.

2. That all allotments set apart under the provisions of this act shall be selected by the Indians, heads of families selecting for their minor children, and the agents shall select for each orphan child, and in such manner as to embrace the improvements of the Indians making the selection. Where the improvements of two or more Indians have been made on the same legal subdivision of land, unless they shall otherwise agree, a provisional line may be run dividing said lands between them, and the amount to which each is entitled shall be equalized in the assignment of the remainder of the land to

which they are entitled under this act: Provided, That if any one entitled to an allotment shall fail to make a selection within four years after the President shall direct that allotments may be made on a particular reservation, the Secretary of the Interior may direct the agent of such tribe or band, if such there be, and if there be no agent, then a special agent appointed for that purpose, to make a selection for such Indian, which selection shall be allotted as in cases where selections are made by the Indians, and patents shall issue in like manner.

3. That the allotments provided for in this act shall be made by special agents appointed by the President for such purpose, and the agents in charge of the respective reservations on which the allotments are directed to be made, under such rules and regulations as the Secretary of the Interior may from time to time prescribe, and shall be certified by such agents to the Commissioner of Indian Affairs, in duplicate one copy to be retained in the Indian Office and the other to be transmitted to the Secretary of the Interior for his action, and to be deposited in the General Land Office.

4. That where any Indian not residing upon a reservation, or for whose tribe no reservation has been provided by treaty, act of Congress, or executive order, shall make settlement upon any surveyed or unsurveyed lands of the United States not otherwise appropriated, he or she shall be entitled, upon application to the local land office for the district in which the lands are located, to have the same allotted to him or her, and to his or her children, in quantities and manner as provided in this act for Indians residing upon reservations, and when such settlement is made upon unsurveyed lands, the grant to such Indians shall be adjusted upon the survey of the lands so as to conform thereto; and patents shall be issued to them for such lands in the manner and with the restrictions as herein provided. And the fees to which the officers of such local land office would have been entitled had such lands been entered under the general laws for the disposition of the public lands shall be paid to them, from any moneys in the Treasury of the United States not otherwise appropriated, upon a statement of an account in their behalf for such fees by the Commissioner of the General Land Office, and a certification of such account to the Secretary of the Treasury by the Secretary of the Interior.

5. That upon the approval of the allotments provided for in this act by the Secretary of the Interior, he shall cause patents to issue therefor in the name of the allottees, which patents shall be of the legal effect, and declare that the United States does and will hold the land thus allotted, for the period of twenty-five years, in trust for the sole use and benefit of the Indian to whom such allotment shall have been made, or, in the case of his decease, of his heirs according to the laws of the State or Territory where such land is located, and that at the expiration of said period the United States will convey the same by patent to said Indian, or his heirs as aforesaid, in fee, discharged of said trust and free of all charge or incumbrance whatsoever: Provided, That the President of the United States may in any case in his discretion extend the period. And if any conveyance shall be made of the lands set apart and allotted as herein provided, or any contract made touching the same, before the expiration of the time above mentioned, such conveyance or contract shall be absolutely null and void: Provided, That the law of descent and partition in force in the State or Territory where such lands are situate shall apply thereto after patents therefor

have been executed and delivered, except as herein otherwise provided; and the laws of the State of Kansas regulating the descent and partition of real estate shall, so far as practicable, apply to all lands in the Indian Territory which may be allotted in severalty under the provisions of this act:

And provided further, That at any time after lands have been allotted to all the Indians of any tribe as herein provided, or sooner if in the opinion of the President it shall be for the best interests of the tribe, it shall be lawful for the Secretary of the Interior to negotiate with such Indian tribe for the purchase and release by said tribe, in conformity with the treaty or statute under which such reservation is held, of such portions of its reservation not allotted as such tribe shall, from time to time, consent to sell, on such terms and conditions as shall be considered just and equitable between the United States and said tribe of Indians, which purchase shall not be complete until ratified by Congress, and the form and manner of executing such release shall also be prescribed by Congress: Provided however, That all lands adapted to agriculture, with or without irrigation so sold or released to the United States by any Indian tribe shall be held by the United States for the sole purpose of securing homes to actual settlers and shall be disposed of by the United States to actual and bona fide settlers only in tracts not exceeding one hundred and sixty acres to any one person, on such terms as Congress shall prescribe, subject to grants which Congress may make in aid of education: And provided further, That no patents shall issue therefor except to the person so taking the same as and for a homestead, or his heirs, and after the expiration of five years occupancy thereof as such homestead; and any conveyance of said lands so taken as a homestead, or any contract touching the same, or lien thereon, created prior to the date of such patent, shall be null and void. And the sums agreed to be paid by the United States as purchase money for any portion of any such reservation shall be held in the Treasury of the United States for the sole use of the tribe or tribes of Indians; to whom such reservations belonged; and the same, with interest thereon at three per cent per annum, shall be at all times subject to appropriation by Congress for the education and civilization of such tribe or tribes of Indians or the members thereof. The patents aforesaid shall be recorded in the General Land Office, and afterward delivered, free of charge, to the allottee entitled thereto. And if any religious society or other organization is now occupying any of the public lands to which this act is applicable, for religious or educational work among the Indians, the Secretary of the Interior is hereby authorized to confirm such occupation to such society or organization, in quantity not exceeding one hundred and sixty acres in any one tract, so long as the same shall be so occupied, on such terms as he shall deem just; but nothing herein contained shall change or alter any claim of such society for religious or educational purposes heretofore granted by law. And hereafter in the employment of Indian police, or any other employes in the public service among any of the Indian tribes or bands affected by this act, and where Indians can perform the duties required, those Indians who have availed themselves of the provisions of this act and become citizens of the United States shall be preferred.

6. That upon the completion of said allotments and the patenting of the lands to said allottees, each and every member of the respective bands or tribes of Indians to whom allotments have been made shall have the benefit of and be subject to the laws, both civil

and criminal, of the State or Territory in which they may reside; and no Territory shall pass or enforce any law denying any such Indian within its jurisdiction the equal protection of the law. And every Indian born within the territorial limits of the United States to whom allotments shall have been made under the provisions of this act, or under any law or treaty, and every Indian born within the territorial limits of the United States who has voluntarily taken up, within said limits, his residence separate and apart from any tribe of Indians therein, and has adopted the habits of civilized life, is hereby declared to be a citizen of the United States, and is entitled to all the rights, privileges, and immunities of such citizens, whether said Indian has been or not, by birth or otherwise, a member of any tribe of Indians within the territorial limits of the United States without in any manner impairing or otherwise affecting the right of such Indian to tribal or other property.

7. That in cases where the use of water for irrigation is necessary to render the lands within any Indian reservation available for agricultural purposes, the Secretary of the Interior be, and he is hereby, authorized to prescribe such rules and regulations as he may deem necessary to secure a just and equal distribution thereof among the Indians residing upon any such reservations; and no other appropriation or grant of water by any riparian proprietor shall be authorized or permitted to the damage of any riparian proprietor.

8. That the provision of this act shall not extend to the territory occupied by the Cherokees, Creeks, Choctaws, Chickasaws, Seminoles, and Osage, Miamies and Peorias, and Sacs and Foxes, in the Indian Territory, nor to any of the reservations of the Seneca Nation of New York Indians in the State of New York, nor to that strip of territory in the State of Nebraska adjoining the Sioux Nation on the south added by executive order.

9. That for the purpose of making the surveys and resurveys in section two of this act, there be, and hereby is, appropriated, out of any moneys in the Treasury not appropriated, the sum of one hundred thousand dollars, to be repaid proportionately out of the proceeds of the sale of such land as may be acquired from the Indians under the provisions of this act.

10. That nothing in this act contained shall be so construed as to affect the right and power of Congress to grant the right of way through any lands granted to an Indian, or a tribe of Indians, for railroads or other highways, or telegraph lines, for the public use, or to condemn such lands to public uses, upon making compensation.

11. That nothing in this act shall be so construed as to prevent the removal of the Southern Ute Indians from their present reservation in Southwestern Colorado to a new reservation by and with the consent of a majority of the adult male members of said tribe.

Only two senators, Henry Moore Teller of Colorado and John Tyler Morgan of Alabama, spoke out against passage of the Dawes Act. Teller's arguments are among the most persuasive ever delivered on the floor of the U.S. Senate: "Now, divide up this land and you will in a few years deprive the Indians a resting-place on the face of this continent; and no man who has studied this question intelligently, and who has the Indian interest at heart, can talk about dividing this land and giving them tracts in severalty till they have made such progress in civilization that they know the benefits and the advantages of land in severalty, and of a fee-simple absolute title; and the whole Presbyterian Church and all other churches all over this country cannot convince me, with an observation of twenty years, and, I believe, a heart that beats as warmly for the Indians as that of any other man living, that that is in the interest of the Indians. It is in the interest of speculators; it is in the interest of the men who are clutching up this land, but not in the interest of the Indians at all; and there is the baneful feature of it that when you have allotted the Indians land on which they cannot make a living the Secretary of the Interior may then proceed to purchase their land, and Congress will, as a matter of course, ratify the purchase, and the Indians will become the owners in a few years in fee, and away goes their title, and, as I said before, they are wanderers over the face of this continent, without a place whereon to lay their heads. And yet every man who raises his voice against a bill of this kind is charged with not looking to the interest of the Indians, and I am met by the astonishing argument that because the Secretary of the Interior, and because chairman of the Committee on Indian Affairs (for whose opinion I have due and proper respect), and because public sentiment say that they should have land in severalty, I am running amuck against all the intelligence and all the virtue of the country, and therefore I must be wrong.

"Mr. President, what I complain of in connection with this Indian business is that practical common sense is not applied to it. Sentiment does not do the Indians any good. It does not educate them and feed them for us to pass high-sounding resolutions and to put upon the statute-book enactments that declare they shall be protected in their rights. Furthermore, it does not accomplish the great purpose of civilization to send a few wild Indians down to Hampton and a few to Carlisle [noted nineteenth-century schools for Indians]. The Indians cannot be educated by such methods. We must put the schools in the Indian community; we must bring the influences where a whole Indian tribe or a whole band will be affected and influenced by

The General Allotment Act (1887) stated that tribal lands would be allotted to individuals. Many sold their allotments, opening Indian lands to white settlement. On 16 September 1893 over 6 million acres of the Cherokee Outlet in Oklahoma Territory were thrown open to white settlement. Here, some of the 100,000 participants race to stake claims.

them. It is folly to suppose that this will civilize them.

"If I stand alone in the Senate, I want to put upon the record my prophecy in this matter, that when thirty or forty years shall have passed and these Indians shall have parted with their title, they will curse the hand that was raised professedly in their defense to secure this kind of legislation, and if the people who are clamoring for it understood Indian character, and Indian laws, and Indian morals, and Indian religion, they would not be here clamoring for this at all.

This is a bill that, in my judgment, ought to be entitled 'A bill to despoil the Indians of their lands and to make them vagabonds on the face of the earth,' because, in my view, that is the result of this kind of legislation."

As the editors of *Felix Cohen's Handbook of Federal Indian Law* write, "The original Dawes Act allotted 160 acres to each head of household and 40 acres to minors. Married women were given no separate rights to land, a fact that soon aroused protest. It was also argued that the young and able-bodied should not have less land than the old and affirm. Equalization was demanded. In 1891, Congress amended the Dawes Act to provide allotments of 80 acres of agricultural land, or 160 acres of grazing land, to each Indian." Scholar Arrell Morgan Gibson wrote in 1987 on the centennial of the act, "The General Allotment Act answered the demands of well-intentioned but naive 'Friends of the Indian' and federal bureaucrats who believed that granting each Indian a homestead from the tribal estate would by some mystical process transform him into a hybrid American yeoman-style farmer, adequately assimilated into the larger society. More realistically the law answered the strident demands of homeseekers who would be permitted to settle the surplus tribal lands and those of railway company executives seeking land grants for constructing their lines across the Indian Territory, as well as bankers and business interests in border towns who would prosper from an enlarged population in this nature-endowed southwestern province [Oklahoma]."

See also Burke Act; Curtis Act; Dawes, Henry Laurens; Indian Reorganization Act; Meriam Report; Morgan, John Tyler; Section 483a of Title 25 (United States Code).

References Gibson, Arrell Morgan, "The Centennial Legacy of the General Allotment Act." *Chronicles of Oklahoma* 65 (3); Senator Teller's remarks in *Congressional Record: Containing the Proceedings and Debates of the Forty-Sixth Congress, Third Session* (1881), 11: 934–35; Strickland, Rennard, ed., *Felix Cohen's Handbook of Federal Indian Law* (1982).

Ghost Dance

This movement is considered to be the impetus for the massacre that occurred at Wounded Knee in 1890. Initiated by the Paiute prophet Wovoka (also known as Jack Wilson), it was a revival of the Native American character, a prophecy that a spirit would come to Earth and reclaim their lands for them and rid the world of whites who had come to take it.

In 1890, ethnologist James Mooney traveled to the reservations of the western United States to study the origins of the Ghost Dance and its implications to the Wounded Knee tragedy. As he wrote in 1890, "The great underlying principle of the Ghost-dance doctrine is that the time will come when the whole Indian race, living and dead, will be reunited upon a regenerated earth, to live a life of aboriginal happiness, forever free from death, disease, and misery. On this foundation each tribe has built a structure from its own mythology, and each apostle and believer has filled in the details according to his own mental capacity or ideas of happiness, with such additions as come to him from the trance. Some changes, also, have undoubtedly resulted from the transmission of the doctrine through the imperfect medium of the sign language. The differences of interpretation are precisely such as we find in Christianity, with its hundreds of sects and innumerable shades of individual opinion. The white race, being alien and secondary and hardly real, has no part in this scheme or aboriginal regeneration, and will be left behind with the other things of earth that have served their temporary purpose, or else will cease entirely to exist."

Turn of the century artist Mary Irvin Wright combined information from photographs by anthropologist James Mooney to document an Arapaho Ghost Dance. The late nineteenth-century movement offered hope that Indian lands could be reclaimed and that the whites who had taken them would go away.

Writer Paul Bailey pens, "The ingredient that fed the Ghost Dance was despair. To a whipped, broke, defrauded people—herded into barren reservations by the unfeeling and victorious white man—it promised one desperate and final hope. The world would again be renewed, the grass would grow high and luxuriant. The buffalo, the elk, the antelope, would return in the manner once known. There would be food, warmth and comfort in place of hopelessness, disgrace, and poverty. The dead would come alive again, brave men would walk one more in dignity, and the cruel and avaricious white man would vanish in the convulsions of the world of evil he had wrought."

In his report on the "causes of the outbreak," Commissioner of Indian Affairs Thomas Jefferson Morgan wrote, "In stating the events which led to this outbreak among the Sioux, the endeavor too often has been merely to find some opportunity for locating blame. The causes are complex, and many are obscure and remote."

See also Mooney, James, Jr.; Wounded Knee (1890); Wovoka.

References Bailey, Paul, *Ghost Dance Messiah* (1986); Mooney, James, "The Ghost Dance Doctrine and an Opening Arapaho Ghost Dance Song, 1890." In Albert L. Hurtado and Peter Iverson, eds., *Major Problems in American Indian History: Documents and Essays* (1994); U.S. Congress, House of Representatives, *Annual Report of the Commissioner of Indian Affairs for the Year 1891*, House Executive Document No. 1, 52d Congress, 1st Session (serial 2934).

Gillespie v. Oklahoma (257 U.S. 501, 66 L.Ed. 338, 42 S.Ct. 171 [1922])

In this Supreme Court case, decided in 1922, the court held that "the income of the lessee from a lease of restricted Indian lands...cannot be taxed by the state as profits or income, since a tax on such profits is a direct hamper of the effort of the United States to make the best terms that it can for its wards." When the state of Oklahoma sought to levy taxes on the income from the leases of allotted lands, F. A. Gillespie (he is not identified as to being an Indian or not) sued in the District Court for the Eastern District of Oklahoma to enjoin the state from collecting the tax. The district court prohibited the collection of the tax, and, at first, the Supreme Court of Oklahoma affirmed. Later, upon reconsideration, it reversed, sending the case to the U.S. Supreme Court. Justice Oliver Wendell Holmes held for a divided court (justices Mahlon Pitney, Louis Brandeis, and John Hessin Clarke dissented) on 30 January 1922 in reversing the judgment of the Supreme Court of Oklahoma. Justice Holmes explained, "Whether this property could be taxed in any other form or not, it cannot be reached as profits or income from leases such as those before us. The same considerations that invalidate a tax upon the leases invalidate a tax upon the profits of the leases, and, stopping short of theoretical possibilites, a tax upon such profits is a direct hamper upon the effort of the United States to make the best terms that it can for its wards."

Gleason et al. v. Wood et al. (224 U.S. 679 [1912])

This was a companion case to *Choate v. Trapp*, which held that under the Curtis Act (30 Stat. 497, at 505), enacted 28 June 1898, Congress affirmed that allotments held by the original Indian allottee were to remain untaxable by states. In this case, *Michael H. Gleason, Minnie Love, Henry McGee et al., Plaintiffs in Error, v. J. I. Wood, County Treasurer of Pittsburg County, Oklahoma et al.*, the Indians were taxed by the state for their allotments, and they sued for relief in the Superior Court for Pittsburg County. The court refused to stop Wood from enforcing the taxes, and the Supreme Court of Oklahoma affirmed. The U.S. Supreme Court agreed to hear the case, and arguments were heard on 23 February 1912. Justice Joseph Rucker Lamar, as in *Choate*, held that Wood's imposition of the taxes was illegal. In a one-paragraph opinion, Lamar wrote, "The complaint alleges that the plaintiffs are Choctaws owning homesteads and surplus [land] granted under the terms of the Atoka Agreement. Their applications to enjoin the officers of the state of Oklahoma from assessing their lands for taxation for the year 1909 were denied. All of the questions involved are disposed of by the decision in *Choate v. Trapp*, just rendered. The judgment, therefore, is reversed, and the case remanded, with directions for further proceedings not inconsistent with that opinion. Reversed." Another case in this vein decided at the same time was *English v. Richardson*.

See also *Choate v. Trapp;* Curtis Act; *English v. Richardson.*

Goat v. United States (224 U.S. 458 [1912])

In this U.S. Supreme Court case, decided in 1912, the court held that Congress had the right to place restrictions on the alienation of conveyances, the right to sell one's allotted land. Alfred F. Goat was among several Seminoles allotted lands under the act of 1 July 1898 (30 Stat. 567); however, the Congress established several restrictions involved in the act to make sure that minor Indians did not alienate, or sell, their allotments. Goat and others sold their conveyances in violation of the law. The U.S. government sought in court to cancel the sales by Goat and the others. The Circuit Court for the Eastern District of Oklahoma struck down the restrictions as unconstitutional; however, the Circuit Court of Appeals for the Eighth Circuit reversed the decision. Goat and the others appealed to the U.S. Supreme Court. Arguments were held before the court on 12 and 13 October 1911, and a decision was handed down on 29 April 1912, the same day the court decided the joint case of *Deming Investment Company v. United States*. Justice Charles Evan Hughes delivered the unanimous decision of the court; he held that lands allotted to minor Seminoles could have restrictions placed upon them, and that these restrictions placed upon the conveyances were constitutional. Hughes did rule, however, that the lower courts would have to consider the violations on a case by case basis, and that surplus tribal lands that had been allotted were exempt from the restrictions. The Supreme Court decided three other cases dealing with this same issue in 1912. For them, refer to *Deming Investment Company v. United States; Heckman v. United States; Mullen v. United States.*

GOON Squads

These "Guardians of the Oglala Nation" squads were composed of Oglala Sioux tribal policemen on the Pine Ridge Reservation in South Dakota under the command of tribal chairman Richard Wilson. The tactics of the GOON squads included harassment and abuse of tribal members who opposed Wilson's authority. The struggle of Wilson's opponents came to a head in February 1973, when some 300 supporters of the American Indian Movement (including so-called traditionals, who supported a return to ancestral Oglala customs), objecting to Wilson's reign, occupied the village of Wounded Knee inside the Pine Ridge Reservation for 71 days, a siege that ended when the government representatives promised an investigation into Wilson's administration.

See also Wounded Knee (1973).

Goudy v. Meath (203 U.S. 146, 51 L.Ed. 130, 27 S.Ct. 48 [1906])

Indians granted citizenship are allowed to be taxed because they are now under the laws and privileges of a state which makes that as its law, the Supreme Court held in this 1906 decision. James Goudy, a Puyallup Indian of Washington State, claimed that under a treaty with the Puyallups of 16 March 1854 (10 Stat. 1043), "No state legislature shall remove the restrictions [upon sale, levying of taxes, and alienation] herein provided for without the consent of Congress." However, under section 6 of the General Allotment Act of 8 February 1887 (24 Stat. 388), it was declared "that upon the completion of said allotments and the patenting of the lands to said allottees, each and every member of the respective bands or tribes of Indians to whom allotments have been made shall have the benefit of and be subject to the laws, both civil and criminal, of the State or Territory in which they may reside." When Edward Meath, assessor of Pierce County, Washington, tried to levy taxes on Goudy's allotment, Goudy sued in the Superior Court for Pierce County to enjoin, or stop, the enforcement. The court denied Goudy's claim, and the Supreme Court of Washington State affirmed the judgment. Goudy appealed to the U.S. Supreme Court. Justice David Josiah Brewer held for a unanimous court on 19 November 1906 that the General Allotment Act made Goudy a citizen, eligible under the state's laws and regulations to be taxed like every other citizen. Justice Brewer wrote, "Among the laws to which the plaintiff as a citizen became subject were those in respect to taxation. His property, unless exempt, became subject to taxation in the same manner as property belonging to other citizens, and the rule of exemption for him must be the same as for other citizens—that is, that no exemption exists by implication, but must be clearly manifested."

Greenwood, Alfred Burton (1811–1889)

Biographer Gary L. Roberts writes, "Alfred Burton Greenwood was the victim of history, for he had the misfortune of serving as commissioner of Indian Affairs during the dissolution of the Union. A man of undoubted ability and long experience in Indian matters, he seemed an auspicious choice to head the Indian office when he was appointed by President James Buchanan in 1859, but he was soon enmeshed in the sectional politics which dominated Buchanan's administration. Although he personally supported the Union, his attention was diverted by his Southern sympathies and his political ambitions. He ultimately gave his support to the Confederacy when his own state, Arkansas, seceded, and left office bitterly, his aspirations thwarted and his political career shattered." He was born in Franklin County, Georgia, on 11 July 1811, the son of Hugh Greenwood and Elizabeth (née Ingram) Greenwood. He attended schools in Lawrenceville,

Georgia, and, after graduating from the University of Georgia, read the law and was admitted to the bar in 1832. In 1837, he was appointed as an agent to provide supplies to the Cherokee Indians being removed on the "Trail of Tears" from Georgia to the Indian Territory in Oklahoma. He soon made his home in Bentonville, Arkansas, and was elected to the state legislature for two terms. He served as a prosecuting attorney and circuit court judge before winning election in 1852 to the U.S. House of Representatives, where he served for four terms until his retirement in 1859.

After the resignation of Commissioner of Indian Affairs James W. Denver in March 1859, Buchanan turned to Greenwood, then a virtual unknown outside of his congressional experience, to fill the position. On 27 April of that year Greenwood wrote to Secretary of the Interior Jacob Thompson, "Your favor of the 16th inst[ant], advising me that you had been instructed to by the President to tender for my acceptance the Office of Commissioner of Indian Affairs, has been received. In reply I beg leave to say that although I am now, and have ever been an ardent supporter of the present administration, the position tendered was wholly unexpected, for I am sure that I never have either directly or indirectly intimated that I desired or would accept such a distinguished position, not am I aware that any friend suggested my name either to you or the President. I conclude therefor that my appointment has been made, alone with a view to the public service. I therefore cheerfully accept the position so generously tendered, I do so the more readily for the reason you advise me that the appointment was made with your cordial assent and approval. I shall proceed to Washington at the earliest practical moment to enter upon the discharge of its duties." Greenwood's tenure, from April 1859 until April 1861, made him the eighth man to occupy the commissionership since June 1849, and that fact alone showed the shambles of national Indian policy and the seeming inability of the commissioner to affect real change. During his short tenure, Greenwood supported the reservation policy that had been put into effect a few years earlier. In his annual report for 1859, only one of two that he produced, he called on the federal government to support this idea so as to prevent "hostilities and a costly Indian war, involving the loss of many lives, and the expenditure of a much larger amount of money than would be required to colonize them on reservations, and to furnish them with the necessary facilities and assistance to enable them to change their mode of life." When antislavery missionaries began to invade the Cherokee Nation and help slaves escape from their Cherokee masters, Greenwood angrily condemned in the 1860 annual report these men "who are charged [by abolitionists] with interfering with the institution of slavery in the Cherokee nation." Because of this proslavery tilt by both Greenwood and his superior, Secretary of the Interior Jacob Thompson, both men were viewed suspiciously by the northern-dominated Congress and were basically considered untrustworthy.

The crisis that was to become the Civil War began when President Buchanan sent the ship *Star of the West* to resupply Fort Sumter in South Carolina, and Secretary of the Interior Thompson resigned to join his native Mississippi, which had seceded from the Union. Buchanan then asked Greenwood to serve as the interim secretary of the interior until the new president, Abraham Lincoln, could fill the spot. When Lincoln cleaned the Interior Department of Democrats, in a dismissive tone Greenwood wrote to newly installed Secretary of the Interior Caleb Blood Smith on 6 March 1861, "Presuming it is the purpose of the President to place his political friends at the head of the different bureaus, and not wishing him to feel the least embarrassment in regard to the position I hold, I have the honor to tender him through you this resignation as Commissioner of Indian Affairs." He then returned to Arkansas, and served as a recruiter of Cherokees and Creeks to side with the Confederacy. He also served for two terms in the Confederate Congress, and as a tax collector for Arkansas. With the end of the war, he retired to Bentonville and was a practicing attorney. He died there on 6 October 1889, at the age of 78.

See also Bureau of Indian Affairs.

References Greenwood to Caleb Blood Smith, 6 March 1861, Box 43, Records of the Appointments Division, Commissioner of Indian Affairs, RG 48, National Archives; Greenwood to Secretary of the Interior Jacob Thompson, 27 April 1859, Box 43, Records of the Appointments Division, Commissioner of Indian Affairs, RG 48, National Archives; Roberts, Gary L., "Alfred Burton Greenwood." In Robert M. Kvasnicka and Herman J. Viola, eds., *The Commissioners of Indian Affairs, 1824–1977* (1979); U.S. Congress, Senate, *Annual Report of the Commissioner of Indian Affairs for the Year 1859*, Senate Executive Document No. 2, 36th Congress, 1st Session (serial 1023); U.S. Congress, Senate, *Annual Report of the Commissioner of Indian Affairs for the Year 1860*, Senate Executive Document No. 1, 36th Congress, 2d Session (serial 1078).

Gritts v. Fisher **(224 U.S. 640 [1912])**

In this case, the U.S. Supreme Court held that Congress had a plenary power over Indian affairs, and thus could change the wording of an agreement as to allotments to include Indian children born after a specific date. Under the act of 1 September 1902, Congress allowed allotments to the Cherokee Nation to proceed, and by the act gave the Cherokee council until 1906 to complete the work of allotting the lands. Further, implied the 1902 act, "all persons not living" at the time could not partake in the allotments. By 1906, the Cherokee council had yet to complete its work. Under the act of 21 June 1906, the Congress expanded those allowed to share in the allotments to include "children who were minors living March 4, 1906." Levi B. Gritts and two other Cherokees sued Secretary of the Interior Walter L. Fisher and Secretary of the Treasury Franklin MacVeagh in the Court of Appeals for the District of Columbia, to enjoin them from distributing allotments to those children not covered by the 1902 act because more people sharing in the allotments would leave a smaller portion given to themselves. The district court held for Fisher and MacVeagh; Gritts and his two unnamed partners appealed to the U.S. Supreme Court. Arguments in the case were held on 10 and 11 January 1912, and the court's decision was handed down on 13 May of that same year. Speaking for a unanimous court, Justice Willis Van Devanter held that under Congress' plenary, or unrestricted and unlimited, power over Indian affairs, it had the right to set new definitions for those eligible for allotments as per the 1906 act. As Justice Van Devanter wrote regarding the 1906 act,

> It is not proposed to disturb the individual allotments made to members living [on] September 1, 1902, and enrolled under the act of 1902, and therefore we are only concerned with whether children born after September 1, 1902, and living [on] March 4, 1906, should be excluded from the allotment and distribution. The act of 1902 required that they be excluded, and the legislation in 1906, as we have seen, provides for their inclusion. It is conceded, and properly so, that the later legislation is valid and controlling unless it impairs or destroys rights which the act of 1902 vested in members living [on] September 1, 1902, and enrolled under that act. As has been indicated, their individual allotments are not affected. But it is said that the act of 1902 contemplated that they alone should receive allotments and be the participants in the distribution of the remaining lands, and also of the funds, of the tribe. No doubt such was the purport of the act. But that, in our opinion, did not confer upon them any vested right such as would disable Congress from thereafter making provision for admitting newly born members of the tribe to the allotment and distribution. The difficulty with the appellants' contention is that it treats the act of 1902 as a contract, when it is only an act of Congress, and can have no greater effect.

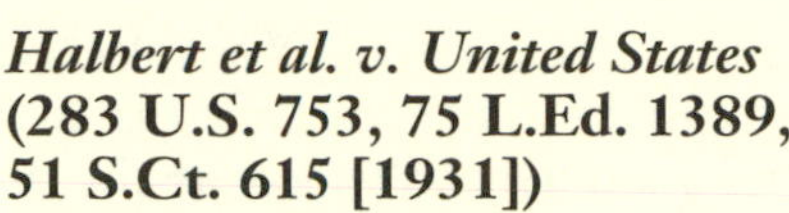

***Hagen v. Utah* (510 U.S.—, 127 L.Ed. 2d 252, 114 S.Ct. 958 [1994])**

In this Supreme Court case, the court held: "Utah courts...have jurisdiction over [an] Indian as to crime on land within original reservation boundaries, based on [a] ruling that Congress diminished [the] reservation, placing [such] land outside Indian country." Petitioner Robert Hagen, a Uintah Indian, was indicted in a Utah court for distributing a controlled substance in the town of Myton, Utah, which now lies on land that had once been part of the Uintah Reservation, established by President Lincoln in his Executive Order 38–1 of 3 October 1861. In 1903, following the Supreme Court's decision in *Lone Wolf v. Hitchcock* that Congress can alter the boundaries of Indian reservations unilaterally, the Congress ordered that the Uintah Reservation be opened for allotment; in 1905, President Theodore Roosevelt ordered that all unallotted lands "shall be restored to the public domain." Myton now sits on these lands. Hagen originally pled guilty to his offense, but later withdrew the plea, claiming that because the crime occurred in "Indian country," he was not subject to the jurisdiction of the state's courts. The trial court denied his motion to withdraw the plea, but a state appellate court reversed, holding that Myton was still to be considered "Indian country." The Utah Supreme Court itself reversed, claiming that since Congress had diminished the reservation, those lands were no longer to be considered "Indian country." On certiorari, the U.S. Supreme Court, on 23 February 1994, affirmed. Holding for a 7–2 decision (justices Harry Blackmun and David Souter dissenting), Justice Sandra Day O'Connor held that since Congress has plenary power over Indians, and made clear its intention in 1903 to diminish the reservation, such lands were now not in "Indian country," and the state had jurisdiction to try Hagen.

***Halbert et al. v. United States* (283 U.S. 753, 75 L.Ed. 1389, 51 S.Ct. 615 [1931])**

Are mixed-blood Indians, of relations between Indians and whites, entitled to allotments of an Indian reservation? This was the issue at hand in this Supreme Court case, decided in 1931. Hilary Halbert, Jr., among more than a dozen plaintiffs, sued in the District Court for the Western District of Washington to be included in the lists for allotment of the Quinaielt reservation in the southwestern part of the state. Although the plaintiffs were admittedly of Indian blood, some had white fathers and Indian mothers and were members of the Chehalis, Chinook, and Cowlitz tribes. In 1855, the Quinaielt, Quillchute (also called Quileute), Chehalis, Chinook, Quits, Ozette, and Chehalis tribes, all known as the "fish-eating Indians," were neighbors in the southwestern portion of what is now Washington state. Although a potential 1855 treaty failed to unite these tribes in one reservation, in 1873 President Ulysses S. Grant signed an executive order placing all of the fish-eating Indians on one reservation. By an act of Congress of 4 March 1911 (36 Stat. 1345), Congress instructed the secretary of the interior to divide the reservation into allotments among these diverse tribes. The original bill called for a division among the "Hoh, Quileute and Ozette tribes," with no provision for the others so mentioned; the final bill, however, included an added provision for all members of the other tribes. However, when the U.S. government started to allot the lands to persons of that reservation, it excluded members of the Chehalis, Chinook, and Cowlitz tribes, asserting that their descendants were not to be considered as members of the original tribe because they were the relatives of a white man and an Indian woman. Halbert, as well as the others, sued in the district court for relief. The court gave the plaintiffs the decrees for the allotments, but the U.S. Court of Appeals for the Ninth Circuit reversed. The U.S. Supreme Court granted certiorari; Justice Willis Van Devanter held for a unanimous court on 1 June 1931 that the government must allot lands with those other members included in the allotment scheme. Justice Van Devanter wrote,

The rule is general that, in the absence of provision to the contrary, the right of individual Indians to share in tribal property, whether lands or funds, depends on tribal membership and is terminated when the membership is ended. Under the operation of this rule an Indian woman loses her tribal membership where she marries a white man, separates from the tribe and lives with him among white people. But it is the separation from the tribe rather than the marriage which puts an end to the membership. The marriage usually serves to explain the separation and illustrate that it is intentional and permanent. But where the woman remains in the tribal environment and continues the tribal affiliation the membership is not affected. If the husband be a citizen of the United States, the woman by the marriage becomes also a citizen, but there is no incompatibility between tribal membership and United States citizenship.

Hamilton, Samuel S. (1783? 1784?-1832)

The second head of the Office of Indian Affairs when that bureau was in the War Department, serving from 1830 to 1831, Samuel S. Hamilton had little discernible effect on Indian policy, and his name is more or less omitted from Indian Office histories. Accordingly, little is known of his life. He was born in Maryland about 1783 or 1784, and employed in the War Department (now the Department of Defense) sometime after the War of 1812. With the creation of the Office of Indian Affairs in 1824, he was named as one of two clerks to assist the Office head, Col. Thomas L. McKenney. A slaveholder, Hamilton spent much of his time as chief clerk compiling the correspondence of the office and a history of Indian treaties settled before 1825. In 1829, McKenney was fired from the office, and Hamilton remained a caretaker until a permanent replacement could be named. In 1830, Hamilton became that replacement. He served as head of the Indian Office from 30 September 1830 until 31 August 1831. In his lone annual report to the Congress on the concerns of the Bureau of Indian Affairs, which appeared in 1830, he called on the Congress to "redefine" the boundary of Indian country as it was determined in 1802. (Hamilton did sign the office's annual report in 1827, but, as he wrote, he did it "in the absence of Col. M'Kenney.") "A few remarks in reference to the existing laws relating to Indian affairs, with a view to some change or modification of the provisions of the same, will close this report," Hamilton wrote at the conclusion of the 1830 discourse:

The act to regulate trade and intercourse with the Indian tribes, and to preserve peace on the frontiers, passed in 1802, is the principal one that governs all our relations with the Indian tribes. Since this act was passed, many treaties have been concluded, which, with other causes, growing out of the increase of our population, and with the consequent extension of our settlements, have contributed to produce changes in our Indian relations, which, it would seem, required corresponding changes in the laws governing them. It is believed that the line defined by the act of 1802 as the Indian boundary, and to which its provisions were intended particularly to apply, has long ceased to be so. It is, therefore, respectfully submitted whether the public interest does not, also, require such a modification of the act of 1802 as would better adapt its provisions to the present state of our Indian relations. A judicious modification of this act, and others connected with it, (embracing some specific provision for the adjustment of the claims for depredations, &c., which are provided for by the 4th and 14 sections [of the 1802 act]) would, no doubt, greatly facilitate and open the way for other improvements in the administration of the affairs of the Indian Department, of which the claims for depredations just mentioned form no unimportant or inconsiderable part.

According to historian R. David Edmunds, "After August 1831, after [Secretary of War John] Eaton resigned from the War Department, the new secretary of war, Lewis Cass, replaced Hamilton with Elbert Herring, a former judge and politician from New York. Anticipating his dismissal, Hamilton...lobbied with [President Andrew] Jackson's friends, hoping to regain his former position as a clerk in the Indian office. His efforts proved unsuccessful, and he continued to be employed in the Indian bureau until 1832, when he died, unexpectedly, in his late forties."

For the act referred to in Hamilton's 1830 report, see Trade and Intercourse Act of 1802.

References Edmunds, R. David, "Samuel S. Hamilton." In Robert M. Kvasnicka and Herman J. Viola, eds., *The Commissioner of Indian Affairs, 1824–1977* (1979); U.S. Congress, Senate, *Annual Report from the Office of Indian Affairs for the Year 1827*, Senate Document No. 1, 20th Congress, 1st Session (serial 163).

Handsome Lake Movement

The Handsome Lake Movement was a nativist movement that, like the Ghost Dance, emphasized the revival of traditional Indian beliefs. It was named for the Seneca visionary Handsome Lake (1735?-1815). His half-brother was the famous Seneca chief Cornplanter (c.1735–1836), also known as Gy-ant-wa-ka. The movement began when Handsome Lake, after a lifetime of alcohol abuse, had a vision of atonement for his people. Sam D. Gill writes, "At about the same time [that the movement around the Shawnee prophet Tenskwatawa began to grow] a Seneca, Handsome Lake, whose personal history reflected the state of decay and degradation suffered by his people, arose as a prophet and founded a new religion. Handsome Lake was an alcoholic. He had a miserable existence, not fitting in a world so radically and rapidly changed because of the European-American presence. During an illness he 'died,' and during this experience he had a vision in which he was escorted to heaven, where he encountered spiritual figures of wisdom. They revealed a new road for the people to follow, which contrasted with Christianity yet incorporated and built upon both tribal traditions and elements of Christianity. With this revelation, Handsome Lake proclaimed the *gaiwiio* (good news), the basis for the establishment of the Handsome Lake religion."

References Floyd, Kay A., "Handsome Lake." In Sharon Malinowski, ed., *Notable Native Americans* (1995); Gill, Sam D., "Native American Religions." In Charles H. Lippy and Peter W. Williams, eds., *Encyclopedia of the American Religious Experience: Studies of Traditions and Movements* (1988).

***Harkness v. Hyde* (98 U.S. 476 [1879])**

In this Supreme Court case, the high court held that a summons issued by a court could not be served on a non-Indian who resided on an Indian reservation. Henry O. Harkness, a white who lived on the Shoshone Indian Reservation, was served with a summons to appear in court with the plaintiff, Jordan W. Hyde, so that Hyde could "recover damages for maliciously and without probable cause procuring the seizure and detention of property of the plaintiff under a writ of attachment." Harkness appeared in court, upon where Hyde won a judgment of $3,500 (which was later reduced to $2,500). The judgment was appealed to the Supreme Court of the Idaho Territory, and was affirmed. Harkness sued to the U.S. Supreme Court on the grounds that under an act of Congress of 3 July 1868 (Treaty with the Eastern Band of Shoshones and Bannocks, 15 Stat. 673), the territorial courts had no jurisdiction over peoples residing on Indian reservations, and as such the summons was illegally served. The case was argued before the court on 8 April 1879, and decided on 21 April of that same year. Justice Stephen Johnson Field delivered the unanimous opinion of the court; he held that "the territory reserved...was as much beyond the jurisdiction, legislative or judicial, of the Government of Idaho, as if it had been set apart within the limits of another country or of a foreign State." He struck down the service of the summons, declaring that "there can be no jurisdiction in a court of a Territory to render a personal judgment against anyone upon service made outside its limits." The doctrine enunciated in *Harkness* was overruled the following year in the case of *Langford v. Monteith*.

See also *Langford v. Montieth; Utah & Northern Railway Company v. Fisher*.

Reference Strickland, Rennard, ed., *Felix Cohen's Handbook of Federal Indian Law* (1982).

Harris, Carey Allen (1806–1842)

The second commissioner of the Bureau of Indian Affairs, Carey Allen Harris served at the height of the Removal period from 1836 until 1838. Much of his life is surrounded in mystery; he was born in Williamson County, Tennessee, on 23 September 1806, but orphaned at an early age. His early careers included journalism (he worked with his future father-in-law on the *Nashville Republican)* and law, the latter after obtaining a license in 1827. His name became known to Andrew Jackson, and when Jackson became president, Harris was named a clerk in the War Department. Historian Ronald N. Satz adds that after Harris was promoted to chief clerk, Secretary of War Lewis Cass "frequently left him in charge as acting secretary of war when he was away from Washington."

On 4 July 1836, Jackson appointed Harris as commissioner of Indian Affairs to replace Elbert Herring. Harris subsequently authored two annual reports of the Indian Affairs office: 1836 and 1837. In his latter discourse, he wrote of the obligations that the Indian office had to the entire structure of Indian affairs in the nation. "The increased extent and diversified character of the operations under the direction of this office will prevent my presenting any thing more than a mere outline," he explained.

They embrace negotiations with the tribes east of the Mississippi, for the extinguishment of their titles; with those of the western prairie, for the establishment of friendly relations between them and the United States; and with the indigenous and emigrated tribes beyond the Mississippi and Missouri rivers, for the adjustment of difficulties and the preservation of peace. They include the removal of the Indians in New York, Ohio, Indians, Illinois, Michigan, and Wisconsin, in the north, the west, and the northwest; and in Georgia, North Carolina, Tennessee, Alabama, Mississippi and Florida, in the south and southwest, to new homes southwest of the Missouri river. They comprehend the location and sale of reservations, the investment or payment of the proceeds, and of the proceeds of the lands ceded, with the collection and disbursement of the interest thereon. They involve a supervision of the execution of treaty stipulations, for the subsistence of emigrants, the examination and payments of debts and claims, the education of the young, the supply of agricultural implements and assistance, the employment of interpreters, farmers, mechanics, and laborers. They demand a constant attention to the conduct of numerous agents and officers necessarily employed; commissioners to hold treaties, or to investigate claims; superintendents of emigration, and of the four divisions of the department; agents and subagents. They call for an exact adherence to the laws, and for the adoption, from time to time, of the regulations requisite to give them full effect. They involve the superintendence of the investment of nearly $2,000,000, the annual disbursement of appropriations not less, in the last three years, than $5,000,000, and the disposition of interest to the amount of about $200,000. And they affect the welfare of a population estimated at 330,000, scattered over an immense extent of country.

Harris was a significant factor in the implementation of Jackson's removal policy, and the president's successor, Martin Van Buren, saw Harris's work as so important that he was retained in the new administration when it took office in March 1837. Yet Harris was also rumored to be involved in Indian land frauds, and investigations into the matter led to Harris's embarrassing resignation on 19 October 1838. He moved to Little Rock, Arkansas, and served as president of a local bank. He then returned to Franklin, Tennessee, where sometime in that year he contracted tuberculosis, then called consumption. He died in Franklin on 17 June 1842, aged 35. In his obituary in the *Arkansas Gazette*, 6 July 1842, the paper wrote, "He died surrounded by his friends, and his death will be deeply regretted by all who had the pleasure of knowing him intimately and well."

See also Bureau of Indian Affairs.

References *Arkansas Gazette* (Little Rock), 6 July 1842, 3; Satz, Ronald N., "Carey Allen Harris." In Robert M. Kvasnicka and Herman J. Viola, eds., *The Commissioners of Indian Affairs, 1824–1977* (1979); U.S. Congress, Senate, *Annual Report of the Commissioner of Indian Affairs for the Year 1837*, Senate Document No. 1, 25th Congress, 2d Session (serial 314).

Harrison et al. v. Laveen (67 Arizona 337, 196 Pacific Reporter 2d 456 [1948])

Harrison is widely regarded as the most important case in the establishment of voting rights for Native Americans. When Frank Harrison and Harry Austin, members of the Mohave-Apache tribe of Arizona's Fort McDowell Reservation, sought to register to vote in elections in Maricopa County (which encompasses Phoenix), Roger G. Laveen, the county recorder for Maricopa, refused to allow them to so register. The plaintiffs then brought suit in the superior court of Maricopa County seeking a writ of mandamus and alleging that they "possessed all the qualifications for suffrage as set forth in the constitution and laws of the state of Arizona, and asserted that if they were denied the right to register and vote they would be deprived of the franchises, immunities, rights and privileges which are guaranteed to them under the constitution and laws of both the United States and the State of Arizona." Laveen asked for a dismissal of the case, and the court acquiesced to his request. Harrison and Austin then appealed to the Arizona Supreme Court. On 15 July 1948, Justice Levi S. Udall wrote that the right of Indians to vote in state and federal elections has "again risen, like Banquo's ghost, to challenge us." He then decided for the plaintiffs (he was joined by Chief Justice R.C. Stanford and Justice Arthur T. La Prade), holding that their civil rights, as guaranteed under state and federal law, were being violated when they were denied access to the ballot. He wrote,

> It is axiomatic that if a person is under guardianship he must have a guardian. If an Indian, living on a reservation, is under guardianship the United States presumably must be his guardian. Yet in the instant case the United States is appearing specially in this litigation as *amicus curiae* [friend of the court] to disclaim any intention to treat the plaintiffs as "persons under guardianship." Certainly the state courts cannot make the United States a guardian against its will. Nor do we believe that the "guardianship" referred to in the Arizona constitution, section 2, article 7, was of the type that could be dissolved by merely stepping across an imaginary line—the boundary of an Indian reservation. Furthermore, to ascribe to all Indians residing on reservations the quality of being "incapable of handling their own affairs in an ordinary manner" would be a grave injustice, for amongst them are educated persons as fully capable of handling their own affairs as their white neighbors. This leads us to the conclusion that the framers of the constitution had in mind situations where disabilities are established on an individual rather than a tribal basis.... The trial court erred (though understandably so) in granting defendant's motion to dismiss the plaintiffs' complaint and in entering judgment for defendant. The judgment is reversed and the cause remanded for further proceeding not inconsistent with this opinion.

Hastings, William Wirt (Cherokee) (1866–1938)

Lawyer and politician, William Wirt Hastings represented Oklahoma in the U.S. House of Representatives from 1915 to 1921 and again from 1923 to 1935. In his nine terms, he was a leader in the struggle for Indian rights. Born on Beattie's Prairie, in the Delaware District of the Cherokee Nation, on 31 December 1866, he was the second son and one of three children of

Archibald Yell Hastings, a rural farmer, and Louisa (née Stover) Hastings. According to biographer Angie Debo, "His father Yell Hastings, a native of Arkansas from a Tennessee family of English origin, had served in a Cherokee regiment on the Confederate side in the Civil War. His mother, Louis (Stover) Hastings, was one-sixteenth Cherokee by blood, a descendant of the tribally prominent Ward family." William Hastings attended tribal schools before entering the Cherokee National Male Seminary in Tahlequah, the Cherokee capital; after receiving his Bachelor of Science degree in 1884, he taught in a tribal Baptist school. In 1889, he received his law degree from Vanderbilt University, and with the degree in hand opened a law practice in Tahlequah.

In the decade of the 1890s, Hastings served in several positions for the Cherokee nation, including tribal superintendent of education (1890–91), Cherokee Nation Attorney General (1891–95), and he represented Cherokee interests for a time in Washington, D.C. When Congress abolished Cherokee tribal courts in 1898 under the Curtis Act, Hastings represented Cherokee criminal and civil claims before local and federal courts. In 1905, when the western half of Oklahoma was opened to white settlement and established as a territory, Hastings served as chairman of the Tahlequah Convention, a meeting of Indians of the Five Civilized Nations who were determined to form the independent state of Sequoyah; Hastings himself helped to draw up the new state's constitution. Congress' refusal to accept the code left the Indians forced to assimilate into the white expansion of Oklahoma.

After this experience, Hastings decided to enter national politics, and served as a delegate to the Democratic National Convention in Baltimore in 1912 which nominated Woodrow Wilson for president. In 1914, Hastings ran for Congress and was elected, and, except for a two year period (1921–23), served until his retirement in 1935. In 1920, he was defeated by Alice Mary Robertson, graddaughter of missionary Samuel A. Worcester, but he won the seat back two years later. In his nine terms, he served ably as a member of the House Indian Affairs Committee, and worked to build hospitals and schools for the Indian people. Considered the most important Indian rights politician to serve in the House, he was responsible for most of the legislation dealing with Native Americans in this period. After his retirement, he returned to Tahlequah to continue his law practice and work in land investments. Hastings died in Muskegee, Oklahoma, on 8 April 1938, of a ruptured gall bladder. He was 71 years old.

See also Robertson, Alice Mary.

References Cravens, Dollye Hefner, *Standard Bearer of the Cherokees: The Life of William Wirt Hastings* (Master's thesis, Oklahoma Agricultural and Mechanical College, 1942); Debo, Angie, "Hastings, William Wirt." In Dumas Malone et al., eds., *Dictionary of American Biography* (1930–88).

Hayt, Ezra Ayres (1823–1902)

The twentieth commissioner of Indian Affairs, Ezra A. Hayt resigned in disgrace over corruption in the Indian Office. He was born on 25 February 1823 in Patterson, Putnam County, New York, and at age 21 entered the dry goods business in New York City. He made such a good living at this enterprise that he retired in 1868 at the age of 45. He then served for a time as president of the International Trust Company of Jersey City, New Jersey. He was also a member of the Board of Foreign Missions of the Reformed Church. In 1874, the church recommended Hayt for a seat on the U.S. Board of Indian Commissioners, a philanthropic watchdog group which oversaw the business of the Bureau of Indian Affairs. On 15 August 1874 Hayt was appointed to the board by President Ulysses S. Grant. He served for two and half years, and it was only at the end that he became embroiled in scandal. Positioned to inspect supplies that the government sent to the Indians, Hayt got into a fight with Commissioner of Indian Affairs John Quincy Smith, and for some statements that he was asserted to have made, his resignation was demanded by President Grant, which was fulfilled on 12 January 1877. Hayt was still involved in national Indian affairs. With the election of Rutherford B. Hayes in 1876, newly installed Secretary of the Interior Carl Schurz turned first to Indian Rights Association president Herbert Welsh to head the BIA, then to Hayt when Welsh refused the honor. The *New York Times* reported that Hayt "was confirmed without much opposition."

Hayt produced three annual reports as commissioner: 1877, 1878, and 1879. In the 1878 essay, Hayt examined the consequences of the removal policy toward the Indians. "The question of greatest importance to the present and future welfare of the Indians is that of a uniform and perfect title to their lands," he inscribed. "The constant removals incident to the former land policy of the Indian service has been freighted [burdened] with evil consequences to the Indians. Even when placed upon reservations they have come to consider, notwithstanding the most solemn guarantees from the United States that the same should be kept sacred and remain theirs forever, that the title to their land is without permanency, and that they are subject to be removed whenever the pressure of white settlers upon them may create a demand for their lands either before Congress or the [Interior] department. So fixed has this opinion become among the more civilized tribes, that in the main they decline to make any improvements upon their lands, even after an allotment in severalty has been made, until they have received their patents for the same." In a letter to Secretary of the Interior Schurz, Hayt supported a program of allotting the Indians land in severalty; he wrote, "In the last annual report of this office [for 1878] a brief reference was made to the importance of giving the various Indian tribes of the United States a several, uniform, perfect, and indefeasible title to the lands occupied by them. The insecurity attaching to their settlement upon the various portions of the public domain assigned for their use has, year by year, become more observable, until it appears that all former methods are entirely inadequate to protect the Indians against the encroachments of the whites upon their reservations, or from the acts of the government itself, whenever an active demand is made that the treaty stipulations under which the Indians hold their lands should be abrogated to open the way for white settlements or the active contentions which often arise for the possession of the mineral or timber interests which may exist on their reservations."

Quite possibly from the beginning of his administration, Hayt was involved in shady transactions, dealings that ultimately led to his downfall. He was forced to refute charges which appeared in the St. Paul *Pioneer Press* on 31 October 1878 in a long letter to Secretary of the Interior Carl Schurz entitled "Commissioner of Indian Affairs makes report, refuting charges published in the Pioneer Press of St. Paul, Minn., relative to fraud in the letting of Beef contracts." The *New York Times* began a long investigation which exposed fraud and nepotism by Hayt (he had hired his son to be an Indian agent). Further, mismanagement in the Ute crisis was Hayt's undoing. The White River Utes of Colorado rioted and murdered Indian agent Nathan C. Meeker; subsequent investigations showed that the Indians had not gotten their government annuity and food for some time. When Hayt remarked in congressional testimony that he thought all of the Utes should be moved to Indian territory, he was finished. After General Clinton B. Fisk of the Board of Indian Commissioners sought to have a hearing on his performance, Secretary Schurz asked for his resignation on 20 January 1880 on the grounds that Hayt had refused to supply to the secretary information about affairs at the San Carlos agency in Arizona. The *New York Times* editorialized: "The removal of Mr. Hayt, late Commissioner of Indian Affairs, has not come one day too soon. It is now two weeks since the *Times* was moved, by many aggravating circumstances, to call attention to the fact that the so-called investigation of Mr. Hayt was not intrusted to impartial hands. The Board of Indian Commissioners was not wholly unfriendly to the Commissioner, who stood accused of various irregularities which had resulted in detriment to the service by the provoking of wars and disturbances [by the Indians]. And as was pointed out in these columns, it was not to be expected that the charges preferred by Gen. C. B. Fisk, (the only member of the board who could not consent to be a merely ornamental officer,) should be impartially investigated by an organization more or less compromised by Hayt's mismanagement."

After his resignation, Hayt returned to his hometown of Patterson, where a series of business failures left him destitute. He died quietly there on 12 January 1902, at the age of 79.

See also Bureau of Indian Affairs.

References "Commissioner Hayt's Case." *New York Times*, 14 January 1880, 1; "Died: Hayt, Ezra A." *New York Times*, 14 January 1902, 9; "Executive Session of the Senate." *New York Times*, 14 December 1877, 1; Hayt to Carl Schurz, 24 January 1879, in U.S. Congress, House of Representatives, *Lands to Indians in Severalty*, House Report No. 165, 45th Congress, 3d Session (serial 1866), 1879, 2; Hayt to Secretary of the Interior Carl Schurz, "Commissioner of Indian Affairs Hayt makes report, refuting charges published in the Pioneer Press of St. Paul, Minn., relative to fraud in the letting of Beef contracts," 8 November 1878, Ezra A. Hayt Appointment File, Box 44, Records of the Appointments Division, Commissioner of Indian Affairs, RG 48, National Archives; "Hayt's Alleged Frauds: A Thorough Investigation Promised." *New York Times*, 15 January 1880, 2; Kvasnicka, Robert M. and Herman J. Viola, eds., *The Commissioner of Indian Affairs, 1824–1977* (1979); "National Capital News: Removal of Indian Commissioner Hayt." *New York Times*, 30 January 1880, 1; "Reform in the Indian Bureau." *New York Times*, 30 January 1880, 4; "The San Carlos Agency and Commissioner Hayt's Connection Therewith." *New York Times*, 6 February 1880, 3; U.S. Congress, House of Representatives, *Annual Report of the Commissioner of Indian Affairs for the Year 1878*, House Executive Document No. 1, 45th Congress, 3d Session (serial 1850); U.S. Congress, House of Representatives, *Testimony in Relation to the Ute Indian Outbreak Taken by the Committee on Indian Affairs in the House of Representatives*, House Miscellaneous Document No. 38, 46th Congress, 2d Session (serial 1931).

Heckman v. United States (224 U.S. 413 [1912])

This Supreme Court case dealt with the issue of whether the Congress could extend the period of inalienability (alienability is the right to sell or lease) of Indian allotments; the court had found that such a right existed in *Tiger v. Western Investment Company* (1911). Under the act of 1 July 1902, the Congress allotted lands to the Cherokee Nation with a specified period which outlawed the alienation, or sale, of the allotted lands. By the act of 26 April 1906, the Congress extended the period of inalienability. In *Tiger*, the court held that the subsequent act of 1906, which extended the period of inalienability, covered allotment restrictions which had expired before the enactment of the later act. In *Heckman*, the court was asked to decide whether the United States could sue in federal court to uphold the extension of those restrictions. P. E. Heckman and Robert L. Owen were full-blooded Indians of the Cherokee Nation, and decided to sell their allotment after the initial five-year restriction on alienation lapsed. When Congress extended the period of alienation, the United States sued the two men to reject the sale of their allotments. The Circuit Court of the Eastern District of Oklahoma dismissed the suit of the United States, but the Eighth Circuit Court of Appeals reversed, causing Heckman and Owen to seek relief from the U.S. Supreme Court. Arguments were held on 12 and 13 October 1911, and the case was decided on 1 April 1912. Justice Charles Evans Hughes spoke for the 8–1 judgment of the court (Justice Horace Harmon Lurton dissented on the grounds of jurisdiction) in holding that Congress had the right to enact new restrictions on alienation, and the United States had the right to seek the sustainment of those restrictions in federal court. Hughes explained simply, "Our conclusion is that the suit was well brought."

For the earlier case involving Congress' power to extend the period of the alienation of Indian lands, see *Tiger v. Western Investment Company*.

Herring, Elbert (1777–1876)

Known more for his judicial activities than his tenure as the third and final head of the Office of Indian Affairs and first official commissioner of Indian Affairs, Elbert Herring served from August 1831 until July 1836. Little is known of his life. He was born, according to his biographer, Ronald N. Satz, "in Stratford, Connecticut, on 8 July 1777. After graduating from Princeton College in 1795, he became a prominent New York lawyer. During the 1800s, he held several appointive positions in New York and enjoyed the support of his politically influential, close personal friend, DeWitt Clinton." The only known obituary column on Herring appeared in the *New York Times* on 22 February 1876. In it, the paper covered a court hearing held in tribute to Herring on the announcement of his death. A Judge Curtis said of the deceased judge and commissioner, "His father, being a Whig in this city, at the outbreak of the [American] Revolution, the year [Manhattan] island was occupied by the British forces, was compelled to pass through the American lines, and in consequence of that enforced removal of his parents, Mr. Elbert Herring was born in the state of Connecticut. Early in life he graduated at Princeton College, in the first year of the century, when Gen. [Alexander] Hamilton was a leader at the Bar...All our histories of to-day are insignificant compared with the recollections of this gentleman, whose experience as a barrister extended back seventy-six years...I need say nothing in regard to the political career of Mr. Herring, marked as it was by his energy and consistency as a politician. Nor need I speak of the favor and approval with which Gen. [Andrew] Jackson looked upon him in his last years at the Bar, and who was pleased to have him at Washington at the head of one of the most important bureaus of the Federal Government."

On 12 August 1831, with the firing of Samuel S. Hamilton, head of the Indian Office in the War Department, President Jackson named Herring to replace him. Herring ultimately contributed five annual reports (1831–35) as commissioner, and it was at this time that the U.S. government instituted its policy of removal. In his 1831 report, Herring called removal "th[is] Humane Policy." "Exemplified in the system adopted by the Government with respect to the Indian tribes residing within the limits of the United States, which is now in operation, is progressively developing its good effects; and, it is confidently trusted, will at no distant day, be crowned with complete success," he penned. In his 1832 report, Herring wrote on Indian educational opportunities instituted by the government. "The contributions of the Government to the establishment and maintenance of Indian schools, grounded, as they are, on the most human considerations, cannot fail to be followed by beneficial results," he justified. And in his final report, for the year 1835, Herring gave support to the removal policy by explaining, "Major J. Brookes has succeeded in concluding a treaty with the Caddo Indians, by which they cede their land in Louisiana to the United States, and agree to remove, at their own expense, beyond our territorial limits, never to return. This alternative may possibly save the small remains of the tribe from total extinction—a fate that seemed to be impending on a continued residence in their present location, surrounded by a population that operates on the children of the forest like miasma [poison] on constitutions unused to its baneful influence."

Refused the chance to be renamed to the office, Herring left on 2 July 1836. He served for a brief time as a paymaster for the War Department before returning to New York; although he was called "Judge Herring," there is no evidence that he sat as a magistrate. He died on 20 February 1876, five months shy of his ninety-ninth birthday.

See also Bureau of Indian Affairs; Removal Policy.

References "Law Reports: Tributes to Dead Judges." *New York Times*, 22 February 1876, 2; Satz, Ronald N., "Elbert Herring." In Robert M. Kvasnicka and Herman J. Viola, eds., *The Commissioner of Indian Affairs, 1824–1977* (1979); U.S. Congress, House of Representatives, *Annual Report of the Commissioner of Indian Affairs for the Year 1831*, House Executive Document No. 2, 22d Congress, 1st Session (serial 216); U.S. Congress, House of Representatives, *Annual Report of the Commissioner of Indian Affairs for the Year 1832*, House Executive Document No. 2, 22d Congress, 2d Session (serial 233); U.S. Congress, House of Representatives,

Annual Report of the Commissioner of Indian Affairs for the Year 1835, House Executive Document No. 2, 24th Congress, 1st Session (serial 286).

Holden v. Joy (17 Wallace [84 U.S.] 211, 21 L Ed 525 [1873])

This Supreme Court decision, which included the case of *William H. Warner v. James F. Joy*, held that Indian tribes are considered states, but not foreign states, and not states of the United States as considered by the U.S. Constitution. Further, treaties with the Cherokees that extinguished title to Indian lands were valid, and that such lands were considered public lands under the meaning of the law, and as a result, settlers had a preemptive right to settle on the land. James F. Joy settled on three hundred acres of former Cherokee land in Kansas years after it was ceded by the Indian tribe to the United States. Appellants Peter F. Holden and William H. Warner claimed that the Cherokees had abandoned the land, and thus they had the right, derived from a railroad's former claim to it, to evict Joy and settle on the tract themselves. In separate actions, they sued Joy to have his title extinguished. The Circuit Court of the United States for the District of Kansas held for Joy in both cases, and the Supreme Court granted certiorari (the right to hear both cases) to the appellants. Arguments were heard on 16 and 17 April 1872, and decisions were handed down on 18 November of that same year. Justice Nathan Clifford delivered the opinion of the court in holding for Joy in both cases. Clifford determined that the Cherokee treaty of 29 December 1835 was valid, and the lands were therefore considered the public lands of the United States. In reaching this decision, Clifford held that Indian tribes had the power of states, and were thus able to confer their lands to the United States as separate entities.

Hoover Commission Report

This report, issued under the official title of the Commission on Organization of the Executive Branch of the Government, was released in October 1948 under the auspices of its chairman, former President Herbert Hoover, and is more commonly referred to as the Hoover Commission Report. Convened to look into improving the administration of executive branch offices, the commission comprised a committee on Indian affairs, which studied the BIA and made recommendations; members of the committee included former Commissioner Charles J. Rhoads and educator John R. Nichols, the man who at the time would be the next commissioner. George A. Graham was the committee chairman, and Gilbert Darlington served as the fourth member.

In the introduction, the committee announced, "Indians are people. Indians are citizens. Indians are wage earners and salaried employees. Indians are ranchers, farmers, and businessmen. Indians are property owners. Such obvious facts are so often overlooked that it is desirable to begin any discussion of Indian affairs by calling them to mind. In most parts of the country, nearly everywhere except the Southwest and Alaska, the 'Indian' of popular imagination has all but vanished. The Indian lives much as other men in his region do and makes his living in the same ways. He is of mixed bloods—as are other Americans. He dresses, speaks, looks, and acts very much like his neighbors. He has the same problems, plus others of his own that are the product of his past and of present circumstances. There is in every tribe, however, a group of 'full bloods' who continue some of the tribal customs, speak the tribal language, and perhaps wear some articles of Indian dress, frequently moccasins. Outside of the Southwest and Alaska they are usually a minority varying in size from tribe to tribe, but probably less than twenty-five percent in many. Although referred to as 'full bloods,' many so-called have some Indian blood, and some men of exclusively Indian blood are not thought of as being in the 'full blood' group."

One section of the report dealt with how the government was dealing with Indian affairs in the wake of the groundbreaking Meriam Report of 1928 and the nearly 20 years since the passage of the Wheeler-Howard Act, known more commonly as the Indian Reorganization Act of 1934. Regarding these two important documents, the Hoover Commission report stated, "In the years immediately following the Meriam Report there was marked progress in professionalizing the Indian Service through better personnel, improved methods, and higher professional standards. Indian education was modernized and a stronger and better coordinated economic program got underway. In the 1930s these activities were carried forward vigorously. The Indian Reorganization Act (IRA) has given further impetus to the economic program by authorizing enlargement of Indian lands, extending the lending function, and establishing a policy of scientific range and forest management."

In its section on recommendations, the committee opined, "The thing that has been most lacking and most needed is Indian motivation. For 150 years policies have been imposed by the government. The[se] policies have been Indian policies, not Indians' policies. If Indian tribes resisted, they could win battles, but they always lost the wars. If they retreated and withdrew to the west, they were always overtaken by the tide of westward migration. If they accepted the inevitable, negotiated a treaty, and reached a definitive agreement, nothing was really settled; there were always revisions. Not merely the acreage but the conditions of life were altered; after a century of unbroken recognition of tribal character and cultural autonomy, the doctrine of 'dependent nations' was swept aside, tribal organization was destroyed, and Indian culture was attacked on a wide front. For a people with the philosophical tendencies of the Indians, the experience was profoundly distressing—and debilitating."

See also Nichols, John Ralph.

References Graham, George et al., *Report of the Committee on Indian Affairs to the Commission on Organization of the Executive Branch of the Government.*

Hopkins, Sarah Winnemucca

See Winnemucca, Sarah.

House Concurrent Resolution 108

This nonstatutory expression of congressional intent on Indian affairs was adopted by a unanimous vote on 1 August 1953, paving the way for the era of termination of government supervision over Indian affairs. Indian historian Francis Paul Prucha writes, "In the Eighty-third Congress a fundamental change was made in Indian policy. House Concurrent Resolution 108 declared it to be the policy of the United States to abolish federal supervision over the tribes as soon as possible and to subject the Indians to the same laws, privileges, and responsibilities as other citizens of the United States." Introduced in the House by Wyoming Representative William Harrison and in the Senate by Senator Henry Jackson of Washington State, the resolution reads:

Whereas it is the policy of Congress, as rapidly as possible, to make the Indians within the territorial limits of the United States subject to the same laws and entitled to the same privileges and responsibilities as are applicable to other citizens of the United States, to end their status as wards of the United States, and to grant them all of the rights and prerogatives pertaining to American citizenship; and

Whereas the Indians within the territorial limits of the United States should assume their full responsibilities as American citizens: Now, therefore, be it

Resolved by the House of Representatives (the Senate concurring),

That it is declared to be the sense of Congress that, at the earliest possible time, all of the Indian tribes and the individual members thereof located within the States of California, Florida, New York, and Texas, and all of the following named Indian tribes and individual members thereof, should be freed from Federal supervision and control and from all disabilities and limitations specially applicable to Indians: The Flathead Tribe of Montana, the Klamath Tribe of Oregon, the Menominee Tribe of Wisconsin, the Potowatamie Tribe of Kansas and Nebraska, and those members of Chippewa Tribe who are on the Turtle Mountain Reservation, North Dakota. It is further declared to be the sense of Congress that, upon the release of such tribes and individual members thereof from such disabilities and limitations, all offices of the Bureau of Indian Affairs in the States of California, Florida, New York, and Texas and all other offices of the Bureau of Indian Affairs whose primary purpose was to serve any Indian tribe or individual freed from Federal supervision should be abolished. It is further declared to be the sense of Congress that the Secretary of the Interior should examine all existing legislation dealing with such Indians, and treaties between the Government of the United States and each such tribe, and report to Congress at the earliest practicable date, but not later than January 1, 1954, his recommendations for such legislation as, in his judgment, may be necessary to accomplish the purposes of this resolution.

See also Public Law 280; Termination Policy; Watkins, Arthur Vivian.

Reference Prucha, Francis Paul, ed., *Documents of United States Indian Policy* (1990).

Hunting and Fishing Rights Cases, Indian, U.S. Supreme Court

See *Antoine et ux. v. Washington; Central Machinery Company v. Arizona Tax Commission; Menominee Tribe of Indians v. United States; Merrian v. Jicarilla Apache Tribe; Metlakatla Indian Community, Annette Islands Reserve v. Egan; Montana v. United States; New Mexico v. Mescalero Apache Tribe; Puyallup v. Department of Game of Washington, et al.; United States v. Winans; Washington v. Confederated Tribes of Colville Indian Reservation; White Mountain Apache Tribe et al. v. Bracker et al.*

I

Ickes, Anna Wilmarth Thompson (1873–1935)

Anna Ickes was the first wife of Secretary of the Interior Harold L. Ickes and a lifelong advocate of Native Americans and their culture. The youngest of three daughters of Henry Martin Wilmarth, a wealthy manufacturer and businessman, and Mary Jane (née Hawes) Wilmarth, a suffragist and a reformer in her own right, she was born in Chicago on 27 January 1873. After Henry Wilmarth's death in 1885, Jane Wilmarth helped to organize and served as the first president of the Woman's City Club of Chicago, while assisting in the activities of the Illinois branch of the Consumer's League. A friend of reformer Jane Addams, who later founded the noted Hull House, Mrs. Wilmarth was an active supporter of the settlement movement. Anna Wilmarth was educated in private schools, and spent a year in Paris. In 1893 she enrolled in the University of Chicago and just four years later married a professor, James Westfall Thompson, but their marriage ended in divorce in 1911. She then married a young Chicago attorney, Harold LeClaire Ickes, who was the legislative counsel for the Women's Trade Union League, of which Anna's mother was a member. Both progressive Republicans, they bolted with more liberal elements of their party when Theodore Roosevelt formed the Progressive ("Bull Moose") Party in 1912, and remained in that party even after its demise in 1916 (in 1920, both of the Ickes campaigned for Democrat James M. Cox for president).

In 1924, Illinois Governor Len Small named Anna Ickes as a trustee of the University of Illinois. Four years later, she ran for a seat in the state legislature (her husband served as her campaign manager) and was elected, ultimately serving until 1934. Still the independent, she was interested in civic affairs and reform measures. In 1932, her husband, by now an influential attorney, broke from the Republican party that they had returned to and backed Democrat Franklin D. Roosevelt for president. Anna Ickes continued to serve in the state legislature as a Republican, but her husband's support of FDR (and subsequent appointment as secretary of the interior) led her to forgo a reelection run in 1934. Biographer J. Leonard Bates wrote, "She now devoted herself to her longstanding avocation: the culture, archaeology, and welfare of the American Indian. She had earlier served on the board of the Indian Rights Association of Chicago, and her acquiescence in her husband's support of Roosevelt in 1932 had apparently been influenced by her hope that he might be appointed commissioner of Indian Affairs." The *New York Times*, on her passing, noted, "Her interests were no more limited to politics than her husband's. Indian archaeology was her particular hobby, and she gave it much time. For ten years prior to 1933 she went annually to a desert station near Gallup, New Mexico, and made her research headquarters in an adobe dwelling." In 1933, her book, *Mesa Land*, an examination of the Navajo and Hopi cultures, appeared.

Anna Ickes was in New Mexico studying the Taos pueblo on 31 August 1935, when the car in which she and three friends, including Genevieve Forbes Harrick, a prominent Chicago journalist, were riding was sideswiped by a hit-and-run automobile, forcing it into a ditch. Mrs. Ickes was killed instantly. She was buried in Memorial Park Cemetery in Evanston, Illinois.

References Bates, J. Leonard, "Ickes, Anna Wilmarth Thompson." In Edward T. James, ed., *Notable American Women, 1607–1950: A Biographical Dictionary* (1971); "Mrs. Harold Ickes Dies as Auto Is Forced off New Mexico Highway," *Washington Post*, 1 September 1935, 1, 3; "Mrs. Ickes Dies in Crash of Auto Near Santa Fe," *New York Times*, 1 September 1935, 1, 19.

In re Heff (197 U.S. 488, 49 L. Ed. 848, 25 S. Ct. 506 [1905])

Officially titled *In the Matter of the Application of Albert Heff, for a Writ of Habeas Corpus*, this Supreme Court case dealt with whether a person was allowed to sell an intoxicating liquor to an Indian who, having received his allotment under the General Allotment Act

(act of Congress of 8 February 1887, 24 Stat. 388), was considered to be "a citizen of the United States," and thus not subject to the laws governing Indians. Albert Heff was convicted in the District Court of the District of Kansas for selling two quarts of beer to one John Butler, a Kickapoo Indian who had received his allotment, under the act of Congress of 30 January 1897 (29 Stat. 506), which prohibited the sale of intoxicating liquors to Indians. Heff was sentenced to four months in prison, fined $200, and forced to repay the cost of his prosecution. On appeal, the Court of Appeals for the Eighth Circuit upheld the conviction, and Heff appealed to the U.S. Supreme Court.

The Supreme Court heard arguments in the case on 9 and 10 January 1905, and handed down a decision on 10 April of the same year. In speaking for the court's 8–1 decision (Justice John Marshall Harlan dissented), Justice David Josiah Brewer held that since Butler had received his allotment, he was a U.S. citizen, and Heff was not guilty of violating laws that outlawed selling intoxicating liquors to Indians. "We are of the opinion that, when the United States grants the privileges of citizenship to an Indian, gives him the benefit of, and requires him to be subject to, the laws, both civil and criminal, of the state, it places him outside the reach of police regulations on the part of Congress; that the emancipation from Federal control, thus created, cannot be set aside at the instance of the government without the consent of the individual Indian and the state, and that this emancipation from Federal control is not affected by the fact that the lands it has granted to the Indian are granted subject to a condition against alienation and encumbrance, or the further fact that it guarantees to him an interest in tribal or other property. The district court of Kansas did not have jurisdiction of the offense charged, and therefore the petitioner is entitled to his discharge from imprisonment." Justice Harlan did not publish his dissent. The case was overruled in 1916 in *United States v. Nice*, which held that even though Indians were apportioned allotments, they were still "wards of the nation," and as such the act of 20 January 1897 was valid.

Indian Alcohol and Substance Abuse Prevention and Treatment Act of 1986 (100 Stat. 3207–148)

This federal action of 27 October 1986 was passed as Title IV, part C of the Anti-Drug Abuse Act of 1986. Now codified at 25 U.S.C. 2433, it authorized the Indian Health Service to assume responsibility for "the determination of the scope of the problem of alcohol and substance abuse among Indian people, including the number of Indians within the jurisdiction of the Indian Health Service who are directly or indirectly affected by alcohol and substance abuse and the financial and human cost, an assessment of the existing and needed resources necessary for the prevention of alcohol and substance abuse and the treatment of Indians affected by alcohol and substance abuse, and an estimate of the funding necessary to adequately support a program of prevention of alcohol and substance abuse and treatment of Indians affected by alcohol and substance abuse." The legislation established the Indian Health Service Youth Program "for acute detoxification and treatment for Indian youth who are alcohol and substance abusers," a program of community education, training and involvement to solve the problem of alcohol and substance abuse, and the formation of a Navajo Alcohol Rehabilitation Demonstration Program for the Navajo Indians of Gallup, New Mexico. This action was amended by the Indian Alcohol and Substance Abuse Prevention and Treatment Act Amendment of 1990 (104 Stat. 137), which authorized the purchase of land for emergency shelters.

Indian Appropriations Act of 1871 (16 Stat. 544)

Better known as the End of Treaty Making Act, or the Termination of Treaty Making Process Act, an amendment to this federal legislation of 3 March 1871 ended the U.S.

government's policy of making treaties with the Indian tribes and treating them as separate nations. After this time, all agreements with the tribes were made into statutory law. The pertinent amendment reads:

An Act Making Appropriations for the Current and Contingent Expenses of the Indian Department, And for Fulfilling Treaty Stipulations With Various Indian Tribes, for the Year Eighteen Hundred and Seventy-Two, and for Other Purposes.

For insurance and transportation of goods to the Yanktons, one thousand five hundred dollars: Provided, That hereafter no Indian nation or tribe within the territory of the United States shall be acknowledged or recognized as an independent nation, tribe, or power with whom the United States may contract by treaty.

Reference *U.S. Statutes at Law*, vol. 16 (1871).

Indian Arts and Crafts Board Act (49 Stat. 891)

Supported by Commissioner of Indian Affairs John Collier, and established by the act of Congress of 27 August 1935, the Indian Arts and Crafts Board was enacted "to promote the development of Indian arts and crafts and to create a board to assist therein."

Historian Robert Fay Schrader writes, "In the second half of the nineteenth century, U.S. government interest in American arts and crafts emerged, following and reflecting a surging public interest in age-old crafts. This sweeping popular force was itself the product of an increasing national intellectual concern over the effects of industrialization on the quality of everyday life. As a result, the commissioners of Indian affairs, through their superintendents in the field, began as early as 1863 to praise the Indians' ingenious craft skills. As the years passed, however, the Indian Office came to emphasize the development of Indian crafts into manufacturing industries. Contrary to the popular emphasis on arts and crafts as an antidote to the effects of industrialization, the motivation behind the federal government's early role in Indian arts and crafts was a desire to industrialize the Indians." He adds, "At the eighth annual meeting of the Lake Mohonk Conference of the Friends of the Indian in 1890, a member of the Board of Indian Commissioners, Philip C. Garrett of Philadelphia, called the members' attention to the basis of certain industries, already in operation among the Indians, afforded to educate the Indians and improved their lives."

The 1935 act was the culmination of this push toward government recognition of the arts and crafts ability of the Native Americans. Section 2 of the act outlines the purpose and the functions of the Arts and Crafts Board:

Sec. 2. It shall be the function and the duty of the Board to promote the economic welfare of the Indian tribes and the Indian wards of the Government through the development of Indian arts and crafts and the expansion of the market for the products of Indian art and craftsmanship. In the execution of this function the Board shall have the following powers: (a) To undertake market research to determine the best opportunity for the sale of various products; (b) to engage in technical research and give technical advice and assistance; (c) to engage in experimentation directly or through selected agencies; (d) to correlate and encourage the activities of the various governmental and private agencies in the field; (e) to offer assistance in the management of operating groups for the furtherance of specific projects; (f) to make recommendations to appropriate agencies for loans in furtherance of the production and sale of Indian products; (g) to create Government trade marks of genuineness and quality for Indian products and the products of particular Indian tribes or groups; to establish standards and regulations for the use of such trade marks; to license corporations, associations, or individuals to use them; and to charge a fee for their use; to register them in the U.S. Patent Office without charge; (h) to employ executive officers, including a general manager, and such other permanent and temporary personnel as may be found necessary, and prescribe the authorities, duties, responsibilities, and tenure and fix the compensation of such officers and other employees; (i) as a Government agency to negotiate and execute in its own name contracts with operating groups to supply management, personnel, and supervision at cost, and to negotiate and execute in its own name such other contracts and to carry on such other business as may be necessary for the accomplishment of the duties and purposes of the Board, Provided, That nothing in the foregoing enumeration of powers shall be construed to authorize the Board to borrow or lend money or to deal in Indian goods.

The legislation was amended by the Indian Arts and Crafts Act of 1990 (104 Stat. 4662).

Reference Schrader, Robert Fay, *The Indian Arts & Crafts Board: An Aspect of New Deal Indian Policy* (1983).

Indian Child Protection and Family Violence Prevention Act (104 Stat. 4544)

Now codified at 25 U.S.C. 3201, this federal action of 28 November 1990 was enacted to oversee a new era in the protection of Indian children from abuse. In the act, "the Congress, after careful review of the problem of child abuse on Indian reservations and the historical and special relationship of the Federal Government with Indian people, finds that a) incidents of abuse of children on Indian reservations are grossly unreported, b) such underreporting is often the result of the lack of a mandatory Federal reporting law, c) multiple incidents of sexual abuse of children on Indian reservations have been perpetuated by persons employed or funded by the Federal Government, d) Federal Government investigations of the background of Federal employees who care for, or teach, Indian children, are often deficient." The act set into motion a series of reporting responsibilities for people dealing with Indian children, including health care workers and teachers, instituted a central registry for the collection of information on abused Indian children, and established in the Department of Health and Human Services the Indian Child Abuse Treatment Grant Program.

Indian Child Welfare Act (92 Stat. 3069, 25 U.S.C. 1901–1963)

Enacted as "an Act to establish standards for the placement of Indian children in foster or adoptive homes, to prevent the breakup of Indian families, and for other purposes," this federal legislation enacted on 8 November 1978 was passed because "there is no resource that is more vital to the continued existence and integrity of Indian tribes than their children and that the United States has a direct interest, as trustee, in protecting Indian children who are members of or are eligible for membership in an Indian tribe." Justice William Brennan, writing the majority opinion in *Mississippi Band of Choctaw Indians v. Holyfield* (1989), said, "The Indian Child Welfare Act was the product of rising concern in the mid-1970s over the consequences to Indian children, Indian families, and Indian tribes of abusive child welfare practices that resulted in the separation of large numbers of Indian children from their families and tribes through adoption or foster care placement, usually non-Indian homes. Senate oversight hearings in 1974 yielded numerous examples, statistical data, and expert testimony documenting what one witness called '[t]he wholesale removal of Indian children from their homes…the most tragic aspect of Indian life today." In Section 3 of the act, the Congress declared "that it is the policy of this Nation to protect the best interests of Indian children and to promote the stability and security of Indian tribes and families by the establishment of minimum Federal standards for the removal of Indian children from their families and the placement of such children in foster or adoptive homes which will reflect the unique values of Indian culture, and by providing for assistance to Indian tribes in the operation of child and family service programs." The law fixed permanent regulations in child custody proceedings, and formulated the development of Indian child and family programs.

See also *Mississippi Band of Choctaw Indians v. Holyfield et al.*

Reference *United States Code Congressional and Administrative News,* 95th Congress, 2d Session (1978).

Indian Citizenship Act of 1924 (43 Stat. 253)

This federal action of 2 June 1924 granted the right of citizenship to all Indians to which that privilege had not been bestowed previously. Authored by Senator Charles Curtis, Republican of Kansas, who had written the Curtis Act of 1898, the act reads:

An Act To Authorize the Secretary of the Interior to issue certificates of citizenship to Indians.

Be it enacted...That all non-citizen Indians born within the territorial limits of the United States be, and they are hereby, declared to be citizens of the United States: Provided, That the granting of such citizenship shall not in any manner impair or otherwise affect the right of any Indian to tribal or other property.

Indian Civil Rights Act of 1968 (82 Stat. 73, 77–81)

This federal legislation, enacted with the Omnibus Civil Rights Act of 1968, specifically delineated the civil rights of Indians as protected by the U.S. Constitution and recognized by the federal government and, in effect, extended certain provisions of the Constitution to the Indian tribes. The crucial section of this act, title II, reads:

Sec. 201. For purposes of this title, the term (1) "Indian tribe" means any tribe, band, or other group of Indians subject to the jurisdiction of the United States and recognized as possessing powers of self-government; (2) "powers of self-government" means and includes all governmental powers possessed by an Indian tribe, executive, legislative, and judicial, and all offices, bodies, and tribunals by and through which they are executed, including courts of Indian offenses; and (3) "Indian court" means any Indian tribal court or court of Indian offense.

Sec. 202. No Indian tribe in exercising powers of self-government shall: (1) make or enforce any law prohibiting the free exercise of religion, or abridging the freedom of speech, or of the press, or the right of the people peaceably to assemble and to petition for a redress of grievances; (2) violate the right of the people to be secure in their persons, houses, papers, and effects against unreasonable search and seizures, nor issue warrants, but upon probable cause, supported by oath or affirmation, and particularly describing the place to be searched and the person or thing to be seized; (3) subject any person for the same offense to be twice put in jeopardy; (4) compel any person in any criminal case to be a witness against himself; (5) take any private property for a public use without just compensation; (6) deny to any person in a criminal proceeding the right to a speedy and public trial, to be informed of the nature and cause of the accusation, to be confronted with the witnesses against him, to have compulsory process for obtaining witnesses in his favor, and at his own expense to have the assistance of counsel for his defense; (7) require excessive bail, impose excessive fines, inflict cruel and unusual punishments, and in no event impose for conviction of any one offense any penalty or punishment greater than imprisonment for a term of six months or a fine of $5,000, or both; (8) deny to any person within its jurisdiction the equal protection of its laws or deprive any person of liberty or property without due process of law; (9) pass any bill of attainder or ex post facto law; or (10) deny to any person accused of an offense punishable by imprisonment the right, upon request, to a trial by jury of not less than six persons.

Sec. 203. The privilege of the writ of habeas corpus shall be available to any person, in a court of the United States, to test the legality of his detention by order of an Indian tribe.

President Lyndon Baines Johnson signs the Civil Rights Act of 1968 in the East Room of the White House on 11 April 1968. Title II of the act confirmed the rights of Indians in language of the U.S. Constitution and the Bill of Rights. A month earlier President Johnson delivered an address to Congress titled "The Forgotten American" in which he proposed a policy of "maximum choice for the American Indian: a policy expressed in programs of self-help, self-development, [and] self-determination."

Other portions of the law established a model code governing the courts of Indian offenses, assented to state jurisdiction over criminal and civil actions involving Indians, amended an issue as to offenses within Indian country, allowed for the employment of legal counsel, called for the publication of materials relating to the constitutional rights of Indians, and set policy regarding fair housing regulations for Indians. Further, the action ended termination as a federal policy and expressly repealed the controversial Public Law 280 unless tribal councils specifically requested that states continued to oversee civil and criminal matters involving Indians. Senator Sam Ervin (D-North Carolina) commented that the passage of this act "confer[red] upon the American Indians the fundamental constitutional rights which belong by right to all Americans."

Reference Senator Sam Ervin, *Congressional Record*, 113: 35472 (1974); *United States Code Congressional and Administrative News*, 90th Congress, 2d Session (1968).

Indian Claims Commission

This commission, established by Congress by the act of 13 August 1946 (60 Stat. 1049), oversaw Indian land claims from 1946 until 1978. Established by "An Act to create an Indian Claims Commission, to provide for the powers, duties, and functions thereof, and for other purposes," the commission sat from 1946 until its caseload was transferred to the Court of Claims (now the Claims Court). The legislation enacted on 13 August 1946 conferred on the commission five separate areas of jurisdiction. As the act reads referring to jurisdiction:

Be it enacted by the Senate and House of Representatives of the United States of America in Congress assembled, That:

There is hereby created and established an Indian Claims Commission, hereafter referred to as the Commission.

Sec. 2. The Commission shall hear and determine the following claims against the United States on behalf of any Indian tribe, band, or other identifiable group of American Indians residing within the territorial limits of the United States or Alaska: (1) claims in law or equity arising under the Constitution, laws, treaties of the United States, and Executive orders of the President; (2) all other claims in law or equity, including those sounding in tort, with respect to which the claimant would have been entitled to sue in a court of the United States if the United States was subject to suit; (3) claims which would result if the treaties, contracts, and agreements between the claimant and the United States were revised on the ground of fraud, duress, unconscionable consideration, mutual or unilateral mistake, whether of law or fact, or any other ground cognizable by a court of equity; (4) claims arising from the taking by the United States, whether as a result of a treaty of cession or otherwise, of lands owned or occupied by the claimant without the payment for such lands of compensation agreed to by the claimant; and (5) claims based upon fair and honorable dealings that are not recognized by any existing rule of law or equity. No claim accruing after the date of the approval of this Act shall be considered by the Commission.

As the report on the passage of this act reads, "The bill in its present form is primarily designed to right a continuing wrong to our Indian citizens for which no possible justification can be asserted. Today any white man who has supplied goods or services to the United States under contract may, if the United States has failed to carry out its part of the bargain, go into the Court of Claims or, in certain cases, into the Federal district courts, and secure a full, free, and fair hearing on his claims against the government. This is an integral part of the American system of justice under which the humblest citizen and the highest official are equal before the law. The only American citizen today who is denied such recourse to the courts is the Indian. By virtue of a statute adopted on March 3, 1863, at a time when a good many Indian tribes were engaged in hostilities against the Federal Government, all claims against the United States growing out of Indian treaties were barred from the jurisdiction of the Court of Claims, and from that day to this no Indians have been able to bring their disputes with the Federal Government before the Court of Claims without a special act of Congress permitting them to receive the hearing that is the right of every other American citizen to demand without special legislation."

With the establishment of the commission, tribes were given five years to file claims. However, because of the extensive petitions involved, Congress was forced to extend the deadline several times, until in 1975 it ended the ICC's mandate on 30 September 1978. To handle the load, the original three commissioners were expanded to five. By 1965, more than $100 million in claims had been handed out to various tribes, but no land is returned and after legal fees were deducted, very little was actually paid to individual Native Americans. The ICC Act was the last piece of New Deal legislation involving Indians.

See also *United States v. Dann et al.*

Reference *Indian Claims Commission, Report of the House Committee on Indian Affairs*, House Report 1466, 79th Congress, 2d Session, 1946.

"Indian Commerce Clause" of the U.S. Constitution

From the very beginning of this nation as a constitutional democracy, Indians have been the concern of the government. Under Article 1, section eight, of the U.S. Constitution, the founding fathers who drafted the Constitution placed within that document responsibilities of the U.S. Congress. Among them is the obligation "To regulate Commerce with foreign Nations, and among the several States, and with the Indian tribes," the latter section which is called the Indian Commerce Clause of the Constitution.

Reference Commager, Henry Steele, ed., *Documents of American History* (1949).

Indian Country—Definition

Justice Samuel Freeman Miller reasoned in *Bates v. Clark* (1877), "It follows from this that all the country described by the Act of 1834 [the Trade and Intercourse Act of 1834] as Indian country remains Indian country so long as the Indians retain their original title to the soil, and ceases to be Indian country whenever they lose that title, in the absence of any different provision or by Act of Congress."

Indian Country has been referred to in several U.S. Supreme Court decisions; however, it is now codified at 18 U.S.C. 1151, with that area now being defined as "(a) all land within the limits of any Indian reservation under the jurisdiction of the U.S. Government, notwithstanding the issuance of any patent, and, including rights-of-way running through the reservation; (b) all dependent Indian communities within the borders of the United States whether within the original or subsequently acquired territory thereof, and whether within or without the limits of a state, and (c) all Indian allotments, the Indian titles to which have not been extinguished, including rights-of-way running through the same" (with exceptions made in sections 1154 and 1156 of the title). In *Pronovost v. United States* (232 U.S. 487, 1914), the Supreme Court held that an Indian reservation is Indian country. Further, the cases of *Donnelly v. United States* (228 U.S. 243, 1913) and *Ex parte Wilson* (140 U.S. 575, 1891) held that Indian country is not confined to lands to which the Indians retained their original right of possession, but includes land lawfully set apart for an Indian reservation out of the public domain, and not previously occupied by Indians. In *United States v. Chavez et al.* (1933), the court held that any unceded lands owned or occupied by the Indians are to be considered as Indian country. The Indian Reorganization Act of 1934 for the first time codified the definition of *Indian country* into law.

See also *Bates v. Clark; Dick v. United States; Donnelly v. United States; Ex parte Wilson;* Indian Reorganization Act; *Oklahoma Tax Commission v. Sac and Fox Nation; Pronovost v. United States; United States v. Chavez et al.*

Reference *United States Code Annotated: Title 18: Crimes and Criminal Procedure, Sections 1081 to 1360* (1984).

Indian Crimes Act of 1976 (90 Stat. 585)

See Indian Major Crimes Act.

Indian Education Act of 1972 (86 Stat. 235, 334–345)

Enacted as part of the Education Amendments of 1972, this federal legislation of 23 June 1972 established policy in the Department of Interior as to Indian education. In the act, Congress found that "in recognition of the special educational needs of Indian students in the United States, Congress hereby declares it to be the policy of the United States to provide financial assistance to local educational agencies to develop and carry out elementary and secondary school programs specially designed to meet these special education needs." The legislation authorized the commissioner of Indian Affairs to "carry out a program of making grants to local educational agencies which are entitled to payments under this title and which have submitted, and had approved, applications therefor, in accordance with the provisions of this title." It also authorized the commissioner to establish "planning, pilot, and demonstration projects-which are designed to test and demonstrate the effectiveness of programs for improving educational opportunities for Indian children," including "remedial and compensatory instruction." Programs for the education of adult Indians were created, and an Office of Indian Education was constituted in the Department of the Interior, as well as a National Advisory Council on Indian Education. The legislation was supplemented and amended by the

Indian Education Act of 1988 (102 Stat. 363).

See also Office of Indian Education.

Reference *United States Code Congressional and Administrative News*, 92d Congress, 2d Session (1972).

Indian Financing Act of 1974 (88 Stat. 77)

In this federal action of 12 April 1974, now codified at 25 U.S.C. 1451–1543, the Congress declared it to be the policy of that body "to provide capital on a reimbursable basis to help develop and utilize Indian resources, both physical and human, to a point where the Indians will fully exercise responsibility for the utilization and management of their own resources and where they will enjoy a standard of living from their own productive efforts comparable to that enjoyed by non-Indians in neighboring communities." The legislation established the Indian Revolving Loan Fund, "in order to provide credit that is not available from private money markets," and constituted a program of repayment of loans and financing "from other sources."

Indian Gaming Regulatory Act of 1988 (Public Law 100–497)

Codified at 102 Stat. 2467 and 25 U.S.C. 2701, this federal legislation of 17 October 1988 was enacted "to provide a statutory basis for the operation of gaming by Indian tribes as a means of promoting tribal economic development, self-suffiency, and strong tribal governments; [and] to provide a statutory basis for the regulation of gaming by an Indian tribe adequate to shield it from organized crime and other corrupting influences, to ensure that the Indian tribe is the primary beneficiary of the gaming operation, and to assure that gaming is conducted fairly and honestly by both the operator and players." The key portion of the law was the establishment of the National Indian Gaming Commission, composed of three members (one nominated by the president and subject to the advice and consent of the Senate, and two others named by the secretary of the interior), two of whom would serve for a single three-year term, with the third serving a single-year term. The chairman of the commission was endowed with the power to levy and collect fines for gaming violations, and approve management contracts for certain classes of gaming. The act was challenged before the U.S. Supreme Court in 1996 in *Seminole Tribe v. Florida et al.*

See also National Indian Gaming Commission; *Seminole Tribe of Florida v. Florida et al.*

Reference *United States Code Congressional and Administrative News*, 100th Congress, Second Session (1988), 2: 2467–71.

Indian Health Care Improvement Act (90 Stat. 1400)

This federal action of 30 September 1976, now codified at 25 U.S.C. 1601, was enacted to "implement the Federal responsibility for the care and education of the Indian people by improving the services and facilities of Federal Indian health programs and encouraging maximum participation of Indians in such programs." In passing the legislation, Congress found that "Federal health services to maintain and improve the health of the Indians are consonant [compatible] with and required by the Federal Government's historical and unique legal relationship with, and resulting responsibility to, the American Indian people," and that "A major national goal of the United States is to provide the quantity and quality of health services which will permit the health status of Indians to be raised to the highest possible level and to encourage the maximum participation of Indians in the planning and management of those services." To make the process easier in introducing health care professionals into the Indian health service structure, the legislation created a Health Professions Scholarship Program, and a Health Professions Recruitment Program for Indians, so Indians capable of a medical education can be identified and given assistance in enrolling and paying for medical school, and authorized the secretary of the interior to expend monies for "eliminating backlogs in Indian health care services."

Indian Health Service

The history of the federal government's role in trying to maintain and preserve the health of Indians, particularly on the reservations, is an important facet of Indian-white relations in the history of the United States. When the War Department was first established in 1789, the only Indians who could receive health care from the government were those near military posts. In 1976 a separate committee of the American Indian Policy Review Commission, titled Task Force Six, examined Indian health and the government's response to it. The task force's members wrote, "The War Department's involvement with Indian health lasted almost half a century, from 1803 to 1849 [when the Interior Department assumed responsibility]. During this period, its activity was minimal and its appropriations small. Its main function was to see that Indians were vaccinated for smallpox, more for the protection of military personnel and the white population than for the Indians themselves. Characteristically, the delivery system was inefficient; vaccines often did not arrive and there was a shortage of doctors to administer them, in spite of the fact that Indian agents wrote frequently to Washington seeking both." From 1849 until 1955, jurisdiction over Indian health matters was vested in the Bureau of Indian Affairs in the Department of the Interior; in that latter year, the Division of Indian Health was transferred to the United States Public Health Service. In that 106-year interval, control of Indian health matters passed from military to civil authority. It was not until the tenure of Commissioner of Indian Affairs Francis E. Leupp and his immediate successor, Robert G. Valentine, that a greater emphasis on Indian health was promoted. Under these two men, doctors were sent to the reservations, particularly in the West, where tuberculosis and trachoma were rampant. Indians such as physician Susan La Flesche Picotte (Omaha) took on the enormous task of ministering to their own people.

Professor Gregory Campbell reports, "The health problems Native Americans are confronting today did not arise out of a historical vacuum. Diseases and ill health have a history. Health levels are linked to the social, political, and economic forces present at any historical moment." He adds, "As part of its assimilation program, the Bureau of Indian Affairs took charge of medical care for Native American people. Bureau medical personnel set about treating reservation diseases that had been created by the social and economic conditions engendered by the bureau's policies. The role of reservation medicine therefore was never separate from the political policy of assimilation. Hospitals, for example, were not constructed to isolate infectious Indian people or to provide a sanitary location to perform medical services, but were constructed to 'civilize' sick Indian people away from tribal influences."

In 1981, Dr. Emery A. Johnson, then director of the IHS, said in congressional testimony,

> The Federal government established its philosophy of self-determination for Indian people in Public Law 93–638. Public Law 94–437 authorizes activities to carry out the mandate for self-determination expressed in Public Law 93–638. Further, it defined in law types of programs and levels of service that could be expected by Indian people; in other words the national goal for programs providing services to Indian people. It also requires the secretary of DHHS [Department of Health and Human Services] to report to the Congress periodically on accomplishments made in implementing these programs and to report on the need for additional resources to accomplish the goals defined in the Act. This latter requirement was accomplished with the submission of a National Plan for the improvement of health care to Indian people, to Congress in April, 1980. There now exists a Federal health program for Indians in which ser-

vices are now delivered by tribes and tribal organizations as well as the IHS. Thus, tribes and the IHS are now both components of a system designed to provide needed health services to Indian people. The rate of participation by tribes in the management of their own health programs is accelerating. Although as expected, a few tribes have exercised their options to operate parts of their health systems and a few have taken over major portions of their health care systems. Most tribes view their participation as an incremental phasing [in] of increasing responsibility for the operation of health programs as meaningful experience is gained, and qualified Indian people become available to staff programs.

See also Indian Alcohol and Substance Abuse Prevention and Treatment Act of 1986; Leupp, Francis Ellington; Picotte, Susan La Flesche (Omaha); Valentine, Robert Grosvenor.

References Campbell, Gregory R., "The Changing Dimension of Native American Health: A Critical Understanding of Contemporary Native American Health Issues." *American Indian Culture and Research Journal* 13 (3–4); Dr. Emery A. Johnson's testimony in *Department of the Interior and Related Agencies Appropriations for 1982, Hearings before the Subcommittee on the Department of the Interior and Related Agencies, a Subcommittee of the Committee on Appropriations*, House of Representatives, 97th Congress, 1st Session, 1981, Part 9: 1–2; *Report on Indian Health—Task Force Six: Indian Health."* Report to the American Indian Policy Review Commission, 1976.

Indian Land Consolidation Act (96 Stat. 2515–19)

This federal action of 12 January 1983 was enacted to provide for the consolidation of Indian heirship lands in cases where segmentation resulted in plots too small to be used adequately. The act, Title II, Section 201–11 of the Devils Lake Sioux Reservation—Indian Land Consolidation Act, reads in part:

Sec. 204. (a) Notwithstanding any other provision of law, any tribe, acting through its governing body, is authorized, with the approval of the Secretary [of the Interior] to adopt a land consolidation plan providing for the sale or exchange of any tribal lands or interest in lands for the purpose of eliminating undivided fractional interests in Indian trust or restricted lands or consolidating its tribal landholdings.

Sec. 205. Any Indian tribe may purchase at no less than the fair market value all of the interests in any tract or trust or restricted land within that tribe's reservation or otherwise subjected to that tribe's jurisdiction with the consent of over 50 per centum of the owners or with the consent of the owners of over 50 per centum of the undivided interests in such tract.

Indian Literature

Since the beginning of the United States, Native American writers have been at the forefront in telling autobiographical, biographical, and tribal narratives of their lives, works which have defined their culture and native customs as no other works can. The first Native American to publish a printed work was Samson Occom (Mohegan), whose *A Sermon Preached at the Execution of Moses Paul, an Indian Who was Executed at New Haven on the 2nd of September 1772 for the Murder of Mr. Moses Cook, late of Waterbury, on the 7th of December 1771/ Preached at the Desire of said Paul by Samson Occim, minister of the gospel and missionary to the Indians, New Haven, 1772* was printed in New Haven in 1772; it was a discourse on alcoholism and how it affected one Indian who had killed a white man when drunk. William Apes (Pequot) composed the first Native American autobiography, *A Son of the Forest. The Experience of William Apes, A Native of the Forest. Written by Himself,* which appeared in 1829. A less influential, but nonetheless important Native American writer was George Copway (Ojibwe), a Canadian Indian whose *Life, History and Travels of Kah-ge-ga-hag-bowh; A Young Chief of the Ojebwa Nation, With A Sketch of the Present State of the Ojibwa Nation, in Regard to Christianity*

Mr. Occom's Addreſs

TO HIS INDIAN BRETHREN.

On the Day that MOSES PAUL, an Indian, was executed at NEW-HAVEN, on the 2d of SEPTEMBER, 1772, for the Murder of MOSES COOK.

I.
MY kindred Indians, pray attend and hear,
With great attention and with godly fear;
This day I warn you of that curſed ſin,
That poor, deſpiſed Indians wallow in.

II.
'Tis drunkenneſs, this is the ſin you know,
Has been and is poor Indians overthrow;
'Twas drunkenneſs that was the leading cauſe,
That made poor Moſes break God's righteous Laws.

III.
When drunk he other evil courſes took,
Thus hurried on, he murdered Moſes Cook;
Poor Moſes Paul muſt now be hang'd this day,
For wilful murder in a drunken fray.

IV.
A dreadful wo pronounc'd by God on high,
To all that in this ſin do lie;
O deviliſh beaſtly luſt, accurſed ſin,
Has almoſt ſtript us all of every thing.

V.
We've nothing valuable or to our praiſe,
And well may other nations on us gaze;
We have no money, credit or a name,
But what this ſin does turn to our great ſhame.

VI.
Mean are our houſes, and we are kept low,
And almoſt naked, ſhivering we go;
Pinch'd for food and almoſt ſtarv'd we are,
And many times put up with ſtinking fare.

VII.
Our little children hovering round us weep,
Moſt ſtarv'd to death we've nought for them to eat;
All this diſtreſs is juſtly on us come,
For the accurſed uſe we make of rum.

VIII.
A ſhocking, dreadful ſight we often ſee,
Our children young and tender, drunkards be;
More ſhocking yet and awful to behold,
Our women will get drunk both young and old.

IX.
Behold a drunkard in a drunken fit,
Incapable to go, ſtand, ſpeak, or ſit;
Deform'd in ſoul and every other part,
Affecting ſight! enough to melt one's heart.

X.
Sometimes he laughs, and then a hideous yell,
That almoſt equals the poor damn'd in hell;
When drown'd in drink we know not what we do,
We are deſpiſed and ſcorn'd and cheated too.

XI.
On level with the beaſts and far below
Are we when with ſtrong drink we reeling go;
Below the devils when in this ſin we run,
A drunken devil I never heard of one.

XII.
My kindred Indians, I intreat you all,
In this vile ſin never again to fall;
Fly to the blood of CHRIST, for that alone
Can for this ſin and all your ſins atone.

XIII.
Though Moſes Paul is here alive and well,
This night his ſoul muſt be in heaven or hell;
O! do take warning by this awful ſight,
And to a JESUS make a ſpeedy flight!

XIV.
You have no leaſe of your ſhort time you know,
To hell this night you may be forc'd to go;
Oh! do embrace an offer'd CHRIST to-day,
And get a ſealed pardon while you may.

XV.
Behold a loving JESUS, ſee him cry,
With earneſtneſs of ſoul, "Why will ye die?"
My kindred Indians, come juſt as you be,
Then Chriſt and his ſalvation you ſhall ſee.

XVI.
If you go on and ſtill reject Chriſt's call,
'Twill be too late, his curſe will on you fall;
The Judge will doom you to that dreadful place,
In hell, where you ſhall never ſee his face.

An early example of Native American literature is a summary of a 1772 sermon given by Samson Occom, a Mohichan, who admonished "kindred Indians" to avoid drunkenness. Distributed widely as a broadside, it may be the first published work by a Native American.

and Their Future Prospects reflects, as Indian historian A. LaVonne Brown Ruoff writes, "the traditions of the spiritual confessions as well as of the missionary narratives." The first Native American woman to compose an autobiography was Sarah Winnemucca (Paiute). Her *Life Among the Piutes* (1885) discussed the plight of her people and her support of the allotment of Indian lands. Winnemucca was in fact the only Native American woman to write such a widely distributed book in the nineteenth century. Other authors prominent in this century included John Rollin Ridge (Cherokee), a member of a noted Cherokee family, who wrote *The Life and Adventures of Joaquín Murieta* (1854), and Simon Pokagon's autobiographical *O-gi-kwe Mit-i-gwa-ki (Queen of the Woods); Also a Sketch of the Algaic Language by Chief Pokagon* (1899), which reflected his anger at the taking of Indian land and the misunderstanding of the Ghost Dance, which precipitated the massacre at Wounded Knee in 1890.

It was not until the twentieth century that Indian literature became a major segment in the fight for Native American rights. Gertrude Simmons Bonnin (Yankton), known as Zitkala-Sa, discussed traditional Sioux narratives in *Old Indian Legends* (1901) and *American Indian Stories* (1921). The works of Mourning Dove (Colville) include *Co-ge-wea; the Half Blood* (1927), considered the first novel written by a Native American woman, and *Coyote Stories* (1933). Dr. Charles Eastman (Santee Sioux) described his early life in such works as *Indian Boyhood* (1902) and *From Deep Woods to Civilization* (1916), but he also described Indian customs and traditions in *Red Hunters and Animal People* (1904), *Old Indian Days* (1907), *Wigwam Evenings* (1909), and *The Soul of an Indian* (1911). Among the other leading Native American writers of the twentieth century have been Ella Deloria (Sioux), John N. B. Hewitt (Tuscarora), William Jones (Fox), Francis LaFlesche (Nez Percé), William Morgan (Navajo), and Arthur C. Parker (Seneca). In 1969, author Navarre Scott Momaday was awarded the Pulitzer Prize for his work, *House Made of Dawn.*

See also Apes, William; Bonnin, Gertrude Simmons; Copway, George; Deloria, Vine Victor, Jr.; Eastman, Charles Alexander; Occom, Samson; Winnemucca, Sarah.

References Crane, Fred A., *The Noble Savage in America, 1815–1860: Concepts of the Indian with Special Reference to the Writers of the Northeast* (Ph.D. dissertation, Yale University, 1952); Ruoff, A. LaVonne Brown, *American Indian Literatures: An Introduction, Bibliographic Review, and Selected Bibliography* (1990); Ruoff, A. LaVonne Brown, "On Literature in English: American Indian Authors, 1774–1899." In Andrew Wiget, *Critical Essays on Native American Literature* (1985).

Indian Long Term Leasing Act of 1955 (69 Stat. 539)

This federal action of 9 August 1955 was enacted "to authorize the leasing of restricted Indian lands for public, religious, educational, recreational, residential, business, and other purposes requiring the grant of long term leases." Section one of the act, the most pertinent of the legislation, reads:

> Any restricted Indian lands, whether tribally or individually owned, may be leased by the Indian owners, with the approval of the Secretary of the Interior, for public, religious, educational, recreational, residential, or business purposes, including the development or utilization of natural resources in connection with operations under such leases, for grazing purposes, and for those farming purposes which require the making of a substantial investment in the improvement of the land for the production of specialized crops as determined by said Secretary. All leases so granted shall be for a term of not to exceed twenty-five years, excepting leases for grazing purposes, which shall be for a term of not to exceed ten years. Leases for public, religious, educational, recreational, residential, or business purposes with the consent of both parties may include provisions authorizing their renewal for one additional term of not to exceed twenty-five years, and all leases and renewals shall be made under terms and regulations as may be prescribed by the Secretary of the Interior.

Indian Major Crimes Act (23 Stat. 362)

This federal legislation of 3 March 1885 was enacted by Congress in response to the Supreme Court decision in *Ex parte Kan-gi-Shun-ca (Otherwise known as Crow Dog)*, in which the court held that Indians were not subject to federal or state law in cases in which an Indian murdered another Indian. Under the area of legislation codified now as 18 U.S.C. 1151, the area of the offenses committed under the act has been changed to "Indian country." The act itself is codified at 18 U.S.C. 1153, and now reads as follows:

Any Indian who commits against the person or property of another Indian or other person any of the following offenses, namely, murder, manslaughter, rape, carnal knowledge of any female, not his wife, who has not attained the age of sixteen years, assault with intent to commit rape, incest, assault with intent to kill, assault with a dangerous weapon, assault resulting in serious bodily injury, arson, burglary, robbery, and larceny within the Indian country, shall be subject to the same laws and penalties as all other persons committing any of the above offenses, within the exclusive jurisdiction of the United States.

As used in this section, the offenses of rape and assault with intent to commit rape shall be defined in accordance with the laws of the States in which the offense was committed, and any Indian who commits the offenses of rape or assault with intent to commit rape upon any female Indian within the Indian country shall be imprisoned at the discretion of the court.

As used in this section, the offenses of burglary, assault with a dangerous weapon, assault resulting in serious bodily injury, and incest shall be defined and punished in accordance with the laws of the State in which such offense was committed.

The act was amended by the act of 3 March 1887 (24 Stat. 635) to include adultery among Indians as one of the crimes to be prosecuted, and by the Indian Crimes Act of 1976 (90 Stat. 585), which added kidnapping to the list of offenses, and incorporated sections which indicated how state law could be involved in such cases. Under the terms of the act of 2 May 1890, which established a temporary government in the territory of Oklahoma, the Congress allowed that "the judicial tribunals of the Indian Nations shall retain exclusive jurisdiction in all civil and criminal cases arising in the country in which members of the Nation by nativity or by adoption shall be the only parties."

While the constitutionality of the act was decided in *United States v. Kagama, alias Pactah Billy* (1886), and jurisdictional questions of the original act were resolved in *United States v. Celestine* (1909), the issue of the constitutionality of the 1887 amendment was decided in the U.S. Supreme Court cases of *Ex parte Mayfield* (1891) and *United States v. Quiver* (1916). It was further considered in *Duro v. Reina* (1990). The 1890 act was challenged in 1896 in *Lucas v. United States.* State jurisdiction over Indian offenses in some areas was extended with the passage by Congress of Public Law 280 in 1953. The question of whether an Indian could be charged with a crime not listed in the Major Crimes Act was at issue in *Keeble v. United States* (1973).

See also *Duro v. Reina et al.; Ex parte Crow Dog; Ex parte Mayfield; Keeble v. United States; Lucas v. United States;* Public Law 280; *United States v. Celestine; United States v. John; United States v. Kagama, alias Pactah Billy.*

Indian Peace Commission Act (15 Stat. 17)

This federal legislation of 20 July 1867 established a delegation of politicians and military men to confer with the Indians of tribes "waging war against the United States or committing depredations upon the people thereof," ascertain their reasons for this warfare, and, if the commissioners failed to obtain a peace with the Indians, provided for a swift military advance to crush all Indian resistance. The legislation, which outlined the purposes and objectives of the commission members, reads in total:

An Act to establish Peace with certain Hostile Indian Tribes.

Be it enacted..., That the President of the United States be, and is hereby, authorized to appoint a commission to consist of three officers of the army not below the rank of brigadier general, who, together with N[athaniel] G[reen] Taylor, Commissioner of Indian Affairs, John B. Henderson, chairman of the Committee of Indian Affairs in the Senate, S[amuel] F. Tappan, and John B. Sanborn, shall have the power and authority to call together the chiefs and headmen of such bands or tribes of Indians as are now waging war against the United States or committing depredations upon the people thereof, to ascertain the alleged reasons for their acts of hostility, and in their discretion, under the direction of the President, to make and conclude with such bands or tribes such treaty stipulations, subject to the action of the Senate, as may remove all just causes of complaint on their part, and at the same time establish security for person and property along the lines of railroad now being constructed to the Pacific and other thoroughfares of travel to the western Territories, and such as will most likely insure civilization for the Indians and peace and safety for the whites.

Sec. 2. And be it further enacted, That said commissioners are required to examine and select a district or districts of country having sufficient area to receive all the Indian tribes now occupying territory east of the Rocky mountains, not now peacefully residing on permanent reservations under treaty stipulations, to which the government has the right of occupation or to which said commissioners can obtain the right of occupation, and in which district or districts there shall be sufficient tillable or grazing land to enable the said tribes, respectively, to support themselves by agricultural and pastoral pursuits. Said district or districts, when so selected, and the selected approved by Congress, shall be and remain permanent homes for said Indians to be located thereon, and no person[s] not members of said tribes shall ever be permitted to enter thereon without the permission of the tribes interested, except officers and employees of the United States; *Provided*, That the district or districts shall be so located as not to interfere with travel on highways located by authority of the United States. nor with the route of the Northern Pacific Railroad, the Union Pacific Railroad, the Union Pacific Railroad Eastern Division, or the proposed route of the Atlantic and Pacific Railroad by the way of Albuquerque.

Sec. 3. And be it further enacted, That the following sums of money are hereby appropriated out of any moneys in the treasury, to wit: To carry out provisions of the preceding sections of this act, one hundred and fifty thousand dollars; to enable the Secretary of the Interior to subsist such friendly Indians as may have separated or may hereafter separate themselves from the hostile bands or tribes and seek the protection of the United States, three hundred thousand dollars.

Sec. 4. And be it further enacted, That the Secretary of War be required to furnish transportation, subsistence, and protection to the commissioners herein named during the discharge of their duties.

Sec. 5. And be it further enacted, That if said commissioners fail to secure the consent of the Indians to remove to the reservations and fail to secure peace, then the Secretary of War, under the direction of the President, is hereby authorized to accept the services of mounted volunteers from the Governors of the several States and Territories, in organized companies and battalions, not exceeding four thousand men in number, and for such term of service as, in his judgment, may be necessary for the suppression of Indian hostilities.

Sec. 6. And be it further enacted, That all volunteers so accepted shall be placed upon the same footing, in respect to pay, clothing, subsistence, and equipment, as the troops of the regular army.

Sec. 7. And be it further enacted, That said commissioners report their doings under this act to the President of the

United States, including any such treaties and all correspondence as well as evidence by them taken.

See also Indian Peace Commission; Tappan, Samuel Forster; Taylor, Nathaniel Green.

Indian Peace Commission

Also called the *Great Plains Peace Commission*, this assemblage of congressional and military personnel was gathered to "restore peace to the Great Plains, secure the right-of-way for Pacific railroads, provide protection of frontier settlements, and recommend a permanent Indian policy." The commission, led by Commissioner of Indian Affairs Nathaniel Green Taylor, included Senator John B. Henderson, chairman of the Senate Committee of Indian Affairs, Samuel F. Tappan, an abolitionist writer who had worked on Horace Greeley's New York *Tribune*, and, as part of its military contingent, General John B. Sanborn, Brevet Major General William S. Harney, Lt. General William Tecumseh Sherman, Brevet Major General Christopher Columbus Augur (1821–98, a veteran of the Mexican and Civil Wars), and Brevet Major General Alfred Howe Terry (1827–90, a veteran of the Civil War and Commander of the Dakota Department concerning Indian affairs).

The following, describing a meeting held with the Brulé Sioux, is a verbatim extract of the commission's report, which was presented to President Andrew Jackson on 7 January 1868:

Swift Bear, a Brulé chief, then and now a faithful friend to the whites, had interested himself to induce the hostile bands to come in to this council, and had promised them, if peace were made, that ammunition should be given [to] them to kill game for the winter. This promise was not authorized by the commissioners, but we were assured that it had been made not only by him, but by others of our runners [messengers], and that nothing less would have brought them in. These Indians are very poor and needy. The game in this section is fast disappearing, and the bow and arrow are scarcely sufficient to provide them food. To give one of these Indians powder and ball is to provide them food. To refuse it, in his judgment, dooms him to starvation; and worse than this, he looks upon the refusal, especially after a profession of friendship on his part, as an imputation upon his truthfulness and fidelity. If an Indian is to be trusted at all, he must be trusted to the full extent of his work. If you betray symptoms of distrust, he discovers it with nature's intuition, and at once condemns the falsehood that would blend friendship and suspicion together. Whatever our people may choose to say of the insincerity or duplicity of the Indian would fail to express the estimate entertained by many Indians of the white man's character in this respect. Promises have been so often broken by those with who they usually come in contact, cupidity has so long plied its work deaf to their cries of suffering, and heartless cruelty has so frequently sought them in the garb of charity, that to obtain their confidence our promises must be scrupulously fulfilled and our professions of friendship divested of all appearance of selfishness and duplicity.

Historian Francis Paul Prucha writes, "The commissioners produced a report that is valuable not only for its historical account of important events in the history of Indian-white relations, but also for its administrative recommendations, which included the suggestion that Indian affairs be committed to an independent bureau or department."

See also Tappan, Samuel Forster; Taylor, Nathaniel Green.

References *Proceedings of the Great Peace Commission of 1867–68* (1975); Prucha, Francis Paul, ed., *Documents of United States Indian Policy* (1990); U.S. Congress, House of Representatives, *Report of the Indian Peace Commission*, House Executive Document No. 97, 40th Congress, 2d Session (serial 1337).

Indian Removal Act (4 Stat. 411)

Enacted on 28 May 1830 after one of the most contentious and bitter debates in the

The Indian Removal Act of 1830 enabled the president of the United States to order Indians living in the East to be relocated to lands west of the Mississippi. President Andrew Jackson ordered the Cherokee removal in 1833. Here federal troops escort Cherokees westward in a trip that was so arduous and caused so many deaths that it was called the Trail of Tears, as represented in Robert Lindneux's 1942 painting.

Congress with the exception of the arguments over slavery, the Indian Removal Act proceeded to shift most of the nations of Indians in the eastern United States to what was deemed "Indian country" in what is now Oklahoma. The act, as it was enacted, reads:

An Act to provide for an exchange of lands with the Indians residing in any one of the states or territories, and for their removal west of the river Mississippi.

Be it enacted...That it shall and may be lawful for the President of the United States to cause so much of any territory belonging to the United States, west of the river Mississippi, not included in any state or organized territory, and to which the Indian title has been extinguished, as he may judge necessary, to be divided into a suitable number of districts, for the reception of such tribes or nations of Indians as may choose to exchange the lands where they now reside, and remove there; and to cause each of said districts to be so described by natural or artificial marks, as to be easily distinguished from every other.

Sec. 2. And be it further enacted, That it shall and may be lawful for the President to exchange any or all of such districts, so to be laid off and described, with any tribe or nation of Indians now residing within the limits of any of the states or territories, and with which the United States have existing treaties, for the whole or any part or portion of the territory claimed and occupied by such tribe or nation, within the bounds of any one or more of the states or territories, where the land claimed and occupied by the Indians, is owned by the United States, or the United States are bound to the state within which it lies to extinguish the Indian claim thereto.

Sec. 3. And be it further enacted, That

in the making of any such exchange or exchanges, it shall and may be lawful for the President solemnly to assure the tribe or nation with which the exchange is made, that the United States will forever secure and guaranty to them, and their heirs or successors, the country so exchanged with them; and if they prefer it, that the United States will cause a patent or grant to be made and executed to them for the same: *Provided always*, That such lands shall revert to the United States, if the Indians become extinct, or abandon the same.

Sec. 4. And be it further enacted, That if, upon any of the lands now occupied by the Indians, and to be exchanged for, there should be such improvements as add value to the land claimed by any individual or individuals of such tribes or nations, it shall and may be lawful for the President to cause such value to be ascertained by appraisement or otherwise, and to cause such ascertained value to be paid to the person or persons rightfully claiming such improvements. And upon the payment of such valuation, the improvements so valued and paid for, shall pass to the United States, and possession shall not afterwards be permitted to any of the same tribe.

Sec. 5. And be it further enacted, That upon the making of any such exchange as is contemplated by this act, it shall and may be lawful for the President to cause such aid and assistance to be furnished to the emigrants as may be necessary and proper to enable them to remove to, and settle in, the country for which they may have exchanged; and also, to give them such aid and assistance as may be necessary for their support and subsistence for the first year after their removal.

Sec. 6. And be it further enacted, That it shall and may be lawful for the President to cause such tribe or nation to be protected, at their new residence, against all interruption or disturbance from any other tribe or nation of Indians, or from any other person or persons whatever.

Sec. 7. And be it further enacted, That it shall and may be lawful for the President to have the same superintendence and care over any tribe or nation in the country to which they may remove, as contemplated by this act, that he is now authorized to have over them at their present places of residence: *Provided*, That nothing in this act contained shall be construed as authorizing or directing the violation of any existing treaty between the United States and any of the Indian tribes.

Sec. 8. And be it further enacted, That for the purpose of giving effect to the provisions of this act, the sum of five hundred thousand dollars in hereby appropriated, to be paid out of any money in the treasury, not otherwise appropriated.

Indian scholar Vine Deloria, Jr., writes of this federal action, "The Indian Removal Act was the first general law passed giving authority to the executive branch to negotiate with the tribes to remove westward and avoid conflict with the advancing tide of white settlement. The basic policies adopted during the 1830s, when the act became law, were generally followed throughout the [nineteenth] century. Treaties signed with the far western and plains tribes in the 1850s and 1860s reflect the basic philosophy of the Removal Act."

See also Cherokee Indians, Removal of—Congressional and Governmental Debate; Jackson, Andrew—Message on Indian Removal.

Reference Deloria, Vine, Jr., ed., *Of Utmost Good Faith* (1972).

Indian Reorganization Act (48 Stat. 984)

This landmark federal act of 18 June 1934, now codified at 25 U.S.C. 476 and officially known as the Wheeler-Howard Act, ended the government's policy of allotment and advocated tribal organization on reservations as a formula for the improvement of Indian life. In its 19 sections, it sought to "conserve and develop Indian lands and resources; to extend to Indians the right to form business and other organizations; to establish a credit system for Indians; to grant certain rights of home rule to Indians; [and] to provide for vocational education for Indians." This act for the first time defined "Indian country" and those who resided within its boundaries—section 19 (48 Stat. 988, 25 U.S.C. 479) reads, "The term 'Indian' as used in this Act shall include all persons of Indian descent who are members of any recognized Indian tribe now under Federal jurisdiction, and all persons who are descendants of such members who were, on June 1, 1934, residing within the present boundaries of any Indian reservation, and shall further include all other persons of one-half or more Indian blood. For the purposes of [this Act] Eskimos and other aboriginal peoples of Alaska shall be considered Indians."

In his annual report for 1934, Commissioner of Indian Affairs John Collier, whose brainchild was the IRA, wrote, "The Wheeler-Howard Act, the most important piece of Indian legislation since the [eighteen] eighties, not only ends the long, painful, futile effort to speed up the normal rate of Indian assimilation by individualizing tribal land and other capital assets, but it also endeavors to provide the means, statutory and financial, to repair as far as possible, the incalculable damage done by the allotment policy and its corollaries." He added, "The repair work authorized by Congress under the terms of the act aims at both the economic and spiritual rehabilitation of the Indian race. Congress and the president recognized that the cumulative loss of land brought about by the allotment system, a loss reaching 90,000,000 acres—two-thirds of the land heritage of the Indian race in 1887—had robbed the Indians in large part of the necessary basis for self-support. They clearly saw that this loss and the companion effort to break up all Indian tribal relations had condemned large numbers of Indians to become chronic recipients of charity; that the system of leasing individuals holdings had created many thousands of petty landlords unfitted to support themselves when their rental income vanished; that a major proportion of the red race was, therefore, ruined economically and pauperized spiritually." Lawrence Kelly writes, "Despite the congressional limitations placed upon Indian self-determination and opposition from a sizable number of assimilated Indians who resisted the revival of tribal governments, 174 Indian tribes and bands approved the Indian Reorganization Act; 78 rejected it. Subsequently, 92 tribes adopted constitutions, and 72 did not; only 71 tribes approved articles of incorporation and thereby qualified for access to the credit loan program. The rejection of the Indian Reorganization Act by many Indians and the failure of others to adopt constitutions and articles of incorporation were severe blows to the Indian New Deal and provided congressional opponents of the legislation with telling arguments for future limitation. Despite these reversals, two permanent reforms were achieved: tribal lands were preserved, free from the threat of division and eventual loss; and the potential for limited self-government, to be achieved mainly after World War II, was guaranteed." In 1936, the features of the IRA were extended to the Indians of Oklahoma with the passage of the Thomas-Rogers Act, or, as it is better known, the Oklahoma Indian Welfare Act of 1936.

See also Collier, John; *Mescalero Apache Tribe v. Franklin Jones, Commissioner of the Bureau of Revenue of the State of New Mexico et al.*; Oklahoma Indian Welfare Act of 1936.

References *Annual Report of the Commissioner of Indian Affairs to the Secretary of the Interior for the Fiscal Year Ended June 30, 1934* (1934); Kelly, Lawrence C., "Indian Policy." In Otis L. Graham, Jr., and Meghan Robinson Wander, eds., *Franklin D. Roosevelt, His Life and Times: An Encyclopedic View* (1985).

Indian Rights Association

Founded in 1882 as the first major Indian rights and reform organization, the Indian Rights Association (IRA) began with a meeting in the home of reformer John Welsh, whose brother, William (who was the first chairman of the U.S. Board of Indian Commissioners), and son, Herbert, also attended, as well as Henry S. Pancoast. The compilers of the papers of the IRA write, "The early leaders of the IRA had a twofold purpose: to protect the interests and general welfare of the Indians, and to initiate, support, or oppose government legislation and policies designed to 'civilize' the American Indian. By the term 'civilize,' the IRA in 1882 meant measures designed to educate, Christianize, make economically dependent, and absorb the Indians as individuals into American society." Indian historian Vine Deloria, Jr., writes of this oldest and longest surviving of the Indian rights organizations, "The Association was founded in 1882 when public attention was shifting from the continuous conflicts on the frontier to new ways of assimilating the surviving members of Indian tribes into American society. It was natural, given this context, that the IRA would begin its corporate life pledging to 'secure to our Indian population civil rights and general education, (to) assist the Secretary of the Interior and the Commissioner of Indian Affairs in carrying out the wise and just measures recommended by them in their last report, and in time bring[ing] about the complete civilization of the Indians and their admission to citizenship." Later members included Charles C. C. Painter, Francis Ellington Leupp, and Charles James Rhoads.

In 1885, the association published its "statement of objectives" for the organization. This statement reads:

The Association seeks to secure the civilization of the two hundred and ninety thousand Indians of the United States (inclusive of the thirty thousand natives of Alaska), and to prepare the way for their absorption into the common life of our own people. The Indian as a savage member of a tribal organization cannot survive, ought not to survive, the aggressions of civilization, but his individual redemption from heathenism and ignorance, his transformation from the condition of a savage nomad to that of an industrious American citizen, is abundantly possible. This change can be fully accomplished only by means of legislation. While we fully recognize the absolute necessity of that work which has been performed in the past and is nobly continued to-day in behalf of the civilization of the Indian by teachers in Government and mission schools, by missionaries, by officers of the Army, by Indian Agents and Government employees, by hundreds of right-minded, generous men and women throughout the country, we, nevertheless, confidently assert these individual efforts will have achieved complete success only when certain vital points of legislation have been secured. No man in these United States to-day can be rightly termed civilized, nor can his position be considered a safe one, who is removed from both the protection and the punishment of the law, who is denied a protected title to land and the right of holding it as an individual, or who is deprived of the blessings of a practical education. The Indian is in *all* cases (broadly speaking) destitute of some of these safeguards and advantages, in *some* cases destitute of them all. So long as this condition of affairs exists, the necessity for an Indian Rights Association may be fairly claimed, and that moral and financial support upon which the life of such an organization depends may be justly asked from the general public.

The Indian Rights Association aims to secure for the Indian,

I. Law, and to awaken that spirit of even-handed justice in the nation which will alone make law, when secured, fully operative.
II. Education. Signifying by this broad term the developing for their highest use physical, intellectual, and moral powers.
III. A protected individual title to land. This is the entering-wedge by which tribal organization is to be rent asunder.

These three foundation stones, on which the true civilization of the American Indian can alone securely rest, must be laid by the Congress of the United States. That Congress will never rouse itself for this great work until commanded so to do by the united voice of people may be safely assumed. It is, therefore, the great object of our Association to affect Congress by the only means through which that body can be affected—its constituency. The pressure of business upon Congress is so enormous that measures designed for the welfare of the Indian cannot even gain a hearing unless they shall be emphasized and supported by public sentiment. In the past Indian wars, Indian wrongs, and the expenditure of blood and money, which they always entail, have resulted mainly from public ignorance regarding them. This ignorance is now, to some extent, but by no means entirely, dissipated.

Historian David Holford writes, "The Indian Rights Association in 1890 opposed cession of any land until after a reservation was allotted. The Association took this position because it feared not enough land would remain to allot all eligible members of the tribe. But the Association too was unconcerned about potential problems land cessions would cause future generations of Indians, and maintained that after a reservation was allotted, the tribe could then safely dispose of 'refuse' and surplus real estate. By 1898, the Indian Rights Association did become aware of a population problem of sorts on some reservations and it protested a bill before Congress [which eventually become the Curtis Act] to formalize an agreement with three tribes in Oklahoma to cede their unallotted lands to the government. The Association contended that 160–acre allotments were not large enough to sustain the growing population on those reservations. However, the group was not speaking of human population; it was concerned about the expanding herds of Indian livestock."

In the first years of the twentieth century, the organization's influence can be seen in the appointment of former IRA members Francis E. Leupp (1905) and Charles J. Rhoads (1928) to the position of commissioner of Indian Affairs. The IRA, however, was an organization of non-Indians, and its support of ending Indian dances on reservations and demise of the peyote religion left Indians who supported those cultural aspects of Native American life to form their own, pan-Indian groups, such as the Society of American Indians (1911). The group still survives (in its headquarters in Philadelphia), and the publication of its papers on microfilm in 1975 allows researchers a glimpse into the rise of the oldest and still surviving Indian rights organization. Its mission now, according to the *Native American Information Directory*, a publication of modern Indian rights groups, is to "maintain first-hand knowledge of conditions in Indian communities; keep in touch with governmental Indian affairs; monintor and report on judicial and legislative activities involving Indian concerns; act as a clearinghouse for appeals of all sorts for aid to Indians and for information on all phases of Indian affairs." It "sponsors prominent artists and speakers in programs introducing local communities to Native American cultures."

See also Painter, Charles Cornelius Coffin.

References Deloria, Vine, Jr., "The Indian Rights Association." In Sandra L. Cadwalader and Vine Deloria, Jr., eds., *The Aggressions of Civilization: Federal Indian Policy since the 1880s* (1984); Ericson, Jack T., *Indian Rights Association Papers: A Guide to the Microfilm Edition, 1864–1973* (1975); Furtaw, Julia C., ed., *Native Americans Information Directory* (1993); Holford, David M., "The Subversion of the Indian Land Allotment System, 1887–1934." *Indian Historian* 8 (1); LaPotin, Armand S., "Indian Rights Association (1882)." In LaPotin, Armand S., ed., *Native American Voluntary Organizations* (1987); *Second Annual Report of the Executive Committee of the Indian Rights Association* (1885).

Indian Self-Determination and Education Assistance Act of 1975 (Public Law 93–638, 88 Stat. 2203–2217)

This federal act of 4 January 1975 was established "to provide maximum Indian participation in the Government of the Indian people; to provide for the full participation of Indian tribes in programs and services conducted by the Federal Government for Indians and to encourage the development of human resources of the Indian people; to establish a program of assistance to upgrade Indian education; to support the right of

Indian citizens to control their own educational activities; and for other purposes." In enacting this legislation, Congress found that "the prolonged Federal domination of Indian service programs has served to retard rather than enhance the progress of Indian people and their communities by depriving Indians of the full opportunity to develop leadership skills crucial to the realization of self-government, and has denied to the Indian people an effective voice in the planning and implementation of programs for the benefit of Indians which are responsive to the true needs of Indian communities." This law is known more simply as "638." The editors of *Felix Cohen's Handbook of Federal Indian Law* call this act one of "the most significant laws from the [Native American] self-determination era."

Reference Strickland, Rennard, ed., *Felix Cohen's Handbook of Federal Indian Law* (1982).

Indian Tribal Tax Status Act of 1982 (96 Stat. 2608–11)

In this federal action of 14 January 1983, which was part of the omnibus bill to revise tax and ERISA provisions of the income tax code, the Congress amended the code to allow 1) Indian tribal governments to be treated as states for certain purposes, to allow an income tax deduction for charitable donations to Indians, or whether Indian vehicles may be taxed, and 2) to properly define what is an "Indian Tribal Government." The latter portion, which is section 203 of the enactment, defined tribal government as "the governing body of any tribe, band, community, village, or group of Indians, or (if applicable) Alaska Natives, which is determined by the Secretary [of the Treasury], after consultation with the Secretary of the Interior, to exercise governmental functions."

Indians in Film

In the first several decades after motion pictures appeared, filmmakers often portrayed American Indians as brutes and savages. The quick production of one-reel films and the need to have exciting, interesting subject matter made the Indian a constant theme of many of these earlier films. From Thomas Edison's flickering kinetoscopic images of Native American dances shown to astonished crowds at the 1893 Columbian Exposition in Chicago to Kevin Costner's landmark *Dances with Wolves*, the Indian had undergone an important and dramatic transformation on the movie screen.

Historian Eileen Bowser writes, "Indian films might be considered a branch of Westerns, but in the early years they constituted a separate genre. They could be made in the eastern or southern part of the United States, as well as in the Far East, without departing from authenticity. The attractions of Indian films included the beautiful landscapes and free movements of Western films plus elements of exoticism, nobility, and romance. There was also the allure of nudity (of men only), which had the same respectability as the nakedness of indigenes in travel films from distant lands." Historian Michael Welsh writes, "Griffith shared with Ince a fascination with the story of the Indian and the darker side of westward expansion. In *A Pueblo Legend* (1912), Griffith journeyed to Isleta Pueblo south of Albuquerque, New Mexico, in search of a realistic setting for a story on the decline of the 'noble savage.' Griffith used costume plates and shields, weapons, and accessories loaned by the Museum of Indian Antiquities in Albuquerque to achieve this realism."

The 1970s saw such groundbreaking movies as *A Man Called Horse* (1970) and *House Made of Dawn* (1972), but the most important was Arthur Penn's *Little Big Man.* American Indian Movement activist Dennis Banks wrote in 1994, "In 1970 when the movie *A Man Called Horse* was being released around the country, the American Indian Movement (AIM) called for a national boycott against the film, protesting the degradation of our culture through Hollywood and its films. We [now] do see Native People, both in television and movies, who have roles with character. Floyd 'Red Crow' Westerman has not only been educating the public for several decades through his album *Custer Died for Your Sins*, but he recently moved into Hollywood with performances in many films, including *Dances with Wolves.*"

See also *Dances with Wolves; Little Big Man.*

References Bowser, Eileen, *The Transformation of Cinema, 1907–1915* (1990); Banks, Dennis, "Foreword." In Champaign, Duane, ed., *Native America Portrait of the Peoples* (1994); Welsh, Michael, "Origins of Western Film Companies, 1887–1920." *Journal of the West* 22 (4).

Indians of All Tribes (IAT)

See Alcatraz, Occupation of.

Iowa Insurance Company v. LaPlante et al. (480 U.S. 9, 94 L.Ed. 2d 10, 107 S.Ct. 971 [1987])

The power of tribal courts and joint jurisdiction with state and federal courts were the subjects of this case, decided by the U.S. Supreme Court in 1987. Edward M. LaPlante, a Blackfeet Indian, worked on the Wellman Ranch, located on the Blackfeet reservation in Montana. In 1982, he was injured in a truck accident, and sued the owners of the ranch, the Wellman family, who are also Blackfeet Indians, before the Blackfeet Tribal Court. The Iowa Mutual Insurance Company, which held the policy for the ranch, then moved in the Federal Court for the District of Montana to have them removed from liability in the case, arguing that LaPlante's work as a truck driver was beyond the scope of the coverage of the insurance held by the ranch. The district court dismissed the action on the grounds that (1) the tribal court had to decide whether it had any jurisdiction in the case, and (2) whether the tribal court held singular or dual jurisdiction with the district court. The U.S. Court of Appeals for the Ninth Circuit in San Francisco affirmed, allowing that if the federal court did become involved in the case, it could do so with the opinion of the tribal court in hand. On appeal, the U.S. Supreme Court granted certiorari (the right to hear the case), and heard arguments on 1 December 1986. Less than three months later, on 24 February 1987, Justice Thurgood Marshall spoke for an 8–1 decision (Justice John Paul Stevens dissented) that the district court had the jurisdiction, whether singularly or dually, and could oversee the tribal court's decision involving, in this case, a non-Indian (plaintiff Iowa Insurance Company). Justice Marshall stated simply, "Although petitioner must exhaust available tribal remedies before instituting suit in federal court, the Blackfeet Tribal Courts' determination of tribal jurisdiction is ultimately subject to review. If the Tribal Appeals Court upholds the lower court's determination that the tribal courts have jurisdiction, petitioner may challenge that ruling in the district court. Unless a federal court determines that the Tribal Court lacked jurisdiction, however, proper deference to the tribal court system precludes relitigation of issues raised by LaPlante's bad-faith claim and resolved in the Tribal Courts."

See also *National Farmers Union Insurance Companies and Lodge Grass School District No. 27 v. Crow Tribe of Indians et al.*

Jackson, Andrew—Message on Indian Removal

In his first Annual Message to Congress in December 1829, President Andrew Jackson outlined his plans for the full-scale removal of the Indian nations east of the Mississippi to new reservation west of that river. However, he expressed some reservation as to the prudence of the removal policy as a whole. In the message, Jackson wrote,

The condition and ulterior destiny of the Indian tribes within the limits of some our States have become objects of much interest and importance. It has long been the policy of Government to introduce among them the arts of civilization, in the hope of gradually reclaiming them from a wandering life. This policy, however, has been coupled with another wholly incompatible with its success. Professing a desire to civilize and settle them, we have at the same time lost no opportunity to purchase their lands and thrust them farther into the wilderness. By this means they have not only been kept in a wandering state, but [have] been led to look upon us as unjust and indifferent to their fate. Thus, though lavish in its expenditures upon the subject, Government has constantly defeated its own policy, and the Indians in general, receding farther and farther to the west, have retained their savage habits. A portion, however, of the Southern tribes, having mingled much with the whites and made some progress in the arts of civilized life, have lately attempted to erect an independent government within the limits of Georgia and Alabama. These States, claiming to be the only sovereigns within their territories, extended their laws over the Indians, which induced the latter to call upon the United States for protection.

Under these circumstances the question presented was whether the General Government had a right to sustain those people in their pretensions. The Constitution declares that 'no new State shall be formed or erected within the jurisdiction of any other State' without the consent of its legislature. If the General Government is not permitted to tolerate the erection of a confederate State within the territory of one of the members of the Union against her consent, much less could it allow a foreign and independent government to establish itself there. Georgia became a member of the Confederacy which eventuated in our Federal Union as a sovereign State, always asserting her claim to certain limits, which, having been originally defined in her colonial charter and subsequently recognized in the treaty of peace, she has ever since continued to enjoy, except as they have circumscribed by her own voluntary transfer of a portion of her territory to the United States in the articles of cession of 1802. Alabama was admitted into the Union on the same footing with the original States, with boundaries which were prescribed by Congress. There is no constitutional, conventional, or legal provision which allows them less power over the Indians within their borders than is possessed by Maine or New York. Would the people of Maine permit the Penobscot tribe to erect an independent government within their State? And unless they did would it not be the duty of the General Government to support them in resisting such a measure? Would the people of New York permit each remnant of the Six Nations within her borders to declare itself an independent people under the protection of the United States? Could the Indians establish a separate republic on each of their reservations in Ohio? And if they were so disposed would it be the duty of this Government to protect them in the attempt? If the principle involved in the obvious answer to these questions be abandoned, it will follow that the objects of this Government are reversed, and that it has become a part of its duty to aid in destroying the States which it was established to protect.

Actuated by this view of the subject, I informed the Indians inhabiting parts of

Georgia and Alabama that their attempt to establish an independent government would not be countenanced by the Executive of the United States, and advised them to emigrate beyond the Mississippi or submit to the laws of those States.

Our conduct toward these people is deeply interesting to our national character. Their present condition, contrasted with what they once were, makes a most powerful appeal to our sympathies. Our ancestors found them the uncontrolled possessors of these vast regions. By persuasion and force they have been made to retire from river to river and from mountain to mountain, until some of the tribes have become extinct and others have left but remnants to preserve for a while their once terrible names. Surrounded by the whites with their arts of civilization, which by destroying the resources of the savage doom him to weakness and decay, the fate of the Mohegan, the Narragansett, and the Delaware is fast overtaking the Choctaw, the Cherokee, and the Creek. That this fate surely awaits them if they remain within the limits of the States does not admit of a doubt. Humanity and national honor demand that every effort should be made to avert so great a calamity. It is too late to inquire whether it was just in the United States to include them and their territory within the bounds of new States, whose limits they could control. That step cannot be retraced. A State can not be dismembered by Congress or restricted in the exercise of her constitutional power. But the people of those States and of every State, actuated by feelings of justice and a regard for our national honor, submit to you the interesting question whether something can not be done, consistently with the rights of the States, to preserve this much-injured race.

As a means of effecting this end I suggest for your consideration the propriety of setting apart an ample district west of the Mississippi, and without the limit of any State or Territory now formed, to be guaranteed to the Indian tribes as long as they shall occupy it, each tribe having a distinct control over the portion designated for its use. There they may be secured in the enjoyment of governments of their own choice, subject to no other control from the United States than such as may be necessary to preserve peace on the frontier and between the several tribes. There the benevolent may endeavor to teach them the arts of civilization, and, by promoting union and harmony among them, to raise up an interesting commonwealth, destined to perpetuate the race and to attest the humanity and justice of this Government.

This emigration should be voluntary, for it would be as cruel as unjust to compel the aborigines to abandon the graves of their fathers and seek a home in a distant land. But they should be distinctly informed that if they remain within the limits of the States they must be subject to their laws. In return for their obedience as individuals they will without doubt be protected in the enjoyment of those possessions which they have improved by their industry. But it seems to me visionary to suppose that in this state of things claims can be allowed on tracts of country on which they have neither dwelt nor made improvements, merely because they have seen them from a mountain or passed them in the chase. Submitting to the laws of the States, and receiving, like other citizens, protection in their persons and property, they will ere long become merged in the mass of our population.

A Cherokee, Speckled Snake, replied to Jackson's Indian Removal message in a discourse that was printed in Samuel G. Drake's 1841 work, *The Book of the Indians; or, Biography and History of the Indians of North America, From Its First Discovery to the Year 1841:*

Brothers! We have heard the talk of our great father; it is very kind. He says he loves his red children. Brothers! When the white man first came to these shores, the Muscogees gave him land, and kindled him a fire to make him comfortable; and when the pale faces of the south made war on him, their young men drew the tomahawk, and protected his head from the scalping knife. But when the white man had warmed himself before the Indian's fire, and filled himself with the Indian's hominy, he became very large; he stopped not for the mountain tops, and his feet covered the plains and the valleys. His hands grasped the eastern and the western sea. Then he became our great father. He loved his red children; but he said, "You must move a little farther, lest I should, by accident, tread on you." With one foot he pushed the red man over the Oconee [a river in central Georgia], and with the other he trampled down the graves of his fathers. But our great father still loved his red children, and he soon made them another talk. He said much; but it all meant nothing, but "move a little farther; you are too near to me." I have heard a great many talks from our great father, and they begun and ended the same. Brothers! When he made us a talk on a former occasion, he said, "Get a little farther; go beyond the Oconee and the Oakmulgee [now Ocmulgee, a river in central Georgia]; there is pleasant country." He also said, "It shall be yours forever." Now he says, "The land you live on is not yours; go beyond the Mississippi; there is game; there you may remain while the grass grows or the water runs." Brothers! Will not our great father come there also? He loves his red children, and his tongue is not forked.

References Drake, Samuel G., *The Book of the Indians; or, Biography and History of the Indians of North America, from Its First Discovery to the Year 1841 (1841);* Richardson, ed., *A Compilation of the Messages and Papers of the Presidents (1897–1911).*

Jackson, Helen Maria Fiske Hunt (1830–1885)

Theodore Roosevelt at one time called her a "foolish sentimentalist." American writer, reformer and novelist, Helen Hunt Jackson's most famous works are those sympathetic to American Indians, including *A Century of Dishonor* (1881) and the novel *Ramona* (1885). Little is known about her life, due, according to biographer Thurman Wilkins, to "[her] strong doubts about the propriety of publicizing women and [she] discouraged accounts of her own career." Born Helen Maria Fiske on 15 October 1830 in Amherst, Massachusetts, she was the eldest of the two daughters of Professor Nathan Welby Fiske of Amherst College, and Deborah (née Vinal) Fiske, both of whom died from tuberculosis before their daughters had grown. Helen was educated at the Ipswich Female Seminary in Ipswich and at the Spingler Institute in New York City (she was a schoolmate of the poet Emily Dickinson). When only 22 she married Lieutenant Edward Bissell Hunt, an army engineer. Their first child died of a brain tumor when only an infant, Hunt was killed in an accident in 1863, and two years later their only surviving child died of diphtheria. After their deaths, Helen Hunt lived in Newport, Rhode Island, and traveled to Europe. Her first published work, a poem entitled "Lifted Over" on her grief, appeared in the influential magazine *The Nation* in 1865. In fact, writes biographer Helen M. Bannan, "[Her] early poems won her recognition from the influential Thomas Wentworth Higginson; her subsequent prolific periodical publications gathered a wide popular audience and critical praise, even from [Ralph Waldo] Emerson. [She] supported herself and traveled widely on the profits of her pen. Her generally pious and sentimental treatments of death, love, and nature themes date much of her poetry, but many of her *Verses* (1870) and *Sonnets and Lyrics* (1886) can still be appreciated for their skillful technique and use of language."

After returning to the United States, Helen Hunt settled in Colorado Springs, Colorado, where she met William Sharpless Jackson, a wealthy merchant and railroad speculator, and the two were married in 1875. While in Colorado, and throughout the West, she saw the plight of the American Indians up close, and she initiated a campaign to improve their condition. It was in the pages of the influential newspaper the

New York Tribune that Jackson's letters, signed "H.H.," became some of the greatest protests against the treatment of the Indians of the nation. Following the massacre at Sand Creek, Colorado, in 1864, she had delivered a series of communications to the papers, all published, which detailed "The Slaughter of Friendly Indians." Responding to a particularly vicious attack by Secretary of the Interior Carl Schurz, she angrily responded, "The writer of this letter is, in allusion to the murders and outrages committed by some of the White River Utes, that 'H. H. is the champion of the friends who wrought the ruin.' Have the readers of *The Tribune* so understood my protests against the injustice of punishing the innocent for the crimes of the guilty?"

After hearing the Indian lecturer Susette La Flesche, Jackson began work on the book that ranks among the finest works of exposé literature. In 1881, her *A Century of Dishonor* appeared. Just as Harriet Beecher Stowe's *Uncle Tom's Cabin* had exposed the evils of slavery thirty years earlier, *A Century of Dishonor* uncovered the disaster that was federal Indian policy. She wrote in the conclusion to the work, "It makes little difference, however, where one opens the record of the history of the Indians; every page and every year has its dark stain. The story of one tribe is the story of all, varied only by differences of place and time; but neither time nor place makes any difference in the main facts. Colorado is as greedy and unjust in 1880 as was Georgia in 1830, and Ohio in 1795; and the United States Government breaks promises now as deftly as then, and with an added ingenuity from long practice." Thomas Henry Tibbles wrote of *A Century of Dishonor*, "I strongly doubt if we could have won [the Ponca citizenship case] without her help." Emerson, writer and Transcendentalist, when asked if he thought she was the greatest woman poet on the continent, remarked, "Perhaps we might as well omit woman."

In 1883, Helen Hunt Jackson and Abbot Kinney (1850–1920), a publisher from California with a noted background in local Indian affairs, were both appointed as special agents to travel to California and investigate the plight of the Mission Indians of that state. They submitted their report to Commissioner of Indian Affairs Hiram Price with several recommendations, among them being the surveying and marking of the boundaries of their reservations, the total removal of all white settlers living on the reservation, that the reservation lands be patented to the individual mission tribes, with the trust to be in the United States, the establishment of more schools for the Indians, increased supervision and inspection of the reservations' interests, and the appointment of a lawyer to represent the Indians' interests in court. Her experiences in California led to the composition of her second important work, 1885's *Ramona.* Mrs. Jackson spent the winter of 1883–84 composing *Ramona.* As Thurman Wilkins relates, "[Jackson wrote that] The story came at white heat. 'I did not write 'Ramona'; it was written through me. My life-

Helen Hunt Jackson wrote A Century of Dishonor, *published in 1881, a work that did for Indian reform what Harriet Beecher Stowe's* Uncle Tom's Cabin *did to rouse antislavery sentiment.*

blood went into it—all I had thought, felt and suffered for five years on the Indian question.' It lacked the scope and power of *Uncle Tom's Cabin;* many oversimplifications distorted the intricate problem that it posed, and the anticlimax of its sugary ending weakened its purpose as a novel of protest. Still, *Ramona* was Mrs. Jackson's finest achievement, a romance of genuine vitality about the tottering Spanish society in California and Indians victimized by gringo usurpers. Successful when published in 1884, the book continued to sell steadily, through more than three hundred printings. It has reached the motion picture screen in at least three versions, and in southern California, where it did much to revive the tradition of a Spanish past, it inspires an annual pageant at Hemet. *Ramona*, rather than the poetry once so overpraised, keeps the name of Helen Hunt Jackson still alive." Biographer Jay C. Clancy explains, "*A Century of Dishonor* and *Ramona* were important to the furtherance of the Indian reform movement and are considered Jackson's major works. Near the end of her life, she wrote to Thomas Wentworth Higginson that they were 'the only things I have done for which I am glad now. The rest is of no moment. They will live on and they will bear fruit. They already have." Dying of cancer, she desired her work to make as much of an impact as possible. Just four days before her death she wrote to President Grover Cleveland that he should read *A Century of Dishonor* and "strike the first steady blow toward lifting the burden of infamy from our country and righting the wrongs of the Indian races." Helen Hunt Jackson died in San Francisco on 12 August 1885 at the age of 54. She asked to be buried at the summit of Cheyenne Mountain in Colorado Springs, but overzealous tourists who camped at her gravesite and promoters who charged ten cents to see the grave led her husband to move her body to Evergreen Cemetery in Colorado Springs.

See also Schurz, Carl.

References Bannon, Helen M., "Helen Maria Fiske Hunt Jackson." In Lina Mainero, ed., *American Women Writers: A Critical Reference Guide from Colonial Times to the Present* (1993); Clancy, Jay C., "Jackson, Helen Maria Fiske Hunt." In Alden Whitman, ed., *American Reformers: An H. W. Wilson Biographical Dictionary* (1985); Jackson, Helen Hunt, *A Century of Dishonor: A Sketch of the United States Government's Dealings with Some of the Indian Tribes* (1887); Jackson, Helen Hunt [as "H. H."], *New York Tribune*, 24 February 1880, 2; Jackson, Helen Hunt and Abbott McKinney, *Report of Mrs. Helen Hunt Jackson and Abbot McKinney on the Mission Indians in 1831, Abbreviated* (1887); Kirkpatrick, D. L., ed., *Reference Guide to American Literature* (1987); May, Antoinette, *Helen Hunt Jackson.: A Lonely Voice of Conscience (1987); "Obituary: Helen Fiske Hunt Jackson." New York Tribune*, 14 August 1885, 5; Roosevelt, Theodore, *The Winning of the West* (1906); *Who Was Who In America, 1897–1942* (1981); Wilkins, Thurman, "Helen Maria Fiske Hunt Jackson." In Edward T. James, ed., *Notable American Women, 1607–1950: A Biographical Dictionary* (1971).

Jaybird Mining Company v. Weir (271 U.S. 609 [1926])

In this Supreme Court case, decided in 1926, the court held that a law of Congress which specified that royalties from the extraction of ore from an allotment on an Indian reservation to be paid directly to the secretary of the interior were exempt from state taxes. After a patent for an allotment was issued to Hum-bah-wat-tah, a Quapaw Indian, in 1896, he submitted that restrictions on alienation and lease would remain on the allotment for 25 years. The act of Congress of 3 March 1921 (41 Stat. 1225, at 1248) extended that period for an additional 25 years. Sometime before 1921, the Jaybird Mining Company obtained a lease to mine lead and zinc ores on the allotment (now belonging to Hum-bah-wat-tah's heirs) from the Department of the Interior, with the stipulation that royalties on the mined ore would be paid to the department to be held in trust for the allottee. When Joe Weir, County Treasurer for Ottawa County, Oklahoma, attempted to follow state law and tax these royalties, the mining company paid the tax ($2,319.80) under protest, then sued in district court to retrieve the tax as well as stop further enforcement of the tax. The district court for

Ottawa County held for the company, but on appeal the Supreme Court of Oklahoma reversed. The U.S. Supreme Court agreed to hear the case. Argued on 29 April 1926, Justice Pierce Butler held for the majority (justices Louis Brandeis and James McReynolds dissenting) that a state cannot tax the activity of a federal agency. Justice Butler explained, "The Quapaw Indians are under the guardianship of the United States. The land and Indian owners are bound by restrictions specified in the patent…It is the duty and established policy of the government to protect these dependents in respect of their property. The restrictions imposed are in furtherance of that policy. The lessee is an agency or instrumentality employed by the government for the development and use of the restricted land and to mine ores therefrom for the benefit of the Indian wards. It is elementary that the federal government in all its activities is independent of state control. This rule is broadly applied; and, without congressional consent, no federal agency or instrumentality can be taxed by state authorities."

Jefferson, Thomas—Address on Indian Affairs

President Thomas Jefferson, in a message to the Senate and House of Representatives on 18 January 1803, discussed his thoughts on the growing conflict between whites and Indians and the formulation of a government policy on dealing with the controversy. Jefferson's message reads:

…The Indian tribes residing within the limits of the United States have for a considerable time been growing more and more uneasy at the constant diminution of the territory they occupy, although effected by their own voluntary sales, and the policy had long been gaining strength with them of refusing absolutely all further sale on any conditions, insomuch as this time it hazards their friendship and excites dangerous jealousies and perturbations in their minds to make any overture for the purchase of the smallest portions of their land. A few tribes only are not yet obstinately in these dispositions. In order peaceable [*sic*] to counteract this policy of theirs and to provide an extension of territory which the rapid increase of our numbers will call for, two measures are deemed expedient. First. to encourage them to abandon hunting, to apply to the raising [of] stock, to agriculture, and domestic manufacture, and thereby prove to themselves that less land and labor will maintain them in this better than their former mode of living. The extensive forests necessary to the hunting life will then become useless, and they will see advantage in exchanging them for the means of improving their farms and of increasing their domestic efforts. Secondly. To multiply trading houses among them, and place within their reach those things which will contribute more to their domestic comfort than the possession of extensive but incultivated wilds. Experience and reflection will develop to them the wisdom of exchanging what they can spare and we want for what we can spare and they want. In leading them thus to agriculture, to manufactures, and civilization; in bringing together their and our sentiments, and in preparing them ultimately to participate in the benefits of our Government, I trust and believe we are acting for their greatest good.

Reference Richardson, James, comp., *A Compilation of the Messages and Papers of the Presidents, 1789–1914* (1897–1917).

Jemison, Alice Mae Lee (Seneca-Cherokee) (1901–1964)

Native American activist, Alice Mae Lee Jemison was noted for her association in the 1930s and 1940s with the obscure American Indian Federation, as well as her harsh opposition to the Indian New Deals and government attempts to control the affairs of Native American peoples. She was born Alice Mae Lee at Silver Creek, near the Cattaraugus Reservation of the Seneca in upstate New York, the first of three children of Daniel Lee, a Cherokee, and Elnora Seneca, a Seneca. According to biographer

Laurence M. Hauptman, her father was a Cherokee cabinetmaker, but Alice and her two siblings were brought up "in the matrilineal society of the Senaca, in which her mother's family was prominent." Alice attended a high school off of the reservation and graduated, while at the same time working at odd jobs to help support her family. Soon after graduating, she married LeVerne Leonard Jemison, a steelworker on the Cattaraugus Reservation, but the marriage failed and they were divorced in 1928.

It was at this time that Alice Jemison became a politically important member of the Native American rights community. Beginning as a secretary to her cousin, Seneca Nation of Indians (SNI) President Ray Jemison in 1929, she became a journalist (writing articles for the North American Indian Newspaper Alliance) and a lobbyist in Washington, D.C. The height of her power came during the Roosevelt Administration, when she joined other critics of the New Deal in general and the Indian New Deal in particular, most notably the Indian Reorganization Act of 1934. Besides her criticism of this legislation, she sought to dissolve the Bureau of Indian Affairs, end government controls over the Native American population, and dispose of Indian Commissioner John Collier, who had been a member of the American Civil Liberties Union, a group which Jemison considered to be a Communist organization. Her outspokeness led her to join the American Indian Federation (AIF), an activist group. She worked closely with the AIF's president, Joseph Bruner (Creek), becoming his spokesman and editor of the federation newspaper, *The First American.* Her stands brought her the support of many fascist organizations, including the German-American Bund, which was the leading pro-German organization in the United States prior to World War II and was pro-Hitler. Although Jemison never gave her support to this or any other German group, she was branded as an Indian Nazi, which brought her great disrepute. Her last fight was to oppose Seneca participation in the Selective Service Act against the Indians' wishes. After that, her power waned. She died in Washington on 6 March 1964 and was buried on the Cattaraugus Reservation.

See also American Indian Federation.

References Hauptman, Laurence M., "Alice Jemison: Seneca Political Activist." *Indian Historian* 12 (2); Hauptman, Laurence M., "Jemison, Alice Mae Lee." In James, Edward T., ed., *Notable American Women, 1607–1950: A Biographical Dictionary* (1971–80); Hauptman, Laurence M., "Jemison, Alice Mae Lee." In Malone, Dumas et al., eds., *Dictionary of American Biography* (1930–88); Symes, Martha I., "Alice Mae Jemison." In Malinowski, Sharon, ed., *Notable Native Americans* (1995).

Johnson, Lyndon Baines—Message on Indian Affairs

On 6 March 1968, shortly before he announced to the nation that he would not run for re-election, President Lyndon Baines Johnson sent to Congress a special message on Indian affairs, titled "The Forgotten American." In the preamble to that message, Johnson wrote:

To the Congress of the United States: Mississippi and Utah, the Potomac and the Chattahoochee, Appalachia and Shenandoah.... The words of the Indian have become our words—the names of our states and streams and landmarks. His myths and his heroes enrich our literature. His lore colors our art and our language. For two centuries, the American Indian has been a symbol of the drama and excitement of the earliest America. But for two centuries, he has been an alien in his own land. Relations between the United States Government and the tribes were originally in the hands of the War Department. Until 1871, the United States treated the Indian tribes as foreign nations. It has been only 44 years since the United States affirmed the Indian's citizenship: the full political equality essential for human dignity in a democratic society. It has been only 22 years since Congress enacted the Indian Claims Act, to acknowledge the Nation's debt to the first Americans for their land. But political equality and compensation for ancestral lands are not enough. The American Indian deserves a chance to develop his talents and share fully in the future of our Nation.

There are about 600,000 Indians in America today. Some 400,000 live on or near reservations in 25 States. The remaining 200,000 have moved to our cities and towns. The most striking fact about the American Indians today is their tragic plight:

Fifty thousand Indian families live in unsanitary, dilapidated dwellings: many in huts, shanties, even abandoned automobiles.

The unemployment rate among Indians is nearly 40 percent—more than ten times the national average.

Fifty percent of Indian schoolchildren—double the national average—drop out before completing high school.

Indian literacy rates are among the lowest in the Nation; the rates of sickness and poverty are among the highest.

Thousands of Indians who have migrated into the cities find themselves untrained for jobs and unprepared for urban life.

The average age of death of an American Indian today is 44 years; for all other Americans, it is 65.

The American Indian, once proud and free, is torn now between white and tribal values; between the politics and language of the white man and his own historic culture. His problems, sharpened by years of defeat and exploitation, neglect and inadequate effort, will take many years to overcome.

But recent landmark laws—The Economic Opportunity Act, the Elementary and Secondary Education Act, the Manpower Development and Training Act—have given us an opportunity to deal with the persistent problems of the American Indian. The time has come to focus our efforts on the plight of the American Indian through these and the other laws passed in the last few years. No enlightened nation, no responsible government, no progressive people can sit idly by and permit this shocking situation to continue.

I propose a new goal for our Indian programs: A goal that ends the old debate about "termination" of Indian programs and stresses self-determination; a goal that erases old attitudes of paternalism and promotes partnership [and] self-help. Our goal must be:

A standard of living for the Indians equal to that of the country as a whole.

Freedom of Choice: An opportunity to remain in their homelands, if they choose, without surrendering their dignity; an opportunity to move to the towns and cities of America, if they choose, equipped with the skills to live in equality and dignity.

Full participation in the life of modern America, with a full share of economic opportunity and social justice.

I propose, in short, a policy of maximum choice for the American Indian: a policy expressed in programs of self-help, self-development, self-determination.

To start toward our goal in Fiscal 1969, I recommend that the Congress appropriate one-half a billion dollars for programs targeted at the American Indian—about 10 percent more than Fiscal 1968.

Reference *Public Papers of the Presidents of the United States: Lyndon B. Johnson, Containing the Public Messages, Speeches, and Statements of the President, January 1 to June 30, 1968* (1970).

Johnson and Graham's Lessee v. McIntosh **(8 Wheaton [21 U.S.] 543 [1823])**

This was the first case to come before the U.S. Supreme Court that defined the legal relationship that Indians had with the U.S. government. In 1775, the Piankeshaw Indians of what was to become Illinois ceded land to a speculator named Thomas Johnson. In 1783 Virginia, which previously had claims to the land that would develop into Illinois, ceded its claims to the U.S. government under the Articles of Confederation. The land remained with Johnson. In 1818, one William McIntosh purchased from the U.S. government Johnson's plot as part of a 11,560 acre acquisition. Thomas Johnson died in October 1819, and bestowed upon his son, Joshua Johnson, and his grandson, Thomas J. Graham, the rights to his original acquisition. The two men then sued McIntosh in the District Court of Illinois to eject him from the lands. The court ruled for McIntosh, and the two plaintiffs sued to the U.S. Supreme Court.

The case was argued before the court on 17 February 1823, and decided on 10 March of the same year. Chief Justice John Marshall held for a unanimous court that the Indians had had no right to sell land directly to anyone, and that McIntosh's claim was the only valid one. Under the theory of discovery, the powers that established government on the continent (namely the British and then, as a formality, the Americans) had the absolute power over Indian lands. As the chief justice explained, "The statutes of Virginia, and of all of the other colonies, and of the United States, treat them [Indians] as an inferior race of people, without the privileges of citizens, and under the perpetual protection and pupilage of the government. The act of Virginia of 1662 forbade purchases from the Indians, and does not appear that it was ever repealed. The act of 1779 is rather to be regarded as a declatory act, founded upon what had always been regarded as the settled law. These statutes seem to define sufficiently the nature of the Indian title to lands; a mere right of usufruct [the right to enjoy a thing which belongs to another] and habitation, without power of alienation [the right to sell one's land]. By the law of nature, they had not acquired a fixed property capable of being transferred. The measure of property acquired by occupancy is determined, according to the law of nature, by the extent of men's wants, and their capacity for using it to supply them. It is a violation of the rights of others to exclude them from the use of what we do not want, and they have an occasion for. Upon this principle the North American Indians could have acquired no proprietary interest in the vast tracts of territory which they wandered over, and their right to the lands on which they hunted could not be considered as superior to that which is acquired to the sea by fishing in it." Historian David Wilkins wrote in the *American Indian Law Review* in 1991 that *Johnson v. McIntosh* was one of the "five seminal cases" handed down by the U.S. Supreme Court in its first four decades forming "the political-philosophical-legal basis of tribal-state-federal relations."

Reference Wilkins, David E., "Johnson v. M'Intosh Revisited: Through the Eyes of Mitchel v. United States." *American Indian Law Review* 19 (1).

Johnson et al. v. Gearlds et al. (234 U.S. 422 [1914])

Could federal officers be enjoined from closing saloons in territories ceded to the United States by Indian tribes, on the grounds that those lands were still to be considered as Indian country? This was the issue at question in this Supreme Court case, decided in 1914. Edwin Gearlds, L.J. Krammer, Fred E. Brinkman, and others owned saloons in Belmidji, Minnesota, on land that had once been Chippewa Indian territory, but had been ceded to the United States; article 7 of the treaty with certain bands of Chippewa Indians of 22 February 1855 (10 Stat. 1169) decreed that this territory to be ceded was still subject to the laws of the United States respecting the sale of liquor in the Indian country. When W. E. Johnson, T. E. Brents, H. F. Coggeshall, and others, having been named as special officers of the Interior Department, threatened the defendants named to destroy their liquor and close their place of business because they were in violation of the law, Gearlds et al. sued in the U.S. District Court for the District of Minnesota to enjoin Johnson and the others from enforcing that law; they argued that because they had avoided selling liquor to the Indians, they were not violating the provision involved. The district court sided with Gearlds, forcing Johnson and the other federal officers to appeal directly to the U.S. Supreme Court. Justice Mahlon Pitney held for the court (justices Joseph McKenna and Horace H.

Lurton dissenting) that Gearlds and the others were in violation of the treaty, that the decree enjoining Johnson and the others from enforcing the law was void, and therefore he remanded the case back to the district court with directions to dismiss the action altogether.

Johnson-O'Malley Act of 1934 (48 Stat. 596)

The leading federal legislation dealing with the funding of education for Indian children, the Johnson-O'Malley Act, or JOM, was enacted by Congress on 16 April 1934. Collier biographer Kenneth R. Philp writes, "Collier had great hope for the Johnson-O'Malley measure, but the impact of this reform was minimal, especially in the area of education, for three reasons: 1. the bureau [of Indian Affairs] failed to retain control over its funds; 2. animosity developed between the federal and state administrators; and 3. the public schools refused to establish special Indian programs." The text of the act reads:

An Act Authorizing the Secretary of the Interior to arrange with States or Territories for the education, medical attention, relief of distress, and social welfare of Indians, and for other purposes.

Be it enacted...That the Secretary of the Interior is hereby authorized, in his discretion, to enter into a contract or contracts with any State or Territory having legal authority to do so, for the education, medical attention, agricultural assistance, and social welfare, including relief of distress, of Indians in such State or Territory, through the qualified agencies of such State or Territory, and to expend under such contract or contracts moneys appropriated by Congress for the education, medical attention, agricultural assistance, and social welfare, including relief of distress, of Indians in such State.

Sec. 2. That the Secretary of the Interior, in making any contract herein authorized with any State or Territory, may permit such State or Territory to utilize for the purpose of this Act, existing school buildings, hospitals, and other facilities, and all equipment therein or appertaining thereto, including livestock and other personal property owned by the Government, under such terms and conditions as may be agreed upon for their use and maintenance.

Sec. 3. That the Secretary of the Interior is hereby authorized to perform any and all acts and to make such rules and regulations, including minimum standards of service, as may be necessary and proper for the purpose of carrying the provisions of this Act into effect: *Provided*, That such minimum standards of service are not less than the highest maintained by the States or Territories with which said contract or contracts, as herein provided, are executed.

Sec. 4. That the Secretary of the Interior shall report annually to the Congress any contract or contracts made under the provisions of this Act, and the moneys expended thereunder.

Sec. 5. That the provisions of this Act not apply to the State of Oklahoma.

See also Collier, John.

Reference Philp, Kenneth R., *John Collier's Crusade for Indian Reform, 1920–1954* (1977).

Joint Tribal Council of the Passamaquoddy Tribe et al. v. Morton (388 F. Supp. 649 [1975])

This landmark district court decision, upheld by the First Circuit Court of Appeals, found that Indian tribes, whether recognized by the federal government or not, were part of the trust relationship between the United States and the Indian tribes in the country because of the Indian Nonintercourse Act of 1790. Under that action (1 Stat. 137, now cited as 25 U.S.C. 177), "no purchase, grant, lease, or other conveyance of lands, or of any title or claim thereto, from any Indian nation or tribe of Indians, shall be of any validity in law or equity, unless the same be made by treaty or convention entered into pursuant to the Constitution." The plaintiffs, the Joint Tribal Council of the Passamaquoddy Tribe, alleged that in 1794, four years after this federal action, the Commonwealth of Massachusetts, which at that time owned the area that is now Maine, negotiated a treaty with the Passamaquoddies in which that tribe ceded its lands to the Commonwealth in exchange for 23,000 acres on which the tribal members would live. They further alleged that of that 23,000 acres, the Commonwealth over the years had "sold, leased for 999 years, given easements on, or permitted flooding of approximately 6,000 acres," all in violation of the 1790 Nonintercourse Act. In 1972, the tribe asked the Bureau of Indian Affairs to look into the matter. The commissioner, Louis Rook Bruce, while sympathetic, nonetheless concluded that because the federal government did not recognize the tribe, and thus had no trust relationship with it, "the tribe's proper legal remedy should be sought elsewhere." The tribe then changed its action to ask not for immediate relief but to be considered entitled to "protection under the 1790 [Intercourse] Act." The state of Maine, with Bruce's letter in hand which demonstrated that the tribe was not under federal recognition, asked that the action be dismissed. The tribe's action, suing Secretary of the Interior Rogers C. B. Morton for recognition (the state of Maine was added as an "intervenor" defendant), was heard before the U.S. District Court for the Northern District of Maine. District Judge Edward Gignoux handed down his opinion on 2 January 1975 which held that the Passamaquoddies, whether recognized by the government or not, were entitled to the protections of the 1790 Nonintercourse Act. After discussing the history of the case and precedents in the case law, he wrote, "Applying these rules of construction, the conclusion is inescapable that, as a matter of simple statutory interpretation, the Nonintercourse Act applies to the Passamaquoddies. The literal meaning of the words employed in the statute, used in their ordinary sense, clearly and unambiguously encompasses all tribes of Indians, including the Passamaquoddies; the plain language of the statute is consistent with the Congressional intent; and there is no legislative history or administrative interpretation which conflicts with the words of the Act." He added, "Judgment will be entered for the plaintiffs declaring that the Indian Nonintercourse Act, 25 U.S.C. 177, is applicable to the Passamaquoddy Indian Tribe; that the Act establishes a trust relationship between the United States and the Tribe; and that defendants may not deny plaintiffs' request for litigation in their behalf on the sole ground that there is no trust relationship between the United States and the Tribe."

See also *Cherokee Nation v. Georgia.*

Jones, William Arthur (1844–1912)

More a businessman and local politician than advocate for Indian reform, William A. Jones was one of the longest-serving Indian commissioners, administering the Indian office from 1897 until 1904. He was born at Star, in Pembrokeshire, Wales, on 17 September 1844; when just seven years old, he and his younger brother David Benton Jones emigrated with their parents to Iowa County, Wisconsin, near modern-day Mineral Point. The third and last of the Jones sons, Thomas Davies Jones, was born in Iowa County. Both of William Jones's brothers went on to graduate from Princeton University and were distinguished Illinois attorneys.

William Jones spent his early years on his family's farm; he graduated from Platteville Normal School in 1872, taught school for several terms, and finally became the principal of Mineral Point High School. From 1877 to 1881 he served as superintendent of schools for Iowa County. In the latter year, he entered the banking business, and in 1883 he purchased the Mineral Point Zinc Company, making his brothers David and Thomas president and vice president, respectively, while he himself served as secretary-treasurer. In 1884, Jones helped to organize the First National Bank of Mineral Point, which was still in business when he went to Washington more than a decade later. A Republican, Jones was elected mayor of Mineral Point in 1884, but he served only a year; he was then elected to the state assembly, where he was from 1895 until his selection as Indian commissioner in 1897. Little is known of Jones's work as an assemblyman; historian David P. Thelen notes that Jones was among a group of state legislators who regularly met with a league of reformers who desired to clean up the state's political system. At this time, Jones identified with the emerging Progressive wing of the Republican party.

It was Jones's support of William McKinley, the Republican presidential candidate in 1896, and his business acumen which brought him to the attention of the new administration, and he was nominated to the post of commissioner soon after McKinley was inaugurated. On 3 May 1897, the Senate confirmed him, and he took over the Indian Office soon after. Biographer W. David Baird writes, "Jones assumed his new post at a time when policy affecting the native American seemed beyond question. Congress had some ten years earlier [1887] passed the General Allotment Act, a measure heralded by humanitarians and politicians alike as the final solution to the Indian problem…Given his own belief in the superiority of the Anglo-Saxon race, Jones endorsed the previously established policy of assimilation and saw his official duty as principally the supervision of programs designed to implement it." However, as he progressed into his post, and investigated the abuses perpetrated against the Indians, he attempted to change the system, a daunting task for any person. He wrote of the evils of "the ration system" (the doling out of government rations to the Indians) as part of a larger criticism of the reservation policy as a whole in his annual report for 1900. He described a policy that seemed, in his view, to discourage the self-sufficiency of the Indians. "The ration system is the corollary of the reservation system," he wrote. "To confine a people upon reservations where the natural conditions are such that agriculture is more or less a failure and all other means of making a livelihood limited and uncertain, it follows inevitably that they must be fed wholly or in part from outside sources or drop out of existence. This is the situation of some of the Indian tribes to-day. It was not always so. Originally and until a comparatively recent period the red man was self-supporting. Leading somewhat of a nomadic life, he roamed with unrestricted freedom over the country in pursuit of game, which was plentiful, or located upon those spots fitted by nature to make his primitive agriculture productive. All this is changed. The advent of the white man was the beginning of the end. From east to west, from one place to another, like poor Jo in Bleak House, the Indian has been 'movin' on' until he can go no further. Surrounded by whites, located upon unproductive reservations often in a rigorous climate, he awaits the destiny which under existing conditions he is powerless to avert. Of the causes that led to this or of the wisdom or unwisdom of the policy pursued it is not necessary now to speak. The purpose of this is to discuss the present and not to criticise the past." On 13 January 1902, Jones sent a broadside to Indian agents prohibiting "the wearing of long hair by the male Indian population." To get them to comply, Jones noted in the announcement, published in a form of a poem, "To wear or not to wear hair," that "Not to be shorn; perchance then not to draw annuities." Wilcomb Washburn, noted Indian historian, comments on Jones's 1902 report, "The tone of Commissioner Jones's reports is notably different from that of Commissioner [Thomas Jefferson] Morgan's ten years earlier. The clarity and even poetry of Morgan's reports are absent in Jones's. What is substituted seems to be a pedestrian expression of the less savory characteristics of the age." In his 1903 report, Jones blasted the act of Congress of 28 February 1902, which granted certain railroad companies unrestricted access across numerous Indian reservations, legislation that was signed by the president before Jones himself had even seen it. "The Office ventured the opinion that the provisions granting additional grounds were entirely too liberal, and that certain limitations should be fixed with reference to the lands the use of which might be acquired under the act," he wrote. "From a careful review of the operations of the railroads under this act for the past year the office is convinced that the property rights of Indians the Oklahoma and Indian Territory are in great peril, and that legislation for their protection is immediately necessary."

William Jones eventually served for three months shy of eight years, the second longest (tied with Cato Sells, and behind John Collier's record 11 years 8 months) tenure in that office. After leaving Washington on 1 January 1905, he presided over the merger of the Mineral Point Railroad and Northern Railroad, and served, until his death, as president of the line, as well as General Manager of the Mineral Point Zinc Company. He died on 17 September 1912, ten days shy of his sixty-eighth birthday.

See also Bureau of Indian Affairs.

References Baird, W. David, "William A. Jones." In Robert M. Kvasnicka and Herman J. Viola, eds., *The Commissioners of Indian Affairs, 1824–1977* (1979); Biographical sketch of W. A. Jones, Box 1, William Arthur Jones Papers, Wisconsin State Historical Society, Madison; State Historical Society of Wisconsin, *Dictionary of Wisconsin Biography (1960);* Thelen, David Paul, *The New Citizenship: Origins of Progressivism in Wisconsin, 1885–1900* (1972); U.S. Congress, House of Representatives, *Annual Report of the Commissioner of Indian Affairs for the Year 1900,* House Document No. 5, 56th Congress, 2d Session (serials 4101 and 4102); U.S. Congress, House of Representatives, *Annual Report of the Commissioner of Indian Affairs for the Year 1903,* House Document No. 5, 58th Congress, 2d Session (serials 4645 and 4646); Washburn, Wilcomb E., comp., *The American Indian and the United States: A Documentary History (1979).*

Jones v. Meehan (175 U.S. 1 [1899])

In this Supreme Court decision, the court held that a treaty with Indians, in which a chief is granted an allotment and then passes it on to his heirs, demands that Congress or any other governmental agency not step in to alter or change the treaty's obligations. Moose Dung, or Monsimoh, was the principal chief of the Red Lake band of Chippewa Indians of Minnesota. Under the Treaty of the Old Crossing at Red Lake of 2 October 1863, the tribe was given ancestral lands at Red Lake. In 1872, Moose Dung died, and his son and heir, known as Moose Dung the Younger, leased to the brothers Patrick and James Meehan in 1891 a strip of land at the lake for $10 a year. Later, after the Indian allowed a railroad to move in, the land became more valuable. In 1894, seeing a need to increase his profit, Moose Dung the Younger leased the Meehans' property to one Ray W. Jones of Wisconsin for $200 a year. The secretary of the interior approved this second lease, but only if Jones paid $400 a year. Jones sued in the District Court for the District of Minnesota to have the earlier lease deemed void. The District Court upheld the Meehans' right to title, and Jones sued to the U.S. Supreme Court. After hearing arguments in the case on 27 and 28 April 1898, the court did not hand down a decision until 30 October 1899. In the decision, a unanimous one, Justice Horace Gray wrote, "The title to the strip of land in controversy, having been granted by the United States to the elder chief Moose Dung by the treaty itself, and having descended, upon his death, by the laws, customs, and usages of the tribe, to his eldest son and successor as chief, Moose Dung the younger, passed by the lease executed by the latter in 1891 to the plaintiffs for the term of that lease; and their rights under that lease could not be divested by any subsequent action of the lessor, or by Congress, or of the executive departments."

Jones v. Prairie Oil & Gas Company (273 U.S. 195 [1927])

Although it is not a case dealing with the rights of Indians, this Supreme Court decision did hold that an act of Congress establishing that minor allottees could not sell their allotments was in violation of the Fifth Amendment to the Constitution. Leonard D. Ingram, a Muscogee (Creek) Indian, was 12 years old in 1907 when he received his patent for his allotment. In 1911, while still a minor, his mother, Minerva Ingram, became his guardian as to the allotment and leased the land to the Prairie Oil and Gas Company of Oklahoma for the right to drill for gas and oil. In 1920, Minerva Ingram, now Minerva Jones, sued with Philip A. Lewis and Carter W. Wesley, trustees of Leonard Ingram's affairs, to end the oil and gas leases on the grounds that an act of Congress of 27 May 1908 prohibited the alienation [sale] or lease of allotments of minors. The District Court of the United States for the Northern District of Oklahoma dismissed the suit, and Jones and the Ingram trustees sued to the U.S. Supreme Court.

Arguments were heard on 11 January 1927, and a decision was handed down a mere 13 days later, on 24 January. Speaking for a unanimous court, Justice Oliver Wendell Holmes upheld the leases as constitutional, and argued that the federal act which applied restrictions upon the allotments of minor Indians was "admitted to apply but is said to be ineffective under the Fifth Amendment, as depriving the minor of his property without due process of law."

Josephy Report

At the request of President-elect Richard Nixon, Indian scholar and historian Alvin M. Josephy, Jr., enunciated the concerns of Indians in a report entitled "The American Indian and the Bureau of Indian Affairs: A Study with Recommendations," which was given to the president on 11 February 1969. In it, Josephy outlined possible policy areas that were eventually adopted by the Nixon Administration in July 1970. The report is some 30 pages long; reprinted here are excerpts from the report's recommendations:

It is certain that the worst problems afflicting American Indians will never be ended without programs that are adequately funded. It is accepted that the Indians do not have the funds themselves and that they do not have access to the sources of credit that are usually available to other Americans. But the actual funding of programs for Indians by the government has never approached the level required by the massive dimensions of the problems.

A few of the facts obscured by the promulgation of intentions in President Johnson's Message on Indian Affairs on March 6, 1968, underscore the point. The Message conveyed proposals for many new or expanded programs which, somehow, were to be financed by only a ten per cent increase in federal expenditures for Indians above the appropriations of the previous year. One of the proposals was for a ten per cent increase in funds for health programs, including a number of items that would make available to the Indians greater numbers of trained personnel to help cope with the many serious health problems on the reservations. Before the year was over, the exact opposite had come to pass, and the Public Health Service was pointing out that, under section 201 of the Revenue and Expenditure Control Act of 1968, Public Law 90–364, the Division of Indian Health was facing a reduction of almost 1,000 employees, or one-sixth of its total staff, principally among nursing personnel and other patient care supportive staff in the field. A reduction in staff is now occurring on reservations and in Indian hospitals, not only nullifying the promise held out in President Johnson's Message, but bringing a new crisis to the Indians. (Corrective legislation, it hardly needs pointing out, is required at the earliest possible moment.)

Again, the inadequacy of funding a program to deal effectively with another pressing problem is evidenced in the field of Indian housing. The Presidential Task Force had reported to the White House that at least three-quarters of all Indian houses on reservations were below minimum standards of decency and that over a 10–year period roughly 100,000 units, "of which approximately 80,000 are new, would have to be provided for the housing of the Indian population." The President's response to the Task Force's assertion that this would require a 10–year program costing approximately $1 billion was to propose an increase of only 1,000 new Indian homes (for a total of 2,500) to be built under HUD [Housing and Urban Development] programs in fiscal year '69.

The American taxpayer may wonder with increasing impatience why Indian problems are not solved, and why expenditures for these problems continue to mount each year. One demonstrable answer is that expenditures have never been high enough to much more than keep the problems going. In the years after the Indians' pacification, the appropriations barely met the minimum subsistence needs of the Indians. In more recent years, with an increasing Indian population and a growing complexity of reservation problems, the appropriations have risen, but consistently have stayed well below a level needed to carry out intentions. It may be impossible, because of higher priority needs elsewhere in the federal budget and the consequent requirement for economy in the Indian budget, to attempt to solve the Indians' problems once and for all with same kind of massive appropriations that have characterized the most ambitious aid programs for some of the underdeveloped peoples overseas. But it should be emphasized that the Indians are Americans, and that until a similar approach is adopted for them, Indian programs will continue to limp along, and Indian development will proceed at an unsatisfactory pace. In addition, because of the rapid increase in the Indians' population, there is every prospect that their economic, educational and health levels will drop steadily behind those of the rest of the population, and that each Administration will leave the Indians worse off, in relation to the rest of the American people, than it found them.

Adequate funding, therefore, should be a major concern of every Indian program....

The planning and application of all economic development programs, long- and short-range, should reflect the Indians' own needs, desires and cultural traits. By bringing the Indians into the planning and decision-making process, programs need not fail, as they have in the past....

With minor exceptions, the Indians desire the federal government to continue to provide its trust protection for their lands, and the government must continue to give that protection. But it should be possible, by amending the Indian Reorganization Act and other pertinent statutes, to reduce the number of ancillary obligations and responsibilities of the trustee. In their drive for self-determination and self-government, tribes will press increasingly for the right to program their judgment funds, have authority over their budgets, and assume full responsibility for the management of their income, the making of contracts with attorneys, and the framing of tribal codes, resolutions, and constitutional actions. Without abandoning the trusteeship protection of lands, the government should be in a position to be able to transfer those other responsibilities, piecemeal or full, to tribes deemed ready to assume them. For some tribes, that day may already have arrived, and the continued denial to them of rights they are able to exercise for themselves may be viewed as the most stultifying of all the obstacles that inhibit them on their road to development.

See also Nixon, Richard Milhous—Message on Indian Affairs.

Reference Josephy, Alvin M. Jr., "The American Indian and the Bureau of Indian Affairs: A Study with Recommendations." In Josephy, Alvin M., Jr., *Red Power* (1971).

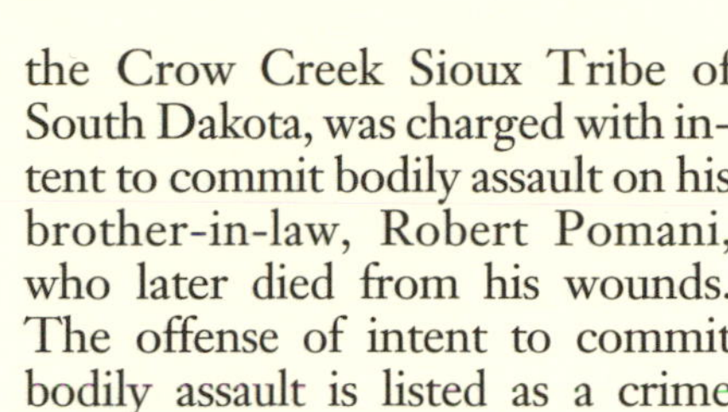

The Kansas Indians (5 Wallace [72 U.S.] 737 [1866])

Although the Supreme Court reporter, William Wallace, consolidated these cases into the single heading of *The Kansas Indians,* they were in fact three separate cases: *Blue Jacket v. Board of Commissioners of Johnson County* (5 Wallace 742), *Yellow Beaver v. Board of Commissioners of Johnson County* (7 Wallace 757) and *Wan-zop-e-ah v. Board of Commissioners of Miami County* (5 Wallace 759). They all dealt with the taxation of Indian lands of three Indian tribes by the state of Kansas: the Weas, Miamis, and Shawnees. Justice David Davis wrote the opinions in all three cases, all of which last for several pages. In *Blue Jacket,* Davis's discourse represents the court's findings in all three cases. Davis opined, "While the general government has a superintending care over their [the Indians'] interests, and continues to treat with them as a nation, the State of Kansas is estopped from denying their title to it. She accepted this status when she accepted the act admitting her into the Union. Conferring rights and privileges on these Indians cannot affect their situation, which can only be changed by treaty stipulation, or a voluntary abandonment of their tribal organization. As long as the United States recognizes their national character they are under the protection of treaties and the laws of Congress, and their property is withdrawn from the operation of State laws."

The underlying constitutional doctrine held in this joint case was upheld by the court in *United States v. Kagama* in 1886.

See also *Fellows v. Blacksmith;* The New York Indians.

Keeble v. United States **(412 U.S. 205, 36 L.Ed. 2d 844, 93 S.Ct. 1993 [1973])**

The question of whether an Indian, on trial under the Indian Major Crimes Act, could have his jury instructed on a lesser charge, one not inscribed in the list of crimes covered by the act, was at issue in this Supreme Court case. Francis A. Keeble, a member of the Crow Creek Sioux Tribe of South Dakota, was charged with intent to commit bodily assault on his brother-in-law, Robert Pomani, who later died from his wounds. The offense of intent to commit bodily assault is listed as a crime under the Indian Major Crimes Act of 1885 (23 Stat. 385, codified at 18 U.S.C. 1153) (IMCA). Keeble asked the judge at the end of trial to instruct the jury to consider the lesser charge of simple assault, a crime not listed in the IMCA. The judge refused on the grounds that the determination of simple assault was a matter for a tribal court, and Keeble was convicted of the higher offense. On appeal, the U.S. Court of Appeals for the Eighth Circuit affirmed the decision, and the U.S. Supreme Court granted certiorari. The case was argued before the court on 27 March 1973, and a decision was handed down on 29 May, two months later. Holding for a six-person majority (justices Potter Stewart, Lewis Powell, and William H. Rehnquist dissenting), Justice William Brennan decided that Keeble deserved the instruction of the lesser included offense, even though Brennan conceded that it was not part of the Indian Major Crimes Act. He explained his decision thus: "We emphasize that our decision today neither expands the reach of the Major Crimes Act nor permits the Government to infringe the residual jurisdiction of a tribe by bringing prosecutions in federal court that are not authorized by statute. We hold only that where an Indian is prosecuted in federal court under the provisions of the Act, the Act does not require that he be deprived of the protection afforded by an instruction on a lesser included offense, assuming of course that the evidence warrants such an instruction. No interest of a tribe is jeopardized by this decision."

See also Indian Major Crimes Act.

Kendall v. Ewert **(259 U.S. 139, 66 L.Ed. 862, 42 S.Ct. 444 [1922])**

The case of *John S. Kendall, Administrator of the estate of George Redeagle v. Paul S. Ewert* dealt with whether government employees who deal with Indian affairs could be prohibited from purchasing allotted lands from Indians. This was the joint case to *Ewert v. Bluejacket.* Paul A. Ewert, an attorney, was appointed as a special assistant to the Attorney General to handle land claims of the Quapaw Indians of Oklahoma. Soon after Ewert arrived to set up his office, one Franklin A. Smith purchased 100 acres of allotted land from George Red-eagle, a full-blood Quapaw. A year later, Smith sold the land to Ewert. Under the Trade and Intercourse Act of 1834 (4 Stat. 729, at 738), it was declared that "no person employed in the Indian department shall have any interest or concern in any trade with the Indians." Redeagle then sued Ewert in district court to return the land, alleging that Smith's purchase was a front for Ewert to skirt the law. The District Court dismissed the petition, and the U.S. Court of Appeals for the Eight Circuit upheld that action. When Redeagle died in November 1918, the administrator of his estate, John S. Kendall, carried on the suit. The U.S. Supreme Court, granting certiorari, heard arguments in the case on 13 March 1922, and handed down a decision on 15 May of the same year. Speaking for the same unanimous court that decided *Ewert v. Bluejacket*, Justice John Hessin Clarke struck down Ewert's purchase of the land as a violation of the 1834 Trade act. Justice Clarke remanded the case back to the Court of Appeals, with an order to dismiss the deed Redeagle sold to Smith, the deed Smith sold to Ewert, and reinstate the deed to Redeagle's estate.

See also *Ewert v. Bluejacket.*

Kennerly and Kennerly, Petitioners, v. District Court of the Ninth Judicial District of Montana et al. (400 U.S. 423, 27 L.Ed. 2d 507, 91 S.Ct. 480 [1971])

This 1971 Supreme Court case further delineated the boundaries of jurisdiction placed in the hands of tribal courts. Petitioners Robert and Helen Kennerly, members of the Blackfeet Indian tribe of Montana, bought food on credit at a grocery store located on the reservation. When the Kennerlys did not pay for their purchases, the grocery store sued in the state courts of Montana for a judgment. The Kennerlys demanded that the suit be dismissed, as only tribal courts had jurisdiction over matters arising on the reservation. When the district court refused to dismiss, the Kennerlys took the action to the Montana State Supreme Court, which affirmed the decision of the lower court. The Kennerlys sued for relief to the U.S. Supreme Court. The case was argued before the court on 18 January 1971, and the court handed down a decision that same day.

The court, by a vote of 7–2 (justices Potter Stewart and Byron White dissenting), vacated the judgment of the Montana State Supreme Court and remanded the case for further action. The opinion handed down expressing the sentiments of the seven members of the majority was *per curiam* (without an acknowledged author). In it, the majority found that while in 1967 the Blackfeet Tribal Council explicitly called for the concurrent, but not exclusive, control over Indian criminal and civil affairs on the reservation, the tribal council did not follow new federal guidelines as to how the state would continue to be allowed this authority as mandated by the Indian Civil Rights Act of 1968. Title IV, Section 406, of the Indian Civil Rights Act of 1968 (25 U.S.C. 1321, at 1326) reads: "State jurisdiction acquired pursuant to this subchapter with respect to criminal offenses or civil causes of action, or with respect to both, shall be applicable in Indian country only where the enrolled Indians within the affected area of such Indian country accept such jurisdiction by a majority vote of the adult Indians voting at a special election held for that purpose." As the opinion noted, "We think the meaning of th[is] provision is clear: the tribal consent that is prerequisite to the assumption of state jurisdiction under the provisions of Title IV of the Act must be manifested by majority vote of the enrolled Indians within the affected areas of Indian country. Legislative action by the Tribal Council does not comport with the explicit requirements of the Act."

Kerr-McGee Corporation v. Navajo Tribe of Indians et al. (471 U.S. 195, 85 L.Ed. 2d 200, 105 S.Ct. 1900 [1985])

The issue of whether Indian tribes could unilaterally impose taxes on companies or businesses operating on Indian lands, or must do so only with the approval of the secretary of the interior, was involved in this Supreme Court case. The Kerr-McGee Corporation was a mineral lessee on the Navajo Indian reservation in Arizona. The Navajos imposed taxes on the company for the use of the lands. The company sued in district court, claiming that such taxes could only be approved by the secretary of the interior. The district court agreed with the corporation and enjoined, or stopped, the tribe from collecting the taxes. On appeal, the U.S. Court of Appeals for the Eighth Circuit reversed, holding that no congressional enactment gave the secretary of the interior such power. The company appealed to the U.S. Supreme Court. After arguments were heard on 25 February 1985, Chief Justice Warren Burger delivered the unanimous opinion of the eight participating members of the court (Justice Lewis Powell did not partake in the decision) in holding that Congress had not enacted legislation requiring the secretary of the interior to approve tax schemes by Indian tribes. As Chief Justice Burger explained, "Even assuming that the Secretary could review tribal laws taxing mineral production, it does not follow that he must do so. We are not inclined to impose upon the Secretary a duty that he has determined is not needed to satisfy [the Indian Mineral Leasing Act of 1938] Act's basic purpose—to maximize tribal revenues from reservation lands."

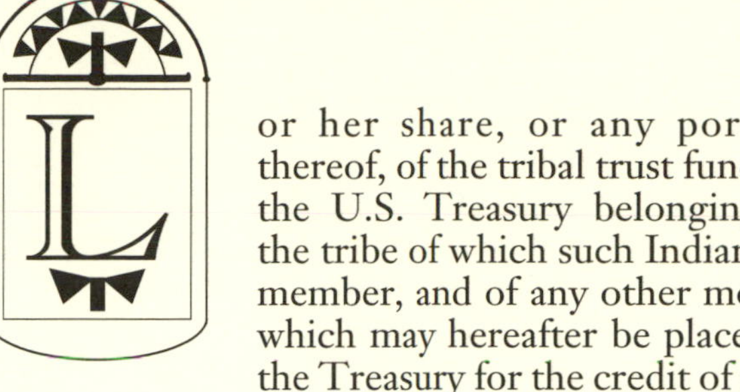

Lacey Act (34 Stat. 1221)
The General Allotment Act (Dawes Act) of 1887 and the Burke Act of 1906 divided Indian reservations into allotments; however, tribal funds held in common by the tribes were separated from these provisions, leaving many Indians unable to retrieve these reserves. Introduced in the House of Representatives by Congressman John Fletcher Lacey of Iowa, this legislative action of 2 March 1907 was intended to fix that situation. The act reads:

An Act Providing for the allotment and distribution of Indian tribal funds.

Be it enacted, That the Secretary of the Interior is hereby authorized, in his discretion, from time to time, to designate any individual Indian belonging to any tribe or tribes whom he may deem capable of managing his or her affairs, and he may cause to be apportioned and allotted to any such Indian his or her pro rata share of any tribal or trust funds on deposit in the Treasury of the United States to the credit of the tribe or tribes of which said Indian is a member, and the amount so apportioned and allotted shall be placed to the credit of such Indian upon the books of the Treasury, and the same shall thereupon be subject to the order of such Indian:

Provided, That no apportionment or allotment shall be made to any Indian until such Indian has first made an application therefor:

Provided further, That the Secretaries of the Interior and of the Treasury are hereby directed to withhold from such apportionment and allotment a sufficient sum of the said Indian funds as may be necessary or required to pay any existing claims against said Indians that may be pending for settlement by judicial determination in the Court of Claims or in the Executive Departments of the Government, at such time of apportionment.

Sec. 2. That the Secretary of the Interior is hereby authorized to pay any Indian who is blind, crippled, decrepit, or helpless from old age, disease, or accident, his or her share, or any portion thereof, of the tribal trust funds in the U.S. Treasury belonging to the tribe of which such Indian is a member, and of any other money which may hereafter be placed in the Treasury for the credit of such tribe and susceptible of division among its members, under such rules, regulations, and conditions as he may prescribe.

LaFlesche Picotte, Susan
See Picotte, Susan LaFlesche.

LaFlesche Tibbles, Susette
See Tibbles, Susette La Flesche.

Lake Mohonk Conferences of the Friends of the Indian
Defining the "Lake Mohonk Spirit Toward Dependent Peoples" in 1909, the *New York Observer* remarked, "Twenty-seven years have passed since the first Lake Mohonk Indian Conference was assembled. Then it was the policy of the nation to push the Indians aside when they were an impediment to national progress; now it is the national policy to incorporate the Indians in the nation and enable them to contribute to the national progress. The most important of the reforms advocated by the Conference have been accepted by the nation, specifically, the abolition of the reservation system, and the application to the Indian service of the Civil Service rules."

Of the attempts at the reform of the way the government dealt with Native Americans, the Lake Mohonk Conferences may be the best known. Under the leadership of philanthropist Albert K. Smiley, named to the U.S. Board of Indian Commissioners by President Rutherford B. Hayes in 1879, reformers from various organizations (including the U.S. Indian Commission, the Women's National Indian Association, and the Indian Rights Association) met at Smiley's resort hotel on Lake Mohonk in upstate New York. Here, at a series of conferences from 1883 to 1916, these reformers, dubbed by Indian historian Paul Prucha as the "friends of the Indian," convened to discuss and argue over the outline of government and private policy towards the Indians, as well as to agree to strategies to advocate and how these could be promoted, both in the public forum and in Congress to enact them into law. Speakers before the conferences included commissioners of Indian Affairs (starting with John DeWitt Clinton Atkins and ending with Robert Grosvenor Valentine).

The journal *The Indian Craftsman*, in its November 1909 edition, stated, "In a recent editorial, *The Outlook* has this to say of the influence wielded by the Mohonk Conference: 'The Lake Mohonk Conference has had an influence on National affairs out of all proportion to the number engaged in it. While the country was still committed to the policy of keeping the Indian shut up in reservations until they had been prepared for freedom, it called for the abandonment of the reservation system and the division of the lands among the Indians in severalty. While the Nation was still leaving the education of the Indians to the voluntary efforts of missionary and philanthropic societies, the Conference called for the establishment by the Federal Government of a system of public schools for the Indians under Federal control. While the offices in the Indian service were still regarded as political, and the agents and inspectors were changed with every changing administration, the Conference declared that they should be brought under the civil service, in order that a continuous and consistent policy might be made possible. Congress successively adopted these reforms, not in compliance with any demand of the Conference, but in obedience to the public opinion which the Conference had both interpreted and helped to create."

References *Indian Craftsman*, 2 (3); *New York Observer*, 4 November 1909, 589; Utley, Robert M., *The Indian Frontier of the American West, 1846–1890 (1984).*

La Motte et al. v. United States (254 U.S. 570 [1921])

The United States has a right to enjoin, or stop, the sale of leases of allotted lands to non-Indians from Indians without the approval of the secretary of the interior, the Supreme Court held in this 1921 decision. Section 7 of the act of Congress of 28 June 1906 (34 Stat. 539) stipulated that "all leases given on said lands for the benefit of the individual members of the tribe…or for their heirs, shall be subject only to the approval of the Secretary of the Interior." George G. La Motte and others were sued by the United States because they had purchased several tracts of allotted lands from Osage Indians of Oklahoma, each with different restrictions placed on it. (Several of the lands were owned by adult Osages, while others were passed down to heirs, while still others had had their restrictions removed.) The district court hearing the case granted the United States the relief it wanted, and the U.S. Court of Appeals for the Eighth Circuit expanded the relief to include more lands. On appeal, the U.S. Supreme Court agreed to hear the case. Submitted on 10 December 1920, Justice Willis Van Devanter spoke for a unanimous court on 24 January 1921 in upholding the enjoinment of some of the sales to La Motte's group, while allowing some sales where restrictions had been removed by Congress. Justice Van Devanter explained, "The right of the United States to maintain the suit, although challenged by the defendants, is not debatable. The Osages have not been fully emancipated, but are still wards of the United States. The restrictions on the disposal and leasing of their allotments constitute an important part of the plan whereby they are being conducted from a state of tribal dependence to one of individual independence and responsibility; and outsiders, such as the defendants, are bound to respect the restrictions quite as much as are the allottees and their heirs. Authority to enforce them, like the power to impose them, is an incident of the guardianship of the United States. That relation and the obligations arising therefrom enable the United States to maintain the suit."

Lane et al. v. Morrison (246 U.S. 214, 62 L.Ed. 674, 38 S.Ct. 252 [1918])
Could the monies held in trust by the United States in the name of Indian tribes be appropriated for the use or the support of those tribes, against the Indians' desires? This was the issue in this Supreme Court case, which was decided in 1918. According to section 8 of the act of Congress of 1 August 1914 (38 Stat. 582, at 590), "The Secretary of the Interior is hereby authorized to withdraw from the Treasury of the United States, at his discretion, the sum of $205,000, or so much thereof as may be necessary…for the purpose of promoting civilization and self-support among the [Chippewa] Indians [of Minnesota]." In 1916, Secretary of the Interior Franklin K. Lane, citing this act, announced his intention to withdraw $160,000 for this purpose. Congress failed to pass an appropriation bill that year, but did enact a joint resolution which supplied much of the same language. John G. Morrison, Jr., whose tribal affiliation was not mentioned (although it was intimated that he was a Chippewa) sued on behalf of the Chippewa Nation of Minnesota to stop Lane, Commissioner of Indian Affairs Cato Sells, and John Burke, secretary of the Treasury, from withdrawing the funds, claiming that Congress did not pass such legislation for fiscal year 1916. A trial court dismissed Morrison's action, but the Court of Appeals for the District of Columbia reversed, holding that the 1916 appropriations bill did not reflect such language as Lane was utilizing. The U.S. Supreme Court, seeking to resolve the issue, granted certiorari. The case was argued on 30 January 1918, and Justice James McReynolds announced the 8–1 decision (Justice Joseph McKenna dissented) in reversing the court of appeals: Justice McReynolds expressed the sentiments of the majority when he wrote, "It seems that 'civilization and self-support' among the Indians cannot be promoted effectively by disconnected efforts, but must be accomplished, if at all, by definite, permanent plans operating through many years. And in view of the long-continued practice of Congress to provide funds for such continuous efforts by annual appropriations, the circumstances under which the Joint Resolution became law, and the studied incorporation therein of the language of former appropriation acts, we think the purpose [of the joint resolution] was to authorize expenditure of $160,000 during 1916, as had been done for 1915. A different construction might have occasioned disruption of well ordered arrangements for advancing the nation's wards, to the great detriment of all concerned; and to such unfortunate consequences experienced legislators probably were not oblivious."

Lane et al. v. Pueblo of Santa Rosa (249 U.S. 110, 63 L.Ed. 504, 39 S.Ct. 185 [1919])
Was an Indian nation recognized by Mexico still an Indian nation after the United States was awarded that territory? And could the secretary of the interior dispose of the lands of that nation as public lands? This 1919 Supreme Court case dealt with the issue of whether the Indians of the Pueblo of Santa Rosa, in southern Arizona, were to be considered a "nation" when the United States received that territory from Mexico. Justice Willis Van Devanter wrote in the Supreme Court's unanimous opinion, "the plaintiff [Pueblo] is an Indian town whose inhabitants are a simple and uninformed people, measurably civilized and industrious, living in substantial houses and engaged in agricultural and pastoral [agrarian] pursuits. Its existence, practically as it is to-day, can be traced back through the period of Mexican rule into that of the Spanish kings." Recognized by Mexico, the pueblo became part of the United States in the Gadsden Purchase (4 August 1854), and it was incorporated into the Territory of New Mexico. On 24 February 1863, the pueblo became part of the Territory of Arizona. When Secretary of the Interior Franklin Knight Lane sought to list these lands for disposal as public lands

of the United States, the pueblo sued in district court to enjoin the secretary. The district court dismissed the suit, but the Court of Appeals for the District of Columbia reversed. The U.S. Supreme Court agreed to hear to the facts in the matter, and rendered its judgment on 3 March 1919; speaking for a unanimous court, Justice Willis Van Devanter held that the court of appeals' judgment permanently enjoining Lane from enforcing the sale was in error, and remanded the case back to district court to allow both sides to properly argue the merits of their cases. In a lengthy discussion, Justice Van Devanter let slip his feelings in the case, arguing, "The defendants assert with much earnestness that the Indians of this pueblo are wards of the United States—recognized as such by the legislative and executive departments—and that in consequence the disposal of their lands is not within their own control, but subject to such regulations as Congress may prescribe for their benefit and protection. Assuming, without so deciding, that this is all true, we think it has no real bearing on the point we are considering. Certainly it would not justify the defendants in treating the lands of these Indians—to which, according to the bill, they have complete and perfect title—as public lands of the United States and disposing of the same under the public land laws. That would not be an exercise of guardianship, but an act of confiscation. Besides, the Indians are not here seeking to establish any power or capacity in themselves to dispose of the lands, but only to prevent a threatened disposal by administrative officers in disregard of their full ownership. Of their capacity to maintain a suit we entertain no doubt. The existing wardship is not an obstacle, as is shown by repeated decisions of this court, of which *Lone Wolf v. Hitchcock*, 187 U.S. 553, 23 S.Ct. 216, 47 L.Ed. 299, is an illustration." He added, "Of course, the Court of Appeals ought not to have directed the entry of a final decree awarding a permanent injunction against the defendants. They were entitled to answer to the merits just as if their motion to dismiss had been overruled in the court of first instance. By the direction given they were denied such an opportunity, and this was a plain and prejudicial error." In 1927, the court heard *Pueblo of Santa Rosa v. Fall et al.*, a continuation of *Lane*, in which the court then held that the secretary of the interior (by then it was Albert Bacon Fall) could not sell the lands of the pueblo without the consent of the tribe through a treaty or law from Congress.

Lane v. United States ex rel. Mickadiet (241 U.S. 201 [1916])

Officially titled *Franklin K. Lane, Secretary of the Interior, Plaintiff in Error, v. United States of America ex relatione Julia Mickadiet, néeTiebault, and Alma Lamere Tiebault*, dealt with whether the secretary of the interior could reopen a matter involving the inheritance of a deceased Indian's allotted land, even though Congress gave him the sole power to make such decisions. Tiebault, a Winnebago Indian, received his allotment under the General Allotment Act of 1887. In 1897, Tiebault proceeded to adopt two girls, both Winnebagos. In 1907, Tiebault's death allowed the two girls, Julia Tiebault Mickadiet and Alma Lamere Tiebault, to ask the secretary of the interior to consider them as Tiebault's heirs. Under the act of 25 June 1910, Congress had conferred final power in the secretary to make such assessments. The secretary, Franklin K. Lane, after hearings, held for the two adopted daughters. At that point, several of Tiebault's nieces and nephews requested that Lane reopen the decision. Lane consented, and asked a district court in Nebraska to make a final determination. Julia Mickadiet and Alma Tiebault asked for a writ of mandamus, asking the courts to prohibit Secretary Lane from acting, claiming that under the 1910 act Lane had no authority to reopen the case. The District Court of the District of Columbia held that Lane had the proper authority; however, the Court of Appeals for the District of Columbia reversed. On appeal, the U.S. Supreme Court granted certiorari (the right to hear the case).

After arguments were held on 10 April

1916, the case was decided on 22 May of that same year. Chief Justice Edward Douglass White held for a unanimous court (Justice James Clarke McReynolds did not participate) that the 1910 act did not preclude Lane from asking for further hearings into the allotment controversy. As White opined, "It follows from what we have said that the court below was without jurisdiction to control the conduct of the Secretary concerning a matter within the administrative authority of that officer, and therefore that the mandamus was wrongfully allowed, and the judgment awarding it must be and it is reversed and the case remanded with directions to affirm the judgment of the Supreme Court of the District of Columbia, dismissing the petition for a writ of mandamus." In 1926, the court ruled in *First Moon v. White Tail* that under the 1910 act, the secretary of the interior's decision in the area of declaring an heir to the allotment was final if he decided not to reopen the case.

See also *First Moon v. White Tail.*

Langford v. Monteith (102 U.S. 145 [1880])

The issue deliberated in this Supreme Court case was whether after a treaty exempts an Indian reservation from a state's authority that state may examine legal issues arising from controversies on that Indian reservation, if the treaty contains such a provision. Charles E. Monteith claimed that he lived on the Nez Percé Indian Reservation under the authority of one John B. Monteith (no relation was established in the case notes), the Indian agent in the area. Charles Monteith claimed that William G. Langford extracted the lease to lands and a house on the reservation by fraud. On orders from Indian agent Monteith, Charles Monteith had Langford forcibly removed from the property. Langford went before a justice of the peace to order that he have his property returned to him. The justice of the peace held for Monteith; a district court, and finally the Supreme Court of the Territory of Idaho, sided against Langford. He sued to the U.S. Supreme Court for relief.

After arguments were heard on 5 April 1880, Justice Samuel Freeman Miller held on 19 April that the original justice of the peace had no jurisdiction to try the case, that he should have sent the case with all its motions to district court, and affirmed the Idaho Territorial Supreme Court's ruling on those narrow grounds. Still, Miller ruled that the court's decision the previous year in *Harkness v. Hyde*, in which it ruled that state courts did not have jurisdiction on matters involving Indian lands, was defective. Wrote Miller, "And this court in the case of *Harkness v. Hyde*, relying upon an imperfect extract from a Treaty with the Shoshonees found in the brief of counsel, inadvertently inferred that it contained a clause against including the lands of the Tribe within a territorial or state jurisdiction like the Treaty with the Shawnees. In this it seems we were laboring under a mistake, and where no such clause or language equivalent to it is found in a treaty with any Indian Tribe within the exterior limits of Idaho, the land held by them is a part of the Territory and subject to its jurisdiction, so that process may run there, however the Indians themselves may be exempt from that jurisdiction. As we are not shown any such treaty with the Nez Percé Tribe, on whose lands the premises in dispute are situated; and as it is a contest between white men, citizens of the United States, the [District] court had jurisdiction of the parties, if the subject-matter was one of which the justice of the peace could take cognizance." The doctrine involved in *Langford* was upheld in *Utah & Northern Railway Company v. Fisher.*

See also *Harkness v. Hyde; Utah & Northern Railway Company v. Fisher.*

Laws of Burgos

These series of reforms of 1512 were enacted by the Spanish under the direction of Dominican priest Bartolomé de las Casas, whose 1542 work "Brevisima relación de la destrucción de las Indias" (A Brief Report on the Destruction of the Indians) was the earliest to call for the humane treatment of the indigenous peoples of North America. They were passed to outlaw the enslavement of Indians and instruct the owners of *encomiendas* (colonial land grants in the New World which included the land of Indian inhabitants) to ameliorate the living and working conditions of the Indians who labored on the lands. It also ordered the Spanish conquistadors to read to any Indians they came across a document called the *Requerimiento* ("Requirements"), which demanded that the Indians become civilized and join the Catholic Church and accept the power of the Spanish crown or be destroyed. The document read, "We ask and require…that you acknowledge the Church…" Without abeyance, the Spanish threatened to "make war against you…subject you to the yoke and obedience of the Church [and Spanish crown]…[and] take you, and your wives, and your children, and…[we will] make slaves of them-take away your goods and…do you all the harm and damage we can."

The domination of the New World by the Spanish, however, continued unabated, and the Laws of Burgos and its subsequent enactment progeny were ignored, leading the way to the continuation of the destruction of much of the Native American way of life for the next 300 years under Spanish rule. The edicts themselves were drafted in the city of Burgos, the capital of Burgos province, located in the Castile-León autonomous community (known as the *comunidad autónoma)* in northern Spain.

Lea, Luke (1810–1898)

The sixth commissioner of Indian Affairs, Luke Lea served for three years and is barely remembered for his tenure. Little is known of his life. He was born in Grainger County, Tennessee, on 16 November 1810; his uncle, also named Luke Lea, fought alongside Andrew Jackson in the Creek and Seminole Wars of 1818, and eventually served two terms in the U.S. House of Representatives (1833–37), while his brother, Pryor Lea, also served two terms in the House (1827–31). About 1836 Luke Lea removed with his brother to Jackson, Mississippi, where they opened a joint law practice which remained in business until 1846. Lea then entered local politics: he served a single term in the state legislature, and ran two unsuccessful races; one for mayor of Jackson, and the other (in which he was overwhelmingly defeated on the Whig ticket) in 1849 for Governor of Mississippi.

With the election of Whig Zachary Taylor to the White House in 1850, Lea sought a political appointment. He must have been surprised when Taylor chose him as commissioner of Indian Affairs, to replace Orlando Brown. Indian historian Robert A. Trennert, Jr., writes, "Lea quickly adopted the idea of reservations for all tribes on the frontier. Only by forcing the Indians to cease their wandering ways, the commissioner believed, could 'the great work of regenerating the Indian race' be accomplished." Lea submitted three annual reports as commissioner: 1850, 1851, and 1852. He advocated the advantages of a reservation system in his 1850 report. "There should be assigned to each tribe, for a permanent home, a country adapted to agriculture, of limited extent and well-defined boundaries; within which all, with occasional exceptions, should be compelled constantly to remain until such time as their general improvement and good conduct may supersede the necessity of such restrictions," he wrote. "In the mean time the government should cause them to be supplied with stock, agricultural implements, and useful materials for clothing; encourage and assist them in the erection of comfortable dwellings, and secure to them the means and facilities of education, intellectual, moral, and religious." In his 1851 discourse, he came to discuss what seemed to be the disturbing question involved with Indians: what could the U.S. government do to alleviate their situation while interfering as little as possible in their affairs and preserving their land for them free of white encroachment? He ended his treatise with these words: "On the general subject of the civilization of the Indians, many and diversified opinions have been put forth; but, unfortunately, like the race to which they relate, they are too wild to be of much utility. The great question, How shall the Indians be civilized? yet remains without a satisfactory answer. The magnitude of the subject, and the manifold difficulties inseparably connected with it, seem to have bewildered the minds of those who have attempted to give it the most thorough investigation. The remark of the late Attorney General Legaré, is not more striking than true, that 'there is nothing in the whole compass of our laws so anomalous, so hard to bring within any precise definition, or any logical and scientific arrangement of principles, as the relation in which the Indians stand towards this government and those of the States.' My own views are not sufficiently matured to justify me in undertaking to present them here. To do would so would require elaborate detail, and swell this report beyond its proper limits. I therefore leave the subject for the present, remarking, only, that any plan for the civilization of our Indians will, in my judgment, be fatally defective, if it do not provide, in the most efficient manner, first, for their ultimate incorporation into the great body of citizen population."

Lea served only three years as Indian commissioner, and left the office in 1853. He returned to Mississippi and quietly engaged in the practice of law. When he died, on 14 May 1898, at the age of 87, Indian policy in the United States had manifested itself several times over.

See also Bureau of Indian Affairs.

References Trennert, Robert A., Jr., *Alternative to Extinction: Federal Indian Policy and the Beginnings of the Reservation System, 1846–1851* (1975); Trennert, Robert A., Jr., "Luke Lea." In Robert M. Kvasnicka and Herman J. Viola, eds., *The Commissioners of Indian Affairs, 1824–1977* (1979); U.S. Congress, House of Representatives, *Annual Report of the Commissioner of Indian Affairs for the Year 1850*, House Executive Document No. 1, 31st Congress, 2d Session (serial 595); U.S. Congress, House of Representatives, *Annual Report of the Commissioner of Indian Affairs for the Year 1851*, House Executive Document No. 2, 32d Congress, 1st Session (serial 636).

Leonard Peltier Defense Committee (LPDC)

See Peltier, Leonard.

Lessee of Margaret Lattimer et al. v. Poteet (14 Peters [39 U.S.] 2 [1840].

"The limits of the Indian country within the State of North Carolina were established by treaties made between the United States and the Cherokee tribe of Indians," wrote Justice John McLean in the majority opinion in this important nineteenth-century case. The court held that states were prohibited from selling land in Indian country or from establishing the boundaries of Indian country. In 1795, one William Cathcart was awarded by the state of North Carolina a grant for land that had been defined by the federal government as belonging to the Cherokee Nation. The lessees of Margaret Lattimer (assumed to be a relative of Cathcart) sued to have William Poteet ejected from the land, estimated to be 49,920 acres. The trial court, which had to interpret the treaties and boundaries established between the United States and the Cherokees, held for Poteet, and Lattimer's lessees sued to the U.S. Supreme Court. The issue came before the court in the January term 1839, and was not decided until 1840. In holding for Poteet, Justice McLean found that any questions as to the treaties should be decided between the parties involved—in this case, the U.S. government and the Cherokee Nation. Justice James Moore Wayne dissented in whole, while Chief Justice Roger Brooke Taney and Justice John Catron dissented in part and concurred in part.

Leupp, Francis Ellington (1849–1918)

The twenty-eighth commissioner of Indian Affairs and a member of the Indian Rights Association and the U.S. Board of Indian Commissioners, Francis E. Leupp was a noted Indian reform advocate who wrote vociferously on the subject. He was born in

New York City on 2 January 1849, the son of John P. Leupp and Emeline (née Loop) Leupp. Little of his early life is known because Leupp ordered that after his death his personal papers be destroyed. He apparently attended local New York City schools and received first a bachelor's degree from Williams College in 1870 and a law degree from Columbia University two years later. Entering the field of journalism, he came under the umbrella of influence of William Cullen Bryant and his son-in-law Parke Godwin when he was made assistant editor of the *New York Evening Post.* Although in 1878, just four years later, he bought a controlling interest in the *Syracuse Herald* (New York), Leupp remained a part of the *Evening Post,* and in 1885 began contributing articles to the paper from Washington; in 1889, he was named the Washington correspondent for the *Post,* a position he held for 15 years.

The last two decades of the nineteenth century bred many reformist movements; among these was the clarion call for civil service reform. Leupp was a major player in this movement, and the election of Grover Cleveland to the White House in 1884 seemed to create a situation that allowed Leupp to editorialize on the issue. He met and became friends with Theodore Roosevelt, an up-and-coming New York politician who shared with Leupp the enthusiasm to correct the abuses in the civil service system. It was at this time, about 1890, that Leupp became interested in Indian affairs—not because of his interest in Indians, but because he saw Indians as victims of Indian agents, hired by the abusive civil service system. In fact, Leupp blamed the Wounded Knee massacre of 1890 on uninformed agents hired for partisan purposes. In February 1895, Leupp's friend, Charles Cornelius Coffin Painter of the Indian Rights Association, the oldest and at the time the largest of the Indian rights organizations, died, and IRA Executive Secretary Herbert Welsh asked Leupp to replace him as the IRA's Washington agent. Leupp biographer Donald L. Parman writes, "Despite his experience with Indian administration, Leupp plunged into his new duties. He soon reported that he had persuaded Interior Secretary Hoke Smith to stop naming only Southern Democrats to field positions and that the quality of appointees had improved. A good portion of Leupp's first work involved the legal defense of two Cheyenne River Sioux policemen unjustly charged with the murder of a white. In June 1895, Leupp visited Durango, Colorado, to investigate the impending removal of the Southern Utes to Utah. He discovered all the elements of a typical Indian scandal—treaty violations, controversial charges, intratribal factionalism, greedy local whites, and removal legislation so repugnant that no one would claim responsibility. He reported [to Welsh] that he was 'cordially hated' by the Durango ring and that he would 'take the keenest enjoyment in hitting back' at the evildoers at the proper time." Smith appointed Leupp to the Board of Indian Commissioners (BIC), an oversight group, in 1896. In 1897 Leupp was considered for Indian commissioner, but the post went to Wisconsin businessman William A. Jones. Leupp clashed with Secretary of the Interior Cornelius Bliss, whom Leupp felt was not interested in civil service reform in the Indian service. Bliss requested Leupp's resignation from the BIC in June 1897 and Leupp complied. For the next year, he spent time in Arizona defending Navajos driven from their homes and an Indian accused of murder. Desiring a return to journalism, Leupp resigned from the IRA in April 1898.

For the next several years, Leupp was not involved in Indian affairs; he did, however, write a 1904 campaign biography, *The Man Roosevelt.* After the resignation of Commissioner of Indian Affairs Jones on 1 January 1905, President Roosevelt turned to his good friend Leupp to fill the open position. Leupp served until 1909 in that post. Independently of the office, Leupp was a leading Indian activist; but once he became part of the establishment, he seemed to become one of the people he had once criticized. Indian historian James Officer writes, "Leupp…was a self-righteous, headstrong individual who has been compared to a later commissioner, John Collier, in temperament and ability. Although an assimilationist, Leupp was more tolerant of Indian culture than his predecessors. Like Collier over a quarter of a century later, however, he was capable of high-handed dealing with Indians, and some of his actions cost him the support of such Indian defense groups as the Indian Rights Association, for whom Leupp had once worked. His former colleagues were particularly upset over the imprisonment of certain Navajos by the arbitrary action of the commissioner. The Indian Rights Association, who maintained that 'the Indian is a person within the meaning of the Constitution and cannot be deprived of his liberty without due process of law,' obtained the Navajos' release in habeas corpus proceedings before the Arizona Supreme Court. Leupp's arrogance appealed to some of his subordinates, however, and during his administration the stereotype of the Indian agent metamorphosed from the light-fingered thief to hard-nosed paternalist." In his first annual report, that for 1905, Leupp wrote of his "Outlines of an Indian Policy," and made perhaps some of the boldest statements ever to come from an Indian commissioner. "The commonest mistake made by his white wellwishers in dealing with the Indian is the assumption that because he is a non-Caucasian he is to be classed indiscriminately with other non-Caucasians, like the negro, for instance," Leupp penned. "The truth is that the Indian has as distinct an individuality as any type of man who has ever lived, and he will never be judged aright till we learn to measure him by his own standards, as we whites would wish to be measured if some more powerful race were to usurp dominion over us."

Perhaps one of the less examined aspects of Leupp's tenure is his work to improve Indian health. As Indian authority Robert A. Trennert, Jr., explains, "The first significant attempt to improve Indian health came during the administration of Indian Commissioner Francis E. Leupp, when medical care and preventive measures received a boost. As the severity of Indian health conditions became more obvious, the Indian Office attempted to determine the extent of the problem. In 1908 Dr. Ales Hrdlicka, a well-known expert on Indian conditions in the Southwest, made an extensive survey of western reservations. Although Hrdlicka's report centered on tuberculosis, his assessment of sanitary conditions, especially at government schools and agencies, indicated that contagious diseases were out of control. Without hesitation Leupp committed the Indian service to protecting the Native population from disease. His 1908 annual report criticized government schools for their unsanitary practices, remarking that strict routine, crowded quarters, overheated buildings, and close confinement 'furnish ideal conditions for the development of germ disease among the race through the forcing process there.'" In that report, Leupp continued, "Great popular interest in the general subject of tuberculosis has been aroused by the International Congress which convened in Washington on September 21, 1908. Discussion of tuberculosis among the Indians was divided between two papers read before the congress. The Indian Office also, in cooperation with the Smithsonian Institution, prepared an exhibit of which the main feature was the charted result of a special and recent investigation by Dr. Ales Hrdlicka of the National Museum and a bacteriologist, who visited five reservations and examined a group of typical families on each. Among the 403 Menominee Indian examined, only 78.5 per cent were found free of all suspicion of tuberculosis; of the 428 Oglala Sioux, 75.5 per cent; of the 62 Quinaielts, 81 per cent; of the 331 Hoopas, 77.6 per cent; of the 357 Mohaves, 88.2 per cent. These figures, as well as other presented by Dr. Hrdlicka, may be regarded as establishing the truth of the assertion founded on many authorities, that although its prevalence may vary greatly in different neighborhoods and groups, yet in general the tuberculosis scourge is the greatest single menace to the future of the red race."

After leaving office in 1909, Leupp spent the last years of his life writing on the Indian situation. He wrote in his 1910 work, *The Indian and His Problem*, "The Indian problem has now reached a stage where its solution is almost wholly a matter of administration. Mere sentiment has spent its day; the moral questions involved have pretty well settled themselves. What is most needed from this time forth is the guidance of affairs by an independent mind, active sympathies free from mawkishness, an elastic patience and a steady hand." He added later, "For twenty-five years I have mixed with Indians. I was more or less intimately acquainted with all my predecessors as Commissioner during that period, and wish here to record my tribute of respect for as conscientious and painstaking a series of officers as could be found in their times of public service. The fact that I did not follow directly in their footsteps must not be interpreted as any disparagement of their motives or their wisdom, but as due to the different conditions obtaining when they and I respectively took charge." Another of Leupp's works in this area was *In Red Man's Land: A Study of the American Indian* (1914); he also published *Walks About Washington*. Francis E. Leupp died at his residence, "Stoneleigh Court," in Washington, D.C., on 19 November 1920, at the age of 69.

See also *Quick Bear v. Leupp et al.*

References "Francis E. Leupp Dies" *New York Times*, 20 November 1918, 15; Leupp, Francis E., *In Red Man's Land: A Study of the American Indian* (1914); Leupp, Francis E., *The Indian and His Problem* (1910); Nevins, Allan, "Leupp, Francis Ellington." In Dumas Malone et al., eds., *Dictionary of American Biography* (1930–1988); Officer, James E., "The Indian Service and Its Evolution." In Sandra L. Cadwalader and Vine Deloria, Jr., eds., *The Aggressions of Civilization Federal Indian Policy since the 1880s* (1984); Parman, Donald L., "Francis Ellington Leupp." In Robert M. Kvasnicka and Herman J. Viola, eds., *The Commissioners of Indian Affairs, 1824–1977* (1979); Trennert, Robert A., Jr., "Indian Sore Eyes: The Federal Campaign to Control Trachoma in the Southwest, 1910–40." *Journal of the Southwest* 32 (2); U.S. Congress, House of Representatives, *Annual Report of the Commissioner of Indian Affairs for the Year 1905*, House Document No. 5, 59th Congress, 1st Session (serials 4959 and 4960); U.S. Congress, House of Representatives, *Annual Report of the Commissioner of Indian Affairs for the Year 1909*, House Document 1046, 60th Congress, 2d Session (serial 5453).

Levindale Lead & Zinc Mining Company v. Coleman (241 U.S. 432, 60 L.Ed. 1082, 36 S.Ct. 644 [1916])

The restriction placed by Congress against the alienation of Indian allotments does not apply to whites who may live on the reservation, the Supreme Court held in this 1916 case. Charles Coleman, the defendant in error, was a white man who was the heir to an allotment granted to his Indian wife, Mary Chesewalla; she died in 1906 intestate (without a will). Under the act of Congress of 28 June 1906 (34 Stat. 539), known as the Osage Allotment Act, heirs to Indian allotments must receive the approval of the secretary of the interior before conveying, or selling, their allotments. In 1909, having divided his land with another of Chesewalla's heirs (her brother), Coleman sold the allotment to the plaintiff in error, the Levindale Lead & Zinc Mining Company. At some point thereafter, Coleman sought to cancel the sale, citing the fact that under the Osage Act, he should have received the approval of the secretary of the interior. When Levindale refused to return the land, Coleman sued the company, as well as its officers (W.H. Aaron and M.L. Levin). The District Court of Osage County, Oklahoma, struck down the conveyance, and the Supreme Court of Oklahoma affirmed. On certiorari, the U.S. Supreme Court declared that it would answer the important question: Was Coleman allowed to convey his land without the approval of the secretary of the interior? On 5 June 1916, the justices held unanimously, in an opinion by Justice Charles Evans Hughes (Justice James McReynolds did not participate) that because Coleman was a white man, the legislation relating to the restrictions upon conveyance did not relate to him. Justice Hughes wrote, "We confine ourselves to the single point presented. There is no controversy whatever as to the authority of the Secretary of the Interior, where there are undivided interests belonging to Indians, adequately to protect those interests according to the statutory provisions to this end. Our conclusion simply is that the act of 1906 placed no restrictions

Dan George, a Salish chief, right, as Cheyenne chief Old Lodge Skins and Dustin Hoffman as Jack Crabbe in Little Big Man, *a 1970 movie based on Thomas Berger's 1964 novel. George won the National Society of Film Critics award for best supporting actor.*

upon the alienation of land, or undivided interests in land, of which white men who were not members of the tribe became owners. The judgment is reversed."

Little Big Man

This 1970 film broke with the "cowboys and Indians" approach to Westerns to portray the wars waged against American Indians by the U.S. government. Based on the work of the same name by Thomas Berger, the film was the fictional story of Jack Crabbe, a 121–year old man brought up among Indians, who becomes the sole white survivor of the defeat of Custer's command at the Battle of the Little Big Horn. Ted Sennett wrote in 1983, "Varying wildly in its approach from slapstick comedy to grim, near-documentary realism, the film was many things (perhaps too many): a jaundiced, satirical view of Western American history, a scalding diatribe against the brutal slaughter of Indian tribes (really the beating heart of the movie), and a comic tall tale related by an old man who had lived as an Indian brave, a con man, and a hermit, and had survived several marriages and a bout with alcoholism." The film changed popular perceptions of the "winning of the West" and virtually put an end to cinematic celebrations of the defeat of American Indians during the years of westward expansion. Directed by Arthur Penn and produced by Stuart Millar, with the screenplay by Calder Willingham, the movie starred Dustin Hoffman as Crabbe, Chief Dan George (the winner of the Best Supporting Actor award of the New York Film Critics Circle) as Cheyenne Chief Old Lodge Skins, Faye Dunaway as Mrs. Pendrake, Martin Balsam as the salesman Allardyce T. Merriweather, Richard Mulligan as Custer, and Jeff Corey as Wild Bill Hickock.

References Ebert, Roger, *Roger Ebert's Video Companion, 1995 Edition* (1994); Maltin, Leonard, *Leonard Maltin's Movie and Video Guide, 1996 Edition* (1995); Sennett, Ted, *Great Hollywood Movies* (1983).

Lone Wolf v. Hitchcock (187 U.S. 553, 47 L.Ed. 299, 23 S.Ct. 216 [1903])

The case of Kiowa chief Lone Wolf and his failed battle against the U.S. government to stop the allotment of the Kiowa reservation was a watershed event in the jurisprudential history of federal government policy toward American Indians. Lone Wolf, according to Kiowa historian N. Scott Momaday, who is Lone Wolf's great-grandson, was called *Guipagho* by the Kiowa; a foster son of Lone Wolf the Elder, his real name was Mamay-day-te. His foster father, for whom the town of Lone Wolf, Oklahoma is named, was imprisoned at Fort Sill and Fort Marion, Florida, from 1875 until 1879, and died a year later on the Kiowa reservation after contracting malaria. By 1892, Lone Wolf the Younger was the chief of the Kiowas. He had spent the past few years battling the government's attempt to extinguish the Kiowa reservation by means of allotment; he had even traveled to Washington, D.C., to protest the General Allotment Act of 1887 but arrived just after its passage by Congress. In 1889, Congress established the Cherokee Commission to travel to the reservations and persuade the tribes to accede to the allotment scheme. Article XII of the Treaty of Medicine Lodge of 1867 (15 Stat. 581, ratified 25 August 1868) between the Kiowas and Comanches and United States provided that further land could be ceded only if "three fourths" of the adult males "occupying same land" agreed to the cession. The three-man Cherokee Commission was led by David H. Jerome and included Alfred M. Wilson and Warren G. Sayre. According to the opinion in *Lone Wolf*, "On October 6, 1892, 456 male adult members of the confederated tribes [the Comanches, Kiowas, and Apaches] signed, with three commissioners representing the United States, an agreement concerning the reservation." [Opinion, at 554.] The terms of the agreement were clear: Jerome offered each Indian of the three nations an allotment of 160 acres, plus two dollars an acre for all of the remaining "surplus" land. The reservation pre-allotment was estimated at 2,968,893 acres, and, allowing for a total of 453,000 acres to be used for allotments, and 350,000 acres considered "barren and worthless," there was left 2,150,000 acres of "surplus" to be used for white settlement, but Jerome said that $2 million was all the government would offer for this surplus. Jerome explained to the Indian representatives, Quanah Parker of the Comanches and White Man of the Kiowas, that $2 million would mean for each Indian of the confederated tribes, "that $665 would buy...25 fat steers...[and] 30 good ponies; it would buy enough blankets and ribbons and pretty things to bury all the Indians on the reservation under. That sum of money will build more houses, dig more wells, plant more orchards, and build more fences than these Indians will use in forty years. This money that we propose to pay you is so much that the Indians would not want it all at one time if they could get it, for they would not know what to do with it." The Indians then signed the agreement after convincing Jerome to make the offer $2.5 million.

The agreement was submitted to Congress in January 1893 by Commissioner of Indian Affairs John DeWitt Clinton Atkins. The following month, the office was taken over by Thomas J. Morgan, who wrote to Secretary of the Interior John Willock Noble, "The Indians upon this reservation seem to believe (but whether from exercise of their own judgment or the advice of others the commission cannot determine) that the surplus land is worth two and one half million dollars, and Congress many be induced to give them that much of it." Almost immediately, ethnologist James Mooney of the Bureau of American Ethnology saw danger in the agreement and wrote to the Indian Rights Association to enlist its aid in fighting the agreement in Congress, calling the matter "urgent and immediate." Herbert Welsh, president of the IRA, enlisted IRA's Washington agent, Charles C. C. Painter, to fight the bill. When Lone Wolf and Quanah Parker went to Washington to denounce the "coercion" used to get the Jerome Agreement, Congress hesitated and consideration of the bill was blocked. The House finally passed the bill in May 1898, but the Senate balked when Commissioner of Indian Affairs William A. Jones asked for it to be defeated because the Indians involved expressed their tenacious resistance to it. As well, Secretary of the Interior Cornelius Bliss reported that upon further investigation, the tribal rolls had not been completed when the agreement had been signed and fewer than three-fourths of the tribal members had signed it. The Indian Rights Association even released in 1899 a pamphlet, "An Appeal on Behalf of the Apaches, Kiowas, and Comanches," designed to communicate the case to the Congress and the American people. The tribes petitioned Congress, asking that the original agreement be scrapped. Nonetheless, the agreement, with several amendments, was attached to a Senate rider and passed as the Act of 6 June 1900 (31 Stat. 672).

Although Parker and the Comanches accepted the allotment, Lone Wolf and the Kiowas, joined by the Apaches, decided to fight it in the courts. They sued Secretary of the Interior Ethan Allen Hitchcock in the Supreme Court of the District of Columbia to enjoin him from allotting the lands. Thus, historian Jill Norgren writes, "The litigation in *Lone Wolf* sought to block congressional ratification of an agreement allotting tribal lands, on the grounds that the allotment violated the 1867 Treaty of Medicine Lodge by failing to obtain the required consent of three-fourths of adult tribal members to land cessions." That court found for Hitchcock, as did the Court of Appeals for the District of Columbia, and Lone Wolf (listed as "Principal Chief of the Kiowas") appealed to the U.S. Supreme Court. The case was argued on 23 October 1902, and a decision was handed down on 5 January 1903. Justice Edward Douglass White held that the agreement was valid. He wrote, "In view of the legislative power possessed by Congress over treaties with the Indians and Indian tribal property, we may specially consider the contentions pressed upon our notice that the signing by the Indians of the agreement of October 6, 1892, was obtained by fraudulent misrepresentations, and concealment, that the requisite three fourths of adult male Indians had not signed, as required by the twelfth article of the treaty of 1867, and that the treaty as signed had been amended by Congress without submitting such amendments to the action of the Indians since all of these matters, in any event, were solely within the domain of the legislative authority, and its action is conclusive upon the courts."

After the decision, the Indian Rights Association angrily editorialized, "It is now distinctly understood that Congress has a right to do as it pleases; that it is under no obligation to respect any treaty, for Indians have no rights which command respect. What is to be hoped for by an appeal to Congress can readily be anticipated by the history of the legislation by which Lone Wolf and his tribe have been deprived of that which had by express treaty stipulation [had] apparently been secured to them." The principle that Congress had an unlimited right to change treaties with Indians without their consent was overturned in 1980 by the court in *United States v. Sioux Nation of Indians*.

See also Congress' Plenary Power over Indian Affairs; *United States v. Sioux Nation of Indians.*

References Indian Rights Association, *Twenty-First Annual Report (1903); Kiowa, Comanche, and Apache Indian Reservation: Letter from the Secretary of the Interior in Response to Resolution of the Senate of January 13, 1899, Relative to Condition and Character of the Kiowa, Comanche, and Apache Indian Reservation, and the Assent of the Indians to the Agreement for the Allotment of Lands and the Ceding of Unallotted Lands,* Senate Document No. 77, 55th Congress, 3d Session (serial 3731); *Message from the President of the United States, Transmitting a Communication from the Secretary of the Interior, with an Agreement of the Comanche, Kiowa, and Apache Indians for the Cession of Certain Lands in the Territory of Oklahoma,* Senate Executive Document No. 17, 52d Congress, 2d Session (1893) (serial 3055); Momaday, N. Scott, *The Names* (1976); Norgren, Jill, "Lone Wolf v. Hitchcock." In Kermit L. Hall, ed., *The Oxford Companion to the Supreme Court of the United States (1992); Proceedings of the Councils Held By the Cherokee Commission at Fort Sill and Anadarko, Indian Territory, beginning September 28, 1892,* Senate Executive Document No. 77, 55th Congress, 3d Session (1899); Wyatt, Kathryn C., "The Supreme Court, *Lyng,* and the *Lone Wolf* Principle." *Chicago-Kent Law Review* 65 (2).

"Longest Walk"

This trek by Indian activists, organized to protest Indian legislation then pending before Congress, recalled the 1973 Trail of Broken Treaties caravan. Approximately 3,000 Native Americans started their trek on 11 February 1978 at Alcatraz Island and ended the march on 15 July in Washington, D.C. Three days later, 25 leaders from Native American organizations met with Vice President Walter Mondale and Secretary of the Interior Cecil Andrus regarding their concerns, but President Jimmy Carter declined to attend the meeting.

Lucas v. United States (163 U.S. 612 [1896])

A black man, murdered in Indian country by an Indian, was an adopted citizen of the Choctaw Nation of Oklahoma by his association with the tribe, the Supreme Court held in this 1896 case. The key legal issue was whether an Indian would be tried under the jurisdiction of a state or a tribal court. Under the act of 2 May 1890 that established a temporary government in the territory of Oklahoma, Congress allowed that "the judicial tribunals of the Indian Nations shall retain exclusive jurisdiction in all civil and criminal cases arising in the country in which members of the Nation by nativity or by adoption shall be the only parties." Defendant Lucas, a Choctaw Indian, was charged with murdering Levy Kemp, a black man, whom Lucas's lawyers contended was an adopted freeman citizen of the Choctaw Nation. The prosecution introduced evidence that before his death Kemp told another man, identified only as Le Flore, that he was from Arkansas, and was not an Indian. When the defense objected, the judge overruled them, and ordered the jury that they must find that Kemp was not an Indian adoptee of the Choctaw Nation. Convicted of murder, Lucas was sentenced to death. The U.S. Supreme Court agreed to hear the issues in the case. On 25 May 1896, just two years after Kemp's murder, Justice George Shiras held for a unanimous court that the evidence that Kemp was not an Indian was hearsay, and that documentation that he had been adopted by the Choctaw Nation should have been introduced. Justice Shiras vacated the conviction and death sentence, and remanded the case back to district court for a new trial.

Native Americans parade past the White House in Washington, D.C., on July 1978 at the end of a five-month cross-country walk that began in California. The demonstration ended with 25 Native American leaders meeting with Vice President Walter Mondale and Secretary of the Interior Cecil Andrus.

Lyng v. Northwest Indian Cemetery Protective Association (485 U.S. 439 [1988])

In this Supreme Court decision, the high court held that the government could not be barred by the Free Exercise Clause of the U.S. Constitution from harvesting timber or building a road on lands in a National Forest used by the Indians for religious purposes. When the U.S. Forest Service, a bureau of the Department of Agriculture, proposed to complete a 75-mile road (known as the Gasquet-Orleans, or G-O, road) between two California towns by building a six-mile segment that crossed through the Chimney Rock section of the Six Rivers National Forest, an area used by some Indians as a religious site, as well as harvesting timber in the area, the three Indian tribes (the Yurok, Karok, and Tolowa) affected sued Secretary of Agriculture Richard E. Lyng to stop the construction. The district court hearing the case held for the Indians, claiming that the decision to build and harvest violated the free exercise of religion clause of the U.S. Constitution, as well as the Federal Water Pollution Control Act (33 U.S.C. 1251) and the National Environmental Policy Act (NEPA) of 1969 (42 U.S.C. 4321). During the appeal to a higher court, Congress enacted the California Wilderness Act of 1984 (98 Stat. 1619), which outlawed timber harvesting in that area, leaving the U.S. Court of Appeals for the Ninth Circuit to hold for the Indians in the area of road construction (the other part of the case being made moot by the congressional action). The U.S. Supreme Court granted certiorari, and heard arguments in the case on 30 November 1987. Justice Sandra Day O'Connor spoke for the court's 5–3 decision (Justices William Brennan, Thurgood Marshall, and Harry Blackmun dissented, while Justice Anthony Kennedy did not participate) in holding that the free exercise clause did not prohibit the federal government from building a road or harvesting timber in the national forest. The dissenters decried the decision bitterly, claiming that the free exercise clause could not be breached in any way.

Reference Wyatt, Kathryn C., "The Supreme Court, *Lyng*, and the *Lone Wolf* Principle." *Chicago-Kent Law Review*, 65 (2).

Madison, James—Letter on Indian Land Rights

In 1817, in a letter to future President James Monroe, President James Madison detailed his thoughts on his policy concerning Indians, a policy that, under Monroe and his successors, became what was to be called the removal policy. Madison's letter of 27 December 1817 is excerpted below:

My quere...relating to the right to Indian lands was suggested by the principle which has limited the claim of the United States to a right of preemption. It seemed also that an *unqualified* right of a Civilized people to land used by people in the hunter-state, on the principle that the earth was intended for those who would make it most conducive to the sustenance & increase of the human race, might imply a right in a people cultivating it with the Spade, to say to one using the plow, either adopt our mode, or let us substitute it ourselves. It might also be not easy to repel the claims of those without land in other Countries, if not our own, to vacant lands within the U.S. likely to remain for a *long* period unproductive of human food. The quere was not meant to contest the doctrine of the Message, under qualifications which were probably entertained without being specified.

Reference Hunt, Gaillard, ed., *The Writings of James Madison* (1908).

Mankiller, Wilma Pearl (Cherokee) (1945–)

The first woman to become chief of the Cherokee Nation, Wilma Mankiller is perhaps the most well-known woman Indian activist in the nation. According to Indian historian Duane Champaign, "She gained an understanding of rural poverty early in life because she witnessed and experienced it. She spent her childhood in the wooded hills of the rural community of Rocky Mountain in Adair County, Oklahoma, where she now lives with her husband,

Wilma Pearl Mankiller, principal chief of the Cherokee, President Ronald Reagan, and Interior Secretary Donald P. Hodel, left, meet with Indian leaders at the White House on 12 December 1988.

Charley Soap, who is involved in community development." Born at Mankiller Flats near Rocky Mountain, Oklahoma, which is close to the former Cherokee Nation capital of Tahlequah, Oklahoma, in November 1945, she grew up there with her parents, Charlie Mankiller, a Cherokee, and mother, Irene, who was Dutch-Irish. In 1956, the family moved to San Francisco under the government's relocation program, which sought to assimilate reservation Indians into American cities and society. Mankiller, in her autobiography, *Mankiller: A Chief and Her People*, called this sojourn "my own Trail of Tears." After a common school education, she attended Skyline Junior College and San Francisco State College. While in San Francisco, she met and became acquainted with the *Indians of All Tribes* (IAT) organization, which staged an occupation of Alcatraz Island in November 1969. At this point, Mankiller relates, she decided that her mission in life was to help her own people. For a time she worked in the office of noted Indian rights attorney Aubrey Grossman in San Francisco.

In 1977, Mankiller returned to Oklahoma and began a decade-long battle against several ailments, including kidney disease (her brother had to donate a kidney when she required a transplant), myasthenia gravis, a muscle disease, and recovery from a serious car accident. In 1983, as an important activist among the Cherokee people, she was asked by Chief Ross Owen Swimmer to be his deputy. When Swimmer was named as head of the Bureau of Indian Affairs in December 1985, Mankiller succeeded him as chief, making her the highest ranking Native American female ever. For her lifetime of work for her people, in 1987, she was named as *Ms.* magazine's Woman of the Year, and in 1994 her name was entered into the Woman's Hall of Fame in New York.

Reference Champaign, Duane, ed., *Native America: Portrait of the Peoples* (1994); Mankiller, Wilma, and Michael Wallis, *Mankiller: A Chief and Her People* (1993); Wilson, Darryl, "Wilma Pearl Mankiller." In Sharon Malinowski, ed., *Notable Native Americans* (1995).

Manypenny, George Washington (1808–1892)

He served as commissioner of Indian Affairs from 1853 until 1857, and in that time made more progress towards calming Indian hostilities on the American frontier than any commissioner before or after. But George Washington Manypenny may be better known for the work he did as chairman of the Sioux Concession Commission, also known as the Manypenny Commission, in 1876. Manypenny was born in 1808 in Uniontown, Pennsylvania, but he lived much of his adult life in Ohio, where he had moved about 1826 to edit the Washington (Ohio) *Republican*. He then bought and edited the *St. Clairsville Gazette*, a local newspaper. After moving to Zanesville, Ohio, he served as a contractor helping to build a local dam. He also served as clerk of common pleas for Muskingum County and, after being admitted to the state bar in 1842, opened his own law practice. After an unsuccessful attempt at a seat on the Board of Public Works, he ran for the Democratic nomination for Governor in 1853, but lost to William Medill who, ironically, served as the commissioner of Indian Affairs from 1845 to 1849. When Franklin Pierce was elected president of the United States in 1853, noted Democrats in Ohio brought Manypenny's name to the new president's attention for a plum patronage position in Washington. On 28 March 1853, less than a month after taking office, Pierce named Manypenny as the seventh Indian commissioner.

The Manypenny administration of the Indian service led to the greatest period of treaty-making in the history of that bureau. The editors of *Felix Cohen's Handbook of Federal Indian Law* write, "On March 24, 1853 [wrong date], George W. Manypenny of Ohio became commissioner of Indian Affairs. The president of the United States authorized him to negotiate with all tribes west of the states of Missouri and Iowa to extinguish Indian title and allow white settlement of tribal lands...Manypenny's first success came with the Otoe and Missouria Tribes on March 15, 1854." In the next two and a half years, culminating in November 1856, Manypenny negotiated over 50 treaties. In his annual report for 1856, while endorsing this work, he did discuss the problems of the Indians in Kansas, which was then fighting over whether to be a free or slave state. As Manypenny elucidated, "The general disorder so long prevailing in Kansas Territory, and the consequent unsettled state of civil affairs there have been very injurious to the interests of many of the Indian tribes in that Territory. The state of affairs referred to, with the influx of lawless men and speculators incident and introductory thereto, has impeded the surveys and the selections for the homes of the Indians, and otherwise prevented the full establishment and proper efficiency of all the means for civilization and improvement within the scope of the several treaties with them. The schools have not been as fully attended, nor the school buildings, agency houses, and other improvements, as rapidly constructed as they might otherwise have been. Trespasses and depredations of every conceivable kind have been committed on the Indians. They have been personally maltreated, their property stolen, their timber destroyed, their possessions encroached upon, and divers [various] other wrongs and injuries done to them." Manypenny is considered by historians at least to have been a southern sympathizer, and he may have even been proslavery. In July 1855, he was instrumental in helping to oust Kansas Territorial Governor Andrew H. Reeder, a former southern supporter who had taken up the cause of the free state movement in Kansas in his short year as Territorial Governor. Larry Gara, a biographer of President Franklin Pierce, writes, "Reeder was vulnerable because of his deep involvement with land schemes. In partnership with two judges, Reeder had contracted for the purchase of large tracts of land that had been reserved for mixed-blood Indians. Indian Commissioner Manypenny, himself sympathetic to the southern faction, reported to Washington that the contracts were clearly an attempt to cheat the Indians of valuable lands, and the report provided an excuse [for Pierce to dismiss Reeder]. Apparently, Manypenny was genuinely trying to protect Indian rights as well as catering to the South."

Although Democrat James Buchanan was elected president in 1856, he desired his own people in office, and Manypenny was forced out. He returned to Ohio, where he became the co-owner of the *Ohio Statesman*. In 1876, he was named by Republican President Ulysses S. Grant to the "commission appointed to obtain certain concessions from the Sioux Indians," known as the Sioux Commission or the Manypenny Commission. Although Manypenny did not want to agree to more Indian removals, he acceded to the demands of the government that the Sioux be removed to more agriculturally advantageous areas. More important, however, was the commission's strong recommendation, concluded just after the massacre of Custer's troops at Little Big Horn, that the Bureau of Indian Affairs remain a civilian agency and not be transferred to the Department of War. The Sioux Commission report went largely ignored, and Manypenny sought to confront supporters of such a move with the publication of his work, *Our Indian Wards* (1880), which outlined Indian-white affairs and sought to expose the government's mishandling of the whole situation. Angered by the broken promises and removals, Manypenny included on the cover page a quote from a Chief Ouray: "Is not the Government strong enough to keep its agreements with us?" As an appendix to the reprinted edition of Manypenny's *Our Indian Wards*, there was enclosed a letter, entitled "A Word About Indians," which the former Indian commissioner had written to the Cincinnati *Gazette* in anger over the seriousness of the Doolittle Report of 1867. Dated 31 January 1867, the letter reads,

We are accustomed to read, at short intervals, terrible stories in the newspapers about the depredations and murders committed by Indians, but we never get the other side of the question; the one side is highly colored, but we never get the other side. Indian

Grocer Wolfe Londoner of Denver, Colorado, incorporated white sentiment against the Utes in an advertisement for his store following the Meeker Massacre in 1879. George Washington Manypenny served on the Ute Commission that orchestrated the removal of Utes from their traditional hunting grounds in the Colorado Rocky Mountains to arid lands in Utah territory and eastern Colorado.

massacres and depredations are terrible, and their mode of warfare to us civilized people very revolting; notwithstanding, I have no hesitation in saying that no "Indian massacre" occurs, no "Indian depredation" is committed, without cause, and that cause, viewed and judged by Indian law, is defensible. Some act previous to the massacre or depredation has been committed by the whites justifying the subsequent conduct of the Indians, according to their law, notwithstanding the Indians may destroy the property or take the lives of innocent whites, for they do not recognize individual responsibility for crimes committed, but take compensation or visit retribution on the race or tribe to whom the offenders belong. Thus it is not unfrequent that the injury and wrong done to Indians by unprincipled whites is revenged by the murder of purely innocent and unoffending persons, without regard to age or sex. If the reckless and unprincipled white men who push themselves into the Indian country in advance of the regular settlements, and the more reckless scoundrels who contrive to get up Indian disturbances for the gain that is found in Indian wars, were all excluded from the Indian country, it would be a rare occurrence when we should be startled with "Indian hostilities."

In his final years, Manypenny served on the Ute Commission, designed to settle the question of the removal of the Utes from Colorado following a series of murders. In 1885 his third wife, Mary Woods Manypenny (sister of Associate Justice of the U.S. Supreme Court William Burnham Woods) tried to get him appointed as commissioner of Indian Affairs, but failed. Manypenny died at his residence near Bowie, Maryland, on 15 July 1892, in his eighties.

See also Manypenny Commission; *United States v. Sioux Nation of Indians.*

Reference "Death of George W. Manypenny." *Washington Evening Star*, 16 July 1892, 6; Fritz, Henry E., "Introduction." In Manypenny, George W., *Our Indian Wards* (1880); Gara, Larry, *The Presidency of Franklin Pierce* (1991); Kvasnicka, Robert M., "George W. Manypenny." In Robert M. Kvasnicka and Herman J. Viola, eds., *The Commissioners of Indian Affairs, 1824–1977* (1979); Manypenny, George W., *Our Indian Wards* (1972); Strickland, Rennard, ed., *Felix Cohen's Handbook of Federal Indian Law* (1982); U.S. Congress, House of Representatives, *Annual Report of the Commissioner of Indian Affairs for the Year 1856*, House Executive Document No. 1, 34th Congress, 3d Session (serial 893).

Manypenny Commission

Known officially as the Sioux Concession Commission, this delegation was sent West to negotiate with the Sioux for the relinquishment of the Black Hills of South Dakota. (Why the commission was established and how are detailed in the entry on "*United States v. Sioux Nation.*") The members of the commission were: chairman, former Commissioner of Indian Affairs George W. Manypenny; the Reverend Henry Benjamin Whipple; General Henry Hastings Sibley; Dr. Jared W. Daniels; Col. Albert G. Boone; Henry C. Bulis; Assistant Attorney General Augustine S. Gaylord; Newton Edmunds; and Samuel D. Hinman, acting as official interpreter. Charles M. Hendley served as commission secretary.

On 24 August 1876, Commissioner of Indian Affairs John Quincy Smith wrote to the men, "Gentlemen: You have been appointed by the president as members of the commission to negotiate with the Sioux Indians, pursuant to the following provisions contained in the Indian appropriation act for the current fiscal year: '*Provided*, That none of said sums appropriated for said Sioux Indians shall be paid to any band thereof while said band is engaged in hostilities against the white people, and hereafter there shall be no appropriation made for the subsistence of said Indians unless they shall first agree to relinquish all right and claim to any country outside the boundaries of the permanent reservation established by the treaty of 1868 [the Fort Laramie Treaty] for said Indians; and also so much of their said permanent reservation as lies west of the one hundred and third meridian of longitude, and shall also grant right of way over said reservation to the country thus ceded for wagon and other roads from convenient and accessible points on the Missouri River, in all not more than three in number; and unless they will receive all such supplies herein provided for by said treaty of 1868 at such points and places on their said reservation and in the vicinity of the Missouri River as the president may designate." He then went to explain that the Sioux must agree "1st. To relinquish all right and claim to any country outside the boundaries of the permanent reservation established by the treaty of 1868. 2d. To relinquish all rights and claim to so much of their said permanent reservations lies west of the one hundred and third meridian of longitude. 3d. To grant right of way over the permanent reservation to that part thereof which lies west of the one hundred and third meridian of longitude for wagon and other roads from convenient and accessible points on the Missouri River, not exceeding three in number. 4th. To receive all such supplies as are provided for by said act and by said treaty of 1868, at such points and places of their said reservation, and in the vicinity of the Missouri River, as the President may designate," or all subsistence from the government would be cut off.

The travels of the members of the Manypenny Commission were numerous and lasted for about a month, from 28 August 1876 (when Manypenny reports that "we held our first meeting in Omaha" on that date) until 27 October of that same year, when the treaty with the Sioux was initialed. On 7 September, the commission members met with Red Cloud and his chiefs, representing more than 4,900 Sioux. After a period of consultation with their council, Red Cloud's band of Oglalla Sioux signed the accord on 20 September. On the 23 September, the Brulé Sioux initialed the treaty. On 11 October, the "Yanctonais, Uncpapas, and Blackfeet Sioux" signed the agreement. The Sans Arcs, Two Kettles, Minneconjou, and Blackfeet Sioux (the latter of the Cheyenne agency) approved the compact on 16 October. The Lower Yanktons of the Crow Creek agency signed on 21 October, the Lower Brulé of the Lower Brulé agency finalized the settlement on 24 October, and the final group, the Santee Sioux, endorsed the treaty on 27 October.

In his letter to Commissioner Smith, submitting the approved agreements, Manypenny penned,

> Your commission respectfully urge[s] that every effort shall be made to secure the ratification and faithful fulfillment of the agreement which we have made by direction of the Government with this hapless people. We entered into upon this work with full knowledge that those who had heretofore made treaties with these Indians had seen their promises broken. We accepted the trust as a solemn duty to our country, to the perishing, and to God. The Indians trusted us. There were times when we trembled as we heard their earnest words of confidence and trust. Said a chief who signed this agreement, as he handed a pipe to our chairman, "Give this pipe of peace to the Great Father. When we give and another receives a pipe we regard it the same as when a white man swears on the Bible in court. If they do not speak the truth, bad will happen." We are confident that this agreement contains provisions which, if faithfully carried out, will save these Indians and redress some of the wrongs which furnish the darkest page of our history. It is an eternal law of the government of God that whatsoever a nation sows, that and nothing but that shall it reap. If we sow broken faith, injustice, and wrong, we shall reap in the future, as we have reaped the past, a harvest of sorrow and blood. We are not simply dealing with a poor perishing race; we are dealing with God. We cannot afford to delay longer fulfilling our bounden duty to those from whom we have taken that country, the possession of which has placed us in the forefront of the nations of the earth. We make it our boast that our country is the home of the oppressed of all lands. Dare we forget that there are also those whom we have made homeless, and to whom we are bound to give protection and care? We are aware that many of our people think that the only solution of the Indian problem is in their extinction. We would remind such persons that there is only One who can exterminate. There are too many graves within our borders over which the grass has hardly grown, for us to forget that God is just. The Indian is a savage, but he is also a man. He is one of the few savage men who clearly recognize the existence of a Great Spirit. He believes in the immortality of the soul. He has a passionate love for his children. He loves his country. He will gladly die for his tribe. Unless we deny all revealed religion, we must admit that he has the right to share in all the benefits of divine revelation. He is capable of civilization. Amid all the obstacles, the wrongs, and evils of our Indian policy, there are no missions which show richer rewards. Thousands of this poor race, who were once as poor and degraded as the wild Sioux, are to-day civilized men, living by the cultivation of the soil, and sharing with us in those blessings which give to men home, country, and freedom. There is no reason why these men may not be led out of the darkness to light. If the men of past generations had reasoned as this generation reasons, none of us would rejoice in the blessings of Christian civilization. . . . A great crisis has arisen in Indian Affairs. The wrongs [done to] the Indians are admitted by all. Thousands of the best men in the land feel keenly the nation's shame. They look to Congress for redress. Unless immediate and appropriate legislation is made for the protection and government of the Indians, they must perish. Our country must forever bear the disgrace and suffer the retribution of its wrong-doing. Our children's children will tell the sad story in hushed tones, and wonder how

their fathers dared so to trample on justice and trifle with God.

The Congress subsequently enacted the Manypenny agreement as the act of 28 February 1877 (19 Stat. 254), which in effect abrogated the Fort Laramie Treaty made between the Sioux and the government in 1868. In 1980, the U.S. Supreme Court, in *United States v. Sioux Nation*, held that because the Manypenny Commission did not obtain the necessary support of three-fourths of all of the Sioux involved, and not just their chiefs, the agreements were void.

See also Manypenny, George Washington; *United States v. Sioux Nation of Indians*; Whipple, Henry Benjamin.

Reference U.S. Congress, Senate, *Message from the President of the United States, Communicating the Report and Journal of Proceedings of the Commission Appointed to Obtain Certain Concessions from the Sioux Indians*, Senate Executive Document No. 9, 44th Congress, 2d Session, 1876.

Maricopa & Phoenix Railroad v. Territory of Arizona (156 U.S. 347 [1895])

A railroad, lacking congressional consent to be exempt from taxation when granted a right-of-way through an Indian reservation, can be taxed by a state or territory—so held the U.S. Supreme Court in this case, decided in 1895. When Arizona was organized as a territory, certain lands were set aside for the Pima and Maricopa Indians as a reservation, a tract known as the Gila (pronounced "heela") River Reservation. The Maricopa and Phoenix Railroad purchased 24.16 miles of land for a track, 6.24 miles of which ran through the Gila River reservation. Under its newly instituted tax laws, the territory levied a $7,000 tax on the total of 24.16 miles of track. The company agreed to pay for the 6.24 miles located outside of the reservation, but refused the rest. The Arizona Territorial Supreme Court ordered that the company pay for the entire tax, and property belonging to it be sold to recover the money if it refused. The company then appealed to the U.S. Supreme Court. On 4 March 1895, Justice Edward Douglass White held for a unanimous court in upholding the right of Arizona to levy a tax on the full 24.16 miles:

> It is wholly immaterial whether the rights vested in the corporation by an act of Congress were rights of ownership, or merely those which result from the grant of an easement. Whatever they were, they were taken out of the reservation by virtue of the grant, and came, to the extent of their withdrawal, under the jurisdiction of the territorial authority. The fact that Congress reserved the power to alter, amend, or repeal the statute in no way affected the authority of the territory over the rights granted, although the duration of that authority may depend on the exercise by Congress of the rights reserved.

Mattz v. Arnett (412 U.S. 481, 37 L.Ed. 2d 92, 93 S.Ct. 2245 [1973])

The issue in this Supreme Court case was whether an Indian reservation still existed after being open for allotment, and whether that land could be considered "Indian country" as defined. Petitioner Raymond Mattz, a Yurok, or Klamath River, Indian, had five nylon gill nets seized by the state game warden; Mattz asserted that he was fishing within the Klamath River reservation, and that he was within "Indian country" when the nets were seized. In a proceeding in which Mattz sued G. Raymond Arnett, the Director of the California Department of Fish and Game, a state superior court ordered the nets forfeited, ruling that because by an act of Congress of 17 June 1892 (27 Stat. 52, known as "An Act to provide for the disposition and sale of lands known as the Klamath River Indian Reservation"), the reservation no longer existed, and Mattz was not within "Indian country" as defined by 18 U.S.C. 1151. The California Court of Appeal affirmed the lower court's ruling, and the California Supreme Court refused to hear the case. On appeal, the U.S. Supreme Court granted Mattz certiorari, and arguments were held on 27 and 28 March 1973. Holding for a unanimous court on 11 June of the same year that reversed the decision of the court of appeals, Justice Harry Blackmun ruled that the act of 17 June 1892, while opening the reservation up for allotment, did not terminate its reservation status. Thus Mattz was within "Indian country" as defined by 18 U.S.C. 1151. Blackmun argued that Congress must express a clear intent that a reservation is to be terminated (in one such example, it held that "the Smith River Reservation is hereby discontinued." 15 Stat. 221 [1868]) and that the act of 17 June 1892 did not include that intent. He added, "Our conclusion that the 1892 Act did not terminate the Klamath River Reservation is reinforced by repeated recognition of the reservation status of the land after 1892 by the Department of the Interior and by Congress. In 1904 the Department, in *Crichton v. Shelton*, 33 I.D. 205 [33 Interior Department decisions 205], ruled that the 1892 Act reconfirmed the continued existence of the reservation. In 1932 the Department continued to recognize the Klamath River Reservation, albeit as part of the Hoopa Valley Reservation, and it continues to do so today. And Congress has recognized the reservation's continued existence by extending the period of trust allotments for this very reservation by the 1942 Act [Act of 24 December 1942, 56 Stat. 1081, codified at 25 U.S.C. 348a], and by restoring to tribal ownership certain vacant and undisposed-of ceded lands in the reservation."

See also Indian Country—Definition.

McBratney Exception

Under the Indian Major Crimes Act (23 Stat. 362) of 3 March 1885, Congress established all offenses by non-Indians on Indian territory as federal crimes. However, the Supreme Court carved out a notable exception in the case of *United States v. McBratney* in 1882. In this case, a white man, Jack McBratney, was tried for the murder of Thomas Casey, another white man, on the Ute Reservation in Colorado. As per Congress' intention, McBratney was convicted under federal law. McBratney sued to the U.S. Supreme Court that the state, and not the federal government, had jurisdiction. The Court, in a unanimous decision, agreed with McBratney that only states had jurisdiction over the crimes of non-Indians on Indian reservations. The Court has upheld the exception through such cases as *New York ex rel. Ray v. Martin* and *Draper v. United States*, yet limited it in the 1913 case of *Donnelly v. United States.*

See also *Donnelly v. United States*; *Draper v. United States*; *United States v. McBratney*.

McCarran Amendment (66 Stat. 560)

Codified at 43 U.S.C. 666, this legislative addition "waived the sovereign immunity of the United States as to comprehensive state water rights adjudications," according to the majority opinion of Justice William Brennan in *Montana et al. v. Northern Cheyenne Tribe of the Northern Cheyenne Indian Reservation et al.* (1983). Although not an enactment which deals directly with Indian Affairs, the amendment was at issue in two Supreme Court cases involving Indian water rights: the above-mentioned *Montana*, and *Colorado River Water Conservation District v. United States* (1976).

The relevant section of the act reads:

Consent is hereby given to join the United States as a defendant in any suit (1) for the adjudication of rights to the use of water of a river system or other source, or (2) for the administration of such rights, where it appears that the United States is the owner of or is in the process of acquiring water rights by appropriation under State law, by purchase, by exchange, or otherwise, and the United States is a necessary party to such suit. The United States, when a party to any such suit, shall (1) be deemed to have waived any right to plead that the State laws are inapplicable or that the United States is not amenable [agreeable] thereto by reason of its sovereignty, and (2) shall be subject to the judgments, orders and decrees of the court having jurisdiction, and may obtain review thereof, in the same manner and to the same extent as a private individual under like circumstances.

See also *Colorado River Water Conservation District v. United States*; *Montana et al. v. Northern Cheyenne Tribe of the Northern Cheyenne Indian Reservation et al.*

McClanahan, etc. v. State Tax Commission of Arizona (411 U.S. 164, 36 L.Ed. 2d 129, 93 S.Ct. 1257 [1973])

In this Supreme Court case, the court held that Indians on reservations were not subject to state income taxes except those called for by an explicit act of Congress. Rosalind McClanahan, an enrolled member of the Navajo tribe, sued in the Superior Court of Apache County, Arizona, to have her state income tax for the year 1967 returned by the state, and at the same time have the state income tax imposed on reservation Indians as unlawful. A trial court dismissed McClanahan's claim, and the Arizona State Court of Appeals affirmed. McClanahan then appealed to the U.S. Supreme Court for relief. After arguments were heard on 12 December 1972, the court's unanimous decision, written by Justice Thurgood Marshall, was handed down on 27 March 1973. In reversing the court of appeals' determination, Marshall held that Indians and Indian property on an Indian reservation are not subject to state taxation except if an act of Congress explicitly calls for such taxation. "We hold that by imposing the tax in question on this appellant, the State has interfered with matters which the relevant treaty and statutes leave to the exclusive province of the Federal Government and the Indians themselves. The tax is therefore unlawful as applied to reservation Indians with income derived wholly from reservation sources," Justice Marshall wrote.

See also *Oklahoma Tax Commission v. Sac and Fox Nation*; *Oklahoma Tax Commission v. Citizen Band Potawatomi Indian Tribe of Oklahoma.*

McKenney, Thomas Loraine (1785–1859)

Biographer James Horan called him the "Shadow Catcher of the Indians." He was perhaps the greatest advocate for the Indians in the earliest years of the nineteenth century, and he spent much of his life in the pursuit of what he perceived was fairness for the Native Americans still struggling against the expansionism of the young American nation. Thomas Loraine McKenney, the first head of the Office of Indian Affairs in the War Department (he was not officially considered the "commissioner" of Indian Affairs, as that specific office was not established until 1832), was born on 21 March 1785 on his father's estate at Hopewell, in Somerset County, Maryland, the son, and one of five sons and two daughters, of William McKenney, a prosperous mercantile businessman, and Anne (née Barber or Barbour) McKenney. Anne McKenney died in 1795, and her husband remarried Hannah Hines, with whom he had seven more children. Hannah Hines McKenney raised Thomas, her step-son, as her own. Thomas himself was named after his father's great-uncle Thomas Loraine, a sea captain who lived in Chestertown, Maryland. In addition, his maternal grandmother was Sarah Grub Barber, an eminent Quaker preacher in the eighteenth century, and Thomas' mother Anne raised her son in the first years of his life prior to her death in the Quaker religion, to which he adhered to for the rest of his life. McKenney attended school at Chestertown, Maryland, and for a time studied medicine, but decided in the end to enter his father's mercantile business.

Historian and writer Herman J. Viola is McKenney's biographer; in his work on McKenney, the Indian activist, Viola writes, "He probably would have spent his life as an Eastern Shore merchant had not the premature death of his father forced the sale of the family business." Carl Waldman writes, "About four years later [when he was 23], McKenney opened two dry-goods businesses" in the nation's capital. "He became well-known in political circles." During the

War of 1812 he served in the local militia, rising to the rank of major (although later in life he was elevated to colonel). It was at this time that McKenney became interested in the field of Indian trade, and it was with the influence of Secretary of War John C. Calhoun that McKenney was named in 1816 as the first Superintendent of Indian Trade, in which he was in charge of the series of forts across the western part of the country that traded with the Indians, as well as claims by and against the Indians. McKenney directed this office for eight years. In his *Memoirs, Official and Personal; with Sketches of Travels among the Northern and Southern Indians; Embracing a War Excursion and Descriptions of Scenes along the Western Borders* (1846), McKenney wrote, "I owe my first connection with our Indian relations, and the first civil trust conferred upon me, to the confidence of President Madison, who, unsolicited by myself, and, so far as I know, by any one for me, honored me, on the 2d April, 1816, with the commission of 'Superintendent of the United States Indian Trade with the Indian Tribes.' I had been informed, a few days previous, of the intention of President Madison to call me to the discharge of the duties of this office, but had never spoken to him on the subject, nor he to me. My commission was brought to me by Hon. William Jones, Secretary of the Navy."

On 11 March 1824, Calhoun wrote to McKenney, "Sir: To you are assigned the duties of the Bureau of Indian Affairs in this Department, for the faithful performance of which you will be responsible. Mr. [Samuel] Hamilton and Mr. Miller are assigned to you, the former as chief, and the latter as assistant clerk. You will take charge of the appropriations for annuities, and of the current expenses, and all warrants on the same will be issued on your requisitions on the Secretary of War, taking special care that no requisition be issued, but in cases where the money previously remitted has been satisfactorily accounted for, and on estimates in detail, approved by you, for the sum required. You will receive and examine the accounts and vouchers for the expenditure thereof, and you will pass them over to the proper Auditor's Office for settlement, after examination and approval by you; submitting such items for the sanction of this department as may require its approval. The administration of the fund for the civilization of the Indian is also committed to your charge, under the regulations extablished by the Department. You are also charged with the examination of the claims arising out of the law regulating the intercourse with Indian Tribes, and will, after examining and briefing the same, report them to this Department, endorsing a recommendation for their allowance or disallowance. The ordinary correspondence with the superintendents, the agents, and the sub-agents, will pass through your Bureau."

McKenney served as head of the Indian Office from its inception in 1824 until he was fired in 1829. His annual reports, as requested by Calhoun, were short and to the point, unlike later commissioners whose reports sometimes went on for hundreds of pages. As to the establishment of schools for the education of Indian children, McKenney wrote in the 1824 treatise, "The returns shew [*sic*] that 32 Schools are now in operation, containing 916 children. The Reports of the Superintendents are highly satisfactory. They certainly demonstrate that no insuperable [impossible] difficulty is in the way of a complete reformation of the principles and pursuits of the American Indian." His 1826 report, dated 20 November and sent to Secretary of War James Barbour, declared that spending for Indian education "is $13,783.33 1/3." "It is respectfully, but earnestly recommended," he added, "that the sum be increased. The personal inspection which I have been able to make during the last Summer of some of the schools, that, for example, at Michilimackinac, and that near Buffalo, in the State of New York, on the Seneca Reserve, has confirmed all my previous convictions of the vast benefits which the Indian children are deriving from these establishments." McKenney further wrote to Barbour on 14 February 1826, regarding the placement of Indian trading sites per the act of 25 May 1824, "The chief object of the Congress in adopting this provision [the trading sites act] was, doubtless, the protection of the Indians. In this point of view, the provision is as just as it is humane. Just, because the Indians have claims upon the Government for protection; and humane, because, without its interference, all experience testifies that they must be injured."

Manuscript collections of McKenney's apparently do not exist; however, he was a prolific letter writer, and many of those pieces of correspondence are preserved in the collections of the many people he communicated with. To Joseph Vallence Bevan of Savannah, Georgia, he wrote, "Sir: Your letter to the Secretary of War of the 8th inst[ant] is received, and I am directed to give you, or your agent, access to any papers in the Department touching the policy pursued by our Government towards the Creek and Cherokee Nations of Indians. I will take an early opportunity and examine and let you know if there be any, and would be very happy to cause extracts and copies to be made for you, but the constant and heavy press of duties upon the clerks in this office, forbids it." His most abundant communications were apparently with Reverend Dr. Philip Milledoler, who seems to have taken an intense interest in the welfare of his fellow man, as well as the Indians, and corresponded with McKenney quite frequently. On 13 February 1828 McKenney wrote to him, "My dear friend, I enclose you a pamphlet—It contains what I hold to be the skeleton of the only just system of commercial intercourse with our Indians. If you think so, use it in the best manner you can to bring out the <u>public opinion.</u> And should it be deemed proper to memorialize the Congress at its next session, let this be the basis."

In 1830, McKenney became caught up in the controversy to remove the Cherokee Indians from their native homes in and around Georgia to Oklahoma, and the episode cost him his job in the Indian Office. In the 1820s, while traveling through Creek Territory, he adopted two orphaned Indian children, and after his dismissal requested that he be allowed to take them to Philadelphia. President Jackson refused the request, and they were returned to the Creeks. (One was later accused of murder, and forced to flee to the Seminole Nation in Florida; the other was never heard from again.) This firing left McKenney, in the latter part of his life, unable to render further assistance to the Indians through his government position. However, throughout his life, and even after his firing, he collected information on the Indians, even commissioning artist Charles Bird King to travel west and paint some of the Native Americans he came across. Utilizing the talents of King and such other artists as James Otto Lewis, McKenney collaborated with historian James Hall to put together the three-volume *History of the Indian Tribes of North America, with Biographical Sketches and Anecdotes of the Principal Chiefs* (Philadelphia: D. Rice and J.G. Clark, 1837–44). McKenney's travels west resulted in his own two-volume *Memoirs, Official and Personal; with Sketches of Travels among the Northern and Southern Indians; Embracing a War Excursion and Descriptions of Scenes along the Western Borders* (New York: Paine and Burgess, 1846). He also authored *Sketches of a Tour to the Lakes, of the Character and Customs of the Chippeway Indians and of Incidents Connected with the Treaty of Fond du Lac* (Baltimore: Fielding Lucas, Jun'r., Printer, 1827). At the end of his life, although broke and unable to care for himself, McKenney nonetheless continued to speak out on behalf of the Indians, and donated a share of the proceeds of his speeches to help various Indian tribes. He died in poverty and alone in Brooklyn, New York, on 20 February 1859.

Herman Viola, in considering McKenney's place in history, writes, "It is easy enough to discuss Indian policy—beginning with Secretary of War Calhoun and extending through the administration of Andrew Jackson—as a heartless expulsion of the Indians from their ancestral homes in the East to new wilderness abodes west of the Mississippi. But what does such an interpretation do about such men as Thomas L. McKenney? I suggest that McKenney (with his views about the Indians and his proposals for their education and civilization) was too powerful a force in a crucial period of Indian relations to be ignored, that he supplied an important ingredient in Indian policy, and that his proposals were forerunners of policies that later became dominant."

See also Cherokee Indians, Removal of—Congressional and Governmental Debate.

References Calhoun to McKenney, 11 March 1824, *U.S. Office of Indian Affairs, Annual Reports of the Commissioner of Indian Affairs, 1824–1831* (1976); Horan, James D., *The McKenney-Hall Portrait Gallery of American Indians* (1972); Lowrie, Walter, and Matthew St. Clair Clarke, eds., *American State Papers: Documents, Legislative and Executive, of the Congress of the United States, from the First to the Third Session of the Thirteenth Congress, Inclusive, Commencing March 3, 1789 and Ending March 3, 1815* (1832); McKenney to Joseph Vallence Bevan, 23 February 1825, Thomas McKenney Miscellaneous Papers, New York Public Library; McKenney to Philip Milledoler, 13 February 1828, Milledoler Papers, New-York Historical Society, New York; McKenney, Thomas L., *Memoirs, Official and Personal, with Sketches of Travels among the Northern and Southern Indians, Embracing a War Excursion and Descriptions of Scenes along the Western Border* (1973); U.S. Congress, Senate, *Annual Report from the Office of Indian Affairs for the Year 1824*, Senate Document No. 1, 18th Congress, 2d Session (serial 108); U.S. Congress, Senate, *Annual Report from the Office of Indian Affairs for the Year 1826*, Senate Document No. 1, 19th Congress, 2d Session (serial 144); Viola, Herman J., "From Civilization to Removal: Early American Indian Policy." In Jane F. Smith and Robert M. Kvasnicka, ed., *Indian-White Relations: A Persistent Paradox* (1976); Viola, Herman J., *Thomas L. McKenney: Architect of America's Early Indian Policy: 1816–1830* (1974); Viola, Herman J., "Thomas L. McKenney, 1824–30." In Robert M. Kvasnicka and Herman J. Viola, eds., *The Commissioners of Indian Affairs, 1824–1977* (1979); Waldman, Carl, *Who Was Who in Native American History: Indians and Non-Indians from Early Contacts through 1900* (1990).

Meacham, Alfred Benjamin (1826–1882)

Alfred B. Meacham, founder of the *Council Fire*, was among the most active and dedicated of the Indian rights reformers of the nineteenth century. He was the son of Anderson Meacham, a farmer and landowner, and Lucinda Meacham (née Wasson), in Orange County, Indiana, on 29 April 1826. Anderson Meacham was descended from a Quaker sect that abandoned North Carolina because of its hatred of slavery, but he seems to have also turned to Methodism, in which his son, Alfred, took a lifelong interest. Nothing is known of Alfred's education, but it is assumed that when his father lost everything in the Panic of 1837 and moved the family to Iowa City, Iowa, Meacham attended local schools. According to biographer Dan Thrapp, "In 1845 he assisted in removing the Sauk and Fox Indians to a reservation they had been assigned to following the Black Hawk War."

In 1869, he was named superintendent of Indian Affairs in Oregon. As superintendent in Oregon, he wrote a highly distinguished paper to the acting Commissioner of Indian Affairs, Henry R. Clum, entitled "Notes on Snakes, Paiutes, Nez Percés at Malheur Reservation." He befriended the Modoc Indians of Oregon and they seemed to have trusted him. His arguments to that tribe to avoid hostilities led them to settle on the Klamath Reservation, which they came to hate. Meacham was in Washington, D.C., when the Modoc War, a reaction by the Modoc against their assignment to the Klamath Reservation, began. President Grant named Meacham to head a delegation to talk with the Modocs. An Indian woman, Tobey Riddle, warned Meacham that the Modocs no longer trusted him and that he and other commissioners would be killed. Meacham went with General Edward Richard Sprigg Canby and the Reverend Eleazar Thomas, but on 11 April 1873, at a conference, several Indians, including Captain Jack and Boston Charley, attacked the party, killing Canby and Thomas and seriously wounding Meacham, who escaped with his life. The *Council Fire* of September 1879 relates that Meacham was left "half paralyzed, with brain congested, spirit broken, helpless, hopeless and friendless in a great city" from the attack. Captain Jack was subsequently executed (with two other Modoc leaders, Black Jim and Boston Charley) on 3 October 1873.

To further his effort in Indian reform,

Meacham established the *Council Fire* in December 1877 (the first was dated January 1878, however) as "a monthly journal, of 10 Royal Quarto pages, devoted to the History, Character, Social Life, Religious Traditions, Government, Current Legends, &c., of the American Indian, including also a full Discussion of our Relations to Him as a People and a Government." In the first issue, Meacham editorialized,

> After years of repeated importunities by the friends of the Indian, I have consented to establish a journal devoted to his interest, assured that my own race are willing to do right whenever convinced of the right, and that the other stands ready to bury the tomahawk and scalping knife forever, whenever justice is guaranteed to them. I have given all my time to this cause for four years, have been kindly received by the people and the press everywhere, and have been assured that my efforts were productive of good results. I do not come to this work with "sickly sentimentality" about the "noble red man" being a superior man. I know him to be a savage, but I know that he is a man of noble attributes, as well as savage propensities; a man of fine mental endowments as well as warlike prowess. I know him to be true to friendship, as well as bitter and revengeful to his foes. I know that he will keep his compacts with those who live faithfully to their promises; that he responds to the treatment he receives, whether good or bad. I know whereof I speak. I have suffered at his hand as no other man of my race ever suffered; and survived; but I remember that the broken promises of my government, and of its citizens, impelled these savages to deeds of violence. My convictions on this question have not changed. I shall endeavor to perform what to me is a sacred duty, with dear of none but God, and relying upon the good will and justice of both races for financial support, and hope that, aided by able friends who have consented to assist me in this labor of love and justice to humanity, to merit the appreciation of all good men and women, without regard to church or sect, society or party, race or color.

He worked on the paper until his death on 16 February 1882, which was caused most likely by the wounds he had suffered in 1873. His friend, Thomas A. Bland, carried on the publication of the journal, and three years after Meacham's death founded the National Indian Defense Association (NIDA). Among Meacham's published works on Indians are *Wigwam and Warpath, or The Royal Chief in Chains* (1875), and *Wi-ne-ma (The Woman Chief) and Her People* (1876).

See also Bland, Thomas Augustus; National Indian Defense Association.

References Phinney, Edward Sterl, *Alfred B. Meacham: Promoter of Indian Reform* (Ph.D. dissertation, University of Oregon at Salem, 1963); Thrapp, Dan L., *Encyclopedia of Frontier Biography* (1990); U.S. Congress, House of Representatives, *Annual Report of the Commissioner of Indian Affairs for the Year 1871*, House Executive Document No. 1, 42nd Congress, 2d Session (serial 1505).

Means, Russell Charles (Oglala Dakota) (1939–)

Russell Means is among the most important of the Indian activists to come out of the militancy of the American Indian Movement. Means was born on the Pine Ridge Reservation in South Dakota on 10 November 1939, the eldest of four sons of Harold ("Hank") Means and Theodora Feather Means. Hank Means' grandfather, Gus Means, worked for the Bureau of Indian Affairs in the nineteenth century. After the onset of World War II, Hank Means moved with his family to California to work as a welder at the Mare Island Navy Yard near San Francisco. Russell Means thus attended local schools in Vallejo, California, but was subjected to racial discrimination in high school. As a result, reports biographer Raymond Wilson, "he became a juvenile delinquent and experimented with drugs. [He] moved to Los Angeles and kicked the drug habit, but became an alcoholic." He worked at a series of dead-end jobs. In 1964, exhibiting some of the militancy he would demonstrate in the 1970s, he joined some other Indian activists to unsuccessfully "occupy" Alcatraz Island in San Francisco. He

Activist Russell Charles Means, a founder of the American Indian Movement, speaks at a news conference in Lansing, Michigan, in 1987.

then served first for a period of time on the tribal council of the Rosebud Reservation in South Dakota, then as director of the American Indian Center in Cleveland, Ohio.

It was in Cleveland that he met Dennis Banks, one of the founders of the American Indian Movement (AIM), one of the most militant Indian civil rights organizations of the period. Attired in his native outfit and braids, he appeared at a Thanksgiving Day parade in Massachusetts to demonstrate against the holiday. He thus became the ultimate figurehead for AIM. He participated in a protest at Mount Rushmore to protest the government's refusal to hand back the Black Hills, which had been confiscated from the Lakota in the nineteenth century. His work in South Dakota to bring attention to the cause of the Native American rights struggle made him the enemy of many white people suspicious of his rhetoric.

In February 1972, in response to what he believed to be a cover-up of the murder of an Oglala, Raymond Yellow Thunder, Means directed a protest march which influenced local authorities to open the investigation and led to the prosecution of two whites for manslaughter. Means was also a member of the Trail of Broken Treaties caravan which protested government policy towards Indians in Washington, D.C. He was an avowed enemy of Dick Wilson, the Pine Ridge tribal chairman, and his so-called GOON squads. To protest the death of Wesley Bad Heart Bull, Means, Banks, and others rioted at the courthouse at Custer, South Dakota, an action which led to Means serving a jail term. On 27 February 1973, Means and other AIM activists occupied a church at Wounded Knee on the Pine Ridge Reservation to call attention to Wilson's dictatorial leadership. The siege, which lasted for 73 days, left Means facing trial for his involvement, but the judge dismissed all charges. Means had faced Wilson in an election for tribal chairman, but Wilson won in a contested election that included charges of vote fraud and threats. In 1974, Means served a jail term for the riot at the Custer courthouse.

In the 1980s, Means turned to environmental protection of Indian lands as the chief focus of his advocacy. He established Camp Yellow Thunder, a spiritual site, in the Black Hills to protest the government's refusal to hand the area back to the Indians. In 1992, Jim Carrier of the *Denver Post* called him the "Last of the Militants."

In November 1991, Means, at that time chairman and CEO of the American Indian Anti-Defamation Council, opened the organization's new office in Denver, Colorado. The objective of the AIADC is "the establishment and operation of a national and international network of education and communication dedicated to the protection, enhancement, and prosperity of the indigenous peoples of the Western Hemisphere. Toward that end, the Council will actively work for the elimination of prejudice, racism, and racial discrimination directed at American Indians, and will actively oppose any human rights and civil rights violations against American Indians." In 1992, he played the role of Chingachgook in the motion picture remake of *The Last of the Mohicans*; in 1995, he published his autobiography, *Where White Men Fear to Tread.*

See also American Indian Movement; Banks, Dennis J.; Wounded Knee (1973).

References D'Emilio, John, "Means, Russell Charles." In Eleanora W. Schoenebaum, ed., *Political Profiles: The Nixon/Ford Years* (1979); Means, Russell, and Marvin J. Wolf, *Where White Men Fear to Tread: The Autobiography of Russell Means* (1995); Moritz, Charles, ed., *Current Biography 1978* (1978); Utter, Jack, *American Indians: Answers to Today's Questions* (1993); Wilson, Raymond, "Russell Means." In David DeLeon, ed., *Leaders from the 1960s: A Biographical Sourcebook of American Activism* (1994); Zimmerman, Karen P., "Russell C. Means." In Sharon Malinowski, ed., *Notable Native Americans* (1995).

Medill, William (1801? or 1802?–1865)

Historian Robert A. Trennert, Jr., writes of William Medill, the fourth commissioner of the Bureau of Indian Affairs, "Medill's tenure as Commissioner of Indian Affairs in the Polk Administration came at the critical time of continental expansion which resulted in forceful removal of the Indian from lands desired by white settlers. Soon after he took office Medill attempted to make some basic reforms in policy governing relations with the Indians. One of the most controversial aspects of his reforming activities as commissioner revolved around his determination to crack down on the rampant abuses in the Indian trade. The difficulties he encountered demonstrate the grip private trading firms held on governmental policy relative to Indian Affairs." Little is known of his life. He was born in New Castle County, Delaware, in either 1801 or 1802, according to most sources on his life. He graduated from Delaware College in 1825, and studied the law. Richard H. Faust, in writing of Medill's mysterious life, elucidates, "The exact date of [Medill's] birth is unknown; and although the date often cited is 1802, different dates from 1801 to 1805 are used. It is sometimes said that Medill studied law at Newark Academy (the ancestral institution of Delaware College and the University of Delaware), but this is doubtful according to University of Delaware archivist John M. Clayton, Jr., who can find no mention of Medill in any of the records [of the college]." At this time, Medill opened a private academy or school at White Clay Creek Hundred in Delaware before eventually removing to Lancaster, Ohio, about 1830. In 1832 he was admitted to the Ohio bar, and entered Democratic party politics thereafter. Three years later, he was elected to the Ohio state legislature and served as Speaker of the state House in 1836. After four years in the state House, he was elected to the U.S. House of Representatives in 1838, and served two brief terms. After losing a bid for reelection in 1842, he returned to his private law practice.

With the election of Martin Van Buren in 1844, Medill, a supporter, was considered for the post of assistant Postmaster General, but instead he was asked to replace Indian Commissioner Thomas Hartley Crawford, who had held the commissionership for eight years and was a Jackson man of some repute. Still, on 28 October 1845, Van Buren named Medill as the fourth Indian commissioner. His service, from 1845 until 1849, was marked by an age of reform of the Indian trade system and the Indian Bureau as a whole. In his annual report for 1847, Medill discussed the role of missionary groups and teachers in the education of Indians. He wrote, "In every system which has been adopted for promoting the cause of education among Indians, the Department has found its most efficient and faithful auxiliaries and laborers in the societies of the several Christian denominations." His discourse for 1848 discussed the situation of the Indian up until that time: "Stolid and unyielding in his nature, and inveterately wedded to the savage habits, customs and prejudices in which he has been reared and trained, it is seldom the case that full blood Indian of our hemisphere can, in immediate juxtaposition with a white population, be brought farther within the pale of civilization than to adopt its vices; under the corrupting influences of which, too indolent [lazy] to labor, and too weak to resist, he soon sinks into misery and despair."

Medill's attempt to end the sale of liquor to the Indians met with contempt from the rest of the government apparatus which was either too busy to care or was cashing in on the trade. With the election of Whig Zachary Taylor as president in 1848, Medill's days as Indian commissioner were numbered. Taylor replaced him soon after the inauguration with Orlando Brown. Medill's career accelerated after he left government. In 1850 he served as president of the Ohio state constitutional convention, as Ohio's lieutenant governor in 1852 and 1853, and as acting governor (upon the resignation of Reuben Wood) from 1853 until he was elected to a single term as governor in 1854. With the return of the Democrats to power in 1856, he was picked by President James Buchanan to be the first comptroller of the U.S. Treasury (1857–61). He never married, and when he died on 2 September 1865, in his sixties, he left a large estate.

See also Bureau of Indian Affairs.

References Faust, Richard H., "William Medill: Commissioner of Indian Affairs, 1845–1849." *Old Northwest* 1 (2); "Medill, William." *National Cyclopedia of American Biography* (1898–1977); Trennert, Robert A., Jr., *Alternative to Extinction: Federal Indian Policy and the Beginnings of the Reservation System, 1846–1851* (1975); Trennert, Robert A., Jr., "William Medill." In Robert M. Kvasnicka and Herman J. Viola, eds., *The Commissioners of Indian Affairs, 1824–1977* (1979); Trennert, Robert A., Jr., "William Medill's War with the Indian Traders, 1847." *Ohio History* 82 (1); U.S. Congress, Senate, *Annual Report of the Commissioner of Indian Affairs*, Senate Executive Document 1, 30th Congress, 1st session, 1847 (serial 503); U.S. Congress, Senate, *Annual Report of the Commissioner of Indian Affairs for the Year 1848*, House Executive Document No. 1, 30th Congress, 2d Session (serial 537).

Menominee Restoration Act of 1973 (87 Stat. 770)

This federal action of 22 December 1973 was enacted to repeal the Menominee Termination Act of 1954, which ended federal control and jurisdiction over the Menominee Indian tribe of Wisconsin. Section 3, subsections (a), (b), and (c) explain the act's importance:

Sec. 3. (a) Notwithstanding the provisions of the Act of June 17, 1954 (68 Stat. 250; 25 U.S.C. 891–902) [the Menominee Termination Act], as amended, or any other law, Federal recognition is hereby extended to the Menominee Indian Tribe of Wisconsin and the provisions of the Act of June 18, 1934 (48 Stat. 984; 25 U.S.C. 461 et seq.) [the Indian Reorganization Act], as amended, are made applicable to it.

(b) The Act of June 17, 1954 (68 Stat. 250; 25 U.S.C. 891–902), as amended, is hereby repealed and there are hereby reinstated all rights and privileges of the tribe or its members under Federal treaty, statute, or otherwise which may have been diminished or lost pursuant to such Act.

(c) Nothing contained in this Act shall diminish any rights or privileges enjoyed by the tribe or its members now or prior to June 17, 1954, under federal treaty, statute, or otherwise, which are not inconsistent with the provisions of the Act.

See also Menominee Termination Act of 1954.

Reference *United States Code Congressional and Administrative News*, 93d Congress, First Session.

Menominee Termination Act of 1954 (68 Stat. 250)

Enacted on 17 June 1954, this act terminated the federal relationship with the Menominee tribe of Wisconsin; the law explains that "the purpose of this Act is to provide for orderly termination of Federal supervision over property and members of the Menominee Indian Tribe of Wisconsin." The pertinent section of the act, in which the funds of the tribe held in trust by the United States were to be divided among the members of the tribe, is section 5:

Sec. 5. The Secretary [of the Interior] is authorized and directed, as soon as practicable after the passage of this Act, to pay from such funds as are deposited to the credit of the tribe in the Treasury of the United States $1,500 to each member of the tribe on the rolls of the tribe on the date of this Act. Any other person whose application for enrollment on the rolls of the tribe is subsequently approved, pursuant to the terms of section 3 hereof, shall, after enrollment, be paid a like sum of $1,500: Provided, That such payments shall be made first from any funds on deposit in the Treasury of the United States to the credit of the Menominee Indian Tribe drawing interest at the rate of 5 per centum, and thereafter from the Menominee judgment fund, symbol 14X7142.

See also Menominee Restoration Act of 1973; *Menominee Tribe of Indians v. United States*; Public Law 280.

Menominee Tribe of Indians v. United States (391 U.S. 404, 20 L.Ed. 2d 697, 88 S.Ct. 1705 [1968])

The issue of the preservation of fishing and hunting rights by a tribe whose federal supervision had been terminated was at hand in this Supreme Court case. An 1854 pact (known as the Wolf River Treaty) between the Menominee tribe of Wisconsin and the federal government granted a reservation to the Indians "to be held as Indian lands are held." In 1954, the Congress passed the Menominee Termination Act, which established 1961 as the end of federal supervision over tribal affairs. In 1962, three members of the Menominee tribe were arrested and convicted of violating state laws involving hunting and fishing. The tribe, representing the three members, sued in Wisconsin District Court to be compensated for the loss of the tribe's hunting and fishing rights. The Court held that these rights were extinguished by the Menominee Termination Act. On appeal, the Wisconsin Supreme Court upheld the judgment, and a divided Court of Claims asked the U.S. Supreme Court to hear the case.

In a 6–2 decision (Justices Potter Stewart and Hugo Black dissented and Justice Thurgood Marshall did not participate), the high court handed down its decision on 27 May 1968. Written by Justice William O. Douglas, the court's opinion held that the government allowed hunting and fishing rights to be preserved by the 1854 treaty and Public Law 280, passed by Congress in 1954, and that the termination act did not extinguish these rights, although they may have been curtailed under state law. As Justice Douglas wrote, "What the precise nature and extent of those hunting and fishing rights were we need not at this time determine. For the issue tendered by the present decision of the Court of Claims is whether those rights, whatever their precise extent, have been extinguished." Later in the decision he explained, "As amended Public Law 280 granted designated States, including Wisconsin, jurisdiction 'over Indian offenses committed by or against Indians in the areas of Indian country' named in the Act, which in the case of Wisconsin was described as 'All Indian country within the State.' But Public Law 280 went on to say that 'Nothing in this section…shall deprive any Indian or any Indian tribe, band, or community of any right, privilege, or immunity afforded under Federal treaty, agreement, or statute with respect to hunting, trapping, or fishing or the control, licensing, or regulation thereof.'"

See also *New Mexico v. Mescalero Apache Tribe*; Public Law 280.

Reference Goldberg, Carole E., "Public Law 280: The Limits of State Jurisdiction over Reservation Indians." *UCLA Law Review* 22.

Meriam Report

Historian Frederick J. Stefon writes, "Perhaps the most important investigation into the social and economic conditions of the Indians—the *Report* uncovered horrible conditions of impoverishment, disease, social and economic degeneration among the native population." He was speaking of the Meriam Report, edited by Lewis Meriam of the University of Chicago. Officially named *The Problem of Indian Administration*, the report ushered out the era of allotment and directed the government towards a reinstitution of the reservation system and a protection of Indian rights.

The report was highly censorious of the allotment policy established under the General Allotment Act (Dawes Act) of 1887. The editors explained,

When the government adopted the policy of individual ownership of land on the reservations, the expectation was that the Indians would become farmers. Part of the plan was to instruct and aid them in agriculture, but this vital part was not pressed with vigor and intelligence. It almost seems as if the government assumed that some magic in individual ownership of property would in itself prove an educational civilizing factor, but unfortunately this policy has for the most part operated in the opposite direction. Individual ownership has in many instances permitted Indians to sell their allotments and to live for a time on the unearned income resulting from the sale. Individual ownership brought promptly all the details of inheritance, and frequently the sale of property of the deceased Indians to whites so that the estate could be divided among heirs. To the heirs the sale brought further unearned income, thereby lessening the necessity for self-support. Many Indians were not ready to make effective use of their individual allotments. Some of the allotments were of such a character that they could not be effectively used by anyone in small units. The solution was to permit the Indians through the government to lease their lands to the whites. In some instances government officers encouraged leasing, as the whites were anxious for the use of the land and it was far easier to administer property leased to whites than to educate and stimulate Indians to use their own property. The lease money, though generally small in amount, gave the Indians further unearned income to permit the continuance of a life of idleness.

Surplus land remaining after allotments were made was often sold and the proceeds placed in a tribal fund. Natural resources, such as timber and oil, were sold and the money paid either into tribal funds or to individual Indians if the land had been allotted. From time to time per capita payments were made to the individual Indians from tribal funds. These policies all added to the unearned income of the Indian and postponed the day when it would be necessary for him to go to work to support himself.

References Meriam, Lewis, ed., *The Problem of Indian Administration* (1928); Stefon, Frederick J., "Significance of the Meriam Report of 1928." *Indian Historian* 8 (3).

Merrion et al. v. Jicarilla Apache Tribe (455 U.S. 130, 71 L.Ed. 2d 21, 102 S.Ct. 894 [1982])

In this Supreme Court case, the justices held that a severance tax imposed by an Indian tribe on oil and gas removed from the reservation was authorized by the tribe's inherent authority to tax as part of its power of self-government, and that such a tax was not violative of the Commerce Clause of the U.S. Constitution. Petitioners J. Gregory Merrion, Robert L. Bayless, the Amoco Production Company, and the Marathon Oil Company, just a few of the 21 total petitioners, signed long-term leases with the Jicarilla Apache Tribe of northwestern New Mexico. As part of its revised Constitution, which the Jicarilla Apaches submitted to the secretary of the interior for approval, the tribe levied a severance tax against oil and gas severed from tribal lands, excluding any oil and gas used to develop the leases or that were received by the tribe as royalty payments. The plaintiffs, Merrion et al., then sued in the District Court for the District of New Mexico to enjoin, or stop, enforcement of the tax. The court consolidated the cases (officially making it Merrion et al.), and then enjoined the tax, holding that an Indian tribe lacked the authority to tax, a power it decided was reserved to the government and the states. On appeal, the U.S. Court of Appeals for the Tenth Circuit overturned the ruling, instead deciding that the taxing power is an "inherent attribute" of tribal sovereignty granted by the Indian Reorganization Act of 1934, and that such power had not be preempted by any treaty or Federal statute. On appeal, the U.S. Supreme Court granted certiorari. Arguments in the case were heard before the court on 30 March 1981, and were reargued on 4 November 1981.

Justice Thurgood Marshall delivered the 6–3 decision of the court (Chief Justice Warren Burger and Justices John Paul Stevens and William H. Rehnquist dissenting) which held the tax to be constitutional, that the tribe's inherent power to tax came from its right of self-government, and that the tax did not violate the Commerce Clause. Justice Marshall explained, "In *Worcester v. Georgia*, 6 Peters, at 559, 8 L.Ed. 483, Chief Justice Marshall observed that Indian tribes 'had always been considered as distinct, independent political communities, retaining their original natural rights.' Although the tribes are subject to the authority of the Federal Government, the 'weaker power does not surrender its independence—its right to self-government, by associating with a stronger, and taking its protection....Adhering to this understanding, we conclude that the Tribe did not surrender its authority to tax the mining activities of petitioners, whether this authority is deemed to arise from the Tribe's inherent power of self-government or from its inherent power to exclude nonmembers. Therefore, the Tribe may enforce its severance tax unless and until Congress divests this power, an action that Congress has not taken to date. Finally, the severance tax imposed by the Tribe cannot be invalidated on the ground that it violates the 'negative implications' of the Commerce Clause. Affirmed." Chief Justice Burger and Justices Stevens and Rehnquist dissented on the grounds that the tax was an ex post facto tax—that when the leases were signed with the lessees, the tribe did not retain the right to impose additional conditions on the companies.

***See** Cotton Petroleum Corp. v. New Mexico.*

***Mescalero Apache Tribe v. Franklin Jones, Commissioner of the Bureau of Revenue of the State of New Mexico et al.* (411 U.S. 145, 36 L.Ed. 2d 114, 93 S.Ct. 1267 [1973])**

The question involved in this Supreme Court case was whether the Indian Reorganization Act (IRA) of 1934 (48 Stat. 984 [codified as 25 U.S.C. 476]) exempted reservation businesses from taxes imposed by states. The Mescalero Indian tribe of New Mexico leased space off their reservation from the U.S. Forest Service, purchased materials, and built a ski resort. The New Mexico Bureau of Revenue imposed a use tax on the materials, and a tax on the resort's gross receipts, to be used for the state school budget. Under protest, the tribe paid a total of $26,086.47. After the taxes were imposed, the tribe asked Franklin Jones, Commissioner of Revenue, to remove the tax assessment; when he refused, the tribe sued to the State Court of Appeals, which affirmed Jones' decision. The Mescalero tribe, after the New Mexico Supreme Court denied to hear the case, appealed for relief from the U.S. Supreme Court. After the case was argued on 12 December 1972, the court handed down the 6–3 decision (Justices William O. Douglas, William Brennan, and Potter Stewart dissenting) upholding the tax on gross receipts but striking it down on the construction materials. Speaking for the majority, Justice Byron White explained, "The Indian Reorganization Act of 1934 neither requires nor counsels us to recognize this tribal business venture as a federal instrumentality. Congress itself felt it necessary to address the immunity question and to provide tax immunity to the extent it deemed desirable." He continued, "The intent and purpose of the Reorganization Act of 1934 was 'to rehabilitate the Indian's economic life and to give him a chance to develop the initiative destroyed by a century of oppression and paternalism'...The Act did not strip Indian tribes and their reservation lands of their historic immunity from state and local control. But, in the context of the Reorganization Act, we think it unrealistic to conclude that Congress conceived of off-reservation tribal enterprises 'virtually as an arm of the Government'...On the contrary, the aim was to disentangle the tribes from the official bureaucracy. The Court's decision in *Organized Village of Kake*, which involved tribes organized under the Reorganization Act, demonstrates that off-reservation activities are within the reach of state law."

Metlakatla Indian Community, Annette Islands Reserve v. Egan (369 U.S. 45 [1962])

The case of the *Metlakatla Indian Community of Alaska v. William Egan, the Governor of Alaska*, dealt with how much power a state could have in outlawing fish traps used by Indian reservations in violation of state laws. It was a joint case with *Organized Village of Kake, and Angoon Community Association v. Egan*, which had to do with the same issues. Under the White Act (act of Congress of 6 June 1924, 43 Stat. 464, codified as amended at 48 U.S.C. 221–28), the secretary of commerce "from time to time may set apart and reserve fishing areas in any of the waters of Alaska over which the United States has jurisdiction, and within such areas may establish closed seasons during which fishing may be limited or prohibited as he may prescribe." The State of Alaska, under the authority of Gov. William Egan, threatened to enforce its ordinance outlawing fishing traps used by the Metlakatla Indians, who utilized such traps in reservation waters, and the Thlinget Indians, who claimed fishing rights under the White Act. The Metlakatlas and two incorporated Thlinget communities sued Egan and the state in 1959 seeking to enjoin, or stop, the state from enforcing the regulations. In the first *Metlakatla* case (363 U.S. 555, 4 L.Ed. 2d 1397, 80 S.Ct. 1321 [1960], the justices of U.S. Supreme Court held (6–2, with Chief Justice Earl Warren, and Justices Hugo Black and William O. Douglas dissenting) that the Alaska state courts must decide the controversy before the high court could intervene. The parties then sought a decision from the U.S. Court for the District of Alaska, which dismissed the complaints of the Indians; pending a decision by the full Court, Supreme Court Justice William Brennan issued an injunction against the state. While affirming jurisdiction, the U.S. Supreme Court nonetheless passed the case on to the Alaska state supreme court, which upheld the district court's dismissal while upholding the state's right to enjoin the use of such fishing traps. The U.S. Supreme Court then granted certiorari, and arguments were heard on 13 and 14 December 1961.

On 5 March 1962, Justice Felix Frankfurter held for a unanimous court that the secretary of the interior must decide the final disposition of the matter, that while he had no authority under the White Act or the Alaska Statehood Act to prohibit the state from exercising control over those fishing regulations contrary to state law, he did have the power under the act which created the Metlakatla Reservation to allow those Indians to fish within the reservation with traps of their choosing. Justice Frankfurter, in a lengthy review, wrote,

Alaska does not expressly argue that the Secretary's power was destroyed by the Statehood Act. She does, however, contend that control of all fishing was transferred to the State with no exception for Indian fishing, and that only the exclusiveness of Metlakatla's fishing rights was preserved. But legislative history makes clear that the transfer of jurisdiction over fishing was subject to rights reserved in section 4 [of the Alaska Statehood Act, 72 Stat. 339]... Clearly this section does not protect only "recognized" Indian rights—those the taking of which would be compensable by the United States. Committee reports demonstrate the aim of Congress to preserve the status quo as to a broader class of "right," including, in the case of land, mere possession or occupancy...We need not here explore the remoter reaches of this protection. The Metlakatla Reservation was Indian property within section 4. Whether or not the "absolute jurisdiction" retained by the United States in section 4 is exclusive of state authority, the statute clearly preserves federal authority over the reservation. Federal authority was lodged in the Secretary [of the Interior] in 1891, and it was not dislodged by the Statehood Act . . . However, in issuing the present regulations the Secretary relied not on the White Act and the Statehood Act, neither of which authorized his action. In a letter to the Solicitor General, filed by the United States as an Appendix to its brief as *amicus curiae* [friend of the court], the Secretary left no doubt that in issuing the regulations he acted under compulsion of what he conceived to be his duty under the Statehood Act to preserve the status quo. He deemed himself, as it were, to be a mere automaton. The exercise of any authority that the Secretary has under the reservation statute to allow fish traps necessarily involves his judgment on a complex of facts, his evaluation of the relative weights of the Indians' needs for traps and of the impact of traps at Metlakatla on the State's interest in conservation. We cannot make this determination for him. The appropriate course is to vacate the judgment of the Supreme Court of Alaska and remand the case there to be held to give ample opportunity for the Secretary of the Interior with all reasonable expedition to determine prior to the 1963 salmon fishing season what, if any, authority he chooses to exercise in light of this opinion. Should the Secretary fail so to act, the parties may apply to the Alaska court for further proceedings not inconsistent with this opinion.

Military, Indians in the

Commissioner of Indian Affairs Cato Sells wrote in his annual report for 1918 as to the Indians' participation in the World War I, "They have signally honored themselves and their country by entering some branch of the Army or Navy; by offering their money in war loans to the Government; by increasing the product of the country's foodstuffs and complying with the public food regulations; by swelling the ranks of wage earners in periods of labor depletion; by generous and eager contributions in money and service to every phase of organized relief."

The issue of the participation of American Indians in the U.S. military has not been studied in great depth, and the records (excepting old entrance rolls of the military) on the matter are few and far between. On 4 January 1855, Secretary of War (and, later, president of the Confederate States of America) Jefferson Davis wrote to Senator Albert Gallatin Brown of Mississippi, chairman of the Senate Committee on Indian Affairs, "I regret to state that the very few muster rolls of such Indians on file in this office will only enable me to furnish to a very limited extent the information desired. In most cases where Indian warriors have been used [by the military], they were not regularly mustered into service and, generally after their discharge, rolls for their payment only have been made. These rolls the paymaster forwarded as vouchers to their accounts, and it is presumed they are filed in the proper offices of the Treasury Department."

The participation of Indians in the world wars, as seen from Commissioner Sells' comment above, as well as subsequent military actions, has been better documented. During World War II, for example, in which an estimated 25, 000 Indians served, Kitus Tecumseh, a descendant of Chief Tecumseh and himself a veteran of World War I, in which he was injured, tried to reenlist. Ira Hayes, a Pima Indian from Arizona, was among those who raised the American flag on Mount Suribachi on Iwo Jima. And it was the skills and heroism of the Navajo Code Talkers, a select group of Navajos utilized for their special ability to speak in a coded language that the Japanese could not understand, which helped turn the tide towards American victory in the battle for Okinawa.

See also Navajo Code Talkers.

References "The Bureau of Indian Affairs Lauds Indian Participation in World War II, 1942." In Albert L. Hurtado and Peter Iverson, eds., *Major Problems in American Indian History: Documents and Essays* (1994); Jefferson Davis to Senator Albert G. Brown, 4 January 1855, Records of the House of Representatives, RG 233, Committee on Indian Affairs, file HR 33A-D7.5, "Indians in the Service of the U.S. Military"; U.S. Congress, House of Representatives, *Annual Report of the Commissioner of Indian Affairs for the Year 1918*, House Document No. 1455, 65th Congress, 3d Session (serial 7498).

Minnesota v. United States (305 U.S. 382, 83 L.Ed. 235, 59 S.Ct. 292 [1939])

When a state desires to condemn Indian properties with the fee held in the United States, the federal government is an "indispensable party" to the proceedings—so held the U.S. Supreme Court in this 1939 decision. The act of Congress of 3 March 1901 (31 Stat. 1084) permitted states to condemn Indian allotments with the fee in severalty held by the United States, with just compensation to be conferred upon the affected allottee. The State of Minnesota moved to condemn nine parcels of land on the Grand Portage Indian Reservation, given to the Band of Chippewa Indians of Lake Superior, to be used for a highway in the District Court of Minnesota, naming as defendants the Indian allottees, the Superintendent of the Consolidated Chippewa Agency, and the United States as holder of the allotment fee for the nine parcels. In court, the U.S. Attorney moved that the United States be removed as a defendant because it did not consent to be sued. The state court ordered removal, and a federal court agreed. However, the U.S. Court of Appeals for the Eighth Circuit reversed, holding that the act of 3 March 1901 made it necessary for the secretary of the interior, the constitutional officer in charge of Indian Affairs, to approve the condemnation, and his input made the United States a necessary party to the proceedings. The U.S. Supreme Court then agreed to hear appeals in the case (Minnesota appealing the denial of its rights to condemn, and the United States still demanding to be removed from the case), and arguments were heard on 10 November 1938. It was Justice Louis D. Brandeis who held for a unanimous court on 3 January 1939 that the United States was an "indispensable party" to the proceedings since its held the fee in severalty, and that Minnesota required the consent of the secretary of the interior to approve the condemnation before it took place. He reiterated that the topic of trust allotments was "a subject within the exclusive control of the federal government."

See also Section 357 of Title 25 (United States Code). Another case decided with this section in mind is *United States v. Clarke et al.*

Mission Indian Act of 1891 (26 Stat. 712)

See *Arenas v. United States.*

Mississippi Band of Choctaw Indians v. Holyfield et al. (490 U.S. 30, 104 L.Ed. 2d 29, 109 S.Ct. 1597 [1989])

The case of the *Mississippi Band of Choctaw Indians v. Orrey Curtiss Holyfield, et ux., J.B., Natural Mother, and W.J., Natural Father,* presented the Supreme Court with an important question: are Indian children not born on the reservation considered "domiciled" on the reservation anyway, to allow tribal courts to have jurisdiction over their adoption as per the Indian Child Welfare Act of 1978? Orrey Curtiss Holyfield and his wife Vivian desired to adopt two Indian children, named B.B. and G.B. for this case. Both children were born out of wedlock in 1985; their parents, named as J.B. and W.J., desired that Holyfield adopt the children and, to assure that the tribal authorities did not have jurisdiction over the adoption proceedings, left the Choctaw reservation in Mississippi so that the Indian Child Welfare Act of 1978 (ICWA), which governs such placements, would not govern in the matter. After the children were born, the Indian parents moved to have their parental rights extinguished, and named the Holyfields as the adoptive parents of their choice; the Holyfields subsequently filed adoption papers. Two months later the tribe moved in a Chancery court to have the adoption voided and have the children returned to the tribe. The Chancery court denied the motion, holding that the natural parents had made efforts to have their children born outside the reservation, and that the children were not born on the reservation as required by the ICWA. The Supreme Court of Mississippi affirmed, holding that for ICWA to apply, the children must have been "domiciled" for a period of time on the reservation. The tribe appealed to the U.S. Supreme Court, and the court granted certiorari. Orrey Holyfield died during the appeal, but his widow continued the petition.

Arguments in the case were heard before the court on 11 January 1989 and a decision was delivered on 3 April of that same year. Speaking for a sharply divided court (Chief Justice William H. Rehnquist and Justices John Paul Stevens and Anthony Kennedy dissented), Justice William Brennan held that for "domicile" to be considered under federal law, in which the Indian children come under the provisions of the act, tribal jurisdiction could not be "defeated" by the actions of the natural parents, and that the Chancery Court had no jurisdiction. Explaining the decision, Justice Brennan added,

> We are not unaware that over three years have passed since the twin babies were born and placed in the Holyfield home, and that a court deciding their fate today is not writing on a blank slate in the same way it would have in January 1986. Three years' development of family ties cannot be undone, and a separation at this point would doubtless cause considerable pain. Whatever feelings we might have as to where the twins should live, however, it is not for us to decide the question. We have been asked to decide the legal question of *who* should make the custody determination concerning these children—not what the outcome of that determination should be. The law places that decision in the hands of the Choctaw tribal court. Had the mandate of the ICWA been followed in 1986, of course, much potential anguish might have been avoided, and in any case the law cannot be applied so as automatically to "reward those who obtain custody, whether lawfully or otherwise, and maintain it during any ensuing (and protracted) litigation." It is not ours to say whether the trauma that might result from removing these children from their adoptive family should outweigh the interest of the Tribe—and perhaps the children themselves—in having them raised as part of the Choctaw community. Rather, "we must defer to the experience, wisdom, and compassion of the [Choctaw] tribal courts to fashion an appropriate remedy."

See also Indian Child Welfare Act of 1978.

"Mitchell Cases"

See *United States v. Mitchell.*

Mix, Charles E. (1810–1878)

A merchant and clerk in the Office of Indian Affairs for a number of years, Charles E. Mix served as commissioner of Indian Affairs for less than five months between the administrations of James W. Denver. Mix was born in Connecticut on 4 February 1810 and by the age of 20 was a noted merchant in Washington, D.C. When his business failed in the wake of the financial panic of 1837, Mix found employment as a clerk in the Bureau of Indian Affairs, where he worked until 1869. In those years, he advanced to become the right-hand man of a series of Indian commissioners. Indian historian Robert M. Utley notes that Mix enthusiastically supported the idea of Commissioner William Medill that Indians should exist on "colonies" surrounded by white settlements.

When Commissioner James William Denver became governor of the Kansas Territory in 1858, Mix ably stepped into his shoes, although there is controversy over whether Mix should be considered as the commissioner or as an interim administrator. In his lone annual report in his position as Indian commissioner, for the year 1858, Mix wrote,

> Experience has demonstrated that at least three serious, and, to the Indians, fatal errors

have, from the beginning, marked our policy towards them, viz: their removal from place to place as our population advanced; the assignment of them of too great an extent of country, to be held in common; and the allowance of large sums of money, as annuities, for the lands ceded by them. These errors, far more than the want of capacity on the part of the Indian, have been the cause of the very limited success of our constant efforts to domesticate and civilize them. By their frequent changes of position and the possession of large bodies of land in common, they have been kept in an unsettled condition and prevented from acquiring a knowledge of separate and individual property, while their large annuities, upon which they have relied for a support, have not only tended to foster habits of indolence and profligacy, but have constantly made them the victims of the lawless and inhuman sharper and speculator.

When Denver returned from Kansas, Mix was reinstated to his position as chief clerk, although, in an 1874 study by Commissioner of Indian Affairs Edward P. Smith, Mix had served as acting commissioner for 1,579 days during his entire tenure in the bureau. Although he retired in 1869, he worked for the rest of his life specializing ion Indian land claims. He died at his residence in the Georgetown section of Washington, D.C., of a "paralysis" on 15 January 1878 at the age of 67, and was buried in Georgetown's Oak Hill Cemetery.

See also Bureau of Indian Affairs.

References Charles E. Mix File, Peabody Room, District of Columbia Library, Washington, D.C.; Kelsey, Harry, "Charles E. Mix." In Robert M. Kvasnicka and Herman J. Viola, eds., *The Commissioners of Indian Affairs, 1824–1977* (1979); U.S. Congress, House of Representatives, *Annual Report of the Commissioner of Indian Affairs for the Year 1858*, House Executive Document No. 2, 35th Congress, 2d Session (serial 997); U.S. Congress, House of Representatives, *Destitution of Sioux Indians: Letter from the Secretary of the Interior [Orville H. Browning], Transmitting A Copy of a Communication from the Acting Commissioner of Indian Affairs [Charles E. Mix] Relative to the Great Destitution of the Sioux Indians, near Devil's Lake, Dakota Territory*, House Executive Document No. 76, 40th Congress, 2d Session, 1868; Utley, Robert M., *The Indian Frontier of the American West, 1846–1890* (1984).

Moe, etc. et al. v. The Confederated Salish and Kootenai Tribes of the Flathead Reservation et al. (425 U.S. 463, 48 L.Ed. 2d 96, 96 S.Ct. 1634 [1976])

In this case, the U.S. Supreme Court held that states could not impose certain taxes on Indian reservations. There were two separate cases melded into this single case: the defendants-appellants, John C. Moe and others, were the director of Montana's Department of Revenue and sheriffs in counties which had arrested several Indians for refusing to pay certain taxes; Joseph Wheeler, a member of the Confederated Salish and Kootenai Tribes located on the Flathead Reservation of Montana, which embraces four counties (Lake, Sanders, Missoula, and Flathead), leased from the tribes a piece of land on which he opened several "smoke shops" where cigarettes and other tobacco products could be sold minus state taxes. Sheriffs from the several counties, on orders from the State Department of Revenue, arrested Wheeler for not possessing a cigarette retail license and selling untaxed cigarettes, both misdemeanors under state law. Wheeler, joined by the tribe, sued to a three-judge district court to have the tax measures declared null and void against the Indians. In a separate action, the tribe sued to the same court to have state personal taxes, notably a tax on motor vehicles owned by tribal members, ruled invalid. By a 2-to-1 vote, the district court struck down the tax schemes based on the Supreme Court's 1973 decision in *McClanahan v. Arizona State Tax Commission*, although it ruled that the state could require that a tax on cigarettes be collected from non-Indians purchasing cigarettes on an Indian reservation. Moe and the others sued to the U.S. Supreme Court for relief.

In the case argued before the court on 20 January 1976 and decided on 27 April of that same year, the nine justices sustained the district court rulings and held unanimously that the personal tax could not be levied against the Indians, that the requirement for a license fee was invalid, and that the imposition of a small tax against non-

Indian cigarette purchasers was a "minimal burden" against Indian tobacco dealers. Delivering the court's opinion, Justice William Rehnquist cited several cases, including *McClanahan, etc. v. State Tax Commission of Arizona* (1973) and *Mescalero Apache Tribe v. Franklin Jones, Commissioner of the Bureau of Revenue of the State of New Mexico et al.* (1973). Regarding *Moe*, Rehnquist wrote,

The State's requirement that the Indian tribal seller collect a tax validly imposed on non-Indians is a minimal burden designed to avoid the likelihood that in its absence non-Indians purchasing from the tribal seller will avoid payment of a concededly lawful tax. Since this burden is not, strictly speaking, a tax at all, it is not governed by the language of Mescalero…dealing with the "special area of state taxation." We see nothing in this burden which frustrates tribal self-government,…or runs afoul of any federal enactment dealing with the affairs of reservation Indians, [see] *United States v. McGowan*, 302 U.S. 535 (1938). We therefore agree with the District Court that to the extent that the "smoke shops" sell to those upon whom the State has validly imposed a sales or excise tax with respect to the article sold, the State may require the Indian proprietor simply to add the tax to the sales price and thereby aid the State's collection and enforcement thereof. For the foregoing reasons, the judgments of the District Court are affirmed.

See also *McClanahan, etc. v. State Tax Commission of Arizona*; *Mescalero Apache Tribe v. Franklin Jones, Commissioner of the Bureau of Revenue of the State of New Mexico et al.*; *Williams v. Lee*.

Montana et al. v. Blackfeet Tribe of Indians (471 U.S. 759, 85 L.Ed. 2d 753, 105 S.Ct. 2399 [1985])

In this Supreme Court case, determined in 1985, the court decided that "application of state taxes to [an] Indian tribe's royalty interests in oil and gas produced under leases issued by the tribe [are] held [to be] not authorized by federal law." Under the Indian Mineral Leasing Act of 1938 (52 Stat. 347, now codified at 25 U.S.C. 396a et seq.), Indian tribes were allowed to issue oil and gas leases to nonmember Indians with the approval of the secretary of the interior; there was no state taxation ability built into the legislation. However, under the act of Congress of 29 May 1924 (43 Stat. 244), states were authorized to tax the royalty interests of Indian tribes on the mineral resources produced within reservation borders. Under the former act, Montana applied several state taxes to the income derived from the leases on the Blackfeet reservation. The tribe instituted an action in the U.S. District Court for the District of Montana to enjoin the state from levying the taxes. The district court sided with the state, claiming that under the 1924 act, such taxes were permissible. The U.S. Court of Appeals for the Ninth Circuit reversed in part, claiming that while the 1938 act did not allow for state taxation, it did not repeal the 1924 act, and thus all leases prosecuted after 1924 but before 1938 could be taxed.

Both sides then appealed to the U.S. Supreme Court to hear the facts in the case and decide the law. Argued on 15 January 1985 (and reargued on 23 April), it was Justice Lewis F. Powell who held for the majority (Justices Byron White, William H. Rehnquist, and John Paul Stevens dissented) on 3 June 1985 that because the 1938 act did not incorporate such language as to the state taxation of Indian reservation mineral leases, the state action was a violation of that act. Justice Powell reasoned, "Nothing in either the text or legislative history of the 1938 Act suggests that Congress intended to permit States to tax tribal royalty income generated by leases issued pursuant to that Act. The statute contains no explicit consent to state taxation. Nor is there any indication that Congress intended to incorporate implicitly in the 1938 Act the taxing authority of the 1924 Act." He added, in a footnote, "In fact, the legislative history suggests that Congress intended to replace the 1924 Act's leasing scheme with that of the 1938 Act."

Montana et al. v. Northern Cheyenne Tribe of the Northern Cheyenne Indian Reservation et al. (463 U.S. 545, 103 S.Ct. 3201 [1983])

Combined with the joint cases of *Arizona et al. v. San Carlos Apache Tribe of Arizona et al.* and *Arizona et al. v. Navajo Tribe of Indians et al.*, this Supreme Court case dealt with the issue of whether the McCarran Amendment (66 Stat. 560, 43 U.S.C. 666) allows for state, and not federal, court jurisdiction over state water rights adjudications, even involving Indian reservations under U.S. government trust authority. Justice William Brennan wrote in the Supreme Court's majority opinion, "These consolidated cases form a sequel to our decision in *Colorado River Water Conservation District v. United States*." In the Montana case, a district court dismissed a suit by the federal government and the Northern Cheyenne Tribe to allow for the federal adjudication of water right allocation on the grounds that state courts had the sole jurisdiction in the matter. On appeal, the U.S. Court of Appeals for the Ninth Circuit reversed. In the two Arizona cases, two suits, brought by the government in cooperation with the San Carlos Apache Tribe and the Navajo Tribe, were dismissed by the district court, but the U.S. Court of Appeals for the Ninth Circuit reversed. The U.S. Supreme Court granted certiorari in all three cases, and coalesced them into one suit, known as *Montana*. Arguments were heard on 23 March 1983, and a decision was handed down on 1 July 1983. Speaking for the 6–3 decision of the court (Justices Thurgood Marshall, John Paul Stevens, and Harry Blackmun dissenting), Justice William Brennan held that the McCarran Amendment clearly allowed for state, and not federal, court jurisdiction over water adjudications, even involving Indian reservations. However, Justice Brennan cautioned,

> Nothing we say today should be understood to represent even the slightest retreat from the general proposition we expressed so recently in *New Mexico v. Mescalero Apache Tribe*, 462 U.S, at 332, 76 L.Ed. 2d 611, 103 S.Ct. 2378: "Because of their sovereign status, [Indian] tribes and their reservation lands are insulated in some respects by a 'historic immunity from state and local control,' *Mescalero Apache Tribe v. Jones*, 411 U.S. 145, [at] 152, 36 L.Ed. 2d 114, 93 S.Ct. 1267 (1973), and tribes retain any aspect of their historical sovereignty not 'inconsistent with the overriding interests of the National Government.' *Washington v. Confederated Tribes*, 447 U.S. 134, [at] 153, 65 L.Ed. 2d 10, 100 S.Ct. 2069 (1980)." Nor should we be understood to retreat from the general proposition, expressed in *Colorado River*, that federal courts have a "virtually unflagging obligation...to exercise the jurisdiction given them." 424 U.S., at 817, 47 L.Ed. 2d 483, 96 S.Ct. 1236. But water rights adjudication is a virtually unique type of proceeding, and the McCarran Amendment is a virtually unique federal statute, and we cannot in this context be guided by general propositions. We also emphasize, as we did in *Colorado River*, that our decision in no way changes the substantive law by which Indian rights in state water adjudications must be judged. State courts, as much as federal courts, have a solemn obligation to follow federal law. Moreover, any state court decision alleged to abridge Indian water rights protected by federal law can expect to receive, if brought for review before this Court, a particularized and exacting scrutiny commensurate with the powerful federal interest in safeguarding those rights from state encroachment.

See also *Colorado River Water Conservation District v. United States*; McCarran Amendment.

Montana v. United States (450 U.S. 544, 67 L.Ed. 2d 493, 101 S.Ct. 1245 [1981])

The editors of *Felix Cohen's Handbook of Federal Indian Law* write of this landmark case, "In *Montana*, the [Supreme] Court held that the Crow tribe lacked inherent civil authority to regulate fishing by non-Indians on non-Indian lands within reservation boundaries when no important tribal interests were directly affected." By a tribal resolution, the Crow Tribe of Montana prohibited fishing and hunting on reservation lands, mostly the bed of the Big Horn River, by nonmembers of the tribe. The State of Montana declared that it had the right to assert its jurisdiction over nonmembers. The United States filed suit in the District Court for the District of Montana asking that the United States, as trustee, and the Crow Tribe had sole and exclusive authority to regulate fishing and hunting on the reservation. The district court denied the United States relief, holding that when Montana entered the Union, the title to the Big Horn passed to Montana, and that the state had the authority to regulate hunting and fishing activities by non-Indians. On appeal, the U.S. Court of Appeals for the Ninth Circuit held that the Second Treaty of Fort Laramie of 1868 (15 Stat. 649) authorized the United States to hold the bed of the Big Horn in trust for the Crow Tribe, and therefore the Indians could regulate hunting and fishing. The United States granted certiorari after the State of Montana appealed the Appeals Court's finding. Arguments were heard on 3 December 1980, and a decision was handed down on 24 March 1981. Speaking for the majority's 6–3 decision (Justices Harry Blackmun, William Brennan, and Thurgood Marshall dissenting), Justice Potter Stewart held that the Second Treaty of Fort Laramie expressly allowed the title to the river bed to pass to the State of Montana upon its admission to the Union. Justice Stewart explained,

A tribe may…retain inherent power to exercise civil authority over the conduct of non-Indians on fee lands within its reservation when that conduct threatens or has some direct effect on the political integrity, the economic security, or the health and welfare of the tribe.…No such circumstances, however, are involved in this case. Non-Indian hunters and fishermen on non-Indian fee land do not enter any agreements or dealing with the Crow Tribe so as to subject themselves to tribal civil jurisdiction. And nothing in this case suggests that such non-Indian hunting and fishing so threaten the Tribe's political or economic security as to justify tribal regulation. The complaint in the district court did not allege that non-Indian hunting and fishing on fee lands imperil the subsistence or welfare of the Tribe. Furthermore, the District Court made express findings, left unaltered by the Court of Appeals, that the Crow Tribe has traditionally accommodated itself to the State's "near exclusive" regulation of hunting on fee lands. And the district court found that Montana's statutory and regulatory scheme does not prevent the Crow Tribe from limiting or forbidding non-Indian hunting and fishing on lands still owned by or held in trust for the Tribe or its members.

Reference Strickland, Rennard, ed., *Felix Cohen's Handbook of Federal Indian Law* (1982).

Montezuma, Carlos (Yavapai) (1866? 1867? or 1869?-1923)

His name was *Wassaja*, which roughly translates into "Beckoning" or "Signaling," a name which he used in his writings for the remainder of his life. A physician and Indian rights advocate and activist, he remains barely known outside of the Indian community. He was born between 1866 and 1869 (while many sources say 1866 or 1867, his tombstone says 1869) near the Four Peaks in the Superstition Mountains in central Arizona, the son of Co-cu-ye-vah and Thil-ge-ya, both Yavapai. Sometime in 1871, he was captured by Pima Indians at Iron Top Mountain who sold him to an Italian photographer, Carlos Gentile, for $30. Gentile took the young man, whom he named Montezuma after the ancient ruins in Arizona to give him some semblance of an Indian heritage and identity, to Washington, D.C., and Chicago, where he attended public schools. Before Gentile committed suicide in 1877 because of financial setbacks, he gave the boy to the Reverend George W. Ingalls of the American Baptist Home Mission Society, who entrusted the youth to W. H. Stedman, a Baptist missionary in

Urbana, Illinois. After a year of private tutoring, Montezuma entered the University of Illinois and was awarded a bachelor of science degree in 1884. While working as a druggist in Chicago, he enrolled at the Chicago Medical College, from which he earned his medical degree in 1889.

After establishing a private practice in Chicago, he went to work as a physician-surgeon in the Indian Service, serving at the Fort Stevenson Indian School in North Dakota, the Western Shoshone Agency in Nevada, and the Colville Agency in Washington State. In 1894, he began to work closely with Richard Henry Pratt, head of the Carlisle Indian School in Pennsylvania, and writer and activist Gertrude Simmons Bonnin (Zitkala-Sa) to improve Indian education and health. Two years later, he returned to Chicago and reopened his medical practice, specializing in the treatment of intestinal diseases. It was at this time that Montezuma started to speak out on behalf of Native American rights. He railed against the failures of the Bureau of Indian Affairs and the reservation system it had created, and demanded American citizenship for Indians. In 1911, Montezuma, along with other noted Indian activists, helped found the Society of American Indians, the first pan-Indian rights organization. In a speech before the Society in Lawrence, Kansas, on 30 September 1915, Dr. Montezuma raged,

> In the bloody and gloomy days of Indian history public sentiment was against the Indians, that they could not be civilized; they could not be educated; they were somewhat like human beings, but not quite within the line of human rights; the only hope was to let the bullets do the work, cover up the bloody deeds, and say no more—God and humanity were forgotten…Patient, silent, and distant the Indian race has been these many years. There comes a time in human events when abandonment of racial responsibilities becomes very oppressive, unbearable, intolerable, and there seems to be no hope—then man must exert himself, speak, and act.…Brothers, that time has come to our race. The society of American Indians is not free. We are wards; we are not free! In a free country we are not free; our heritage is freedom, but we are not free. Wake up, Indians, all over America! We are hoodwinked, duped more and more every year; we are made to feel that we are free when we are not. We are chained hand and foot; we stand helpless, innocently waiting for the fulfillment of promises that will never be fulfilled in the overwhelming great ocean of civilization.

For the remainder of his life, Montezuma worked to alleviate the difficult and often tragic conditions afflicting Indian people. Although he called for assimilation, he was proud to be an Indian and felt other Indians should feel the same. In addition to his published books, including *The Indian of Today and Tomorrow* (1906) and *Let My People Go* (1914), he was the editor, from 1916 until his death, of the journal *Wassaja*, which was

Wassaja, a Yavapai, pictured here at about age seven, was captured by Pima Indians and sold to Carlos Gentile in the early 1870s. Named Carlos Montezuma, he later became an activist and a founder of the Society of American Indians.

subtitled *Freedom's Signal for the Indians*. Biographer Peter Iverson opines, "Like other 'progressive' Indian leaders of his time, Montezuma accepted parts of the white value system, such as formal education, the work ethic, and individual enterprise. Because his paper championed these virtues, it probably appealed more to educated Indians and their white sympathizers than to many members of the reservation communities. Yet Montezuma provided important leadership during these years, not only as a major proponent of the pan-Indian movement, but also as a spokesman for Indian rights who tried to make the public aware of the bad conditions on the reservations." Suffering from diabetes and tuberculosis, Montezuma returned to his native land and settled on the Fort McDowell Indian Reservation near Phoenix, where he died on 31 January 1923.

See also Society of American Indians.

References Armstrong, Virginia Irving, comp., *I Have Spoken: American History through the Voices of the Indians* (1971); Carlos Montezuma Collection, Department of Archives and Manuscripts, Arizona State University, Tempe; Iverson, Peter, "Carlos Montezuma." In R. David Edmunds, ed., *American Indian Leaders: Studies in Diversity* (1980); Iverson, Peter, *Carlos Montezuma and the Changing World of American Indians* (1982); Waldman, Carl, *Who Was Who in Native American History: Indians and Non-Indians from Early Contacts through 1900* (1990); Waldman, Henry, et al, eds., *Dictionary of Indians of North America* (1978).

Montoya v. United States (180 U.S. 261, 45 L.Ed. 52, 21 S.Ct. 358 [1901])

The case of Eutemio Montoya, like that decided the same day before the Supreme Court of Milton Conners, Jr., dealt with whether the United States could be held liable for Indian depredations. Montoya, the surviving partner of the firm E. Montoya and Sons located at Nogal, in Sorocco County, New Mexico, about eight miles west of San Antonio, Texas, sued the United States in the Court of Claims for damages arising out of depredations caused by Indians from the Mescalero Apache tribe of New Mexico who had joined a marauding band of Chiricahua Indians, known as "Victoria's Band." Because the Mescaleros were in amity with the United States, Montoya sued the United States for compensation for lost livestock. Under the Act of 3 March 1891, Congress established that the Court of Claims had jurisdiction and could adjudicate "all claims for property of citizens of the United States taken or destroyed by Indians belonging to any band, tribe or nation in amity with the United States, without just cause or provocation on the part of owner or agent in charge, and not returned or paid for." However, the court dismissed Montoya's suit and he appealed to the U.S. Supreme Court. The case was heard on 14 and 17 December 1900 and the court handed down a decision on 11 February 1901 in conjunction with its decision in *Conners*. As with that other case, the court ruled because the Indians involved in the depredations had split from the tribal majority considered in amity, the U.S. government was not liable. Speaking for a unanimous court, Justice Henry Brown wrote, "The property in question was stolen and driven away, or destroyed, by certain Mescalero Apache Indians, who were at that time allied with Victoria's band for the purpose of hostility and war as aforesaid, and the band so constituted was not in amity with the United States, although the Mescalero tribe, which was then upon its reservation about 100 miles distant from the scene of the depredation, and to which the Mescaleros who committed the depredation had belonged before they joined Victoria's band, was in amity with the United States."

See also *Conners v. United States.*

Mooney, James, Jr. (1861–1921)

Considered by some to be the premier ethnologist of the Cherokee people, James Mooney was also a foremost chronicler of Native American messianic movements. He was born on 10 February 1861 in Richmond, Indiana, the son and third child of James Mooney, Sr., and Ellen Mooney (née Devlin), both Irish immigrants who emigrated to the United States from Liverpool,

England, in the early 1850s. Sometime in 1861, shortly after the birth of his son, James Mooney, Sr., succumbed to pneumonia, and his young widow undertook to raise three children. Biographer William M. Colby writes that in 1879, "eight[een] year old James helped to supplement the family income by taking a part time job in the printing office of the *Richmond Palladium*. Although his father had worked for the Indiana Central Railroad, young Mooney preferred newspaper work. He advanced from type-setting to reporting and editorial writing, until he left for Washington, D.C. in 1885."

Mooney's interest in Indians can be traced back to about 1873. Writing the introduction for a reprint of his *Myths of the Cherokee*, George Ellison said, "In 1893, Lida Rose McCabe, writing for Chicago's *Inter-Ocean Illustrated Supplement*, reported in an article titled 'Indian Man' that Mooney 'dated his interest in Indians from hearing a chance remark in 1873, at the time of the Modoc War in northern California and southern Oregon, that every little Indian uprising brought to light another unknown tribe. It was then at twelve, that he decided to learn the names and locations of all the tribes in the Americas.'" In 1882, he first applied to join the Bureau of Ethnology of the Smithsonian Institution but was turned down. Although he was finally accepted in 1885, he was put in an unsalaried position and sent to study the Cherokee people. Curtis M. Hinsley, Jr., who wrote about the bureau, reports, "Throughout his career in anthropology he was associated and concerned with politically and culturally oppressed peoples—Irish or Native American—and was fascinated by modes of communication. From these roots came the central question of his anthropology: How do oppressed people transmit the binding

Ethnologist James Mooney, center, with Jesse Bent, right, and Ben Beveridge, left

elements of their culture from one generation to the next? How do those who are defeated and dispersed nonetheless preserve identity and tradition?" This was the basis of Mooney's work, which included such works as *The Sacred Formulas of the Cherokees* (1891), *The Siouan Tribes of the East* (1894), *Myths of the Cherokee* (1900), and *The Swimmer Manuscript: Cherokee Sacred Formulas and Medicinal Prescriptions* (1932). Among Mooney's more influential works was *The Ghost Dance Religion and the Sioux Outbreak of 1890* (1896), which studied the underlying causes of the movement that led ultimately to the Wounded Knee massacre in 1890. His interest in the Ghost Dance led him to meet with the Paiute mystic Wovoka, whose visions began the movement.

In 1911, Mooney, suffering from poor health, moved to Washington, but after two years returned to his fieldwork among the Cherokees. A supporter of the Native American Church and its ritualistic use of peyote, Mooney came under attack from anti-peyote activists and was forbidden to set foot on Indian reservations by Commissioner of Indian Affairs Cato Sells in 1918. Mooney was perhaps the first white man to participate in a peyote ceremony, and is considered the first anthropologist to describe the practice. Retired to Washington, and refused permission to visit the Cherokee people he loved and studied, Mooney died on 22 December 1921 at the age of 60.

See also Ghost Dance; Wovoka.

References Colby, William Munn, *Routes to Rainy Mountain: A Biography of James Mooney, Ethnologist* (Ph.D. dissertation, University of Wisconsin at Madison, 1977); Ellison, George, ed., *James Mooney's History, Myths, and Sacred Formulas of the Cherokees* (1992); Hinsley, Curtis M., Jr., *The Smithsonian and the American Indian: Making a Moral Anthropology in Victorian America* (1981); Mooney, James, *The Ghost Dance Religion and the Sioux Outbreak of 1890*, 14th Annual Report of the Bureau of American Ethnology, 1892–93 (1896); Mooney, James, *Myths of the Cherokee*, Nineteenth Annual Report of the Bureau of American Ethnology, 1897–98 (1900), part 1; Moses, Lester George, "James Mooney and Wovoka: An Ethnologist's Visit with the Ghost Dance Prophet." *Nevada Historical Society Quarterly* 23 (2); Moses, Lester George, *The Indian Man: A Biography of James Mooney* (1984); Moses, Lester George, and Margaret Connell Szasz, "'My Father, Have Pity on Me!': Indian Revitalization Movements of the Late-Nineteenth Century." *Journal of the West* 23 (1).

Morgan, John Tyler (1824–1907)

John Tyler Morgan is not known for his concern for Indian welfare or rights, but his was an important voice raised in the U.S. Senate against the General Allotment Act of 1887, known as the Dawes Allotment Act. Morgan was born in Athens, in McMinn County, Tennessee, on 20 June 1824, the son of George Morgan and Frances (née Irby) Morgan, a relative of the Tyler family of Virginia which includes President John Tyler. Morgan attended rural schools, where he received a classical education in Greek and Latin, and grew up among the Indians, experience that he used later as chairman of the Senate Committee on Indian Affairs. He studied the law in a private office and was admitted to the bar in 1845. Ten years later he moved to Selma, Alabama, a city with which he was identified for the rest of his life. In 1861, he was a member of the state secessionist convention in which Alabama left the Union. Preferring military service to the political forum, he enlisted in the "Catawba Rifles," a unit formed at Catawba, Alabama, and saw action at Chickamauga and Knoxville, actions for which he was eventually commissioned as a brigadier general. By the end of the war, he attempted to raise a platoon of freed slaves as soldiers in the southern cause.

With the end of the war, Tyler picked up his old law practice but fought against black suffrage and for the reestablishment of white government in the South. In 1876 he was elected to the United State Senate, and although there was a move afoot to prevent him from taking his seat, he was admitted, and served until his death. His first vote, ironically, was an affirmative one to seat the black orator Frederick Douglass as marshal of the District of Columbia. As mentioned, he was a leader as chairman of the Senate Committee on Indian Affairs. On 10 June 1881, Senator Morgan took to the floor of the U.S. Senate to deliver a constitutional argument against the allotment act. As Indian historian Vine Deloria, Jr., wrote in 1970, "Many of the arguments raised by Senator Morgan should be raised in the courts today." Morgan argued,

So much respect has been paid to the communal idea, the tribal government of these Indians in our treaty relations with them and in our statutory enactments heretofore, that we have not seen proper to disturb anything of that kind; and I venture to say that plenty of instances can be found of treaties solemnly entered into between us and Indian tribes which will be plainly violated if this law [the General Allotment Act] is put in force. Therefore, whether we have the power or not we should not do it in a broad and sweeping enactment of this kind, but we should take up the particular case of a particular tribe and adapt our legislation to them. If we do pause in our movement, if we are not a little more circumspect in our treatment of the Indians, a little less heroic in our treatment of this subject, we shall have ample leisure to repent either that we have done ourselves gross injustice in the violation or abuse of our treaty obligation, or that we have compelled a poor people who have suffered enough to suffer more or else fight in defense of their rights. We shall have leisure to repent of this law after we have passed it. We shall have ample time to understand that this committee [on Indian Affairs], able as it is, had not the power, as no living set of men to-day have the power, to grasp this great and magnificent problem and to solve it in the form of a bill of such dimensions as this.

Although the bill passed, Morgan remained a staunch and supportive friend of the Indian. His work in the Senate continued right up until his death on 11 June 1907, just nine days shy of his eighty-third birthday. His body was returned to Alabama for interment in Selma's Live Oak Cemetery.

See also General Allotment Act.

References Anders, James M., *The Senatorial Career of John Tyler Morgan* (Ph.D. dissertation, George Peabody College, 1956); Deloria, Vine, Jr., ed., *Of Utmost Good Faith* (1972); Garrison, Curtis W., "Morgan, John Tyler." In Dumas Malone et al., eds., *Dictionary of American Biography* (1930–88); "Morgan, John Tyler." *Biographical Directory of the U.S. Congress, 1774–1989, Senate Document 100–34, 100th Congress, Second Session* (1989); "Morgan Passes Away." *Washington Evening Star*, 12 June 1907, 6; Radke, August C., Jr., *John Tyler Morgan: An Expansionist Senator, 1877–1907* (Ph.D. dissertation, University of Washington, 1953); "U.S. Senator J. T. Morgan of Alabama Passes Away." *Commercial Appeal* [Memphis], 12 June 1907, 1.

Morgan, Thomas Jefferson (1839–1902)

The twenty-fifth commissioner of Indian Affairs, Thomas J. Morgan enunciated a clear program of education for Indian children and was the principal force in the effort to assimilate the Indians into American society. Born in Franklin, Indiana, on 17 August 1839, the son of the Reverend Lewis Morgan, an antislavery advocate and educator, and his third wife, Mary (née Causey or Cansey) Morgan. Thomas Morgan attended Franklin College but left in 1861 to join the Union army. He was commissioned a first lieutenant in the 70th Indiana Volunteer Infantry in 1862, and served for three years, becoming the lieutenant colonel of the Fourteenth U.S. Colored Infantry, an all-black unit, with which he saw action at Nashville. He was breveted a brigadier general shortly before the end of the war. Instead of returning home, he entered the Rochester Theological Seminary in New York, from which he graduated in 1868, the following year being ordained as a Baptist minister.

For the next 20 years Morgan served in various capacities as principal of various religious schools. In 1888 he came to the attention of the Harrison administration to head the Office of Education. On 26 November 1888, from his office in Providence, where he was the principal of the Rhode Island State Normal School, Morgan wrote to President Benjamin Harrison, "As my name has been suggested to you in connection with the office of United States Commissioner of Education I wish to say just a word about it. The suggestion did not originate with me. The thought had not occurred to me until I was asked in Boston if I would like to have the place? I just said no! but in further reflection I think if you are willing to appoint me I would like to undertake the work, especially if I could have your help in making the office an effective agency in developing the educational interests of the country." Instead, Harrison turned to Morgan to fill the position of commissioner of Indian Affairs, vacated by John H. Oberly. The Boston *Evening Traveller* editorialized on his selection, "In the appointment of General Morgan as Commissioner of Indian Affairs, President Harrison has selected a man in whom the public has unbounded confidence, one well known in the West and South as well as in the East, a man of affairs as well as a scholar, one who has identified himself closely with the Indian work, one whose trustworthiness and good judgment are attested by numerous experiences." Morgan assumed his office on 1 July 1889, and delivered his first annual report to the Congress three short months later. Indian historian Alvin M. Josephy, Jr., writes, "Like many of his predecessors and successors in that office, Morgan knew little about Indians or their needs as they themselves perceived them." Morgan's 1889 annual report would be the first of four such essays. In that first report, the new commissioner explained that with the passage of the General Severalty Act (Dawes Act) two years earlier, he foresaw that the allotment in severalty system would abolish the reservation system. He wrote:

I entered upon the discharge of the duties of this office July 1, 1889. I have had not time as yet to familiarize myself fully with the details of office administration nor to make myself acquainted by personal observation with the practical workings of the Indian field-service. As soon as practicable, I hope to do both.

Unexpectedly called to this responsible position, I entered upon the discharge of its duties with a few simple, well-defined, and strongly cherished convictions:

First. The anomalous position heretofore occupied by the Indians in this country can not much longer be maintained. The reservation system belongs to a "vanishing state of things" and must soon cease to exist.

Second. The logic of events demands the absorption of the Indians into our national life, not as Indians, but as American citizens.

Third. As soon as a wise conservatism will warrant, the relations of the Indians to the Government must rest solely upon the full recognition of their individuality. Each Indian must be treated as a man, be allowed a man's rights and privileges, and be held to the performance of a man's obligations. Each Indian is entitled to his proper share of the inherited wealth of the tribe, and to the protection of the courts in his "life, liberty, and pursuit of happiness." He is not entitled to be supported in idleness.

Fourth. The Indians must conform to "the white man's ways," peaceably if they will, forcibly if they must. They must adjust themselves to their environment, and conform their mode of living substantially to our civilization. This civilization may not be the best possible, but it is the best the Indians can get. They can not escape it, and must either conform to it or be crushed by it.

Fifth. The paramount duty of the hour is to prepare the rising generation of Indians for the new order of things thus forced upon them. A comprehensive system of education modeled after the American public-school system, but adapted to the special exigencies of the Indian youth, embracing all persons of school age, compulsory in its demands and uniformly administered, should be developed as rapidly as possible.

Sixth. The tribal relations should be broken up, socialism destroyed, and the family and the autonomy of the individual substituted. The allotment of lands in severalty, the establishment of local courts and police, the development of a personal sense of independence, and the universal adoption of the English language are means to this end.

Seventh. In the administration of Indian Affairs there is need and opportunity for the exercise of the same qualities demanded in any other great administration—integrity, justice, patience, and good sense. Dishonesty, injustice, favoritism, and incompetency have no place here any more than elsewhere in the Government.

Eighth. The chief thing to be considered in the administration of this office is the character of the men and women employed to carry out the designs of the Government. The best system may be perverted to bad ends by incompetent or dishonest persons employed to carry it into execution, while a very bad system may yield good results if wisely and honestly administered.

In his 1890 discourse, he discussed the allotment policy of the government. "It has become the settled policy of the Government to break up reservations, destroy tribal relations, settle Indians upon their own homesteads, incorporate them into the national life, and deal with them not as nations or tribes or bands, but as individual citizens," he wrote. "How far this process has advanced during the past year will be shown under the head of the reduction of reservations and allotment of lands." Further, writes historian Frederick Hoxie, Morgan stressed improved education for Indian children. "Morgan's educational system consisted of four stages, each of which complemented the others, and all of which were aimed at the enhancement of 'civic culture,'" he explains. "At the basic level, he proposed establishing day schools in every Indian community. These schools would provide an 'impressive object lesson' on the virtues of civilized living and would prepare children for primary schools. The mission of the primary schools was to lay 'the foundation work' of Indian children. To accomplish this goal, Morgan proposed locating boarding facilities at agencies and population centers, and urged that students be enrolled at as early an age as possible, 'before camp life has made an indelible stamp upon them.' At about ten years of age, Indian students would advance to grammar schools, where they would begin to learn trades and where the emphasis on a rigid daily schedule would accustom them to systematic habits. Finally, at about fifteen years of age, academically inclined students would enter government high schools. The high schools, Morgan explained, 'should lift the Indian students to so high a plane of thought and aspiration as to render the life of the camp intolerable to them.' By so doing, the high schools would serve as gateways 'out from the desolation of the reservation into assimilation with our national life.'" Morgan's program was eventually taken apart by successive commissioners.

With the defeat of Benjamin Harrison in the election of 1892, Morgan's days as Indian commissioner were numbered. After leaving office on 1 March 1893, he served as corresponding secretary of the Baptist Home Mission Society and as editor of *Home Mission Weekly*. Among his writings are *Indian Education* (1890), and *The Present Phase of the Indian Question* (1891). A few weeks before his death, he delivered an address titled "Indian Education" before the American Social Science Association in Washington, D.C., where he defended his program as Indian commissioner. Morgan died in Washington on 13 July 1902.

See also Ghost Dance.

References "General T. J. Morgan." *Evening Traveller* (Boston), 11 June 1889, 4; Hoxie, Frederick E., "Redefining Indian Education: Thomas J. Morgan's Program in Disarray." *Arizona and the West* 24 (Spring 1982); Josephy, Alvin M., Jr., *Now That the Buffalo's Gone: A Study of Today's American Indians* (1989); Moehlman, Conrad Henry, "Morgan, Thomas Jefferson." In Dumas Malone et al., eds., *Dictionary of American Biography* (1930–88); Morgan to Halford, 14 January 1889, Morgan Appointment File, Box 44, Records of the Appointments Division, Commissioner of Indian Affairs, RG 48, National Archives; Morgan to Harrison, 26 November 1888, Morgan Appointment File, Box 44, Records of the Appointments Division, Commissioner of Indian Affairs, RG 48, National Archives; Prucha, Francis Paul, "Thomas Jefferson Morgan." In Robert M. Kvasnicka and Herman J. Viola, eds., *The Commissioners of Indian Affairs, 1824–1977* (1979); U.S. Congress, House of Representatives, *Annual Report of the Commissioner of Indian Affairs for the Year 1889*, House Executive Document No. 1, 51st Congress, 1st

Session (serial 2725); U.S. Congress, House of Representatives, *Annual Report of the Commissioner of Indian Affairs for the Year 1890*, House Executive Document No. 1, 51st Congress, 2d Session (serial 2841).

Morris et al. v. Hitchcock, Secretary of the Interior et al. **(194 U.S. 384 [1904])**
Laws and regulations proclaimed by the secretary of the interior as authorized by an act of Congress do not violate the Constitution—so held the U.S. Supreme Court in this case, decided in 1904. Defendants Edwin T. Morris and nine other unnamed persons owned cattle and horses that grazed on lands of the Chickasaw Nation in Oklahoma, lands rented to them by individual members of that nation. When Secretary of the Interior Ethan Allen Hitchcock stepped in to enjoin, or stop, Morris and the others from using the land, Morris sued Hitchcock; Commissioner of Indian Affairs William A. Jones; J. George Wright, Indian inspector; and J. Blair Schoenfelt, U.S. Indian agent, to enjoin interference. Hitchcock charged that by a law passed by the Chickasaw legislature, such non-Indians must pay a tax, that Morris' refusal to pay the tax was a violation of the law, and that as secretary of the interior, the constitutional officer with the power over Indian Affairs, he was allowed to carry out this order with the consent of Congress. The Supreme Court of the District of Columbia dismissed Morris' suit, and the Court of Appeals for the District of Columbia affirmed.

Morris appealed to the U.S. Supreme Court, and the case was submitted on 29 April 1904. It was Justice Edward Douglass White who spoke for a unanimous court on 16 May of that same year when he upheld Hitchcock's right to carry out the will of the Chickasaw legislature. Justice White explained, "While it is unquestioned that, by the Constitution of the United States, Congress is vested with paramount power to regulate commerce with the Indian tribes, yet it is also undoubted that in treaties entered with the Chickasaw Nation, the right of that tribe to control the presence within their territory assigned to it of persons who might otherwise be regarded as intruders has been sanctioned, and the duty of the United States to protect the Indians 'from aggression by other Indians and white persons, not subject to their jurisdiction and laws,' has also been recognized. Treaty [of] June 22 1855. art[icle]s. 7 and 14 (11 Stat. 611); Treaty [of] April 28 1866, art. 8 (14 Stat. 769). And it is not disputed that, under the authority of these treaties, the Chickasaw Nation has exercised the power to attach conditions to the presence within its borders of persons who might otherwise not be entitled to remain within the tribal territory."

Morton, Secretary of the Interior, v. C. R. Mancari et al. and Amerind v. C. R. Mancari et al. **(417 U.S. 535, 41 L.Ed. 2d 290, 94 S.Ct. 2474 [1974])**
In this joint case, the Supreme Court held that a provision of the Indian Reorganization Act (IRA) of 1934 giving preference to Indians in hiring in the Bureau of Indian Affairs was not in violation of the Equal Employment Opportunities Act of 1972. In June 1972, the commissioner of the Bureau of Indian Affairs, Louis Rook Bruce, issued an order (with the approval of Secretary of the Interior Rogers C. B. Morton) declaring the policy of the BIA to be to give preference not only in hiring but in promotions to Indians over other employees in the bureau. Plaintiff C. R. Mancari, who is identified only as a "non-Indian" who works in the bureau as a "teacher…or programmer, in computer work," joined others similarly situated and sued Morton, claiming that such a directive was illegal under the Equal Employment Opportunities Act of 1972, as well as violative of the due process clause of the Fifth Amendment to the U.S. Constitution. The U.S. District Court for the District of New Mexico convened a three-judge federal panel, which ruled that the preference in the 1934 act was overruled by the 1972 act, which outlawed discrimination in hiring in government on the basis of race. On appeal, the U.S. Supreme Court granted certiorari.

After the case was argued on 24 April 1974, a decision was handed down on 17 June of that same year; speaking for a unanimous court, Justice Harry Blackmun upheld the preference provision of the IRA and dismissed claims that it violated the due process clause of the Fifth Amendment. Discussing the issue historically, Justice Blackmun wrote, "The Federal policy of according some hiring preference to Indians in the Indian service dates at least as far back as 1834 [Act of 30 June 1834, 4 Stat. 737]. Since that time, Congress repeatedly has enacted various preferences of the general type here at issue. The purpose of these preferences, as variously expressed in the legislative history, has been to give Indians a greater participation in their own self-government; to further the Government's trust obligation toward the Indian tribes; and to reduce the negative effect of having non-Indians administer matters that affect Indian tribal life."

Morton, Secretary of the Interior, v. Ramon Ruiz et ux. (415 U.S. 199, 39 L.Ed. 2d 270, 94 S.Ct. 1055 [1974])

In this Supreme Court case, the court held that the Snyder Act (42 Stat. 208) of 1921 did allow general assistance benefits to be given to needy Indians even if they lived off the reservation, as long as they maintained "close economic and social ties" with that reservation. The Snyder Act was enacted to provide appropriated monies for the benefit, care, and general assistance of Indians in the United States. Ramon Ruiz and his wife, Anita, were full-blooded Papago Indians who at one time lived on the Papago Indian reservation in Arizona. When Ramon Ruiz obtained work for a nearby copper mine, the couple left the reservation and took up residence in the general population. When there was a strike at the mine, Ruiz and his wife applied to the Bureau of Indian Affairs for general assistance benefits under the Snyder Act. The bureau refused, claiming that under the act, the benefits were for those Indians "on reservations." The Ruizes sued in district court, claiming that the eligibility requirements were unconstitutional. The District Court ruled for the defendant, Secretary of the Interior Rogers C.B. Morton, but the U.S. Court of Appeals for the Ninth Circuit reversed. On appeal, the U.S. Supreme Court agreed to hear the case.

Arguments were held before the court on 5 and 6 November 1973; a decision was handed down on 20 February 1974. Speaking for a unanimous court, Justice Harry Blackmun held that because the Ruizes did not break their social and economic contacts with the reservation, they could not be denied benefits under the Snyder Act, explaining, "The overriding duty of our Federal Government is to deal fairly with Indians wherever located has been recognized by this Court on many occasions." However, he added, "We emphasize that our holding does not, as was suggested at oral argument, make general assistance available to all Indians 'throughout the country.' Even respondents [Ruizes] do not claim this much. The appropriation, as we see it, was for Indians 'on or near' the reservation. This is broad enough, we hold, to include the Ruizes who lived where they found employment in an Indian community only a few miles from their reservation, who maintain their close economic and social ties with that reservation, and who are unassimilated. The parameter of their class will be determined, to the extent necessary, by the district court on remand of the case. Whether other persons qualify for general assistance will be left to cases that arise in the future."

See also Snyder Act.

Muskrat and Dick v. United States (219 U.S. 346 [1911])

This Supreme Court case, officially titled *David Muskrat and J. Henry Dick, on Their Own Behalf, etc. Appellants, v. United States*, and decided jointly with *William Brown and Levi B. Gritts, on Their Own Behalf, and on Behalf of All Other Cherokee Citizens Having*

Like Interests in the Property Allotted under the Act of July 1, 1902, Appellants, v. United States, held that certain acts of Congress were invalid as to the jurisdiction of Indian claims. The cases of Muskrat and Dick dealt with the act of Congress of 26 April 1906, amended by the act of 21 June 1906, which sought to increase the number of persons entitled to share in the final disposition of lands and funds of the Cherokee Nation. By an act of Congress on 1 July 1902 (32 Stat. 716), those Cherokees enrolled by 1 September 1902 could only share in the settlement of lands and funds, and the two appellants in this case requested that the later act be declared invalid. The case of Brown and Gritts also involved the act of 1 July 1902; in their case, however, both men had received their allotments. The act of 11 March 1904 (33 Stat. 65) authorized the secretary of the interior to grant right-of-way licenses to companies to run pipe lines through allotted Indian lands. Another act, that of 26 April 1906, extended the period barring the alienation (sale), lease, or rental of allotments for an additional 25 years. On 1 March 1907, Congress passed legislation conferring jurisdiction upon the Court of Claims to decide these cases.

The parties in both suits took their grievances to the Court of Claims, which now had jurisdiction, but which in both cases dismissed the litigation. The Supreme Court agreed to hear the cases. Arguments were heard on 30 November and 1 and 2 December 1910, and a decision was handed down on 23 January 1911 in both cases. Speaking for a unanimous court, Justice William Rufus Day held on the narrow issue that the federal legislation conferring authority on the Court of Claims to adjudicate the matters in these cases was invalid. As Justice Day questioned, "Is such a determination within the judicial power conferred by the Constitution, as the same has been interpreted and defined in the authoritative decisions to which we have referred? We think not." He added, "The judgments will be reversed and the cases remanded to the Court of Claims, with directions to dismiss for want of jurisdiction."

Myer, Dillon Seymour (1909–1982)

Dillon S. Myer's service as commissioner of Indian Affairs from 1950 to 1953 is overshadowed by his previous work as head of the War Relocation Agency when he oversaw the relocation of some 110,000 Japanese from their homes in California to internment camps, yet he had a long and distinguished career in the government. The son and fourth child of John Hyson Myer and Harriett Estella (née Seymour) Myer, he was born on his family's farm in Hebron, Ohio, on 4 September 1891, a place he later called "a typical corn belt farm of 135 acres in central Ohio." He attended Ohio State University, where he earned a bachelor's degree in Business Administration in 1914, and as well was awarded a master's degree from Columbia University in 1924. For two years after he graduated from Ohio State he taught agronomy at the Kentucky Agricultural College. In 1916 he entered the Department of Agriculture's Extension Service, and from then until 1942 he held a series of positions in that department related to agriculture, including posts at Ohio State University and Purdue. In 1934 he went to work in the department's headquarters in Washington, D.C., where he remained until 1942.

In that year, President Franklin D. Roosevelt asked Myer to head the War Relocation Authority (WRA), a program to handle the removal and relocation of Japanese Americans to internment camps during World War II. Under Myer's command, more than 110,000 Japanese were moved to 10 camps that were modeled on army camps to stave off a possible invasion by Japanese troops. The work of the WRA has been criticized by many historians as the worst example of a violation of the civil rights of American citizens in the nation's history. After the war, Myer was appointed director of the Federal Public Housing Authority, a post which he served in from 1946 to 1947, to reconvert the wartime bureau to the peacetime National Housing Agency. In 1947, Myer was named as president of the Institute of Inter-American Affairs, at that time a State Department office which handled education and health matters in friendly countries in the Western Hemisphere.

On 5 May 1950, President Harry S Truman named Myer as the commissioner of Indian Affairs, to succeed Dr. John Ralph Nichols, who had resigned. Myer's first mistake after taking over the Indian Bureau was to hire many of the men who had worked with him at the WRA; thus, those in charge of the BIA had experience handling the affairs of Japanese Americans, but not Native Americans. Within a few months of his taking office, he was barraged from all sides by harsh criticism over his handling of Indian affairs. Perhaps the greatest denunciation came from attorney Felix S. Cohen, who had drafted the Indian Reorganization Act of 1934. In an article in the *Yale Law Journal* in February 1953, Cohen blasted Myer in terms seldom used, accusing the commissioner of restricting the freedom of Indians, forcing changes in Indian health care that would hurt them in the long run, and refusing them the right to control their reservations. By the end of his administration, Myer was pushing for the termination of Indian tribes. Dwight D. Eisenhower's election as president, however, was the denouement to his work. On 19 March 1953, he resigned. In the years after his retirement from the Indian office, Myer served as director of the Group Health Association in Washington. He died of cardiac arrest in a nursing home in Silver Spring, Maryland, on 21 October 1982 at the age of 91.

See also Bureau of Indian Affairs.

References Cohen, Felix S., "The Erosion of Indian Rights, 1950–53: A Case Study in Bureaucracy." *Yale Law Journal* 62 (3); Dicke, William, "Dillon S. Myer, Who Headed War Relocation Agency, Dies." *New York Times*, 25 October 1982, D11; Drinnon, Richard, *Keeper of the Concentration Camps: Dillon S. Myer and American Racism* (1987); Myer, Dillon S., *Uprooted Americans* (1971); "Myer, Dillon Seymour." In Anne Rothe, ed., *Current Biography* 1947 (1947); Ourada, Patricia K., "Dillon Seymour Myer" in Robert M. Kvasnicka and Herman J. Viola, eds., *The Commissioners of Indian Affairs, 1824–1977* (1979).

***Nadeau et al. v. Union Pacific Railroad Company* (253 U.S. 442 [1920])**

After an Indian tribe has ceded lands to the United States, the period between that cession and the allotment in severalty makes those lands public lands, and the United States may grant a right-of-way to a railroad to pass through them, the Supreme Court held in this 1920 decision. In 1846 the Potawatomie Indians of Kansas ceded all of the lands of their reservation to the United States; in 1861, the government agreed to allot these lands back to those Indians in severalty. However, in 1862, before the allotment could take place, the government granted a right-of-way through these lands to the Leavenworth, Pawnees and Western Railroad Company (which later became part of the Union Pacific Railroad Company, the defendant in error in this case). Joseph E. Nadeau, a member of the Potawatomie, sued in the District Court of the United States for the District of Kansas to have the lands returned. The district court held for the railroad, and Nadeau appealed to the U.S. Supreme Court. Justice James McReynolds held for a unanimous court on 7 June 1920 that during the period between cession and allotment, the Potawatomie lands were to be considered as "public lands," and Congress had the right to grant the railroads a right-of-way. Justice McReynolds explained, "Until actually allotted in severalty [in 1864], the lands were but part of the domain held by the tribe under the ordinary Indian claim—the right of possession and occupancy—with fee in the United States. *Beecher v. Wetherby*, 95 U.S. 517, [at] 525, 24 L.Ed. 440. The power of Congress, as guardian for the Indians, to legislate in respect to such lands is settled. *Cherokee Nation v. Southern Kansas Railway Company*, 135 U.S. 641, [at] 653, 10 S.Ct. 965, 34 L.Ed. 295."

***Naganab v. Hitchcock* (202 U.S. 473 [1906])**

The case of *Joseph Naganab, Appellant, v. Ethan Allan Hitchcock, Secretary of the Interior*, decided in 1906, dealt with whether Congress could authorize the secretary of the interior to sell surplus Indian pinelands as public lands. In 1889, Congress established an allotment schedule for the lands of the Chippewa Indians of Minnesota. At the time, 1.5 million acres were classified as pinelands. By the act of Congress of 27 June 1902 (32 Stat. 400), the remaining pinelands (estimated in 1902 at 600,000 acres) not yet allotted or sold were established as a forest reservation, and authorized the secretary of the interior to sell the lands without the consent of the Chippewas. Complainant Joseph Naganab, a Chippewa, sued Secretary of the Interior Ethan Allan Hitchcock to stop him from selling these surplus lands. The Supreme Court of the District of Columbia dismissed Naganab's suit, and the Court of Appeals for the District of Columbia affirmed the decision. Naganab appealed to the U.S. Supreme Court. Holding for a unanimous court on 21 May 1906, Justice William Rufus Day decided that the Act of 27 June 1902 had lawfully redesignated the surplus pinelands as a forest reservation and, because such a redesignation left the fee in the United States and not the Indians, authorizing the secretary of the interior (whom Justice Day held was not really a party to this litigation) to sell the lands without the consent of the Indians was part of Congress' plenary, or absolute, power over Indian tribes. Citing *Oregon v. Hitchcock* (202 U.S. 60 [1906]), a similar case, Justice Day wrote, "In this case as in the Oregon Case, the legal title to all the tracts of land in question is still in the government, and the United States, the real party in interest herein, has not waived in any manner its immunity, or consented to be sued concerning the lands in question, and there is no act of Congress in anywise authorizing this action. Upon the Oregon Case we hold that there is no jurisdiction to maintain the present suit."

***See also** Oregon v. Hitchcock.*

Nash, Philleo (1909–1987)

An anthropologist rather than a career expert in Indian policy, Philleo Nash was appointed commissioner of Indian Affairs in 1961. The last non-Indian to hold that position, Nash's work was hampered by Congress and by a president who was apathetic toward his program. Born in Wisconsin Rapids, Wisconsin, on 25 October 1909, Nash's father was the head of the Biron Cranberry Company, and his grandfather, T. E. Nash, founded the Nekoosa-Edwards Paper Company. He received a common school education, then attended the University of Wisconsin at Madison, from which he earned a bachelor's degree in anthropology in 1932. In a speech in 1986, Nash said, "My own professional life came of age with 'acculturation' and 'applied anthropology.' I was lucky enough to have been one Ralph Linton's first students at the University of Wisconsin; Lauriston Sharp and Sol Tax were just ahead of me." He was awarded a Ph.D. degree in anthropology from the University of Chicago in 1937. According to Stephen Labaton, "After spending a year on an Indian reservation in Oregon, he wrote his doctoral dissertation examining the Klamath Indian Ghost Dance of 1870, which he contended was a response to the tribe's contact with white men." After leaving Chicago, he taught anthropology for several years at the University of Toronto and at his alma mater, the University of Wisconsin. In 1942, just after the United States entered World War II, Nash went to Washington to work as a special assistant to Elmer Davis, head of the Office of War Information (OWI), where he wrote propaganda leaflets such as "The Command of Negro Troops" and "Enemy Japan." With the end of the war, he served in the Truman Administration as a special liaison to the president on minority affairs in the Department of the Interior (1946–52), where he supported fair employment practices and an end to discrimination against black Americans in the military. In January 1952, Senator Joseph McCarthy of Wisconsin accused Nash of being a Communist, but Nash called the charge "a contemptible lie" and President Truman came to his defense. With Dwight D. Eisenhower's election as president, Nash returned to Wisconsin, where he chaired the state Democratic party. In 1958, he ran with Gaylord Nelson (later a U.S. senator and the founder of Earth Day) and was elected lieutenant governor, but was defeated for reelection in 1960.

The 1960 election brought John F. Kennedy to the White House and a new attitude toward American Indians in the federal government. John Crow was acting commissioner of Indian Affairs, but he was unpopular among Native Americans and Kennedy was looking for a commissioner who could be effective. In June 1961, the American Indian Chicago Conference was held calling for an end to termination. Kennedy appointed Secretary of the Interior Stewart L. Udall to the Kennedy Task Force on Indian Affairs, known as the Udall Commission, to visit the Indians and ask for their input into policy decisions. Among the members of this commission was the chairman, W. W. Keeler of the Cherokee Nation; William Zimmerman, Jr., who had served for several years as acting commissioner during Truman's administration; James E. Officer, an anthropologist from Arizona; and Nash. After the report of the task force was delivered to the president, Kennedy chose Nash as Indian commissioner on 31 July 1961; Officer was appointed assistant commissioner. In his five years as Indian commissioner, Nash attempted to undue the effects of termination, and began a drastic program of invigorating poverty-stricken reservations with economically self-sufficient measures. In a speech entitled "American Indians and The American Society," delivered at Fisk University in Nashville, Tennessee in 1965, Nash said, "For those who prefer to continue tribal life, I stand firmly on the ground that they have every right to do so—and that the U.S. Government, at the same time, has an obligation to see that the penalty for being an Indian is not abject poverty. Therefore, we wrest with the economic obstacles in development of Indian lands. We encourage the tribal governments to make wise use of their tribal funds—which may come from land leasing; tribal enterprises, such as ranching or recreational development; or from awards in settlement of claims against the United States for land-takings in the last century."

Faced with opposition in Congress, particularly from Senator Clinton P. Anderson of New Mexico, and without support from President Lyndon Johnson, Nash resigned his office. He wrote, "I resigned voluntarily on March 15, 1966, having had a little less than five years of spirited and—on the whole—successful activity. When I left I had general support among the tribes and within the Bureau of Indian Affairs; no support from the Chairmen of the Congressional Committees exercising oversight of Indian Affairs; I had lost the support of the Secretary of the Interior; the President of the United States was indifferent. Continuing in office could only damage the programs that were just beginning to be effective. By resigning when I requested I could avoid a fruitless confrontation, protect my programs, and open the way to an Indian person who was qualified, a friend from my own state. The decision was painful, but the course was clear." President Johnson then selected Robert LaFollette Bennett (Oneida) of Wisconsin as the first Native American commissioner since Ely S. Parker in 1871. Nash remained in Washington to run his own consulting business until 1977, then returned to Wisconsin to head his family's cranberry business. In 1986, shortly before his death, he was the recipient of the Malinowski Award of the Society for Applied Anthropology, given "in recognition of his efforts to understand and serve the needs of the world through social science." Nash died the following year, on 12 October 1987, in Marshfield, Wisconsin, at the age of 77.

See also Bureau of Indian Affairs.

References Labaton, Stephen, "Philleo Nash at 77; Was a U.S. Official in 3 Administrations." *New York Times*, 27 October 1987, D35; Nash, Philleo, "American Indians and the American Society," a speech before Fisk University, Nashville, Tennessee, 29 June 1965, a publication of the Department of the Interior (1965); Nash, Philleo, *The Place of Religious Revivalism in the Formation of the Intercultural Community on Klamath Reservation* (Ph.D. dissertation, University of Chicago, 1937); Nash, Philleo, "Science, Politics, and Human Values: A Memoir." *Human Organization* 45:3; Papers of Philleo Nash, Harry S Truman Library, Independence, Missouri; Philp, Kenneth R., ed., *Indian Self-Rule: First-Hand Accounts of Indian-White Relations from Roosevelt to Reagan* (1986); Szasz, Margaret Connell, "Philleo Nash." In Robert M. Kvasnicka and Herman J. Viola, eds., *The Commissioners of Indian Affairs, 1824–1977 (1979).*

National Congress of American Indians

The oldest and largest national pan-Indian and Indian rights organization in the United States, the National Congress of American Indians (NCAI) was founded in 1944 to promote treaty rights, advocate and protect the traditional, property and cultural rights of the Native American, while at the same time promote the advancement of Indian education and economic development among the American Indian people. The idea of D'Arcy McNickle (Salish-Kutenai), an Indian writer and historian, who approached Commissioner of Indian Affairs John Collier in the 1940s for help in forming a national pan-Indian organization, the NCAI was born when delegates from 27 states representing 50 tribes came together at the Cosmopolitan Hotel in Denver, Colorado, from 15 to 18 December 1944 and established the council. The platform of the first congress follows:

Charles E. Trimble, executive director of the oldest national pan-Indian rights organization, the National Congress of American Indians, holds a press conference in 1972.

This convention formulated and adopted a platform and program consisting of the following points:

1. The Aboriginal Races of North America. This organization shall work toward the promotion of the common welfare of aboriginal races in North America, including the natives of Alaska, protect the rights, develop and advance the better values in these races.

2. People of High Degree Indian Blood. It shall be the first order of business of this organization to give thought to the situation of the higher degree Indian blood members of the Indian race—to the end that all possible effort be made to safeguard their property and to make provision for the continuation of appropriate services to such members of the various tribes.

3. Legal Aid Service. Realizing that many tribes, and the members thereof, do not have the financial means that are necessary with which to employ attorneys to represent them before the various branches of the Federal Government in Washington, this organization purports to establish a Legal Aid Service through which the cause of such tribes, or members thereof, may be properly represented.

4. News Letter. In order that information concerning legislation pending in the Congress of the United States, the activities of the Indian Bureau and information of general interest to the Indians may be regularly available, it is proposed that this organization shall publish and distribute as often as possible a News Letter dealing with such matters.

5. Indian Claims Commission Bill. This organization shall advocate and take the necessary steps to prevail upon the Congress of the United States to create an Indian Claims Commission authorized to hear, consider and settle the claims of the various Indian tribes of the United States and Alaska against the Federal Government.

6. Employment of Indians in the Indian Service. The Secretary of the Interior and the Commissioner of Indian Affairs shall be called upon to give real and meaningful preference to Indians in filling all positions in the Indian Service under Section 12 of the Indian Reorganization Act—and shall advocate in-service training of Indians for Government Career Service.

7. Franchise for Indians. This organization shall use its influence and exert its efforts toward securing the right to vote for Indians in the several states where voting privileges are being denied them—if and when this organization is requested by the Indians affected to assist them in vitalizing this right of American citizens.

8. Consultation with Indians Relative to Indian Legislation. The Congress of the United States shall be called upon to adopt a policy of consulting with Indians, through their daily appointed representatives, before enacting any legislation directed specifically or prescriptively at Indians, their lives or their property.

9. Adherence to Charters of Indian Organizations. The Department of the Interior and the Commissioner of Indian Affairs shall be urged to examine fully into the provisions of charters that have been granted to Indian organizations under existing law and to give proper regard, consideration and adherence to the provisions of such charters.

10. Poll of Indian Opinion. The Executive Council of this organization shall take such steps as may be necessary to bring about a cooperative arrangement with the National Opinion Research Center of Denver, Colorado, in conducting a poll of Indian opinion regarding the policies and actions of the Office of Indian Affairs.

One of its early leaders was Robert L. Bennett (Oneida), who served as a treasurer and was later commissioner of Indian Affairs. Among the organization's accomplishments were the advancement of the creation of the Indians Claims Commission in 1946, the end of the termination policy of the Congress in the 1960s, and the Indian Self-Determination and Education Act, which was enacted in 1975. Its current president is Gaiashkibos (Chippewa) and in

1996 the organization had a membership of nearly 200 tribes. Its publications include the *NCAI News* and the *Sentinel.*

References O'Brien, Sharon, "National Congress of American Indians (1944)." In Armand S. La Potin, ed., *Native American Voluntary Organizations* (1987); "The Platforms of the First Two Annual Conventions of the National Congress of American Indians, 1944, 1945: The First Annual Convention." In Hurtado, Albert L., and Peter Iverson, eds., *Major Problems in American Indian History: Documents and Essays* (1994).

National Farmers Union Insurance Companies and Lodge Grass School District No. 27 v. Crow Tribe of Indians et al. (471 U.S. 845, 85 L.Ed. 2d 818, 105 S.Ct. 2447 [1985])

In this Supreme Court case, decided in 1985, the court held that for a non-Indian to utilize the federal courts against an Indian defendant in a civil case, that non-Indian must "exhaust...[all] tribal court remedies" before going to a state court. In 1982, Leroy Sage, a minor, and member of the Crow Tribe of Indians of Montana, was hit by a motorcycle in the parking lot of the Lodge Grass Elementary School, which, though on the Crow reservation, was owned by the state. Sage, through his guardian, Flora Not Afraid, filed a suit for damages and medical expenses in the Crow tribal court. The School Board did not respond, and Sage won a default judgment. Later that year, the School Board, backed by its insurance company, the National Farmers Insurance Companies, filed suit in the District Court for the District of Montana to enjoin, or stop, Sage from enforcing the default. These defendants cited 28 U.S.C. 1331, which provides that federal district courts "shall have original jurisdiction of all civil actions arising under the Constitution, laws, or treaties of the United States." The district court, on this basis, granted a permanent injunction against the tribal court because that court did not have original jurisdiction. On appeal, the U.S. Court of Appeals for the Ninth Circuit reversed; while it did not reach a conclusion as to the fitness of the Tribal Court opinion, it did hold that 28 U.S.C. 1331 did not apply in this case. On certiorari, the U.S. Supreme Court heard arguments on 16 April 1985, and handed down a decision on 3 June of the same year. In an opinion by Justice John Paul Stevens, expressing the unanimous view of the court, it was held that while 28 U.S.C. 1331 may apply to this case, the school board and insurance company must exhaust all tribal court remedies before taking the case to district court. In remanding the case back to district court, Justice Stevens explained, "The question whether an Indian tribe retains the power to compel a non-Indian property owner to submit to the civil jurisdiction of a tribal court is one that must be answered by reference to federal law and is a 'federal question' under [section] 1331."

National Indian Defense Association

An Indian rights organization founded by Thomas Augustus Bland and others in Washington, D.C., in 1885, the National Indian Defense Association (NIDA) sought to gain for Indians rights held by other American citizens. Influenced by the exposé of abuse in the government's dealings with the Indians as detailed in activist Helen Hunt Jackson's *A Century of Dishonor*, the organization arose out of the obscure but influential journal of reform, the *Council Fire*, founded by Bland's mentor, Alfred B. Meacham, an Oregon Indian superintendent. After Meacham's death, Bland and his wife Cora underwrote the costs and continued the work on the *Council Fire* and just three years later helped found the NIDA. Members included Bland, Charles Rhoads, Reverend Alexander Kent, and Professor Bernard T. Janney. The preamble of the organization's charter follows:

The General question presented for the consideration of this Association is, whether an exigency is presented by the state of relations between the Government of the United States and the Indians calling for organized effort to secure the application of sound principles to those relations.

The development of this question involves the ascertainment of the principles upon which those relations should be based; whether there is a necessity for organized effort in that behalf, whether the present time is opportune for such effort, and what should be the scope and character of an organization adapted to that end.

Until within a few years the Indian tribes were treated by our Government as alien sovereignties, tolerated under treaty stipulations, within our territorial limits, creating anomalous political relations, inconvenient, but of assumed temporary duration. It is impossible to resist the conclusion that such a national policy ultimately rested on the idea that at no distant day the Indian, as societies of men, would disappear, leaving only fragmentary remnants of the race, of inconsiderable magnitude, capable of being absorbed, or eliminated in the ordinary processes of national growth.

Under the pressure for increased landed areas for cultivation, that threatened to place the entire support of the Indians upon the Government, the original Indian policy at length gave way and the Indians were subjected to the general authority of Congress, their proprietary right, as against the Government, being defined by agreements made with the tribal authorities. Although Congress asserted the possession of general governmental authority over the Indians, as tribes and as persons, they had failed to exercise that authority by extending the laws of the United States for the protection of person and property, over the Territory and persons of the Indians, or to recognize, explicitly and definitely, municipal authority in the tribes for that purpose, but has constituted executive agencies for the administration of federal interests among the Indians, that have assumed authority, both legislative and judicial, over them.

The combined influence of the weight of support of the Indians upon the treasury, the pressure of portions of the Indians' domain, and a misdirected sentiment favorable to the advance of the Indians in civilization has precipitated the discussion of a policy that, if prevalent, would at once destroy the tribal authority and influence, clothe the individual Indian with such proprietary rights as Congress might see fit to confer upon him, and thrust him into competition with all the interests clashing with his own. In this scheme education is looked to as the means of conserving the interests of the Indian.

At this moment pressure is being brought to bear upon the legislative and executive government to induce the immediate adoption of the policy of dissolving the tribal relations, conferring land in severalty upon the Indians, and absorbing him into the body of the population, with rights and obligations such as are common to all other citizens.

The NIDA platform was both a summary of the organization's policies and a series of recommendations:

First. That the immediate dissolution of the tribal relation would prove to be an impediment to the civilization of the Indians by depriving them of a conservative influence tending to preserve order, respect for person and property, and repress vagrancy and vagabondage. That it would diminish the available protection for the rights of the Indians, and depress his industry by depriving him of the mutual assistance of those conditioned like himself in an organized form.

Second. That in the present condition of the mass of the Indians to confer upon him the title to his lands in severalty would not supply to him the motive and means of industry adequate to contend with the disadvantages of his condition and surroundings, while the motives to part with his land would be in the great majority of cases irresistible. That if his title should be made available for a long term of years that fact would not afford protection unless his capacity to transfer or relinquish the occupancy of his lands was likewise taken away, and in that event he would be placed in an anomalous condition, unlike any that has been the concomitant of any known civilization.

Third. That whatever education may do for the next generation it cannot combat the evils threatening the present generation, so that the patrimony of the Indian may be gone before his capacity for managing it is developed.

The present time is believed to be favorable for an effort in behalf of a sound policy, as a reactive tendency appears against precipitate measures for advancing the civil condition of the Indians. That an effort in that direction would be materially assisted by organization is obvious, while the fact that powerful organizations are already advocates of the policy to be opposed renders it necessary that the effort to counteract their influences should be an organized effort also.

Your committee have [*sic*] given consideration to the objects that should be pursued in an organized effort for the rectification of our Indian policy, and submit the results of their conclusions in the following resolutions:

Resolved, That an organization be formed for the purpose of protecting and assisting the Indians of the United States in acquiring the benefits of civilization, and in securing their territorial and proprietary rights.

Resolved, That such organization accept as its fundamental purpose, the following propositions:

First. That the laws of the United States for the protection of persons and property should be extended over the Indian reservations, as far as consistent with the obligations of the United States to the Indians, and with that degree of exercise of the rights of self government that is essential to their development, and with such modifications, especially as regards the administration of justice, as the case may demand.

Second. The tribal condition should be maintained to the extent demanded by the interests of good government within the reservations, with such modifications as may be necessary to eventually merge it into some political institution in harmony with the general system of our Government.

Third. Such lands as are intended for the perpetual use of the Indians should be patented to the tribes, in trust, to secure permanent individual occupation and industrial use, and ultimately to enure in severalty, to the Indians on a principle of distribution according to age and numbers.

Historian Armand S. La Potin writes, "Initially, Bland worked closely with [Indian Rights Association head Herbert] Welsh, [Women's National Indian Association leader Amelia] Quinton, and other reformers in advocating measures to encourage the allotment of Indian lands from tribal to individual ownership. They believed that the division of reservation holdings would encourage industry and initiative." From 1885 until its demise sometime after the *Council Fire* stopped publication in 1889, the National Indian Defense Association was the only national Indian reformist organization which opposed forced assimilation, but it was against a rising tide. Its last fight, to preserve Sioux land rights in South Dakota, ended with the massacre at Wounded Knee in December 1890.

See also Bland, Theodore Augustus; Meacham, Alfred Benjamin.

References Behrens, Jo Lea Wetherilt, "In Defense of 'Poor Lo': National Indian Defense Association and *Council Fire's* Advocacy for Sioux Land Rights." *South Dakota History* 24 (3–4); Bland, Thomas Augustus, *A Brief History of the Late Military Invasion of the Home of the Sioux* (1891); La Potin, Armand S., "National Indian Defense Association." In Armand S. La Potin, ed., *Native American Voluntary Organizations* (1987); Prucha, Francis Paul, ed., *Americanizing the American Indians: Writings by the "Friends of the Indian," 1880–1890* (1973).

National Indian Gaming Commission

Established by the Indian Gaming Regulatory Act of 1988 (Public Law 100–497, 102 Stat. 2467), the National Indian Gaming Commission (NIGC) is a regulatory agency located within the Department of the Interior, whose sole mission is to oversee the gaming industry conducted on Indian reservations nationwide.

See also Indian Gaming Regulatory Act of 1988.

National Indian Policy Center

Established with an appropriation of $1,000,000 by section 11 of an act of Congress of 24 May 1990 (104 Stat. 206, at 211) as the National Center for Native American Studies and Policy Development, this Bureau of the Department of Health and Human Services was located at George Washington University in Washington, D.C. Considered a "think tank" on Indian policy matters, it presented a final report to the Senate Select Committee on Indian Affairs in 1992 entitled *Report to Congress: Recommendations for the Establishment of a National Indian Policy Center* to help initiate essential Indian legislation.

Reference Utter, Jack, *American Indians: Answers to Today's Questions* (1993).

National Indian Youth Council (NIYC)

This grassroots Indian rights and reform organization was established in 1961 to "help protect traditional tribal rights and values through education and litigation." Indian historian and writer Vine Deloria, Jr., writes, "The NIYC is the SNCC [Student Nonviolent Coordinating Committee, a youth-oriented group that fought for civil rights for black Americans] of Indian Affairs. Organized in 1961, it has been active among the post-college group just entering Indian Affairs. Although NIYC has a short history, it has been able to achieve recognition as a force to be reckoned with in national Indian Affairs. Generally more liberal and excitable than the National Congress of American Indians, the NIYC inclines to the spectacular short-term project rather than the extended program. The rivalry between the two groups is intense." For its first three years, the NIYC published an official journal, *ABC: Americans Before Columbus*. One of the prime movers behind the creation of the NIYC, Clyde Warrior (Ponca), used the pages of *ABC* to rail against the Indian establishment (he called them "Uncle Tomahawks"). Other founders included Herbert Blatchford (Navajo), Melvin Thom (Nevada Paiute), and Bruce Wilkie (Washington Makah).

In 1964, NIYC activists organized the first "Fish-in" in the Quillayute River in Washington State to fish in violation of state ordinances and to assert treaty rights. Originally conceived as a civil rights organization, the NIYC evolved in the 1970s into an environmental association, pushing for the rights of Indians involved in cleaning up environmental damage to the land; by the 1980s, it had expanded the scope of its mission to include protecting the freedom of Indian religion, voting rights for Indians and increased voter participation, and hemispheric Indian protection. Presently, its national headquarters is located in Albuquerque, New Mexico.

See also Fish-In.

References Deloria, Vine, Jr., *Custer Died for Your Sins: An Indian Manifesto* (1970); Utter, Jack, *American Indians: Answers to Today's Questions (1993).*

Native American Graves Protection and Repatriation Act (Public Law 101–601, 104 Stat. 3048)

Now codified at 25 U.S.C. 3001, this federal legislation of 16 November 1990 was enacted "to protect Native American burial sites and the removal of human remains, funerary objects, sacred objects, and objects of cultural patrimony on Federal, Indian and Native Hawaiian lands. The Act also sets up a process by which Federal agencies and museums receiving federal funds will inventory holdings of such remains and objects and work with appropriate Indian tribes and Native Hawaiian organizations to reach agreement on repatriation or other disposition of these remains and objects." In the House report (101–877), considered on 15 October 1990, a summary of the act is discussed. "The Native American Grave[s] Protection and Repatriation Act achieves two main objectives," it maintains.

The first objective deals with Native American human remains, funerary objects, sacred objects and objects of cultural patrimony which are excavated or removed from Federal or tribal lands after the enactment of the Act. The Act calls for any persons who wish to excavate such items or other archaeological items to do so after receiving a permit pursuant to the Archaeological Resources Protection Act [of 1979, 93 Stat. 721]. If any of such remains or objects are found on Federal lands and it is known which tribe is closely related to them, that tribe is given the opportunity to reclaim the remains or objects. If the tribe does not want to take possession of the remains or objects, the Secretary of the Interior will determine the disposition of the remains or objects in consultation with Native American, scientific and museum groups...The second main objective addressed in the Act deals with collections of Native American human remains, associated and unassociated funerary objects, sacred objects, and objects of cultural patrimony currently held or controlled by Federal agencies and museums. Within five years of enactment, all Federal agencies and all museums which receive federal funds, which have possession of, or control over, any Native American human remains or associated funerary object..., are to compile an inventory of such remains or objects and, with the use of available information they have, attempt to identify them so as to geographical and cultural affiliation. Upon completion of the inventory, the appropriate tribe or Native Hawaiian organizatiuon is to be contacted. If it is clear which tribe or Native Hawaiian organization is related to the remains or objects and that tribe of organization wishes return of the items, they are to be returned.

Reference U.S. Congress, House of Representatives, *Native American Graves Protection and Reparation Act*, a report of the House Interior and Insular Affairs Committee to accompany H.R. 5237, House Report 101–877, 15 October 1990.

Native American Languages Act (104 Stat. 1153)

This legislation of 30 October 1990 was enacted in response to the finding that "the status of the cultures and languages of Native Americans is unique and the United States has the responsibility to act together with Native Americans to ensure the survival of these unique cultures and languages." Its chief aim is "(1) to preserve, protect, and promote the rights and freedom of Native Americans to use, practice, and develop Native American languages; (2) allow exceptions to teacher certification requirements for Federal programs, and programs funded in whole or in part by the Federal Government, for instruction in Native American languages when such teacher certification requirements hinder the employment of qualified teachers who teach in Native American languages, and to encourage State and territorial governments to make similar exceptions; (3) encourage and support the use of Native American languages as a medium of instruction in order to encourage and support—(A) Native American language survival, (B) educational opportunity, (C) increased student success and performance, (D) increased student awareness and knowledge of their culture and history, and (E) increased student and community pride; (4) encourage State and local education programs to work with Native American parents, educators, Indians tribes, and other Native American governing bodies in the implementation of programs to put this policy into effect; (5) recognize the right of Indian tribes and other Native American governing bodies to use the Native American languages as a medium of instruction in all schools funded by the Secretary of the Interior; (6) fully recognize the inherent right of Indian tribes and other Native American governing bodies, States, territories, and possessions of the United States to take action on, and give official status to, their Native American languages for the purpose of conducting their own business."

In order to implement these recommendations, "the President shall direct the heads of the various Federal departments, agencies, and instrumentalities to (1) evaluate their policies and procedures in consultation with Indian tribes and other Native

American governing bodies as well as traditional leaders and educators in order to determine and implement changes needed to bring the policies and procedures into compliance with the provisions of this title; (2) give the greatest effect possible in making such evaluations, absent a clear specific Federal statutory requirement to the contrary, to the policies and procedures which will give the broadest effect to the provisions of this title; and (3) evaluate the laws which they administer and make recommendations to the President on amendments needed to bring such laws into compliance with the provisions of this title."

Native American Rights Fund

Founded in 1970, the Native American Rights Fund, located in Boulder, Colorado, is the leading national organization working for the legal rights of Native Americans. Led by Executive Director John Echohawk, the group works in "five priority areas: preservation of tribal existence, protection of tribal natural resources, promotion of human rights, accountability of governments to Native Americans, and development of Indian Law. Two cases in which the fund has played an important role are the Boldt decision (Washington State fishing rights) and *Solem v. Bartlett*. Aside from maintaining the National Indian Law Library, which was founded as a national clearinghouse in 1972, the fund publishes the *NARF Legal Review*.

See also *United States v. Washington.*

References Campisi, Jack, "Native American Rights Fund (1970)." In Armand S. La Potin, ed., *Native American Voluntary Organizations* (1987); Hirschfelder, Arlene, and Martha Kreipe de Montaño, *The Native American Almanac: A Portrait of Native America Today* (1993).

Navajo Code Talkers

The code talkers of World War II were "an elite force of Navajos who transmitted secret military information in their native language and then translated it into English for military officials." Carl Gorman, one of 32 Navajo code talkers among some 25,000 Native Americans who served in the war, said that "they created a series of short, quick messages using basic words from the Navajo language. For example, military ships were referred to and distinguished by different kinds of fish. Planes were spoken of as birds, such as 'hawk' and 'eagle.'"

The actions of the Navajo code talkers are all the more remarkable in light of their tribe's history with the U.S. government. After a series of skirmishes between Navajo warriors and Army soldiers in the early 1860s, the government decided to crush the Navajos permanently. General James Carleton instructed Colonel Christopher "Kit" Carson to move into Navajo territory and either force them to surrender and submit to removal or exterminate them. Carson burned fields and slaughtered the Indians' animals, eventually forcing the Navajos to give up and relocate to Fort Sumner, New Mexico. On the three-week journey of some 300 miles, known today as the "Long Walk," hundreds of Navajos died.

Still, Navajos served in the military. During World War I, according to historian Nathan Aaseng, "Company D of the 141st Infantry had used eight Choctaw Indians to send and translate orders by telephone. The experiment had worked well enough on a limited basis against the Germans that the U.S. military continued to recruit Oneidas, Chippewas, Sac & Fox, and Comanches for signal corp work at the start of World War II." The Navajos were organized as the code talkers, officially the 382d Platoon, U.S. Marine Corps. A sample of the alphabet that they utilized, at least for the first few letters of the alphabet, follows:

Letter	Navajo Translation	Coded Letter
A	Wol-la-chee	Ant
B	Shush	Bear
C	Moasi	Cat
D	Be	Deer
E	Dzeh	Elk
F	Ma-e	Fox

In the code, a dive bomber was *gini* (chicken hawk), a torpedo plane was *tas-chizzie* (swallow), and an observation plane was *ne-as-jah* (owl).

In describing the work of this select

Volume 21, No.2 Summer/Fall 1996

300,000 INDIANS SUE FEDERAL GOVERNMENT FOR MISMANAGING THEIR MONEY

Class Action to Address Largest Financial Scandal Ever Involving Federal Government — Billions of Dollars Potentially at Stake —

Introduction

The Native American Rights Fund, along with other attorneys, filed a class action lawsuit on June 10, 1996 against the federal government. The lawsuit was filed on behalf of 300,000 Indians, to seek redress for government mismanagement of trust funds through which billions of dollars in Indian money has flowed over the years. The suit charges Secretary of the Interior Bruce Babbitt, Assistant Interior Secretary for Indian Affairs Ada Deer, and Secretary of the Treasury Robert Rubin with illegal conduct in what is viewed as the largest and most shameful financial scandal ever involving the United States government.

The federal government is required by law to manage the Indians' money, held in what is known as trust accounts. Although the money in question is processed by the Interior Department and deposited in the U.S. treasury, it is the Indians' own money, derived largely from income produced from leases of Indian lands. In a sense, the law requires the Indians to use the federal government as their bank. The Government Accounting Office (GAO) and a big six accounting firm have independently concluded that the government-managed trust fund is in total disarray and hopelessly broken.

"The Bureau of Indian Affairs (BIA) has spent more than 100 years mismanaging, diverting and losing money that belongs to Indians," said John Echohawk, Executive Director of the Native American Rights Fund. "They have no idea how much has been collected from the companies that use our land and are unable to provide even a basic, regular statement to Indian account holders. Every day the system remains broken, hundreds of thousands of Indians are losing more and more money."

Continued on page 3

CALL TO ACTION:

STOP GOVERNMENT MISMANAGEMENT AND LOSS OF INDIANS' MONEY

See Page 2

NARF LEGAL REVIEW

The Native American Rights Fund (NARF) produces the bimonthly NARF Legal Review as part of its mission to defend the legal rights of Native Americans. The masthead includes a Hopi prayer feather, a representation of the group's first token of appreciation received shortly after the organization's founding in 1970.

group of heroes, Major Howard M. Conner said, "Were it not for the Navajos, the Marines would never have taken Iwo Jima!"

See also Military, Indians in the.

References Aaseng, Nathan, *Navajo Code Talkers* (1992); Hafford, William E., "The Navajo Code

Navajo marines baffled Japanese on the South Pacific island of Bougainville in 1943. Like Choctaw soldiers during World War I, World War II units with Hopi and Navajo marines and soldiers mystified enemy intelligence by sending and receiving messages in their native languages.

Talkers." *Arizona Highways* 65 (2); Paul, Doris A., *The Navajo Code Talkers* (1973); "Statue Honors WWII Navajo Code Talkers." *Arizona Republic*, 12 November 1995, B3.

Navajo-Hopi Rehabilitation Act (64 Stat. 44)

This act "to promote the rehabilitation of the Navajo and Hopi Tribes of Indians and a better utilization of the resources of the Navajo and Hopi Indian Reservations" was enacted on 19 April 1950 to end the termination of these two tribes. The legislation authorized the secretary of the interior "to undertake, within the limits of the funds from time to time appropriated pursuant to this Act, a program of basic improvements for the conservation and development of the resources of the Navajo and Hopi Indians, the more productive employment of their manpower, and the supplying of means to be used in their rehabilitation, whether on of the Navajo and Hopi Indian Reservations." The action appropriated moneys for irrigation projects, surveys of timber and other natural resources on the reservations, the development of industrial and other business-related enterprises, the formation of roads and trails, the establishment of telephone and radio communication systems, and for the construction of hospitals and other health facilities.

Reference *United States Code Congressional Service*, 81st Congress, Second Session (1951).

Nevada et al. v. United States et al. (463 U.S. 110, 77 L.Ed. 2d 509, 103 S.Ct. 2906 [1983])

Jointly decided with *Truckee-Carson Irrigation District v. United States et al.* and *Pyramid Lake Paiute Tribe of Indians v. Truckee-Carson Irrigation District*, this case, which came before the Supreme Court in 1983, upheld the ruling that a decree between a state and the federal government over the water rights of Indians cannot be undone to seek additional water rights for those Indians. In 1913, the United States government sued to have the Pyramid Lake Paiute Tribe of Nevada adjudicated certain water rights upon the completion of the Newlands Reclamation Project. In 1944, 31 years later, the U.S. District Court for the District of Nevada entered into a final decree with respect to the amount of water this Indian tribe would receive. In 1973, the United States sought to have the decree modified, with new water to be added for the Indians' Pyramid Lake fishery from the Truckee River, one of three principal rivers flowing through west-central Nevada. The defendants—the state of Nevada and the Truckee-Carson Irrigation District (TCID)—claimed that the theory of *res judicata* ("a matter adjudged," "a thing acted upon or decided,") prevented the United States and the Indians from opening up the decree. The U.S. District Court for the District of Nevada, hearing this case, held that the decree was final. On appeal, the U.S. Court of Appeals for the Ninth Circuit affirmed in part and reversed in part, upholding the theory of *res judicata* as to those originally involved in the lawsuit, but holding that owners of land within the reclamation project who had not been litigants in the original suit could be sued. The state of Nevada, seeking to overturn this final holding, appealed to the U.S. Supreme Court. On 24 June 1983, Justice William H. Rehnquist, speaking for a unanimous court, held that *res judicata* prevented the United States and the Indians from reopening the final decree as to any litigants, whether they were part of the original decree or not.

Reference Florio, Roger, "Water Rights: Enforcing the Federal-Indian Trust after *Nevada v. United States*." *American Indian Law Review* 13 (1).

New Mexico v. Mescalero Apache Tribe (462 U.S. 324, 76 L.Ed. 2d 611, 103 S.Ct. 2378 [1983])

The issue of the federal pre-emption of state laws regulating hunting and fishing on the Mescalero Apache reservation for nonmembers of the Mescalero Apache Tribe of New Mexico was at issue in this Supreme Court case. Prohibited by federal law from setting hunting and fishing regulations as to Indians on the reservation, the State of New Mexico applied its regulations to nonmembers hunting and fishing on the reservation. The Mescalero Apache Tribe filed suit in the U.S. District Court for the District of New Mexico to enjoin the state from enforcing its regulations. The Court enjoined the regulations, and, on appeal, the U.S. Court of Appeals for the Tenth Circuit upheld the lower court's holding. The Supreme Court granted certiorari to hear the case. Arguments were held on 19 April 1983, with a decision being handed down on 13 June of that same year.

Speaking for a unanimous court, Justice Thurgood Marshall upheld the decision of the Court of Appeals and ruled that federal law pre-empted the application of state regulations regarding hunting and fishing on Indian reservations. Justice Marshall explained, "In this case the governing body of an Indian Tribe, working closely with the Federal Government and under the authority of federal law, has exercised its lawful authority to develop and manage the reservation's resources for the benefit of its members. The exercise of concurrent jurisdiction by the State would effectively nullify the Tribe's unquestioned authority to regulate the use of its resources by members and nonmembers, interfere with the comprehensive tribal regulatory scheme, and threaten Congress' firm commitment to the encouragement of tribal self-sufficiency and economic development. Given the strong interests favoring exclusive tribal jurisdiction and the absence of state interests which justify the assertion of concurrent authority, we conclude that the application of the State's hunting and fishing laws to the reservation is pre-empted. Accordingly, the judgment of the Court of Appeals is affirmed."

Reference Berk, Robert, "Case Notes: Indian Law—State Preempted from Enforcing Its Hunting and Fishing Regulations against Non-Indians on the Reservation—*New Mexico v. Mescalero Apache Tribe* 103 S.Ct. 2378." *Arizona State Law Journal*, 1984 (1).

The New York Indians (5 Wallace [72 U.S] 761 [1867])

In this landmark case, decided before the Supreme Court in 1867, the court held that "where Indians, being in possession of lands, their ancient and native homes, the enjoyment of which, 'without disturbance by the United States,' has been secured to them by treaty with the Federal government, with the assurance that 'the lands shall remain theirs until they choose to sell them,' the State in which the lands lie has no power to tax them, either for ordinary town and county purposes or for the special purpose of surveying them and opening roads through them." The Supreme Court reporter, William Wallace, gave this particular case its historical designation in his *Reports;* the Lawyer's Edition of the reports lists the case by its official name: *Fellows v. Denniston* (18 L.Ed. 708).

Under the treaty between New York and Massachusetts, signed in 1786, New York ceded to Massachusetts the right to preemption and estate of the four reservations of New York (Cattaraugus, Allegheny, Buffalo Creek, and Tonawanda) while leaving jurisdiction and sovereignty in New York. The treaty held that as long as the property remained part of Massachusetts, the reservations would be "exempt from all taxes whatsoever." However, in 1838, Massachusetts sold the lands to the company of Ogden & Fellows. In 1842, Ogden & Fellows handed two of the reservations, Allegheny and Cattaraugus, back to the Indians. In 1840, acting on the grounds that Massachusetts had ceded the lands, the New York legislature enacted a highway tax on the Allegheny and Cattaraugus reservations and the following year passed new taxes on these two reservations and on the Buffalo Creek reservation. Fellows (Ogden had died) then sued Denniston, the controller of the state of New York, to enjoin him from collecting the taxes. The New York supreme court held for Denniston and the state court of appeals affirmed. The U.S. Supreme Court agreed to hear the case.

Justice Samuel Nelson then held for a unanimous court in holding the state tax on the Indians to be unconstitutional. Justice Nelson wrote simply, "We have already given the answer which we think satisfactory to this ground in support of the judgment below. Until the Indians have sold their lands, and removed from them in pursuance of the treaty stipulations, they are to be regarded as still in their ancient possessions, and are in under their original rights, and entitled to the undisturbed enjoyment of them. This was the effect of the decision in the case of *Fellows v. Blacksmith*." The basis for this case in constitutional law was upheld by the high court in *United States v. Kagama* in 1886.

See also *Fellows v. Blacksmith*; The Kansas Indians.

Reference "Petition of Henry Beard on Behalf of the New York Indians, Feb. 21, 1825, referred to the Committee on Indian Affairs." Records of the House of Representatives, RG 233, Committee on Indian Affairs, file HR 18A-F7.1, folder 1.

New York ex rel. Kennedy v. Becker (241 U.S. 556 [1916])

Known officially as *People of the State of New York in the relation of Walter S. Kennedy, as Next Friend of Fayette Kennedy, Warren Kennedy, and Willis White, Jr., Plaintiffs in Error, v. Frederick W. Becker, as Sheriff of Erie County, New York*, this 1916 Supreme Court case dealt with the treaty-granted rights of Indians to fish on waters outside reservations. Fayette Kennedy, Warren Kennedy, and Willis White, Jr., three Seneca Indians of the Cattaraugus reservation in Erie County, New York, were arrested for spearing fish in Eighteen Mile Creek, outside of the reservation, in violation of state conservation laws. A justice of the peace committed them to the custody of Frederick W. Becker, the Sheriff for Erie County, New York; however, the state supreme court ordered them released, declaring that an Indian treaty signed in 1797 allowed the Indians to fish "in the waters on and in said lands." This pact, the "Treaty of the Big Tree" (7 Stat. 601), was signed on 15 September 1797 and conveyed from the Seneca Indians to one Robert Morris a share of their lands in exchange for money and a promise that they could fish the waters on the lands in the future. The appellate division of the state supreme court reversed the order, and the New York State court of appeals affirmed that judgment. The U.S. Supreme Court agreed to hear the case to decide the applicability of the state conservation law. Chief Justice Edward Douglass White held on 12 June 1916 that the state's interest in conservation outweighed the Indians' interest in fishing on lands that did not belong to their reservation. Chief Justice White added in his opinion that the court was not at that time deciding the question of whether such state laws could be applied fairly to conservation *on* Indian reservations.

Nichols, John Ralph (1898–1968)

Known better as a missionary to Africa, as well as an educator and administrator, John R. Nichols served as the thirty-fifth commissioner of Indian Affairs from 1949 to 1950. Born in New York City on 19 September 1898, he earned a bachelor of science degree from the Oregon State Agricultural College in 1922, a master's degree in education from Stanford University in 1925, a Ph.D. in educational administration from Stanford in 1930, and a master's degree in international administration from Columbia University in 1943. From 1934 until 1947 he was an administrator in the University of Idaho system, including serving as president of the Idaho State College at Pocatello and executive dean of the southern branch of the University of Idaho. From 1947 to 1949 he was president of the New Mexico College of Agriculture and Mechanical Arts.

In 1948, Nichols was a member of the Commission on Organization of the Executive Branch of the Government, also known as the Hoover Commission. In October of that year, the commission released its report on the Indian Service, which called for the rapid assimilation of Indians into mainstream American society. On 10 March 1949, President Harry S Truman tapped Nichols to fill the position of commissioner of Indian Affairs, vacant since June 1948 when William A. Brophy resigned because of poor health, to put into play some of the Hoover Commission's recommendations. In a memorandum on the "Qualifications of Mr. John Ralph Nichols as Commissioner of Indian Affairs," Secretary of the Interior Julius Krug discusses Nichols' credentials for the commissioner's post. "Mr. Nichols has had extensive experience in the education field, which is one of the most important of the activities of the Indian Service, and is fundamental to carrying out the Administration's long-term policies with respect to the Indians," Krug wrote. To President Truman, he penned, "I believe that he would do a creditable job as Commissioner." According to one newspaper, "The Interior Department's Advisory Committee on Indian Affairs unanimously recommended him [Nichols] for the job. Oliver La Farge, committee chairman, told reporters the committee regarded Dr. Nichols as the best qualified candidate for the position." Historian James E. Officer writes, "[Nichols] remained in the office only eleven months, but in his annual report for 1949 he clearly favored withdrawal of the federal government from its special role in Indian Affairs as rapidly as the tribes could be prepared to take over. He cited two instances—those of the Stockbridge-Munsee of Wisconsin and the Saginaw Chippewa of Michigan—wherein tribes organized under the Indian Reorganization Act had requested withdrawal of the Interior Department from supervision of certain of their affairs. Although Nichols obviously viewed these as cases that he would have classified under the heading of 'termination,' they much more closely resemble what we today describe as 'self-determination.' Midway through Nichols' abbreviated term, Congress enacted legislation transferring civil and criminal jurisdiction over the Agua Caliente reservation at Palm Springs to the state of California. From this point on, as an important aspect of preparing tribes for termination, the legislators would give special attention to matters involving jurisdiction." After less that a year as commissioner, Nichols surprisingly resigned. In his letter of resignation, he wrote, "I have served under your appointment as Commissioner of Indian Affairs for nearly a year, but after full consideration of my future long-range plans I have reluctantly reached the conclusion that I should relinquish this post at an early date. I am, therefore, tendering my resignation to be effective at your pleasure."

John Nichols is among the few commissioners whose career outside of the Indian office is better known than his term in the custody of that bureau. From 1952 to 1953 he was director of technical cooperation at the U.S. Embassy in Cairo, Egypt, and simultaneously served as director of the educational and training staff of the Foreign Operations Administration. After a period of time with an animal husbandry farm in California, he joined the Near East Foundation, serving as director of the foundation's Project for Africa (he was a coordinator of cultural activities in such nations as Upper Volta, Tanzania, Kenya, Cameroon, and Niger) from 1965 until his death. He died in New York City on 5 May 1968 at the age of 69.

See also Bureau of Indian Affairs; Hoover Commission Report.

References Dennehy, William J., "John Ralph Nichols." In Robert M. Kvasnicka and Herman J. Viola, eds., *The Commissioners of Indian Affairs, 1824–1977* (1979), 289–92; "Dr. John Nichols of Aid Foundation." *New York Times*, 7 May 1968, 41; Nichols to Truman, 20 March 1950, Papers of Harry S Truman, Official File, Harry S Truman Library, Independence, Missouri; Philp, Kenneth R., ed., *Indian Self-Rule: First-Hand Accounts of Indian-White Relations from Roosevelt to Reagan* (1986); "Qualifications of Mr. John Ralph Nichols as Commissioner of Indian Affairs," 24 February 1949, Harry S Truman Papers, Official File, Harry S Truman Library, Independence, Missouri; Secretary Krug to President Harry S Truman, Papers of Harry S Truman, Official File.

Nixon, Richard Milhous—Message on Indian Affairs

On 8 July 1970, President Richard M. Nixon sent to Congress a special message on Indian Affairs. Nixon actively pursued an interest in the concerns of American Indians following his election to the presidency in November 1968. At that time, as president-elect, he requested that Indian scholar and historian Alvin M. Josephy, Jr., articulate those matters important to Indians that Josephy felt should be addressed by the new administration. Josephy's report, *The American Indian and the Bureau of Indian Affairs: A Study with Recommendations*, was delivered to the president on 11 February 1969, and was the basis of Nixon's special message. In the preamble of the message, Nixon wrote:

To the Congress of the United States: The first Americans—the Indians—are the most deprived and most isolated minority group in our nation. On virtually every scale of measurement—employment, income, education, health—the condition of the Indian people ranks at the bottom.

This condition is the heritage of centuries of injustice. From the time of their first contact with European settlers, the American Indians have been oppressed and brutalized, deprived of their ancestral lands and denied the opportunity to control their own destiny. Even the Federal programs which are intended to meet their needs have frequently proven to be ineffective and demeaning.

But the story of the Indian in America is something more than the record of the white man's frequent aggression, broken agreements, intermittent remorse and prolonged failure. It is a record also of endurance, of survival, of adaptation and creativity in the face of overwhelming obstacles. It is a record of enormous contributions to this country—to its art and culture, to its strength and spirit, to its sense of history and its sense of purpose.

It is long past time that the Indian policies of the Federal government began to recognize and build upon the capacities and insights of the Indian people. Both as a matter of justice and as a matter of enlightened social policy, we must begin to act on the basis of what the Indians themselves have long been telling us. The time has come to break decisively with the past and to create the conditions for a new era in which the Indian future is determined by Indian acts and Indian decisions.

In the other parts of the message, Nixon discussed "Self-Determination without Termination," "The Right [of the Indians] to Control and Operate Federal Programs," "Indian Education," "Economic Development Legislation," "More Money for Indian Health," and "Helping Urban Indians" The president also called for the establishment of an Indian Trust Counsel Authority "to assure independent legal representation for the Indians' natural resource rights." To conclude the message, Nixon wrote:

The recommendations of this Administration represent an historic step forward in Indian policy. We are proposing to break sharply with past approaches to Indian problems. In place of a long series of piecemeal reforms, we suggest a new and coherent strategy. In place of policies which simply call for more spending, we suggest policies which simply call for wiser spending. In place of policies which oscillate between the deadly extremes of forced termination and constant paternalism, we suggest a policy in which the Federal government and the Indian community play complementary roles.

But most importantly, we have turned from the question of whether the Federal government has a responsibility to Indians to the question of how that responsibility can best be fulfilled. We have concluded that the Indians will get better programs and that public monies will be more effectively expended if the people who are most affected by these programs are responsible for operating them.

The Indians of America need Federal assistance—this much has long been clear. What has not always been clear, however, is that the Federal government needs Indians energies and Indian leadership if assistance is to be effective in improving the conditions of Indian life. It is a new and balanced relationship between the United States government and the first Americans that is at the heart of our approach to Indian problems. And that is why we now approach these problems with new confidence that they will successfully be overcome.

See also Josephy Report.

Reference *Public Papers of the Presidents of the United States: Richard Nixon, Containing the Public Messages, Speeches, and Statements of the President, 1970* (1971).

Nofire et al. v. United States (164 U.S. 657 [1897])

In this landmark case, the Supreme Court held that "the jurisdiction of the courts of the Cherokee Nation over offenses committed by one Indian upon the person of another includes not only Indians by birth, but also citizens of the Nation by adoption." Defendants Nofire and his accomplice (who was not named in the opinion) were full-blooded Cherokee Indians indicted and convicted in the Circuit Court for the Western District of Arkansas for the murder in 1895 of one Fred Rutherford, a white man who it was shown was married to a Cherokee in 1894 and was subsequently adopted into the tribe. Nofire and his accomplice challenged the jurisdiction of the court trying them, on the grounds that because Rutherford was an adopted Indian, they should be tried by a tribal court only. Upon conviction, Nofire and his unnamed cohort appealed directly to the U.S. Supreme Court for a dismissal of the charges. The only question before the court was whether Rutherford was an "adopted" member of the Cherokee Nation. In documents reproduced in the opinion, it was shown that according to Cherokee law, "it is evident that Rutherford intended to change his nationality, and become a Cherokee citizen." Thus, Justice David Josiah Brewer held for a unanimous court on 4 January 1897, in dismissing the two convictions, that "the jurisdiction over the offense charged herein is, by the laws of the United States and treaties with the Cherokee Nation, vested in the courts of that nation."

Northern Pacific Railway Company v. Wismer (246 U.S. 283, 62 L.Ed. 716, 38 S.Ct. 240 [1918])

The decisions made by the commissioner of the Bureau of Indian Affairs in the area of the creation of Indian reservations have the same standing as those made by the secretary of the interior, the Supreme Court held in this 1918 decision. An act of Congress of 2 July 1864 (13 Stat. 365) granted the Northern Pacific Railway a right-of-way through several miles of land, in what was then Washington Territory, to the Pacific Ocean. In 1880, the railroad finally picked a parcel of land. Prior to 1877, the Spokane Indians of Washington Territory were among a number of tribes that roamed across the eastern portion of what is now Washington State, and at that time were finding themselves in conflicts with white settlers. On 7 May 1877, Commissioner of Indian Affairs John Quincy Smith directed Col. E.C. Watkins to meet with these Indians and place them, with their consent, on a reservation. After a meeting with Watkins and the chiefs of the Spokane tribe on 16, 17, and 18 August 1877 at Spokane Falls, the Indians agreed to settle on a reservation. On 23 August, Col. Watkins sent to Commissioner Smith the executed agreement; because Smith left office the next month, it was up to newly installed Commissioner Ezra A. Hayt to transmit the agreement to Secretary of the Interior Carl Schurz, who sent it to the Senate on 23 January 1878. The Spokanes settled on the reservation and remained at peace with the United States. An act of Congress of 29 May 1908 (35 Stat. 458) directed the secretary of the interior to divide up the reservation into allotments, with all surplus land to be sold as public lands, and those proceeds to be placed in the Treasury to the credit of the Spokane tribe. In 1913, George F. Wismer purchased one of the lots of unallotted lands, lands which happened to cross onto the lands of the railroad. The railroad then sued to eject Wismer (who later died, making his widow, Emma A. Wismer, the defendant in error) from the land. The District Court for the District of Washington held for Wismer and the U.S. Court of Appeals for the Ninth Circuit affirmed. The railroad sued for relief to U.S. Supreme Court. Justice John Hessin Clarke held for a unanimous court on 4 March 1918 that the commissioner of Indian Affairs' decision to negotiate and reach an agreement with the Spokanes, even without the explicit approval of the secretary of the interior, carried the same power as if the secretary himself had given his approval. Further, argued Justice Clarke, the granting of the reservation to the Indians in 1877 closed the lands from the railroad's use.

Northwestern Bands of Shoshone Indians v. United States (324 U.S. 335 [1945])

In this case, the Supreme Court held that a treaty between the United States and an Indian tribe which established a reservation did not create a title of occupancy for that tribe, and they cannot be awarded damages by the government for the extinguishment of their hold over those lands. Under an act of Congress of 28 February 1929 (45 Stat. 1407), the Congress conferred upon the Court of Claims the authority to settle a dispute between the Northwestern Bands of Shoshone of Utah and the United States. The Indians claimed that the Treaty of Box Elder, signed 30 July 1863, bestowed upon the tribe the right to the title of their lands. When the United States government took 15 million acres of this land, the Indians sought from the Court of Claims a judgment of $15 million. The court dismissed the claim and the Supreme Court granted certiorari. Justice Stanley Reed wrote the court's opinion for the 5–4 decision (Justices Frank Murphy, William O. Douglas, Felix Frankfurter, and Owen Roberts dissenting) in upholding the Court of Claims decision. Justice Reed wrote, "Since *Johnson v. McIntosh*, 8 Wheat. 543, 5 L.Ed. 681, decided in 1823, have rationalization to the appropriation of Indian lands to the white man's government, the extinguishment of Indian title by that sovereignty had proceeded, as a political matter, without any admitted legal responsibility in the sovereign to compensate the Indian for his loss. Exclusive title to the lands passed to the white discoverers, subject to the Indian title with power in the white sovereign alone to extinguish that right by 'purchase or by conquest.'" He added, "It seems to us clear from the circumstances leading up to and following the execution of the Box Elder Treaty that the parties did not intend to recognize or acknowledge by that treaty the Indian title to the lands in question. Whether the lands were in fact held by the Shoshones by Indian title from occupancy or otherwise or what rights flow to the Indians from such title is not involved. Since the rights, if any the Shoshones have, did not arise under or grow out of the Box Elder treaty, no recovery may be had under the jurisdictional act. Affirmed." The Supreme Court then twice denied the Shoshones a rehearing (324 U.S. 890 [1945]; 325 U.S. 840 [1945]).

Oakes, Richard
See Alcatraz, Occupation of.

Oberly, John Hemphill (1837–1899)
Twenty-third Commissioner of Indian Affairs, John H. Oberly served only from 1888 to 1889, leaving little imprint on national Indian policy. Born in Cincinnati, Ohio, probably in January 1837, he was the son of John Oberly and Mary (née Hemphill) Oberly. According to biographer Floyd A. O'Neil, Oberly "spent most of his active career in Illinois, where he engaged in newspaper work. He started the *Cairo Bulletin*, a daily paper at Cairo, Illinois, in 1867, and later owned the *Wayne County Democrat.* Turning to politics, he was elected to the state legislature in 1880 and served as chairman of the Democratic executive committee in 1884. In that year he went to Albany, New York, as a staff contributor on the *Chicago Times.* It was there that he came to the attention of Governor Grover Cleveland." However, according to the *Civil Service Journal*, a publication associated with the civil service reform movement, Oberly's career had a different beginning. "At the beginning of the war, he was editing and publishing a Democratic newspaper in Memphis, Tennessee, in which he advocated vigorously the integrity of the Union; and he now bears a number of scars from wounds received in three or four hand to hand encounters with the apostles of disunion. As a member of the Illinois legislature in 1873–74, he introduced and was prominent in securing the passage of the important measures which now constitute the chief part of the statutory railroad law of that State; and, in 1876, he was appointed, by Governor [Shelby] Cullom, one of the Railroad and Warehouse Commissioners of Illinois." In 1885, with the help of the new president, he was appointed Superintendent of Indian Schools, and, according to one source, "was instrumental in reorganizing them." According to *Harper's Weekly*, he was transferred to the United States Civil Service Commission on 17 April 1886.

On 26 September 1888, Cleveland nominated Oberly for the Indian Affairs post. The *New York Times*, in its edition the next day, headlined "Mr. Oberly Transferred: To Be Commissioner of Indian Affairs...A Great Loss to the Civil Service Commission." "President Cleveland will now have to look for a Civil Service Commissioner to succeed Mr. John H. Oberly, for to-day Mr. Oberly was nominated by the Senate for Commissioner of Indian Affairs in the place of Commissioner [John DeWitt Clinton] Atkins," the paper announced in a somewhat morose tone. "The latter resigned some time ago in order to devote himself to the task of defeating Senator Isham G. Harris in the race for a seat in the Senate from Tennessee. Nobody interested in the matter is surprised at the President's selection of Mr. Oberly. The only doubt about it from the start has been the fact that Mr. Oberly has made such an excellent Civil Service Commissioner that the President has been loth [*sic*] to make a change. Mr. Oberly's value on the Civil Service Commission has been recognized and admitted by all friends of the merit system, who know that to him and to Commissioner [Charles] Lyman belong the credit for the steady growth of the reform which it is the Commission's special duty to foster." Approved by the Senate, Oberly took charge of the bureau on 10 October 1888.

As commissioner, Oberly contributed a single annual report, in 1888. In the essay, prepared quite hastily (it was released on 3 December 1888, seven weeks after Oberly assumed the position as commissioner), its most important section detailed the rise in appropriations for Indian office operations, including those allocations for fulfilling treaties with Indian tribes permanently, and for the support of Indian schools. Oberly penned, "I have no doubt that under the favorable conditions of an Indian service in which the evils of what is known as the party spoils system of appointment and dismissal would be minimized and in which intelligent and zealous action might confidently anticipate the support of the Government, in which, too, devotion and efficiency might labor, assured of the applause of the people, and honest administration do its perfect work promptly on all occasions without rebuke or fear or prosecution." The *New York Times* reported that "the Commissioner favors the extension of the provisions of the civil service law to the Indian service, and says that he would advise that its extension be made immediately if he were not fearful that, if taken now [the Democrats had just lost the presidential election], it would be robbed of much of its effectiveness by being attributed to partisan motives."

One of the Oberly's strongest critics may have been editor George Bird Grinnell. Historian William T. Hagan, in discussing Theodore Roosevelt's relationship with Herbert Welsh, founder of the Indian Rights Association, who wanted Roosevelt to help push for Indian reform, writes, "Although Welsh contacted Roosevelt immediately after the latter's become Civil Service commissioner, it took a year and a half for the relationship to solidify. Indeed, it got off to a poor start. In May 1889, Welsh was in the midst of a campaign to ensure the retention, by newly elected President Benjamin Harrison, of Commissioner of Indian Affairs John H. Oberly, a Cleveland appointee. Roosevelt responded to Welsh's request for help by telling him that he would not oppose Oberly, but neither could he support him. Roosevelt had been prejudiced against Oberly by George Bird Grinnell, the editor of *Forest and Stream* and a student of Indians, who objected to Oberly's failure to remove an incompetent Indian agent."

Oberly's short tenure in office in which he did not demonstrably change national Indian policy was marked for termination when President Cleveland was defeated for reelection in 1888. The Indian commissioner submitted his resignation on 6 June 1889, and left office on 30 June. He did not return to politics. Instead, he went back to journalism, going to work for the *Daily People and Patriot*, a Democratic newspaper in Concord, New Hampshire. Oberly died there on 15 April 1899, and his body was returned to Washington, D.C., for burial.

See also Atkins, John DeWitt Clinton; Bureau of Indian Affairs.

References *Fifty United States Civil Service Commissioners: Biographical Sketches, Biographical Sources, Writings* (1971); Hagan, William T., "Civil Service Commissioner Theodore Roosevelt and the Indian Rights Association." *Pacific Historical Review*, 44: 189–90; "Indian Service Reform: Commissioner Oberly Suggests Some Changes." *New York Times*, 14 January 1889, 2; "Mr. Oberly Transferred." *New York Times*, 27 September 1888, 1; O'Neil, Floyd A., "John H. Oberly." In Robert M. Kvasnicka and Herman J. Viola, eds., *The Commissioners of Indian Affairs, 1824–1977* (1979); U.S. Civil Service Commission, *Sixth Report of the United States Civil Service Commission* (1 July 1888–30 June 1889); U.S. Congress, House of Representatives, *Annual Report of the Commissioner of Indian Affairs for the Year 1888*, House Executive Document No. 1, 50th Congress, 2d Session (serial 2637); Untitled article, *Harper's Weekly* 30 (1527) (27 March 1886).

Occom, Samson (Mohegan) (1723–1792)

Samson Occom (or Occum) was, as one source noted, "certainly not the last of the Mohegans," but he was the first Native American to write and publish a work in the English language and a noted preacher of his time. He was born in 1723, the son of Joshua Tomockham (also spelled Ockham or Aucum) and Sarah, who, Indian historian A. LaVonne Brown Ruoff relates, "was reputed to descend from the famous Mohegan chief Uncas." Joshua was also known as "The Great Hunter," while Occom's brother Jonathan served in both the French and Indian War and the Revolutionary War. Discovered in the archives of Dartmouth College in 1982, Occom's "autobiography," a short text of ten pages on his life written in Boston and dated 28 November 1765, was first published in Bernd Peyer's *The Elders Wrote: An Anthology of Early Prose by North American Indians, 1768–1931* (1982). As Occom related, "I was Born a Heathen and Brought up in Heathenism, till I was between 16 & 17 years of age, at a place Calld Mohegan, in New London, Connecticut, in New England. My Parents Livd a wandering life, for did all the Indians at Mohegan, they Chiefly Depended upon

Hunting, Fishing & Fowling for their Living and had no Connection with the English, excepting to Traffic with them in their small Trifles; and they Strictly maintained and followed their Heathenish Ways, Customs & Religion, though there was Some Preaching among them. Once a Fortnight, in ye Summer Season, a Minister from New London used to come up, and the Indians to attend; not that they regarded the Christian Religion, but they had Blankets given to them every Fall of the Year and for these things they would attend and there was a Sort of School kept, when I was quite young, but I believe there never was one that ever Learnt to read any thing,—and when I was about 10 Years of age there was a man who went among the Indian Wigwams, and wherever he Could find the Indian Children, would make them read; but the Children Used to take Care to keep out of his way."

Occom converted to Christianity in 1741 and subsequently studied under the Episcopal minister Eleazar Wheelock at Windham, Connecticut, teachings that led him to become an instructor in 1749 among the Montauk Indians on New York's Long Island. Wheelock may be considered on his own an important figure in Indian rights during this period. With funds received from various philanthropic sources, he established Dartmouth College in New Hampshire as the first major institution of higher learning in the colonies for the education of Native Americans. For two decades, Occom and Wheelock worked on demonstrating Wheelock's Indian Charity School as a formative organization for Indian education. The two men split over Wheelock's paternalism and Occom's overt pride in his race.

In 1772, Occom was asked to speak to a crowd on the occasion of the execution of Moses Paul, an Indian who while drunk had murdered a white man. Occom used the opportunity to lecture the whites on the evils of alcohol—particularly on its pernicious effects among the Indians, and he condemned the whites for providing it. The strength of Occom's discourse was so powerful that it was published later that year as "A Sermon Preached at the Execution of Moses Paul, an Indian Who was Executed at New Haven on the 2d of September 1772 for the Murder of Mr. Moses Cook, late of Waterbury, on the 7th of December 1771, Preached at the Desire of Said Paul by Samson Occom, Minister of the Gospel and Missionary to the Indians, New Haven, 1772." This was the first English work published by a Native American. Occom followed the work with two hymnals: *Awaked by Sinai's Awful Sound* and *Now the Shades of Night are Gone*, both published in 1774.

After these works appeared, Occom and his wife Mary Fowler Occom, one of his students at Wheelock's Indian Charity School, settled down with their children in the Stockbridge Oneida community in New York. He spent the rest of his life defending Oneida land rights and writing. It was just after completing a passage for an article that he collapsed at his desk and died on 14 July 1792 at the age of 69.

References Occom, Samson, "A Short Narrative of My Life." In Arnold Krupat, ed., *Native American Autobiography: An Anthology* (1994); Ruoff, A. LaVonne Brown, "On Literature in English: American Indian Authors, 1774–1899." In Andrew Wiget, *Critical Essays on Native American Literature* (1985); Waldman, Henry, et al., eds., *Dictionary of Indians of North America* (1978); Welburn, Ron, "Occom, Samson." In Sharon Malinowski, ed., *Notable Native Americans* (1995).

Office of Indian Education

This division of the Department of Education, established by Congress in the Indian Education Act of 1972 (86 Stat. 235, 334–345), "oversees funding distribution for special programs designed to provide educational opportunities for Indian children and adults, and to address culturally related academic needs of Indian children."

See also Indian Education Act of 1972.

Reference Utter, Jack, *American Indians: Answers to Today's Questions* (1993).

Oglala Civil Rights Organization

See Wounded Knee (1973).

Oklahoma Indian Welfare Act of 1936 (49 Stat. 1967)

Known by its official name, the Thomas-Rogers Act, this legislation of 26 June 1936 officially extended the provisions of the Indian Reorganization Act of 1934 to the Native Americans of Oklahoma, who had resisted being brought into the jurisdiction of the 1934 act. Titled "An Act to Promote the General Welfare of the Indians of the State of Oklahoma, and for other purposes," the most pertinent section reads:

Sec. 3. Any recognized tribe or band of Indians residing in Oklahoma shall have the right to organize for its common welfare and to adopt a constitution and bylaws, under such rules and regulations as the Secretary of the Interior shall prescribe. The Secretary of the Interior may issue to any such organized group a charter of incorporation, which shall become operative when ratified by a majority vote of the adult members of the organization voting: Provided, however, That such election shall be void unless the total vote cast be at least 30 per centum of those entitled to vote. Such charter may convey to the incorporated group, in addition to any powers which may properly be vested in a body corporate under the laws of the State of Oklahoma, the right to participate in the revolving credit fund and to enjoy any other rights or privileges secured to an organized Indian tribe under the Act of June 18, 1934 (48 Stat. 984): Provided, That the corporate funds of any such chartered group may be deposited in any national bank within the State of Oklahoma or otherwise invested, utilized, or disbursed in accordance with the terms of the corporate charter.

Oklahoma Tax Commission v. Citizen Band Potawatomi Indian Tribe of Oklahoma (498 U.S. 505, 112 L.Ed. 2d 1112, 111 S.Ct. 905 [1991])

A state was empowered to collect taxes on the sales of cigarettes to non-Indians on Indian reservations, but Indians themselves were immune from such taxes, even though that state had not asserted jurisdiction over the Indians as per Public Law 280. In 1987, the petitioner, the Oklahoma Tax Commission, presented the Potawatomi Indian tribe of that state with a bill for $2.7 million, taxes on cigarettes to non-Indians that the state claimed the Indians did not collect. After the Indians sued to enjoin enforcement of the claim, the state countersued, asking that the Indians be forced to stop selling cigarettes until they paid the taxes on future sales to non-Indians. The district court subsequently found that the Indians were immune from such suits by the state and thus could not be fined directly for the unpaid taxes, but that the tribe must tax nonmembers and submit those funds to the state. The United States Court of Appeals for the Tenth Circuit reversed, claiming that the state lacked any authority to tax any sale that occurred on reservations. Wishing to hear the questions in the controversy, the U.S. Supreme Court granted certiorari, holding arguments in the case on 7 January 1991. In handing down its decision less than two months later, on 26 February, Chief Justice William H. Rehnquist spoke for a unanimous court (Justice John Paul Stevens concurred; however, he agreed on different grounds and issued his own opinion) in holding that while the tribe was immune from paying the past taxes directly, it was not exempt from collecting the taxes on nonmembers as to future sales. On this second point, Chief Justice Rehnquist opined, "Although the doctrine of tribal sovereign immunity applies to the Potawatomis, that doctrine does not excuse a tribe from all obligations to assist in the collection of validly imposed state sales taxes…Oklahoma argued that the Potawatomis' tribal immunity notwithstanding, it has the authority to tax sales of cigarettes to nonmembers of the Tribe at the Tribe's convenience store. We agree." The Chief Justice also argued that even though the state did not assert its authority over Indian Affairs as per Public Law 280, the tribe was not immune from being forced to collect taxes on nonmembers.

See also *Department of Taxation and Finance of New York et al. v. Milhelm Attea & Bros., Inc., etc. et al.*

Oklahoma Tax Commission v. Sac and Fox Nation (508 U.S.-, 124 L.Ed. 2d 30, 113 S.Ct. 1985 [1993])

In this Supreme Court case, it was held that states were without jurisdiction, absent explicit congressional authority, to tax members of an Indian tribe living on a reservation. The Sac and Fox Nation of Oklahoma moved in the District Court for the Western District of Oklahoma to enjoin, or stop, the state from collecting taxes on 1) income of Indians working on the reservation, as well as nonmembers working on the reservation, and 2) motor vehicles owned and operated by reservation members who live and work on the reservation under the tribe's jurisdiction. The tribe itself imposed these taxes, and claimed such state imposition would amount to double taxation. The state contended that under Oklahoma law, all persons residing in the state who received income in the state were subject to state income taxes, as well as an excise tax on all transfers of ownership of vehicles or use of vehicles registered in the state. Further, it argued, an 1891 treaty disestablished the reservation, making none of its present lands "Indian country." The district court found that the state could tax the income earned by non-Indian members on trust lands, but not that of tribal members on those same lands, and that the state could not have as a prerequisite the payment of excise taxes before issuing a state vehicle title. Both sides appealed to the Tenth Circuit Court of Appeals, which upheld the judgments. The U.S. Supreme Court agreed to hear the case, and arguments in the matter were heard on 23 March 1993.

On 17 May of that same year, Justice Sandra Day O'Connor, speaking for a unanimous court, struck down the state taxes on tribal members as being outside the parameter of state action, but upheld those on nonmembers. Justice O'Connor, in a lengthy explanation of what is Indian country and what is not, angrily dismissed the arguments of the Oklahoma Tax Commission, which had been before the court in 1991 with a similar case against a different Indian tribe. She wrote,

> To determine whether a tribal member is exempt from state income taxes under *McClanahan* [*McClanahan, etc. v. State Tax Commission of Arizona* (411 U.S. 164, 36 L.Ed. 2d 129, 93 S.Ct. 1257) [1973])], a court first must determine the residence of the tribal member. To the extent that the Court of Appeals ruled without such a reference, it erred. The Commission, however, contends that the relevant boundary for taxing jurisdiction is the perimeter of a formal reservation, not merely land set aside for a tribe or its members. In the Commission's view, Indian sovereignty serves as a "backdrop" only for those tribal members who live on the reservation, and all others fall outside McClanahan's presumption against taxation. It is true that we began our discussion in McClanahan by emphasizing that we were not "dealing with Indians who have left or never inhabited reservations set aside for their exclusive use or who do not possess the usual accoutrements of tribal self-government." [Opinion], at 167–68, 36 L.Ed. 2d 129, 93 S.Ct. 1257. Here, in contrast, some of the Tribe's members may not live within a reservation; indeed, if the Commission's interpretation of the 1891 Treaty is correct and the Reservation was disestablished, none do... Nonetheless, in *Oklahoma Tax Commission v. Citizen Band Potawatomi Indian Tribe of Oklahoma* [498 U.S. 505, 112 L.Ed. 2d 1112, 111 S.Ct. 905 [1991]], we rejected precisely the same argument—and from precisely the same litigant. There the Commission contended that even if the State did not have jurisdiction to tax cigarette sales to tribal members on the reservation, it had jurisdiction to tax sales by a tribal convenience store located outside the reservation on land held in trust for the Potawatomi. 498 U.S., at 511, 112 L.Ed. 2d 1112, 111 S.Ct. 905. We noted that we have never drawn the distinction

Oklahoma urged. Instead, we ask only whether the land is Indian country. . . Absent explicit congressional direction to the contrary, we presume against a State's having the jurisdiction to tax within Indian country, whether the particular territory consists of a formal or informal reservation, allotted lands, or dependent Indian communities. Because the Court of Appeals did not determine whether the tribal members on whom Oklahoma attempts to impose income and motor vehicle taxes live within Indian country, its judgment is vacated. We remand this case for further proceedings consistent with this opinion.

See also *McClanahan, etc. v. State Tax Commission of Arizona*; *Oklahoma Tax Commission v. Citizen Band Potawatomi Indian Tribe of Oklahoma.*

Oklahoma Tax Commission v. United States (319 U.S. 598, 87 L.Ed. 1612, 63 S.Ct. 1284 [1943])

Congressional intent to leave Indian estates free of state taxation as to inheritance was the issue of this Supreme Court case, decided in 1943. Three separate cases came before the court, and were consolidated. In their decision, the justices held 5–4 that "where restricted Indian lands, exempt from direct taxation [by the state], were exempt from state inheritance taxes but personal property[,] cash and securities were subject to state inheritance taxes, judgment and insurance policy which constituted part of [the] estate of [a] deceased Indian were to be treated in a class with the 'personal property' and 'cash and securities' and were subject to state inheritance taxes." The opinion of the court, delivered by Justice Hugo Black on 14 June 1943, with Chief Justice Harlan Fiske Stone joined by Justices Frank Murphy, Stanley Reed, and Felix Frankfurter in dissent, did not identify the parties involved in this litigation. The majority did find that the act of Congress of 27 January 1933 (47 Stat. 777), introduced in the House of Representatives by Representative William Wirt Hastings of Oklahoma, did not "exempt Indians' cash and securities from Oklahoma's estate taxes."

Oliphant and Belgarde v. The Suquamish Indian Tribe et al. (435 U.S. 191, 55 L.Ed. 2d 209, 98 S.Ct. 1011 [1978])

As the Supreme Court summary in this decision declared, "this case presented the question whether Indian tribal courts have inherent criminal jurisdiction over non-Indians." Appellants-defendants Mark David Oliphant and Daniel B. Belgarde, both non-Indians, were arrested for nonviolent offenses on Indian tribal land. When the Suquamish Indian Tribal Court announced its intention to try the two men in separate actions, they appealed for relief from the U.S. District Court for the Western District of Washington State, on the grounds that the tribal court did not have jurisdiction over their cases. The Indians, answering the charge, cited the case of *Morton v. Mancari* (417 U.S. 535, 41 L.Ed. 290, 94 S.Ct. 2474 [1974]), which described Indian tribes as "quasi-sovereign entities." Agreeing with the tribe, the district court refused to grant the appellants relief. On appeal, the U.S. Court of Appeals for the Ninth Circuit upheld the denial in one case; however, on hearing the question, the U.S. Supreme Court granted certiorari (the right to hear the cases) in both situations. Arguments were held on 9 January 1978. On 6 March 1978, the Supreme Court delivered its opinion: by a 6–2 vote (Justice William Brennan did not participate), the court held that Indian tribal courts, because of the limited power given to reservations by Congress, did not have the jurisdiction to try non-Indians for offenses committed on Indian land. Writing for the court was Justice William Rehnquist, joined by Justices Byron White, John Paul Stevens, Potter Stewart, Harry Blackmun, and Lewis Powell, Jr. In the decision, Rehnquist cited *In re Mayfield* (141 U.S. 107 [1891]), in which the court confirmed Congress' power to "reserve jurisdiction over non-Indians for the federal courts." In *Oliphant*, Rehnquist stated that "while Congress never expressly forbade Indian tribes to impose criminal penalties on non-Indians, we now express our implicit conclusion of nearly a century ago that Congress consistently believed this to be the necessary result of its repeated legislative actions." Chief Justice Warren Burger, along with Justice Thurgood Marshall, dissented.

Oneida Indian Nation of New York State et al. v. County of Oneida, New York (414 U.S. 661, 39 L.Ed. 2d 73, 94 S.Ct. 772 [1974])

The first of two cases involving the Oneida Indian Nation of New York and the county of Oneida, New York, Oneida dealt with the narrow issue of whether a federal issue was involved in a land cession case. The Oneida Nation of Indians ceded to the State of New York some 5 million acres, with about 300,000 being reserved for a reservation for the Oneidas. The Indians then ceded a strip of its reservation lands in 1795. In 1970, the Oneidas of New York and the Oneidas of Wisconsin sued to have damages awarded for the taking of these lands and their use by the counties of Oneida and Madison, New York, on the grounds that the Nonintercourse Act of 1790 (1 Stat. 137) prohibited any cession of land from Indians without approval and consent from the United States. The district court dismissed the suit, claiming that the issue was a state question, not a federal one. The United States Court of Appeals for the Second Circuit affirmed, holding that the issue was one dealing with the illegal possession of property under state law. The U.S. Supreme Court, granting certiorari, agreed to hear the appeal. Arguments were held on 6 and 7 November 1973, with the case being decided on 21 January 1974. Speaking for a unanimous court, Justice Byron White held that under 28 U.S.C. 1331, which confers jurisdiction to federal district courts of cases rising from constitutional questions and laws, and treaties, and 28 U.S.C. 1362, which confers federal jurisdiction on federal district courts in all cases involving Indian tribes where the controversy is in regards to constitutional questions or treaties, the issues in this case must be resolved in federal court. The case was then remanded for further consideration. The issues in this case came before the court again the case of *County of Oneida, New York et al. v. Oneida Indian Nation of New York State et al.*

See also *County of Oneida, New York et al., v. Oneida Indian Nation of New York State et al.*

Oregon Department of Fish and Wildlife et al. v. Klamath Indian Tribe (473 U.S. 753, 87 L.Ed. 2d 542, 105 S.Ct. 3420 [1985])

The question involving the cession of Indian lands and whether states can institute regulations on those ceded lands was at issue in this Supreme Court case. The Klamath Indians of Oregon signed the Treaty of 14 October 1864 (ratified by the U.S. Senate on 2 July 1866, it was proclaimed by President Ulysses S Grant on 17 February 1870), which created a reservation for that tribe, and secured to the tribe "the exclusive right of taking fish in the streams and lakes, included in said reservation." In 1901, the Klamaths, through the 1901 Cession Agreement, ceded certain lands to the United States. In 1982, the tribe filed a claim against the State of Oregon's Department of Fish and Wildlife for interfering with the fishing rights of members fishing on the lands ceded in the 1901 agreement. The District Court for the District of Oregon held for the tribe, ruling that the 1901 agreement did not abrogate Indian rights to fish and hunt on those lands. On appeal, the United States Court of Appeals for the Ninth Circuit affirmed, and on further appeal, the U.S. Supreme Court agreed to hear the case. Arguments were heard on 27 February 1985, and Justice John Paul Stevens delivered the court's opinion on 2 July of the same year. In expressing the majority 6–2 decision (Justices Thurgood Marshall and William Brennan dissented and Justice Lewis F. Powell did not participate), Justice Stevens held that the tribe's "exclusive right to hunt and fish on the lands reserved to the tribe by the 1864 Treaty did not survive as a special right...after the 1901 Agreement." Justice Stevens explained,

"Thus, even though 'legal ambiguities are resolved to the benefit of the Indians,' *DeCoteau v. District County Court*, 420 U.S. 425, [at] 447, 43 L.Ed. 2d 200, 95 S.Ct. 1082 (1975), courts cannot ignore plain language that, viewed in historical context and given a 'fair appraisal'...clearly runs counter to a tribe's later claims. Careful examination of the entire record in this case leaves us with the firm conviction that the exclusive right to hunt, fish, and gather roots, berries and seeds of the lands reserved to the Klamath Tribe by the 1864 Treaty was not intended to survive as a special right to be free of state regulation in the ceded lands that were outside the reservation after the 1901 Agreement. The judgment of the Court of Appeals is therefore reversed."

Oregon et al. v. Smith et al. (494 U.S. 872 [1990])

Known as "Oregon II," this case was the second time this issue came before the Supreme Court. In the first case, two men, Alfred L. Smith and Galen W. Black, both American Indians, were refused state unemployment benefits because they had been fired for using peyote. They appealed the denial to the U.S. Supreme Court, which remanded the case and refused to rule on whether the use of that drug is protected by the Constitution. On remand, the Supreme Court of Oregon held that the sacramental use of peyote was not protected from state laws prohibiting drug use, but such a prohibition was in conflict with the Free Exercise Clause of the Constitution. The U.S. Supreme Court agreed to hear the case a second time. Justice Antonin Scalia held for the majority of the court (Justices Harry Blackmun, William Brennan, and Thurgood Marshall dissenting) on 17 April 1990 that "the Free Exercise Clause permits the State to prohibit sacramental peyote use and thus to deny unemployment benefits to people discharged for such use." In 1994, in response to this decision, Congress passed the American Indian Religious Freedom Amendments of 1994.

See also American Indian Religious Freedom Act; Peyotism.

Oregon v. Hitchcock (202 U.S. 60, 50 L.Ed. 935, 26 S.Ct. 568 [1906])

In this Supreme Court case, decided in 1906, the court held that "the courts cannot interfere with the allotment and patenting by the Land Department [General Land Office] of swamp lands within the limits of an Indian reservation, while the legal title is still in the Federal government." The State of Oregon filed a lawsuit against Secretary of the Interior Ethan Allen Hitchcock and Commissioner of the General Land Office William A. Richards to enjoin, or stop, the men from allotting and patenting to the Indians swamplands located on the Klamath Indian Reservation in that state, claiming that the two men could only allot to Indians lands which were occupied, and that such remaining lands should be given to the state. By an act of Congress of 28 September 1850 (9 Stat. 519), Congress granted to Arkansas and all other states all lands within their respective borders, including "swamp and overflowed lands." Because Oregon did not enter the Union until 1859, an act of 12 March 1860 (12 Stat. 3) extended the provisions of the swamp act to that new state. The U.S. Supreme Court heard the original bill (no lower court had yet heard the case) on 5 and 6 April 1906, and handed down a decision 17 days later, on 23 April. Speaking for a unanimous court, Justice David Josiah Brewer (the son of missionary parents, he was born in Asia Minor, now modern day Turkey) held that because the fee involving the swampland was in the United States, the General Land Office had complete jurisdiction over its disposition. Wrote Justice Brewer, "It must be noticed that the legal title to all these tracts of land is still in the government. No patents or conveyances of any kind have been executed...Under those circumstances it is not a province of the courts to interfere with the Land Department in its administration."

See also *Naganab v. Hitchcock.*

***Oregon v. Smith and Oregon v. Black* (485 U.S. 660, 99 L.Ed. 2d 753, 108 S.Ct. 1444 [1988])**

Officially titled *Employment Division, Department of Human Resources of the State of Oregon et al., Petitioners, v. Alfred L. Smith* (which includes the joint case of *Employment Division, Department of Human Resources of the State of Oregon et al., Petitioners, v. Galen W. Black*), and known as "Oregon I," this controversial case dealt with the issue of the use of peyote by Native Americans. Original plaintiffs Alfred L. Smith and Galen W. Black, both American Indians, were employed as drug counselors by the Douglas County, Oregon, Council on Alcohol and Drug Abuse Prevention and Treatment (ADAPT). Both men were admitted former drug and alcohol abusers. As part of their religious ritual with the Native American Church, both men used quantities of peyote, a hallucinogenic drug, for sacramental purposes. ADAPT discovered this fact, and fired both men. They then applied to the Employment Division of the state of Oregon's Department of Human Resources for unemployment compensation, but were denied on the grounds that their terminations came about as a result of misconduct on their part at work. On an appeal to the Oregon Court of Appeals, the court held that the denial of benefits to persons fired for engaging in a religious act was a violation of their rights to the free exercise of their religion. The Oregon Supreme Court upheld the judgments, and the Department of Human Resources appealed to the U.S. Supreme Court.

Arguments were heard in the case on 8 December 1987, and a decision was handed down on 27 April 1988. Justice John Paul Stevens delivered the 5–3 opinion of the court (Justices William Brennan, Thurgood Marshall, and Harry Blackmun dissented, while Justice Anthony Kennedy did not participate) in holding that the fact that peyote was used in a religious act was irrelevant, and the men could not receive unemployment benefits. As Justice Stevens wrote, "Because we are uncertain about the legality of the religious use of peyote in Oregon, it is not now appropriate for us to decide whether the practice is protected by the Federal Constitution. The possibility that respondents' conduct would be unprotected if it violated the State's criminal code is, however, sufficient to counsel against affirming the state court's holding that the Federal Constitution requires the award of benefits to these respondents. If the Oregon Supreme Court's holding rests on the unstated premise that respondents' conduct is entitled to the same measure of federal constitutional protection regardless of its criminality, that holding is erroneous. If, on the other hand, it rests on the unstated premise that this conduct is not unlawful in Oregon, the explanation of that premise would make it more difficult to distinguish our holdings in Sherbert, Thomas, and Hobbie [previous cases]. We therefore vacate the judgments of the Oregon Supreme Court and remand the cases for further proceedings not inconsistent with this opinion."

***See also** Oregon et al. v. Smith et al.*; Peyotism.

***Organized Village of Kake, and Angoon Community Association v. Egan* (309 U.S. 60 [1962])**

***See** Metlakatla Community, Annette Islands Reserve v. Egan.*

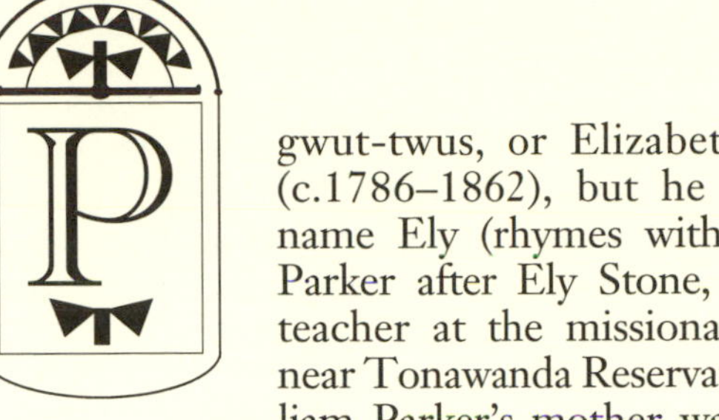

Painter, Charles Cornelius Coffin (?–1895)

Indian historian and authority Francis Paul Prucha called Professor Charles C. Painter "one of the most powerful men in the movement for Indian reform." His premature death in 1895 cut short an important career in the battle for Indian rights. Little is known of his life. What is established is that as an agent for the Indian Rights Association, he worked tirelessly in the last two decades of the nineteenth century to promote Indian rights and the reform of government policy. In his landmark report, *The Condition of Affairs in Indian Territory and California* (1888), Painter examined abuses among Indian traders, and he penned, "Whether abuses are greater under the present administration than under previous ones is not a question that concerns the friends of the Indians so much as the more pertinent and pressing one, whether the abuses of the system itself shall be continued?" Among his works are *Facts Regarding the Recent Opening to White Settlement of Crow Creek Reservation in Dakota* (1885), *A Visit to the Mission Indians of Southern California, and Other Western Tribes* (1886), *The Dawes Land in Severalty Bill and Indian Emancipation* (1887), and *The Oklahoma Bill, and Oklahoma* (1889), all publications of the Indian Rights Association. He died in 1895.

References Painter, Charles Cornelius Coffin, *The Condition of Affairs in Indian Territory and California: A Report by Prof. C. C. Painter, Agent of the Indian Rights Association* (1888); Prucha, Francis Paul, ed., *Americanizing the American Indians: Writings by the "Friends of the Indian," 1880–1890* (1973).

Parker, Ely Samuel (Seneca) (c.1828–1895)

Ely S. Parker was the first Native American to serve as commissioner of Indian Affairs, the sixteenth commissioner overall, and the first of four to serve under President Ulysses S Grant. A Seneca chief, Parker was born with the name Ha-sa-no-an-da, or "Leading Name," at Indians Falls near Pembroke, New York, about 1828, the son of Jo-no-essto-wa ("Dragon Fly"), also known as William Parker (c.1793–1864), and Ga-ont-gwut-twus, or Elizabeth Parker (c.1786–1862), but he took the name Ely (rhymes with "freely") Parker after Ely Stone, a Baptist teacher at the missionary school near Tonawanda Reservation. William Parker's mother was a white woman who had been captured by the Iroquois, making his son Ely one-fourth white; William Parker's two brothers, after being adopted by whites, took the names Henry Parker and Samuel Parker, and all three Parker men fought for the United States in the War of 1812. Elizabeth Parker's father, Jimmy Johnson, was descended from the Seneca leaders Handsome Lake and Cornplanter. Parker's mother was a niece of the Seneca chief Red Jacket (Sagoyewatha, "He keeps them awake"). Anthropologist Lewis Henry Morgan, who knew Parker's parents, wrote of Mrs. Parker that she was "the very picture of goodness of heart and natural kindness...a very dignified, industrious and noble looking woman."

Ely Samuel Parker, a Seneca, served as President Ulysses S. Grant's commissioner of Indian Affairs from 1869 to 1871.

Starting at a young age, Ely Parker fought to live "in two worlds." He attended the Baptist school on the reservation, spent some time on an Iroquois reservation in Ontario to learn woodcrafting, went to Yates Acdemy in Yates, New York, then to Cayuga Academy in Aurora, New York. While in Albany in 1844, he met and was befriended by anthropologist Morgan, and later co-wrote Morgan's book, *League of the Ho-de-no-sau-nee or Iroquois* (1851). In 1850, Parker became chief of the Senecas; he was renamed Do-ne-ho-gawa ("Keeper of the Western Door of the Long House of the Iroquois"). In that role, he fought to preserve the lands of New York's Senecas and was involved in the landmark Supreme Court case *Fellows v. Blacksmith* in 1857. Denied admission to the New York bar because he was not white, Parker instead attended the Rensselaer Polytechnic Institute in Troy, New York, where he studied civil engineering; thereafter, he was employed in a series of government positions, including, from 1858 to 1861, as superintendent of construction of government works at Galena, Illinois, where he met Ulysses S. Grant.

With the outbreak of the Civil War, Parker hoped to raise a regiment of Iroquois soldiers to fight for the Union, but he was refused. Instead, through his friendship with Grant, he was commissioned as captain of engineers in the Seventh Corps and fought next to Grant at Vicksburg. Distressed at the Indian problem, Parker wrote a letter in January 1864 to Grant expressing his views on how to settle "all matters of difference" between the United States and the Indians. In it, he outlined the idea that eventually led to creation of the Board of Indian commissioners. That letter reads:

General: In compliance with your request, I have the honor to submit the following proposed plan for the establishment of a permanent and perpetual peace, and for settling all matters of differences between the United States and the various Indian tribes.

First. The transfer of the Indian Bureau from the Interior Department back to the War Department, or military branch of the government, where it originally belonged, until within the last few years.

The condition and disposition of all the Indians west of the Mississippi river, as developed in consequence of the great and rapid influx of immigration by reason of the discovery of the precious metals throughout the entire west, renders it of the utmost importance that military supervision should be extended over the Indians. Treaties have been made with a very large number of the tribes, and generally reservations have been provided as homes for them. Agents appointed from civil life have generally been provided to protect their lives and property, and to attend to the prompt and faithful observance or treaty stipulations. But as the hardy pioneer and adventurous miner advanced into the inhospitable regions occupied by the Indians in search of the precious metals, they found no rights possessed by the Indians that they were bound to respect. The faith of treaties solemnly entered into were totally disregarded, and Indian territory wantonly violated. If any tribe remonstrated against the violation of their natural treaty rights, members of the tribe were inhumanely shot down and the whole treated as mere dogs. Retaliation generally followed, and bloody Indian wars have been the consequence, costing many lives and much treasure. In all troubles arising in this manner the civil agents have been totally powerless to avert the consequences, and when too late the military have been called in to protect the whites and punish the Indians, when if, in the beginning, the military had had the supervision of the Indians, their rights would not have been improperly molested, or if disturbed in their quietude by any lawless whites, a prompt and summary check to any further aggressions could have been given. In cases where the government promises the Indians the quiet and peaceable possession of a reservation, and precious metals are discovered or found to exist upon it, the military alone can give the Indians the needed protection and keep the adventurous miner from encroaching upon the Indians until the government has come to some understanding with them. In such cases the civil agent is absolutely powerless.

Most...Indian treaties contain stipulations for the payment annually to Indians of annuities, either in money or goods, or both, and agents are appointed to make these payments whenever government furnishes them the means. I know of no reason why officers of the army could not make these payments as well as civilians. The expense of agencies would be saved, and, I think, the Indians would be more honestly dealt by. An officer's honor and interest is at stake, which impels him to discharge his duty honestly and faithfully, while civil agents have none of these incentives, the ruling passion with them being generally to avoid all trouble and responsibility, and to make as much money as possible out of their offices.

In the retransfer of this bureau I would provide for the complete abolishment of the system of Indian traders, which, in my opinion, is a great evil to Indian communities. I would make government the purchaser of all articles usually brought in by Indians, giving them a fair equivalent for the same in money or goods at cost prices. In this way it would be an easy matter to regulate the sale of issue of arms and ammunition to Indians, a question which of late has agitated the minds of the civil and military authorities. If the entry of large numbers of Indians to any military post is objectionable, it can easily be arranged that only limited numbers shall be admitted daily...

Second. The next measure I would suggest is the passage by Congress of a plan of territorial government for the Indians, as was submitted last winter, or a similar one. When once passed it should remain upon the statute-books as the permanent and settled policy of the government. The boundaries of the Indian territory or territories should be well defined by metes and bounds, and should remain inviolate from settlement by any except Indians and government employees.

The subject of the improvement and civilization of the Indians, and the maintenance of peaceful relations with them, has engaged the serious consideration of every administration since the birth of the American republic; and, if I recollect aright, President Jefferson was the first to inaugurate the policy of removal of the Indians from the States to the country west of the Mississippi; and President Monroe, in furtherance of this policy, recommended that the Indians be concentrated, as far as was practicable, and civil governments established for them, with schools for every branch of instruction in literature and the arts of civilized life. The plan of removal was adopted as the policy of the government, and, by treaty stipulation, affirmed by Congress; lands were set apart for tribes removing into the western wilds, and the faith of a great nation pledged that the homes selected by Indians should be and remain their homes forever, unmolested by the hand of the grasping and avaricious white man; and, in some cases, the government promised that the Indian homes and lands should never be incorporated within the limits of any new State that might be organized. How the pledges so solemnly given and the promises made were kept, the history of the western country can tell. It is presumed that humanity dictated the original policy of the removal and concentration of the Indians in the west to save them from threatened extinction. But to-day, by reason of the immense augmentation of the American population, and the extension of their settlements throughout the entire west, covering both slopes of the Rocky mountains, the Indian races are more seriously threatened with a speedy extermination than ever before in the history of the country. And, however much such a deplorable result might be wished for by some, it seems to me that the honor of a Christian nation and every sentiment of humanity dictate that no pains should be spared to avert such an appalling calamity befalling a portion of the human race. The establishment of the Indians upon any one territory is perhaps impracticable, but numbers of them can, without doubt, be consolidated in separate districts of country, and the same system of government made to apply to each. By the concentration of tribes, although in several and separate districts, government can more readily control them and more economically press and carry out the plans for their improvement and civilization, and a better field be offered for philanthropic aid and Christian instruction. Some system of this kind has, at different periods in the history of our government, been put forward, but never successfully put into execution. A renewal of the attempt, with proper aids, it seems to me cannot fail of success.

Third. The passage by Congress of an act authorizing the appointment of an inspection board, or commission, to hold office during good behavior, or until the necessity for their services is terminated by the completion of the retransfer of the Indian Bureau to the War Department. It shall be the duty of this board to examine the account of the several agencies, see that every cent due the Indians is paid to them promptly as may be promised in treaties, and that proper and suitable goods and implements of agriculture are delivered to them when such articles are due; to make semi-annual reports, with such suggestions as, in their judgment, might seem necessary to the perfect establishment of a permanent and friendly feeling between the people of the United States and the Indians.

This commission could undoubtedly be dispensed with in a few years, but the results of their labors might be very important and beneficial, not only in supervising and promptly checking the delinquencies of incompetent and dishonest agents, but it would be a most convincing proof to the Indians' mind that the government was disposed to deal honestly and fairly by them. Such a commission might, indeed, be rendered wholly unnecessary if Congress would consent to the next and fourth proposition which I submit in this plan.

Fourth. The passage of an act authorizing the appointment of a permanent Indian commission, to be a mixed commission, composed of such white men as possessed in a large degree the confidence of their country, and a number of the most reputable educated Indians, selected from different tribes. The entire commission might be composed of ten members, and, if deemed advisable, might be divided so that five could operate north and five south of a given line, but both to be governed by the same general instructions, and impressing upon the Indians the same line of governmental policy. Its shall be made their duty to visit all the Indian tribes within the limits of the United States, whether, to do this, it requires three, five, or ten years. They shall hold talks with them, setting forth the great benefits that would result to them from a permanent peace with the whites, from their abandonment of their nomadic mode of life, and adopting agricultural and pastoral pursuits, and the habits and modes of civilized communities. Under the directions of the president the commission shall explain to the various the advantages of their consolidation upon some common territory, over which Congress shall have extended the ægis of good, wise, and wholesome laws for their protection and perpetuation. It would be wise to convince the Indians of the great power and number of the whites; that they cover the whole land, to the north, south, east and west of them. I believe they could easily understand that although this country was once wholly inhabited by Indians, the tribes, and many of them once powerful, who occupied the countries now constituting the States east of the Mississippi, have, one by one, been exterminated by their abortive attempts to stem the western march of civilization.

They could probably be made to comprehend that the waves of population and civilization are upon every side of them; that it is too strong for them to resist; and that, unless they fall in line with the current of destiny as it rolls and surges around them, they must succumb and be annihilated by its overwhelming force. In consequence of the gradual extinction of the Indian races, and the failure of almost every plan heretofore attempted for the amelioration of their condition, and the prolongation of their national existence, and also because they will not abandon their savage tastes and propensities, it has of late years become somewhat common, not only for the press, but in the speeches of men of intelligence, and some occupying high and responsible positions, to advocate the policy of their immediate and absolute extermination. Such a proposition, so revolting to every sense of humanity and Christianity, it seems to me could not for one moment be entertained by any enlightened nation. On the contrary, the honor of the national character and the dictates of a sound policy, guided by the principles of religion and philanthropy, would urge the adoption of a system to avert the extinction of a people, however unenlightened they may be. The American government can never adopt the policy of a total extermination of the Indian race within her limits, numbering, perhaps, less than four hundred thousand, without a cost of untold treasure and lives of her people, beside exposing herself to the abhorrence and censure of the entire civilized world.

On 26 August 1864, Grant asked Secretary of War Edwin M. Stanton to appoint Parker as his military secretary with the rank of lieutenant colonel to replace William R. Rowley, who had resigned because of ill health. Parker served at Grant's side throughout the rest of the war and at Appomattox Ely Parker helped draft the papers that Confederate general Robert E. Lee signed to surrender the Army of Virginia. With the surrender, Parker was promoted to brigadier general of volunteers, and for the next four years, as he traveled throughout the western United States, he held the rank of brigadier general, the highest-ranking Native American officer in the army.

A little more than four years after the end of the war, Grant was elected president of the United States and named Parker as his first commissioner of Indian Affairs. Parker served in this post for two years and three months, supervising the establishment of the Board of Indian commissioners, an oversight group composed of white philanthropists. In his first annual report, dated 23 December 1869, Parker wrote, "Among the reports of the superintendents and agents herewith, there will be found information, with views and suggestions of much practical value, which should command the earnest attention of our legislators, and all others who are concerned for the future welfare and destiny of the remaining original inhabitants of our country. The question is still one of deepest interest, 'What shall be done for the amelioration and civilization of the race?' For a long period in the past, great and commendable efforts were made by the government and the philanthropist, and large sums of money expended to accomplish these desirable ends, but the success never was commensurate with the means employed. Of late years a change in policy was seen to be required, as the cause of failure, the difficulties to be encountered, and the best means of overcoming them, became better understood. The measures to which we are indebted for an improved condition of affairs are, the concentration of the Indians upon suitable reservations, and the supplying them with means for engaging in agricultural and mechanical pursuits, and for their education and moral training. As a result, the clouds of ignorance and superstition in which many of this people were so long enveloped have disappeared, and the light of a Christian civilization seems to have dawned upon their moral darkness, and opened up a brighter future. Much, however, remains to be done for the multitude yet in their savage state, and I can but earnestly invite the serious consideration of those whose duty it is to legislate in their behalf, to the justice and importance of promptly fulfilling all treaty obligations, and the wisdom of placing at the disposal of the department adequate funds for the purpose, and investing it with powers to adopt the requisite measures to be set apart for their use and occupancy."

In 1870, William Welsh, formerly of the Board of Indian commissioners, with which Parker had developed a stormy relationship, accused the Indian commissioner of criminal action. A congressional committee heard the charges and found Parker innocent, but his good name was stained. Further, Parker found that the Bureau of Indian Affairs bureaucracy was so oppressive that few if any of his reforms would ever be given a chance. He submitted his resignation effective 1 August 1871. Because Parker resigned in August, and his replacement, Francis A. Walker, did not fill the position until November of that same year, acting commissioner Henry R. Clum wrote and signed the annual report of the bureau for that year.

Ely Parker lived for 24 years after serving as Indian commissioner, spending much of his time as a civil engineer and small businessman, in the process going broke several times. His last employment was with the New York City police department; he was working there just three days before his death on 31 August 1895 at his summer home at Fairfield, Connecticut, at the age of 67.

See also *Fellows v. Blacksmith*; The New York Indians; "Peace Policy" of President Ulysses S Grant.

References "Ely Samuel Parker." In Robert M. Kvasnicka and Herman J. Viola, eds., *The Commissioners of Indian Affairs, 1824–1977* (1979); Parker, Arthur C., *The Life of General Ely S. Parker, Last Grand Sachem of the Iroqouis and General Grant's Military Secretary* (1919); U.S. Congress, House of Representatives, *Annual Report of the Commissioner of Indian Affairs for the Year 1869*, House Executive Document No. 1, 41st Congress, 2d Session (serial 1414); Waldman, Carl, *Who Was Who in Native American History: Indians and Non-Indians from Early Contacts through 1900* (1990); Waltmann, Henry G., Armstrong, William H., *Warrior in Two Camps: Ely S. Parker, Union General and Seneca Chief* (1978).

"Peace Policy" of President Ulysses S. Grant

Marked most importantly by the creation of the United States Board of Indian Commissioners and the ascension of Ely Samuel Parker to the post of commissioner of Indian Affairs, the first Native American to hold that office, the period from 1869 until Grant left office in 1877 is considered to be one of the greatest of reform of Indian policy prior to the New Deal of the 1930s. Henry G. Waltmann writes, "President Grant has enjoyed considerable acclaim in the annals of United States-Indian relations for the celebrated Peace Policy of the post-Civil War years. Despite an otherwise unfavorable political image, historians have repeatedly depicted Grant as a forceful and imaginative Indian reformer, a crusader for justice, and an enemy of the spoilsmen who perennially preyed upon the Indian service." However, Indian historian David M. Holford writes, "Grant's 'Peace Policy' was designed to isolate the Indians on reservations where federal agents, farmers, craftsmen, teachers, and clergymen could work with maximum results to alter the red man's social patterns and behavior. However, these efforts to restructure Indian society on the white man's model were unsuccessful because reformers generally failed to break down tribal loyalty and custom."

President Grant discussed his new policy in his Second Annual Message to Congress, delivered on 5 December 1870:

> Reform in the management of Indian Affairs has received the special attention of the Administration from it inauguration to the present day. The experiment of making it a missionary work was tried with a few agencies given to the denomination of Friends, and has been found to work most advantageously. All agencies and superintendencies not so disposed were given to officers of the Army. The act of Congress reducing the army renders army officers ineligible for civil positions. Indian agencies being civil offices, I determined to give all the agencies to such religious dominations as had heretofore established missionaries among the Indians, and perhaps to some other denominations who would undertake the work on the same terms—*i.e.*, as a missionary work.

The societies selected are allowed to name their own agents, subject to the approval of the Executive, and are expected to watch over them and aid them as missionaries, to Christianize and civilize the Indian, and to train him in the arts of peace. The Government watches over the official acts of these agents, and requires of them as strict an accountability as if they were appointed in any other manner. I entertain the confident hope that the policy now pursued will in a few years bring all the Indians upon reservations, where they will live in houses, and have schoolhouses and churches, and will be pursuing peaceful and self-sustaining avocations [occupations], and where they may be visited by the law-abiding white man with same impunity [freedom] that he visits the civilized white settlements. I call special attention to the report of the Commissioner of Indian Affairs for full information on this subject.

In his annual report for 1886, Commissioner of Indian Affairs John DeWitt Clinton Atkins wrote of Grant's Peace Policy, "Another year's experience and practical trial of this 'humanitarian and peace system' only adds cumulative testimony to the superiority of its methods of Indian civilization over any others yet tried." He added, "A benign policy on the part of the Government toward the Indian race, dictated by a love of humanity, one in which both political parties have fortunately and exceptionally agreed, is a proud national distinction. It speaks well for the great heart of the people which lies back of and behind this Government that they order and command their representatives to foster a policy which alone can save the aborigines from destruction—from being worn away by the attrition of the conflicting elements of Anglo-Saxon civilization." In a letter to President Chester A. Arthur, praising the work of Commissioner of Indian Affairs Hiram Price, the officers of the American Missionary Association penned, "The Peace Policy inaugurated by Gen. Grant was an honor to the nation and an unspeakable boon to the Indians. It met the wishes and conscientious feelings of a large share of the Christian people of America, and while assuming to be neither denominational nor distinctly religious, yet carried with it the blessings of education and Christian civilization."

See also Parker, Ely Samuel.

References Holford, David M., "The Subversion of the Indian Land Allotment System, 1887–1934," *Indian Historian* 8 (1); M. E. Strieby, Corresponding Secretary et al., of the American Missionary Association to President Arthur, 8 April 1882, Hiram Price Appointment File, Box 44, Records of the Appointments Division, Commissioner of Indian Affairs, RG 48, National Archives; Richardson, James, comp., *A Compilation of the Messages and Papers of the Presidents, 1789–1914* (1897–1917); U.S. Congress, House of Representatives, *Annual Report of the Commissioner of Indian Affairs for the Year 1886*, House Executive Document No. 1, 49th Congress, 1st Session (serial 2467); Waltmann, Henry G., "Circumstantial Reformer: President Grant & The Indian Problem." *Arizona and the West* 13 (4).

Peltier, Leonard (Lakota-Ojibwa) (1944–)

He remains perhaps the most controversial figure of the American Indian Movement and its fight for civil rights for Native Americans; also known by his Indian name, *Gwarth-ee-lass* (He Leads the People), he was convicted in 1977 of killing two F.B.I. agents, and is now serving two consecutive life sentences. But voices of protest have been raised that the conviction was political and not criminal in nature. Leonard Peltier was born on 12 September 1944 in Grand Forks, North Dakota, the son of Leo Peltier, a mixed-blood (three-quarters Ojibwa and one-quarter French) and Alvina Showers, whose mother was a full-blood Lakota Sioux. Peltier had a limited education (he spent some time at a reservation school); when his parents separated, he moved with his sister to live with his paternal grandparents. When they moved to Montana, Peltier looked for work in the mines and logging areas of Montana. After he was racially harassed, he returned to the Wahpeton Reservation in North Dakota. He became interested in traditional Indian medicine and dances after he went to live with his father on the Turtle Mountain Reservation, but when he practiced the illegal sun dance on Turtle Mountain, he was arrested. After he moved to the West Coast and opened an auto body shop in Seattle, he became an activist with the American Indian Movement to protest fishing rights violations in Washington State. He participated in the takeover of former Indian land at Fort Lawton, near Seattle, in 1970. After that, he began to travel with AIM activists Dennis Banks, Russell Means, and the Bel-

Canadian officials escort activist Leonard Peltier to a helicopter in Vancouver, British Columbia, in 1976. Accused of murdering two Federal Bureau of Investigation officers, Peltier's controversial trial led to his being sentenced to life imprisonment.

lecourt brothers, and participated in the Trail of Broken Treaties march and caravan in 1972.

The activists of AIM were targeted by the government, and Peltier was one of the first. He was arrested in Milwaukee in 1972 for carrying an unloaded gun, but instead of waiting for trial he fled to the Dakotas. After AIM "occupied" the site of Wounded Knee for 71 days in 1973 to protest the tribal government of Pine Ridge Reservation, tribal leaders called on Peltier to establish a "spiritual camp" at the site in 1975. On 26 June 1975, FBI agents Jack Coler and Ronald Williams crossed onto the Pine Ridge Reservation to serve a warrant on an Oglala Sioux named Jimmy Eagle. In an action that remains controversial to this day, a firefight broke out, leaving agents Coler and Williams, as well as a Coeur d'Alene Indian, Joe (Killsright) Stuntz, dead. The FBI immediately charged Peltier in the deaths of the federal officers, although the evidence was thin. After a raid of Pine Ridge on 5 September, Peltier and AIM activists Jimmy Eagle, Dino Butler, and Bob Robideau were indicted for the murders of Coler and Williams. Peltier fled to Canada, because, as he said later, "I realized the possibility of getting a fair trial was very slim." On 6 February 1976, he was arrested in Canada. The FBI tried to get AIM member Anna Mae Aquash to testify that she witnessed Peltier killing the two agents; she refused and several days later was shot to death. The FBI then got another activist, Myrtle Poor Bear, to testify; when she did, the Canadian government sent Peltier back for trial. Poor Bear later claimed that the FBI had threatened her if she had not signed the statement.

The trial of Leonard Peltier can be best characterized as one of the worst miscarriages of justice in American history. In 1982, columnist Jack Anderson reported that the "FBI Shopped for Its Judge in Indian Case." He wrote that while "'shopping' for a friendly judge is an old, if not particularly honorable, practice in the American system of justice...the FBI and federal prosecutors carried it to an unsavory extreme in the murder trial of American Indian activist Leonard Peltier." After a trial in which evidence that the FBI started the firefight was excluded, Peltier was found guilty and sentenced to two consecutive life terms. In 18 April 1991, Judge Gerald W. Heaney of the Eighth Circuit Court of Appeals, which had heard two of Peltier's appeals, wrote in a letter to Sen. Daniel Inouye (D-Hawaii), then chairman of the Senate Select Committee on Indian Affairs, "The United States government must share the responsibility with the Native Americans for the June 26 [1975] firefight....The government's role in escalating the conflict into a firefight...can properly be considered as a mitigating circumstance....The FBI used improper tactics in securing Peltier's extradition from Canada and in otherwise investigating and trying the Peltier case." Now imprisoned in the Marion Federal Penitentiary in Illinois, Peltier is the subject of two documentaries: *Warrior: The Life of Leonard Peltier* and *Incident at Oglala.*

See also American Indian Movement; Wounded Knee (1973).

References Anderson, Jack, "FBI Shopped for Its Judge in Indian Case." *Washington Post,* 28 December 1982, C-14; Carter, Christina E., "Leonard Peltier." In Sharon Malinowski, ed., *Notable Native Americans* (1995); Matthiessen, Peter, *In the Spirit of Crazy Horse*" (1991); Utter, Jack, *American Indians: Answers to Today's Questions* (1993).

***Peoria Tribe of Indians of Oklahoma et al. v. United States* (390 U.S. 468, 20 L.Ed. 2d 39, 88 S.Ct. 1137 [1968])**
Can an Indian tribe collect damages from the United States if lands that the tribe ceded to the government for sale at auction had been sold to private investors, at a lower price, in violation of a treaty? In 1854, by a treaty between the Peoria Tribe of Indians of Oklahoma (formerly known as the Confederated Tribe of the Peoria, Kaskaskia, Wea and Piankeshaw Indians) and the United States (10 Stat. 1082), the Peorias placed a portion of their lands in trust, to be held by the United States government, with the remainder to be sold at auction, with the tribe receiving the proceeds of the sale. Instead, in 1857, the government sold most of

the land, 207,759 acres, by private sales, which yielded lower profits for the Indians. The Indian Claims Commission, hearing the Peorias' grievance, held that the sales netted $172,726 less than if the treaty's obligations had been fulfilled. The Peorias asked the Court of Claims that not only should this amount be awarded, but that damages, allowing if the moneys had been invested in 1857, also be conferred. The Court of Claims rejected the Peorias' request, and the tribe appealed to the U.S. Supreme Court to settle the question. After arguments were heard on 15 January 1968, Justice Potter Stewart held for a unanimous court (Justice Thurgood Marshall did not participate) on 1 April 1968 that while it is a general rule that the United States is not liable for interest on claims against it, such a rule does not apply when the government violates a treaty. Justice Stewart remanded the case back to the Court of Claims and the Indian Claims Commission, holding that the original award must be recalculated to allow for a 5 percent yearly return on the monies that would have been received had the treaty's obligations been fulfilled.

Perrin v. United States (232 U.S. 478 [1914])

This case was but another in the long line of decisions handed down by the U.S. Supreme Court in the area of the prohibition of intoxicating substances on Indian reservations and the Congress' ability to ban such sales. In this case, Sam Perrin was convicted of selling intoxicating liquors upon lands that had been part of an Indian reservation but had been ceded to the United States after they remained unallotted. The government, in a treaty with the Yankton Sioux Indians of South Dakota, specifically declared that any such ceded lands would remain under the laws of the United States, and as such would be free from intoxicating substances. Perrin's conviction was upheld by the District Court for the District of South Dakota, and Perrin appealed to the U.S. Supreme Court. After being submitted on 13 January 1914, a decision was handed down on 24 February of that same year. Speaking for a unanimous court, Justice Willis Van Devanter upheld Perrin's conviction, holding that the Congress had the final authority on what laws would apply on the former reservation lands. As Justice Van Devanter explained, "The power of Congress to prohibit the introduction of intoxicating liquors into an Indian reservation, wheresoever situate, and to prohibit traffic in such liquors with tribal Indians, whether upon or off a reservation and whether within or without the limits of a state, does not admit of any doubt. It arises in part from the clause in the Constitution investing Congress with the authority 'to regulate commerce with foreign nations, and among the several states, and the Indian tribes,' and in part from the recognized relation of tribal Indians to the Federal government."

Peyotism

The use of peyote by Native Americans is an old and enduring tradition, but its history and its links to the Native American Church are little known outside the Indian community. Peyotism is in some ways the essence of the religion itself, the elevation of the plant and its use to the sacramental status of bread and wine in Christian churches. It serves, as one source notes, as "a unifying influence in Indian life, providing the basis for ceremonies, friendships, social gatherings, travel, marriage, and much more."

Writer Weston La Barre writes that the "first of modern students to describe the peyote rite was James Mooney, who visited the Kiowa, Comanche, Tarahumari, and 'a number of other tribes, among them the Mexican tribe of the Sierra Madre, and as far south as the City of Mexico.' But at his death he had published no further study of peyote; ethnographers of the period were in general concerned with preserving complete records of older native cultures and ignored or paid scant attention to the modern cult of peyote. Mooney himself gave little notice to the rite in his monographs on the Cheyenne and the Kiowa, although at the time he was undoubtedly the authority on the subject."

This issue was discussed in *People v. Woody* (40 California Reporter 60, 394 Pacific Reporter 2d 813 [1964]), a California Supreme Court case in which Justice Tobriner, speaking for that court, held that the state of California could not apply its law against the use of illegal drugs to peyote because it was "a sacramental symbol similar to bread and wine used in Christian churches." Because Woody is the leading case to involve peyote and discuss it to some length, a portion of the opinion is reprinted here:

The plant *Lophophora williamsii*, a small, spineless cactus, found in the Rio Grande Valley of Texas and northern Mexico, produces peyote, which grows in small buttons on the top of the cactus. Peyote's principal constituent is mescaline. When taken internally by chewing the buttons or drinking a derivative tea, peyote produces several types of hallucinations, depending primarily upon the user. In most subjects it causes extraordinary vision marked by bright and kaleidoscopic colors, geometric patterns, or scenes involving humans or animals. In others it engenders hallucinatory symptoms similar to those produced in cases of schizophrenia, dementia praccox [the ancient term for schizophrenia], or paranoia. Beyond its hallucinatory effect, peyote renders for most users a heightened sense of comprehension; it fosters a feeling of friendliness toward other persons.

Peyote, as we shall see, plays a central role in the ceremony and practice of the Native American Church, a religious organization of Indians. Although the church claims no official prerequisites to membership, no written membership rolls, and no recorded theology, estimates of its membership range from 30,000 to 250,000, the wide variance deriving from differing definitions of a "member." As the anthropologists have ascertained through conversations with members, the theology of the church combines certain Christian teachings with the belief that peyote embodies the Holy Spirit and that those who partake of peyote enter into direct contact with God.

Peyotism discloses a long history. A reference to the religious use of peyote in Mexico appears in Spanish historical sources as early as 1560. Peyotism spread from Mexico to the United States and Canada; American anthropologists describe it as well established in this country during the latter part of the nineteenth century. Today, Indians of many tribes practice Peyotism. Despite the absence of recorded dogma, the several tribes follow surprisingly similar ritual and theology; the practices of Navajo members in Arizona practically paralleled those of adherents in California, Montana, Oklahoma, Wisconsin, and Saskatchewan.

The "meeting," a ceremony marked by the sacramental use of peyote, composes the cornerstone of the peyote religion. The meeting convenes in an enclosure and continues from sundown Saturday to sunrise Sunday. To give thanks for the past good fortune or find guidance for future conduct, a member will "sponsor" a meeting and supply to those who attend both the peyote and the next morning's breakfast. The "sponsor," usually but not always the "leader," takes charge of the meeting; he decides the order of events and the amount of peyote to be consumed. Although the individual leader exercises an absolute control of the meeting, anthropologists report a striking uniformity of its ritual.

A meeting connotes a solemn and special occasion. Whole families attend together, although children and young women participate only by their presence. Adherents don their finest clothing, usually suits for men and fancy dresses for the women, but sometimes ceremonial Indian costumes. At the meeting the members pray, sing, and make ritual use of drum, fan, eagle bone, whistle, rattle and prayer cigarette, the symbolic emblems of their faith. The central event, of course, consists of the use of peyote in quantities sufficient to produce an hallucinatory state.

At an early but fixed stage in the ritual

the members pass around a ceremonial bag of peyote buttons. Each adult may take four, the customary number, or take none. The participants chew the buttons, usually with some difficulty because of the extreme bitterness; later, at a set time in the ceremony any member may ask for more peyote; occasionally a member may take as many as four more buttons. At sunrise on Sunday the ritual ends; after a brief outdoor prayer, the host and his family serve breakfast. Then the members depart. By morning the effects of the peyote disappear; the user suffers no aftereffects.

Although peyote serves as a sacramental symbol similar to bread and wine in certain Christian churches, it is more than a sacrament. Peyote constitutes in itself an object or worship; prayers are directed to it much as prayers are devoted to the Holy Ghost. On the other hand, to use peyote for nonreligious purposes is sacrilegious. Members of the church regard peyote also as a "teacher" because it induces a feeling of brotherhood with other members; indeed, it enables the participant to experience the Deity. Finally, devotees treat peyote as a "protector." Much as a Catholic carries his medallion, an Indian G.I. often wears around his neck a beautifully beaded pouch containing one large peyote button.

Congress enacted the American Indian Religious Freedom Amendments of 1994, which recognized the use of peyote as part of a protected religious ceremony.

See also Mooney, James, Jr.; *Oregon v. Smith* and *Oregon v. Black*.

References La Barre, Weston, *The Peyote Cult* (1969); *People v. Woody* (40 Cal. Rep. 60, 394 Pac. Rep. 2d 813 [1964]); Stewart, Omer C., *Peyote Religion: A History* (1987);

Picotte, Susan La Flesche (Omaha) (1865–1915)

Reformer, activist, and missionary among the Omahas, Susan La Flesche Picotte was also a noted Indian physician. She was born in Omaha, Nebraska, on 17 June 1865, the youngest of three children of Joseph La Flesche (Insta Maza, or "Iron Eye"), the half-Indian and half-white who became chief of the Omahas in 1853, and Mary (née Gale) La Flesche, who was also known as Hinnungsnun, or "One Woman." Susan was the younger sister of activist Susette La Flesche Tibbles and half-sister of ethnologist Francis La Flesche. According to historian Frederick J. Dockstader, "She followed her sister's path at the Elizabeth Institute for Young Ladies and then graduated in 1886 from the Hampton Institute. But she undertook a quite different career by entering the Women's Medical College of Pennsylvania, where she graduated in 1889, becoming the first female Indian physician. For the next five years she was the government physician to the Omaha, traveling around the reservation on horseback." Her *Report of Physician for Omahas*, written at Omaha Agency in 1893, is considered by historians as an important discourse on Indian health in the late nineteenth century.

In 1894, Susan La Flesche married Yankton storyteller Henry Picotte, who was an alcoholic even though his wife was a strong advocate for prohibitionism among Native Americans. In fact, she spent most her 11 year marriage to Picotte advocating an end to the sale of alcohol to the Omaha Indians, a stance that made her unpopular among her people. Still she wrote, "I know that I shall be unpopular for a while with my people, because they will misconstrue my efforts, but this is nothing, just so I can help them for their own good." After Henry Picotte's death (probably from an alcohol-related disease), Picotte was appointed as a missionary to the Omaha people by the Presbyterian Board of Home Missions, and in the intervening years she worked to build a hospital at Walthill, Nebraska. Until her death in 1915, she remained a staunch and unwavering advocate for her people and their well-being.

See also Tibbles, Susette La Flesche.

References Canon, Charles, "Susan La Flesche Picotte." In Sharon Malinowski, ed., *Notable Native Americans* (1995); Dockstader, Frederick J., *Great North American Indians: Profiles in Life and Leadership* (1977); La Flesche, Susan, "Report of Physician for Omahas." In U.S. Congress, House of Representatives, *Annual Report of the Commissioner of Indian Affairs for the Year 1893*, House Executive Document No. 1, 53rd Congress, 2d Session (serial 3210).

Pierce, Maris Bryant (Seneca) (1811–1874)

His Indian name was *Ha-dya-no-doh* ("Swift Runner"); known as Maris Pierce, he was a leader for most of his life in the fight against the removal of the Senecas from New York. He was born in 1811 on the Allegheny Reservation in upstate New York. According to biographer H. A. Vernon, "He attended a Quaker primary school as a child and was later sent to Fredonia Academy. Later still, he transferred to another academy in Homer, Cortland County, after which he spent some time in Rochester. While in Rochester, he was converted to Christianity by the Presbyterian church. His precollegiate studies ended in a school located in Thetford, Vermont, following which he was admitted to Dartmouth College." Indian historian Carl Waldman adds that Pierce became an activist while in college by taking a stand against the Treaty of Buffalo Creek of 1838, which allowed the Seneca lands in New York to be sold and the Indians to be removed to Kansas. "Pierce made numerous speeches on behalf of his tribe before church and civil groups. He also helped the tribe draft a letter to President Martin Van Buren and hire legal counsel in Washington, D.C." Pierce's views on the treaty and its effects on his people are contained in a letter not from Pierce but from Seneca chiefs Big Kettle, William Kronse, and John Kennedy, addressed to Representative Samuel Prentis, chairman of the House Committee on Indian Affairs. In that letter of 2 March 1838, the men wrote:

Sir—Your letter to Maris B. Pierce was received in due season, and he having meanwhile changed his views, and signed the treaty, (as he says, in consequence of regarding the case of his people as hopeless, by reason of the bribery and intimidation practised upon the chiefs, and because the only hope of being any service to his nation seemed to lie in securing some new advantage in the treaty, which he had an opportunity to do by signing,) he made known your views to one of our number, still strong in opposition to the treaty. This man, conceiving that the only prospect of success was in following your suggestions, called a council of such chiefs as could be in a little time assembled, and who are regarded by all our party as having power to act in their behalf, and laid the matter before us; whereupon we resolved to forward you the enclosed statement of our affairs, with the earnest request that you would befriend us to the most of your ability, and, if possible, secure us the possession of our rights. You will lay us under great obligations, and our people, also, by making such a use of these facts, either in the Senate of before the Committee on Indian Affairs, or with individuals in private, as in your judgment will best promote our interests. Many affidavits, substantiating these statements, have already forwarded to Mr. [Henry] Clay, and others, with whom, should you find it necessary, we shall be happy to have you consult, in devising measures for our benefit. Messrs. Robinson, Blacksmith, Kennedy, and Jimison [*sic*] whom we shall desire to confer with you in respect to all their movements, and whom we now wish the privilege of commending to your kindness. They will stand in great need of advice and aid, for they have a weighty responsibility resting upon them, and they are unacquainted with the arts of political intrigue. Your kindness to them may save a distressed and down-trodden people from destruction. They will give you particular information why no more delegates have been sent from our party, and why these have been so long delayed.

May Almighty God aid you in every effort to rescue us from injustice and oppression; and may his rich blessing reward abundantly all your labors in the cause of human rights.

The controversy over the sale made it expedient for the company trying to buy the

Seneca lands, the Ogden Land Company, to renegotiate in 1842. The new agreement resulted in the sale of some of the acreage, including the Buffalo Creek reservation, but saved for the Senecas the Allegheny, Cattaraugus, and Tonawanda Reservations.

In his last years, Pierce was a secretary for the Seneca nation and helped bring about tribal government in 1848. He died in 1874. Vernon writes of his legacy, "Pierce can…be considered a leader in the breadth of his views concerning the Native Americans and the problems they faced in white, nineteenth-century America. Pierce concerned himself not only with the fate of the Seneca Nation, but also with the fate of other nations in the Iroquois Confederacy and among fellow 'Indians' throughout the country. He made common cause with the chiefs of the four Seneca reservations, involved himself in the concerns of the League, and more than once spoke as an interpreter of Indian culture and civilization to other Americans. On such occasions he continually referred to the 'Aborigines of America' and 'American Indians.'"

References *The Case of the Seneca Indians in the State of New York.* (1840); Vernon, H. A., "Maris Bryant Pierce: The Making of a Seneca Leader." In Lester George Wilson and Raymond Wilson, eds., *Indian Lives: Essays on Nineteenth- and Twentieth-Century Native American Leaders* (1985); Waldman, Carl, *Who Was Who in Native American History: Indians and Non-Indians from Early Contacts through 1900* (1990).

Poafpybitty et al. v. Skelly Oil Company (390 U.S. 265, 19 L.Ed. 2d 1238, 88 S.Ct. 982 [1968])

The case of *Frank P. Poafpybitty et al. v. Skelly Oil Company* involved the issue of whether Indian allottees who had executed oil and gas leases on their allotted lands could sue for breaches of the lease. In 1947 petitioners, Comanche Indians of Oklahoma, received an approval from the Acting Commissioner of Indian Affairs, William Zimmerman, Jr., to lease oil and gas reserves on their allotments to the Skelly Oil Company. The company sank its first well in 1956, and soon operated seven wells. In 1961, petitioners retained lawyers to sue the company, alleging that their mismanagement had wasted natural gas and had diminished the petitioners' royalties in violation of the leases. The District Court of Oklahoma County, Oklahoma, dismissed the suit as demanded by the respondent, the oil company, on the grounds that the Indians, allottees, had no right to sue. The Supreme Court of Oklahoma affirmed, and the U.S. Supreme Court granted certiorari to decide the question. Arguments were held on 24 January 1968, and the case was decided on 18 March of the same year. In an opinion by Chief Justice Earl Warren expressing the unanimous view of the court (Justice Thurgood Marshall did not participate), it was held that since the Indian allottees had received the expressed approval of the secretary of the Interior to execute the leases, they had the right to sue for breach of contract, and that such a denial "unduly restricts the right of the Indians to seek judicial relief for a claimed injury to their interests."

Presidential Commission on Indian Reservation Economies

This presidential committee was established by President Ronald Reagan with Executive Order 12401 of 14 January 1983. The functions of the Commission, as established by section 2 of the order, were to "advise the President on what actions should be taken to develop a stronger private sector of Federally recognized Indian reservations, lessen tribal dependence on Federal monies and programs and reduce the Federal presence in Indian Affairs. The underlying principles of this mission are the government-to-government relationship, the established Federal policy of self-determination and the Federal trust responsibility." The order required that the Commission focus on the following areas: 1) Defining the existing Federal legislative, regulatory, and procedural obstacles to the creation of positive economic environments on Indian reservations; 2) Identifying and recommending changes or other remedial actions necessary to remove these obstacles; 3) Defining the obstacles at the State, local and tribal government levels which impede both Indian and non-Indian private sector investments on reservations; 4) Identifying actions which these levels of government could initiate to rectify the identified problems; and 5) Recommending ways for the private sector, both Indian and non-Indian, to participate in the development and growth of reservation economies, including capital formation. One of the commission members, Ross Swimmer (Cherokee), was named assistant secretary for Indian Affairs in 1985, just after the commission's final report was submitted to the president.

See also Swimmer, Ross Owen.

Reference "Executive Orders." *United States Code Congressional and Administrative News*, 98th Congress, 1st Session, 1983 (1984).

Preston-Engle Report (1930)

Officially titled *Report of Advisors on Irrigation on Indian Reservations*, this document, prepared for the Indian Irrigation Service, appeared as part six of *Survey of Conditions of Indians in the U.S.: Hearings before a Subcommittee of the Senate Committee on Indian Affairs* (seventy-first Congress, second Session). It was prepared by Porter J. Preston of the Bureau of Reclamation and Charles A. Engle, Supervisory Engineer for the Bureau of Indian Affairs. Anthropologist Thomas R. McGuire writes, "Engle and Preston visited the large, glamorous Indian irrigation projects, those which, presumably, should have received the most thought in planning, the most care in engineering. Each of the fifteen operations toured in 1927 had their own peculiarities, but all showed similar problems. A common failing was the appalling discrepancy between information and design, which was due not to the inherently tricky problem of gauging and predicting long-term stream flows but was rather the result of behavior in organizations. This, Engle and Preston observed: 'In some cases it seems apparent, as the result of over optimism, coupled with a desire to demonstrate the feasibility of a project and thus bring about its contruction, there has been a surrender on the part of the investigating engineer to the inherent human tendency to minimize difficulties and swell the irrigable acreage by the inclusion of lands that in all probability can never be profitably used.'"

References McGuire, Thomas R., "Illusions of Choice in the Indian Irrigation Service: The Ak Chin Project and an Epilogue." *Journal of the Southwest* 30 (2); U.S. Congress, Senate, *Report of Advisors on Irrigation on Indian Reservations*, vol. 6 of *Survey of the Conditions of the Indians in the United States*, Hearings before a Subcommittee of the Committee on Indian Affairs, U.S. Senate, 71st Session, 2d Session; 1930.

Price, Hiram (1814–1901)

Iowa congressman, banker, and Methodist layman, Hiram Price's tenure as commissioner of Indian Affairs is little remembered nor noted in histories of that government bureau. He is so obscure that no manuscript collections of his exist, and only one letter from him outside of his regular correspondence as commissioner of Indian Affairs could be found. Born in Washington County, Pennsylvania, on 10 January 1814, he was the son of a farmer. He received an education in the common schools of rural Pennsylvania and engaged in agricultural pursuits on his father's farm. Before he was thirty, he worked as a bookkeeper near Pittsburgh and learned the mercantile trade. In 1844, he removed to Davenport, Iowa, a city with which he was identified the rest of his life. After serving on the school board he was named treasurer and recorder of Scott County, Iowa. In the 1850s he was heavily involved in the construction of a railroad from Davenport to Council Bluffs. He was politically active, helping to draft a state prohibition law and joining the new Republican party in 1856.

Biographer Floyd O'Neil writes, "In 1863 Price was elected to Congress on the Republican ticket. In the House of Representatives he supported proposals to reform Indian policy and joined a group that advocated the set of reforms which later evolved into Grant's Peace Policy." He left Congress in 1869, and was reelected in 1877. In the intervening years, he had served as president of the Davenport and St. Paul Railroad Company. In 1881, after just two terms in Congress, Price was asked by President James A. Garfield and Secretary of the Interior Samuel J. Kirkwood to fill the commissioner of Indian Affairs post left vacant by the sudden resignation of a dying Roland E. Trowbridge. Price accepted and took office on 6 May 1881. He served until 1885. During this time he served as a stabilizing influence in the bureau and contributed four annual reports as commissioner. His examinations did little but push for a major severalty bill to be enacted by the Congress.

In his 1881 essay, he explained, "In the outset, I desire to urge with earnestness the absolute necessity for a thorough and radical change of the Indian policy in some respects, and in so doing I shall touch upon points which will be referred to more at length hereafter under special headings." Continuing, he added, "It is claimed and admitted by all that the great object of the government is to civilize the Indians and render them such assistance in kind and degree as will make them self-supporting, and yet I think no one will deny that one part of our policy is calculated to produce the very opposite result. It must be apparent to the most casual observer that the system of gathering the Indians in bands or tribes on reservations and carrying them victuals [provisions] and clothes, thus relieving them of the necessity of labor, never will and never can civilize them. Labor is an essential element in producing civilization. If white men were treated as we treat the Indians the result would certainly be a race of worthless vagabonds. The greatest kindness the government can bestow upon the Indian is to teach him to labor for his own support, thus developing his true manhood, and, as a consequence, making him self-relying and self-supporting." Later in that same report, Price wrote, "The allotment system tends to break up tribal relations. It has the effect of creating individuality, responsibility, and a desire to accumulate property. It teaches the Indian habits of industry and frugality, and stimulates them to look forward to a better and more useful life, and, in the end, it will relieve the government of large annual appropriations. As stated in the annual report of this office for the year 1880, the desire to take lands in severalty is almost universal among the Indians." In his 1882 treatise, Price discussed the role of religious societies in the formation of Indian policy. "One very important auxiliary in transforming men from savage to civilized life is the influence brought to bear upon them through the labors of Christian men and women as educators and missionaries," Price explained. "This, I think, has been forcibly illustrated and clearly demonstrated among the different Indian tribes by the missionary labors of the various religious societies in the last few years. Civilization is a plant of exceeding slow growth, unless supplemented by Christian teaching and influences. I am decidedly of the opinion that a liberal encouragement by the government to all religious denominations to extend their educational operations among the Indians would be of immense benefit."

By 1884, Price, now 70 years old and desiring of retirement, asked to be relieved of his post if a suitable replacement could be found. In his letter of resignation to Secretary of the Interior Schurz, Price penned, "I have not found the position [of Commissioner] to be a 'bed of roses,' but I have endeavored to give to the discharge of the duties connected with the office my best thought and effort, with an earnest desire to subserve the best interests of the Government—the Indians. I am now desirous of retiring and I therefor hereby respectfully tender to the President through you my resignation." Although there was a search, no one was found. The election of a Democrat, Grover Cleveland, in 1884 and his desire to install John DeWitt Clinton Atkins as Indian Commissioner made the search moot. Price left office on 26 March 1885, but stayed on in Washington. In the years before his death, he wrote several articles for leading magazines, including "The

Government and the Indians" (*The Forum*, February 1891), and "Recollections of Iowa Men and Affairs" (*Annals of Iowa*, April 1893). Price died in Washington on 30 May 1901 at the age of 87, and his body was returned to to Iowa for interment in Davenport's Oakdale Cemetery.

See also Bureau of Indian Affairs.

References *Biographical Directory of the United States Congress, 1774–1989*, Senate Document 100-34, 100th Congress, Second Session (1989); Haynes, Fred E., "Price, Hiram." In Dumas Malone et al., eds., *Dictionary of American Biography* (1930–88); O'Neil, Floyd A., "Hiram Price." In Robert M. Kvasnicka and Herman J. Viola, eds., *The Commissioners of Indian Affairs, 1824–1977* (1979); Price to Secretary of the Interior Henry Moore Teller, 15 March 1884, Box 44, Records of the Appointments Division, Commissioner of Indian Affairs, RG 48, National Archives; U.S. Congress, House of Representatives, *Annual Report of the Commissioner of Indian Affairs for the Year 1881*, House Executive Document No. 1, 47th Congress, 1st Session (serial 2018); U.S. Congress, House of Representatives, *Annual Report of the Commissioner of Indian Affairs for the Year 1882*, House Executive Document No. 1, 47th Congress, 2d Session (serial 2100).

Pronovost v. United States (232 U.S. 696 [1914])

In this case, the U.S. Supreme Court held that under an act of Congress of 30 January 1897 (29 Stat. 506), "the introduction of liquors, such as whisky [*sic*], wine and beer, into the Indian country, [is] an offense against the United States, and prescribes its punishment." Joseph Pronovost, the plaintiff in error, was prosecuted for introducing such intoxicating liquors into the Flathead Indian Reservation in Montana. Tried, he was convicted by a jury, and subsequently appealed his conviction to the District Court of the District of Montana but that court upheld the conviction as legal under 29 Stat. 506. Pronovost appealed to the U.S. Supreme Court. He did not argue his case before the court. Instead, he submitted the case arguments on 15 January 1914, and the court handed down its judgment a month later, on 24 February 1914. Speaking for a unanimous court, Justice Willis Van Devanter held that since the defendant admitted that he had introduced the liquors onto the reservation, and that the court found 29 Stat. 506 to bear constitutional muster, Pronovost's conviction must stand, and he had no legal standing to challenge it.

Public Law 280 (67 Stat. 588)

Passed in the era of the termination of federal responsibilities over Indian tribal affairs, this federal action of 15 August 1953 was meant to consent to state jurisdiction over criminal and civil matters dealing with Indians from terminated tribes. Justice William Brennan wrote in *Bryan v. Itasca County* (1976), "The primary concern of Congress in enacting Public Law 280 that emerges from its sparse legislative history was with the problem of lawlessness on certain Indian reservations, and the absence of adequate tribal institutions for law enforcement." The law was repealed with the passage of the Indian Civil Rights Act of 1968. Known as 280, the law conferred jurisdiction on the states of California, Minnesota, Nebraska, Oregon, and Wisconsin "with respect to criminal offenses and civil causes of action committed or arising on Indian reservations within such States."

See also *Bryan v. Itasca County*; *Washington et al. v. Confederated Bands and Tribes of the Yakima Indian Nation.*

Reference Goldberg, Carole E., "Public Law 280: The Limits of State Jurisdiction Over Reservation Indians." *UCLA Law Review* 22.

Pueblo of Santa Rosa v. Fall (273 U.S. 315, 71 L.Ed. 658, 47 S.Ct. 361 [1927])

See *Lane et al. v. Pueblo of Pueblo of Santa Rosa.*

Puyallup Tribe, etc. v. The Department of Game of Washington et al. (391 U.S. 392, 20 L.Ed. 2d 689, 88 S.Ct. 1725 [1968])

The first in a series of three Supreme Court cases dealing with the fishing rights of reservations, *Puyallup*, decided jointly with the case of *Nugent Kautz et al. v. The Department of Game of Washington*, held that "treaty provisions did not preclude the state from regulating the manner of fishing and restricting commercial fishing in the interest of conservation, provided that such regulation was a reasonable and necessary exercise of the state's police power and did not discriminate against the Indians." Under article III of the Treaty of Medicine Creek (10 Stat. 1133), made in 1854 with the Puyallup and Nisqually Indians of what would become Washington State, "the right of taking fish, at all usual and accustomed grounds and stations, is further secured to said Indians, in common with all citizens of the Territory, and of erecting temporary houses for the purposes of curing, together with the privilege of hunting, gathering roots and berries, and pasturing their horses on open and unclaimed lands." In the 1960s, to formulate conservation measures to protect the rapidly dwindling stocks of salmon (four types: chinook, silver, chum, and pink) and steelhead trout in the Puyallup River, the Washington State legislature prohibited the use by all persons, including Indians, of certain nets used to catch a large number of fish at one time. Members of the two tribes, in violation of the legislation, set up their nets anyway. The Washington Department of Game sued in the state courts to force the Indians to conform to the law, and was rewarded with an injunction against further use of the nets by the Indians. The Washington State Supreme Court held that such regulations were within the purview of the state's police power over its natural resources; the two tribes appealed to the Supreme Court.

Argued on 25 and 26 March 1968, the case was decided on 27 May of that same year with a unanimous decision of the court. In an opinion delivered by Justice William O. Douglas, the court held that under the police power of the state, Washington State had a right to regulate fishing by all persons if done in the name of conservation. Justice Douglas explained, "Another forerunner of *Tulee* [*Tulee v. Washington*, 315 U.S. 681, 86 L.Ed. 1115, 62 S.Ct. 862 (1942)] was *Kennedy v. Becker*, 241 U.S. 556, 60 L.Ed. 1166, 36 S.Ct. 705], which also involved a nonexclusive grant of fishing rights to Indians. Indians were charged with the spearing of fish contrary to New York law, their defense being the fishing rights granted by a treaty. The Court, in sustaining the judgments of conviction, said: 'We do not think that it is a proper construction of the reservation in the conveyance to regard it as an attempt either to reserve sovereign prerogative or so to divide the inherent power of preservation as to make its competent exercise impossible. Rather are we of the opinion that the clause is fully satisfied by considering it a reservation of a privilege of fishing and hunting upon the granted lands in common with the grantees, and others to whom the privilege might be extended but subject nevertheless to that necessary power of appropriate regulation, as to all those privileged, which inhered in the sovereignty of the State over the lands where the privilege was exercised.'"

See also *Puyallup Tribe v. The Department of Game of the State of Washington et al.* (Puyallup II, 1973); *Puyallup Tribe Inc. and Ramona Bennett v. The Department of Game of Washington et al.* (Puyallup III, 1977); *Tulee v. Washington.*

Puyallup Tribe, Inc., and Ramona Bennett v. The Department of Game of the State of Washington et al. (433 U.S. 165 [1977])

Known as *Puyallup III*, this case involves, like its two predecessors, the fishing rights of the Puyallup Indian tribe of Washington State. In 1973, the Supreme Court, in *Puyallup Tribe v. The Department of Game of the State of Washington et al.*, held that the Treaty of Medicine Creek (10 Stat. 1133) prohibited a complete ban on the catching of steelhead trout by the Puyallup Indians from the Puyallup River, and ordered the case remanded (returned) to the lower court which had originally heard the action to determine the number of fish the Indians could catch in the interest of conservation. This court, the Superior Court of the State of Washington for Pierce County, then held that the court had jurisdiction to regulate the number of fish the tribe may catch, and demanded a listing of those tribal members who intended to fish. The Washington State Supreme Court, after modifying the judgment slightly, affirmed. The Puyallup tribe appealed the district court's judgment to the Supreme Court for the third time. Arguments were heard on 18 April 1977, and a decision was delivered by Justice John Paul Stevens on 23 June of that same year. In the 7–2 decision (Justices William Brennan and Thurgood Marshall dissenting), the majority held that while the doctrine of "sovereign immunity" disallowed the lower court from exercising jurisdiction over the tribe as a whole, such a ruling did not stop the court from regulating the catching of fish by individual tribal members; further, the state could regulate the fishing industry on the Puyallup reservation, and that a fixed total placed on the number of fish caught by the Indians was not improper. Justice Stevens explained,

> A practical problem is presented by our disposition. The limitation on the size of the new catch applies to all members of the Tribe. The respondent has no interest in how the catch is allocated among the Indians; its concern is with the total number of steelhead netted during each season, with obtaining information to make it possible to recommend a proper allocation in succeeding years, and with enforcement against individuals who may net fish after the allowable limit has been reached. On the other hand, the Tribe has a separate interest in affording equitable treatment to its members and protecting those members from any mistaken enforcement efforts. For that reason, although it properly resists the authority of the state court to order it to provide information with respect to the status of enrolled members of the Tribe and the size of their catch, it may find that its members' interests are best served by voluntarily providing such information to respondent and to the court in order to minimize the risk of an erroneous enforcement effort. The state courts must continue to accord full respect to the Tribe's right to participate in the proceedings on behalf of its members as it has in the past without treating such participation as qualifying its right to claim immunity as a sovereign. The judgment is vacated, and the case is remanded to the Supreme Court of Washington for further proceedings not inconsistent with the opinion.

Justice Harry Blackmun, while he concurred in the result, nonetheless wrote, "I join the Court's opinion. I entertain doubts, however, about the continuing vitality in this day of the doctrine of tribal immunity as it was enunciated in United States Fidelity & Guaranty Co., 309 U.S. 506, 84 L.Ed. 894, 60 S.Ct. 653 (1940). I am of the view that that doctrine may well merit re-examination in an appropriate case."

See also *Puyallup Tribe v. The Department of Game of Washington et al.* (Puyallup I, 1968); *Puyallup Tribe v. The Department of Game of the State of Washington et al.* (Puyallup II, 1973).

Puyallup Tribe v. The Department of Game of the State of Washington et al. (414 U.S. 44, 38 L.Ed. 2d 254, 94 S.Ct. 330 [1973])

Known as *Puyallup II*, this case was a continuation of a long-standing dispute between the Puyallup Indians and the state of Washington, which intended to institute some sort of fishing regulations against the Indians to protect steelhead trout in the Puyallup River. After the Supreme Court held in the first case in 1968 that while the Indians' fishing rights were protected by treaty, the state had the right to make "reasonable, necessary, and nondiscriminatory regulations affecting the manner of the Indians' fishing" if the state sought to conserve fish stocks, the case was remanded (returned) to the original court for a rehearing. Ultimately, the Supreme Court of Washington State upheld Department of Game regulations which banned all net fishing for steelhead trout, allowing only hook-and-line sports fishing in order to preserve the species. The Supreme Court granted certiorari to review the new regulations. After arguments were heard on 10 October 1973, Justice William O. Douglas delivered the unanimous opinion of the court on 19 November 1973; he held that the regulations "improperly discriminated" against the Indians because they used nets rather than hooks and lines. However, Justice Douglas cautioned in the court's opinion, "We do not imply that these fishing rights persist down to the very last steelhead in the river. Rights can be controlled by the need to conserve a species; and the time may come when the life of a steelhead is so precarious in a particular stream that all fishing should be banned until the species regains assurance of survival. The police power of the State is adequate to prevent the steelhead from following the fate of the passenger pigeon; and the Treaty does not give the Indians a federal right to pursue the last living steelhead until it enters their nets." Justice Douglas remanded the case back to the original court for more hearings.

See also *Puyallup Tribe v. The Department of Game of Washington et al.* (Puyallup I, 1968); *Puyallup Tribe, Inc. and Ramona Bennett v. The Department of Game of Washington et al.* (Puyallup III, 1977).

Q

***Quick Bear v. Leupp et al.* (210 U.S. 50 [1908])**
Officially titled *Reuben Quick Bear, Ralph Eagle Feather, and Charles Tackett, on Behalf of Themselves and All Other Members of the Sioux Tribe of Indians of the Rosebud Agency, South Dakota, Appellants, v. Francis E. Leupp, Commissioner of Indian Affairs; James Rudolph Garfield, Secretary of the Interior; George Bruce Cortelyou, Secretary of the Treasury et al.*, this Supreme Court case dealt with the issue of the public funding of Indian sectarian schools. By article 7 of the Sioux treaty of 29 April 1868, and continued for twenty additional years under the act of 1 July 1889, a fund (known as the Sioux Treaty Fund) was established for the schooling of Sioux children. The act of 3 March 1905 (33 Stat. 1048, at 1055) appropriated $225,000 for this fund. When Commissioner of Indian Affairs Francis E. Leupp attempted to sign a contract with the Bureau of Catholic Indian Missions of Washington, D.C., for a number of Rosebud Sioux to be sent to the missions' St. Francis Boarding School on the Rosebud reservation, the Rosebud Sioux sued to enjoin, or stop, Leupp from signing the contract. The tribe claimed that Leupp was violating the law; under the act of 7 June 1897 (30 Stat. 62, at 79), it was "declared to be the settled policy of the government to hereafter make no appropriation whatever for education [of Indian children] in any sectarian school." The Supreme Court of the District of Columbia, where the suit was filed, held for the Rosebud Sioux, but the court of appeals reversed. The Supreme Court agreed to hear the Indians' appeal. After arguments were heard on 26 and 27 February 1908, a decision was handed down on 18 May of the same year. Chief Justice Melville Weston Fuller held for a unanimous court in affirming the lower courts and siding with Leupp. Fuller declared in reading the court's opinion that when the government decided to "make no appropriation whatever for education" of Indian children in sectarian schools, it was talking about "gratuitous appropriations," and not funds appropriated for a treaty obligation. As Chief Justice Fuller explained,

This "trust fund" is held for the Indians, and not distributed *per capita*, being held as property in common. The money is distributed in accordance with the discretion of the Secretary of the Interior, but really belongs to the Indians. The President declared it to be the moral right of the Indians to have this "trust fund" applied to the education of the Indians in the schools of their choice, and the same view was entertained by the supreme court of the District of Columbia and the court of appeals of the District. But the "treaty fund" has exactly the same characteristics. They are moneys belonging really to the Indians. They are the price of land ceded by the Indians to the government. The only difference is that, in the "treaty fund," the debt to the Indians created and secured by the treaty is paid by annual appropriations. They are not gratuitous appropriations of public moneys, but the payment, we repeat, of a treaty debt in installments. We perceive no justification for applying the proviso or declaration of policy to the payment of treaty obligations, the two things being distinct and different in nature, and having no relation to each other, except that both are technically appropriations.

See also Leupp, Francis Ellington.

Quinton, Amelia Stone (1833–1926)
It was the alliance of Mary Bonney Rambaut and Amelia Stone Quinton which formed the Women's National Indian Association in 1879, one of the leading white-led Indian reform organizations of the nineteenth century. Yet Amelia Stone Quinton was the lessen known of the two, and her life of trying to reform American society for American Indians and in the area of temperance has been little studied. She was born Amelia Stone in Janesville, New York, on 31 July 1833, the daughter of Jacob Benjamin Stone and Mary (née Bennett) Stone. Of

them, prohibitionists Frances E. Willard and Mary Livermore wrote in 1893, "She comes of English ancestry and is directly descended from both Pilgrim and Puritan New England stock. Her father was a man of noble nature, of great conciousness and of musical gifts, while her mother was endowed with energy, executive ability and courage." Both were devout Baptists; her maternal grandfather, Asa Bennett, a Baptist deacon, had been part of the Revivalist movement of the eighteenth century. Amelia grew up in nearby Homer, New York, and attended Cortland Academy in that town. She taught for a period of time at a small school near Syracuse, New York, before moving on to a position in a seminary school in Madison, Georgia. There she met the Reverend James Franklin Swanson and married him. They were united but a few years; Swanson became ill and died when Amelia was eighteen. Widowed before her twentieth birthday, Amelia moved to Philadelphia, where she got a position as a teacher at Mary Bonney's Chestnut Street Female Seminary. There she befriended Bonney, who was an advocate for the poor and Native Americans. Amelia later went to New York City, where she worked in almshouses (established for debtors and the poor) and for prison reform.

In the 1870s, Amelia Stone was a leading voice in the prohibition movement, and as a member of the Woman's Christian Temperance Union she became overworked and had to travel to Europe to recover her precarious health. In England, she met Professor Richard Quinton, and with him toured churches in England delivering temperance lectures. While there she married Quinton, and when they returned to United States in 1878 they settled in Philadelphia. Quinton then approached her friend Mary Bonney with stories of massacres of Indians and their brutal treatment at the hands of the government. The women then formed the Committee on Ways and Means, a committee of correspondence designed to encourage other womens' groups to participate in a call for Indian reform. They circulated a petition among the leading citizens of the city to be sent to Congress, calling on the reform of the government's agenda toward Native Americans. The petition, bearing 13,000 signatories, was delivered to President Rutherford B. Hayes at the White House in February 1880. In 1879, the Committee on Ways and Means became first the Central Indian Committee, then the Indian Treaty-Keeping and Protective Association, and then the National Indian Association. In 1883, it got its final name: the Women's National Indian Association (WNIA), with Mary Bonney as president and Quinton as vice president. Further petitions, including one delivered to Senator Henry L. Dawes of Massachusetts in 1882, contained 100,000 signatures. This appeal, calling for improved Indian education, Indian citizenship, allotment in severalty of and Indian lands, and full rights for Native Americans, was written by Quinton herself.

The WNIA was the leading women's Indian reform group at the time; the Indian Rights Association, as well as the Lake Mohonk Conferences of the Friends of the Indians, were male in character and membership. The WNIA distinguished itself by sending missionaries to live among the Indians and "civilize" them. Amelia Quinton toured the Indian reservations in the western United States, and organized white women into "auxiliaries" of the WNIA to rally Congress to change its laws. She wrote articles in some 800 periodicals, drafted petitions to Congress, and traveled to England to lobby for international attention to her cause. In 1887, Richard Quinton died, but his widow continued her work. For many years she edited the WNIA's journal, *The Indian's Friend.* It was her idea that for the WNIA to expand its constituency, men should be allowed to join, and the organization's name was changed to the National Indian Association. In 1907 she moved to Los Angeles to continue her work there, but moved back east, to Ridgefield Park, New Jersey, and continued to work until felled by illness. She suffered a cerebral hemorrhage and died at her home on 23 June 1926, just a month shy of her ninety-fourth birthday. She was buried in Homer, New York. Irene

Joanne Westing writes of her, "To the end she had remained confident that 'the *right* thing…can be done; for the right is God's way.' A humanitarian innocent of any sense of cultural relativism, she had in long, unpaid service demonstrated her belief that 'barbarism has no claim upon us, but barbarians have.' Seeing 'no per se dependent races,' recognizing that all races 'with opportunity, witness the same results,' she had striven to give Indians a chance to become like everyone else."

See also Rambaut, Mary Lucinda Bonney; Women's National Indian Association.

References Fenichell, Lois F., "Quinton, Amelia Stone." In Alden Whitman, ed., *American Reformers: An H. W. Wilson Biographical Dictionary* (1985); Hardy, Gail J., "American Women Civil Rights Activists: Biobibliographies of 68 Leaders, 1825–1992" (1993); Westing, Irene Joanne, "Quinton, Amelia Stone." In Edward T. James, ed., *Notable American Women, 1607–1950: A Biographical Dictionary* (1971); Willard, Frances E., and Mary Livermore, eds., *A Woman of the Century: Fourteen Hundred-Seventy Biographical Sketches Accompanied by Portraits of Leading American Women in All Walks of Life* (1893).

R

***Ramah Navajo School Board et al. v. Bureau of Revenue of New Mexico* (458 U.S. 832, 73 L.Ed. 2d 1174, 102 S.Ct. 3394 [1982])**

Were the gross receipts gathered by a nonreservation corporation from the construction of an Indian school on a reservation subject to state taxes, or were such taxes in violation of the federal-Indian trust relationship? The Ramah Navajos, a chapter of the Navajo Indian Nation, live on their reservation in west central New Mexico. Prior to 1979, the children of the Ramah tribe did not have a reservation school to attend; however, in 1974, and continuing for five years, the separate Ramah Navajo School Board, Inc., a nonprofit organization, hired co-plaintiff Lembke Construction Company to design and build an on-reservation school. For the five years of construction, Lembke paid a state tax on nonreservation construction companies, levied on its gross receipts, and Lembke was reimbursed by the school board. While paying the tax, both Lembke and the tribe protested the imposition of the tax. In 1978, after arguing with the state for four years, both the company and the tribe filed suit against the state Bureau of Revenue for $232,264.38, which if refunded would go to the tribe. The District Court ruled in favor of the state Bureau of Revenue, holding that the tax was not imposed on the tribe but on the non-Indian construction company. On appeal, the Court of Appeals for the State of New Mexico affirmed. The U.S. Supreme Court granted certiorari (the right to hear the case).

Arguments were heard on 28 April 1982, with a decision being handed down on 2 July of the same year. In a ruling by Justice Thurgood Marshall (Justices William H. Rehnquist, Byron White, and John Paul Stevens dissenting), the 6–3 majority held that under such federal laws as the Indian Self-Determination and Education Assistance Act of 1975 (88 Stat. 2203–2217) and the Indian Financing Act of 1974 (25 U.S.C. 1451–1543), both of which "encourag[ed] tribal self-sufficiency in the area of education," federal law pre-empted such state taxes. Justice Marshall explained, "The State's ultimate justification for imposing this tax amounts to nothing more than a general desire to increase revenues. This purpose, as we held in *White Mountain [Apache Tribe v. Bracker]*, 448 U.S. [136], at 150, 65 L.Ed. 2d 665, 100 S.Ct. 2578, is insufficient to justify the additional burdens imposed by the tax on the comprehensive federal scheme regulating the creation and maintenance of educational opportunities for Indian children and on the express federal policy of encouraging Indian self-sufficiency in the area of education. This regulatory scheme precludes any state tax that 'stands as an obstacle to the accomplishment of the full purposes and objectives of Congress.'"

Rambaut, Mary Lucinda Bonney (1816–1900)

The *Philadelphia Public Ledger* remembered her on her death with a small announcement in its 25 July 1900 edition: "Obituary: Mrs. Mary L. Bonney Rambaut, for thirty-three years one of the Principals of Miss Bonney's and Miss Dillaye's Chestnut Street Female Seminary, and one of the founders of the Ogontz School, died, aged 84 years." The paper did not mention that Mary Bonney Rambaut was a woman whose life was dedicated to reform, including aiding the Indians in the last years of the nineteenth century. The daughter and the fourth of six children (only two survived infancy) of Benjamin Bonney, a veteran of the Revolutionary War, and Lucinda (née Wilder) Bonney, she was born in Hamilton, Madison County, New York, on 8 June 1816. Mary Bonney attended Hamilton Academy, then graduated in 1835 from Emma Willard's Troy (New York) Female Seminary. Afterwards she taught in several schools from New York City to South Carolina. After teaching in Philadelphia, she and a fellow schoolmate from the Troy Seminary, Harriette Dillaye, founded the Chestnut Street Female Seminary in that city in 1850. The school, comments Gayle Hardy, "was dedicated to producing clear, independent, principled thinkers."

Sometime in the 1850s, Bonney served as a member of the Philadelphia branch of the Woman's Union Missionary Society of America for Heathen Lands, an organization which she had assisted in its organization, and the Woman's Home Missionary Committee of the First Baptist Church to work for the betterment of the American Indian. For the next twenty years she worked tirelessly to advance Indian rights. When Congress declared its intention to open up Indian lands to whites in Oklahoma, she wrote, "A moral wrong upon our Government! It took hold of me!" Her activism led to her establishment, with her friend Amelia Stone Quinton, of a women's Indian rights organization. Named at first the Committee of Ways and Means, they changed it the Central Indian Committee, the Indian Treaty-Keeping and Protective Association, and the National Indian Association. In 1883, it was finally called the Women's National Indian Association (WNIA), and Bonney served as its second president. Angered at the Sand Creek Massacre and the government's overall attitude towards the Indians, Bonney and Quinton signed a protest which they delivered to the White House on 14 February 1880. A second protest, with 50,000 signatures, was sent to Senator Henry L. Dawes of Massachusetts, pleading with him to preserve Indian land rights and respect all treaties made with them. In 1882, a third petition, this time with 100,000 signatures, called on President Chester A. Arthur to grant citizenship to the Indians and give them their land in allotments. This declaration became the basis for Dawes' support for the General Allotment Act, which was enacted in 1887. Thus the WNIA became the most influential female Indian rights group in the nineteenth century.

Mary Bonney married the Reverend Dr. Thomas Rambaut, a longtime friend, in 1888, and she never had any children. After traveling to England and Ireland (she resigned from the WNIA in 1884), she and her husband settled in Hamilton, New York. Their married life was short, as her husband died in October 1890, and she lived in Hamilton for the remainder of her life with her brother, Benjamin Franklin Bonney. She died in Hamilton on 24 July 1900 at the age of 84.

See also Quinton, Amelia Stone; Women's National Indian Association.

References "Bonney, Mary Lucinda." In Robert McHenry, ed., *Famous American Women: A Biographical Dictionary from Colonial Times to the Present* (1980); Fenichell, Lois F., "Bonney, Mary Lucinda." In Alden Whitman, ed., *American Reformers: An H. W. Wilson Biographical Dictionary* (1985); Hardy, Gail J., *American Women Civil Rights Activists: Biobibliographies of 68 Leaders, 1825–1992* (1993); "Obituary." *Philadelphia Public Ledger*, 25 July 1900, 1; "Rambaut, Mrs. Mary L. Bonney." In Frances E. Willard and Mary Livermore, eds., *A Woman of the Century: Fourteen Hundred-Seventy Biographical Sketches Accompanied by Portraits of Leading American Women in All Walks of Life* (1893), 595; Westing, Irene Joanne, "Bonney, Mary Lucinda." In Edward T. James, ed., *Notable American Women, 1607–1950: A Biographical Dictionary* (1971).

Reagan, Ronald—Statement of Indian Policy

On 24 January 1983, President Ronald Reagan released a statement of Indian policy for his administration. The following, a portion of that statement, is perhaps the fullest of any modern president on his goals for the handling of Indian Affairs.

This administration believes that responsibilities should be restored to the governments which are closest to the people served. This philosophy applies not only to State and local governments but also to federally recognized American Indian tribes.

When European colonial powers began to explore and colonize this land, they entered into treaties with sovereign Indian nations. Our new nation continued to make treaties and to deal with Indian tribes on a government-to-government basis. Throughout our history, despite periods of conflict and shifting national policies the government-to-government relationship between the United States and Indian tribes has endured. The Constitution, treaties, laws, and court decisions have consistently recognized a unique political relationship between Indian tribes and the United States which this administration pledges to uphold.

In 1970 President Nixon announced a national policy of self-determination for Indian tribes. At the heart of the new policy was a commitment by the federal government to foster and encourage tribal self-government. That commitment was signed into law in 1975 as the Indian Self-Determination and Education Assistance Act.

The principle of self-government set forth in this act was a good starting point. However, since 1975 there has been more rhetoric than action. Instead of fostering and encouraging self-government, federal policies have inhibited the political and economic development of the tribes. Excessive regulation and self-perpetuating bureaucracy have stifled decisionmaking, thwarted Indian control of Indian resources, and promoted dependency rather than self-sufficiency.

This administration intends to reverse this trend by removing the obstacles to self-government and by creating a more favorable environment for the development of healthy reservation economies. Tribal governments, the Federal Government, and the private sector will all have a role. This administration will take a flexible approach which recognizes the diversity among tribes and the right of each tribe to set its own priorities and goals. Change will not happen overnight. Development will be chartered by the tribes, not the Federal Government.

This administration honors the commitment this nation made in 1970 and 1975 to strengthen tribal governments and lessen Federal control over tribal governmental affairs. This administration is determined to turn these goals into reality. Our policy is to reaffirm dealing with Indian tribes on a government-to-government basis and to pursue the policy of self-government for Indian tribes without threatening termination.…

Tribal governments, like State and local governments, are more aware of the needs and desires of their citizens than is the Federal Government and should, therefore, have the primary responsibility for meeting those needs. The only effective way for Indian reservations to develop is through tribal governments which are responsive and accountable to their members.

Early in this nation's dealings with Indian tribes, Federal employees began to perform Indian tribal government functions. Despite the Indian Self-Determination Act, major tribal government functions—enforcing tribal laws, developing and managing tribal resources, educating children—are frequently still carried on by Federal employees. The Federal Government must move away from this surrogate role which undermines the concept of self-government.

It is important to the concept of self-government that tribes reduce their dependence on Federal funds by providing a greater percentage of the cost of their self-government. Some tribes are already moving in this direction. This administration pledges to assist tribes in strengthening their governments by removing the Federal impediments to tribal self-government and tribal resource development. Necessary Federal funds will continue to be available. This administration affirms the right of tribes to determine the best way to meet the needs of their members and to establish and run programs which best meet those needs.

For those small tribes which have the greatest need to develop core governmental capacities, this administration has developed, through the Assistant Secretary of the Interior for Indian Affairs, the Small Tribes Initiative. This program will provide financial support necessary to allow these tribes to develop basic tribal administrative and management capabilities.

In keeping with the government-to-government relationship, Indian tribes are defined by law as eligible entities and receive direct funding, if they wish, in five block programs administered by the Department of Health and Human Services. These and other blocks to the States consolidated dozens of categorical Federal domestic assistance programs to reduce fragmentation and overlap, eliminate excessive Federal regulation, and provide for more local control. This administration now proposes that Indian tribes be eligible for direct funding in the Title XX social services block, the block with the largest appropriation and greatest flexibility in service delivery.

In addition, we are moving the White House liaison for federally recognized tribes from the Office of Public Liaison to the Office of Intergovernmental Affairs, which maintains liaison with State and local governments. In the past several administrations, tribes have been placed along with vital interest groups, such as veterans, businessmen, and religious leaders. In moving the tribal government contact within the White House Intergovernmental Affairs staff, this administration is underscoring its commitment to recognizing tribal governments on a government-to-government basis.

Further, we are recommending that the Congress expand the authorized membership of the Advisory Commission of Intergovernmental Relations (42 U.S.C. 4273) to include a representative of Indian tribal governments. In the interim, before federal action, we are requesting that the Assistant Secretary for Indian Affairs join the Commission as an observer. We also supported and signed into law the Indian Tribal Governmental Tax Status Act which provides tribal governments with essentially the same treatment under Federal tax laws as applies to other governments with regard to revenue raising and saving mechanisms.

In addition, this administration calls upon Congress to replace House Concurrent Resolution 108 of the 83rd Congress, the resolution which established the now discredited policy of terminating the Federal-tribal relationship. Congress has implicitly rejected the termination policy by enacting the Indian Self-Determination and Education Assistance Act of 1975. However, because the termination policy declared in H. Con. Res. 108 has not been expressly and formally repudiated by a concurrent resolution of Congress, it continues to create among Indian people an apprehension that the United States may not in the future honor the unique relationship between the Indian people and the Federal Government. A lingering threat of termination has no place in this administration's policy of self-government for Indian tribes, and I ask Congress to again express its support of self-government.

These actions are but the first steps in restoring control to tribal governments. Much more needs to be done. Without sound reservation economies, the concept of self-government has little meaning. In the past, despite good intentions, the Federal Government has been one of the major obstacles to economic progress. This administration intends to remove the impediments to economic development and to encourage cooperative efforts among the tribes, the Federal Government, and the private sector in developing reservation economies....

The economies of American Indian reservations are extremely depressed, with unemployment rates among the highest in the country. Indian leaders have told this administration that the development of reservation economies is their number one priority. Growing economies provide jobs, promote self-sufficiency, and provide revenue for essential services. Past attempts to stimulate growth have been fragmented and largely ineffective. As a result, involvement of private industry has been limited, with only infrequent success. Developing reservation economies offers a special challenge: devising investment procedures consistent with the trust status, removing legal barriers which restrict the type of contracts tribes can enter into, and reducing the numerous and complex regulations which hinder economic growth.

Tribes have had limited opportunities to invest in their own economies, because often there has been no established resource base for community investment and development. Many reservations lack a developed physical infrastructure, including utilities, transportation, and other public services. They also often lack the regulatory, adjudicatory, and enforcement mechanisms necessary to interact with the private sector for reservation economic development. Development on the reservation offers potential for tribes and individual entrepreneurs in manufacturing, agribusiness, and modern technology, as well as fishing, livestock, arts and crafts, and other traditional livelihoods.

Natural resources such as timber, fishing, and energy provide and avenue of development for many tribes. Tribal governments have the responsibility to determine the extent and the methods of developing the tribe's natural resources. The Federal Government's responsibility should not be used to hinder tribes from taking advantage of economic development opportunities.

With regard to energy resources, both the Indian tribes and the Nation stand to gain from the prudent development and management of the vast coal, oil, gas, uranium, and other resources found on Indian lands. As already demonstrated by a number of tribes, these resources can become the foundation for economic development on many reservations, whule lessening our nation's dependence on imported oil. The Federal role is to encourage the production of energy resources in ways consistent with Indian values and priorities. To that end, we have strongly supported the use of creative agreements such as joint ventures and other nonlease agreements for the development of Indian mineral resources.

It is the free market which will supply the bulk of the capital investments required to develop tribal energy and other resources. A fundamental prerequisite to economic development is capital formation. The establishment of a financial structure that is a part of the Indian reservation community is essential to the development of Indian capital formation.

Red Bird v. United States (203 U.S. 76 [1906])

See Cherokee Intermarriage Cases.

Red Power Movement

Created to imitate the achievements of black Americans and their "black power" movement of the 1960s, this movement by American Indians started over fishing rights in Washington State. On the river banks of the northwestern part of that state throughout 1964 and 1965, Indians native to the area, as well as journalists, clergy in sympathy with the Indians, and such personalities as Marlon Brando and Dick Gregory assembed in "fish-ins" to protest the state's refusal to let them fish according to their treaty rights. It was the start of the Indian rights movement of the era. Robert Allen Warrior writes, "By defying state law in full view of media and law-enforcement personnel, these Natives were among those initiating a new way of bringing their political struggles to the attention of the United States and the world. The series of events in Washington and other places continues to affect Native politics and intellectual discourse to the present day." As part of the movement, there was a rebellion against elders who these radicals felt "collaborated" with the government—so-called "Uncle Tomahawks"—and with the government itself, an attitude which led to the standoff with government troops at Wounded Knee in 1973. The last major event of the Red Power movement was the "Longest Walk" in July 1978, when several hundred Indian activists marched for five months from San Francisco to Washington, D.C., to protest government inaction towards the problems of Native Americans. However, the Red Power movement did induce the government to enact several major pieces of legislation in the 1970s, particularly those passed in response to recommendations from the

American Indian Policy Review Commission; these include the Alaska Native Claims Settlement Act (1971), the Indian Financing Act of 1974, the Indian Self-Determination and Education Assistance Act of 1975, and the Rhode Island Indian Claims Settlement Act of 1978, which brought a final disposition to the claims of Indians in that state.

Indian historian and writer Alvin Josephy, Jr., writes, "Red Power, as it has been taken up in the intervening years by Indians throughout the United States (as well as Canada), today reflects a determined and patriotic fight for freedom—freedom from injustice and bondage, freedom from patronization and oppression, freedom from what the white man cannot and will not solve."

See also Alaska Native Claims Settlement Act; American Indian Policy Review Commission; Fish-In; Indian Financing Act of 1974; Indian Self-Determination and Education Assistance Act of 1975; "Longest Walk"; National Indian Youth Council.

References Champagne, Duane, ed., *The Native North American Almanac: A Reference Work on Native North Americans in the United States and Canada* (1994); Josephy, Alvin M., Jr., *Red Power: The American Indians' Fight for Freedom* (1971); Warrior, Robert Allen, *Tribal Secrets Recovering American Indian Intellectual Traditions* (1995).

Reifel, Benjamin (Brulé Sioux) (1906–1990)

He served less than two months as the last official commissioner of Indian Affairs, but the name of Benjamin Reifel remains an outstanding one in the fight for Native American rights. Born on the Rosebud Reservation in South Dakota on 19 September 1906, he was the son of William M. ("Shorty") Reifel, a German-American farmer, and Lucy Burning Breast, a full-blood Brulé Sioux. (Brulé means "Burnt Thigh.") Reifel was known as Wiyaka Wanjila ("Lone Feather"), but his father called him Ben. The Reifel family life was difficult: William Reifel spoke in a heavy German accent, and his wife spoke only Sioux. In an interview in 1986, Reifel explained, "While I was a boy growing up on the Rosebud Indian Reservation, we had the most sickening poverty that one could imagine. Tuberculosis was a killer of Indians. The people in the Pine Ridge Reservation and at Oglala were eating their horses to survive. Impoverishment was everywhere." He attended the Indian day school on the reservation, and looked for ways to educate himself. "I grew up on the reservation," he said later, "speaking Sioux all the time. Why did not the other Indians respond [to educational opportunities] as I did?" He went to South Dakota State College in Brookings, where he majored in chemistry and dairy science, and earned his bachelor's degree in 1932. He was then hired by the Bureau of Indian Affairs to act as the farm extension agent for the Pine Ridge Reservation in South Dakota. According to biographer Karen P. Zimmerman, "In 1935, he was transferred to Pierre, South Dakota, where he served as Organization Field Agent for North Dakota, South Dakota, Nebraska, Montana, and Kansas under the Indian Reorganization Act. Reifel's role was to help tribes develop organizational skills in order to improve tribal business management." During World War II, he served as a military policeman in the U.S. Army with the rank of lieutenant; after the landings in Europe, he saw limited action on the continent while training troops for combat. When he was discharged from the army, he had advanced to the rank of major.

When he returned home, Reifel went back to work for the BIA, serving in various positions. In 1952 he received a Ph.D. degree in public administration from Harvard University. Three years later, he was named as Aberdeen (South Dakota) area director. In 1960, he ran for a seat representing South Dakota's First District in the U.S. House of Representatives, was elected, and served for five terms until his retirement in 1971. Considered as a replacement for resigning Commissioner of Indian Affairs Louis Rook Bruce, Jr., in 1972, he returned to South Dakota, where he strove for economic independence for the Indian people of that state.

On 7 December 1976, as he neared the end of his administration, President Gerald Ford named Reifel as commissioner of Indian Affairs to succeed the resigning Morris Thompson. It was a recess appointment, so called because Congress was not due to return until after the inauguration of Jimmy Carter as president the following 20 January and the new commissioner would not be confirmed by the Senate. Reifel assumed that Carter would retain him until a new commissioner could be found, but instead the new president asked for Reifel's resignation on 28 January 1977 after less than two months on the job. His ranks as the shortest term in Indian Office history. Biographer Michael Smith relates, "Such a short tenure in office did not permit Reifel to make any major changes in Indian policy. Brief as it was, however, his administration showed that a man with a no-nonsense manner who was respected by the Indian people, the Congress, and the bureau employees, could revitalize the bureau and imbue its personnel with a new sense of purpose." Reifel was ultimately succeeded by acting commissioners Raymond Butler (Blackfeet), Martin Seneca, Jr. (Seneca), and William E. Hallett (Chippewa), but Reifel was officially the last commissioner of Indian Affairs. In September 1977 the powers of the office were invested in the assistant secretary for Indian Affairs, of whom Forrest J. Gerard (Blackfeet) was first; six persons, all Native Americans, have thus far, as of this writing, served in that position.

Following his short reign, Reifel retired to his home in South Dakota. He died in Sioux Falls, South Dakota, on 2 January 1990.

See also Bureau of Indian Affairs.

References Fielder, Mildred, *Sioux Indian Leaders* (1975); Philp, Kenneth R., ed., *Indian Self-Rule: First-Hand Accounts of Indian-White Relations from Roosevelt to Reagan* (1986); Smith, Michael T., "Benjamin Reifel." In Robert M. Kvasnicka and Herman J. Viola, eds., *The Commissioners of Indian Affairs, 1824–1977* (1979); Zimmerman, Karen P., "Ben Reifel." In Sharon Malinowski, ed., *Notable Native Americans* (1995).

Relocation

During the 1950s, the policy of relocation was one of the three legs of the federal government's administration of Indian tribes, the others being termination and the transfer (through Public Law 280) of federal responsibility over Indian civil and criminal matters to state jurisdiction. The goal of relocation was to establish pockets of Indian communities away from reservations so that the old Indian ways would die out and these new "urbanized" Indians would integrate more easily into American society. The Bureau of Indian Affairs established the Voluntary Relocation Program (also known as the Employment Assistance Program) in 1952 to pay for the training, moving, and settlement of Indians willing to move to large urban areas. Also included in the program were educational and vocational benefits. By 1960, more than 35,000 Native Americans had taken advantage of this program, but many soon returned to their reservations and the program was ended.

Removal Policy

Beginning in 1830, the Indian tribes in the East who had survived more than two centuries of white encroachment were subjected to a systematic effort by the federal government to remove them westward. The legislation that started this effort was the Removal Bill, which became known as the Indian Removal Act (4 Stat. 411), enacted on 28 May 1830. The underlying reason for the bill's introduction was that farmland occupied by the Indians was coveted by the growing white population. After its introduction, the arguments for and against the bill rose to fever pitch on the floor of the House and Senate. The chief record of the debate over removal was published in five volumes in 1830 as *Indian Removal* (Senate Document 512, twenty-third Congress, first session). The removal era, which spanned some 50 years, was characterized not only by the forced relocation of whole Indian nations but also by a shift in federal policy toward the "management" of native populations on reservations. As a government policy, removal was replaced after more than 50 years by a policy of dividing the reservations "in severalty" for assignment to individuals, a process that also cost the Indians land.

See also Brown, Orlando; Cherokee Indians, Removal of—Congressional and Governmental Debate; Crawford, Thomas Hartley; Formative or Treaty Era; Herring, Elbert; Indian Removal Act; Jackson, Andrew—Message on Indian Removal; Medill, William.

Reference Priest, Loring Benson, *Uncle Sam's Stepchildren: The Reformation of United States Indian Policy, 1865–1887* (1942).

Revitalization Movements, Native American

See Ghost Dance; Handsome Lake Movement; Peyotism.

Rhoads, Charles James (1872–1954)

A banker who took an interest in the welfare of Indians for his entire life, Charles J. Rhoads, a Quaker, was the thirty-second commissioner of Indian Affairs in the Hoover administration. The son of noted Indian reformist James E. Rhoads, he was born in Germantown, Pennsylvania, on 4 October 1872. His father, a dedicated member of the Society of Friends, known as the Quakers, was one of the original members of the Indian Rights Association when it was founded in 1882, was its president from 1885 to 1894, and later was president of Bryn Mawr College. Charles Rhoads was educated at the prestigious William Penn Charter School and Haverford College, from which he graduated in 1893. Starting his career as a clerk in the Girard Trust Company of Philadelphia that same year, he was promoted to treasurer in 1900 but resigned fourteen years later to become the first governor of the Federal Reserve Bank in Philadelphia, established with the passage of the Federal Reserve Act of 1913. With the outbreak of World War I and America's entry in 1917, Rhoads became the chairman of the YMCA War Prisoner's Aid Service in Switzerland, and chief of the Society of Friends Bureau of the American Red Cross in which he oversaw relief and reconstruction work in war-torn France. During his service with the Quaker organization, he met and befriended Herbert Hoover, a fellow Quaker whose interest was relief work. The two became fast friends. After the war, Rhoads, who had been a member of the Indian Rights Association since 1897, was named president in 1927.

The resignation of Commissioner of Indian Affairs Charles Henry Burke on 9 March 1929 set off a mad scramble to fill his post. Cato Sells, commissioner under Woodrow Wilson, was suggested for the spot, but he told the New York *Daily News* that he was not interested. Finally, after "weeks of search," Hoover, now president, offered the post to Rhoads, who accepted on the condition that he be allowed time to make arrangements for leave with his banking firm. At his thirteenth news conference, held on 16 April 1929, President Hoover said, "Mr. Rhoads has accepted the appointment as chief of the Indian Bureau, which I think is rather a notable case of public service from a man who makes a very large sacrifice to leave one of the most important posts a man can have in his local community to take over a bureau in Washington." Secretary of the Interior Ray Lyman Wilbur, in his *Memoirs*, wrote of Rhoads,

> He [President Herbert Hoover] and I gave special attention to the appointment of Mr. Charles J. Rhoads as Commissioner of Indian Affairs and J. Henry Scattergood as Assistant Commissioner. Mr. Hoover had become well acquainted with these two Quakers from Philadelphia and the fine work done by them in the Friends' reconstruction service in France following World War I, in connection with the American Red Cross and the Y.M.C.A. They showed excellent teamwork. Both were men of high integrity and purpose who had long taken a constructive interest in and had a real knowledge of Indian problems, in the work of the Indian Rights Association and in other ways. It was because of their very real desire to be helpful to the Indians that we were able to persuade them, even though it would be at great personal sacrifice in the leaving of large business interests, to undertake this otherwise thankless task.

Rhoads's one prerequisite for taking the position was that he must be allowed to follow the recommendations of the Meriam Commission, which released its report in 1928. In fact, Rhoads's administration was so widely applauded that John Collier, later to be Indian commissioner and a critic of Indian Bureau policy in the 1920s, worked hand in hand with Rhoads. The two men deviated when Rhoads felt that Congress should enact legislation on it own to aid the Indians, while Collier wanted Rhoads to take charge of the entire legislative program. One of Rhoads's proposals, the creation of an Indian court of claims, was not enacted by Congress until 1946 with the establishment of the Indian Claims Commission. Another, the commission of a report on irrigation and reclamation policy on Indian reservations, came to fruition in the Report of Advisors on Irrigation on Indian Reservations, known as the Preston-Engle Report, released in 1930. Rhoads also called for increased independence for tribal councils, an notion embodied in the Indian Reorganization Act of 1934. Rhoads was also deeply involved in reforming the Indian education system.

With the election of Franklin D. Roosevelt in 1932, the Indian Rights Association asked for Rhoads to be retained as Indian commissioner, but he was passed over in favor of Collier. For the rest of his life, Rhoads spoke out in favor of assimilation for the Native American. Impressed by his hard work, when former President Hoover was named in 1947 to assemble a staff to look into ways to improve the executive branch, he named Rhoads to the Indian Bureau Committee. Their report maintained Rhoads's original position that "assimilation must be the dominant goal of public policy" of the government. Soon after, the goal of termination became that of the Congress. Rhoads retired to Bryn Mawr, Pennsylvania, where he died on 2 January 1954 at the age of 81.

See also Bureau of Indian Affairs.

References Kvasnicka, Robert M. and Herman J. Viola, eds., *The Commissioners of Indian Affairs, 1824–1977* (1979); *Public Papers of the President of the United States: Herbert Hoover, Containing the Public Messages, Speeches, and Statements of the President, March 4 to December 31, 1929* (1974); "Rhoads Selected to Succeed Burke." *Washington Evening Star*, 11 April 1929, 23; Robinson, Edgar Eugene, and Paul Carroll Edwards, eds., *The Memoirs of Ray Lyman Wilbur, 1875–1949* (1960); "Successor to Burke Is Sought by Hoover." *Daily News* (New York), 13 March 1929, 5.

Rhode Island Claims Settlement Act (92 Stat. 813)

In 1975, the Narragansett Indian Tribe of Rhode Island filed suit in district court for the return of 3,200 acres of former tribal land that is now the site of Charlestown, Rhode Island, claiming that between 1790 and 1880 the state of Rhode Island stole the land from the tribe. The tribe claimed that the subjugation of the land was in violation of the Trade and Intercourse Act of 1790, codified in 1834 as 4 Stat. 730: "No purchase, grant, lease, or other conveyance of lands, or of any title or claim thereto, from any Indian nation or tribe of Indians, shall be of any validity in law or equity, unless the same be made by treaty or convention entered into pursuant to the Constitution." The purpose of the 1978 Rhode Island Claims Settlement Act was to trade the Narragansetts the disputed land and any further claims to it in exchange for 900 acres of state land and 900 additional acres of private land to be purchased by the federal government for $3.5 million.

References "Legislative History of the Rhode Island Claims Settlement Act." *United States Code Congressional and Administrative News*, 95th Congress, 2d Session (1978); *United States Code Congressional and Administrative News*, 95th Congress, 2d Session (1978).

Rice v. Olson (324 U.S. 786 [1945])

In *Rice v. Olson*, decided by the Supreme Court in 1945, it was held that even though Indians were wards of the nation, they were entitled to the same constitutional right to the assistance of counsel in a criminal matter as other citizens. Richard Rice, an Indian (his tribe was not identified), pled guilty to a charge of burglary in the District Court of

Thurston County, Nebraska, and was sentenced to a term of one to seven years in prison. He then sued Neil Olson, Warden of the Nebraska State Penitentiary of Lancaster, located in Lancaster County, Nebraska, in another district court for a writ of habeas corpus releasing him from prison because he was not provided with counsel prior to his plea of guilty, and he had been deprived of due process when the trial court failed to inform him that he had a right to counsel and to call witnesses in support of his case, and that the conviction was void because it had been heard in a state court and the crime occurred on an Indian reservation, which was exclusively within federal jurisdiction. This second district court rejected Rice's petition, and on his own he sued for relief to the Nebraska Supreme Court. That court, too, rejected his arguments, and the U.S. Supreme Court, citing "important constitutional rights" involved in the case, granted certiorari, and arguments were heard in 1 February 1945 with Barton H. Kuhns of Omaha arguing for petitioner Rice. On 23 April, Justice Hugo Black spoke for an 6–3 decision (Justices Felix Frankfurter, Owen J. Roberts, and Robert H. Jackson dissenting) in striking down Rice's conviction. Justice Black admitted in the court's opinion that "it must be conceded that the petition is not a skillfully drawn pleading, but as it was not attacked in the district court it must receive a liberal construction here." The "shabbiness" of the petitioner's first appeal, argued Justice Black, was evidence to the majority of the court that Rice did not have proper counsel.

Rice v. Rehner (463 U.S. 713, 77 L.Ed. 2d 961, 103 S.Ct. 3291 [1983])

The question of whether an Indian trader, selling alcohol to off-reservation persons, should be required to obtain a state liquor license was at issue in this 1983 Supreme Court case. Eva Rehner was a federally licensed Indian trader who operated a liquor store on the Pala Reservation in San Diego, California. The Palas had adopted a tribal ordinance that allowed Rehner to sell liquor on the reservation provided that the sales conformed to state law, an ordinance approved by the secretary of the interior. Rehner then asked the state for an exemption from the requirement that she obtain a state liquor license to sell liquor consumed off the reservation. The state of California refused, and Rehner filed suit against Baxter Rice, the Director of the Department of Alcoholic Beverage Control of the state, asking that she be allowed to sell liquor consumed off reservation without being forced to obtain a state liquor license. The U.S. District Court for the Southern District of California, on appeal from the state, dismissed the suit, claiming that under 18 U.S.C. 1161, defining Indian country, the federal government had approved the tribal ordinance if such sales conformed with state law. On appeal, the U.S. Court of Appeals for the Ninth Circuit reversed, claiming that 1161 prohibited state action in the area of intoxicating beverages sold on reservations. On an appeal from Rice, the U.S. Supreme Court granted certiorari.

After arguments were held on 21 March 1983, the court handed down its decision on 1 July of the same year. In an opinion delivered by Justice Sandra Day O'Connor (Justices Harry Blackmun, William Brennan, and Thurgood Marshall dissenting), the court held that because the state was interested only in liquor that was to be consumed off the reservation, it had the right to require a liquor license. Justice O'Connor explained, "We conclude that 1161 was intended to remove federal discrimination that resulted from the imposition of liquor prohibition on Native Americans. Congress was well aware that the Indians never enjoyed a tradition of tribal self-government insofar as liquor transactions were concerned. Congress was also aware that the States exercised concurrent authority insofar as prohibiting liquor transactions with Indians was concerned. By enacting 1161, Congress intended to delegate a portion of its authority to the tribes as well as to the States, so as to fill the void that would be created by the absence of the discriminatory federal prohibition. Congress did not intend to make tribal members 'super citizens' who could trade in a traditionally regulated substance free from all but self-imposed regulations. Rather, we believe that in enacting 1161, Congress intended to recognize that Native Americans are not 'weak and defenseless,' and are capable of making personal decisions about alcohol consumption without special assistance from the Federal Government. Application of the state licensing scheme does not 'impair a right granted or reserved by federal law.'"

Robertson, Alice Mary (1854–1931)
Indian reformer and Congresswoman in her own right, Alice Mary Robertson was the granddaughter of the well-known Indian missionary, the Reverend Samuel Austin Worcester, for whom the famous Supreme Court decision *Worcester v. Georgia* was named. Born at Tullahassee Mission, on the Creek Nation, Indian Territory (now Tullahassee, Oklahoma) on 2 January 1854, she was the daughter of William Schenck Robertson and Ann Eliza (née Worcester) Robertson, both missionaries to the Creeks who had devoted their lives to the cause of Indians. William Schenck Robertson (1820–1881) was a Presbyterian missionary who worked as a teacher among the Creek Indians at Tullahassee from 1849 to 1861 and then after 1866, while Ann Eliza Robertson was the daughter of noted Cherokee missionary Samuel A. Worcester, who had been jailed rather than give up his life among the Cherokee people before they were removed from Georgia. When the Civil War broke out, Alice was seven years old, and her parents moved to Wisconsin and Kansas, where she attended rural schools. In 1866, the Robertsons returned to the Creek Nation, and Alice was tutored by her father. At age 17 she enrolled at Elmira College in New York, but left before graduating to help her ailing sister (she was subsequently awarded an honorary master's degree in 1886).

From 1873 to 1880, Robertson worked in the main office of the Bureau of Indian Affairs in Washington as a clerk, and from 1880 until 1882 worked for Captain Richard H. Pratt's Carlisle Indian School in Pennsylvania. In 1882, she left for Indian Territory when her father died and her mother became ill. She then taught at an Indian school at Ocmulgee, and, when an Indian school at Tullahassee burned down, raised money for the construction of the Nuyaka Creek Mission school, which was eventually moved to Tulsa and renamed the University of Tulsa. Before it was moved, it was called Henry Kendall College, and Robertson worked at various posts there, including teaching English and civics, until 1899. In 1900 she was appointed as the first government administrator of the Creek education program, and her work in that position led her friend, Theodore Roosevelt, to name her postmistress of

Alice Mary Robertson of Muskogee, Oklahoma, upon her election to the U.S. Congress in November 1920

Muskogee, where she served from 1905 to 1913. Until 1920, she worked at her farm (where she operated a local dairy) near Muskogee and her feeding of hungry veterans of World War I made her a leading candidate for a political career. In 1920, she ran for a seat in the U.S. House of Representatives as a Republican and defeated a popular Cherokee politician, William Wirt Hastings. She served on the House committees on Indian Affairs and expenditures in the Department of the Interior, and on the Committee on Woman Suffrage. She supported the program of President Warren G. Harding, opposing the Veteran's Bonus Bill and joined southern politicians in opposing the Anti-Lynching Bill. These stands cost her her seat when she ran for reelection, defeated by Hastings in 1922. For the remaining years of her life, she worked at the Veterans' Hospital in Muskogee and as a correspondent in Washington for the *Muskogee News*. Her last job was as a researcher for the Oklahoma Historical Society, but ill health cut her work there short. She died in Muskogee on 1 July 1931 at the age of 77. Robertson Hall at the University of Oklahoma is named in her honor.

See also Hastings, William Wirt; Worcester, Samuel Austin.

References Dale, Edward E., "Robertson, Alice Mary." In Dumas Malone et al., eds., *Dictionary of American Biography* (1930–88); McHenry, Robert, ed., *Famous American Women: A Biographical Dictionary from Colonial Times to the Present* (1980); "Robertson, Alice Mary." *Biographical Directory of the United States Congress, 1774–1989*, Senate Document 100–34, 100th Congress, Second Session (1989); Spaulding, Joe Powell, *The Life of Alice Mary Robertson* (Ph.D. dissertation, University of Oklahoma, 1959).

Roff v. Burney (168 U.S. 218 [1897])

The U.S. Supreme Court held in this case that Indian councils may annul a grant of citizenship to American citizens, but that this annulment in no way prevented Americans from suing in American courts of law. Plaintiff A. B. Roff, an American citizen, married Matilda Bourland, who was granted citizenship by the Chickasaw Nation in 1876. By a treaty with the Chickasaw Nation of 28 April 1866, "every white person who, having married a Choctaw or Chickasaw, resides in the said Choctaw or Chickasaw nation, or who has been adopted by the legislative authorities, is to be deemed a member of said nation." In 1883, the legislature of the Chickasaw Nation annulled Matilda Bourland's citizenship as a Chickasaw. When Roff attempted to sue Louisa Burney, administratrix of the estate of one B.C. Burney, in a United States court, Burney claimed that Roff was still an Indian, and could only bring his suit in an Indian court. The U.S. Court for the Indian Territory agreed, and Roff appealed to the U.S. Supreme Court.

The case was submitted to the court on 15 October 1897 and decided on 29 November of that same year. Writing for the unanimous court, Justice David Josiah Brewer held that because Mrs. Roff's citizenship as a Chickasaw had been annulled, Roff himself was no longer considered an Indian, while still retaining his rights as an American citizen that he had not repudiated. Brewer returned the case to the lower court for reconsideration.

Roosevelt, Theodore—Statement on Indians

As part of his first annual message to Congress, delivered on 3 December 1901 just after he had taken office following the assassination of President William McKinley, President Theodore Roosevelt wrote at length on federal-Indian Affairs.

In my judgment the time has arrived when we should definitely make up our minds to recognize the Indian as an individual and not as a member of a tribe. The General Allotment Act is a mighty pulverizing engine to break up the tribal mass. It acts directly upon the family and the individual. Under its provisions some sixty thousand Indians have already become citizens of the United States. We should now break up the tribal funds, doing for them what allotment does for the tribal lands; that is, they should be divided into individual holdings. There will be a transition period during which the funds will in many cases have to be held in trust. This is the case also with the lands. A stop should be put upon the indiscriminate permissions to Indians to lease their allotments. The effort should be steadily to make the Indian work like any other man on his own ground. The marriage laws of the Indians should be made the same as those of the whites.

In the schools the education should be elementary and largely industrial. The needs of higher education among the Indians is very, very limited. On the reservations care should be taken to try to suit the teaching to the needs of the particular Indian. There is no use in attempting to induce agriculture in a country only suited for cattle raising, where the Indian should be made a stock grower. The ration system, which is merely the corral and the reservation system, is highly detrimental to the Indians. Its promotes beggary, perpetuates pauperism, and stifles industry. It is an effectual barrier to progress. It must continue to a greater or less degree as long as tribes are herded on reservations and have everything in common. The Indian should be treated as an individual—like the white man. During the change of treatment inevitable hardships will occur; but we should not because of them hesitate to make the change. There should be a continuous reduction in the number of agencies.

In dealing with the aboriginal races few things are more important than to preserve them from the terrible physical and moral degradation resulting from the liquor traffic. We are doing all we can to save our own Indian tribes from this evil. Wherever by international agreement this same end can be attained as regards races where we do possess exclusive control, every effort should be made to bring it about.

Reference *Congressional Record*, Senate, 3 December 1901.

Rosebud Sioux Tribe v. Kneip (430 U.S. 584 [1977])

Congress' intent as to the disposition of allotted lands from a reservation, and whether this intent was in violation of a treaty between the United States and the Indians involved, was the subject of this Supreme Court decision. In June 1972, the Rosebud Sioux tribe of South Dakota sued in district court to obtain a declaratory judgment against the United States government alleging that through several acts of Congress, the reservation as originally carved out was "diminished," and thus the government was liable for damages. Under a treaty with the Rosebuds of 29 April 1868 (15 Stat. 635), the land set aside for the reservation included "all land in South Dakota west of the Missouri River" (opinion, at 589). Congress then passed three acts: act of 23 April 1904 (33 Stat. 254); act of 2 March 1907 (34 Stat. 1230); and act of 30 May 1910 (36 Stat. 448), all of which opened the reservation to allotment, and set aside unallotted lands to be used to create several new counties. The Indians sued on the grounds that the three federal acts "diminished" the reservation, a violation of the 1868 treaty. The district court denied the Rosebud Sioux relief, and the U.S. Court of Appeals for the Eight Circuit affirmed. The tribe appealed to the U.S. Supreme Court.

After the case was argued on 12 January 1977, and decided on 4 April of the same year, Justice William H. Rehnquist spoke for the court in the 6–3 decision (Justices Thurgood Marshall, William Brennan, and Potter Stewart dissenting) that Congress excluded the reservation from the three federal acts, that they cannot be construed to "diminish" the reservation as it was later reconfigured, and thus were not unconstitutional. Rehnquist used the term "deestablish" to describe the federal intent so as not to break the treaty. "These clear provisions, as well as the clear legislative history of the 1910 Act, reflect strongly the continued intent to diminish the reservation boundaries," Rehnquist wrote. "We conclude that the 1910 Act continued the policies of the two prior Acts, and Mellette County was thereby detached from the Reservation. The intent of Congress in the 1904, the 1907, and the 1910 Acts was to change the boundaries of the original Rosebud Reservation. Much has changed since then, and if Congress had it to do over again it might well have chosen a different course. But, as we observed in *DeCoteau v. District County Court* 420 U.S., at 449, 43 L.Ed. 300, 95 S.Ct. 1082: '[O]ur task here is a narrow one...[W]e cannot remake history.' Affirmed."

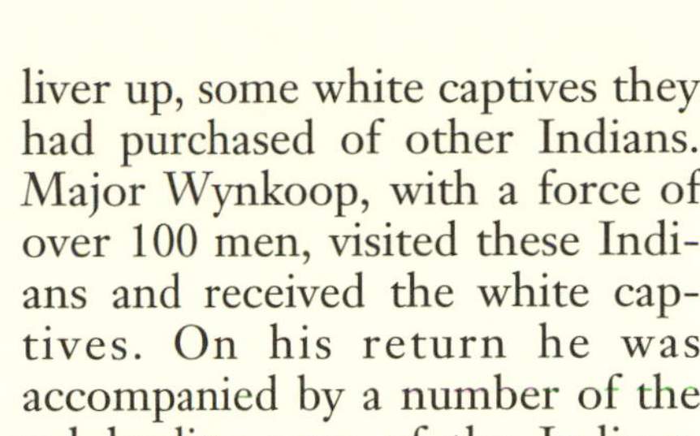

Sand Creek Massacre
On the morning of 29 November 1864, a force of Colorado troops under the command of Colonel John Chivington, in violation of a series of peaceful agreements and understandings, attacked Black Kettle's village of Southern Cheyenne and Arapaho Indians at Sand Creek, Colorado. What followed was the wanton butchery of about 150 Indians, mostly women and children. The atrocity was examined in a report of the Joint Committee on the Conduct of the War. This committee, assembled during the Civil War and consisting of members from both houses of Congress and chaired by Senator Benjamin F. Wade, Republican of Ohio, was dispatched to investigate the massacre. One of the writers of the report who was not a member of Congress was Samuel Forster Tappan. Ultimately, Tappan's report would excoriate Colonel John Chivington for his role in the slaughter. Indian historian Robert M. Utley wrote of Tappan, "He…[was] a long-time crusader for humanitarian causes whose investigation of Colonel Chivington…earned him some notoriety as a friend of the Indian." In 1865, the committee released its report, which called for the punishment of the Army officers responsible. However, no one was ever charged. The report, which discusses the facts which led to the massacre, is reproduced below:

In the summer of 1864, Governor [John] Evans, of Colorado Territory, as acting superintendent of Indian Affairs, sent notice to the various bands and tribes of Indians within his jurisdiction that such as desired to be considered friendly to the whites should at once repair to the nearest military post in order to be protected from the soldiers who were to take the field against the hostile Indians.

About the close of the summer, some Cheyenne Indians, in the neighborhood of the Smoke Hills, sent word to Major [Edward W.] Wynkoop, the commandant of the post of Fort Lyon, that they had in their possession, and were willing to deliver up, some white captives they had purchased of other Indians. Major Wynkoop, with a force of over 100 men, visited these Indians and received the white captives. On his return he was accompanied by a number of the chiefs and leading men of the Indians, whom he had invited to visit Denver for the purpose of conferring with the authorities there in regard to keeping peace. Among them were Black Kettle and White Antelope of the Cheyennes, and some chiefs of the Arapahoes. The council was held and these chiefs stated that they were very friendly to the whites, and always had been, and that they desired peace. Governor Evans and Colonel Chivington, the commander of that military district, advised them to repair to Fort Lyon and submit to whatever terms the military commander there should impose. This was done by the Indians, who were

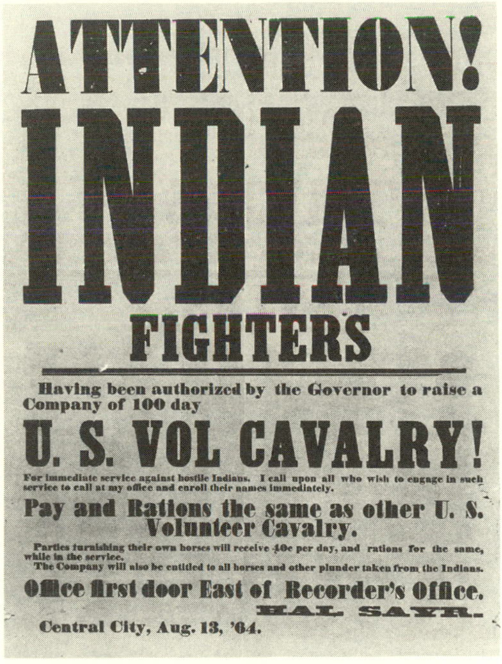

A poster from Central City, Colorado, advertises three-month enlistments into the volunteer Colorado cavalry. Members of the unit under Colonel John M. Chivington massacred Cheyenne men, women, and children as they slept at a peaceful encampment on Sand Creek, a dry wash in Colorado Territory, on 29 November 1864.

treated somewhat as prisoners of war, receiving rations, and being obliged to remain within certain bounds.

All the testimony goes to show that the Indians, under the immediate control of Black Kettle and White Antelope of the Cheyennes, and Left Hand of the Arapahoes, were and had been friendly to the whites, and had not been guilty of any acts of hostility or depredation. The Indian agents, the Indian interpreter and others examined by your committee, all testify to the good character of those Indians. Even Governor Evans and Major [Scott A.] Anthony, though evidently willing to convey to your committee a false impression of the character of those Indians, were forced, in spite of their prevarication, to admit that they knew of nothing they [the Indians] had done which rendered them deserving of punishment.

A northern band of the Cheyennes, known as the Dog Soldiers, had been guilty of acts of hostility; but all the testimony goes to prove that they had no connexion [*sic*] with Black Kettle's band, but acted in spite of his authority and influence. Black Kettle and his band denied all connexion [*sic*] with or responsibility for the Dog Soldiers, and Left Hand and his band of Arapahoes were equally friendly.

These Indians, at the suggestion of Governor Evans and Colonel Chivington, repaired to Fort Lyon and placed themselves under the protection of Major Wynkoop. They were led to believe that they were regarded in the light of friendly Indians, and would be treated as such so long as they conducted themselves quietly.

The treatment extended to those Indians by Major Wynkoop does not seem to have satisfied those in authority there, and for some cause, which does not appear, he was removed, and Major Scott J. Anthony was assigned to the command of Fort Lyon; but even Major Anthony seems to have found it difficult at first to pursue any different course toward the Indians he found there. They were entirely within the power of the military. Major Anthony having demanded their arms, which they surrendered to him, they conducted themselves quietly, and in every way manifested a disposition to remain at peace with the whites. For a time even he continued issuing rations to them as Major Wynkoop had done; but it was determined by Major Anthony (whether upon his own motion or as the suggestion of others does not appear) to pursue a different course towards these friendly Indians. They were called together and told that rations could no longer be issued to them, and they had better go where they could obtain subsistence by hunting. At the suggestion of Major Anthony (and from one in his position a suggestion was the equivalent to a command) these Indians went to place on Sand Creek, about thirty-five miles from Fort Lyon, and there established their camp, their arms being restored to them. He told them that he then had no authority to make peace with them; but in case he received such authority he would inform them of it. In his testimony he says:

"I told them they might go back on Sand creek, or between there and the headwaters of the Smoky Hill, and remain there until I received instructions from the department headquarters, from General [Samuel R.] Curtis; and that in case I did receive any authority to make peace with them I would go right over and let them know it. *I did not state to them that I would give them notice in case we intended to attack them.* They went away with that understanding, and in case I received instructions from department headquarters I was to let them know it."

To render the Indians less apprehensive of any danger, One Eye, a Cheyenne chief, was allowed to remain with them to obtain information for the use of the military authorities. He was employed at $125 a month, and several times brought to Major Anthony, at Fort Lyon, information of proposed movements of other, hostile bands. Jack Smith, a half-breed son of John S. Smith, an Indian interpreter, employed by the government, was also there for the same purpose. A U.S. soldier was allowed to remain there, and two days before the massacre Mr. Smith, the interpreter, was permitted to go there with goods to trade with the Indians. Everything practicable seems to have been done to remove from the minds of the Indians any fear of approaching danger; and when Colonel Chivington commenced his movement he took all of the precautions in his power to prevent these Indians learning of his approach. For some days all travel on that route was forcibly stopped by him, not even the mail being allowed to pass. On the morning of 28 November he appeared at Fort Lyon with over 700 mounted men and two pieces of artillery. One of his first acts was throw a guard around the post to prevent any one from leaving it. At this place Major Anthony joined him with 125 men and two pieces of artillery.

That night, the entire party started from Fort Lyon, and, by a forced march, arrived at the Indian camp, on Sand creek, shortly after daybreak. The Indian camp consisted of about 100 lodges of Cheyennes, under Black Kettle, and from 8 to 10 lodges of Arapahoes under Left Hand. It is estimated that each lodge contained five or more persons, and that more than one-half were women and children.

Upon observing the approach of the soldiers, Black Kettle, the head chief, ran up to the top of his lodge an American flag, which had been presented to him some years before by Commissioner [of Indian Affairs Alfred B.] Greenwood, with a small white flag under it, as he had been advised to do in case he met with any troops on the prairies. Mr. Smith, the interpreter, supposing that they might be strange troops, unaware of the character of the Indians encamped there, advanced from his lodge to meet them, but was fired upon, and returned to his lodge.

And then the scene of murder and barbarity began—men, women, and children were indiscriminately slaughtered. In a few minutes all the Indians were flying over the plain in terror and confusion. A few who endeavored to hide themselves under the bank of the creek were surrounded and shot down in cold blood, offering but feeble resistance. From the sucking babe to the old warrior, all who were overtaken were deliberately murdered. Not content with killing women and children, who were incapable of offering any resistance, the soldiers indulged in acts of barbarity of the most revolting character; such, it is to be hoped, as never before disgraced the acts of men claiming to be civilized. No attempt was made by the officers to restrain the savage cruelty of the men under their command, but they stood by and witnessed these acts without one word of reproof, if they did not incite their commission. For more than two hours the work of murder and barbarity was continued, until more than one hundred dead bodies, three fourths of them women and children, lay on the plain as evidences of the fiendish malignity and cruelty of the officers who had sedulously and carefully plotted the massacre, and of the soldiers who had so faithfully acted out the spirit of their officers.

It is difficult to believe that beings in the form of men, and disgracing the uniform of United States soldiers and officers, could commit or countenance the commission of such acts of cruelty and barbarity as are detailed in the testimony, but which your committee will not specify in the report. It is true that there seems to have existed among the people inhabiting the region of country a hostile feeling towards the Indians. Some of the Indians had committed acts of hostility towards the whites; but no effort seems to have been made by the authorities there to prevent these hostilities, other than by the commission of even worse acts. The hatred of the whites to the Indians would seem to have been inflamed and excited to the utmost; the bodies of persons killed at a great distance—whether by Indians or not, is not certain—were brought to the capital of the Territory and exposed to the public gaze for the purpose of inflaming still more the already excited feeling of the people. Their cupidity was appealed to, for the governor in a proclamation calls upon all, "either individually or in such parties as they may organize," "to kill and destroy as enemies of the country, whatever they may be found, all such hostile Indians," authorizing them to "hold to their own private use and benefit all the property of said hostile Indians that they may capture." What Indians he would ever term friendly it is impossible to tell. His testimony before your committee was characterized by such prevarication and shuffling as has been shown by no witness they have examined during the four years they have been engaged in their investigations; and for the evident purpose of avoiding admission that he was fully aware that the Indians massacred so brutally at Sand Creek, were then, and had been, actuated by the most friendly feelings towards the whites, and had done all in their power to restrain those less friendly disposed.

The testimony of Major Anthony, who succeeded an officer disposed to treat these Indians with justice and humanity, is sufficient of itself to show how unprovoked and unwarranted was this massacre. He testifies that he found these Indians in the neighborhood of Fort Lyon when he assumed command of that post; that they professed their friendliness to the whites, and their willingness to do whatever he demanded of them; that they delivered their arms up to him; and they went to and encamped upon the place designated by him; that they gave him information from time to time of acts of hostility which were meditated by other and hostile bands, and in every way conducted themselves properly and peaceably, and yet he says it was fear and not principle which prevented his killing them while they were completely in his power. And when Colonel Chivington appeared at Fort Lyon, on his mission of murder and barbarity, Major Anthony made haste to accompany him with men and artillery, although Colonel Chivington had no authority whatever over him.

As to Colonel Chivington, your committee can hardly find fitting terms to describe his conduct. Wearing the uniform of the United States, which should be the emblem of justice and humanity; holding the important position of commander of a military district, and therefore having the honor of the government to that extent in his keeping, he deliberately and executed a foul and dastardly massacre which would have disgraced the veriest savage among those who were the victims of his cruelty. Having full knowledge of their friendly character, having himself been instrumental to some extent in placing them in their position of fancied security, he took advantage of their inapprehension and defenceless condition to gratify the worst passions that ever cursed the heart of man. It is thought by some that desire for political preferment prompted him to this cowardly act; that he supposed that by pandering to the inflamed passions of an excited population he could recommend himself to their regard and consideration. Others think its was to avoid the being sent where there was more of danger and hard service to be performed; that he was willing to get up a show of hostility on the part of the Indians by committing himself acts which savages themselves would never premeditate. Whatever may have been his motive, it is to be hoped that the authority of this government will never again be disgraced by acts such as he and those acting with him have been guilty of committing.

There were *hostile* Indians not far distant, against which Colonel Chivington could have led the force under his command. Major Anthony testifies that but three of four days' march from his post were several hundreds of Indians, generally believed to be engaged in acts of hostility towards the whites. And he deliberately testifies that only the fear of them prevented him from killing those who were friendly and entirely within his reach and control. It is true that to reach them required some days of hard marching. It was not to be expected that they could be surprised as easily as those on Sand creek; and the warriors among them were almost, if not quite, as numerous as the soldiers under the control of Colonel

Chivington. Whatever influence this may have had upon Colonel Chivington, the truth is that he surprised and murdered in cold blood, the unsuspecting men, women, and children on Sand Creek, who had every reason to believe they were under the protection of the United States authorities, and then returned to Denver and boasted of the brave deeds he and the men under his command had performed.

The Congress of the United States, at its last session, authorized the appointment of a commission to investigate all matters relating to the administration of Indian Affairs within the limits of the United States. Your committee most sincerely trust that the result of their inquiry will be the adoption of measures which will render impossible the employment of officers, civil and military, such as have heretofore made the administration of Indian Affairs in this country a byword and reproach.

In conclusion, your committee are of the opinion that for the purpose of vindicating the cause of justice and upholding the honor of the nation, prompt and energetic measures should be at once taken to remove from office those who have thus disgraced the government by whom they are employed, and to punish, as their crimes deserve, those who have been guilty of these brutal and cowardly acts.

One of the survivors of the Sand Creek massacre, George Bent (Cheyenne), gave testimony as to what he witnessed at the creek on the day of the massacre. Published by noted writer George Bird Grinnell, the attestation did not appear until Grinnell's work was published in 1956. Bent stated, "at the beginning of the attack Black Kettle, with his wife and White Antelope, took their position before Black Kettle's lodge and remained there after all others had left the camp. At last Black Kettle, seeing that it was useless to stay longer, started to run, calling out to White Antelope to follow him; but White Antelope refused and stood there ready to die, with arms folded, singing his death song: 'Nothing lives long, Except the earth and the mountains,' and he was shot down by the soldiers."

U.S. Senator Ben Nighthorse Campbell sponsored a resolution when he served in the Colorado legislature to erect a sign on the site of the massacre. The sign reads:

November 29, 1864, was an unforgettable day for the Cheyenne and Arapaho on the banks of Sand Creek. 8 miles north and 1 mile east of here, stood a camp of about 100 Cheyenne and 10 Arapaho lodges established, by what may have been taken as the order of the U.S. Army commander at nearby Fort Lyon. According to Indian tradition, early that morning Cheyenne hunters reported that soldiers were approaching. Black Kettle, a leader and spokesman for the camp, hoisted an American flag to convey that the camp was peaceful. Ignoring the signal, volunteer militia, led by Colonel John M. Chivington, attacked, killing all in their path. With many of the men away, organized resistance was impossible. When the tragic day was over, more than 137 Indian people, mostly women and children, lay dead, their bodies mutilated. The brutal attack was denounced in congressional hearings, but none of the participants was punished.

Author Helen Hunt Jackson, a noted nineteenth-century Indian-rights advocate and reformer, discussed in a series of letters to the *New York Tribune* in 1880 her revulsion at the government's inability to punish those involved. Her anger later led to her publishing her landmark work, *A Century of Dishonor* (1881).

See also Doolittle Commission; Jackson, Helen Maria Fiske Hunt; Schurz, Carl; Tappan, Samuel Forster.

References Grinnell, George Bird, *The Fighting Cheyennes* (1956); *Massacre of Cheyenne Indians*, Report of the Joint Committee on the Conduct of the War, 38th Congress, 2d Session (1865); Utley, Robert M., *Frontier Regulars: The United States Army and the Indian, 1866–1891* (1973).

Sanders, Elizabeth Elkins (1762–1851)

Elizabeth Elkins Sanders was an important reformer on behalf of Indian civil rights in the early nineteenth century. She was born Elizabeth Elkins on 12 August 1762 in Salem, Massachusetts, the daughter of Thomas Elkins and Elizabeth (née White) Elkins. Little is known about her early life, except that her father died when his daughter was two. In 1782, she married Thomas Sanders, a Gloucester merchant. The beginning of her interest in Indians or concern for their treatment remains undated; in 1828 her first writing on the matter, *Conversations, Principally on the Aborigines of North America*, did not include her name (none of her writings were credited to her), but which is considered to have written by her. Biographer Ernest S. Dodge writes, "*Conversations* [was]...a 179–page expression of admiration for Indian culture, indignation over its destruction, and contempt to the 'sanguinary [bloody] chieftain' [Andrew] Jackson." The pamphlet entitled *Circular Addressed to Benevolent Ladies of the United States: The Present Crisis in the Affairs of the Indian Nations in the United States, Demands the Immediate and Interested Attention of All Who Make Any Claims to Benevolence or Humanity* (Boston: Printed by Crockett and Brewster, 1829), may have been written by her, but concrete evidence is lacking. She definitely did write *The First Settlers of New England* (1829), which discusses her disdain for the government's policy toward Native Americans. She also discussed her hatred of slavery—a theme she continued in *Second Part of a Tract in Missions* (1845) and *Remarks on the "Tour Around Hawaii," by the Missionaries, Messrs. Ellis, Thurston, Bishop, and Goodrich, in 1823* (1848). All of these tracts were signed "A Lady," considered to be her *nom de plume*.

Elizabeth Elkins died of what may be emphysema in Salem on 19 February 1851 at the age of 88. Marianne Silsbee wrote of her in 1887, "She was the centre of a prosperous and happy family, performing well the duties of life, liberally bestowing its blessings on the less fortunate, filling existence with all the graces of hospitality, the ornament of a large circle of friends and the light of home. She was a reformer and a philanthropist; reformer of doctors too liberal in the use or abuse of drugs, a homeopathist unawares; philanthropic in the case of the Indian, whom she regarded as the dethroned sovereign of the land."

References Dodge, Ernest S., "Elizabeth Elkins Sanders." In Edward T. James, ed., *Notable American Women, 1607–1950: A Biographical Dictionary* (1971); Hardy, Gail J., *American Women Civil Rights Activists: Biobibliographies of 68 Leaders, 1825–1992* (1993); Silsbee, Marianne C. D., *A Half Century in Salem* (1887).

Santa Clara Pueblo v. Martinez (436 U.S. 49 [1978])

Did the equal protection clause of the United States Constitution extend to Indians, even on reservations? And did the 1968 Indian Civil Rights Act extend these rights beyond the federal courts' ability to intervene in such matters? In *Santa Clara Pueblo*, decided by the Supreme Court in 1978, these questions became a major issue for the court to resolve. Julia Martinez and her daughter sued the Santa Clara Pueblo of New Mexico after the tribal council refused to give her daughter tribal membership. As part of a tribal ordinance, membership was refused to the children of female tribal members who married outside of the tribe, while the children of male members who married outside the tribe were recognized. Martinez sued in the U.S. District Court for the District of New Mexico that since the 1968 Indian Civil Rights Act (ICRA), 25 U.S.C. 1301–1303) extended the principles of the U.S. Constitution to Indian tribes, such an ordinance was a violation of the equal protection clause. The district court upheld the ordinance as valid under the ICRA, but concluded that the court lacked jurisdiction to intervene in inter-tribal affairs. On appeal, the U.S. Court of Appeals for the Tenth Circuit reversed. The Santa Clara Pueblo appealed to the U.S. Supreme Court. Argued on 29 November 1977, the court handed down its decision on 15 May 1978. In holding for the tribe, Justice Thurgood Marshall, in the 7–1 judgment (Justice Byron White dissented and Justice Harry Blackmun did not participate) found on the narrow issue that nothing in Title I of the

ICRA, the relevant section litigated, allowed Indian tribes to be subjected to lawsuits in nontribal courts because such suits were barred by the tribe's sovereign immunity. Justice Marshall explained, "Title I of the ICRA does not expressly authorize the bringing of civil actions for declaratory relief to enforce its substantive provisions. The threshold issue in this case is thus whether the Act may be interpreted to impliedly authorize such actions, against a tribe or its officers, in the federal courts...[W]e hold that the Act cannot be so read." He added, "Indian tribes have long been recognized as possessing the common-law immunity for suit traditionally enjoyed by sovereign powers. *Turner v. United States*, 248 U.S. 354, 358, 63 L.Ed. 291, 39 S.Ct. 109 (1919); *United States v. United States Fidelity and Guaranty Co.*, 309 U.S. 506, 512–13, 84 L.Ed. 894, 60 S.Ct. 653 (1940); *Puyallup Tribe v. Washington Department of Game*, 433 U.S. 165, 172–73, 53 L.Ed. 2d 667, 97 S.Ct. 2616 (1977). This aspect of tribal sovereignty, like all others, is subject to the superior and plenary control of Congress. But 'without congressional authorization,' the 'Indian Nations are exempt from suit.' *United States v. United States Fidelity and Guaranty Co.*, supra, at 512, 84 L.Ed. 894, 60 S.Ct. 653."

Schoolcraft, Henry Rowe (1793–1864)

An ethnologist who spent much of his life studying American Indians, Henry R. Schoolcraft was also an author, explorer, Indian agent, geologist, and, to some extent, the creator of the Smithsonian Institution's Bureau of American Ethnology. He was born in Albany County, New York, on 28 March 1793, and spent his youth learning the trade of glassmaking from his father, Lawrence Schoolcraft. He attended Union College and Middlebury College, but economic misfortune led him to travel west. On his way through Missouri, he traveled down the Ohio river and explored that state's mineral resources, studies which became the focus of his first known published work, *A View of the Lead Mines of Missouri* (New York: Charles Wiley, 1819). In 1820 he accompanied Michigan's territorial Governor Lewis Cass (later secretary of war) on an expedition to Lake Superior and the upper reaches of the Mississippi Valley of the Northwest Territory. Impressed with the knowledge and capacity for learning of this young man, Cass recommended that Secretary of War John Calhoun hire Schoolcraft for a government position. The young explorer was named as the Indian agent for the tribes of Sault Ste. Marie in the Lake Superior region, a position he served in from 1822 until 1841. As he later wrote in *Personal Memoirs of a Residence of Thirty Years with the Indian Tribes on the American Frontier* (1851), "I had now attained a fixed position; not such as I desired at the outset, and had striven for, but one that offered an interesting class of duties, in the performances of which there was a wide field of honorable exertion, if it was embraced, also of historical inquiry and research."

While an Indian agent, Schoolcraft also served in the Legislative Council of the Michigan Territory (1828–32), and led an expedition in 1832 that found the source of the Mississippi River, which led to his second work, *Narrative of an Expedition Through the Upper Mississippi to Itasca Lake* (New York: Harper, 1834). Named superintendent for Indian Affairs for Michigan, he began work on the first of what are considered his two greatest works, *Algic Researches, Comprising Inquiries Respecting the Mental Characteristics of the North American Indian; First Series, Indian Tales and Legends* (New York: Harper; two volumes, 1839), in which he wrote, "The Indians could never be made to appreciate the offers of education and Christianity by one portion of the community, while others were arrayed against them in arms. Their idea of government was, after all, the Western notion of a unity or despotism, in which everything emanates from the governing power, and is responsible to it....Owing to illiterate interpreters and dishonest men, the parties have never more than half understood each other. Distrust and the misapprehension have existed by the century together, and it is, therefore, no cause for astonishment, that the whole period of our contemporary history should be filled up with so many negotiations and cessions, wars and treaties." The work was published in a second edition in 1856 as *The Myth of Hiawatha and Other Oral Legends* (Philadelphia: J.B. Lippincott).

After a voyage to Europe, Schoolcraft returned and wrote *Oneota, or the Red Race of America* (New York: Burgess, Stringer, 1845). In 1845, he was named as an agent for counting the number of Iroquois for the state of New York. The result of that work was *Notes on the Iroquois* (New York: Bartlett & Welford, 1846). Of his time there, Curtis Hinsley, Jr., historian of the Bureau of American Ethnology, writes, "In August 1846, the New Confederacy of the Iroquois assembled around the light of their 'emblematic council fire' in Rochester, New York, to hear the respected ethnologist Henry Rowe Schoolcraft. In a stirring paean to American distinctiveness, Schoolcraft urged Lewis Henry Morgan and the other young men of Rochester to devote themselves to the study of America's 'free, bold, wild, independent, native race.'"

By this time, Schoolcraft was considered the leading national authority on the ethnology of the American Indian. By an act of Congress of 3 March 1847, he was authorized "to collect and digest such statistics and materials as may illustrate the history, present condition and future prospects of the Indian tribes of the United States." The six volumes, published over a 6 years period, did not appear until 1851. This greatest of his works, entitled *Historical and Statistical Information Respecting the History, Condition and Prospects of the Indian Tribes of the United States: Collected and Prepared under the Direction of the Bureau of Indian Affairs, Per Act of Congress of March 3d, 1847*, was published in Philadelphia by Lippincott, Grambo & Company. *Historical and Statistical Information* is considered one of the finest works on the ethnology of Indians. In his letter to Commissioner of Indian Affairs Luke Lea on 22 July 1850, transmitting the report to Congress, Schoolcraft wrote, "Time was required in order to place an inquiry so comprehensive in its character on a proper basis. Misapprehensions on the part of the Indians, with respect to the object of the collection of their statistics, were to be met. The additional duties required of the agents of Indian Affairs presupposed so intimate an acquaintance with the history and languages of the tribes and the distinguishing traits of races, that few of this class of officers were prepared to undertake them. The investigation in these particulars was therefore extended to embrace gentlemen of experience, observation, and learning, in various parts of the Union; including numerous teachers and missionaries employed in moral and intellectual labors among them. Facts were, indeed, solicited from all who had facts to communicate." Historian David L. Marden writes, "*Information Respecting the History, Condition, and Prospects of the Indian Tribes of the United States* may be described as ethnocentric and pseudoscientific, although it contains an extensive collection of engravings on Indian art and architecture. What is significant about Schoolcraft's work is that in spite of his ethnocentrism he found much to admire in his subjects, and he urged the formulation of an Indian policy designed to alleviate some of the inequities of the then-current system." It was reissued in 1860 as *Archives of Aboriginal Knowledge* (Philadelphia: Lippincott).

His other works include *Journal of a Tour Into the Interior of Missouri and Arkansas* (London: Phillips, 1821), and Scenes and Adventures in the Semi-Alpine Region of the Ozark Mountains of Missouri and Arkansas (Philadelphia: Lippincott, Grambo, 1853). His last position with the government was as an interpreter (he could speak fluent Chippewa) with the Bureau of Indian Affairs. After spending the last three years in bed (he was paralyzed with what seems to be a stroke in 1849), Schoolcraft died in Washington, D.C., on 10 December 1864 at 71. Robert Bieder, a biographer, writes, "His ethnology was heavily influenced by his personality, his changing attitudes toward Indians, and his concern for their welfare. It was also shaped first by Schoolcraft's romanticism and later by his religious experience, which led to his moralistic and eventually pessimistic outlook."

References Bieder, Robert E., *Science Encounters the Indian, 1820–1880* (1986); Bremer, Richard G., *Indian Agent and Wilderness Scholar: The Life of Henry Rowe Schoolcraft* (1987); Freeman, John Finley, *Henry Rowe Schoolcraft, 1793–1864* (Ph.D. dissertation, Harvard University, 1960); Hinsley, Curtis M., Jr., *The Smithsonian and the American Indian: Making a Moral Anthropology in Victorian America* (1981); "Letters from the Allegheny Mountains, History of the Cherokees—Continued," Henry Rowe Schoolcraft Papers, Reel 66, Library of Congress; Marden, David L., "Anthropologists and Federal Indian Policy Prior to 1940." *Indian Historian,* 5 (4); Schoolcraft, Henry Rowe, *Algic Researches, Comprising Inquiries Respecting the Mental Characteristics of the North American Indian. First Series: Indian Tales and Legends* (1839); Schoolcraft, Henry Rowe, *Historical and Statistical Information Respecting the History, Condition and Prospects of the Indian Tribes of the United States Collected and Prepared under the Direction of the Bureau of Indian Affairs, Per Act of Congress of March 3d, 1847* (1851–57); Schoolcraft, Henry Rowe, *Personal Memoirs of a Residence of Thirty Years with the Indian Tribes on the American Frontier* (1851).

Schurz, Carl (1829–1906)

Indian writer and historian Francis Paul Prucha called Carl Schurz "one of the notable reformers of the second half of the nineteenth century." Leader of the Liberal Republican movement of the 1870s, which stressed civil service reform as its banner, Schurz spent years as secretary of the interior, where he formulated national policy on the environment and, as the head of the agency overseeing the Bureau of Indian Affairs, framed government attitudes toward the Indians. Born in the town of Liblar, on the Rhine River near Cologne, Germany, on 2 March 1829, he entered the University of Bonn at the age of 17. Two years later, the revolution of 1848 broke out across Europe and Schurz participated under the influence of Professor Gottfried Kinkel. After an armed confrontation at the fortress of Rastatt, which he escaped when Prussian troops invaded the stronghold, he went to France but returned to rescue Kinkel from a life sentence in a German prison. Exiled from France because of his revolutionary activities, Schurz lived in England for a time but then moved on to the United States, where he eventually made his home. After three years in Philadelphia, he made his way to Wisconsin, where he read the law and was admitted to the bar. Drawn into politics, he campaigned for John Charles Fremont, the Republican candidate for president, in 1856 because of that party's stand against slavery. In 1858, he campaigned for Abraham Lincoln in his unsuccessful Senate race against Stephen A. Douglas and against the anti-immigrant Know Nothing Party.

Considered but rejected for the Republican nomination for governor of Wisconsin in 1860, he instead campaigned for Lincoln's presidential campaign that year. Following Lincoln's election, Schurz was appointed minister to Spain. Schurz was not there long: in 1862 he was given command of a division of Union troops and breveted a brigadier general. He saw action at the Second Bull Run and Chancellorsville. After the war, he left the army and became a journalist, working for Horace Greeley's *New York Tribune*, the *Detroit Post*, and a German-language weekly in St. Louis. Still active in the Republican party, he delivered the keynote address at the 1868 Republican National Convention. When he returned home, the Wisconsin state legislature appointed him to the U.S. Senate and he took his seat on 4 March 1869. Opposing many of the policies of the Grant administration, he advocated the creation of a civil service system to end corruption in the selection of government employees. His dislike for Grant, on the one hand, and his hatred for the Democrats, on the other, eventually compelled him to bolt from the Republican party to form, with such notables as Greeley and Charles Francis Adams, the Liberal Republican party. The party nominated Greeley for president in 1872 but was trounced at the polls. Schurz lost his Senate seat in 1875 and pursued his journalistic career. In 1876, however, he returned to the Republican party, supporting Rutherford B. Hayes' successful campaign for the presidency; as a reward for his endorsement

Secretary of the Interior Carl Schurz with Ute representatives, left to right, Ignacio, Ouray, Chipeta, and, standing, Woretiz and Agent Charles Adams in January 1880. The Utes in this case wanted to assure whites in Washington that what was called the Meeker Massacre in 1879 was an unfortunate and isolated incident. Whites adopted the phrase "The Utes Must Go," and the Indians were eventually removed from their traditional hunting grounds in the Rocky Mountains to arid lands in Utah's Great Basin and the plains of Colorado.

Schurz was appointed secretary of the interior in the new administration.

Schurz is considered by historians to have been "enlightened" in his treatment of the Indians, but it was on his watch that many reformers of the time sprang to action to denounce government Indian policy. Schurz got into a "shouting match" in the newspapers with Helen Hunt Jackson, among the greatest of the white reformers, whose *Century of Dishonor* spawned the reform era. In an article titled, "The Indian Problem: How Secretary Schurz Would Solve It," which appeared in the *New York Tribune* in February 1880, a reporter wrote, "Mr. Schurz then went on to say [after responding to charges of mismanagement from Mrs. Helen Hunt Jackson] that in his opinion the only certain way to secure the Indians in their possessions and to prevent their being a race of paupers and vagabonds forever was to transform their tribal title into an individual title, inalienable for a certain period; in other words, to settle them in severalty and give them by patent an individual fee simple in the lands actually occupied by them; the rest of their lands to be sold for their benefit."

In "Present Aspects of the Indian Problem," an article that appeared in the July 1881 issue of the highly respected journal *North American Review*, Schurz wrote,

I am profoundly convinced that a stubborn maintenance of the system of large Indian reservations must eventually result in the destruction of the red men, however faithfully the Government may endeavor to protect their rights. It is only a question of time.... What we can and should do is, in general terms, to fit the Indians, as much as possible, for the habits and occupations of civilized life, by work and education; to individualize them in the possession and appreciation of property, by allotting to them lands in severalty, giving them a fee simple title individually to the parcels of land they cultivate, inalienable for a certain period, and to obtain their consent to a disposition of that part of their lands which they cannot use, for a fair compensation, in such a manner that they no longer stand in the way of the development of the country as an obstacle, but form part of it and are benefitted by it.

The circumstances surrounding them place before the Indians this stern alternative: extermination or civilization. The thought of exterminating a race, once the only occupant of the soil upon which so many millions of our own people have grown prosperous and happy, must be revolting to every American who is not devoid of all sentiments of justice and humanity. To civilize them, which was once only a benevolent fancy, has now become an absolute necessity, if we mean to save them.

Can Indians be civilized? The question is answered in the negative only be those who do not want to civilize them. My experience in the management of Indian Affairs, which enabled me to witness the progress made even among the wildest tribes, confirms me in the belief that it is not only possible but easy to introduce civilized habits and occupations among Indians, if only the proper means are employed. We are frequently told that Indians will not work. True, it is difficult to make them work as long as they can live upon hunting. But they will work when their living depends upon it, or when sufficient inducements are offered to them.

Indian rights advocate William Justin Harsha responded to Schurz with an article in the March 1882 *North American Review* entitled "Law for the Indians." In that discourse, Harsha proclaimed that the government must extend the full rights and guarantees of the U.S. Constitution to the Indians before they could be granted their lands in severalty. Harsha wrote, "The larger proportion of Secretary Schurz's article...is taken up with a discussion of the three elements entering into his programme for the elevation of the Indians. With his wise and humane suggestion we have not the slightest quarrel. But we do most earnestly insist that, upon the testimony of the agents in every part of our Indian country, it has been shown that the three things he advocates can only be secured, in any worthy degree, by the immediate extending of legal protection to those we desire to benefit."

After leaving the cabinet in 1881, Schurz again turned to journalism, making his mark both as an editor and as a regular correspondent of *Harper's Weekly*. In the last years of his life, he supported Democrats Grover Cleveland and William Jennings Bryan for president and called for the establishment of civil service reform leagues. He died at his home in New York City on 14 May 1906 at the age of 77.

References "Carl Schurz Is Dead after a Week's Illness." *New York Times*, 15 May 1906, 9; Harsha, William Justin, "Law for the Indians." *North American Review* 134 (3); "The Indian Problem." *New York Tribune*, 12 February 1880, 2; Prucha, Francis Paul, ed., *Americanizing the American Indians: Writings by the "Friends of the Indian," 1880–1890* (1973); Schurz, Carl, "Present Aspects of the Indian Problem." *North American Review* 133 (7); Villard, Oswald Garrison, "Schurz, Carl." In Dumas Malone, ed., *Dictionary of American Biography* (1930–88).

Section 357 of Title 25 (United States Code)

This important federal action of 3 March 1901 (31 Stat. 1084) was enacted to allow for the condemnation of Indian lands allotted in severalty to be used for public purposes, with just compensation to be awarded to the allottee. The legislation, now codified at 25 U.S.C. 357, reads: "Lands allotted in severalty to Indians may be condemned for any public purpose under the laws of the State or Territory where located in the same manner as land owned in fee may be condemned, and the money awarded as damages shall be paid to the allottee." The issue of this law came before the U.S. Supreme Court in two important cases: *Minnesota v. United States* and *United States v. Clarke*.

See also *Minnesota v. United States*; *United States v. Clarke*.

Reference *United States Code Annotated Title 25—Indians* (1983).

Section 483a of Title 25 (United States Code)

Until 1956, Indian allottees, under provisions of the General Allotment Act of 1887, did not have the power to take out mortgages or deeds on their allotments. Writing in the *American Indian Law Review*, Colorado attorney John Fredericks explained, "It was against the background of the General Allotment Act that Congress in 1956 enacted section 483a of title 25 of the United States Code, which allowed individual Indian owners of trust land to execute a mortgage or deed of trust to such land. All mortgages were made subject to the approval of the Secretary of the Interior."

The text of 483a reads:

The individual Indian owners of any land which either is held by the United States in trust for them or is subject to a restriction against alienation imposed by the United States are authorized, subject to approval by the Secretary of the Interior, to execute a mortgage or deed of trust to such land. Such land shall be subject to foreclosure or sale pursuant to the terms of such mortgage or deed of trust in accordance with the laws of the State or Territory in which the land is located. For the purpose of any foreclosure or sale proceeding the Indian owners shall be regarded as vested with an unrestricted fee simple title to the land, the United States shall not be a necessary party to the proceeding, and any conveyance of the land pursuant to the proceeding shall divest the United States of title to the land. All mortgages and deeds of trust to such land heretofore approved by the Secretary of the Interior are ratified and confirmed.

No Supreme Court cases have yet been decided as to section 483a.

See also General Allotment Act.

Reference Fredericks, John, III, "Indian Lands: Financing Indian Agriculture: Mortgaged Indian Lands and the Federal Trust Responsibility." *American Indian Law Review* 16 (1).

Self-Determination

Described as the rights of Indians to handle their own affairs with as little government intervention as possible, the doctrine of self-determination is a current policy recently instituted in the last 40 years by the government. The height of the "era" of self-determination came with the termination action brought by the U.S. Congress between 1947 and 1973, a time when Indians were expected to live largely without government assistance.

In *New Mexico v. Mescalero Apache Tribe* (1982), the Supreme Court cited several federal enactments which it declared promoted tribal self-determination; that among these was the Indian Reorganization Act of 1934, the Indian Civil Rights Act of 1968, the Indian Financing Act of 1974, and the Indian Self-Determination and Education Assistance Act of 1975, as well as Public Law 280, enacted in 1954.

See also Indian Civil Rights Act of 1968; Indian Financing Act of 1974; Indian Reorganization Act; Indian Self-Determination and Education Assistance Act of 1975; Public Law 280.

Sells, Cato (1859–1948)

Born in Vinton, Iowa, on 6 October 1859, Cato Sells attended Cornell College, a religious school, in Mount Vernon, Iowa, and read law. Before being admitted to the state bar in 1884, he was elected as a Democrat as city attorney and mayor of La Porte, Iowa. He later served as county attorney (1891–94),

U.S. district attorney (1894–99), and as a delegate to three Democratic national conventions. After a career in the law, he retired to Cleburne, Texas, to found a small bank. In 1912, he supported Woodrow Wilson for president, and upon election Wilson turned to the Sells to fill the position of commissioner of Indian Affairs. There is no evidence that Sells knew much about American Indians; his was a political appointment. Yet Sells served for over seven years as Indian commissioner. In his 1918 report, Sells wrote of Indian participation in the World War I. "We have endeavored to give the Indians a clear understanding of their relation to the war and their part in its prosecution, whether at home or abroad, and have seen them fall in line with marked intelligence and inspiring patriotism for service in every kind of activity to which the white man responds. They have signally honored themselves and their country by entering some branch of the Army or Navy; by offering their money in war loans to the Government; by increasing the product of the country's foodstuffs and complying with the public food regulations; by swelling the ranks of wage earners in periods of labor depletion; by generous and eager contributions in money and service to every phase of organized relief." In his 1914 work, *The American Indian in the United States: Period 1850–1914*, historian Warren K. Moorehead wrote, "The Indian policy the past two or three years has appreciably changed for the better. If the reforms instituted by Honorable Cato Sells can be carried out as planned, we shall conserve much of the Indian property that remains."

With the election of Republican Warren G. Harding in 1920, Sells left the Indian Office and returned to his bank in Texas. In the 1920s he turned against the "wet" (antiprohibition) policies of the national Democratic party and for a time became a supporter of Republican Herbert Hoover. Sells died in Cleburne on 30 December 1948 and is buried there.

See also Bureau of Indian Affairs.

References Kelly, Lawrence C., "Cato Sells." In Robert M. Kvasnicka and Herman J. Viola, eds., *The Commissioners of Indian Affairs, 1824–1977* (1979); Moorehead, Warren K., *The American Indian in the United States: Period 1850–1914* (1914); U.S. Congress, House of Representatives, *Annual Report of the Commissioner of Indian Affairs for the Year 1918*, House Document No. 1455, 65th Congress, 3d Session (serial 7498).

Seminole Nation v. United States (316 U.S. 286 [1942]); _Seminole Nation v. United States_ (316 U.S. 310 [1942])

These were the last two in a series of three Seminole Indian cases that came before the U.S. Supreme Court starting in 1936. After the U.S. Supreme Court held in 1937 that any claims made by the Seminole Nation after a certain date set by Congress for land claims were void, Congress, by an Act of 16 August 1937 (50 Stat. 650), removed the restriction as to the date of claims. At that time, the Seminole Nation refiled its complaint as to the six claims turned down by the Supreme Court. The Court of Claims then decided that of those six new claims, three would be dismissed, two would be considered in part, and one in full; as to these, the claims court added an additional $18,388.30 to the previous judgment to be awarded to the Seminoles. However, the act of Congress of 12 August 1935 (49 Stat. 417, at 431) allowed for any awards to Indian tribes to "be set aside" by any gratuity [compensation] paid for by the United States government. The Court decided that these gratuities amounted to $705,337.33, and dismissed the Seminoles' new claims. The U.S. Supreme Court then decided to grant certiorari to hear as to the correctness of the disallowance of three of the claims, and as to some of the gratuities included by the government. In a major opinion written by Justice Frank Murphy (Justice Robert H. Jackson dissented, and Justice Stanley Reed did not participate) on 11 May 1942, the court held that while the court was correct to dismiss several of the claims, it should reexamine the gratuitous offsets demanded by the government, and remanded the case.

Justice Murphy also delivered the opinion in the third *Seminole* case, announced on 11 May 1942 as well, in which the court held (again, Justice Robert H. Jackson dissented) that a certain land purchase by the United States could not be considered a gratuitous charge because it offset a deficiency in the boundaries of the land originally set aside for the Seminoles. Justice Murphy, in his opinion, reversed the Court of Claims decision and remanded the case for further hearings.

Seminole Tribe of Florida v. Florida et al. (116 S.Ct. 1114, 134 L.Ed. 2d 252 [1996])

In this Supreme Court case, the court determined that the states could not be sued under the Indian Gaming Regulatory Act. In 1988, the Congress enacted the Indian Gaming Regulatory Act (25 U.S.C. 2702 et seq.) "in order to provide a statutory basis for the operation and regulation of gaming by Indian tribes." Part of the act obligated the states to negotiate "in good faith" with the Indian nations inside their jurisdictions to provide for the proper disposition of Indian gaming. Under section 25 U.S.C. 2710(d)(7)(A)(i) and (B)(i) of the act, "(A) The United States district courts shall have jurisdiction over...(i) any cause of action initiated by an Indian tribe arising from the failure of a State to enter into negotiations with the Indian tribe for the purpose of entering into a Tribal-State compact...or to conduct such negotiations in good faith." In 1991, the Seminole Tribe of Florida brought suit in district court against the state of Florida and its governor, Lawton Chiles, alleging that the state and governor had "refused to enter into any negotiation for inclusion of (certain gaming activities) in a tribal-state compact." The state of Florida asked the court to dismiss the suit, arguing that such an action violated the State's "sovereign immunity from suit in a federal court." The district court refused to dismiss the action, and, before a hearing could be heard, the state appealed to the Court of Appeals for the Eleventh Circuit, which reversed the lower court's ruling. The Seminole Tribe then sought relief from the U.S. Supreme Court. After arguments were heard on 11 October 1995, the court handed down its decision on 27 March 1996. Holding for a divided 5–4 court, Chief Justice William H. Rehnquist found that "the Eleventh Amendment to the Constitution prevents Congress from authorizing suits by Indian tribes against States to enforce legislation enacted pursuant to the Indian Commerce Clause." The chief justice wrote, "...We have found that Congress does not have authority under the Constitution to make the State suable in federal court under 2710(d)(7)....The Eleventh Amendment prohibits Congress from making the State of Florida capable of being sued in federal court...The Eleventh Circuit's dismissal of petitioner's suit is hereby affirmed." In their dissent, which included Justices John Paul Stevens, David Souter, Ruth Bader Ginsburg, and Stephen Breyer, the minority argued that in such cases as *Chisholm v. Georgia*, which was the precedent for the enactment of the Eleventh Amendment, the Supreme Court found that Congress could grant such power to allow states to be sued.

See also Indian Gaming Regulatory Act of 1988.

Sequoyah (Sequoya) (ca. 1770–1843)

Indian rights advocate and originator of the Cherokee alphabet, which helped thousands of Indians to learn to read, Sequoyah ("Sparrow" or "Principal Bird") was also known as George Gist or George Guess. He was born about 1770 (it could have been as early as 1760), the son of a Cherokee mother, Wurteh, and a white father, probably the white trader and Revolutionary War soldier Nathaniel Gist. He became an accomplished farmer and silversmith and, after he fought with Andrew Jackson in the Creek War of 1813–14, he moved with his Cherokee wife, Sarah (or Sally) to Arkansas. Sequoyah is considered to have begun the invention of an alphabet for his people about 1809. Of his creation of the Cherokee syllabary, John Ehle writes that Sequoyah tried to demonstrate his capacity for inventing such a language for his people.

Sequoyah, a Cherokee, adapted the English alphabet to his language and developed the first written form of a North American Indian language. Charles Bird King's portrait shows him with the alphabet that was used to publish newspapers and books among the Cherokee.

His friends laughed at him for saying that he could make stones speak and told him he would not find stones to be entertaining company, anyway. Not only can I make them speak, but I can make characters you can understand, he told them. One morning he took a pin, and on a stone he made many marks, each intended to represent a sentence, such as: "I made a journey," "I am well," "The children are well," "When arrive you here?" "I arrive before the snows." Within a few days there were too many marks to be remembered, even though he was not nearly through, so he began to make marks that represented words. Here again, the mass of signs overcame him, and their combination in sentences was complicated. Next he came upon the idea of devising a character for each sound. These sounds, when combined, could convey words. He decided that there were eighty-six distinct sounds in Cherokee use. He made a simple sign for each, borrowing them from a copy of the Bible, the McGuffey Reader, and a Greek text.

He finished the work about 1821 and demonstrated it by writing letters in the new language. It was used most notably by Reverend Samuel A. Worcester in the 1820s in the publication of the first Indian language newspaper, the *Cherokee Phoenix*. The language was also used to teach thousands of Indian children to read. He moved to Arkansas in 1829 and served as president of the Cherokees (those that moved from Georgia to Indian Territory), where he was instrumental in uniting the two factions of the confederacy with the signing of the Cherokee Act of Union in 1839. In 1842 he went with a number of Cherokees to the western United States to study Indian languages, particularly a lost band of Cherokees rumored to have settled in the west, but he became sick and died near San Fernando, Tamaulipas, Mexico, in 1843, possibly in his seventies or eighties. In 1917, his name was honored when the state of Oklahoma sent his statue (by law, a state may send two) to the U.S. Capitol to be deposited in Statuary Hall. He is also honored by Sequoyah County, Oklahoma, and the great genus of redwood trees found only in California, the sequoia redwood.

References Ehle, John, *Trail of Tears: The Rise and Fall of the Cherokee Nation* (1988); Waldman, Carl, *Who Was Who in Native American History: Indians and Non-Indians from Early Contacts through 1900* (1990).

Seymour v. Superintendent of Washington State Penitentiary (368 U.S. 351, 7 L.Ed. 2d 346, 82 S.Ct. 424 [1962])

In *Seymour*, the Supreme Court held that Indians convicted of offenses on Indian land are under the jurisdiction of Indian tribal courts. This case in effect was the standard used in the later case of *Oliphant and Belgarde v. The Suquamish Indian Tribe et al.* (1978), in which non-Indians involved in offenses on Indian lands were found not to be under the jurisdiction of Indian tribal courts. Paul Seymour, an acknowledged member of the Colville Indian tribe of

Washington State, was convicted of burglary on what had once been the southern half of the Colville reservation, and sentenced to 7 1/2 years in the state penitentiary. Seymour petitioned the Washington State Supreme Court to void his conviction because he had been convicted of an offense committed on Indian land. The state of Washington countered that the land was no longer part of the Indian reservation. The state Supreme Court denied Seymour relief, and he sued to the U.S. Supreme Court. Arguments were heard on 13 December 1961.

On 15 January 1962, the Supreme Court handed down a unanimous decision which declared the land to still be Indian reservation land, and as such Seymour was subject to Indian tribal court jurisdiction. Justice Hugo L. Black delivered the court's opinion. Under an act of Congress of 22 March 1906, the land under question was utilized for homestead entry and settlement. A presidential proclamation in 1916 ordered that any lands not sold, be disposed of as part of the Homestead Act of 1862. The court concluded that the lower court had read the act to mean that the southern half of the reservation had been turned into public lands. Wrote Justice Black, "Time and time again in statutes enacted since 1906, Congress has explicitly recognized the continued existence as a federal Indian reservation of this South Half or diminished Colville Indian Reservation. As recently as 1956, Congress enacted a statute which provides that 'the undisposed-of lands of the Colville Indian Reservation, Washington, dealt with by the Act of March 22, 1906 (34 Stat. 80) are hereby restored to tribal ownership to be held in trust by the United States to the same extent as all other tribal lands *on the existing reservation*, subject to any existing valid rights."

See also *Oliphant and Belgarde v. The Suquamish Indian Tribe et al.*

Smith, Edward Parmelee (1827–1876)

More a preacher and missionary than a politician, Edward P. Smith stepped ably into the chair of the commissioner of the Bureau of Indian Affairs for two years just as Ulysses S Grant's "Peace Policy" was being put into action. Smith was born on 3 June 1827 at South Britain, Connecticut, the son of the Reverend Noah Smith and Laura (née Parmelee) Smith. Noah Smith died when his son was three, and he was sent to live with his paternal grandparents on their farm in Hanover, New Hampshire. He received his education at Thetford Academy in Thetford, Vermont, and the Chandler School in Hanover. He attended Dartmouth College and Yale University, the latter institution awarding him a bachelor's degree in 1849, and, after he taught for a period of time, was studied at the Yale Theological Seminary in New Hampshire, Connecticut; the Union Theological Seminary in New York City; and received his divinity degree from the Andover Theological Seminary in Andover, Massachusetts, in 1855. He was the pastor of a church in Pepperell, Massachusetts until 1864. That year, he joined the U.S. Christian Commission as a delegate with the Army of the Potomac to preach to the Union troops during the Civil War. He also worked as a field agent for the commission with the Army of the Cumberland. After the war, he served as the commission's field secretary in its central office in Philadelphia. Starting in 1871, Smith was an agent in the Chippewa and Pillager Indian tribes on the White Earth Reservation in northern Minnesota by Commissioner of Indian Affairs Ely S. Parker to fulfill President Ulysses S. Grant's "Peace Policy" in appointing religious men to oversee Indian Affairs on the reservations. The following year, Parker selected Smith to accompany General Oliver Otis Howard on his peace mission to the Apache Indians of Arizona and New Mexico. Howard later wrote in his report that Smith's "patience and unflagging energy" during the mission aided the members in their "long and tedious effort at reconciliation."

On 26 December 1872, Commissioner of Indian Affairs Francis A. Walker resigned, and it was not until March that President Grant filled the position. On 12 March, he named Smith to succeed Walker, and after being confirmed by the Senate took over eight days later. He contributed three annual reports, 1873, 1874, and 1875, as Indian commissioner. His most important discourse was for 1874, in which he called for a complete overhaul of federal legislation dealing with Indians. He elaborated, "In my judgment, whatever failure has attended the management of Indian Affairs in the past has been largely attributable to this fundamental failure to recognize and treat the Indian as a man capable of civilization, and, therefore, a proper subject of the Government and amenable to its laws." In the treatise, he detailed several enactments that he felt if passed would change the situation of the Indian in America. Among these suggestions were:

First. A suitable government of Indians.

(1.)By providing that the criminal laws of the United States shall be in force upon Indian reservations, and shall apply to all offenses, including offenses of Indians against Indians, and extending the jurisdiction of the United States courts to enforce the same.

(2.)By declaring Indians amenable to the police laws of the State or Territory for any act committed outside a reservation.

(3.)By conferring upon the President authority, at his discretion, to extend the jurisdiction of the State courts, or any portion of them, to any reservation, whenever, in his judgment, any tribe is prepared for such control.

(4.)By providing a sufficient force of deputy marshals to enforce law and order among and in behalf of Indians.

(5.)By giving authority to the Secretary of the Interior to prescribe for all tribes prepared, in his judgment, to adopt the same, an elective government, through which shall be administered all necessary police regulations of a reservation.

(6.)By providing a distinct territorial government, of United States court, wherever Indians are in numbers sufficient to justify it.

Second. Legislation for the encouragement of individual improvement:

(1.)By providing a way into citizenship for such as desire it.

(2.)By providing for holding lands in severalty by allotment for occupation, and for patents with an ultimate fee, but unalienable for a term of years.

(3.)By providing that wherever per capita distribution provided by treaty has proved injurious or without benefit to its recipients, a distribution of the same may, in the discretion of the President, be made only in return for labor of some sort." Over the next 50 years, Smith's proposals became the Indian Major Crimes Act of 1885, the General Allotment Act of 1887, and the Indian Citizenship Act of 1924.

At the end of his term, Smith was confronted by the growing crisis over the Sioux Indians in South Dakota, which ultimately led to the destruction of George Armstrong Custer's Seventh Cavalry at the Little Big Horn just seven months later. On 6 December 1875, Smith demanded that the Sioux under Sitting Bull return to their reservation or face extermination. Five days later, he resigned and was immediately sent by the American Missionary Association to Africa to begin to lay the groundwork for their new mission there. He died on or about 13 June 1876 aboard ship off the west coast of Africa of an unknown illness. His most significant published work was *Incidents of the United States Christian Commission* (1869).

See also Bureau of Indian Affairs.

References Armstrong, William H., *A Friend to God's Poor: Edward Parmelee Smith* (1993); Crawford, Richard C., "Edward Parmelee Smith." In Robert M. Kvasnicka and Herman J. Viola, eds., *The Commissioners of Indian Affairs, 1824–1977* (1979); Register of the Edward Parmelee Smith Papers, Amistad Research Center, New Orleans, Louisiana; "Smith, Edward Parmelee." In James Grant Wilson and John Fiske, eds., *Appletons' Cyclopædia of American Biography* (1888–1900); U.S. Congress, House of Representatives, *Annual Report of the Commissioner of Indian Affairs for the Year 1874*, House Executive Document No. 1, 43rd Congress, 2d Session (serial 1639).

Smith, John Quincy (1824–1901)

Although he served in the U.S. House of Representatives and was the commissioner of Indian Affairs for two years, the name of John Quincy Smith remains virtually unknown. He was born near Waynesville, in Warren County, Ohio, on 5 November 1824, and received an education in the common schools of that rural area and Miami University in Oxford, Ohio. A farmer, he served in the Ohio state Senate in 1860 and 1861 and the state House of Representatives in 1862 and 1863, and again in 1872 and 1873. Elected to the U.S. House of Representatives in 1873, he served a single term in the Forty-third Congress. In 1874, he was an unsuccessful candidate for reelection. Biographer Edward E. Hill reports that he was then named commissioner of Indian Affairs upon the recommendation of Senator John Sherman of Ohio (brother of Civil War General William Tecumseh Sherman) to replace, ironically, Commissioner Edward P. Smith, who had resigned. Smith's lone annual report appeared in 1876; historian Wilcomb Washburn declares that "no more insensitive report of an Indian commissioner is on record than the 1876 report of Commissioner Smith." Speaking harshly on all facets of Indian life and policy towards the tribes, Smith wrote, "From the fact that for so long a period Indian civilization has been retarded, it must not be concluded that some inherent characteristic in the race disqualifies it for civilized life. It may well be doubted whether this be true of any race of men. Surely it cannot be true of a race, any portion of which has made the actual progress realized by some of our Indians. They can and do learn labor; they can and do learn to read. Many thousands to-day are engaged in civilized occupations. But the road out of barbarism is a long and difficult one. Even in enlightened Europe there are millions of people whose ancestors a few generations ago were as ignorant and poor and degraded as our most civilized Indian tribes now are. Civilization is a vague, indefinite, comparative term. Our children's grand children may look upon our civilization as very rude and imperfect. It is not my wish to give any rose-colored view of the present condition of our Indians. Many of them are as miserable and degraded as men can be; but it cannot be denied that others are making reasonably satisfactory progress."

There is evidence that Smith was not well liked within the Indian office. In an undated, anonymous letter, someone inside the office wrote, "Mr. Smith, the Comm. of Ind. Aff.s, has the common reputation of being an imbecile, so far as it respects any attitude on discharging the duties of the position which he occupies. He was a complete nobody in the H. of R. [House of Representatives] and, although a member of the Committee on Claims, his principal official act consisted in agreeing to report a Bill recommended by the Secretary of War. When the Committee reported he went to another M.C. [member of Congress], placed his face near the M.C.'s ear, and whispered, 'won't you offer this?' When Mr. Smith came here to take charge of the Indian Office he questioned several persons who knew the facts respecting that office, and he was very fully informed about it, but of all the men who were anxious of reform in, and the purification of that office, he has not taken one of them into his confidence, but has struck at them directly and indirectly."

Having had a limited career before the Indian Office, Smith served after it only as the United States consul general to Montreal, Canada, from 1878 to 1882, when he resigned and returned to private life in Ohio. He died in Oakland, in Clinton County, Ohio, on 30 December 1901, and was buried in Miami Cemetery in his native Waynesville.

See also Bureau of Indian Affairs.

References *Biographical Directory of the United States Congress, 1774–1989*, Senate Document 100–34, 100th Congress, Second Session (1989); Hill, Edward E., "John Quincy Smith." In Robert M. Kvasnicka and Herman J. Viola, eds., *The Commissioners of Indian Affairs, 1824–1977* (1979); Kinney, J. P, *A Continent Lost—A Civilization Won: Indian Land Tenure in America* (1937); U.S. Congress, House of Representatives, *Annual Report of the Commissioner of Indian Affairs for the Year 1876*, House Executive Document No. 1, 44th Congress, 2d Session (serial 1749); Washburn, Wilcomb E., comp., *The American Indian and the United States: A Documentary History* (1979).

Smith v. United States (151 U.S. 50 [1894])

Known more commonly as *Famous Smith v. United States*, this Supreme Court case upheld the doctrine that "the federal courts have no jurisdiction of a crime committed by one Indian against another in the Indian Territory." Famous Smith, a Cherokee Indian (whether he was full-blooded or not is in dispute, but the opinion notes that "he was born and raised in the Cherokee Nation"), was indicted and convicted of murdering one James Gentry, who, although alleged by several witnesses to have been a Cherokee, was pronounced by the court to have been a white man. The controversy before the Supreme Court, which had the direct appeal from the Circuit Court of the United States for the western district of Arkansas, was this: What evidence did Smith have that showed Gentry was an Indian, and should the district court have dismissed the indictment without considering its strength? Gentry, witnesses related, looked like an Indian (he had "the dark hair, eyes, and complexion of an Indian, and he was generally recognized as one," stated the opinion) and his reputed father, Kajo Gentry, was either a full-blood Cherokee or of mixed Cherokee-Creek blood. The only testimony that he was not an Indian was that he had not been allowed to vote in an election held in the Cherokee Nation, but Smith's attorneys showed that it was because he had not lived in the district long enough to qualify as a voter. In spite of this, the judge hearing the case qualified to the jury that Gentry must be considered a white man, and Smith was convicted. The U.S. Supreme Court agreed to hear the case and on 3 January 1894 Justice Henry Brown held that because of the overwhelming evidence that Gentry was an Indian, the jury should have been instructed so, with the indictment then being dismissed. Justice Brown wrote, "It was held in this court in *Elk v. Wilkins*, 112 U.S. 94, 5 S.Ct. 41, that an Indian, born a member of one of the Indian tribes within the United States, which still exists and is recognized as a tribe by the government of the United States, who has voluntarily severed himself from his tribe, and taken up residence among the white citizens of a state, but who has not been naturalized, taxed, or recognized as a citizen, either by the state or by the United States, is not a citizen of the United States, within the fourteenth amendment of the constitution. Much more is that the case where it appears that the Indian was but temporarily a resident of a state, the length of his residence not being shown, and that he had done nothing to indicate his intention to sever his tribal relations."

Snyder Act (42 Stat. 208)

This federal action of 2 November 1921 established a system of annual appropriations for the Bureau of Indian Affairs (BIA). In the Supreme Court decision *Morton v. Ruiz* (1974), Justice Harry Blackmun wrote, "The Snyder Act, approved November 2, 1921, provides the underlying congressional authority for most BIA activities including, in particular and importantly, the general assistance program. Prior to the Act, there was no such general authorization. As a result, appropriation requests made by the House Committee on Indian Affairs were frequently stricken on the House floor by point-of-order objections.... The Snyder Act was designed to remedy this situation. It is comprehensively worded for the apparent purpose of avoiding these point-of-order motions to strike. Since the passage of the Act, the BIA has presented its budget requests without further interruption of that kind and Congress has enacted appropriation bills annually in response to the requests."

Now codified as 25 U.S.C. 13, the act reads:

The Bureau of Indian Affairs, under the supervision of the secretary of the interior, shall direct, supervise, and expend such moneys as Congress may from time to time appropriate, for the benefit, care, and assistance of the Indians throughout the United States for the following purposes:

General support and civilization, including education.

For the relief of distress and conservation of health.

For industrial assistance and advancement and general administration of Indian property.

For extension, improvement, operation, and maintenance of existing Indian irrigation systems and for the development of water supplies.

For the enlargement, extension, improvement and repair of the buildings and grounds of existing plants and projects.

For the employment of inspectors, supervisors, superintendents, clerks, field matrons, farmers, physicians, Indian police, Indian judges, and other employees.

For the suppression of traffic in intoxicating liquor and deleterious drugs.

For the purchase of horse-drawn and motor-propelled passenger-carrying vehicles for official use.

And for general and incidental expenses in connection with the administration of Indian Affairs.

Roger C. Wolf, a critic of the Snyder Act who also represented the Ruiz family in the case of *Morton, Secretary of the Interior, v. Ramon Ruiz et ux.*, wrote of the act, "The Snyder Act is a familiar and somewhat distressing occurrence in the history of Indian Affairs. As in other instances, Congress enacted a very general measure and left the rest up to the secretary of the interior and the BIA. The result is that the structure of the welfare system is the BIA's own creation. The regulatory scheme is contained in the departmental manual which remains inaccessible except for a few social workers and persistent attorneys."

See also *Morton, Secretary of the Interior, v. Ramon Ruiz et ux.*

References *Morton, Secretary of the Interior, v. Ramon Ruiz et ux.* (415 U.S. 199 [1974]), at 205–06; Wolf, Roger C., "Needed: A System of Income Maintenance for Indians." *Arizona Law Review* 10 (6).

Society of American Indians

This association of educated Indians desirous to formulate a reformist program for the American Indian in the United States lasted from 1911 until its dissolution some time after 1923. The main influences behind the formation of this pan-Indian organization were Dr. Charles Alexander Eastman (Santee) and Dr. Carlos Montezuma (Yavapai). Indian historian and Charles Eastman biographer Raymond Wilson penned, "It was during the era of Progressivism, when many of the injustices in American society were under attack, that Eastman and others who comprised the small number of educated Indians in American met in an effort to form a pan-Indian organization which would extend the ideals of change and progress to include improvements among their own race. As early as 1899, Eastman, his brother John, and the Reverend Sherman Coolidge, an Arapaho Episcopal minister, had discussed the possibilites of organizing such a group. They decided against it because such a body might be misunderstood by Indians and whites and would undoubtendly cause the Indian Bureau to view suspiciously a meeting of educated Indians as conspiratorial. By 1911, these fears had vanished."

On 3 April 1911, in a meeting that lasted for two days at Ohio State University in Columbus, Ohio, six Indians, Eastman, Montezuma, attorney Thomas L. Sloan (Omaha), Henry Standing Bear (Sioux), Supervisor of Employment in the Bureau of Indian Affairs Charles E. Dagenett (Peoria), and Laura M. Cornelius (Oneida), gathered under the auspices of a non-Indian, Fayette McKenzie, a professor at Ohio State in economics and sociology who had written on Indians for many years, and who belived that there was a need for an Indian organization somewhat like the National Association for the Advancement of Colored People, a black civil rights group formed in 1909. Initially calling itself the American Indian Association (AIA), the organization stated, in the preamble to its charter, "The time has come when the American Indian race should contribute, in a more united way, its influence and exertion with the rest of the citizens of the United States in all lines of progress and reform for the welfare of the Indian race in particular, and humanity in general."

The group met again in Columbus from 12 to 17 October 1911 to expand the organization and to rename it the Society of American Indians (SAI). It was declared that although non-Indians could join, only Native Americans had voting and officeholding rights. The gathering was addressed by Commissioner of Indian Affairs Robert G. Valentine, and several papers were delivered on national Indian problems. Among the people who eventually worked closely with the organization was Representative Charles D. Carter (Chickasaw), a congressman from Oklahoma and chairman of the House Committee on Indian Affairs; Arthur C. Parker (Seneca), editor of the association journal, the *American Indian Magazine*, from 1913 to 1918; and Gertrude Bonnin (Yankton Lakota).

Raymond Wilson, in a short history of the SAI, writes, "Having such an auspicious start, the Society of American Indians believed that they could help Indian people as well as convince non-Indians to respect Indian achievements and recognize the potential of Indians as functioning members of the larger American society. The organization called for better Indian educational programs and improved conditions in reservations. In 1913, they began publishing *Quarterly Journal of the Society of American Indians*, renamed *American Indian Magazine* in 1916, under the editorial guidance of Arthur C. Parker. Subsequent conferences were held in Denver in 1913; Madison, Wisconsin, in 1914; Lawrence, Kansas, in 1915; Cedar Rapids, Iowa, in 1916; Pierre, South Dakota, in 1918; Minneapolis in 1919; St. Louis in 1920; Detroit in 1921; and Chicago in 1923."

Soon after its creation, the SAI split over several issues, including its view toward the Bureau of Indian Affairs and the use of peyote. However, Indian historian Wilcomb E. Washburn wrote of the main problem of the SAI: "The moderate position of the Society was not accepted by all its members. Over the years a more militant group, led by one of the founders, Dr. Montezuma..., increasingly criticized the leadership of the Society for its tendency—in Montezuma's view—to *discuss* problems rather than *act* on them. The Society, which had set up its headquarters in Washington in order to be able to bring it influence to bear on legislation affecting the Indian, preferred to act by persuasion rather than by assault." This more aggressive attitude was expressed by Montezuma at a conference of the Society in Lawrence, Kansas, on 30 September 1915, when he thundered, "What is the Society of American Indians good for? Dare we shy? Dare we run? Dare we cower? And dare we hide when our duty is so plainly written before us? As a society with the greatest object for our people, it should be no longer possible to evade the issue; the reponsibility rests with us to be the message runners to every camp and to let every Indian know that it remains with every individual Indian to be free."

Historian David L. Marden writes, "The activist focus of the SAI did little to attract the support of white anthropologists. With few exceptions, such as Alanson Skinner of New York, anthropologists and social scientists exhibited minimal interest in the SAI until the 1920, when the SAI's magazine, the *American Indian Magazine*, changed its format. At that time, the *American Indian Magazine* began soliciting more articles from white anthropologists such as Clark Wissler of the American Museum of Natural History and Stewart Culin of the Brooklyn Institute of Arts and Sciences. This change in contributors led to a corresponding change in subject matter emphasis, as the new contributors concentrated on Indians of the past at the expense of topics of more immediate concern. This was consistent with the anthropological mandate to study primitive peoples, but the new emphasis apparently had little appeal to Indian readers, and the career of the *American Indian Magazine* soon sputtered to a close." The organization ceased operating soon after. Some of its members started the American Indian Association (AIA) in 1922, but that group did not last long. Its official journal was the *Indian Teepee*, which ceased publication in 1928.

See also Eastman, Charles Alexander; Montezuma, Carlos.

References Marden, David L., "Anthropologists and Federal Indian Policy Prior to 1940." *Indian Historian*, 5 (4); Montezuma speech, 30 September 1915, Congressional Record, 64th Congress, 1st Session (1915); Washburn, Wilcomb E., "The Society of American Indians." *Indian Historian* 3 (1); Wilson, Raymond, *Dr. Charles Alexander Eastman (Ohiyesa), Santee Sioux* (Ph.D. dissertation, University of New Mexico at Albuquerque, 1977); Wilson, Raymond, "Society of American Indians." In Armand S. La Potin, ed., *Native American Voluntary Organizations* (1987).

Solem v. Bartlett (465 U.S. 463, 79 L.Ed. 2d 443, 104 S.Ct. 1161 [1984])

The issue involved in this Supreme Court case was whether, after Congress opens an Indian reservation for settlement by non-Indians, crimes committed by Indians on that reservation are still under the jurisdiction of the Indian Major Crimes Act, or fall under state jurisdiction. John Bartlett, an enrolled member of the Cheyenne River Lakota tribe of South Dakota, was convicted of attempted rape and sentenced to ten years in the state penitentiary at Sioux Falls. Bartlett sued Herman S. Solem, warden of the prison, and Mark V. Meierhenry, South Dakota state Attorney General, for a writ of habeas corpus on the grounds that even though the Congress opened the entire reservation for settlement by non-Indians by the act of 29 May 1908 (35 Stat. 460), also known as the Cheyenne River Act, the lands therein were still to be considered "Indian country" as defined by 18 U.S.C. 1151. The district court hearing the writ agreed with Bartlett; on appeal, the U.S. Court of Appeals for the Eight Circuit affirmed the lower court's decision. The Supreme Court granted certiorari and arguments were heard on 7 December 1983.

Justice Thurgood Marshall delivered the court's unanimous decision on 22 February 1984, holding that although the act of 29 May 1908 opened the Cheyenne River Lakota reservation for settlement by non-Indians, Congress did not explicitly diminish the reservation, and as such the area must still be considered "Indian country." As Justice Marshall wrote, "[What is] clear is the historical fact that the opening of the Cheyenne River Sioux Reservation was a failure. Few homesteaders perfected claims on the lands, due perhaps in part to the price of the land but probably more importantly to the fact that the opened area was much less fertile than the lands in southern South Dakota opened by other surplus land acts. As a result of the small number of homesteaders who settled on the opened lands and the high percentage of tribal members who continue to live in the area, the population of the disputed area is now evenly divided between Indian and non-Indian residents. Under these circumstances, it is impossible to say that the opened areas of the Cheyenne River Sioux Reservation have lost their Indian character. Neither the Act of 29 May 1908, the circumstances surrounding its passage, nor subsequent events clearly establish that the Act diminished the Cheyenne River Sioux Reservation. The presumption that Congress did not intend to diminish the reservation therefore stands, and the judgment of the Eighth Circuit is affirmed." In addition, Justice Marshall cited the case of *DeCoteau v. The District County Court for the Tenth Judicial District* (420 U.S. 425 [1975]), in which Congress expressly enacted legislation that diminished a reservation's boundaries, and thus ended the right to call that area "Indian country."

See also *DeCoteau v. The District County Court for the Tenth Judicial District*; Indian Country—Definition.

South Carolina v. Catawba Indian Tribe (476 U.S. 498, 90 L.Ed. 2d 490, 106 S.Ct. 2039 [1986])

The issue decided in this Supreme Court case was the narrow one of whether a terminated tribe must file lawsuits against a state with a state statute of limitations in effect in the case. By the Catawba Indian Tribe Division of Assets Act of 1959 (25 U.S.C. 931–938), the assets of the Catawba Indian tribe were disposed of and federal responsibility over the tribe was terminated; section 5 of the act provided that state laws enacted to apply to non-Indians would apply to those Indians from terminated tribes as well. In 1980, the Catawbas filed suit for trespass and to recover a 225 square mile tract, located near the northern border of the South Carolina, from the state; in 1840, the tribe has ceded most of this tract to the state, and in 1980 some 27,000 people were living on it. The tribe contended that by the Trade and Intercourse Act of 1790, the Indians could not cede land to the state without the consent of the United States. The relevant section of that legislation reads:

Sec. 4. And be it enacted and declared, That no sale of lands made by any Indians, or any nation or tribe of Indians within the United States, shall be valid to any person or persons, or to any state, whether having the right of pre-emption to such lands or not, unless the same shall be made and duly executed at some public treaty, held under the authority of the United States.

The District Court for the District of South Carolina held for the state, but the U.S. Court of Appeals for the Fourth Circuit reversed, opining that 1) the land cession was illegal in 1840, 2) that the Catawba Indian Tribe Division of Assets Act of 1959 did not extinguish the tribe's trust relationship with the federal government, and 3) that the state statute of limitations could not be applied to the tribal suit. The state appealed and the U.S. Supreme Court granted certiorari. After the case was argued on 12 December 1985, Justice John Paul Stevens spoke for a divided court (Justices Harry Blackmun, Thurgood Marshall, and Sandra Day O'Connor dissenting) in holding narrowly that the Catawba Indian Tribe Division of Assets Act allowed for the state statute of limitations to be applied; the court did not address the other issues, preferring to remand the case to the court of appeals for a rehearing. Justice Stevens wrote, "The specific question presented to us is whether the State's statute of limitations applies to the Tribe's claim. The answer depends on an interpretation of a statute enacted by Congress in 1959 to authorize a division of Catawba tribal assets. We hold that the State's statute applies, but we do not reach the question whether it bars the Tribe's claim."

See also Termination Policy.

Standing Bear v. Crook (25 Federal Cases 695 [No. 14,891] [1879])

Officially known as *United States ex relatione* [in the relation of] *Standing Bear v. Crook* this landmark case, decided before the United States Circuit Court for the District of Nebraska in 1879, held that Indians were "persons" within the meaning of the Constitution and thus could sue in federal courts for writs of habeas corpus. The story behind *Standing Bear* started in 1868, when, in an egregious blunder, lands that were given to the Ponca tribe of northern Nebraska in 1858 were ceded to the Sioux under the Fort Laramie Treaty of 1868. Chief Standing Bear, whose Indian name was Ma-chu-nah-zha, and his members fought Sioux incursions into the area, but the Sioux complained to the government that the land was now theirs. To rectify the problem, the government sought to remove the Poncas to Indian Territory (now Oklahoma). After removal, Chief Standing Bear found the new lands to be unacceptable; when told that he must accept them, he stole away with his people and returned to their nation on the Niobrara River in Nebraska. The remaining Poncas were removed to Indian Territory. When Standing Bear's son died from disease, the chief decided that he had nothing to lose and led his people on a trek back towards their territory, settling for a time with the Omahas. Officials in Washington, D.C. then ordered Brigadier General George Crook to go to the Omaha Reservation and arrest the Poncas. Crook, considered an Indian sympathizer, nonetheless arrested the band but allowed them to stop at Fort Omaha to rest. It was there that the plight of these Indians came to the attention of a local reporter, Thomas Henry Tibbles, assistant editor of the *Omaha Daily Herald*, who took pity on the Indians and hired two local attorneys, John L. Webster and Andrew L. Poppleton, to sue on behalf of Standing Bear and the Poncas that they had been deprived of their liberty, and that they desired a court trial to order their release with a writ of habeas corpus.

After a lengthy trial, Circuit Court Judge Elmer Dundy delivered a stunning verdict: Indians were "persons" within the meaning of the Constitution, and as such had the right to sue for a writ of habeas corpus, and that the military did not have the right to remove them from their lands in Nebraska to the Indian Territory. He wrote, "During the fifteen years in which I have been engaged in administering the laws of my country, I have never been called upon to hear or decide a case that appealed so strongly to my sympathy as the one now under consideration." Judge Dundy's conclusion, partly reprinted here, reflects this thinking, coming 17 years before the U.S. Supreme Court held in *Plessy v. Ferguson* that black Americans could be segregated.

The reasoning advanced in support of my views leads me to conclude:

1. That an Indian is a "person" within the meaning of the laws of the United States, and has, therefore, the right to sue out a writ of habeas corpus in a federal court, or before a federal judge, in all cases where he may be confined or in custody under color of authority of the United States, or where he is restrained of liberty in violation of the constitution or laws of the United States.
2. That General George Crook, the respondent, being commander of the military department of the Platte, has the custody of the relators, under color of authority of the United States, and in violation of the laws thereof.
3. That no rightful authority exists for removing by force any of the relators to the Indian Territory, as the respondent has been directed to do.
4. That the Indians possess the inherent right of expatriation, as well as the more fortunate white race, and have the inalienable right to "life, liberty, and the pursuit of happiness," so long as they obey the laws and do not trespass on forbidden ground. And,
5. Being restrained of liberty under color of authority of the United States, and in violation of the laws thereof, the relators must be discharged from custody, and it is so ordered.

At the May term of the U.S. Supreme Court, Justice Samuel Freeman Miller refused to overturn Judge Dundy's decision on appeal by the United States because the Indians involved in the case had returned to their land and were not available for the hearing. On 29 February 1980, Standing Bear was enshrined in the Nebraska Hall of Fame—the first Native American to be so honored. In 1988 public television highlighted the case in *The Trial of Standing Bear*.

See also Tibbles, Thomas Henry.

References Lake, James A., Sr., "Standing Bear! Who?" *Nebraska Law Review* 60 (3); Mardock, Robert Winston, *The Reformers and the American Indian* (1971); *United States ex rel. Standing Bear v. Crook*, 25 Federal Cases 695 (1879).

Stephens v. Cherokee Nation (174 U.S. 445 [1899])

Officially titled *Stephens et al. v. Cherokee Nation* and combined with the cases of *Choctaw Nation v. Robinson*, *Johnson et al. v. Creek Nation*, and *Chickasaw Nation v. Wiggs et al.*, this important Supreme Court case involved the constitutionality of the Commission to the Five Civilized Tribes in the Indian Territory, also known as the Dawes Commission, and whether Congress had the authority to establish such a commission. The four named suits were actually only four of 166 total actions filed for hearings by the Supreme Court. These cases were all attached because they all dealt with the same question: could the Congress establish laws that in effect overruled treaties that had been signed in good faith between the federal government and the Indian tribes? Plaintiffs involved in this action were all desirous of citizenship to be granted by the Dawes Commission, established by the sixteenth section of the Indian Appropriations act of 3 March 1893 (27 Stat. 612, at 645), with rolls for citizenship to be completed as required by the Curtis Act of 28 June 1898 (30 Stat. 497). The Indian Appropriation act of 1 July 1898 (30 Stat. 545) allowed for citizenship controversies to be settled in the U.S. Supreme Court directly from United States courts in Indian territory. When the tribal councils of the Five Civilized Nations denied certain applicants citizenship, they appealed to the U.S. Supreme Court.

In all 166 cases, the Supreme Court granted certiorari, both to review the denial of citizenship and the constitutionality the Dawes Commission and the Curtis Act. Chief Justice Melville Weston Fuller, after reviewing the facts of the case, delivered the judgment of the court on 15 May 1899. In holding for the 7–2 decision (Justices Edward Douglass White and Joseph McKenna dissenting), Fuller upheld the constitutionality of both the Dawes Commission and the Curtis Act, thereby opening the way for the plaintiffs to be granted citizenship. As Chief Justice Fuller explained simply, "As we hold the entire legislation constitutional, the result is that all the judgments must be affirmed." Justices White and McKenna dissented on the grounds that the Supreme Court did not have the jurisdiction to hear such cases involving Indian citizenship.

See also Commission to the Five Civilized Tribes in the Indian Territory.

Stigler, William Grady (1891–1952)

Representative Carl Albert of Oklahoma said of William Stigler, one of the leading voices for Indians in the U.S. Congress in the 1940s and 1950s, "[He] was truly one of Oklahoma's finest citizens and public servants. He has left behind him a long and noble record of service to his State and Nation." Born in Newton, Indian Territory (now Stigler, Oklahoma) on 7 July 1891, William Grady Stigler was the son of Joseph S. Stigler and Mary Jane (née Folsom) Stigler. William Stigler, by birth, was one fourth Choctaw, and was later enrolled as a member of the Choctaw Nation. He received his education at Northeastern State College at Tahlequah, Oklahoma, which awarded him a teaching certificate in 1912, and the University of Oklahoma at Norman, where he studied the law but did not earn a degree. In 1917 he attended officers' training school, and later served as a second lieutenant in the 357th Infantry of the 90th Division of the U.S. Army, seeing action at the battles of St.-Mihiel and at the Meuse-Argonne in France during World War I. He remained in France following the end of the war and attended the University of Grenoble. Upon his return, he was admitted to the Oklahoma bar and began his practice in Newton, now renamed Stigler. He served as Stigler's city attorney (1920–24) and four years later was elected to the Oklahoma state senate, where he sat from 1924 to 1932 (he was president pro tempore in 1931). After service as a lieutenant colonel in the Forty-fifth Division, Oklahoma National Guard (1925–38), he also served as the national attorney for the Choctaw Nation, 1937–44.

In 1944, Stigler was elected the U.S. House of Representatives to fill the seat of a resigning Jack Nichols. In his four full terms (1944–52), Stigler became a trusted friend of the Indians. Although as a member of the House Appropriations Committee and the Agriculture Appropriations Subcommittee he championed the cause of farmers and veterans, he worked to improve the lot of Native Americans. Known as "Stigler from Stigler," one of his first speeches in the House was on the sale of coal and asphalt deposits in the Choctaw and Chickasaw nations of Oklahoma. In asking the Congress to limit the taxes paid by individuals who could purchase these minerals, thus benefitting the Indians, Stigler said, "As a consequence the Choctaws and Chickasaws are here again today asking Congress to authorize the Secretary of the Interior to negotiate with the tribal officials for the sale of these deposits to our Government. Our people have been coming here for more than 40 years asking Congress to keep its word—a solemn pledge it made in 1902."

William Stigler may have known that he was ill when he refused to run for reelection in 1952. Hospitalized in August of that year in Walter Reed Hospital in Washington, D.C., he was moved to his home in Stigler and died a week later on 21 August 1952 at the age 61. Biographer Ronald A. Mulder wrote of him, "He successfully championed the causes of farmers and veterans, but his central concern was the status of the American Indian. He lobbied for additional aid for the reservations; he watched the Interior Department, to be sure that it properly spent appropriated funds and protected the legal rights of Indians; and he fought for adequate compensation for natural resources extracted from tribal lands." Carl Albert memorialized Stigler, "He knew more about Indian problems and accomplished more in this body in the field of Indian legislation, affecting the Five Civilized Tribes, than any other Member of Congress in the history of our State."

References *Biographical Directory of the United States Congress, 1774–1989*, Senate Document 100–34, 100th Congress, Second Session (1989); "The Late Honorable William G. Stigler, A Representative from the State of Oklahoma," comments by Representative Carl Albert. *Congressional Proceedings and Debates of the Eighty-Third Congress, First Session* (1953); Mulder, Ronald A., "William Grady Stigler." In Dumas Malone, ed., *Dictionary of American Biography* (1930–88); "William G. Stigler, Representative, 61." *New York Times*, 22 August 1952, 21.

Swimmer, Ross Owen (Cherokee) (1943–)

Ross Owen Swimmer was principal chief of the Cherokee Nation from 1975 until he was named in 1985 as assistant secretary for Indian Affairs in the Interior Department, the fourth Native American to hold that position. Born in Oklahoma City, Oklahoma, on 26 October 1943, he is the son of Robert Owen Swimmer, a half-blood Cherokee and attorney, and Virginia (née Pounder) Swimmer, who like her husband was also a lawyer. After a common school education, Ross Swimmer enrolled at the University of Oklahoma in 1961 and was awarded a bachelor's degree in political science in 1965. He then attended the university's law school, where he earned a law degree in 1969. After being admitted to the bar, he joined the Oklahoma City firm of Hansen, Peterson, and Thompkins. He was there only two years when Chief W. W. Keeler of the Cherokee Nation asked him to serve as general counsel for the Cherokee Nation of Oklahoma, which he did from 1972 to 1975. Keeler retired in 1975 and Swimmer was elected as principal chief of the Cherokee Nation. Important during his tenure was the return of the old Cherokee Capitol building at Tahlequah (which had been used by the state for a courthouse) to the Cherokee people.

Chief Wilma Mankiller wrote of Swimmer in 1993,

> In 1983, history was made when Ross Swimmer asked me to run as his deputy chief in the next election. Just the year before, he had been deserted by most of his closest political supporters, partly because he had been diagnosed with lymphatic cancer. Those supposed allies of Swimmer's had little courage or loyalty. One of the reasons they decided to challenge him as chief was because they considered that he was too ill to remain in office, since he was out much of the time taking chemotherapy treatments. They wrote him off as a dead man. So the following year when the time came for Swimmer to announce his bid for reelection for another four year term, he remembered me. I suppose he trusted me, and was satisfied with my work and my allegiance to my tribe. He asked me if I would consider being on the ticket as his deputy. By that time, Swimmer had recovered much of his health. The chemotherapy treatments had been effective. His prognosis was good, but he had also chosen to seek internal Cherokee healing from William Smith, a traditional medicine person, and from the Seven Medicine Men at the ceremonial grounds. He stepped inside the cir-

Cherokee Ross Owen Swimmer in Tahlequah, Oklahoma, upon his election as principal chief of the Cherokee in December 1975

cle and asked for their help. I recall that Chief Swimmer made the point that he did not seek the traditional Cherokee healing as a symbolic gesture, but because he believed in its power.

Swimmer served in the federal government when President Ronald Reagan appointed him as co-chairman of the Presidential Commission on Indian Reservation Economies, which he served on from 1983 to 1984. On 26 September 1985, Reagan nominated Swimmer to fill the position of assistant secretary for Indian Affairs in the Interior Department to succeed Kenneth L. Smith (Blackfeet), who had announced his intention to resign. Swimmer was a controversial figure in that he wanted to end the bureau's grip on Indian life, a stance that earned him great enmity from his fellow Indians. Marjane Ambler writes, "During Reagan's second term, the National Congress of American Indians (NCAI) called for the resignation of Reagan's assistant Interior Secretary for Indian Affairs, Ross Swimmer. A former tribal leader himself, Swimmer understood the role of tribal governments and reservations better than [Interior Secretary James] Watt and also took a stronger stand defending tribal natural resources. Nevertheless, when he attempted to reduce the involvement of the BIA in tribal affairs, many Indian tribes believed that Swimmer was trying to terminate their relationship with the federal government. Swimmer advocated phasing out BIA, and although some Indians agreed that it should be abolished, most reservations believed the Bureau was the only thing standing between them and termination of their reservations' special status." After only a year as head of the BIA, Swimmer resigned. He returned to Oklahoma, where he started and now runs Cherokee Nation Industries, which produces products made by Cherokee Indians and provides employment to the reservation.

See also Mankiller, Wilma Pearl.

References Ambler, Marjane, "The Importance of Economic Development on the Reservation." In Albert L. Hurtado and Peter Iverson, eds., *Major Problems in American Indian History: Documents and Essays* (1994); Mankiller, Wilma and Michael Wallis, *Mankiller: A Chief and Her People* (1993); *Public Papers of the Presidents of the United States: Ronald Reagan* (1988); Viles, Philip H., "Ross Swimmer." In Sharon Malinowski, ed., *Notable Native Americans* (1995).

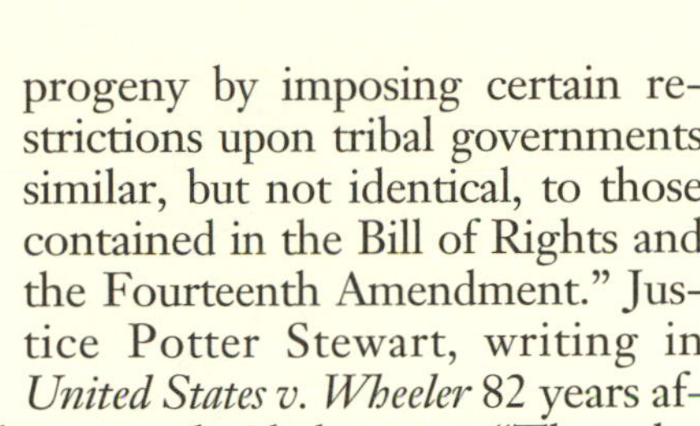

Talton v. Mayes (163 U.S. 376 [1896])

This important Supreme Court case involved the rights and sovereignty of the Cherokee Nation. Bob Talton, a Cherokee, was arrested for a murder committed on another unnamed Indian on the Cherokee reservation. A Cherokee tribal court found Talton guilty and, on 31 December 1882, sentenced him to death by hanging on 28 February 1883. Thirteen days before his execution, Talton appealed to the Circuit Court of the United States of the Western District of Arkansas on the grounds that under the Indian Major Crimes Act (23 Stat. 362) of 1885, Indians were subject to federal or state laws if they murdered another Indian. Talton sued Wash Mayes, high sheriff of the Cherokee Nation, on the grounds that he was being denied the due process of the law. The district court denied Talton relief and he appealed to the U.S. Supreme Court. On 18 May 1896, Justice Edward Douglass White delivered the opinion of the court, decided by an 8–1 vote (Justice John Marshall Harlan dissented). In his opinion, Justice White declared in denying Talton's appeal that "the crime of murder committed by one Cherokee Indian upon another within the jurisdiction of the Cherokee Nation is an offense, not against the United States, but against the local laws of the Cherokee Nation." White explained, however, that "the Indian tribes are subject to the dominant authority of Congress, and that their powers of local self-government are also operated upon and restrained by the general provisions of the constitution of the United States."

Talton has had an effect on future legislation and court action in the area of self-government of Indians. In 1978, in *Santa Clara Pueblo v. Martinez*, the court held that, "As the Court in *Talton* recognized, however, Congress has plenary authority to limit, modify or eliminate the powers of self-government which the tribes otherwise possess...In 25 U.S.C. section 1302 [the Indian Civil Rights Act of 1968], Congress acted to modify the effect of *Talton* and its progeny by imposing certain restrictions upon tribal governments similar, but not identical, to those contained in the Bill of Rights and the Fourteenth Amendment." Justice Potter Stewart, writing in *United States v. Wheeler* 82 years after Talton was decided, wrote, "The relevance of *Talton v. Mayes* to the present case is clear. The Court at that time held that when an Indian tribe criminally punishes a trib[al] member for violating tribal law, the tribe acts as an independent sovereign, and not as an arm of the Federal Government."

See also *Santa Clara Pueblo v. Martinez*; *United States v. Wheeler*.

References *Santa Clara Pueblo v. Martinez* (436 U.S. 56 [1978]); *United States v. Wheeler* (435 U.S. 313 [1978]).

Tappan, Samuel Forster (1830–1913)

One of the most important Indian reformers of the nineteenth century, Samuel Forster Tappan spent years working to alleviate the situation of American Indians. A chairmaker, philanthropist, soldier, and journalist, Tappan was born in 1830 in Manchester, Massachusetts. His education is unknown, but he became a newspaperman at a young age and befriended such men as William Lloyd Garrison, Wendell Phillips, and Theodore Parker, all giants of the abolitionist movement of the first half of the nineteenth century. Tappan became an intimate of Horace Greeley, famed editor of the influential *New York Tribune*, and Greeley sent him to Kansas to cover the fighting in that territory over the slavery issue, where Tappan became a friend of radical John Brown. Tappan, after serving as assistant clerk of the 1855 Kansas constitutional convention and to the U.S. House of Representatives, became a gunrunner for abolitionist forces.

Around 1859 or 1860, Tappan left the fight in Kansas and followed the gold rush to Colorado, where he worked as assistant editor of the *Denver Herald* and continued to report for Greeley's *Tribune*. When the Civil War broke out, he enlisted in Company B of the First Colorado Volunteers

Samuel Forster Tappan, 1862

and saw action in New Mexico. When his superior resigned, Tappan, a lieutenant colonel, was slated for the position, but it went instead to Col. John Chivington, with whom Tappan would later clash. On 29 November 1864, troops under the command of Chivington and Major Scott J. Anthony, a Chivington supporter, attacked a band of peaceful Cheyenne Indians at Sand Creek and murdered more than one hundred of them. Tappan adopted an orphan from the massacre, but she later died in a girls' school in New York. He was directed by Congress to investigate the slaughter and, although denounced by Chivington as prejudiced, found the colonel and his inferiors to be completely responsible for the Sand Creek atrocity, although none of those responsible were ever punished. Tappan also served as a member of the Indian Peace Commission, which looked into ways white settlement on the plains could be better handled so as to avoid clashes with the Indians. His writings make him one of the unsung heroes of the Native American rights movement. Historian Henry Fritz writes of Tappan, "[His] activity lends weight to the thesis that Indian reform was largely a matter of Christian conscience, nurtured in the East, reacting in the West."

On 29 January 1866, Tappan wrote a lengthy memorandum to Commissioner of Indian Affairs Dennis Nelson Cooley "in reference to the policy to be pursued towards the Indians, and recommending that proper provision be made, to secure a better class of officers, to adjust Indian difficulties." In the letter, addressed to "Judge Cooley, Commissioner of Indian Affairs," Tappan wrote:

Permit me to make a few suggestions as to what in my opinion should be done to secure a permanent and honorable peace with the various Indian tribes within the boundaries of the United States, and end the troubles which have existed for the last five years and the dreadful scenes to which they have led.

The fruitful source of all the difficulties with the Indians has been on account of the Indians having no legal protection from depredations upon them by the whites. It is a well established fact that the whites are very much prejudiced against the Indians and demand the extermination of the whole race, which had induced many of them to consider the Indians as having 'no rights which a whiteman is bound to respect' [these words are meant to mimic Chief Justice Roger Taney's from his opinion in *Dred Scott v. Sandford* [1857]], as having no claims whatever to considerations as human beings, but fit subjects for assassination and mutilation. To shoot an Indian woman was not more criminal than to kill [a] wolf. To trample upon and assassinate a pappose [*sic*] no greater offense against the laws and honor of the country than to 'bruise the serpent's head,' but on the contrary demanded by the highest interests of civilization to kill and mutilate Indians whenever and wherever an opportunity occurred. These things has [*sic*] led to outrages upon the Indians which they have not been slow in retaliating upon our people, not upon the guilty parties, but often upon those who were inocent [*sic*]. The first white man they overtook must answer with his life [for] the crime of some scoundrel who had preceded him in the Indian country, and committed an outrage upon [an] Indian family.

Then again, the salaries allowed your Indian agents has [*sic*] not been sufficient to induce an honest man to accept the position, and men who have taken the office have so often done so for the 'stealings' more than the salary.

The later evil I warned remedy by an incursion of compensation and the former by making such agents judicial officers to adjudicate and determine all matters of difference and difficulty between the Indians and also between the whites and Indians, arrest, try and to punish offenders and administer justice to all parties. Permit the Indians to give evidence as witnesses, and to receive it as such. Keep a faithful record of all trials, evidence taken, the statute or statutes by authority of which the trial was had.

The only appeal from these judicial officers to a higher court should be upon the record of the case, and the law, and no court prevented from receiving the evidence of the Indians should have the right of revising or reversing the order of the Commissioner.

In his last years, Tappan remained at the forefront of Indian reform, serving as a member of philanthropist Peter Cooper's privately financed United States Indian Commission. He died in Washington, D.C., where he had spent the last quarter century of his life, on 6 January 1913, and was buried in Arlington National Cemetery.

See also Indian Peace Commission; United States Indian Commission.

References Dennis Nelson Cooley to James Harlan, 16 March 1866, Records of the House of Representatives, RG 233, Committee on Indian Affairs, file HR 39A-F11.5; Fritz, Henry E., *The Movement for Indian Assimilation*, 1860–1890 (1963); James Harlan to William Windom, Chairman of the House Committee on Indian Affairs, 3 February 1866, Records of the House of Representatives, RG 233, Committee on Indian Affairs, file HR 39A-F11.5; Hoig, Stan, *The Sand Creek Massacre* (1961); Thrapp, Dan L., *Encyclopedia of Frontier Biography* (1990); Whitford, William Clarke, *Colorado Volunteers in the Civil War: The New Mexico Campaign in 1862* (1906); Waldman, Carl, *Who Was Who in Native American History: Indians and Non Indians from Early Contacts through 1900* (1990).

Taylor, Nathaniel Green (1819–1887)

He was the commissioner of Indian Affairs for two short years, but in that period Nathaniel G. Taylor pursued a peace policy toward the Indians that made him one of the more important administrators of that office. He was born in Happy Valley, Carter County, Tennessee, on 29 December 1819, the son of James P. Taylor, a leading attorney in the state and Attorney General for Tennessee's First Judicial District, and Mary (née Carter) Taylor. James Taylor's father, General Nathaniel Taylor, was a noted soldier who commanded, under the authority of General Andrew Jackson, a Tennessee regiment at the Battle of New Orleans. Mary Carter Taylor's grandfather, John Carter, was one of the founders of the first settlement of the state and, with his son, Landon (for whom Carter County was named), served in several state constitutional conventions. Nathaniel G. Taylor attended Washington College near Jonesboro, Tennessee, and graduated from Princeton University in 1840. He studied the law, was admitted to the Tennessee bar in 1841, and opened a law practice in Elizabethton, Tennessee (named after his grandmother, Elizabeth Carter). Overcome by the death of his sister, who was struck by lightning, Taylor became a Methodist minister at the age of 23. In 1849, he broke family tradition and ran as a Whig (his family were Jacksonian Democrats) for Congress against Andrew Johnson, who would later succeed Abraham Lincoln as president of the United States. Unsuccessful in this race, he ran again in 1853 but was defeated by Democrat Brookins Campbell. Upon Campbell's unexpected death, Taylor was elected to fill his seat (he sat in the thirty-third Congress), but was defeated for reelection in 1854.

At this point, Taylor turned to the Constitutional Union party, a short-lived entity that sought to preserve the Union while avoiding a national fight over slavery. Taylor served as an elector for the party, which nominated John Bell and Edward Everett for president and vice president in 1860 against Abraham Lincoln. During the Civil War, Tennessee was occupied by both the Union and the Confederacy and poverty reigned in Taylor's native state. At the end of 1863 he went to New York with Everett (who delivered the keynote address at the Gettysburg dedication ceremony) to raise funds for the people there. Their work produced some $250,000, which helped many Tennesseans avoid starvation. Taylor rode the popularity from this act to a seat in Congress in 1865, when he ran as a Unionist Republican. Taylor served in the thirty-ninth Congress but his work there was undistinguished. On 12 March 1867, the Senate refused to confirm Lewis Vital Bogy as Indian commissioner and President Andrew Johnson turned to his former political rival Taylor for the post. On 29 March, the Senate confirmed Taylor as the sixteenth Indian commissioner. According to historian Robert M. Utley, "The Senate apparently withheld confirmation of Bogy as part of the conflict building between Congress and President Johnson. Secretary [of the Interior Orville Hickman] Browning regarded it as a calamity. He urged [the appointment] of Henry H. Sibley of Minnesota as Bogy's successor but had to defer to the President's insistence on Taylor, whom he viewed as unqualified. [Browning wrote,] 'I now have a Methodist preacher at the head of the Bureau. I will do the best I can with him.'" Taylor was at constant loggerheads with Secretary Browning over the powers of the office of the commissioner. In a 15-page letter that Taylor wrote to President Andrew Johnson on 15 June 1867, which Taylor biographer William E. Unrau calls "perhaps the single most comprehensive statement by an Indian commissioner to that time on the frustrating constitutional position of the office of Indian commissioner," Taylor penned,

The duties I owe to the public service, to my own official responsibility, and to your Administration, in the faithful management of this Bureau in its conduct towards the civilized and savage wards of the nation committed to its care, impel me to address you upon the grave differences existing between the Secretary of the Interior and myself as to our respective rights, duties and responsibilities in the management of Indian Affairs under the organic acts and the regulations which have been prescribed from time to time by the President, by virtue of the authority invested in him by Congress… At a time far less urgent, your illustrious predecessor, President Jackson, declared what his will was, and his will became law. The power is still confided to you, and I again earnestly ask that any proper position may be defined, my power prescribed, and my rights and duties made known in the form of regulations, by virtue of the authority confided upon you by the Organic Act. Believing that you are controlled by the same patriotic motives and the same fixed devotion to right and firmness in duty that distinguished your illustrious predecessor, above named, I have the honor herewith to submit for your action, certain regulations which I believe embody the letter and spirit of the law, and the regulations, heretofore prescribed, and which, in my judgment, are absolutely essential to the successful management of the difficult matters committed to my charge.

An act of Congress of 20 July 1867 established the Indian Peace Commission, also called the Taylor Commission or Great Plains Peace Commission, designed to converse with the Indian tribes "waging war against the United States or committing depredations upon the people thereof" and to determine what it would take to end the warfare. Members included Senator John B. Henderson, chairman of the Senate Committee on Indian Affairs, Indian rights advocate Samuel F. Tappan, General John B. Sanborn, Brevet Major General William S. Harney, Lieutenant General William Tecumseh Sherman, Brevet Major General Christopher Columbus Augur, and Brevet

Major General Alfred Howe Terry. The commission's report, delivered to President Andrew Johnson on 7 January 1868, explained that mistreatment of the Indians had led to the warfare in the west and suggested that the Indian Bureau be made an independent department of the government. In his single report as Indian commissioner, in 1868, Taylor confronted the issue of whether the Bureau of Indian Affairs should be transferred to the control of the War Department so that a military campaign to eradicate the Indians could be instituted by proponents of such a policy. In his discourse, Taylor reported, "I yield to none in admiration and love of the gallant officers and soldiers of our army." However, he added later in the treatise, "It is inhuman and unchristian, in my opinion, leaving the question of economy out of view, to destroy a whole race by such demoralization and disease as military government is sure to entail upon our tribes."

Taylor's conflict with Browning pushed him toward resignation. As word spread that Taylor's time in the Indian office was growing short, several persons sympathetic to him deluged President Grant with messages to retain him. Jay S. Backus, corresponding secretary of the American Baptist Home Mission Work in North America and E. E. L. Taylor, corresponding secretary of the organization's Indian Missions section, wrote to the president on 1 March 1869, "We take pleasure in stating that Commissioner N. G. Taylor has in all our business transactions with him shown an intimate acquaintance and thorough knowledge of Indian matters, and a Christian sympathy for the Indians, and has uniformly adjusted our business matters on principles of fairness and freedom from sectarian bias, though he is a member of another religious denomination." They added, "Our Board has never before addressed any President of the United States on this subject, but believing Commissioner Taylor to be eminently qualified for his post and fearing that a change may be injurious to the highest interests of the Indians we have written this, without solicitation from any source." The massacre of peaceful Southern Cheyenne Indians under Black Kettle by George A. Custer's Seventh Cavalry at the Washita River in November 1868 shattered whatever chance Taylor's peace policy had of success. When the Indian commissioner sided with noted Indian rights activists Samuel Tappan, Maria Lydia Child, and Peter Cooper in denouncing Custer, Taylor was finished. On 25 April 1869, he resigned.

In his final years, Taylor resumed a quiet life of farming and lawyering. On 31 January 1880, Felix Reeve wrote to Senator John Sherman of Ohio, "I have been requested by my friend the Hon. N. G. Taylor to solicit your attention to his claims for the office of Commissioner of Indian Affairs recently vacated by the removal of Mr. [Ezra] Hayt—an office which Mr. Taylor filled with ability and integrity for two years under the administration of President Johnson." Taylor was passed over instead for Rowland E. Trowbridge. Seven years later, Taylor died at his home in Happy Valley, on 1 April 1887, at the age of 67.

See also Bureau of Indian Affairs; Indian Peace Commission Act; Indian Peace Commission.

References Augsburg, Paul D., *Bob and Alf Taylor: Their Lives and Lectures* (1925); *Biographical Directory of the United States Congress, 1774–1989*, Senate Document 100–34, 100th Congress, Second Session (1989); Crutchfield, James, *Timeless Tennessee* (1984); Felix H. Reeve to John Sherman, 31 January 1880, Box 43, Records of the Appointments Division, Commissioner of Indian Affairs, RG 48, National Archives; Jay S. Backus and E. E. L. Taylor to Grant, 1 March 1869, Box 43, Records of the Appointments Division, Commissioner of Indian Affairs, RG 48, National Archives; Robert L. Taylor to President Johnson, 15 June 1867, Selected Classes of Letters Received by the Indian Division of the Office of the Secretary of the Interior, 1867–69, RG 48, National Archives Microfilm Publication M825, roll 1, frames 0534–48; Taylor, James P., *Life and Career of Sen. Robert Love Taylor* (1913); U.S. Congress, House of Representatives, *Annual Report of the Commissioner of Indian Affairs for the Year 1868*, House Executive Document No. 1, 40th Congress, 3d Session (serial 1366), 1868; U.S. Congress, House of Representatives, *Report of the Indian Peace Commission*, House Executive Document No. 97, 40th Congress, 2d Session (serial 1337); Unrau, William E., "Nathaniel Green Taylor." In Robert M. Kvasnicka and Herman J. Viola, eds., *The Commissioners of Indian Affairs, 1824–1977 (1979); Utley,*

Robert M., Frontier Regulars: The United States Army and the Indian, 1866–1891 (1973).

Taxation of Indians and Indian Property, Supreme Court Cases

See *Childers v. Beaver et al.*; *Choate v. Trapp*; *Department of Taxation and Finance of New York et al. v. Milhelm Attea & Bros., Inc. etc. et al.*; *Gillespie v. Oklahoma*; *Gleason et al. v. Wood et al.*; *Goudy v. Meath*; *Jaybird Mining Company v. Weir*; The Kansas Indians; *McClanahan, etc. v. State Tax Commission of Arizona*; *Moe, etc. et al. v. The Confederated Salish and Kootenai Tribes of the Flathead Reservation et al.*; The New York Indians; *Oklahoma Tax Commission v. Citizen Band Potawatomi Indian Tribe of Oklahoma*; *Oklahoma Tax Commission v. Sac and Fox Nation*; *Oklahoma Tax Commission v. United States*; *Thomas et al. v. Gay et al.*; *United States v. Mason*; *United States v. Rickert*; *Wagoner et al. v. Evans et al.*; *White Mountain Apache Tribe et al. v. Bracker et al.*; *Williams v. Lee.*

Tee-Hit-Ton Indians, an Identifiable Group of Alaska Indians, v. United States (348 U.S. 273 [1955])

In this Supreme Court case, the court held that since Congress had not recognized an Indian tribe's assertions of ownership of certain lands that it claimed were part of its ancestral lands, the government was not responsible to compensate those Indians for the taking of timber from those disputed lands. The Tee-Hit-Ton Indians of Alaska, a clan of Tlinglit Indians, sued the U.S. government for taking timber from more than 350,000 acres of land that it claimed were part of its reservation. The Court of Claims, which heard the case, dismissed the lawsuit on the grounds that the Indians' use of the lands where the timber was located was the same as the use of the "nomadic" tribes of the Indians in the contiguous United States, and that such title making the Indians the owners of the land must come from Congress. The Tee-Hit-Ton Indians appealed to the U.S. Supreme Court. After arguments were heard on 12 November 1954, the court handed down its judgment on 7 February 1955. Speaking for a fractured 6–3 court (Chief Justice Earl Warren and Justices William O. Douglas and Felix Frankfurter dissented), Justice Stanley Reed upheld the Court of Claims decision that since Congress did not recognize the Tee-Hit-Ton Indians' right to their lands, such takings by the federal government were not liable for compensation. As Justice Reed wrote, "The line of cases adjudicating Indian rights on American soil leads to the conclusion that Indian occupancy, not specifically authorized by Congress, may be extinguished by the Government, without compensation. Every American schoolboy knows that savage tribes of this continent were deprived of their ancestral ranges by force and that, even when the Indians ceded millions of acres by treaty in return for blankets, food and trinkets, it was not a sale but a conquerors' will that deprived them of their land. The duty that rests on this Nation was adequately phrased by Mr. Justice [Robert H.] Jackson in his concurrence, Mr. Justice [Hugo L.] Black joining, in *Northwestern Bands of Shoshone Indians v. United States*, 324 U.S. 335 at 355, 65 S.Ct. 690 at 700, 89 L.Ed. 985, a case that differentiated 'recognized' from 'unrecognized' Indian title, and held the former only compensable."

Termination Policy

Defined in this context as "the cessation of all federal services and programs to the Indian reservations," termination was started by Congress in 1944, when a House Select Committee recommended that a "final solution to the Indian problem" be enacted, and ended in 1973, with the passage of the Menominee Restoration Act, making that Wisconsin tribe the first to have its federal services "restored." One of its leading congressional proponents was Senator Arthur V. Watkins of Utah. Termination as law was set into stone with the Congressional intent involved in House Concurrent Resolution 108, and the passage of Public Law 280, both in 1953. While 108 was a nonbinding resolution, with no actual force in law, it gave way to 280, which transferred federal jurisdiction over law and order on reservations to the states. Although this era lasted from 1954 to 1958 and included only a few tribes (the Menominees and the Klamath tribe in Oregon being the most striking examples), it nonetheless took many years to overcome and change. On 18 September 1958 Secretary of the Interior Fred Seaton announced that while he was in office no other Indian tribes would be terminated, and by the time he left in 1961 the era had passed. A recent Supreme Court case which dealt with issues surrounding termination issues is *South Carolina v. Catawba Indian Tribe* (1986).

See alsoMenominee Restoration Act of 1973; Menominee Termination Act of 1954; Public Law 280; *South Carolina v. Catawba Indian Tribe*; Watkins, Arthur Vivian.

Thomas-Rogers Act of 1936

See Oklahoma Indian Welfare Act of 1936.

Thomas et al. v. Gay et al. (169 U.S. 264, 42 L.Ed. 740, 18 S.Ct. 340 [1898])

The dual cases of *A. M. Thomas and Others, Commissioners of Kay County, etc., v. Gay and Reed et al.*, and *Gay and Reed et al., v. A. M. Thomas and Others, Commissioners of Kay County, etc.* dealt with the issue of whether the Congress could change a treaty with Indian nations with a simple act of Congress. In two treaties with the Cherokees (6 May 1828 [7 Stat. 311] and 29 December 1835 [7 Stat. 478]), the government agreed to recognize their rights to a reservation in what is now Oklahoma, and that the lands could not, without the consent of the Cherokees, be "included within the territorial limits or jurisdiction of any state or territory." A subsequent treaty, that of 19 July 1866 (14 Stat. 799, at 801) stipulated that Indians friendly to the Cherokees that had been removed from other parts of the country could be placed on the Cherokee lands if the Cherokees were properly reimbursed by the government. The Osage and Kansas Indians were later moved to these lands, and the Cherokees were compensated. However, the government, in the act of Congress of 2 May 1890 (26 Stat. 81), which established the territory of Oklahoma, included the lands of the Osage and Kansas tribes within the geographical limits of the new territory. Then, on 5 March 1895, the Oklahoma legislature passed a law taxing the cattle that grazed or were kept by the Indians of these two affected tribes. Appellants Gay and Reed were not Indians; they were, in fact, nonresidents of Oklahoma entirely. They did, however, graze their cattle on the lands of the Osage and Kansas nation, and as such they were taxed by the territory. Backed by the Indians, they sued A. M. Thomas, Commissioner of Kay County, Oklahoma, to enjoin, or stop, him from collecting the tax on the grounds that the legislature was without power to impose a tax on Indians lands and that such a tax was violative of the Interstate Commerce Clause of the United States Constitution. The District Court of Kay County held that the tax was valid, as well as other "territorial taxes" imposed by the county; the Oklahoma Territorial Supreme Court, however, while upholding the cattle tax, did not agree with the territorial taxes. Both sides in this controversy then submitted the case to the U.S. Supreme Court under the consolidated name of *Gay v. Thomas*.

Justice George Shiras, Jr., held for a unanimous court on 21 February 1898 in reversing the Oklahoma Territorial Supreme Court's decision as to territorial taxes, and upholding the cattle tax. Justice Shiras noted particularly the sixth section of the act that created the Oklahoma Territory: "Nothing in this act shall be construed to impair any right now pertaining to any Indians or

Indian tribe in said territory under the laws, agreements, and treaties of the United States, or to impair the rights of person or property pertaining to said Indians, or to affect the authority of the government of the United States to make any regulation or to make any law respecting said Indians, their lands, property, or other rights, which it would have been competent to make or enact if this act had not been passed." He explained in his opinion, "It is well settled that an act of Congress may supersede a prior treaty, and that any questions that may arise are beyond the sphere of judicial cognizance, and must be met by the political department of the government [referring to Congress]." This case was upheld in the same court term in *Wagoner et al. v. Evans*.

See also *Wagoner et al. v. Evans et al.*

Three Affiliated Tribes of the Fort Berthold Reservation v. Wold Engineering, P.C. et al. (467 U.S. 138, 81 L.Ed. 2d 113, 104 S.Ct. 2267 [1984])

Known as "Three Tribes I," this Supreme Court case dealt with the issue of whether state courts had jurisdiction over civil matters between Indian tribes and non-Indians. In 1974, the Three Affiliated Tribes of the Fort Berthold Reservation in North Dakota hired the engineering firm of Wold Engineering, P.C., to design and build the Four Bears Water System Project, a water supply complex entirely within the reservation. After the project was completed in 1977, the tribe became dissatisfied with its performance and moved in the North Dakota state courts in 1980 to sue the firm for negligence and breach of contract. The trial court held that even though Public Law 280 (67 Stat. 588) gave the states jurisdiction over Indian civil matters, it was repealed by the Indian Civil Rights Act of 1968, which forced states to get tribal consent before assuming jurisdiction over these civil matters, and dismissed the suit. The North Dakota Supreme Court affirmed, further holding that any state jurisdiction of tribal civil matters must come only if the Indian citizens of that reservation vote to accept state jurisdiction. Further, it decided that a state statute—known as 27–19—passed in the wake of the 1968 Civil Rights Act, disclaimed state jurisdiction over Indian civil matters. The Three Affiliated Tribes appealed the decision to the U.S. Supreme Court.

After arguments were heard on 29 November 1983, a decision was handed down on 29 May 1984. Voting to reverse the holding of the North Dakota Supreme Court and remand the case for reconsideration by a 7–2 decision (Justices William H. Rehnquist and John Paul Stevens dissenting), the court, with Justice Harry Blackmun speaking for the majority, held that the state court's original decision may have been based on "the misapprehension that state court jurisdiction was inconsistent" with Public Law 280's provisions. It remanded, or returned, the case for further consideration.

See also *Three Affiliated Tribes of the Fort Berthold Reservation v. Wold Engineering, P.C. et al.* ("Three Tribes II")

Three Affiliated Tribes of the Fort Berthold Reservation v. Wold Engineering, P.C. et al. (476 U.S. 877, 90 L.Ed. 2d 881, 106 S.Ct. 2305 [1986])

Known as "Three Tribes II," this case was the second time that the parties in this action came before the Supreme Court. After the Supreme Court reversed the original holding of the North Dakota state Supreme Court and remanded the case for reconsideration, the state Supreme Court again held against the Indian tribe, claiming that the state statute in question—known as 27–19—specifically disclaimed all state jurisdiction over Indian civil matters. On appeal, the U.S. Supreme Court, for the second time in three years, granted certiorari to hear the case. Arguments were held on 24 March 1986, and the court decided the case on 16 June of that same year. Speaking for the 6–3 decision of the court (original *Three Tribes I* dissenters William H. Rehnquist and John Paul Stevens this time were joined by Justice William Brennan), Justice Sandra Day O'Connor held that even though Public Law 280 (67 Stat. 588) did not address the issue of whether a state could eventually disclaim its jurisdiction over Indian civil matters, such a disclaimer was inconsistent with the federal statute, and was "unduly burdensome" to the Indian tribes. Dissenters, led by Justice Rehnquist, expressed the will that if the federal statute did not address the subject of a state disclaiming jurisdiction, the court could not infer the "congressional intent" if such a disclaimer were to be enacted by a state.

Tibbles, Susette La Flesche (Omaha) (1854–1902)

Her Indian name was *Inshtatheamba*, yet to the world she was known as Susette La Flesche, or "Bright Eyes." Before and after her marriage to white Indian reformer Thomas Henry Tibbles, she was a nationally known figure, an important voice in the latter half of the nineteenth century on behalf of American Indian rights. She was born on the Omaha Reservation in 1854 near what today is Bellevue, Nebraska, the daughter and one of several children of Chief Joseph La Flesche *(Istamaza*, or "Iron Eye"), head of the Omahas from 1853 to 1866, and his half-white, half-Omaha wife, Mary Gale *(Hinnuagsnun*, or "One Woman"). Susette's siblings included Susan La Flesche (later Picotte), the first female Indian physician, and her half-brother, the anthropologist Francis La Flesche. She attended the Presbyterian mission school on the Omaha reservation, and then the Elizabeth Institute for Young Ladies, from which she graduated in 1875. It then took two years for her to obtain a licence to teach in the reservation school, where she worked from 1877 to 1879.

It was at this time that the plight of the Ponca tribe of Nebraska became national news. By a government mistake, the lands of the Poncas were allotted to the Sioux under the Fort Laramie Treaty of 1868, and the Poncas were forcibly removed to the Indian Territory (now Oklahoma). When Standing Bear, chief of the Poncas, and his people attempted to return to their grounds at the junction of the Niobrara River and Keya Paha River (now on the border between Nebraska and South Dakota), they were arrested. Thomas Henry Tibbles, a white reporter for the Omaha *Herald*, reported on the case and traveled through the eastern United States bringing the situation of the Poncas to public attention. Susette La Flesche, her half-brother Francis, and Standing Bear joined Tibbles on the tour, in which Susette spoke to civic groups and literary organizations. On the tour, her eloquence on behalf of the Poncas brought her to the attention of such people as Helen Hunt Jackson (who would later write the Indian exposé *Century of Dishonor)* and ethnologist Alice Cunningham Fletcher. Two years after Tibbles' first wife died in 1879, he and Susette married, and they became a two-person lobbying team on behalf of Native American rights. In a discourse entitled "First lecture delivered by Bright Eyes in Boston" (Tibbles apparently later rectified the fact, correcting it as to be the "most reported meeting"), delivered some time in 1880, Bright Eyes explained,

> My people have made desperate struggles, year after year, for their lives and for their liberty. They have writhed under the hand of a powerful oppressor. It has been said that "The Government system has been one of alternate pauperizing and butchery." From time to time during three hundred years, there have arisen king men and just men, judges and senators, who have tried to compel the Government to right these wrongs and to change its system. From time to time parties have arisen like this to insist that these wrongs be righted, and compel the Government to change its course for the future, but they have always been beaten, and it remains to be seen whether we are or not. It has been said that you cannot compel the Government to right a wrong unless the people demand it. I do not know whether it is because the people do not know enough or care enough to demand justice for a handful of

helpless people in the absolute control of one Government official who has unlimited authority to kill and butcher if they do not obey his imperious will, or whether it is because this one Government official is greater than the people who elect him, or he is so great in himself that he can afford to defy public opinion, or he has made money out of it. It is your place to find out which.

During the last three years three tribes, the Nez Percés, the Poncas and the Cheyennes have been forcibly removed from their homes into strange lands, where many had died in hopeless anguish. What did these tribes do in their defence? You known they would have been less than men if they had submitted meekly like slaves to the authority of this one Government official at Washington. The Nez Percé resisted, and there are now a feeble remnant of them left in the Indian Territory, to which they were forced to go. Of the Cheyennes who resisted not a man is left to tell the tale. What did the Poncas do? They went into the courts with the writ of habeas corpus in their hand, claiming their liberty like men. This one Government official sent an order to his attorney to dismiss the case, that they [the Indians] were not persons, and were not entitled to the right of liberty. When the Cheyennes fought to maintain their rights, they were exterminated. When the Poncas claimed the protection of the courts, the great Secretary of the Interior tried to kick them out. Whether he will succeed or not, it is for you to say.

We offer a solution to the Indian problem. This solution will end all wars; it will end the shedding of the blood of innocent women and children; it will stop all these wrongs which have gone on month after month, year after year, for a hundred years. The solution of the Indian problem, as it is called, is citizenship. Like all great questions which have agitated the world, the solution is simple—so simple that men cannot understand it. They look for something complicated, something wonderful, as the answer to a question which has puzzled the wisest heads for a hundred years. The question, I believe, is, "What shall be done with the Indian?" One part of the American people try to solve it by crying "exterminate him." The answer to such people is, that he has a Creator who will avenge his extermination. The other part cry "civilize him." Forthwith they go to work, tell him that his land shall be his "as long as grass grows and the waters run." We all know that "the grass grows and the waters run" only as long as it pleases the Secretary of the Interior. They say to him, "You must not pass beyond this line without the permission of this man, your agent, whom we place over you," thus effectually preventing him from seeing or moving in any civilization but his own. This, you see, is a lesson in freedom and liberty, their first lesson in the art of civilization.

From the time they married until Susette's death on 26 May 1903, the Tibbleses traveled to England and Scotland to lecture, and reported on the massacre at Wounded Knee in December 1890. Her contributions to Tibbles' populist newspaper, the *Independent*, were the first for a Native American woman.

See also *Standing Bear v. Crook;* Picotte, Susan La Flesche; Tibbles, Thomas Henry.

References "Bright Eyes, Lecture in Boston, 3 December 1880[?]" Box 42, Folder 7, Thomas Henry Tibbles Papers, Archives of the National Museum of the American Indian, New York; Clark, Jerry E. and Martha Ellen Webb, "Susette and Susan LaFlesche: Reformer and Missionary." In James A. Clifton, ed., *Being and Becoming Indian: Biographical Studies of North American Frontiers* (1989); James, Edward T., ed., *Notable American Women, 1607–1950: A Biographical Dictionary* (1971); Parins, James W., "LaFlesche Tibbles, Susette." In Gretchen M. Bataille, ed., *Native American Women: A Biographical Dictionary* (1993); Wilson, Dorothy Clarke, *Bright Eyes: The Story of Susette LaFlesche, An Omaha Indian* (1974).

Tibbles, Thomas Henry (1840–1928)

Historian Charles Q. DeFrance, an intimate of Thomas H. Tibbles, wrote in 1932, "Leonine! That's the only adjective I can find that aptly describes the great shock of snowy white hair, the ruddy, almost bronze complexion, the square determined jaw, and the steely eyes of Thomas H. Tibbles as I came to know him. But Tibbles was a good-natured, a kindly lion, even when he was launching his invectives against the predatory elements of humanity, the satraps and minions of Wall Street." A newsman who was one of the most important Indian reformers of the nineteenth century, Thomas Henry Tibbles was born near Athens, in Washington County, Ohio, on 22 May 1840, the son of William and Martha (née Cooley) Tibbles. As a youth, he traveled to Kansas and joined a company of antislavery activists led by John Brown. According to Tibbles, he was captured by William Quantrill's raiders and sentenced to death, but was saved by some of Brown's men before the sentence could be carried out. He studied at Mount Union College in Alliance, Ohio, from 1858 to 1861. With the outbreak of the Civil War, he headed west, working as an itinerant preacher and as a newspaper man and journalist. He saw military service later in the war, seeing action at Pea Ridge and in battles near Memphis. After the war, he went to Nebraska and during the grasshopper-induced famine of 1874 he traveled to the East Coast to raise money for the starving farmers and their families. From 1874 until 1879 he worked as a reporter for the Omaha *Herald*, eventually reaching the position of editor.

When the Ponca Indians of Nebraska were being forced to relocate to Indian Territory, away from their homes on Nebraska's Niobrara River, Tibbles went into action and used the pages of the *Herald* to call attention to their plight. He raised money for their defense and hired attorneys John L. Webster and Andrew L. Poppleton to litigate in court on behalf of the Poncas. On 2 June 1879, Bishop Robert H. Clarkson, Bishop of Nebraska, wrote to President Rutherford B. Hayes. "I beg leave to commend to you to your kind attention the Rev. T. H. Tibbals [*sic*] of this city, who has most nobly interested himself in the case of the poor unfortunate Ponkas. I feel sure that your kind Excellency can not be personally acquainted with the history of the wrongs done to this helpless tribe. Mr. Tibbals [*sic*] is in possession of all the facts concerning their removal from their reservation, their sickness and trials in the Indian Territory, their present deplorable situation, and their great anxiety for one more change for life and health. I beg of you, Mr. President, to give a patient hearing to the sad story, and there can be no doubt that justice will be accorded them. Mr. Tibbals [*sic*] is a citizen of Omaha, very highly respected in the community, and [in] every way worthy of confidence." Tibbles' work led to a favorable decision from Judge Elmer Dundy, which held that the Indians were persons in the meaning of the U.S. Constitution. It was a landmark decision and Tibbles was its chief cause. His first wife having died, Tibbles courted Susette La Flesche, or Bright Eyes, the daughter of a former chief of the Omaha Indians. Tibbles and Bright Eyes were married in 1882, but not before going on a whirlwind speaking tour of the eastern United States and bringing the message of the plight of the Indian to unknowing audiences. In 1893, the couple founded a newsweekly, the *Nonconformist*, and later the *Independent*, which became the official journal of the small but growing Populist Party. Bright Eyes died in 1903. The following year, Tibbles was chosen as the vice presidential candidate on the Populist ticket headed by Thomas E. Watson of Georgia. Although Tibbles toured the United States, the ticket drew only 100,000 votes in the election that year.

Tibbles' *Buckskin and Blanket Days: Memoirs of a Friend of the Indians Written in 1905*, is a record of Tibbles' efforts on behalf of the Indians. He also wrote *The Ponca Chiefs: An Account of the Trial of Standing Bear* (1880), *Hidden Power* (1881), an exposé of the "Indian Ring" and corruption in the Indian Bureau, and *The American Peasant* (1892), which dealt with the problems of Western farmers, the last three under the pen name "Zylyff." Tibbles died on 14 May 1928.

See also Tibbles, Susette La Flesche.

References DeFrance, Charles Q., "Some Recollections of Thomas H. Tibbles." *Nebraska History Magazine* 13 (4). Mardock, Robert Winston, *The Reformers and the American Indian* (1971); "Populists Name Watson; Nominated for President at Springfield Convention." *New York Times*, 1 July 1904, 3; "Robert H. Clarkson to Rutherford B. Hayes, 2 June 1879, Box 42, File 6, Thomas Henry Tibbles Papers, Archives of the National Museum of the American Indian, New York; "Thomas H. Tibbles, Populist Leader, Dies." *New York Times*, 15 May 1928, 27; "The Thrilling Experiences of Thomas H. Tibbles." *Sunday Boston Herald Magazine*, 17 December 1905.

Tiger v. Western Investment Company (221 U.S. 286 [1911])

Congress' plenary, or absolute, right over Indian Affairs and how they may be conducted allows Congress to extend the period of alienation of the sale of allotted lands, according to this U.S. Supreme Court case. On two occasions in 1907, Marchie Tiger, a full-blooded Creek Indian, sold his allotments (without the approval of the secretary of the interior before the end of the trust period) to members of the Western Investment Company under the name of the Coweta Realty Company, a real estate company in Oklahoma. Tiger had received the allotment, or conveyance, as an heir to the allotments of his deceased brother and sister. A total of $5,000 was settled upon, but the Western Investment Company only paid Tiger a total of $2,558. At some point, Tiger offered to return the money in exchange for the restoration of the allotment to himself. The company refused. Congress, in an act of 26 April 1906, allowed all adult members of the Creek Nation to sell their conveyances "with the approval of the Secretary of the Interior," while section 29 repealed all legislation inconsistent with this new law. Marchie Tiger sued in the United States Court for the Western District of Indian Territory for the return of his land. The district court held for Tiger, but on appeal the Oklahoma Supreme Court reversed, holding that Congress did not have the power to add new restrictions to previous legislation. On appeal, the U.S. Supreme Court granted certiorari.

Arguments were held on 30 November and 1 and 2 December 1910, and were held a second time, after rearguments were ordered, on 1 and 2 March 1911. A decision was handed down on 15 May 1911; speaking for a unanimous court, Justice William Rufus Day held that "Congress, in pursuance of the long-established policy of the government, has a right to determine for itself when the guardianship which has been maintained over the Indians shall cease." As Justice Day explained,

> Conceding that Marchie Tiger, by the act conferring citizenship, obtained a status which gave him certain civil and political rights, inhering in the privileges and immunities of such citizenship, unnecessary to here discuss, he was still a ward of the nation so far as the alienation of these lands was concerned, and a member of the existing Creek Nation. The inherited lands, though otherwise held in fee, were inalienable without the consent of the Secretary of the Interior, until August, 1907, by virtue of an act of Congress. In this state of affairs Congress, with plenary power over the subject, by a new act permitted alienation of such lands at any time, subject only to the condition that the Secretary of the Interior should approve the conveyance. . . Upon the matters involved, our conclusions are that Congress has had at all times, and now has, the right to pass legislation in the interest of the Indians as a dependent people; that there is nothing in citizenship incompatible with this guardianship over the Indian's lands inherited from allottees, as shown in this case; that in the present case, when the act of 1906 was passed, the Congress had not released its control over the alienation of lands of full-blood Indians, the consent of the Secretary of the Interior to a proposed alienation of lands such as are involved in this case; that it rests with Congress to determine when its guardianship shall cease; and while it still continues, it has the right to vary its restrictions upon alienation of Indian lands in the promotion of what it deems the best interest of the Indian.

See also Heckman v. United States.

The Problem of Indian Administration
See Meriam Report.

Title VIII of the Headstart, Economic Opportunity, and Community Partnership Act of 1974 (88 Stat. 2291, 2323)

The pertinent section of this federal action of 4 January 1974, designated Title VIII, was enacted "to promote the goal of economic and social self-sufficiency for American Indians, Hawaiian Natives and Alaskan Natives." In title VIII, the secretary of the interior was authorized "to provide financial assistance to public and nonprofit private agencies, including, but not limited to, governing bodies of Indian tribes on Federal and State reservations, Alaskan Native villages and regional corporations established by the Alaska Native Claims Settlement Act, and such public and nonprofit private agencies serving Hawaiian Natives, and Indian organizations in urban or rural nonreservation areas, for projects pertaining" to the advancement of Indian economic and social self-sufficiency. The act continues, "In determining the projects to be assisted under this title, the Secretary shall consult with other Federal agencies for the purpose of eliminating duplication or conflict among similar activities or projects and for the purpose of determining whether the findings resulting from those projects may be incorporated into one or more programs for which those agencies are responsible." The act also authorized the secretary to provide technical assistance and training funding, appropriations for research, demonstration, and pilot projects in Indian communities.

***Tooahnippah, Administratrix et al. v. Hickel et al.* (397 U.S. 598, 25 L.Ed. 2d 600, 90 S.Ct. 1316 [1970])**

The narrow issue decided in this Supreme Court case was whether under 25 U.S.C. 373 (section 2 of the act of Congress of 25 June 1910, which provides that no will disposing of any interest in an allotment held by an Indian or other property held in trust by the United States was valid unless approved of by the secretary of the interior), an administrative decision regarding the final disposition of an Indian's will was subject to judicial review. George Chahsenah, a Comanche Indian, died on 11 October 1963, leaving no immediate relatives except an illegimate daughter, Dorita High Horse, and a niece, Viola Atewooftakewa Tate, and her three children. As per his will, Chahsenah left his allotment and other property to Tate and her children, specifying in his will that he had never been close with High Horse but had had a loving relationship with Tate. As per section 2 of the Act of 25 June 1910 (36 Stat. 856; now codified at 25 U.S.C. 373), all wills involving the disposition of Indian allotments or other property held in trust by the United States must be approved by the secretary of the interior. At a hearing before the Department's Examiner of Inheritance, Dorita High Horse contended that because of acute alcoholism, cirrhosis of the liver, and diabetes, Chahsenah was incompetent to make a will. The examiner approved the will, finding that Chahsenah had lived with Tate and established a "familial relationship" with her and her children, while at the same time having "virtually no contact" with High Horse or her family. A regional solicitor, called to hear an appeal of the case by the secretary of the interior, Walter J. Hickel, overturned the examiner's ruling on the grounds that it failed to provide for High Horse. Tate and her family sued to the U.S. District Court for the Western District of Oklahoma, which held that the regional solicitor's decision was wrong, and at the same time subject to the court's judicial review. The U.S. Court of Appeals for the Tenth Circuit reversed, claiming that under 25 U.S.C. 373, the secretary of the interior's word was final as to the disposition of the will. On appeal, Julia Tooahnippah, the administratrix of Chahsenah's estate, appealed to the Supreme Court for a hearing whether the court could intervene and review the secretary of the interior's actions.

The court heard arguments in the case on 14 January 1970, and handed down its decision on 27 April of the same year. Speaking for a unanimous court (Justices John Marshall Harlan and Hugo Black concurred but filed separate opinions expressing some dissatisfaction with the court's holding), Chief Justice Warren Burger held that under 25 U.S.C. 373, the secretary of the interior's opinion did not "constitute final and unreviewable agency action [and] was subject to judicial review"; further, the disapproval of the will by the regional solicitor was "arbitrary and capricious" and that "power was not vested in a government official to revoke or rewrite a will which reflected a rational testamentary scheme, providing for a relative who had befriended the testator and omitting one who had not, simply because of a subjective feeling that the disposition of the estate was not 'just and equitable.'" The chief justice remanded the case back to the court of appeals, with orders to "reinstate the District Court's judgment," in effect holding for the sustainment of Chahnesah's will.

Trade and Intercourse Act of 1790 (1 Stat. 137)

This federal action of 22 July 1790 was enacted "to regulate trade and intercourse with the Indian tribes." Indian historian Francis Paul Prucha writes of this legislation, "Continuing the pattern set in the Ordinance of 1786 and earlier colonial legislation, the law first of all provided for the licensing of traders and established penalties for trading without a license. Then it struck directly at the frontier difficulties. To prevent the steady erosion of the Indian Country by individuals who privately acquired lands from the Indians, it declared the purchase of lands from the Indians invalid unless made by a public treaty with the United States. To put a stop to the outrages committed against the Indians by whites who aggressively invaded the Indian Country, the act made provisions for the punishment of murder and other crimes committed by whites against the Indians in the Indian Country." One of the first laws of the new American nation to deal with Indian matters, the act reads:

Section 1. Be it enacted...That no person shall be permitted to carry on any trade or intercourse with the Indian tribes, without a license for that purpose under the hand and seal of the superintendent of the [War] department, or of such other person as the President of the United States shall appoint for that purpose; which superintendent, or other person so appointed, shall, on application, issue such license to any proper person, who shall enter into bond with one or more sureties, approved of by the superintendent, or person issuing such license, or by the President of the United States, in the penal sum of one thousand dollars, payable to the President of the United States for the time being, for the use of the United States, conditioned for the true and faithful observance of such rules, regulations and restriction, as now are, or hereafter shall be made for the government of trade and intercourse with the Indian tribes. The said superintendents, and persons by them licensed as aforesaid, shall be governed in all things touching the said trade and intercourse, by such rules and regulations as the President shall prescribe. And no other person shall be permitted to carry on any trade or intercourse with the Indians without such license as aforesaid. No license shall be granted for a longer term than two years. Provided nevertheless, That the President may make such order respecting the tribes surrounded in their settlements by the citizens of the United States, as to secure an intercourse without license, if he may deem it proper.

Sec. 2. And be it further enacted, That the superintendent, or person issuing such license, shall have full power and authority to recall all such license as he may have issued, if the person so licensed shall transgress any of the regulations or restrictions provided for the government of trade and intercourse with the Indian tribes, and shall put in suit such bonds as he may have taken, immediately on the breach of any condition in said bond: Provided always, That if it shall appear on trial, that the person from whom such license shall have been recalled, has not offended against any of the provisions of this act, or the regulations prescribed for the trade and intercourse with the Indian tribes, he shall be entitled to received a new license.

Sec. 3. And be it further enacted, That every person who shall attempt to trade with the Indian tribes, or be found in the Indian country with such merchandise in his possession as are usually vended to the Indians, without a license first had and obtained, as in this act prescribed, and being thereof convicted in any court proper to try the same, shall forfeit all the merchandise so offered for sale to the Indian tribes, or so found in the Indian country, which forfeiture shall be one half to the benefit of the person prosecuting, and the other half to the benefit of the United States.

Sec. 4. And be it enacted and declared, That no sale of lands made by any Indians, or any nation or tribe of Indians within the United States, shall be valid to any person or persons, or to any state, whether having the right of pre-emption to such lands or not, unless the same shall be made and duly executed at some public treaty, held under the authority of the United States.

Sec. 5. And be it further enacted, That if any citizen or inhabitant of the United States, or of either of the territorial districts of the United States, shall go into any town, settlement or territory belonging to any nation or tribe of Indians, and shall there commit any crime upon, or trespass against, the person or property of any peaceable and friendly Indian or Indians, which, if committed within the jurisdiction of any state, or within the jurisdiction of either of the said districts, against a citizen or white inhabitant thereof, would be punishable by the laws of such state or district, such offender or offenders shall be subject to the same punishment, and shall be proceeded against in the same manner as if the offence had been committed within the jurisdiction of the state or district to which he or they may belong, against a citizen or white inhabitant thereof.

Sec. 6. And be it further enacted, That for any of the crimes or offences aforesaid, the like proceedings shall be had for apprehending, imprisoning or bailing the offender, as the case may be, and for recognizing the witnesses for their appearance to testify in the case, and where the offender shall be committed, or the witnesses shall be in a district other than that in which the offence is to be tried, for the removal of the offender and the witnesses or either of them, as the case may be, to the district in which the trial is to be had, as by the act to establish the judicial courts of the United States, are directed for any crimes or offences against the United States.

Sec. 7. And be it further enacted, That this act shall be in force for the term of two years, and from thence to the end of the next session of Congress, and no longer.

Reference Prucha, Francis Paul, *American Indian Policy in the Formative Years: The Indian Trade and Intercourse Acts, 1790–1834* (1970).

Trade and Intercourse Act of 1793 (1 Stat. 329)

This federal legislation, enacted on 1 March 1793, was designed to improve on the Trade and Intercourse act decreed three years earlier. The law was established in reaction to a report from President George Washington, who told Congress that the original act was not working and needed to be strengthened. As historian Francis Paul Prucha explains, "The [1793] law was a considerably stronger and more inclusive piece of legislation than its predecessor of 1790. The seven sections of the earlier law were expanded to fifteen. Part of the increase came from the new sections authorizing the president to give goods and money to the tribes to 'promote civilization…and to secure the continuance of their friendship,' and from a long section that aimed to stop horse stealing, but the bulk of the augmentation came from the detailed provision enacted to stop criminal attacks of whites against the Indians and irregular acquisition of their lands. This act, too, was a temporary one, having the same limitations as the first trade and intercourse act."

Reference Prucha, Francis Paul, *American Indian Policy in the Formative Years: The Indian Trade and Intercourse Acts, 1790–1834* (1970).

Trade and Intercourse Act of 1802 (2 Stat. 139)

Thomas Jefferson, in his annual message in 1801, called for a permanent renewal of the several trade and intercourse acts that had been enacted in the previous congresses. Historian Francis Paul Prucha writes, "Accordingly, on March 30, 1802, a new trade and intercourse act became law. It was for the most part merely a restatement of the laws of 1796 and 1799, but by now the period of trial was over. The act of 1802 was no longer a temporary measure; it was to remain in force, with occasional additions, as the basic law governing Indian relations until it was replaced by a new codification of Indian policy in 1834."

Reference Prucha, Francis Paul, *American Indian Policy in the Formative Years: The Indian Trade and Intercourse Acts, 1790–1834* (1970).

Trade and Intercourse Act of 1834 (4 Stat. 729)

Enacted on 30 June 1834, this was the last of several such federal acts to "regulate trade and intercourse with the Indian tribes, and to preserve peace on the frontiers." Running for 30 sections, the most important portion of the act, section 1, reads:

Be it enacted by the Senate and House of Representatives of the United States of America, in Congress assembled, That all that part of the United States west of the Mississippi, and not within the states of Missouri and Louisiana, or the territory of Arkansas, and, also, that part of the United States east of the Mississippi river, and not within any state[,] to which the Indian title has not been extinguished, for the purposes of this act, be taken and deemed to be the Indian country." [The bracketed comma was added by the Supreme Court in the case of *Bates v. Clark* to clarify the legislation's meaning.]

See also *Bates v. Clark*.

Trail of Broken Treaties (1972)

Indian historian Vine Deloria, Jr., calls this procession of Indian rights supporters to Washington, D.C., in 1972, "an Indian Declaration of Independence." *Akwesasne Notes*, the official journal of the Mohawk Nation, wrote, "The concept for the Trail of Broken Treaties Caravans took shape during the annual late summer festival of the Rosebud Sioux in the third week of August [1972]. There, a number of individuals, some Rosebud Sioux residents, and some members of the American Indian Movement, discussed continuing failures in the administration of Indian Affairs, the upcoming national elections, and the outlines of a truly workable Indian policy on the part of both political parties." Eight Indian organizations were involved in putting together the caravans: The National Indian Brotherhood (a Canadian organization), the Native American Rights Fund, the American Indian Movement, the National Indian Youth Council, the National American Indian Council, the National Council on Indian Work, National Indian Leadership Training, and the American Indian Committee on Alcohol & Drug Abuse.

The Indians released a manifesto, "The Twenty Points," in which they enumerated their grievances with the government and their demands to have them changed. These twenty points included the restoration of constitutional treaty-making authority, the establishment of a treaty commission to make new treaties, the call for an address to the American people and joint session of Congress, and the creation

Native Americans occupy the Bureau of Indian Affairs office in Washington, D.C., in November 1972 as part of the Trail of Broken Treaties protest. The protest pointed to the federal government's continuing inability to address grievances arising from broken agreements with Native Americans.

of a commission to review treaty commitments and violations.

References Deloria, Vine, Jr., *Behind the Trail of Broken Treaties: An Indian Declaration of Independence* (1974); *Trail of Broken Treaties: B.I.A. I'm Not Your Indian Anymore* (1976); "The Twenty Points." In Betty Ballantine and Ian Ballantine, eds., *The Native Americans: An Illustrated History* (1993).

Tribally Controlled Schools Act (102 Stat. 385)

In this federal action, enacted on 28 April 1988 as Part B of the Augustus F. Hawkins-Robert T. Stafford Elementary and Secondary School Improvement Amendments of 1988, Congress found that the Indian Self-Determination and Education Assistance Act of 1975 (Public Law 93–638, 88 Stat. 2203–2217), "which was the product of the legitimate aspirations and a recognition of the inherent authority of Indian nations, was and is a crucial positive step towards tribal and community control," that "the Federal administration of education for Indian children has not effected the desired level of educational achievement nor created the diverse opportunities and personal satisfaction which education can and should provide," and that "the time has come to enhance the concepts made manifest in the Indian Self-Determination and Education Assistance Act." "Congress recognizes the obligation of the United States to respond to the strong expression of the Indian people for self-determination by assuring maximum Indian participation in the direction of educational services so as to render such services more responsive to the needs and desires of those communities," the act continues. The act then authorized the secretary of the interior to provide grants to Indian tribes and tribal organizations which operate tribally controlled schools, for use in school operations, academic, educational, residential, guidance and counseling, and administrative purposes for these schools, as well as support services (such as transportation).

See also Indian Self-Determination and Education Assistance Act of 1975.

Trowbridge, Rowland Ebenezer (1821–1881)

Although history credits Rowland E. Trowbridge for his work as the twenty-first commissioner of Indian Affairs, he only served 17 days more than a year and for much of that time he was ill. His sole annual report as commissioner was in fact written by another. He was born on 18 June 1821 in Horseheads, in Chemung County, New York, the son of Stephen and Elizabeth Trowbridge. Just after their son's birth the Trowbridges moved to Oakland County, Michigan, where his father served as state senator and where Roland grew up. Although pursuing farming instead of the law, he graduated from Kenyon College in Gambier, Ohio, in 1841, and subsequently held a series of elective offices, including state senator (1856–60). A Republican, he was elected to the thirty-seventh Congress in 1860 and served one term until defeated for reelection; in 1864, he ran for the seat again and was elected, this time serving two terms (1865–69). When he was not renominated, he returned to farming.

Biographer Michael A. Goldman writes, "Nothing in his background indicates that Trowbridge had any interest in Indians. More important for his selection as Indian Commissioner were his college years. At Kenyon College…Trowbridge formed a close and lasting relationship with a younger classmate, Rutherford B. Hayes." It was this connection that secured the Indian commissionership for Trowbridge. In 1880, Secretary of the Interior Carl Schurz and Hayes, then president, needed a man for the Indian office with a clear record. The office had just undergone two bruising scandals in which two commissioners, John Quincy Smith and Ezra A. Hayt, were forced to resign. Trowbridge was nominated on 20 February 1880, confirmed within the week, and he took office on 2 March. His health began to fail by July 1880 and in August he accompanied his friend President Hayes back home to Michigan. Historian Henry E. Fritz mentions him in a short paragraph, explaining that at one point the commissioner solicited from various religious societies who were running schools and appointing agents on the various reservations their views on whether the rule prohibiting two different societies from operating on the same reservation should be lifted. When an overwhelming number wrote back to him asking that that rule be upheld, Trowbridge left it in place. The annual report of the commissioner for 1880 was in fact written by acting commissioner E. M. Marble; his discourse deals more with the failures of the Hayt administration than any conceivable Trowbridge policymaking. Marble discussed Indian education, Indian police, transportation by Indians, the use of wagons for farming and freighting, and stock cattle, and examined how current policies were working on the San Carlos, Ute, and Sioux reservations. In concluding his report on supplies utilized by the bureau for the benefit of Indians, Marble wrote, "It is gratifying to state that less difficulty has been experienced this year, in the matter of deliveries of goods, &c., by contractors, than in any former year. But few attempts have been made to force upon the department supplies inferior to those contracted for, which fact is, in my opinion, entirely due to the rigid inspection to which all goods are subjected, and the well-known policy of rejecting all that do not conform to contract requirements."

From August 1880 until March 1881, Trowbridge struggled to recover, but slipped closer to death. On 19 March 1881, he wrote to Secretary of the Interior Samuel J. Kirkwood, "My dear sir: Being unable by reason of sickness to attend to the duties of the office of Commissioner of Indians Affairs, I hereby respectfully tender my resignation to take effect upon the appointment of my successor." A month later, on 20 April 1881, Trowbridge succumbed from his illness. He was two months shy of his sixtieth birthday.

See also Bureau of Indian Affairs.

References *Biographical Directory of the United*

States Congress, 1774–1989, Senate Document 100-34, 100th Congress, Second Session (1989); Fritz, Henry E., *The Movement for Indian Assimilation, 1860–1890* (1963); Marble, E. M., *Annual Report of the Commissioner of Indian Affairs to the Secretary of the Interior for the Year 1880* (1880); Goldman, Michael A., "Roland E. Trowbridge." In Robert M. Kvasnicka and Herman J. Viola, eds., *The Commissioners of Indian Affairs, 1824–1977* (1979); Trowbridge to Kirkwood, 19 March 1881, Box 44, Records of the Appointments Division, Commissioner of Indian Affairs, RG 48, National Archives.

"Trust Responsibility" of the Federal Government

See *Cherokee Nation v. Georgia.*

Tulee v. Washington (315 U.S. 681 [1942])

In *Sampson Tulee v. the State of Washington* the Supreme Court held that a state had the right to impose restrictions, for conservation purposes, on the rights of Indians to fish but had no right to charge a fee for a fishing license. According to the court opinion, "appellant Sampson Tulee, a member of the Yakima tribe of Indians, was convicted in the Superior Court of Klickitat County, Washington State, for catching salmon without first having obtained a license as required by state law." In article 3 of a Treaty with the Yakimas of 18 April 1859 (12 Stat. 951), the Indians were guaranteed that "the exclusive right of taking fish in all streams, where running through or bordering said reservation, is further secured to said confederated tribes and bands of Indians, as also the right of taking fish at all usual and accustomed places, in common with the citizens of the Territory…" The State of Washington countered that prior court law, including the cases of *Geer v. Connecticut* (1916) and *Ward v. Race Horse* (1896), gave it "broad powers to conserve game and fish within its borders." The Washington state supreme court affirmed Tulee's conviction and he appealed to the U.S. Supreme Court. After arguments were heard on 3 March 1942, it was Justice Hugo L. Black who handed down the court's unanimous decision just 27 days later on 30 March in reversing Tulee's conviction. Reasoned Justice Black, "In determining the scope of the reserved rights of hunting and fishing, we must not give the treaty [of 1859] the narrowest construction it will bear. In *United States v. Winans*, 198 U.S. 371, 49 L.Ed. 1089, 25 S.Ct. 662, this Court held that, despite the phrase 'in common with the citizens of the territory,' Article 3 conferred upon the Yakimas continuing rights, beyond those which other citizens may enjoy, to fish at their 'usual and accustomed places' in the ceded area; and in *Seufert Bros. Co. v. United States*, 249 U.S. 194, 63 L.Ed. 555, 39 S.Ct. 203, a similar conclusion was reached even with respect to places outside the ceded area." He added, "Viewing the treaty in this light we are of the opinion that the state is without power to charge the Yakimas a fee for fishing."

Turner v. United States (248 U.S. 354 [1919])

Was the United States government, as trustee of funds for an Indian nation, liable for mob violence committed by members of that nation? In 1890, Clarence W. Turner, with an unnamed partner and one hundred Creek Indians, formed the corporation called Pussy, Tiger, & Company, designed to establish a cattle-grazing pasture of about 256,000 acres on the Creek Nation in Oklahoma. Turner contracted with a local judge to build a fence of approximately 80 miles in length to encircle the pasture. Soon after construction on the fence began, many local Creeks, shut out of the decision involving both the pasture and fence, began to issue threats. Turner obtained an injunction against several Creek officials, including L.C. Perryman, principal Chief of the Creek nation, from interfering or damaging the fence. As the barrier neared completion, three bands of Creeks set about and tore it down, causing about $10,000 in damage. The Creek Tribal Council voted to offer Turner compensation, but Perryman vetoed the claim and his veto was upheld. Over the next several years, Turner attempted to get restitution, but failed. By an act of Congress of 29 May 1908 (35 Stat. 444, at 457), the Court of Claims was authorized to settle the matter. Because the Creek Tribal Council had dissolved in 1906, Turner, now holding all rights of his partners, sued the United States government as trustee of the Creek Nation's funds. The Court of Claims dismissed the action (51 Ct. Cl. 125), and the United States Supreme Court granted certiorari to hear the issues in the case. On 7 January 1919, Justice Louis D. Brandeis spoke for a unanimous court against Turner, holding that the Creek Nation was free of liability from the suit and that the United States had not consented to be a target of the action. Justice Brandeis wrote, "The Creek Nation was recognized by the United States as a distinct political community, with which it made treaties, and which, within its own territory, administered its internal affairs. Like other governments, the Creek Nation was free from liability for injuries to persons or property due to mob violence or failure to keep the peace." Brandeis further argued that while Perryman's actions were not *colore officii* [Latin, "by color of office"; the acts of an officer authorized by his or her office], they did not alter the facts in the case.

United States Board of Indian Commissioners
This group served as a civilian watchdog agency over the Bureau of Indian Affairs from 1869 until its demise in 1933; established in the wake of a series of scandals over the inefficiency of the bureau and its inhumane treatment of the Indians in a policy that seemed to be more attuned to bureaucracy that to helping the Native American, the board (known as the BIC) was comprised of philanthropists and humanitarians who desired to reform governmental Indian policy without entering government service. Comments historian Henry E. Fritz, "Under the act of 1869, the ten philanthropists, who served without pay, were authorized to exercise joint control with the Secretary of the Interior in disbursing Indian appropriations, and they were to investigate and make recommendations regarding all issues that concerned Indian Affairs." On 10 April 1869, President Ulysses S. Grant issued an executive order that created the board (a federal action that same day appropriated monies for its existence) and "authorized it to inspect the records of the Indian Office and to obtain full information as to the conduct of all parts of the affairs thereof; gave to its members full power to inspect Indian agencies, to be present at payments of annuities, at consultations or councils with Indians; to advise agents respecting their duties; to be present at purchases of goods for Indian purposes; to inspect said purchases, advising the Commissioner of Indian Affairs in regard thereto; and to advise respecting instructions to agents and changes in the methods of purchasing goods or of conducting the affairs of the Indian Bureau proper," according to Indian historian Frederick W. Hodge.

In a letter to the men, Commissioner of Indian Affairs Ely S. Parker wrote to the commissioners on 26 May 1869 with instructions regarding their duties:

Gentlemen: You have been solicited by the President, under the provision of the fourth section of the act of Congress, approved April 10, 1869, entitled "An Act making appropriation for the current and contingent expenses of the Indian Department," &c., for the year ending June 30, 1870, for the purpose of enabling the President to exercise the power conferred by said act, and being authorized by the same to exercise, under the direction of the President, joint control with the Secretary of the Interior over the disbursement of the appropriations made by said act, or any part thereof that the President may designate, and having been convened in the city for the purpose of organizing for the execution of your duties, and believing that, in common with the President and other officers of the government, you desire the humanization, civilization, and Christianization of the Indians, I respectfully, after consultation with the Secretary of the Interior, submit the following questions, which, with a view to proper and intelligent action in the future relation of the government with the Indians, I deem it important should receive your early consideration and suggestion, viz: A determination or settlement of what should be the legal status of the Indians; a definition of their rights and obligations under the laws of the United States, of the States and Territories and treaty stipulations; whether any more treaties shall be stipulated with the Indians, and if not, what legislation is necessary for those with whom there are existing treaty stipulations, and what for those with whom no such stipulations exist; should the Indians be placed upon reservations, and what is the best method to accomplish this object; should not legislation discriminate between the civilized and localized Indians, and the united roving tribes of the plains and mountains; what changes are necessary in existing laws relating to purchasing goods and provisions for the Indians, in order to prevent fraud, &c.; should any change be made in the method of paying the money annuities; and if so, what. Great mischief, evils and frequently serious results follow from friendly Indians leaving the reservations, producing conflicts between the citizens, soldiers, and

Indians. At what time and point shall the civil rule cease and the military begin? Is any change required in the intercourse laws by reason of the present and changed condition of the country? I respectfully suggest that inspection should be made by your commission of as many Indian tribes, especially the wild and roving ones, as the time of the honorable commissioners will permit, and their conditions and wants be reported on, with any suggestions that each case may seem to require. Also, the accounts of superintendents and agents should be examined, and the efficiency or inefficiency of those officers should be reported on. All suggestions, recommendations, and reports from the commission should be made to the honorable Secretary of the Interior, to be by him submitted, when necessary, to the President and Congress.

William Welsh, a noted Indian reformer and advocate who was later founder and president of the Indian Rights Association, was the first chairman of the BIC, but he resigned within a month over a difference of opinion over the power of the board. Other members included William Earl Dodge (who was also a founder and member of the United States Indian Commission, a private reformist group founded by philanthropist Peter Cooper in 1868), General Clinton B. Fisk (who was the Prohibition Party's Presidential candidate in 1888), Merrill Edwards Gates, Francis E. Leupp (Commissioner of Indian Affairs, 1905–09), and Charles J. Bonaparte, first head of the Bureau of Investigation, the forerunner of the modern F.B.I. Headquartered in the Corcoran Building in Washington, D.C., the Board clashed with Secretaries of the Interior and commissioners of Indian Affairs alike for their investigative practices to root out corruption and fraud in the Indian office, most notably Commissioner Ezra A. Hayt, a clash which led to Hayt's resignation from the Indian Office.

In 1933, after 64 years, the board was dismantled by an executive order signed by President Franklin D. Roosevelt, who felt that the board had done its business and that oversight was no longer necessary. This paved the way for the dominating administration of Commissioner John Collier during the period 1933–45.

See also Gates, Merrill Edwards; Parker, Ely Samuel; "Peace Policy" of President Ulysses S Grant.

References Fritz, Henry E., "The Board of Indian Commissioners and Ethnocentric Reform, 1878–1893." In Jane F. Smith and Robert M. Kvasnicka, eds., *Indian-White Relations: A Persistent Paradox* (1976); Hodge, Frederick Webb, ed., *Handbook of American Indians North of Mexico* (1907–10); Moody, Marshall Dwight, *A History of the Board of Indian Commissioners and Its Relationship to the Administration of Indian Affairs, 1869–1900* (Master's thesis, American University, 1951); U.S. Congress, House of Representatives, *Annual Report of the Commissioner of Indian Affairs for the Year 1869*, House Executive Document No. 1, 41st Congress, 2d Session (serial 1414).

United States ex rel. Standing Bear v. Crook

See *Standing Bear v. Crook.*

United States ex rel. West v. Hitchcock (205 U.S. 80 [1907])

Could a white man, married to an Indian and considered by an Indian tribe as an adopted member, be denied an allotment given to other Indians of that reservation? This was the question before the U.S. Supreme Court in 1907. Willis C. West, a white man, was married to a member of the Wichita and Affiliated Bands of Indians. By several articles of the act of Congress of 2 March 1891 (29 Stat. 876, at 895–97), these Indians ceded their lands to the government and were to be allotted 160–acre parcels, with the fee in severalty to be held in the United States. The fourth article requires that the lands "shall have been selected and taken aforesaid, and approved by the Secretary of the Interior." Secretary of the Interior Ethan Allen Hitchcock examined West's application, then ruled against his receiving an allotment as he was not to be considered a member of the tribe. The Supreme Court of the District of Columbia held in Hitchcock's favor, and the court of appeals affirmed; West appealed to the U.S.

Supreme Court, which heard arguments on 30 January 1907. Justice Oliver Wendell Holmes delivered the opinion of a unanimous court on 4 March of the same year in upholding Hitchcock's denial of West's claim. As Justice Holmes explained, "The approval of the Secretary, required by the agreement, must include, as one of its elements, the recognition of the applicant's right. If a mere outsider were to make a claim, it would have to be rejected by someone, and the Secretary is the natural, if not the only, person to do it." He added, "We doubt if Congress meant to open an appeal to the courts in all cases where an applicant is dissatisfied. Of course the promise of the United States that there shall be allotted 160 acres to each member of the Wichita band may be said to confer an absolute right upon every actual member of the band. But someone must decide who the members are. We already have expressed the opinion that the primary decision must come from the Secretary. There is no indication of an intent to let the applicants go farther. There are insuperable [insurmountable] difficulties in the way of at least this form of suit, and the Department of the Interior generally has been the custodian of Indian rights. Judgment affirmed."

United States Indian Commission

This privately financed Indian reform group was officially formed by philanthropist Peter Cooper of New York in 1868, and among its members were Howard Crosby, president; Vincent Colyer, secretary; Henry Bergh (founder of the American Society for the Prevention of Cruelty to Animals); Samuel F. Tappan, a wealthy New England philanthropist and Indian rights advocate; William Earl Dodge, a successful New York merchant and himself later a member of the U.S. Board of Indian Commissioners; and the Reverend Henry Ward Beecher. (There may be some dispute as to the date of founding; on 1 July 1864, the *New York Times* reported that "at a meeting of the Indian Commission Society [*sic*], in the Cooper Institute, Rev. Dr. Crosby strongly denounced the frauds usually practiced by white men in their dealings with the red men. Mr. Beecher also said some strong, true things, in his own direct way, declaring that the Indian trader was a Satanic fellow, and the Indian Department of the Government a very corrupt one." The editorial closed with, "It is to be hoped the Indian Commission will obtain for the natives something like fair play.") The origin of the commission is poorly known; however, historian Armand La Potin writes that Cooper founded the organization after reading abolitionist and reform advocate Lydia Maria Child's *An Appeal for the Indians* (1868). He writes, "The creation of the U.S. Indian Commission marked the beginning of the post-Civil War movement for reform and established a pattern of direct and persistent involvement in the administration that other organizations emulated. Consequently, the organization's significance is as much if not more in its procedures for implementing its goals as in the goals themselves." The commission played a key role in the formation of Grant's peace policy.

In a memorial presented to Congress in 1869, the group wrote the following, a portion of the full text:

To the Senate and House of Representatives in Congress assembled:

Your memorialists, on behalf of the general committee of the United States Indian Commission, beg leave to call the attention of your honorable bodies to the condition and treatment of our Indian tribes.

We are the more encouraged to make this appeal by the humane spirit which has been so distinctly manifested in your recent legislation. The appointment, amid of the excitement of impending hostilities, of the Peace Commission, and the gratifying results of that commission in averting an apparently inevitable and general Indian war, one year since, afford assurance of a deep desire to do justice, and a willingness to make sacrifices for that end, which it gives us the most sincere pleasure to acknowledge.

It has long been the conviction of the

humane amongst us, that our aboriginal inhabitants have been the victims of great wrongs, cruelties and outrage[s]; but it is only recently that the particular nature, the atrocious character, and the frightful results of these crimes have been brought distinctly before us. The recent reports of the Indian Peace commissioners, and of the joint special committee of the two houses of Congress, have in some degree disclosed the nature and sources of them; and the disclosure is at once so painful and humiliating as to call for the most prompt and vigorous measures or redress and remedy, for the reason that it concerns alike the honor and the interests of the nation.

We stand charged before the civilized world, by the testimony of our own witnesses, with having been "uniformly unjust to the Indians"; and it is stated by General [William Tecumseh] Sherman and his associate commissioners, that this injustice has been the cause of all the wars which they have waged against us.

Among the chief causes of these wars, which have entailed the loss of many lives, and been the pretext upon which the people of the United States have been robbed of millions of hard-earned treasure, we enumerate the following:

1. The dissatisfaction of the Indians in consequence of having sometimes been betrayed into the cession of their lands by pretended treaties.
2. The constant failure of the government to fulfill in good faith its treaty obligations with the tribes.
3. The frequent and unprovoked outrages and murders of Indians by soldiers and white citizens.
4. The impossibility of obtaining justice in local courts, or of punishing white criminals, for the reason that the testimony of Indians is not allowed in those courts.
5. The unlawful occupation, by the whites, of lands not ceded nor treated for.
6. The shameful fact, that of all the appropriations made by Congress for their benefit but a small part ever reaches them.

There is no exact date for the dissolution of the U.S. Indian Commission, although by the early 1880s it was surpassed in influence by such organizations as the Lake Mohonk Conferences of the Friends of the Indian and the Indian Rights Association.

See also American Indian Aid Association; Tappan, Samuel Forster.

References La Potin, Armand S., "United States Indian Commission (1868)." In Armand S. La Potin, ed., *Native American Voluntary Organizations* (1987); *New York Times*, 1 July 1864, 4; U.S. Congress, House of Representatives, *Annual Report of the Commissioner of Indian Affairs for the Year 1869*, House Executive Document No. 1, 41st Congress, 2d Session (serial 1414); Utley, Robert M., *The Indian Frontier of the American West, 1846–1890* (1984).

United States v. Algoma Lumber Company (305 U.S. 415, 83 L.Ed. 260, 59 S.Ct. 267 [1939])

The Supreme Court held in this case that "under treaty with Klamath Indians, setting apart [their] reservation, the Indians have substantial beneficial ownership, as it existed before the treaty, of the land and the timber standing upon it and of the proceeds of their sale, subject to the plenary power of control by the United States, to be exercised for the benefit and protection of the Indians." In a Treaty with the Klamath Indians of 17 February 1870 (16 Stat. 707), timber on allotted and unallotted lands could be sold to private parties with the consent of the secretary of the interior. The act of Congress of 25 June 1910 (36 Stat. 855, at 857) requires that the secretary of the interior fix the prices to be paid for the timber, and that the proceeds from such sales be deposited in a trust "for the benefit of the Indians." The Algoma Lumber Company, as well the Forrest Lumber Company and the Lamm Lumber Company, sued the United States and Secretary of the Interior Harold L. Ickes to recover overcharges that it claims it paid for the timber based on prices set by Secretary of the Interior Franklin K. Lane in 1917. The Court of

Claims held that the prices set by Lane were excessive, and that the United States was liable for the overcharges. The United States appealed, and the U.S. Supreme Court granted certiorari. Justice Harlan Fiske Stone held for a unanimous court (Justices James McReynolds and Owen J. Roberts did not participate) which reversed as to the charges and deeming the prices set to be fair. Justice Stone stated flatly, "Since none of the contracts in suit were contracts or obligations of the United States, it is plain that receipt, by the Treasury of the United States, of payments made under them to the Superintendent for 'the use and benefit' of the Indians, even though made under protest, gave rise to no contract for repayment implied in fact on the part of the United States, and that the cause of action, if any, is not within the jurisdiction of the Court of Claims."

United States v. Antelope et al. (430 U.S. 641, 51 L.Ed. 2d 701, 97 S.Ct. 1395 [1977])

In this case, the U.S. Supreme Court held that federal laws covering Indians for crimes such as murder superseded state laws covering the same crimes. Gabriel Francis Antelope and brothers Leonard and William Davison, all Coeur d'Alene Indians, were tried and convicted of a murder of a non-Indian woman. Since the murder took place within the boundaries of the Coeur d'Alene Indian Reservation in Idaho, the crime was subject to federal jurisdiction under the Indian Major Crimes Act (23 Stat. 362, 18 U.S.C. 1153, 3 March 1885) and the three men were convicted with what is considered a lesser form of proof (state law requires proof of premeditation and deliberation). On appeal, according to the case notes, the defendants claimed that due to "racial discrimination," they had been convicted of a federal crime, whereas a non-Indian who had committed the same exact crime would have been subject to state law. The United States Court of Appeals for the Ninth Circuit in San Francisco agreed, vacating the convictions by holding that the disparities in the sentences between state and federal law denied the defendants due process as described in the Fifth Amendment to the U.S. Constitution. On certiorari, the U.S. Supreme Court reversed the court of appeals' holding. In a unanimous opinion issued by Chief Justice Warren Burger, the court held that the tribal community is considered a "federal enclave" subject to federal regulation only, and that if the defendants had been white, they were still subject to that law because of the place of the murder, not the race of the defendants. Burger cited *Morton v. Mancari* (417 U.S. 535 [1974]) and *Fisher v. District Court* (424 U.S. 382 [1976]) when he wrote, "...the Court unanimously concluded in Mancari: 'The preference, as applied, is granted to Indians not as a discrete racial group, but, rather, as members of quasi-sovereign tribal entities...' ...Last term, in *Fisher v. District Court*..., we held that members of the Northern Cheyenne Tribe could be denied access to Montana state courts in connection with an adoption proceeding arising on their reservation." In deciding *Antelope*, Burger wrote, "The challenged statutes [of the Major Crimes Act] do not otherwise violate equal protection. We have previously observed that Indians indicted under the Major Crimes Act enjoy the same procedural benefits and privileges as all other persons within federal jurisdiction."

See also *Fisher v. The District Court of the Sixteenth Judicial District of Montana, In and For the County of Rosebud;* Indian Major Crimes Act; *Morton v. Mancari*; *United States v. Ramsey et al.*

United States v. Blackfeather (155 U.S. 180 [1894])

In this case, a companion to *Cherokee Nation v. Journeycake*, the U.S. Supreme Court held that an Indian tribe incorporated into another tribe had equal rights to proceeds from land sales. In *Journeycake*, the Cherokee Nation allowed the Delaware Indians to become full Cherokee citizens after being removed from their native lands. Later, after the Cherokees sold some lands to the federal government, they refused to share the proceeds with the Delawares. The

U.S. Supreme Court, affirming a lower court ruling, held that the Cherokees, by their treaty with the Delawares, must share the proceeds of the sale. In this case, officially titled *United States and the Cherokee Nation, Appellants, v. Johnson Blackfeather, Principal Chief of the Shawnee Indians*, the same issue was decided. In pursuance of a treaty of 19 July 1866, the Shawnee Indians, removed from their ancestral lands, were incorporated as full citizens into the Cherokee Nation. When the Cherokees sold a strip of land called the Cherokee Outlet, among other lands, to the United States, the Shawnees, as did the Delawares, demanded a portion of the proceeds. The Cherokees refused and the Shawnees sued in the U.S. Court of Claims. The court held for the Shawnees against the respondents, the Cherokee Nation, and the United States, and these respondents sued for relief to the U.S. Supreme Court. The high court heard arguments in the case on 18 October 1894, and handed down a decision on 19 November of that same year. Holding for a unanimous court (as he did in *Journeycake,)* Justice David Josiah Brewer sustained the Court of Claims judgment. Brewer cited "the express stipulation" in the 1866 treaty "that the said Shawnees shall be incorporated into and ever after remain a part of the Cherokee Nation, on equal terms in every respect, and with all the privileges and immunities of native citizens of said Cherokee Nation."

***See also** Cherokee Nation v. Journeycake.*

United States v. Board of County Commissioners of Osage County, Oklahoma (251 U.S. 128 [1919])

The United States, as "protector and guardian" of Indians under allotment restrictions, does not exhaust its right to continue to protect the Indians even after they are given allotments and the restrictions on those allotments have run out—so held the U.S. Supreme Court in this case, decided in 1919. Under the act of Congress of 28 June 1906 (34 Stat. 539), the government presented each Osage Indian of Oklahoma with three allotments of 160 acres each, with one of three allotments to be used as a homestead and the others for farming. The allotments were to remain inalienable for 25 years and untaxable for 3 years, during which the United States would remain as trustee of the allotments, subject to the Indians being considered competent by the secretary of the interior. In 1917, the U.S. district attorney for the District of Oklahoma sued the Board of Commissioners of Osage County in the name of incompetent members of the Osage Nation for taxes on their lands. Secretary of the interior Franklin K. Lane became so incensed at the taxes that he asked, and got, Congress to enact the Act of 2 March 1917 (29 Stat. 983), which required the secretary to determine the amount the Osages had overpaid in taxes. The District Court of Oklahoma held that Congress allowed for taxes to be levied after 3 years and that the board was within its rights to collect them. On appeal, the U.S. Circuit Court of Appeals added that the plaintiff, the United States, had no interest in the lands since they had passed from its hands to the Indians. The U.S. Supreme Court granted certiorari, and arguments were heard on 16 April 1919. On 15 December of that year Chief Justice Edward Douglass White held for a unanimous court in reversing the court of appeals' decision and holding that the lands could not be subject to taxation and that the United States still had an interest in their protection even after the restrictions on alienation and taxation were lifted. Chief Justice White explained, "Certain is it that as the United States as guardian of the Indians had a duty to protect them from spoliation [devastation] and, therefore, the right to prevent their being illegally deprived of the property rights conferred under the act of Congress of 1906, the power existed in the officers of the United States to invoke relief for the accomplishment of the purpose stated. Indeed the act of Congress of 1917, providing for the appraisement of the lands in question, by necessary implication, if not in express terms, treated the power of the officers of the United States to resist the illegal assessments as undoubted."

United States v. Candelaria et al. (271 U.S. 432 [1926])

In *Candelaria*, the U.S. Supreme Court held that "state courts have jurisdiction to entertain suits involving title to lands of Pueblo Indians." In 1922 the United States sued in federal court to have Jose Candelaria and several others vacate lands it contended had belonged to the Pueblo Indians of New Mexico on the theory that the Indians were "wards" of the United States. Candelaria, who had purchased his land from the Indians, insisted that the Indians were not wards, and that they had the right to live on the land as well as that of selling to another party. Candelaria relied on *United States v. Joseph* (1877), in which the court held that the Pueblo Indians were "civilized," not under the protection of the laws of the United States like other Indian tribes, and thus able to sell their land. Although the court had in one area (the prohibition of the selling of alcohol on Indian reservations) overturned *Joseph* in *United States v. Sandoval*, by granting certiorari to hear *Candelaria* the court seemed to be asking to examine the matter completely and either overturn the edict or uphold it. After hearing arguments in the case on 18 and 19 November 1925, the court issued its opinion on 1 June 1926. Writing for a unanimous court, Justice Willis Van Devanter overturned the precedent set in *Joseph* and ruled against Candelaria. Citing the court's decision in Sandoval, Van Devanter wrote, "While we recognized in that case that the Indians of each pueblo, collectively as a community, have a fee-simple title to the lands of the pueblo, we held that their lands, like the tribal lands of other Indians owned in fee under patents from the United States, are 'subject to the legislation of Congress enacted in the exercise of the government's guardianship' over Indian tribes and their property."

The editors of *Felix Cohen's Handbook of Federal Indian Law* write, "Since 1790 federal Indian Intercourse Acts have rendered transfers of land 'from any Indian nation or tribe of nations' absolutely void unless approved by the federal government." The intent of the *Candelaria* decision was upheld in an important case decided by the First Circuit Court of Appeals in 1975, *Joint Tribal Council of the Passamaquoddy Tribe v. Morton* (388 F. Supp. 649 [D. Maine, 1975]).

See also *United States v. Joseph*; *United States v. Sandoval.*

Reference Strickland, Rennard, *Felix Cohen's Handbook of Federal Indian Law* (1982).

United States v. Celestine (215 U.S. 278 [1909])

An Indian having received an allotment is still under federal jurisdiction as to crimes committed on those lands, and cannot consider himself under state jurisdiction—so held the U.S. Supreme Court in this case, decided in 1909. Bob Celestine, a member of the Tulalip Reservation in the state of Washington, attacked and murdered one Mary Chealco, another member of the Tulalip Reservation, with an axe. The Indian Major Crimes Act of 1885 (23 Stat. 385) required that federal courts have jurisdiction over crimes committed by Indians on reservations. Celestine pled that the federal courts did not jurisdiction over his case, because he had been awarded an allotment certificate, which he claimed made him "a citizen of the United States, and therefore subject to the laws of the territory and state of Washington." As well, he argued, Mary Chealco was also awarded a certificate, and as such was also a citizen. The federal court accepted Celestine's argument and dismissed the charge, a decision which was upheld by the Circuit Court of the United States for the Western District of Washington. On appeal, the U.S. Supreme Court agreed to hear arguments in the case, which took place of 14 October 1909. Justice David Josiah Brewer held for a unanimous court that Celestine could not be considered a citizen of the United States just because he received his certificate and that the federal courts still had jurisdiction. Justice Brewer argued, "Notwithstanding the gift of citizenship, both the defendant and the murdered woman remained Indians by race, and the crime was committed by one Indian upon the person of another, and within the limits of a reservation. Bearing in mind the rule that the legislation of Congress is to be construed in the interest of the Indian, it may fairly be held that the statute does not contemplate a surrender of jurisdiction over an offense committed by one Indian upon the person of another Indian within the limits of a reservation; at any rate, it cannot be said to be clear that Congress intended, by the mere grant of citizenship, to renounce entirely its jurisdiction over the individual members of this dependent race. There is not in this case in terms of a subjection of the individual Indian to the laws, both civil and criminal, of the state; no grant to him of the benefit of those laws; no denial of the personal jurisdiction of the United States."

United States v. Chavez et al. (290 U.S. 357 [1933])

Indian country extends to any unceded lands owned or occupied by Indians—so held the U.S. Supreme Court in this case, decided in 1933. Gregario Chavez and Jose Martin Chavez (there is no indication of whether they were related) were charged with stealing livestock from the Pueblo of Isleta in New Mexico. The men asked for a dismissal of federal charges, claiming that the pueblo could not be considered Indian country, and even if it was, only an Indian committing an offense in Indian country can be charged with a federal crime. The District Court for the District of New Mexico dismissed the charge, holding that the offense was a subject for state jurisdiction. The United States appealed directly to the Supreme Court, which granted certiorari, and arguments were heard on 6 and 7 November 1933. Justice Willis Van Devanter spoke for a unanimous court on 11 December of that same year in reversing the lower court's dismissal. He wrote, "It follows from what has been said that the people of the pueblo of Isleta are Indian wards of the United States; that the lands owned and occupied by them under their ancient grant are Indian country...; that the United States, in virtue of its guardianship, has full power to punish crimes within the limits of the pueblo lands by or against the Indians or against their property, even though, where the offense is against the Indian or his property, the offender be not an Indian.... Judgment reversed."

United States v. Choctaw Nation (119 U.S. 1 [1886])

***See** Choctaw Nation v. United States.*

United States v. Choctaw Nation and Chickasaw Nation (179 U.S. 494 [1900])

Joined with the cases of *Wichita and Affiliated Bands of Indians, Appellants, v. Choctaw Nation, Chickasaw Nation, and United States,* and *Choctaw Nation and Chickasaw Nation, Appellants, v. United States and Wichita and Affiliated Bands of Indians,* this litigation involved the question of whether an Indian tribe, band, or nation could voluntarily abrogate a treaty in which it had ceded land to other Indians, land that was later returned by these other Indians to the United States. A treaty between the United States and the Wichita and Affiliated Bands of Indians of Oklahoma, signed 4 June 1891 (28 Stat. 876, at 895), established that a certain section of lands held by the Wichitas would be ceded to the United States and, by the act of Congress of 8 February 1887 (24 Stat. 388), the General Allotment Act, these lands would be ceded back to individual Wichitas in parcels of 160 acres each, to be held in trust for a period of twenty five years. The land formally held by the Wichitas was surrounded by the Choctaw and Chickasaw Nations, and when the land was parceled out for allotment, some remained. The Choctaw and Chickasaw nations demanded that these lands, which before the Wichitas were removed to them, belonged to these two nations, be returned to them. When the United States refused, the two tribes sued in the Court of Claims. The court held that the government must return these lands to the Indians; the United States appealed to the U.S. Supreme Court.

Arguments were heard on 7, 8, and 9 March 1900 and the case was decided on 10 December of that same year. Holding for a unanimous court, Justice John Marshall Harlan held that when the Choctaws and Chickasaws accepted the new boundaries to make way for the Wichitas, they sanctioned the parceling out of the land and new treaties signed with the Wichitas. Harlan wrote, "Under the views we have expressed, the Choctaws and Chickasaws have had no interest in the particular lands in dispute since the absolute cession made by them to the United States in the treaty of 1866. They have therefore no concern in the questions that have arisen between the United States and the Wichita and Affiliated Bands of Indians as to the disposition of those lands."

United States v. Clarke et al. (445 U.S. 535, 63 L.Ed. 2d 373, 100 S.Ct. 1127 [1980])

This Supreme Court action dealt with the issue of the condemnation of lands allotted to Indians held in trust, and whether 25 U.S.C. 357 allowed for state action in the area of the condemnation and taking. Bertha Mae Tabbytite, an American Indian (her nation and status was not mentioned in the opinion), was awarded an allotment in the Chugach Mountains south of Anchorage, Alaska. Her attempts to receive the land with an unrestricted fee title (sole ownership in her name) were unsuccessful, and she settled for a trust patent in which the United States retained the title in trust. In 1958, Glen M. Clarke and his family moved onto an 80–acre plot next to the Tabbytite plot. Two months later, without permission, they constructed a road which crossed onto Tabbytite's allotment but became the only access to their property. In 1961, the Clarkes subdivided their land into 40 parcels of 2 acres each, selling most of them but retaining a few for themselves. In June 1961, the 40 parcels were incorporated as the Alaskan city of Glen Alps. In 1969, the U.S. government sued on behalf of Tabbytite in district court, asking the court to enjoin the Glen Alps residents from using the road and to award damages to Tabbytite. Although the district court claimed that closing the road would be "hardship" to the Glen Alps residents, and denied the motion of the United States as to enjoining the use of the road (it did award Tabbytite damages for "trespass"), the U.S. Court of Appeals for the Ninth Circuit overturned the decision, claiming that no one, except the federal government, had the right to use Tabbytite's land without her permission (529 Federal Reports 2d 984 [1976]). In September 1975, the municipality of Anchorage annexed Glen Alps and condemned Tabbytite's allotment under what it claimed was its right under 25 U.S.C. 357, which allows state action in this area. A district court hearing the case held that under 25 U.S.C. 357, the state was allowed to condemn the property and pay just compensation; on appeal, the Ninth Circuit Court of Appeals affirmed the decision. The U.S. Supreme Court granted certiorari.

Arguments in the case were heard before the court on 15 and 16 January 1980 and a decision was handed down on 18 March of that same year. Speaking for a 7–2 majority (Justices Harry Blackmun and Byron White dissenting), Justice William H. Rehnquist held that 25 U.S.C. 357 only allowed a condemnation after hearings were held and a plan of compensation approved, and that "condemnation by occupation" was not acceptable. Justice Rehnquist wrote, "Respondent municipality of Anchorage argues that the action authorized by the Court of Appeals here should be regarded as one in condemnation because Alaska allows the 'exercise of the power of eminent domain through inverse condemnation or a taking in the nature of inverse condemnation.' But we do not reach questions of Alaska law here because 25 U.S.C. 357, although prescribing that allotted lands 'may be condemned for any public purpose under the laws of the State or Territory where located,' requires that they nonetheless be 'condemned.' It is conceded that there has never been a formal condemnation action instituted in this case. Since we construe such an action to be an indispensable prerequisite for the reliance of any State or Territory on the other provisions of this section, we therefore reverse the judgment of the Court of Appeals."

United States v. Dann et al. (470 U.S. 39, 84 L.Ed. 2d 28, 105 S.Ct. 1058 [1985])

The Supreme Court held in this 1985 case that once an Indian tribe is paid according to a settlement with the United States because of a judgment in the Court of Claims, the Indians' claim to the land in controversy is extinguished and does not necessarily require a federal plan for the distribution of the funds to tribal members. The United States brought suit against two sisters, Mary and Carrie Dann, for allegedly grazing livestock illegally on land formerly belonging to the Shoshone Tribe in Nevada. In 1951, the Shoshones had sued in the Court of Claims for loss of aboriginal title; 11 years later, the court awarded the Shoshones $26 million in compensation and the United States deposited the funds into an account in the Treasury that, by the time this case reached the Supreme Court, had grown to $43 million with the accumulation of interest. The Danns argued that the land still belonged to the tribe because the secretary of the interior had yet to approve a plan for the distribution of the funds to the tribal members. The U.S. District Court for the District of Nevada held that the title to the land was extinguished when Congress appropriated the funds to the Treasury account; the U.S. Court of Appeals for the Ninth Circuit reversed, holding that until the secretary of the interior issued a distribution plan, the Court of Claims decision had not yet been fulfilled. On appeal, the U.S. Supreme Court granted certiorari. In an opinion issued by Justice William Brennan on 20 February 1985, which expressed the view of a unanimous court, the Supreme Court reversed the decision of the court of appeals, finding that under section 22 of the Indian Claims Commission Act [25 U.S.C. 70u(a)], once the money was appropriated and placed in the Treasury account, the title to the land was extinguished. Justice Brennan reasoned, "The common law recognizes that payment may be satisfied despite the absence of actual possession of the funds by the creditor. Funds transferred from a debtor to an agent or trustee of the creditor constitute payment, and it is of no consequence that the creditor refuses to accept the funds from the agent or the agent misappropriates the funds."

United States v. Dawson (15 Howard [56 U.S.] 467 [1853])

In this eighteenth-century Supreme Court case, the issue decided was whether, when Congress created a separate judicial district from the one set up to try offenses in Indian country, the original court lost its jurisdiction. James L. Dawson, a white man, was indicted for the murder of Seaborn Hill, another white man, on 8 July 1844 in the Creek Nation of Oklahoma. Another white man, John R. Baylor, was indicted for aiding Dawson in the crime. The previous month, Congress had established that the Circuit Court of the United States for the District of Arkansas was vested with the power to try offenses committed within the Indian country. On 3 March 1851, Congress constituted a separate judicial district, dividing Arkansas into Eastern and Western judicial districts. In April 1853, Dawson's case came up for trial; Baylor had yet to be tried. Dawson, with Baylor as his co-plaintiff in error, claimed that because his crime had been committed in the western portion of the state, the subsequent federal act denied the court before him jurisdiction, and demanded that both mens' indictments be dismissed. Justice Peter Vivian Daniel was sitting on the case as part of his circuit duties; he split with another judge as to whether the indictments should be dismissed and asked the full Supreme Court to rule on the matter. Justice Samuel Nelson delivered the opinion of the court (Justice John McLean dissented) when he held that Congress did not extinguish the powers of the Eastern court to try Indian country offenses when it devised the Western District Court. McLean argued in his dissent that the splitting of the courts led him to dispute the Western District's jurisdiction over the matter.

United States v. Dion (476 U.S. 734, 90 L.Ed. 2d 767, 106 S.Ct. 2216 [1986])

An Indian is not protected by his tribe's treaty with the United States when hunting endangered eagles in violation of the Endangered Species Act—so said the U.S. Supreme Court in this 1986 case. Dwight Dion, Sr., a member of the Yankton Sioux Tribe of South Dakota, was convicted in the District Court for the Southern District of South Dakota for shooting bald eagles on the Yankton Sioux Reservation in violation of the Endangered Species Act (87 Stat. 884, as amended at 16 U.S.C. 1531 et seq.). He was also convicted of selling parts of the carcasses of the eagles and other endangered birds in violation of the Migratory Bird Treaty Act (40 Stat. 755, amended at 16 U.S.C. 703 et seq.) On appeal, the U.S. Court of Appeals for the Eighth Circuit struck down the convictions, declaring that under the Treaty with the Yanktons of April 1858 (11 Stat. 743) there were no restrictions placed on hunting by the Indians on lands within the reservation. The federal government appealed and the U.S. Supreme Court granted certiorari. After arguments were heard on 25 March 1986, Justice Thurgood Marshall spoke for a unanimous court on 11 June of that same year in reinstating the convictions. Justice Marshall held that the Bald Eagle Protection Act (54 Stat. 250, as amended at 16 U.S.C. 668 et seq.) is to be read as abrogating the rights of Indians to hunt bald or golden eagles. Justice Marshall declared,

Dion…asserts a treaty right to take bald eagles as a defense to his Endangered Species Act prosecution. He argues that the evidence that Congress intended to abrogate treaty rights when it passed the Endangered Species Act is considerably more slim than that relating to the Eagle Protection Act. The Endangered Species Act and its legislative history, he points out, are to a great extent silent regarding Indian hunting rights. In this case, however, we need not resolve the question of whether the Congress in the Endangered Species Act abrogated Indian treaty rights. We conclude that Dion's asserted treaty defense is barred in any event . . . Dion asserts that he is immune from Endangered Species Act prosecution because he possesses a treaty right to hunt and kill bald eagles. We have held, however, that Congress in passing and amending the Eagle Protection Act divested Dion of his treaty right to hunt bald eagles. He therefore has no treaty right to hunt bald eagles that he can assert as a defense to an Endangered Species Act charge. We do not hold that when Congress passed and amended the Eagle Protection Act, it stripped away Indian treaty protection for conduct not expressly prohibited by that statute. But the Eagle Protection Act and the Endangered Species Act, in relevant part, prohibit exactly the same conduct, and for the same reasons. Dion here asserts a treaty right to engage in precisely the conduct that Congress, overriding Indian treaty rights, made criminal in the Eagle Protection Act. Dion's treaty shield for that conduct, we hold, was removed by that statute, and Congress' failure to discuss that shield in the context of the Endangered Species Act did not revive that treaty right.

United States v. Fernandez (10 Peters [35 U.S.] 303 [1836])

In one of the earliest cases to be decided by the U.S. Supreme Court regarding Indian land rights and cessions, the court held in this 1836 decision that land titles granted to persons by the Spanish crown, before the territory became part of the United States, remained valid after the United States acquired that region. Before Florida became a territory of the United States, it belonged to Spain. In 1817, Stephen D. Fernandez (his nationality is not identified) was granted a title to 16,000 acres of Indian land by the Spanish governor of what was then called East Florida. The United States was later awarded Florida by Spain and when Fernandez refused to relinquish his claim to the land, the government sued him in the Superior Court of the District of East Florida, which held for Fernandez. The United States then sued to the U.S. Supreme Court. Justice Henry Baldwin spoke for a unanimous court in declaring that Fernandez' title was valid. He wrote simply, "On the general question, therefore, of the validity of grants of lands in East Florida in possession of the Indians, we are of the opinion that they were good to pass the right of the crown; the grant of the governor severed them from the royal domain, so that they became private property, which was not ceded to the United States by the treaty with Spain."

United States v. 43 Gallons of Whiskey

See *United States v. Lariviere.*

United States v. Jim et al. (409 U.S. 80, 34 L.Ed. 2d 282, 93 S.Ct. 261 [1972])

Congress may modify a law that changes the pool of Indian beneficiaries, the Supreme Court held in this 1972 decision. In a class action lawsuit brought in the name of James Jim, the residents of the Aneth extension of the Navajo Reservation in Utah challenged a federal act. On 1 March 1933, Congress passed an act (47 Stat. 1418) that took lands from the public domain and established the Aneth extension, on the condition that if oil or gas were found on those lands, 37.5 percent of the net royalties would be set aside by the state of Utah, to be used for "the tuition of Indian children in white schools and/or the building or maintenance of roads across the lands described in section 1 hereof, or for the benefit of the Indians residing therein." Then, Congress passed the act of 17 May 1968 (82 Stat. 121), which deleted the passage quoted and substituted "for the health, education, and general welfare of the Navajo Indians in San Juan County." The Aneth Navajos claimed that by changing the meaning of the action, Congress was extending the number of people benefitting from the mineral royalties. The U.S. District Court for the District of Utah struck down the 1968 action as unconstitutional. On direct appeal, the U.S. Supreme Court granted certiorari, and handed down a decision on 20 November 1972. In a *per curiam* opinion (without an acknowledged author) expressing the views of eight members of the court (Justice William O. Douglas dissented), the court held that because the 1933 act did not confer any "property" in the Fifth Amendment sense to the Aneth residents, the Congress had the power to alter the action in 1968. The opinion stated, "Congress has not deprived the Navajos of the benefits of mineral deposits on their tribal lands. It has merely chosen to re-allocate the 37.5 percent of royalties which flow through the State in a more efficient manner. This was well within the power of Congress to do."

United States v. John (437 U.S. 634 [1978])

As Justice Harry Blackmun explained at the beginning of his opinion in this difficult Supreme Court case, "These cases present issues concerning state and federal jurisdiction over certain crimes committed on lands within the area designated as a reservation for the Choctaw Indians residing in central Mississippi. More precisely, the questions presented are whether the lands are 'Indian country' as that phrase is defined in 18 U.S.C. 1151 and as it was used in the Major Crimes Act of 1885, being section 9 of the Act of March 3, 1885, 23 Stat. 385, later codified as 18 U.S.C. 1153, and, if so, whether these federal statutes operate to preclude the exercise of state criminal jurisdiction over the offenses." In October 1975, Smith John and his son Harry Smith John were indicted by a federal grand jury for assault with intent to kill. (Harry Smith John died on 18 February 1978, and, although he was considered as part of the case—the two cases being *United States, Petitioner, v. Smith John and Harry Smith John, Appellants* [No. 77–836] and *Smith John and*

Harry Smith John, Appellants, v. State of Mississippi [No. 77–575]—the issues surrounding him were declared to be moot). On trial, they were convicted of the lesser charge of simple assault, sentenced to 90 days in jail, and fined $900. Before the U.S. Court of Appeals for the Fifth Circuit could hear the appeal, the grand jury for Leake County, Mississippi, where the crime took place, indicted the Johns for violating state law as to aggravated assault and they were convicted in May 1976 of that crime. The court of appeals then ruled in the federal case, holding that because the area where the crime took place was not considered "Indian country" as defined by 18 U.S.C. 1151, the Indian Major Crimes Act, codified at 18 U.S.C. 1153, did not apply in this case, and dismissed the indictment and conviction. On appeal for the state case, the Supreme Court of Mississippi upheld the conviction, finding that the federal court did not have jurisdiction to try the Johns, and as such their arguments against a lack of state jurisdiction were without merit. In both cases, the U.S. Supreme Court granted certiorari to hear the matters.

After arguments were held on 19 April 1978, the court handed down its decision on 23 June of that same year. Expressing the views of a unanimous court, Justice Harry Blackmun reversed and remanded the federal case and reversed the state case. As Justice Blackmun stated, "The State [of Mississippi]...argues that the Federal Government may not deal specifically with Indians within the State's boundaries because to do so would be inconsistent with the Treaty of Dancing Rabbit Creek [the treaty that terminated the Choctaw reservation in Mississippi]....And even if that treaty were the only source regarding the status of these Indians in federal law, we see nothing in it inconsistent with the continued federal supervision of them under the Commerce Clause. It is true that this treaty anticipated that each of those electing to remain in Mississippi would become 'a citizen of the States,' but the extension of citizenship status to Indians does not, in itself, end the powers given Congress to deal with them....We therefore hold that section 1153 provides a proper basis for federal prosecution of the offense involved here, and that Mississippi has no power similarly to prosecute Smith John for that same offense. Accordingly, the judgment of the Supreme Court of Mississippi in No. 77–575 is reversed; further, the judgment of the United States Court of Appeals for the Fifth Circuit in No. 77–836 is reversed, and that case is remanded for further proceedings consistent with this opinion."

See also "Indian Commerce Clause" of the U.S. Constitution; Indian Country—Definition; Indian Major Crimes Act.

United States v. Joseph (94 U.S. 614 [1877])

The concept later overturned in such cases as *United States v. Sandoval* and *United States v. Candelaria et al.* was first held in the case of *United States v. Antonio Joseph* —the idea that the Pueblo Indians of New Mexico, formerly part of Mexico, had no title to their lands, were not a tribe of Indians recognized by the United States, and that their occupancy did not fall under the laws of the United States that covered other nations of Indians. Antonio Joseph purchased land from the Pueblo Indians of New Mexico and proceeded to build a house on the tract. Section 2118 of the Revised Statutes, enacted on 30 June 1834, holds that any person who settles on land belonging, secured, or granted by treaty with the United States to any Indian tribe is liable to pay a penalty of $1,000. Joseph was arrested and fined $1,000 for building on his 10–acre plot, which had been part of the Taos, New Mexico, pueblo. On appeal to the New Mexico Territorial Supreme Court, the indictment and fine were dismissed, the court holding that the Taos Pueblo Indians were not recognized by the United States.

On appeal, the U.S. Supreme Court granted certiorari. The case was argued on 20 April 1877 and decided less than three weeks later, on 7 May 1877. Justice Samuel Freeman Miller held that because these Indians were not recognized as a tribe under the protection of the laws of the United States, the act of 30 June 1834 could not pertain to them. "At the time the act of 1834 was passed there were no such Indians as these in the United States, unless it be one or two Reservations or Tribes, such as the Senecas or Oneidas of New York, to whom, it is clear, the 11th section of the statute could have no application. When it became necessary to extend the laws regulating intercourse with the Indians over our new acquisitions from Mexico, there was ample room for the exercise of those laws among the nomadic Apaches, Comanches, Navajoes, and other Tribes whose incapacity for self-government required both for themselves and for the citizens of the country this guardian care of the General Government." A portion of *Joseph*, involving whether Congress had the right to regulate the sale of alcohol on Indian reservations to include the Pueblo Indians, was overturned in *United States v. Sandoval* (1913). The Court overturned *Joseph* completely in *United States v. Candelaria et al.* (1926).

See also *United States v. Candelaria et al.*; *United States v. Sandoval.*

United States v. Kagama, alias Pactah Billy (118 U.S. 375, 30 L.Ed. 228, 6 S.Ct. 1109 [1886])

This landmark case, decided in 1886, upheld the Indian Major Crimes Act, passed the previous year, which empowered state and territorial courts to handle Indian offenses committed in those states and territories, while providing that the federal government would have jurisdiction over crimes perpetrated on Indian reservations. Kagama, alias Pactah Billy, an Indian (the opinion does not state what nation he belonged to), was charged in Humboldt County, California, with the murder of Iyouse, alias Ike, another Indian, on the Hoopa Valley Reservation in California; also charged was Mahawaha, alias Ben, another Indian, who was indicted for aiding and abetting in the murder. Under section 9 of the Indian Major Crimes Act of 1885 (26 Stat. 362), it was considered a federal offense if an Indian committed a crime on the reservation, but a state matter if the offense occurred on state territory. Congress had enacted this legislation in response to the 1885 case of *Ex parte Crow Dog*, in which the court held that in the absence of federal intent, crimes committed by Indians could only be punished by tribal courts. Kagama was convicted of murder in the Circuit Court for the District of California, but he appealed the conviction on the ground that the 1885 action was an unconstitutional and invalid law, repugnant to the U.S. Constitution. The U.S. Supreme Court granted certiorari to answer the question whether the act was legal.

Justice Samuel Freeman Miller spoke for a unanimous court in holding the legislation to be constitutional. Justice Miller explained,

> The Case of Crow Dog, 109 U.S. 556, in which an agreement with the Sioux Indians, ratified by an act of Congress, was supposed to extend over them the laws of the United States and the jurisdiction of its courts, covering murder and other grave crimes, shows the purpose of Congress in this new departure. The decision in that case admits that if the intention of Congress had been to punish, by the United States courts, the murder of one Indian by another, the law would have been valid. But the court could not see, in the agreement with the Indians sanctioned by Congress, a purpose to repeal section 2146 of the Revised Statutes, which expressly excludes from that jurisdiction the case of a crime committed by one Indian against another in the Indian country. The passage of the act now under consideration was designed to remove that objection, and to go further by including such crimes on reservations lying within a State. Is the latter fact a fatal objection to the law? The statute itself contains no express limitation upon the powers of a State or the jurisdiction of its courts. If there be any limitation in either of these, it grows out of the implication arising from the fact that Congress had defined a

crime committed within the State, and made it punishable in the courts of the United States. But Congress has done this, and can do it, with regard to all offenses relating to matters to which the Federal authority extends. Does that authority extend to this case?

It will be seen at once that the nature of the offense (murder) is one which in almost all cases of its commission is punishable by the laws of the States, and within the jurisdiction of their courts. The distinction is claimed to be that the offense under the statute is committed by an Indian, that it is committed on a reservation set apart within the States for residence of the tribe of Indians by the United States, and the fair inference is that the offending Indian shall belong to that or some other tribe. It does not interfere with the process of the State courts within the reservation, nor with the operation of State laws upon white people found there. Its effect is confined to the acts of an Indian of some tribe, of a criminal character, committed within the limits of the reservation.

It seems to us that this is within the competency of Congress. These Indian tribes are the wards of the nation. They are communities dependent on the United States. Dependent largely for their daily food. Dependent for their political rights. They owe no allegiance to the States, and receive from them no protection. Because of the local ill feeling, the people of the States where they are found are often their deadliest enemies. From their very weakness and helplessness, so largely due to the course of dealing of the Federal Government with them and the treaties in which it has been promised, there arises the duty of protection, and with it the power. This has always been recognized by the Executive and by Congress, and by this court, whenever the question has arisen. . . The power of the General Government over these remnants of a race once powerful, now weak and diminished in numbers, is necessary to their protection, as well as to the safety of those among whom they dwell. It must exist in that government, because it never has existed anywhere else, because the theatre of its exercise is within the geographical limits of the United States, because it has never been denied, and because it alone can enforce its laws on all the tribes. We answer the questions propounded to us; that the 9th section of the act of March 1885 is a valid law in both its branches, and that the Circuit Court for the District of California has jurisdiction of the offense charged in the indictment in this case.

United States v. Lariviere (93 U.S. 188, 23 L.Ed. 846 [1876])

In this action, also known by the quaint name, *United States v. 43 Gallons of Whiskey*, the U.S. Supreme Court held that "Congress has the power to exclude spirituous liquors, not only from existing Indian Country, but from that which has ceased to be so by reason of its cession to the United States." According to the case notes, defendants in error Bernard Lariviere and Charles Grant were accused of selling intoxicating liquors on the reservation of the Red Lake and Pembina Band of Chippewa Indians located in Minnesota. The treaty of 2 October 1863, which established the reservation, ceded by the Indians a portion of the lands to the United States. A section of the treaty reads, "The laws of the United States now in force, or that may hereafter be enacted, prohibiting the introduction and sale of spirituous liquors in the Indian Country, shall be in full force throughout the country hereby ceded, until otherwise directed by Congress or the President of the United States." Defendants Lariviere and Grant, whose 43 gallons of whiskey were confiscated, claimed that the allowance for such a stipulation to be included in the treaty was an unconstitutional exercise of congressional powers. The district court hearing the case agreed, and dismissed the case. The United States appealed to the U.S. Supreme Court. After the case was submitted on 19 October 1876, Justice David Davis spoke for a unanimous court on 13 November 1876 in reinstating the indictments and ordering the lower court to try the case. "The power is in nowise affected by the magnitude of the traffic or the extent of the intercourse," Justice Davis wrote.

As long as the Indians remain a distinct people, with existing tribal organizations, recognized by the Political Department of the Government, Congress has the power to say with whom, and on what terms they shall deal and what articles shall be contraband. If liquor is injurious to them inside of a reservation, it is equally so outside of it; and why cannot Congress forbid its introduction into places nearby, which the Indians would be likely to frequent? It is easy to see that the love of liquor would tempt them beyond their borders to obtain it; and that bad white men, knowing this, would seek adjoining localities, where the traffic was not prohibited rather than venture upon forbidden ground. If Congress had the power, as the case we have last cited [United States v. Holliday] decides, to punish the sale of liquor anywhere to an individual member of an Indian tribe, why cannot it also punish the introduction of liquor for a similar purpose into territory in proximity to that where the Indians live? There is no reason for the distinction; and as there can be no divided authority on the subject, our duty to a dependent people would require Congress to impose further restrictions, should country adjacent to Indian reservations be used to carry on the liquor traffic with Indians.

United States v. Mason (412 U.S. 391, 37 L.Ed. 2d 22, 93 S.Ct. 2202 [1973])

Could the United States be forced to pay estate taxes on the allotment of a deceased Indian? That was the issue in this Supreme Court case, joined with *Oklahoma v. Archie L. Mason, Administrator of Margaret R. Mason, etc. et al.* in 1973. Prior to 1906, the Osage Reservation in Oklahoma was totally held in trust by the United States; however, with the passage of the Osage Allotment Act (34 Stat. 539) that year, the tribal lands were equally divided among the members into allotments. One of the allottees was Rose Mason. Upon her death, she was found to be intestate (without a will), and the United States government awarded her allotment to her heirs after paying the state of Oklahoma $8,087.10 in estate taxes. Her decedents, among them Archie L. Mason, sued in the Court of Claims on the grounds that the United States government had breached its fiduciary duty in paying the tax. The Court of Claims ruled that even though the Supreme Court had held in *West v. Oklahoma Tax Commission* (1948) that such estate taxes on restricted Osage properties were valid, the court in the intervening years had "eroded" that decision, and that the United States government had an "obligation" to challenge the validity of these taxes, a challenge the court believed would be successful, and that the government had breached its fiduciary duty by paying the taxes. On certiorari, after hearing arguments on 18 April 1973, the U.S. Supreme Court, in a decision expressing the views of eight members of the court (Justice William O. Douglas concurred, but did not give his reasons in a printed opinion), Justice Thurgood Marshall reversed the Court of Claims decision, holding that the *West* decision was still viable law and that the taxes were not a breach of the government's fiduciary duty.

United States v. Mazurie (419 U.S. 544 [1975])

The Supreme Court held in this case that laws prohibiting the introduction of intoxicating liquors into "Indian country" were not unconstitutionally vague. Defendants Martin Dewalt Mazurie and his wife Margaret, both whites, ran a bar (known as the Blue Bull) on the Wind River Reservation in Wyoming even though they did not obtain a tribal liquor license. Up until 1953, the sale of intoxicating liquors and other such beverages was prohibited on Indian reservations; the act of 15 August 1953 (67 Stat. 686) allowed for Indian nations to control the sale of such beverages with the approval of the secretary of the interior. The Wind River Reservation tribal council adopted the law to fit all state laws. Even though the Blue Bull had a state liquor license, the tribe denied it a tribal liquor license. The Blue Bull closed, but reopened, the proprietors claiming that even though the bar was on the reservation, it was on land considered "non-Indian held," and thus was not under tribal jurisdiction. The Mazuries were then arrested and tried for violating the law. In district court, the two were convicted and fined $100. The United States Court of Appeals for the Tenth Circuit overturned the convictions, holding that the act of 15 August 1953 was an unconstitutional attempt by Congress to delegate authority to Indian tribal councils. The government appealed the judgment to the U.S. Supreme Court.

After arguments were heard on 12 November 1974, the court handed down its decision on 21 January 1975. In expressing the views of a unanimous court, Justice William H. Rehnquist reinstated the convictions of the Mazuries. He held that "Indian country" was constitutionally delineated in 18 U.S.C. 1154 to include non-Indian held lands "within the limits of any reservation." Further, Justice Rehnquist wrote, the act of 15 August 1953 (67 Stat. 586, now codified at 18 U.S.C. 1161) was not an unconstitutional attempt by Congress to grant authority to the tribes to settle issues dealing with intoxicating beverages. "Cases such as Worcester [*Worcester v. Georgia*, 6 Peters [31 U.S.] 515 [1832])] and Kagama [*United States v. Kagama, alias Pactah Billy* (118 U.S. 375, 30 L.Ed. 228, 6 S.Ct. 1109 [1886])], surely establish the proposition that Indian tribes within 'Indian country' are a good deal more than 'private, voluntary organizations,' and they thus undermine the rationale of the Court of Appeals decision. These same cases, in addition, make clear that when Congress delegated its authority to control the introduction of alcoholic beverages into Indian country, it did so to entities which possess a certain degree of independent authority over matters that affect the internal and social relations of tribal life. Clearly the distribution and use of intoxicants is just such a matter."

United States v. McBratney (104 U.S. 621 [1882])

This important case determined that Indians had control over legal affairs on their reservations, including areas of legal matters involving non-Indians, reinforcing the court's earlier decision in the case of *United States v. Rogers*. The case, however, carved a conspicuous exception into the Indian Major Crimes Act. Jack McBratney was tried and convicted of the murder of Thomas Casey on the Ute Reservation in Colorado. The defense and prosecution in this case both conceded that both men were white; the United States, however, argued that it had jurisdiction over legal matters involving non-Indians on Indian lands as per Congress' intention in the Indian Major Crimes Act. McBratney sued to the U.S. Supreme Court to get his conviction overturned on the grounds that the Circuit Court did not have jurisdiction. The case was argued on 18 January 1882, and decided on 6 March 1882. The Supreme Court based its decision on two earlier lower court rulings: *United States v. Ward* (28 Federal Cases 397, Kansas [1863]) and *United States v. Bailey* (24 Federal Cases 937, Tennessee [1834]). Justice Samuel Freeman Miller sat as the circuit judge on *Ward* and on the Supreme Court in *McBratney*, so his participation in the *Ward* case may have held some influence on the court's holding in *McBratney*. In his opinion expressing the will of a unanimous court, Justice Horace Gray held that the circuit court had no jurisdiction to try McBratney for a murder committed on an Indian reservation. Wrote Gray,

> Whenever, upon the admission of a State into the Union, Congress has intended to except out of it an Indian reservation, or the sole and exclusive jurisdiction over that reservation, it has done so by express words. *Case of the Kansas Indians*, 5 Wallace 737.... The State of Colorado, by its admission into the Union of Congress, upon an equal footing with the original States in all respects whatever, without any such exception as had been made in the Treaty with the Ute Indians and in the Act establishing

a territorial government, has acquired criminal jurisdiction over its own citizens and other white persons throughout the whole of the territory within its limits, including the Ute Reservation, and that reservation is no longer within the sole and exclusive jurisdiction of the United States.... The single question that we do or can decide in this case is, that stated in the certificate of division of opinion, namely: whether the Circuit Court of the United States for the District of Colorado has jurisdiction of the crime of murder committed by a white man upon a white man within the Ute Reservation and within the limits of the State of Colorado; and for the reasons above given, *that question must be answered in the negative.*

The case's basis, that non-Indians accused of murder on an Indian reservation must be tried in a state, and not federal, court, was upheld in 1896 in *Draper v. United States.*

See also *Draper v. United States*; The Kansas Indians; *United States v. Rogers.*

United States v. Mitchell (463 U.S. 206, 77 L.Ed. 2d 580, 103 S.Ct. 2961 [1983])

Distinguished from the earlier case in this matter, this decision is known as "Mitchell II." Emboldened by Justice Thurgood Marshall's "invitation" to seek monetary damages for government mismanagement of forest resources on Indian allotments through a law other than the General Allotment Act of 1887, Mitchell et al. refiled in the Court of Claims, asserting that under the timber management statutes (25 U.S.C. 406–407, 466) and statutes governing Indian funds held by the government and government fees (25 U.S.C. 162a and 413), as well as the Tucker Act (28 U.S.C. 1491(a)(1), the latter which gave the Court of Claims the "jurisdiction to render judgment upon any claim against the United States founded either upon the Constitution, or any Act of Congress or any regulation of an executive department," they were owed monetary damages. The Court of Claims upheld its earlier judgment that the federal government was liable and the U.S. Supreme Court granted certiorari. The case was argued on 1 March 1983, and it was Justice Marshall who spoke for a 6–3 majority (Justices Lewis Powell, William H. Rehnquist, and Sandra Day O'Connor dissented) in affirming the Court of Claims decision, six years after the case was first filed. Justice Marshall opined, "Where the Federal Government takes on or has control or supervision over tribal monies or properties, the fiduciary relationship normally exists with respect to such monies or properties...even though nothing is said expressly in the authorizing or underlying statute (or other fundamental document) about a...trust or fiduciary connection."

Reference Fredericks, John, III, "Indian Lands Financing Indian Agriculture Mortgaged Indian Lands and the Federal Trust Responsibility." *American Indian Law Review* 41 (1).

United States v. Mitchell et al. (445 U.S. 535, 63 L.Ed. 2d 607, 100 S.Ct. 1349 [1980])

Known as "Mitchell I," this Supreme Court case held that Indians could not sue under the General Allotment Act to recover money damages for the federal government's alleged mismanagemenmt of timber resources on allotted lands, a violation of the trust doctrine between the government and the Indians. Helen Mitchell, a Quinault Indian of the Quinault Reservation of Washington State, joined others (1,465 Indians, as well as the Quinault Allottees Association) similarly situated when she sued the U.S. government for failing to properly administer the timber resources on lands allotted to the Quinaults. Under the General Allotment Act of 1887 (24 Stat. 388, as amended at 25 U.S.C. 331 et seq.) (GAA), the reservation was allotted to the Indians in severalty; later acts of Congress obligated the secretary of the interior to manage the forests on the allotments, sell the timber, and pay the proceeds of the sales, minus administrative fees, to the alottees. Mitchell's lawsuit alleged, among other matters, (1) that the government failed to obtain a fair price for the timber that was sold; (2) that the government neglected to manage the forests in a sustained-yield program and rehabilitate the forests after logging; (3) that the government charged exorbitant administrative fees. Mitchell sued in the United States Court of Claims for monetary damages under the GAA. The court denied the United States' request to dismiss the claim, and instead ruled that the actions violated the government trust responsibility over the Indians. The U.S. Supreme Court granted certiorari, heard arguments on 3 December 1979, and handed down a decision on 15 April 1980. Holding for a 6–3 majority (Justices Byron White, William Brennan, and John Paul Stevens dissented), Justice Thurgood Marshall held that the GAA does not allow for monetary damages if the law was violated, and that the law created a "limited trust" between the government which does not impose a fiduciary duty on the government. In a keenly worded opinion, Justice Marshall proclaimed, "The General Allotment Act…cannot be read as establishing that the United States has a fiduciary responsibility for management of alloted forest lands. Any right of the respondents to recover money damages for Government mismanagement of timber resources must be found in some source other than that Act." On the basis of that last sentence, the plaintiffs behind Mitchell took the case to court a second time.

See also *United States v. Mitchell* ("Mitchell II").

United States v. Ramsey et al. (271 U.S. 467 [1926])

The issue of the federal trust responsibility over allotments, and whether federal laws, or those of states, covered crimes committed on those allotments, was involved in this Supreme Court case. John Ramsey and another white man, not identified in this case, were convicted of the murder of Henry Roan, a full-blooded Osage Indian, on an allotment belonging to an unnamed woman on the Osage Reservation in Oklahoma. Under Revised Statute 2145, a murder committed in "Indian country" was subject to federal, and not state, law. Attorneys for the defendants argued that since the allotments were given to the Indians, they were no longer under the care of the government, and that their crime was subject to state jurisdiction. The District Court of the United States for the Western District of Oklahoma, hearing the case, dismissed the charges against the men as being of a federal nature. The United States appealed to the Supreme Court. Arguments were heard on 22 April 1926, and the case was decided on 1 June of that same year. Speaking for a unanimous court, Justice George Sutherland held that Indians under the allotment plan were still "wards" of the government, and crimes committed on those allotments against them must be considered federal crimes. As Justice Sutherland explained, "The sole question for our determination, therefore, is whether the place of the crime is Indian country within the meaning of section 2145. The place is a tract of land constituting an Indian allotment, carved out of the Osage Indian reservation and conveyed in fee to the allottee named in the indictment, subject to a restriction of alienation [inability to sell the land] for a period of 25 years. That period has not elapsed, nor has the allottee ever received a certificate of competency authorizing her to sell." He added, "In *United States v. Pelican*, 232 U.S. 442, 34 S.Ct. 396, 58 L.Ed. 676, a case involving the murder of an Indian upon a trust allotment, this court held (at 449, 34 S.Ct. 399) that trust allotments retain 'during the trust period a distinctively Indian character, being devoted to Indian occupancy under the limitations imposed by federal legislation,' and that they are embraced within the term 'Indian country' as used in section 2145."

United States v. Rickert (188 U.S. 432 [1903])

States were prohibited from taxing Indian allotments granted under the General Allotment Act of 1887 (24 Stat. 389)—so held the U.S. Supreme Court in this early test of whether state could levy such taxes. When James A. Rickert, County Treasurer for Roberts County, South Dakota, moved to tax the allotments of Charles R. Crawford, Adam Little Thunder, Solomon Two Stars, and Victor Renville, all Sisseton Indians of South Dakota, the United States moved in state court to enjoin, or stop, Rickert from taxing such improvements to the allotments, or cattle and other livestock on the lands. The state court dismissed the suit on the grounds that the United States had no interest in such subject matter, and the U.S. Circuit Court of Appeals for the Eighth Circuit upheld the decision. The United States then appealed to the U.S. Supreme Court, and arguments were heard on 28 and 29 January 1903. Less than a month later, on 23 February 1903, Justice John Marshall Harlan held for a unanimous court that (1) the taxes were unconstitutional under the General Allotment Act, and (2) the U.S. government, in its guardian-to-ward relationship, had a definite interest in defending the Indians. After deciding the case point by point, Justice Harlan explained, "Some observations may be made that are applicable to the whole case. It is said that the state has conferred upon these Indians the right of suffrage and other rights that belong only to citizens, and that they ought, therefore, to share the burdens of government like other people who enjoy such rights. These are considerations to be addressed by Congress. It is for the legislative branch of the government to say when these Indians shall cease to be dependent and assume the responsibilities attaching to citizenship. That is a political question, which the courts may not determine. We can only deal with the case as it exists under the legislation of Congress."

United States v. Ritchie (17 Howard [58 U.S.] 525 [1855])

The U.S. Supreme Court held in this case that land grants issued to the Indians under Mexican law before the United States took control of areas in California were valid, and must be honored by the United States government. Archibald Ritchie received a land grant in Sonoma, California, in 1842. After California was granted statehood, the federal government declared that Ritchie's grant was void. A Board of Commissioners sitting to hear land claims held for Ritchie; the District Court for the Northern District of California agreed. The United States appealed to the Supreme Court. Arguments in the case were held on 13 February 1855 (led by Attorney General Caleb Cushing for the government), with the case decided on 10 March of that same year. Justice Samuel Nelson held for a unanimous court (Justice Peter Vivian Daniel did not participate) that Ritchie's claims were valid and must be upheld. Justice John Archibald Campbell wrote a concurring but separate opinion.

United States v. Rogers (4 Howard [45 U.S.] 567 [1846])

In this early case, the U.S. Supreme Court held that white men could not become Indians, and such a determination did not shield them from the laws of the United States. In the April 1845 term of an Arkansas grand jury, Williams S. Rogers was indicted for the murder of Jacob Nicholson on the Cherokee Indian reservation in western Arkansas. In an argument in district court over whether the court had jurisdiction, Rogers claimed that although born a white man in the United States, at some point in his life he moved to Osage Territory and married an Indian woman, steps he argued made him an adopted Cherokee Indian. He also argued that Jacob Nicholson had, likewise, been born an American but had also become a Cherokee. Therefore, Rogers' indictment of murder (an indictment he was fighting with a claim of innocence) was null and void. The district attorney, Samuel H. Hempstead, argued in his brief before the court, "1st. That a native born citizen of the United States cannot expatriate himself, so as to owe no allegiance to the United States, without some law authorizing him to do so; 2d. That no white man can rightfully become a citizen of the Cherokee tribe of Indians, either by marriage, residence, adoption, or any other means, unless the proper authority of the United States shall authorize such incorporation; 3d. That the proviso of the act of Congress relating to crimes committed by one Indian upon the property or person of another Indian, was never intended to embrace white persons, whether married and residing in the Indian nation or not." The divided district court justices asked the U.S. Supreme Court for a decision on the matter.

After the case was submitted, Chief Justice Roger B. Taney delivered the unanimous opinion of the court. In his decision, he held that under the strict interpretation of federal intent, William Rogers could never become an Indian, and as such his crime was under the jurisdiction of an American court of law. "...We think it is very clear that a white man, who at [a] mature age is adopted in an Indian tribe, does not thereby become an Indian, and was not intended to be embraced [as such]," Taney wrote, "He may by such adoption become entitled to certain privileges in the tribe, and make himself amenable to their laws and usages. Yet he is not an Indian; [any such definition] is confined to those who by the usages and customs of the Indians are regarded as belonging to their race. [The definition] does not speak of members of a tribe, but of the race generally—of the family of Indians; and it intended to leave them both, as regarded their own tribe, and other tribes also, to be governed by Indian usages and customs." The concept of Indian jurisdiction over tribal court affairs, first delineated in this case, was upheld by the court in 1882 in *United States v. McBratney*.

See also *United States v. McBratney*.

United States v. Sandoval (231 U.S. 28 [1913])

In this case, the Supreme Court held that Congress had the power to "exercise...its control over the Indian tribes [and] could validly prohibit...the introduction of intoxicating liquors into the Indian pueblos of New Mexico." Felipe Sandoval was accused of selling alcohol to the Indians on the Santa Clara Pueblo Reservation in New Mexico. According to the Act of 30 January 1897 (29 Stat. 506), and the act of 20 June 1910 (36 Stat. 557), also known as the New Mexico Enabling Act, it was mandated "a punishable offense to introduce intoxicating liquor into the Indian country." At the same time, under the enabling act, which allowed New Mexico to enter the Union, the state had to set certain conditions for statehood, among them being the inclusion of the laws of New Mexico into the Indian lands. Sandoval was indicted under this act, but the District Court for New Mexico dismissed the complaint because the territorial supreme court had concluded that Indian lands were not the subject of U.S. jurisdiction. The U.S. government, plaintiff in this case, filed an appeal with the Supreme Court.

The case, *United States, Plaintiff in Error, v. Felipe Sandoval*, was argued on 27 February 1913, and Justice Willis Van Devanter announced the unanimous opinion of the court on 20 October of that same year. In the decision, Van Devanter declared that "Congress, in the exercise of its control over the Indian tribes, could validly prohibit...the introduction of intoxicating liquors into the Indian pueblos of the state of New Mexico..." In discussing the passage and approval of certain legislation which gives Congress more control over Indian Affairs than over any other segment of American society, Van Devanter wrote, "It is said that such legislation cannot be made to embrace the Pueblos, because they are citizens. As before stated, whether they are citizens is an open question, and we need not determine it now, because citizenship is not in itself an obstacle to the exercise by Congress of its power to enact laws for the benefit and protection of tribal Indians as a dependent people...Being a legitimate exercise of that power, the legislation in question does not encroach upon the police power of the state, or disturb the principle of equality among the states....The judgment is accordingly reversed." This case thus, in this small area, overruled the court's decision in the 1877 case *United States v. Joseph*. The court later fully overturned *Joseph* in *United States v. Candelaria et al.*

See also *United States v. Candelaria et al.*; *United States v. Joseph.*

United States v. Seminole Nation (299 U.S. 417 [1937])

The Supreme Court held in this 1937 case that Indians were allowed to file petitions for claims within a time period consented to by the Congress, and any petitions filed thereafter were null and void. An act of Congress of 20 May 1924 (43 Stat. 133) conferred upon the Court of Claims (which heard Indian land grievances before the Indian Claims Commission was established in 1946) the right to hear the Seminole Nation's land controversies, if the suits were filed within a five-year period. A joint resolution of 19 February 1929 (45 Stat. 1229) allowed this time period to be extended to 30 June 1930. On 24 February 1930, the Seminole Nation filed its suit as to several causes of action, but asked that it be allowed to amend its complaint at a later date. The amended charge was not filed until 19 September 1934, and included far assertions. The Court of Claims heard the case, and on 2 December 1935 held for the Seminoles in the total of $1,317,087.21. The United States sought relief from the Supreme Court as to damages for charges made after the 30 June 1930 date. The case was argued on 10 December 1936, and it was Justice Pierce Butler who held for a unanimous court (Justice Harlan Fiske Stone did not participate) on 4 January 1937 that all damages awarded after the 30 June 1930 date were void. Justice Butler explained, "The jurisdiction of the lower court was limited to claims sued on before the expiration of the period within which the United States consented to be sued. It did not extend to any cause of action which was not alleged in plaintiff's original petition. As the United States may not be sued without its consent, causes of action not alleged within the period allowed may not be enforced. The amended petition was not filed within the time allowed; no cause of action was by it brought within the power of the court. The judgment may not be sustained as to any item that is not included in a cause of action set up in the original petition."

See also *Seminole Nation v. United States.*

United States v. Sioux Nation of Indians (448 U.S. 371, 65 L.Ed. 2d 844, 100 S.Ct. 2716 [1980])

This landmark Supreme Court case in effect overturned the 77 year old precedent set in *Lone Wolf v. Hitchcock*, which defined that congressional "good faith" in dealings with the Indians precluded any compensation awards to the Indians for the illegal taking of their lands. Under the Treaty of Fort Laramie (15 Stat. 635), signed in 1868, the United States promised that the Great Sioux Reservation, which included the Black Hills of South Dakota, also called *Paha Sapa* by the Lakota people, would be set aside "for the absolute and undisturbed use and occupation of the Sioux." The treaty also pledged that no land would be ceded to the United States unless three fourths of the adult males of the Sioux nation agreed. Over the next seven years, several expeditions (including one lead by Lt. Col. George Armstrong Custer) confirmed that the Black Hills were a rich source of gold, and when word spread miners began to enter the area. To prevent fights from occurring between miners and the Indians, the U.S. Army patrolled the area to keep whites out. To resolve the situation, in 1875 Secretary of the interior Zachariah Chandler asked Senator William Boyd Allison of Iowa to head a commission to negotiate with the Sioux for the cession of the Black Hills. (See the entry "Allison Commission" for further study of that delegation's negotiations with the Sioux.) The Sioux, when asked to relinquish the Black Hills, demanded $70 million; Allison offered $400,000 a year rental, or $6 million for the purchase. The Indians refused, and the negotiations broke down. Edward Lazarus, in his *Black Hills/White Justice: The Sioux Nation Versus the United States, 1775 to the Present*, which documents the events leading up to the 1980 Supreme Court decision, writes, "Senator Allison dutifully reported to

Washington that the Sioux would not sell except for a price that the nation could not even consider. From the moment of his report, whatever remained of the long-standing economic rationale for peaceful relations with the Sioux vanished entirely, and the policy itself was reduced to nothing more than a patina that glossed the administration's rhetoric: 'The occupation of the Black Hills by white men now seems inevitable,' Commissioner of Indian Affairs Edward P. Smith reported after Allison's return, 'but no reason exists for making this inevitability an occasion for wrong or lasting injury to the Sioux.'...Commissioner Smith advised Congress to expropriate the Hills unilaterally; the United States, he reasoned, should receive some consideration for the $1.25 million in gratuitous rations it provided the Sioux each year." Instead, in a secret Executive Order which had been signed by President Ulysses S. Grant on 3 November, the U.S. government ended all resistance to the white miners and in effect appropriated the Black Hills. Commissioner Smith then ordered all Sioux out of the Black Hills and demanded that they return to their reservation by 31 January 1876. On 1 February 1876, Secretary Chandler relinquished all jurisdiction over all Sioux not on the reservation, and the War Department sent out troops, led by now General Custer, to herd them in. This led to the Battle of the Little Big Horn (or, as the Indians call it, the Battle of the Greasy Grass) on 25 June 1876, in which Custer and over 200 of his men were slaughtered. This victory by the Indians was short-lived; most soon surrendered and were returned to the reservation, stripped of their arms and horses. The fight for the Black Hills was effectively over.

In 1876, President Grant established the Manypenny Commission, under the auspices of former Indian Commissioner George Washington Manypenny, to decide the Black Hills issue once and for all. As Justice Harry Blackmun wrote in the *Sioux Nation* opinion, "This commission, headed by George Manypenny, arrived in the Sioux country in early September and commenced meetings with the head men of the various tribes. The members of commission impressed upon the Indians that the United States no longer had any obligation to provide them with subsistence rations. The commissioner brought with them the text of a treaty that had been prepared in advance. The principal provisions of this treaty were that the Sioux would relinquish their rights to the Black Hills and other lands west of the one hundred and third meridian, and their rights to hunt in the unceded territories to the north, in exchange for subsistence rations for as long as they would be needed to ensure the Sioux' survival. In setting out to obtain the tribes' agreement to this treaty, the commission ignored the stipulation of the Fort Laramie Treaty that any cession of the lands contained within the Great Sioux Reservation would have to be joined in by three-fourths of the adult males. Instead, the treaty was presented to just the Sioux chiefs and their leading men. It was [eventually] signed by only 10 percent of the adult male Sioux population." Adds Indian historian Doane Robinson in his 1904 work, *A History of the Dakota or Sioux Indians*, "As will be readily understood, the making of [the] treaty was forced put, so far as the Indians were concerned. Defeated, disarmed, dismounted, they were at the mercy of a superior power and there was no alternative but to accept the conditions imposed upon them. This they did with as good grace as possible under all of the conditions existing." Congress enacted the Manypenny agreement as the Act of 28 February 1877 (19 Stat. 254), which in effect abrogated the Fort Laramie Treaty.

In 1920 Congress passed the Act of 3 June 1920 (41 Stat. 738), which allowed the Sioux to file a claim for damages in the Court of Claims if the United States "misappropriate[d]...any of the funds or lands of said tribe or band or bands thereof." In 1923, the Sioux filed suit, claiming that the Black Hills were appropriated without just compensation, in violation of the Fifth Amendment. In 1942, the court dismissed the Sioux' suit, claiming that it was not required to decide whether the compensation awarded to the Sioux by the Manypenny agreement was adequate. In 1946, the creation of the Indian Claims Commission, the Sioux had a new forum in which to air their grievance, and filed suit in that forum in 1950. Although four years later the ICC dismissed the claim, it reopened the case in 1958. In 1968, it reheard the case; six years later, in a 4–1 vote, it held that the value of the rations given to the Sioux, considered payment for the Black Hills, was so inconsequential as to have no value to the land that was taken, and that Congress was acting under its power of eminent domain, rather than as a trustee, when it passed the 1877 act, and as such it must compensate the Sioux for the taking. The United States appealed to the Court of Claims, which, in 1975, held that "a more ripe and rank case of dishonorable dealings will never, in all probability, be found in our history, which is not, taken as a whole, the disgrace it now pleases some persons to believe" (*United States v. Sioux Nation*, 207 Ct. Cl. 234, at 241, 518 F2d 1298. at 1302 [1975]). However, that court also held that the case was decided *res judicata* ("something decided previously") in 1942 by the Court of Claims, and as such was beyond the scope of further litigation. In 1978, Congress enacted Public Law 95–243 (92 Stat. 153), which allowed the Court of Claims to decide the issues in the case without regard to *res judicata*. In 1979, the Court of Claims held that the Black Hills seizure was a taking without just compensation, and awarded the Sioux $17.5 million, plus 5 percent yearly interest since 1877. The United States appealed to the Supreme Court, claiming that the waiver of *res judicata* was a violation of the separation of powers.

Arguments in the case were heard on 24 March 1980, and the case was decided on 30 June of the same year. Holding for an 8–1 decision (Justice William H. Rehnquist dissented), Justice Harry Blackmun ruled that the congressional waiver was not a violation of the separation of powers, and that the Sioux were entitled to the award of $17.5 million, plus interest, totalling about $106 million. Justice Blackmun wrote, "In sum, we conclude that the legal analysis and factual findings of the Court of Claims fully support its conclusion that the terms of 1877 Act did not effect 'a mere change in the form of investment of Indian tribal property.' Rather, the 1877 Act effected a taking of tribal property, property which had been set aside for the exclusive occupation of the Sioux by the Fort Laramie Treaty of 1868. That taking implied an obligation on the part of the Government to make just compensation to the Sioux Nation, and that obligation, including an award of interest, must now, at last, be paid."

To this day, some 16 years after the Supreme Court ruled in their favor, the Sioux have refused money for the Black Hills, demanding that the land be returned.

See also Allison Commission; Manypenny Commission.

References Lazarus, Edward, *Black Hills/White Justice: The Sioux Nation versus the United States, 1775 to the Present* (1991); Robinson, Doane, *A History of the Dakota or Sioux Indians from Their Earliest Traditions and First Contact with White Men to the Final Settlement of the Last of Them upon Reservations and the Consequent Abandonment of the Old Tribal Life* (1904).

United States v. Southern Ute Tribe (402 U.S. 159, 28 L.Ed. 2d 695, 91 S.Ct. 1336 [1971])

In this complicated case, which the Supreme Court heard in 1971, it was held that an earlier judgment, which awarded a confederated Indian nation damages against the United States, denied a wing of that nation from suing the United States over the same piece of territory. By two acts of Congress, one in 1880 (21 Stat. 203–204) and one in 1895 (28 Stat. 678), the Ute Indians agreed to cede their lands to the United States when promised that lands not sold by the United States would be held in trust for them. In 1950, the Court of Claims held that the United States had neglected its fiduciary responsibility to the Indians under those acts, and awarded the Confederated Bands of Utes of Colorado damages. The following year, the Southern Ute Tribe or

Band of Indians, a wing of the Confederated Bands of Utes who had been part of the first lawsuit, filed suit separately as to damages; the United States claimed that under the theory of *res judicata* (a matter already settled by judgment), the government had already been held accountable for the neglect of the fiduciary responsibility, and asked that the lawsuit be dismissed. It took 16 years before the Indian Claims Commission held that the United States' defense was not valid. The Court of Claims, on appeal, remanded the case for further action, but in 1969 the Indians Claims Commission again rejected the United States' argument, and the Court of Claims affirmed. The Supreme Court granted certiorari, and arguments were heard on 1 March 1971. In an opinion expressing the will of eight justices (Justice William O. Douglas dissenting), Justice William Brennan on 26 April 1971 reversed the Indian Claims Commission holding, agreeing that the claim was *res judicata*, or previously decided, in the earlier lawsuit.

United States v. Sutton et al. (215 U.S. 291 [1909])

The case of *United States, Plaintiff in Error, v. Harvey Sutton and Robert Miller* dealt with whether an act of Congress making it illegal to introduce intoxicating liquors into Indian country made such a violation an injury against the United States. Defendants Harvey Sutton and Robert Miller were indicted in the U.S. District Court for the Eastern District of Washington for introducing "ardent spirits and intoxicating liquor[s]" onto an allotment which had been part of the Yakima Indian Reservation in Washington State. The indictment was based on the Act of 30 January 1897 (29 Stat. 506), which made it illegal for "any person…to introduce any malt, spirituous, or vinous liquor, including beer, ale, and wine, or any ardent or intoxicating liquor of any kind whatsoever into the Indian country, which term shall include any Indian allotment while the title to the same shall be held in trust by the government, or while the same shall remain inalienable by the allottee without the consent of the United States." The defendants, arguing that the introduction of intoxicating liquors did not injure the United States and that the act of 30 January 1897 was unconstitutional, asked for a dismissal of the charges, which was granted. The United States appealed the case directly to the U.S. Supreme Court, which granted certiorari. Speaking for a unanimous court, Justice David Josiah Brewer held that the act of 30 January 1897 was legal, within the power that Congress had over Indian reservations, and as such the dismissal of the indictment must be reversed. Justice Brewer argued simply, "[U]ndoubtedly Congress has the right to forbid the introduction of liquor, and to provide punishment for any violation thereof."

See also Alcohol on Reservations.

United States v. Waller et al. (243 U.S. 452 [1916])

Could the United States government, after removing the restrictions against conveyance held against Indian allotments, sue on behalf of those Indians if their land was taken by fraud? This narrow question was the focus of the case of *United States v. Lucky S. and Mamie S. Waller*. The acts of Congress of 21 June 1906 (34 Stat. 325, also known as the Clapp Amendment) and 1 March 1907 (34 Stat. 1015) removed the restrictions on sale or lease from allotments given to all adult mixed-blood Indians. In December 1907, two Chippewa Indians of the White Earth reservation in Minnesota, Ah-be-daun-ah-quod and Ah-sum, signed a paper with one Lucky S. Waller for the purchase of timber on their allotted lands. After Waller paid them $50 (and later gave them more money, a total of $145), they signed the paper, thinking it was a receipt for the payment for the timber; in fact, they had signed their allotments over to Waller. The United States government estimated that the land was worth no less than $2,500, and the timber no less than $2,000, and, finding that the sum given to the two Indians constituted fraud, instituted a lawsuit in the U.S. District Court for the District of Minnesota to have the Wallers return the deed for the land to the two Indians. The District Court held that the plaintiff, the United States, had no bearing to bring this suit; on appeal, the U.S. Court of Appeals for the Eighth Circuit upheld the judgment. The United States appealed to the Supreme Court. The case was argued before the court on 14 and 15 March 1917, and decided on 9 April of that same year. Speaking for a unanimous court, Justice William Rufus Day upheld the court of appeals holding. "It does not follow that the Indians are without remedy in proper actions brought by themselves or their guardians, if there be such, for the protection of their rights," Justice Day explained.

In *Dickson v. Luck Land Company*, decided at this term and reported in 242 U.S. 371, 61 L.Ed. 371, 37 S.Ct. 167, this court had occasion to deal with rights concerning lands allotted and patented under the Clapp Amendment to admit mixed-blood Chippewa Indians, and speaking of the effect of the removal of the restrictions, this court said, at page 375: "With those restrictions entirely removed and the fee simple patent issued it would seem that the situation was one in which all questions pertaining to the disposal of the lands naturally would fall within the scope and operation of the laws of the state. And that Congress so intended is shown by the Act of May 8, 1906, 34 Stat. 182, which provides that when an Indian allottee is given a patent in fee for his allotment he 'shall have the benefit of and be subject to the laws, both civil and criminal, of the state.' Among the laws to which the allottee became subject, and to the benefit of which he became entitled, under the enactment, were those governing the transfer of real property, fixing the age of majority, and declaring the disability of minors." We reach the conclusion that in this suit the United States was without capacity to bring the action for the benefit of the Indians named, and it follows that the question propounded must be answered in the negative. And so it is ordered.

See also *Brader v. James*; *Dickson v. Luck Land Company*.

United States v. Washington (384 F.Supp. 312 [1974])

In this landmark lower court case the fishing rights of Indians were upheld. The matter originated when activists from the National Indian Youth Council (NIYC) started a "fish-in" in the Quillayute River in Washington state to protest state regulations prohibiting fishing with nets, a method used only by Indians. The Federal Court for the District of Washington State, with Judge George H. Boldt in attendance, heard the case. In 1974, Judge Boldt held for the Indians; his decision runs for 111 pages. In the opinion, the judge states flatly, "Because the right of each Treaty Tribe to take anadromous fish arises from a treaty with the United States, that right is preserved and protected under the supreme law of the land, does not depend on State law, is distinct from rights or privileges held by others, and may not be qualified by any action of the State." [Opinion, at 407.]

The opinion details the situation that led to the case: "In September 1970 the United States, on its own behalf and as trustee for several Western Washington Indians tribes [the Hoh, Makah, Muckleshoot, Nisqually, Puyallup, Quileute, and Skokomish], later joined as intervenor plaintiffs by additional tribes [the Lummi, Quinault, Sauk-Suiattle, Squaxin Island, Stillaguamish, Upper Skagit River, and Yakima Nation], filed the complaint initiating this action against the state of Washington. Shortly later the State Department of Fisheries and the State Game Commission, their repective directors, and the Washington Reef Net Owners Association were included as defendants. By state statute [the State Department of] Fisheries is charged with exercising regulatory authority over fishing for all anadromous food fish. Regulation of anadromous steelhead trout is vested in [the Washington State Game Commission]. Plaintiffs seek a declaratory judgment pursuant to 28 U.S.C. 2201 and 2202 concerning off reservation treaty right fishing within the case area by plaintiff tribes, which long has been and is in controversy, and for injunctive relief to provide enforcement of those fishing rights as they previously have been or herein may be judicially determined. The case area is that portion of the State of Washington west of the Cascade Mountains and north of the Columbia River drainage area, and includes the American portion of the Puget Sound watershed, the watersheds of the Olympic Peninsula north of the Grays Harbor watershed, and the offshore waters adjacent to those areas."

The U.S. Court of Appeals for the Ninth Circuit ultimately upheld Judge Boldt's decision (520 Federal Reporter 676 [1975]) and the Supreme Court refused to hear the case. Historian Judith Harlan writes, "In 1974...in the Washington State Puget Sound 'fish war,' the Supreme Court listened to the arguments in *United States v. Washington,* and took into account the fact that the 1854 treaties signed by the area's Indians were translated from English into 'Chinook,' a language used by Indian people and non-Indians who did not speak each other's languages. Chinook was used to communicate when buying and selling goods. It was a trade medium, not a full language, and it had a limited vocabulary. The Indian leaders signing the treaty, therefore, may not have understood what they were giving away. The Court based its decision [not to review the case] partially on what the Indian leader thought the treaty said, and ruled in favor of the Indian interests." In 1986, the white residents of Washington State put a proposition on the state ballot which would urge Congress to overturn the 1979 Supreme Court decision. Even though the ballot measure passed, the governors of Washington state have refused to send the initiative to Washington. And so the battle goes on.

See also Fish-In; National Indian Youth Council.

References American Friends Service Committee, *Uncommon Controversy: Fishing Rights of the Muckleshoot, Puyallup and Nisqually Indians* (1970); Harlan, Judith, *American Indians Today; Issues and Conflicts* (1987).

United States v. Wheeler (435 U.S. 313, 55 L.Ed. 2d 303, 98 S.Ct. 1079 [1978])

In this Supreme Court case, the court upheld its previous rulings regarding the jurisdiction of crimes committed by Indians as to states and the rights of Indians. In 1886, the Court held in *United States v. Kagama,* "With the Indians themselves these relations are equally difficult to define. They were, and always have been, regarded as having a semi-independent position when they preserved their tribal relations; not as states, not as nations, not as possessed of the full attributes of sovereignty, but as a separate people, with the power of regulating their internal and social relations, and thus not brought under the laws of the Union, or of the state within whose limits they reside." This concept was reinforced by the 1896 decision *Talton v. Mayes.* In *Wheeler,* which was decided 92 years after *Kagama,* the court upheld this principle. Anthony Robert Wheeler, a Navajo, was convicted in a tribal court in Arizona of contributing to the delinquency of a minor. A grand jury sitting for the U.S. District Court for the District of Arizona indicted Wheeler for the higher offense of statutory rape in violation of the Major Crimes Act (23 Stat. 362, 18 U.S.C. 1153, 3 March 1885). The District Court dismissed the indictment, asserting that the indictment was void under the double jeopardy clause of the Fifth Amendment to the U.S. Constitution. On appeal by the United States, the U.S. Court of Appeals for the Ninth Circuit, sitting in San Francisco, upheld the district court's dismissal. On certiorari, the Supreme Court reversed the lower court's decision and remanded the case back for consideration. In a decision written by Justice Potter Stewart, the court held unanimously (Justice William Brennan did not participate) that because Indian tribes were considered separate entities from the United States, their sovereignty over criminal actions did not affect the double jeopardy clause. Stewart wrote that while "tribal courts are important mechanisms for protecting significant tribal interests," they are not an arm of the federal government, and thus any judgment arising from those tribal courts did not prohibit further prosecution in federal courts.

See also *Talton v. Mayes*; *United States v. Kagama, alias Pactah Billy*.

Reference *United States v. Kagama, alias Pactah Billy* (118 U.S. 375, 30 L.Ed. 228, 6 S.Ct. 1109 [1886], at [U.S.] 381 and [S.Ct.] 1109).

United States v. Winans (198 U.S. 371 [1905])

In this Supreme Court case, the court held that "the United States is bound, on the highest compulsions and sanctions controlling human institutions, to deal with the Indians on the most liberal doctrines of construction and the most generous rules of duty and obligation to inferiors known to our national principles and in international law," and must honor all Indian treaties with regard to fishing rights. Officially titled *The United States, Thomas Simpson, and White Swan, Appellants, v. Lineas Winans and Audubon Winans, Partners, Doing Business under the Firm Name of Winans Brothers*, the case hinged on whether the government could honor land patents issued to whites after such land had been secured to Indians under treaties. Under the Treaty of 1859, the Yakima Indians of Washington State secured the fishing rights to the Columbia River. The Winans, respondents, under land patents issued to them by the Washington state government, set up a device called a fishing wheel to take salmon from the Columbia. At the same time, they prohibited the Yakimas from using their ancestral fishing sites. The United States sued on behalf of plaintiffs Thomas Simpson and White Swan to halt the enjoinment. The Circuit Court for the District of Washington dismissed the case, holding that under the Treaty of 1859, the Indians ceded title to their fishing rights. The tribe appealed to the Supreme Court.

The case was argued before the court on 3 and 4 April 1905, and decided on 15 May of that same year. Justice Joseph McKenna delivered the opinion of a unanimous court in holding that the district court had not construed the Treaty of 1859 correctly, and held that the respondents could not keep the Indians from their fishing sites. In effect, it remanded (returned) the case to the lower court for a rehearing. As McKenna wrote, "The license from the state, which respondents plead, to maintain a fishing wheel, gives no power to them to exclude the Indians, nor was it intended to give such power. It was the permission of the state to use a particular device. What rights the Indians had were not determined or limited. This was a matter for judicial determination regarding the rights of the Indians and rights of the respondents. And that there may be adjustment and accommodation of them the Solicitor General concedes and points out the way. We think, however, that such adjustment and accommodation are more within the province of the circuit court in the first instance than of this court."

See also *Antoine et ux. v. Washington; Central Machinery Company v. Arizona Tax Commission; Menominee Tribe of Indians v. United States; Merrian v. Jicarilla Apache Tribe; Metlakatla Indian Community, Annette Islands Reserve v. Egan; Montana v. United States; New Mexico v. Mescalero Apache Tribe; Puyallup v. Department of Game of Washington, et al.; United States v. Winans; Washington v. Confederated Tribes of Colville Indian Reservation; White Mountain Apache Tribe et al. v. Bracker et al.*

Utah & Northern Railway Company v. Fisher (116 U.S. 28, 29 L.Ed. 542, 6 S.Ct. 246 [1885])

In this Supreme Court case, the court held that because Indian reservations are under the taxable jurisdiction of states, railroads built within their parameters are liable for taxes. The Utah & Northern Railway Company built a 69–mile line through the Fort Hill Reservation, which belonged to the Bannock tribe. Under the Treaty of the Eastern Band of Shoshonees [*sic*] and the Bannock Tribe of 3 July 1868, the Indians were declared to be set apart from the Territory of Idaho. When William F. Fisher, Assessor and ex officio Collector of Territorial and County Taxes in and for Oneida County, Idaho Territory, attempted to collect taxes on the railroad line, the line sued arguing that because the reservation was separate from the Territory, the railroad was not liable for taxes. The Idaho Territorial Supreme Court held for Fisher, and the railroad appealed to the U.S. Supreme Court. After arguments were heard on 21 October 1885, Justice Stephen Johnson Field delivered the court's unanimous opinion on 14 December of that same year in upholding Fisher's right to collect the taxes. Field opined simply, "If the plaintiff lawfully constructed and now operates a railroad through the Reservation, it is not perceived that any just rights of the Indians under the Treaty can be impaired by taxing the road and property used in operating it."

See *Harkness v. Hyde*; and *Langford v. Monteith* for other cases in this line decided before Utah.

Valentine, Robert Grosvenor (1872–1916)

Robert G. Valentine was the twenty-ninth commissioner of Indian Affairs and his early death silenced a staunch advocate of Indian interests and a critic of government policy. His administration was marked by a partisan investigation that drove him from office and his last years saw him side with the Progressive wing of the Republican party. Robert G. Valentine was born in West Newton, Massachusetts, on 29 November 1872, the only child of Charles Theodore Valentine and Charlotte Grosvenor (née Light) Valentine. He attended local schools, was prepared for college at the prestigious Hopkinson's School, and graduated from Harvard in 1896. For two periods, 1896–1899 and 1901–1903, he taught English at the Massachusetts Institute of Technology, while in the intervening years he worked at the National City Bank in New York City and for the Union Pacific Railroad in Omaha, Nebraska. From 1903 to 1904, he returned to work in Omaha and campaigned for reformist Seth Low for Mayor of New York, but ill health forced him to retire in 1904.

President Theodore Roosevelt's reelection in 1904 gave Valentine the opportunity to be named as the private secretary to Commissioner of Indian Affairs Francis Ellington Leupp, a position he held until being named as Leupp's assistant in 1908. On 18 June 1909, Commissioner Leupp resigned and Valentine took the oath as Indian commissioner on 19 June. Biographer Felix Frankfurter reports, "His [Valentine's] administration of that office was a notable one. He was resourceful in the protection of the enormous Indian properties against the many attempts at encroachments upon them, and was eager for the development of the best of the Indian cultures. One of his acts as commissioner created considerable difficulties because of the religious susceptibilities [sensitivities] that it awakened. By an Indian Office circular (number 601), he prohibited the wearing of religious garb and the display of religious insignia in what had formerly been religious schools for Indians but had been taken over as government institutions." Valentine's 1909 annual report as commissioner was submitted less than three months into his job. In that report, he wrote, "As the administration of the service thus changed hands in the last month of the fiscal year, the events recorded in this report fall almost entirely within Mr. Leupp's term. I have tried, therefore, to make the record largely a simple statement of fact, uncolored by my own views. For whatever there may be here in the way of indications of future work I alone am responsible." His 1910 treatise reflected this "future work." Valentine discussed the health among Indians (including "increased attention...being given to sanitary inspection" and the treatment of such diseases as trachoma and tuberculosis) and the situation in which the Kickapoos of Oklahoma had been fraudulently cheated out of their allotments. His 1911 discourse, his last, called into question the government's policy of allotment; the commissioner said that the policy was causing the Indians "to bear heavier and heavier, and often seemingly impossible, loads." Valentine also denounced the influence of the cult of the peyote bean, and called for a campaign against its use by Native Americans. Historian James E. Officer writes, "[Valentine] was commissioner in 1910 when Congress passed the greatest legislative impetus to reservation resource development in the long history of federal Indian administration. Although relatively unknown to persons not connected with the Indian Bureau, the Omnibus Act touched on virtually every aspect of Bureau responsibilities related to Indian lands and resources. J. P Kinney, in his history of Indian land tenure, observed that this legislation 'contained so many items...of vital importance...that the fiscal year beginning July 1, 1910 may appropriately be accepted as the first in a new period of Indian administration.' Within ten years after this enactment [36 Stat. 269], the Indian Bureau had acquired a large staff of foresters, irrigation engineers, and real property management specialists." Valentine made an influential impression at the Lake Mohonk Conference in 1909. The New York *Observer*, a noted magazine of that time, editorialized,

The address of R.G. Valentine, the new commissioner of Indian Affairs, was well received. It was his first address at Mohonk and he made a most pleasing impression upon the conference. Mr. Sherman [Vice President James Schoolcraft Sherman] later commended him and his work and said that he would find Congress ready to back practically any movement in behalf of the Indians which he brought before it. Beside speaking, Mr. Valentine introduced a number of his agents and associates, who told what they are doing to better the condition of the Indians on and off the reservations. Mr. Valentine said in part, "The people of the United States ought to know certain things about their Indian Bureau. They know to-day too little about the two or three fundamental principles in the light of which all multiform activities of the Indian service fall into well-ordered array in an advance toward a single goal. In the minds of most people the Indian service is a mere hodgepodge of activity. Indians are going to this or that kind of school, being allotted, raising stock, working in the woods, learning to irrigate, drawing per capita payments in some cases and rations in others, owning banks accounts of all sizes from a few dollars to many thousands, going to church and engaging in pagan rites, dealing shrewdly with traders or becoming an easy mark for them, developing all kinds of diseases, getting drunk and even keeping sober, loafing and making some of the best workmen the United States possesses. All of these various activities are kept in further confusion by the kaleidoscopic changes introduced by the rapidly developing economic and social life of the white people scattered more and more around and through the Indian country."

In early 1912, Representative James M. Graham of Illinois targeted Valentine, investigating the Indian commissioner on several charges including helping to introduce intoxicating liquors into Indian territory. Dismayed at the investigation, Valentine resigned on 10 September 1912. Three months later, in January 1913, the congressional committee looking into the charges (divided into four Democrats and three Republicans) denounced Valentine's handling of the Indian office and called for his dismissal. (The three Republicans on the panel condemned the majority report as a vendetta by vengeful Democrats.) The episode, however, broke Valentine's already frail health. He began to work for the election of Theodore Roosevelt for president on the Progressive party ticket, and served on a board which investigated the impact of a minimum wage in Massachusetts. On 14 November 1916, after advising the mayor of New York during a street railway crisis, Valentine collapsed and died in a restaurant in New York City of a massive heart attack. He was only 43 years old, just two weeks shy of his birthday.

See also Bureau of Indian Affairs.

References Frankfurter, Felix, "Valentine, Robert Grosvenor." In Dumas Malone et al., eds., *Dictionary of American Biography* (1930–88); "A New Voice for the Indians." *New York Observer*, 4 November 1909, 591; Officer, James E., "The Indian Service and Its Evolution." In Sandra L. Cadwalader and Vine Deloria, Jr., eds., *The Aggressions of Civilization Federal Indian Policy since the 1880s* (1984); Putney, Diane T., "Robert Grosvenor." Valentine." In Robert M. Kvasnicka and Herman J. Viola, eds., *The Commissioners of Indian Affairs, 1824–1977* (1979); "Robt. G. Valentine, Labor Arbiter, Dies." *New York Times*, 15 November 1916, 11; U.S. Congress, House of Representatives, *Annual Report of the Commissioner of Indian Affairs for the Year 1909*, House Document No. 107, 61st Congress, 2d Session (serial 5747); U.S. Congress, House of Representatives, *Annual Report of the Commissioner of Indian Affairs for the Year 1910*, House Document No. 1006, 61st Congress, 3d Session (serial 5976); U.S. Congress, House of Representatives, *Annual Report of the Commissioner of Indian Affairs for the year 1911*, House Document No. 120, 62nd Congress, 2d Session (serial 6223).

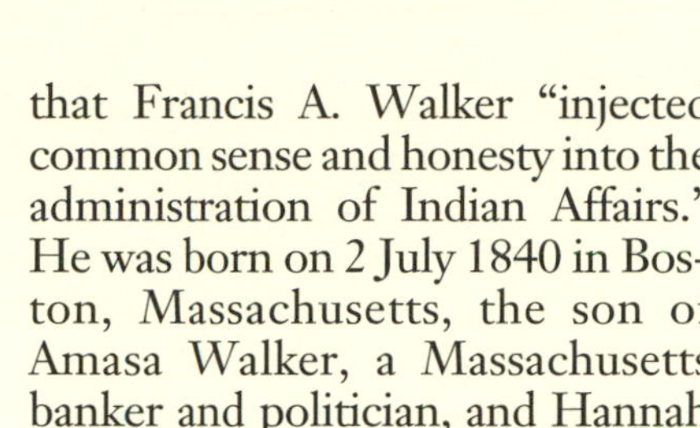

Wade Committee Report

See Sand Creek Massacre.

Wagoner et al. v. Evans et al. (170 U.S. 588 [1898])

This case was decided soon after the Supreme Court found in *Thomas et al. v. Gay et al.* that Indian lands included in a territory when that territory was created could be used to tax non-Indians on cattle grazing on that land. Justice George Shiras, Jr., who composed the opinion in *Thomas*, noted, "The appeal of Wagoner and others, owners of cattle kept by them on the Indian reservation attached to Canadian county, brings up the same questions which were considered and determined by us at the present term in the case of *Thomas v. Gay*." Appellants D. and W.T. Wagoner and S.B. Burnett filed suit in the District Court of Canadian County, Oklahoma Territory, against Neil W. Evans, county treasurer, and I.M. Cannon, county sheriff, to enjoin them from collecting taxes on cattle that the men had grazed on Indian lands that had been included in the territorial scheme. A mixed outcome allowed the two sides to appeal to the Oklahoma Territorial Supreme Court and, when that court affirmed the lower court's ruling, to the U.S. Supreme Court. On 23 May 1898 Justice Shiras held for unanimous court in upholding the earlier decision in *Thomas* and ruling that "Territorial legislatures may impose a tax on cattle belonging to others than Indians, which are grazing on Indian reservations within the territory pursuant to a lease of the land for that purpose made by the Indians with the approval of federal authorities."

See also *Thomas et al. v. Gay et al.*

Walker, Francis Amasa (1840–1897)

Walker is noted in American history for his work as a statistician, educator, and economist who worked as Superintendent of the Tenth Census (1880); his service as commissioner of Indian Affairs lasted little more than a year (November 1871 to December 1872), yet in that time one biographer notes that Francis A. Walker "injected common sense and honesty into the administration of Indian Affairs." He was born on 2 July 1840 in Boston, Massachusetts, the son of Amasa Walker, a Massachusetts banker and politician, and Hannah (née Ambrose) Walker. The senior Walker (1799–1875) was also a successful shoe manufacturer who, after retiring at the age of 41, spent the rest of his life teaching and writing on economic matters, as his son would. Francis Walker was schooled early in his life in the classics (Latin, Greek, as well as mathematics), and at age 15 enrolled in Amherst University, where he came to write his first tract, a treatise on free trade that appeared (signed by "W") in the *National Era* in Washington, D.C., on 29 October 1857.

Although after graduation he entered the law office of Devens & Hoar, a prestigious Worcester, Massachusetts, firm, Walker's career was cut short by the onset of the Civil War. Walker himself immediately volunteered in the Fifteenth Massachusetts Regiment as a sergeant major, was commissioned a captain, and, after being captured by the Confederates, spent time in the South's notorious Libby Prison, where he became ill. Exchanged, he was forced to retire, but not before being promoted to brigadier general. After returning home, he eschewed his law career and instead accepted a position teaching Latin and Greek at the Williston Seminary. In 1868, again changing horses in mid-stream, he entered the domain of journalism and joined the influential newspaper *The Springfield* (Massachusetts) *Republican.*

In 1869, most likely because of his father's influence, Walker was named as chief of the Bureau of Statistics, and a year later promoted to Superintendent of the Ninth Census (1870). A year after that, President Ulysses S. Grant turned to Walker to fill the position of commissioner of Indian Affairs, replacing Ely S. Parker (Seneca), who had resigned in July of that year. On 11 December 1871, the Senate confirmed Walker as Indian commissioner. In his sole report as head of that post, Walker discussed the dual government policy of treating loyal Indian tribes with seeming contempt, while appeasing and even acting with benevolence toward the more hostile tribes. As Indian land authority J. P. Kinney wrote, "When General Walker assumed the office of commissioner, federal Indian administration was being subjected to a storm of criticism. In his report, dated 1 November 1872, Walker presented a vigorous defense of the course that was being pursued by the administration in placating the hostile tribes by methods that were being denounced as inconsistent, ineffective and humiliating to the nation." Wrote Walker, "There is no question of national dignity, be it remembered, involved in the treatment of savages by a civilized power. With wild men, as with wild beasts, the question whether in a given situation one shall fight, coax, or run, is a question merely of what is easiest and safest." He added that "No one certainly will rejoice more heartily than the present Commissioner when the Indians of this country cease to be in a position to dictate, in any form or degree, to the Government; when, in fact, the last hostile tribe becomes reduced to the condition of suppliants for charity. This is, indeed, the only hope of salvation for the aborigines of the continent. If they stand up against the progress of civilization and industry, they must be relentlessly crushed. The westward course of population is neither to be denied nor delayed for the sake of all the Indians that ever called this country their home. They must yield or perish." Biographer James Phinney Munroe notes that Walker's tenure was marked by exposure of massive frauds and abuses in the Indian Bureau. To discuss his administration, Walker composed *The Indian Question* (1874), in which he discussed his solutions to the lack of a cognizant government policy on Indian matters. He did not sign the 1872 report (clerk and aide Henry R. Clum was the signer), and resigned on 26 December 1872 to become the professor of political economy and history at the Sheffield Scientific School at Yale University.

He later served as United States commissioner to the International Monetary Conference, Paris (1878), Superintendent of the Tenth Census (1880), president of the Massachusetts Institute of Technology (1881–97), and president of the American Economic Association (1886). His other publications include *The Science of Wealth* (1866) (which he wrote with his father), *The Wages Question* (1876), *The First Century of the Republic* (1876), *Land and Its Rent* (1883), and *Discussions in Education*, posthumously published in 1899. Walker died at his home in Boston on 5 January 1897 of a stroke at the age of 57. Today, Walker's name is commemorated by the Walker Medal, bestowed by the American Economic Association every five years for the contributions by American economists in outstanding economic thought and study.

See also Bureau of Indian Affairs.

References "Gen. Francis Walker Dead." *New York Times*, 6 January 1897, 9; Kinney, J. P., *A Continent Lost—A Civilization Won: Indian Land Tenure in America* (1937); Miner, H. Craig, "Francis A. Walker." In Robert M. Kvasnicka and Herman J. Viola, eds., *The Commissioners of Indian Affairs, 1824–1977* (1979); Munroe, James Phinney, *A Life of Francis Amasa Walker* (1923); Newton, Bernard, *The Economics of Francis Amasa Walker: American Economics in Transition* (1968); Nichols, Jeannette P., "Francis Amasa Walker." In Malone, Dumas et al., eds., *Dictionary of American Biography* (1930–88); U.S. Congress, House of Representatives, *Annual Report of the Commissioner of Indian Affairs for the Year 1872*, House Executive Document No. 1, 42nd Congress, 3d Session (serial 1560).

Wan-zop-e-ah v. Miami County **(5 Wallace [72 U.S.] 756, 18 L.Ed. 674 [1867])**

See The Kansas Indians.

War Department, Establishment of

With the constitution of the War Department on 7 August 1789, Congress placed the authority of Indian Affairs under its jurisdiction. This power remained with the War Department until the creation of the Interior Department in 1849, where such administration was vested in a separate Bureau of Indian Affairs. The act that established the War Department, which appears at 1 Stat. 49, reads:

An Act to establish an Executive Department, to be denominated the Department of War.

Section 1. Be it enacted...That there shall be an executive department to be denominated the Department of War, and that there shall be a principal officer therein, to be called the Secretary for the Department of War, who shall perform and execute such duties as shall from time to time be enjoined on, or entrusted to him by the President of the United States, agreeably to the Constitution, relative to military commissions, or to the land or naval forces, ships, or warlike stores of the United States, or to such other matters respecting military or naval affairs, as the President of the United States shall assign to the said department, or relative to the granting of lands to persons entitled thereto, for military services rendered to the United States, or relative to Indian Affairs; and furthermore, that the said principal officer shall conduct the business of the said department in such manner, as the President of the United States shall from time to time order or instruct.

Ward, Nancy (Cherokee) (1738?-1824)

The "Beloved Woman" or "Pretty Woman" of the Cherokee people, she was known in her native language as *Ghigau* ("The Beloved Woman"), but she also went by the names *Nan'yehi* ("One Who Goes About") and *Tsistunagiska* ("Wild Rose"). Nancy Ward was born about 1738 at Chota, Tennessee, the "mother town" of the Cherokees. Historian Henry Waldman speculates that her father "was probably a British officer and [her] mother was probably the sister of the [Cherokee] chief Attakullaculla." Virtually nothing is known of her early life, only that she married Kingfisher, a Cherokee warrior whose death notice at the battle of Taliwa in 1755 mentions her name as his widow. Fighting by his side, she rallied the Cherokees to victory over the Creeks, and for her heroism was called Beloved Woman. Her status as a heroine among her people established, she sat as a member of the Cherokee General Council (where biographer Cynthia Kasee mentions that she had a full voice and vote on tribal matters), and acted as a negotiator with whites over treaties, especially the Treaty of Hopewell, 28 November 1785, the first such treaty signed with white settlers. A friend of whites, she warned a colony of them before Cherokee chief Dragging Canoe could attack them, thereby saving their lives. Nancy Ward owned large numbers of cattle and slaves, possibly becoming one of the first women on this continent to have equal rights with men in her tribe in being allowed to own property. She took the English name Nancy Ward when she married Irish (or Scottish) merchant Bryan Ward. The two opened an inn near Chota, on Womankiller Ford on the Ocowee River. She returned to Chota just before she died sometime in 1824 of an unknown illness. Her son, Fivekiller, wrote later that he saw a white light leave his mother's body after she passed away. Today, her name is revered among the Cherokee people, both those of Oklahoma and the eastern band of Cherokees who remained behind after the removal of the tribe to the West.

References Kasee, Cynthia R., "Nancy Ward." In Sharon Malinowski, ed., *Notable Native Americans* (1995); Kasee, Cynthia R., "Ward, Nancy." In Gretchen M. Bataille, ed., *Native American Women: A Biographical Dictionary* (1993); Waldman, Henry, et al, eds., *Dictionary of Indians of North America* (1978).

Ward et al. v. Board of County Commissioners of Love County, Oklahoma (253 U.S. 17 [1920])

The right of Indian allotments to be exempt from taxation, established by an act of Congress, was a federal right to be recognized by all recognized authorities—so held the U.S. Supreme Court in this case, decided in 1920. Under the Curtis Act of 28 June 1898 (30 Stat. 495), "lands allotted [to the Indians] shall be nontaxable while the title remains in the original allottee, but not to exceed twenty-one years." Plaintiffs Coleman J. Ward and 66 other unnamed Choctaw Indians of Oklahoma were awarded their certificates in 1898. However, by an act of Congress of 27 May 1908 (25 Stat. 312), these lands were declared to be "subject to taxation, as though it were the property of other persons than allottees." Under this subsequent act, the commissioners of Love County, Oklahoma, levied taxes against Ward and the others. Ward then instituted a class action suit to recover the taxes, claiming that the second act was unconstitutional. The District Court for Love County found for Ward et al., but the Oklahoma State Supreme Court reversed, and the U.S. Supreme Court granted certiorari. Arguments were heard on 11 March 1920, and a decision was handed down less than two months later, on 26 April. Justice Willis Van Devanter spoke for a unanimous court in holding that the allotments must remain free of taxation for the allocated time period, and could not breached before that. Justice Van Devanter commented, "The right to the exemption was a federal right, and was specially set up and claimed as such in the petition [of the plaintiffs]. Whether the right was denied, or not given due recognition, by the Supreme Court is a question as to which the claimants were entitled to invoke our judgment, and this they have done in the appropriate way."

Ward v. Race Horse (163 U.S. 504 [1896])

The Supreme Court held in this nineteenth-century case that a treaty allowing a tribe of Indians to hunt "on the unoccupied lands of the United States" was void when those lands came under the jurisdiction of a territory or state. Race Horse, a Bannock Indian on the Ft. Hall Reservation located in Idaho, was arrested and convicted of illegal hunting in Wyoming. He sued John H. Ward, sheriff of Uinta county, for a writ of habeas corpus releasing him from custody. Race Horse argued that under Article 4 of the Treaty with the Bannocks of 24 February 1869 (15 Stat. 673), the Indians were granted "the right to hunt upon the unoccupied lands of the United States so long as game may be found thereon..." The court that found Race Horse guilty held that under the act of the Wyoming legislature of 20 July 1895, the killing of game in that state was to be regulated. The Circuit Court of the United States for the District of Wyoming granted Race Horse an order releasing him from custody, and Ward appealed directly to the U.S. Supreme Court. On 25 May 1896, Justice Edward Douglass White held for the 7–1 decision of the court (Justice Henry Brown dissented, and Justice David Josiah Brewer did not participate) in reinstating Race Horse's conviction. Justice White explained, "The power of all the states to regulate the killing of game within their borders will not be gainsaid, yet, if the treaty applied to the unoccupied land of the United States in the state of Wyoming, that state would be bereft of such power, since every isolated piece of land belonging to the United States as a private owner, so long as it continued to be unoccupied land, would be exempt in this regard from the authority of the state. Wyoming, then, will have been admitted into the Union, not as an equal member, but as one shorn of a legislative power vested in all other states of the Union, a power resulting from the fact of statehood and incident to its plenary existence."

Warren Trading Post Company v. Arizona State Tax Commission (380 U.S. 685, 14 L.Ed. 2d 165, 85 S.Ct. 1242 [1965])

In this landmark Supreme Court case, the court held that states, in conflict with federal laws, could not levy taxes on businesses operating on Indian reservations. The state of Arizona levied a 2 percent tax on the gross receipts of companies operating within the state; the tax was then assessed on the Warren Trading Post Company, a retail enterprise doing business with the Navajo Indians on their reservation with the approval of the Bureau of Indian Affairs. The company argued that the tax was inconsistent with federal law, but the Arizona Supreme Court upheld its application on the company. On appeal, the U.S. Supreme Court granted certiorari. Arguments were heard on 9 March 1965, and a decision was handed down less than two months later, on 29 April. Speaking for a unanimous court, Justice Hugo Black struck down the state tax as inconsistent with federal laws governing Indian reservations. In an opinion than runs five short pages, Justice Black explained, "Congress has, since the creation of the Navajo Reservation nearly a century ago, left the Indians on it largely free to run the reservation and its affairs without state control, a policy which has automatically relieved Arizona of all burdens for carrying on those same responsibilities. And in compliance with its treaty obligations the Federal Government has provided for roads, education and other services needed by the Indians. We think the assessment and collection of this tax would to a substantial extent frustrate the evident congressional purpose of ensuring that no burden shall be placed upon Indian traders for trading with Indians on reservations except as authorized by Acts of Congress or by valid regulations promulgated under those Acts. This state tax on gross income would put financial burdens on appellant or the Indians with whom it deals in addition to those Congress or the tribes have prescribed, and could thereby disturb and disarrange the statutory plan Congress set up in order to protect Indians against prices deemed unfair or unreasonable by the Indian Commissioner. And since federal legislation has left the State with no duties or responsibilities respecting the reservation Indians, we cannot believe that Congress intended to leave to the State the privilege of levying this tax."

Washington v. Confederated Bands of the Yakima Indian Nation (439 U.S. 463 [1979])

The question of whether Congress allowed for states to assume only partial jurisdiction over Indian matters as established under Public Law 280 was at issue in this Supreme Court decision. Under the act of Congress of 15 August 1953 (67 Stat. 588), known as Public Law 280, the Congress allowed states to assert jurisdiction over Indian Affairs in the areas of criminal and civil matters, if those particular states mentioned in the act passed statutes claiming jurisdiction in their respective state legislatures. The Washington State legislature's statute covered only partial jurisdiction, leaving other matters to tribal considerations. The Confederated Bands and Tribes of the Yakima Indian Nation then sued in the U.S. District Court for the Eastern District of Washington to have the state statute struck down, claiming that the statute's provisions providing only partial jurisdiction violated the equal protection and due process clauses of the United States Constitution. The district court found for the state; on appeal, however, the United States Court of Appeals for the Eighth Circuit held that Congress did not intend for partial jurisdiction and struck down the statute. The State of Washington then appealed to the U.S. Supreme Court. After the case was argued on 2 October 1978, a decision was handed down on 16 January 1979. Speaking for the 7–2 decision (Thurgood Marshall and William Brennan dissenting), Justice Potter Stewart held that under sections 6 and 7 of Public Law 280, the state could enact "partial jurisdictional" provisions in its statute. In their dissent, Justices Marshall and Brennan held that the language and legislative history of the Act did not "equivocally" authorize states to enact selective jurisdictional legislation.

See also Public Law 280.

Washington v. Confederated Tribes of the Colville Indian Reservation (447 U.S. 134, 65 L.Ed. 2d 10, 100 S.Ct. 2069 [1980])

Combined with the cases of *State of Washington v. United States et al.* and *Confederated Tribes of the Colville Indian Reservation et al. v. State of Washington*, this Supreme Court action dealt with the issue of the state taxation of cigarettes sold on Indian reservations and

Indian vehicles on those same reservations. The Colville, Makah, and Lummi Indians and, in a separate case, the United States on behalf of the Yakima Indians, sued the state of Washington to enjoin, or stop, the implementation of state taxes on the sale of cigarettes sold at on-reservation outlets, as well as certain state excise taxes exacted on motor vehicle and motor homes, camper and travel trailers that were levied against such vehicles on the reservations. A three-judge district court held against both the cigarette taxes and the motor vehicle taxes.

On direct appeal, the U.S. Supreme Court decided to hear the case. Arguments were held on 9 October 1979; a summary judgment was handed down on 10 June 1980. In a far-reaching decision in which the justices were divided, the court held that (1) the state could enforce the sales tax against the sale of cigarettes to nonmembers of the Indian tribes, (2) the state could force an Indian tribe to affix state tax stamps on the cigarettes sold on Indian reservations so that non-Indians could be properly taxed, and (3) the state could not impose the tax on vehicles belonging to the reservation. Speaking for the majority, Justice Byron White wrote, "It can no longer be seriously argued that the Indian Commerce Clause, of its own force, automatically bars all state taxation of matters significantly touching the political and economic interests of the Tribes....That Clause may have a more limited role to play in preventing undue discrimination against, or burdens on, Indian commerce. But Washington's taxes are applied in a nondiscriminatory manner to all transactions within the State. And although the result of these taxes will be to lessen or eliminate tribal commerce with nonmembers [of the tribe], that market existed in the first place only because of a claimed exemption from these very taxes. The taxes under consideration do not burden commerce that would exist on the reservations without respect to the tax exemption." Justices William Brennan, Thurgood Marshall, Potter Stewart, and William Rehnquist concurred in part and dissented in part.

***See also** California State Board of Equalization et al. v. Chemehuevi Indian Tribe.*

Washington v. Washington State Commercial Passenger Fishing Vessel Association (443 U.S. 658, 61 L.Ed. 2d 823, 99 S.Ct. 3055 [1979])

Combined with the cases of *State of Washington et al. v. United States* and *Puget Sound Gillnetters Association et al. v. United States Distirict Court for the Western District of Washington (United States et al., Real Parties in Interest)*, this Supreme Court case dealt with whether treaties allowed Indian tribes to harvest fish that are to be protected by the state because of scarcity. In 1970, the United States sued in the U.S. District Court for the Western District of Washington, seeking to protect seven tribes' share of the anadromous fish run in the Columbia River. Anadromous fish are, according to one source, "fish that are born in fresh water, spend all their lives in salt water, then return to fresh water to spawn." By treaties that the tribes signed with Isaac Stevens, the first Governor of Washington Territory, in 1854 and 1855, the tribes ceded lands to the state in exchange for "the right of taking fish at usual and accustomed grounds and stations...in common with all citizens of the Territory." The district court, hearing the case, held that the Indians were entitled to from 45 to 50 percent of the anadromous fish run. The U.S. Court of Appeals for the Ninth Circuit affirmed and the U.S. Supreme Court denied certiorari. On remand, the Fisheries Department of Washington State enacted new regulations to fit the district court's ruling, but a private fishing group, the Washington State Commercial Passenger Fishing Vessel Association, sued to have the regulations declared null and void. The Supreme Court of the State of Washington held for the private group, opining that the treaties did not guarantee the Indian tribes a share of the fish run. A federal district court, hearing the case, then held that it would supervise the fish runs with the aid of the U.S. Attorney for the district, and the Court of Appeals for the Ninth Circuit affirmed. Asked to decide the issues in this case, the U.S. Supreme Court granted certiorari. The case was argued 28 February 1979, and Justice John Paul Stevens delivered the court's opinion on 2 July 1979 (Justices Lewis F. Powell, Potter Stewart, and William H. Rehnquist dissenting) striking down the opinions of the federal court, the court of appeals, and the Washington State Supreme Court and upholding the right of the Indians, under treaty, to a share of the fish run. Justice Stevens explained, "Whether [the Department of] Games and Fisheries may be ordered actually to promulgate regulations having effect as a matter of state law may well be doubtful. But the District Court may rescind that problem by assuming direct supervision of the fisheries if state recalcitrance or state-law barriers should be continued."

Water Rights Adjudication Cases (McCarran Amendment Cases)

***See** Colorado River Water Conservation District v. United States*; *Montana et al. v. Northern Cheyenne Tribe of the Northern Cheyenne Indian Reservation et al.*

Watkins, Arthur Vivian (1886–1973)

Labeled by historian Nancy Oestreich Lurie as "the main architect of termination," Arthur V. Watkins was a noted U.S. senator from Utah. He was born in Midway, Utah, on 18 December 1886, the son of Arthur Watkins, a rancher and entrepreneur, and Emily Adelia (née Gerber) Watkins; Arthur Watkins' father, John Edward Watkins, was an emigrant from England sometime in the nineteenth century. Arthur Watkins, the subject of this biography, attended local schools before entering Brigham Young University to study political science and Columbia University in New York, the latter institution awarding him a law degree in 1912. He was admitted to the Utah bar that year and opened a practice first in Salt Lake City, then in Provo. He was involved in local civic affairs, such as organizing the Provo River Reclamation Project in 1934. He was assistant county attorney (1914–16), and judge (1928–33) of Utah's Fourth Judicial District. In 1946, two years after serving on the Republican National Committee platform committee, he ran and won a seat as the junior U.S. senator from Utah. He ultimately served two terms. He was highly supportive of the policies of President Dwight D. Eisenhower, but he did serve as chairman of the committee which studied charges of censure against fellow Republican senator Joseph R. McCarthy of Wisconsin. He was a strong critic of NATO and voted in favor of antisegregation measures to be included in federal housing legislation. However, he is most remembered for his stand on Indians. In an article that expressed his feelings on the termination policy, Watkins wrote in the *Annals of the American Academy of Political and Social Science* in May 1957.

> Virtually since the end of the decade of our national life the Indian, as tribesman and individual, was accorded a status apart. Now, however, we think constructively and affirmatively of the Indian as a fellow American. We seek to assure that in health, education, and welfare, in social, political, economic, and cultural opportunity, he or she stands as one with us in the enjoyment and responsibilities of our national citizenship. It is particularly gratifying to know that recent years of united effort, mutual planning, and Indian self-appraisal truly have begun to bear increasing fruit...One facet of this over-all development concerns the freeing of the Indians from special federal restrictions on the property and the persons of the tribes and their members. This is not a novel development, but a natural outgrowth of our relationship with the Indians. Congress is fully agreed upon its accomplishment. By [a] unanimous vote in both the Senate and the House of Representatives, termination of such special federal supervision has been called for as soon as possible. Of course, as with any such major social concern, methods vary in proposed solutions and emotions sometimes

rise as to how the final goal should be reached. A clear understanding of principles and events is necessary...After all, the matter of freeing the Indian from wardship status is not rightfully a subject to debate in academic fashion, with facts marshalled here and there to be maneuvered and countermaneuvered in a vast battle of words and ideas. Much more I see this as an ideal or universal truth, to which all men subscribe, and concerning which they differ only in their opinion as to how the ideal may be obtained and in what degree and during what period of time.

Watkins left the Senate in 1959. He died in Utah on 1 September 1973 at the age of 86.

See also Termination Policy.

References Lurie, Nancy Oestreich, "Menominee Termination." *Indian Historian* 4 (4); Watkins, Arthur V., "Termination of Federal Supervision: Removal of Restrictions over Indian Property and Persons." *Annals of the American Academy of Political and Social Sciences* 311 (5); "Watkins, Arthur Vivian." In Anne Rothe, ed., *Current Biography 1950* (1950); "Watkins, Arthur Vivian." *National Cyclopedia of American Biography* (1898–1977).

Westmoreland v. United States (155 U.S. 645 [1895])

Was a white man, married to an Indian and considered by that nation to be a citizen, to be determined as an Indian before the law? That was the issue in this case, decided by the U.S. Supreme Court in 1895. Thomas Westmoreland, a white man, was convicted in the Circuit Court for the Eastern District of Texas and sentenced to be hanged for the poisoning murder of Robert Green, another white man. Westmoreland, however, was married to an Indian; under article 28 of the Treaty with the Choctaws and Chickasaws of 28 April 1866 (14 Stat. 779), "every white person who, having married a Choctaw or Chickasaw, resides in the Choctaw or Chickasaw Nation, or who has been adopted by [tribal] legislative authorities, is to be deemed a member of said nation, and shall be subject to the laws of the Choctaw and Chickasaw Nations." Upon conviction, Westmoreland appealed directly to the Supreme Court. On 7 January 1895, Justice David Josiah Brewer held for a unanimous court that Westmoreland could not be considered an Indian under the law and the conviction must stand. Brewer explained in the short opinion that because Westmoreland was not a citizen of the Indian Territory (he lived off the reservation), the fact that he had married an Indian was negated.

Whipple, Henry Benjamin (1822–1901)

He was known as "Straight Tongue" by the Indians who knew him for the honest way in which he dealt with them. He wrote in his autobiography, *Lights and Shadows of a Long Episcopate*, "The world and the church have forced me to be the friend of this poor race, which has cost me more anxiety and has brought me more trials than all my other work. But I do not regret it." Born in Adams, New York, on 15 February 1822, Henry Benjamin Whipple was the son and eldest of seven children of John Hall Whipple, a merchant, and Elizabeth (née Wager) Whipple, a relative by marriage of Daniel Webster. After attending Presbyterian mission schools in New York, according to biographer Phillips Endicott Osgood, he studied at Oberlin College in Ohio, from 1838–39, but was compelled to withdraw from the school on account of ill health. However, the *Minneapolis Journal*, in its obituary of the famed minister, reported that he received "a D.D. degree from Hobart and Racine Colleges, and degrees of D.D. and LL.D. from the English universities of Oxford, Cambridge and Durham." After returning home, he worked for his father for a time, then became immersed in local Democratic politics and served for a time as a major in the New York State militia.

In 1843, on a doctor's orders to improve his health, Whipple traveled to Florida, where he saw the mistreatment of the Indian by the American forces fighting the Seminole War. It was at this point that he turned his life's mission to one of helping the red man. Although he spent the years 1857 to 1859 among the poor in Chicago, he then traveled to Minnesota where, as first bishop of Minnesota, he established his home at Faribault, the center of Indian missionary work in that state. Biographer Lois F. Fenichell writes, "While travelling among the Ojibwa and Dakota people of his diocese, Whipple had ample opportunity to observe the operations of the Bureau of Indian Affairs, a complicated network of political appointees and licensed traders who channeled federal appropriations for Indian welfare into the hands of local politicians and businessmen. Appalled by the degrading effects of this system, in 1860 he began a series of appeals to Washington officials for thorough reform modeled on the Canadian system: the government must drop the pretense of tribal sovereignty and frankly acknowledge the Indians as wards; the Indians must be granted individual land allotments; and they must be helped by honest agents and teachers to become civilized—that is, Christian—farmers (the ethnic and religious traditions of native American peoples were felt by many white missionaries and reformers, Whipple included, to be hindrances to their assimilation)." On 6 March 1862, he wrote a carefully drafted letter to President Lincoln, warning him that failings in the administration of Indian Affairs and cruelty toward the Indians were driving them to strike back at whites with reckless unrestraint. The letter, apparently, was never answered.

On 17 August of that year, Whipple's foreshadowed revelation came true, when, in what historian called "an outburst of blind fury...a spontaneous, passionate act of vengeance against the United States" and its citizens, a terror developed. Convinced that the white man had stolen their land and dignity, four warriors attacked a farm and killed five white settlers. Inspired by the attack, the rest of the Sioux arose to slaughter an unknown number of people (some estimate the total to be in the thousands). Col. (later General) Henry H. Sibley was dispatched to quell the riot, and those Indians not slain were put on trial for the murders. After the massacre, Whipple wrote an important article entitled, "The Duty of the Citizens Concerning the Indian Massacre," in which he explained that killing the Indians would extend the life of the Indian-white conflict, and not abate it. "No wonder that deep indignation has been aroused and that our people cry vengeance. But if that vengeance is to be something better than a savage thirst for blood, we must examine the causes which have brought this bloodshed, that our condemnation may fall upon the guilty. No outburst of passion, no temporary expediency, no deed of revenge, can excuse us from the duties which such days of sorrow have thrust upon us." When more than 300 Indians were sentenced to death, it was Whipple who begged Lincoln to spare most of their lives. Eventually, while 38 were executed in the largest mass hanging in American history, Whipple's intervention had saved more than 250 lives. In 1864, Secretary of War Edwin M. Stanton, angered at Whipple's continued persistence at reforming the Indian Bureau, wrote to General Henry Halleck, "What does Bishop Whipple want? If he has come here to tell us of the corruption of our Indian system, tell him that we know it. But the Government never reforms an evil until the people demand it. Tell him that when he reaches the heart of the American people, the Indians will be saved."

Whipple pushed for reform of the Indian system for much of the late nineteenth century but not until President Ulysses S. Grant's "Peace Policy" was instituted did much of Whipple's program come to fruition. Biographer Grace Lee Nute relates, "For the next two decades he fought valiantly for his 'red children,' exposing fraud, building up mission work in the new Chippewa home in Minnesota [on] the White Earth Reservation, and making appeals for them by addresses in America and abroad." In the first edition of the *Council Fire*, which was founded by Indian reformer Alfred B. Meacham and later became the official journal of the National Indian Defense Association, a speech delivered by Whipple in November 1877 in New York before the

Fourth Church Congress was reprinted. In that discourse, Whipple said,

> The North American Indian is the noblest type of a wild man on the earth. He recognizes a Great Spirit. He believes in a future life. He is devoted to his children. He will die for his people. The cry of extermination against such a people is a disgrace to humanity, and an insult to Almighty God. No Christian missions have brought richer rewards. When our Church began this work all was dark as midnight. The Indians were degraded and desperate. Everything which the cupidity of bad white men or the malice of the devil could do, was done to hinder the work. The influence of the Government agents was often against us. For a time the Church stood aloof. Yet to-day we have half a score of Indian clergy, who, far away on the Missouri and in the forests of Minnesota, are preaching the Gospel to their own people. We number our communicants by [the] hundreds, and many whom we met as painted savages are waiting for us in Paradise, and will join in that song which no man can learn but they who were redeemed from among men.

In 1887, Whipple was asked to write the preface for Helen Hunt Jackson's *A Century of Dishonor: A Sketch of the United States Government's Dealings with Some of the Indian Tribes.* In it, he inscribed, "I have been requested to write a preface to this sad story of 'A Century of Dishonor.' I cannot refuse the request of one whose woman's heart has pleaded so eloquently for the poor Red men. The materials for her book have been taken from official documents. The sad revelation of broken faith, of violated treaties, and of inhuman deeds of violence will bring a flush of shame to the cheeks of those who love their country. They will wonder how our rulers have dared to so trifle with justice, and provoke the anger of God. Many of the stories will be new to the reader. The Indian owns no telegraph, employs no press reporter, and his side of the story is unknown to the people."

Whipple spent his last years in Minnesota with his second wife, Evangeline Simpson Whipple, whom he married in 1896 (his first wife Cornelia Wright Whipple had died in 1890), and four of his six children who survived him. He died at his home in Faribault, Minnesota, on 16 September 1901, just days after President William McKinley was assassinated.

See also Jackson, Helen Maria Fiske Hunt; Manypenny Commission.

References "Bishop Whipple on Indians." *Council Fire* 1 (1); "Bishop Whipple Passes Away; The Venerable Prelate, Full of Good Works, Died at 6 O'Clock This Morning." *Minneapolis Journal*, 16 September 1901, 1–2; Nute, Grace Lee, Lois F. Fenichell, and Phillips Endicott Osgood, *Straight Tongue: A Story of Henry Benjamin Whipple, First Episcopal Bishop of Minnesota* (1958); Stanton to Halleck, quoted in Schmeckebier, Laurence F., *The Office of Indian Affairs: Its History, Activities and Organization* (1927); "Whipple, Henry Benjamin." In Alden Whitman, ed., *American Reformers: An H. W. Wilson Biographical Dictionary* (1985); "Whipple, Henry Benjamin." In Dumas Malone et al., eds., *Dictionary of American Biography* (1930–88); Whipple, Henry Benjamin, *Lights and Shadows of a Long Episcopate, Being Reminiscences and Recollections of the Right Reverend Henry Benjamin Whipple, D.D., LL.D, Bishop of Minnesota* (1899); Whipple, Henry Benjamin, "Preface." In Helen Hunt Jackson, *A Century of Dishonor: A Sketch of the United States Government's Dealings with Some of the Indian Tribes* (1887).

White Mountain Apache Tribe et al. v. Bracker et al. (448 U.S. 136, 65 L.Ed. 2d 665 [1980])

Where the federal government has a vested interest in establishing a regulatory scheme to encourage commerce on Indian reservations, state governments are prohibited from levying taxes on any part of those operations—so held the Supreme Court in this case, decided in 1980, and upholding a long-held precedent that states cannot tax such transactions. In 1964, the White Mountain Apache Tribe, whose members reside on their reservation located in a mountainous and forested area of northeastern Arizona, formed the Fort Apache Timber Company (FATCO), with the approval of the secretary of the interior, to harvest and sell timber located on the reservation. In 1968 the tribe contracted with six logging companies, including the Pinetop Logging Company, to carry out operations that FATCO could not; these included hauling the logs from the area where they were cut down to the tribe's sawmill, all activities carried out within the parameters of the reservation. In 1971, respondents Robert M. Bracker, head of the Arizona Highway Commission, and the heads of other state agencies, levied the state's motor carrier license tax and its use fuel tax, on Pinetop. The company paid the taxes under protest and then filed suit in state court to recover the taxes as being illegal under federal law. The company was backed by FATCO, the head forester of the Bureau of Indian Affairs, and the chairman of the White Mountain Apache Tribal Council. The state court held for the state officials, and, on appeal, the Arizona Court of Appeals upheld the judgment and the state Supreme Court refused to review the finding, leaving the Supreme Court to decide the issue.

Arguments were heard on 14 January 1980, and a decision was handed down on 27 June of that same year. Justice Thurgood Marshall held for 6–3 court (Justices John Paul Stevens, Potter Stewart, and William H. Rehnquist dissenting) in reversing the lower court's decision and holding for the White Mountain Apaches and Pinetop. The decision, which was based on the court's earlier precedent in *Warren Trading Post Co. v. Arizona Tax Commission* (1965), held that federal operations schemes which were approved by the secretary of the interior on Indian reservations were beyond the scope of state taxes. Justice Marshall explained,

> Respondents' argument is reduced to a claim that they may assess taxes on non-Indians engaged in commerce on the reservation whenever there is no express congressional statement to the contrary. That is simply not the law. In a number of cases we have held that state authority over non-Indians acting on tribal reservations is pre-empted even though Congress has offered no explicit statement on the subject… The Court has repeatedly emphasized that there is a significant geographical component to tribal sovereignty, a component which remains highly relevant to the preemption inquiry; though the reservation boundary is not absolute, it remains an important factor to weigh in determining whether state authority has exceeded the permissible limits…Moreover, it is undisputed that the economic burden of the asserted taxes will ultimately fall on the Tribe. Where, as here, the Federal Government has undertaken comprehensive regulation of the harvesting and sale of tribal timber, where a number of the policies underlying the federal regulatory scheme are threatened by the taxes respondents seek to impose, and where respondents are unable to justify the taxes except in terms of a generalized interest in raising revenue, we believe that the proposed exercise of state authority is impermissible.

Wilbur v. United States ex rel. Kadrie et al. (281 U.S. 206 [1930])

An officer of the executive branch could revoke the ruling of a predecessor as it relates to persons entitled to annuities as Chippewa Indians, the Supreme Court held in this 1930 case. The act of Congress of 14 January 1889 (25 Stat. 642) established the Chippewa Nation of Minnesota from a state of "dependent wardship to full individual emancipation with its incident rights and responsibilities," with annuities from the sale of lands to the government to be held in trust for the members of the tribe. Before such annuities could be paid, rolls of Indians needed to be fixed. In 1919, Secretary of the Interior Franklin K. Lane held that the children of half-breed Chippewa mothers and white fathers, born after the mother separated from the tribe, could still share in the tribal annuities. The nine minor children of Sarah and Mall Kadrie, who themselves had lived in white communities before the birth of their children, fell under this decision. However, in 1927, Secretary of the Interior Ray Lyman Wilbur reversed Lane's decision, declaring that the children of such a relationship could not share in the annuities. The United States, representing the rights of the Kadrie children, sued Wilbur in the Supreme Court of the District of Columbia for a writ of mandamus to force Wilbur to revoke his decision. Although that court sided with Wilbur, the Court of Appeals for the District of Columbia reversed, and the Supreme Court agreed to hear the case. Arguments were heard on 10 and 13 January 1930. Justice Willis Van Devanter held for a unanimous court on 14 April of that same year in striking down the appeals court ruling and holding for Wilbur. Justice Van Devanter concluded that the decision in 1927 was not controlled by the courts, but by "the character of judgment or discretion [of the particular Secretary] which cannot be controlled by mandamus."

Williams et al. v. Johnson (239 U.S. 414 [1915])

Congress could, in the exercise of its plenary power over Indian Affairs, authorize the secretary of the interior to remove the restrictions on the alienation on Indian allotments if the local Indian agent felt that such removal was to the benefit of the Indians—so held the U.S. Supreme Court in this case. Under the act of Congress of 21 April 1904 (33 Stat. 204), the secretary of the interior was empowered to remove such restrictions, and under that act one Selin Taylor, a member of the Choctaw Nation, was awarded a certificate for his allotment. He then sold the certificate to a number of people before Ben F. Johnson became its final owner. Eli Williams, Elmer Williams, and Charles H. Williams, heirs of Taylor, then sued Johnson to quiet, or dismiss, his title to the land because, as they contended, the restrictions should not have been removed, as per the act of Congress of 1 July 1902 (32 Stat. 641), on a full-blood Indian. The District Court of Grady County, Oklahoma, held for Johnson, and the Oklahoma State Supreme Court affirmed. The Williamses then appealed to the U.S. Supreme Court. The case was submitted on 6 December 1915, and it was Justice Joseph McKenna who held for a unanimous court just two weeks later on 20 December that because Congress had the power to instruct the secretary of the interior to use his judgment to remove or retain restrictions on alienation, the title could not be quieted. Justice McKenna explained, "It has often been decided that the Indians are wards of the nation, and that Congress has plenary control over tribal relations and property, and that this power continues after the Indians are made citizens, and may be exercised as to restrictions upon alienation."

Williams v. Lee (358 U.S. 217 [1959])

State courts, in this case Arizona courts, cannot exercise jurisdiction over a civil suit between a non-Indian and an Indian when the cause of action occurs on an Indian reservation—so held the U.S. Supreme Court in this 1959 case. Respondent Hugh Lee, a non-Indian, owned the Ganado Trading Post on the Navajo Indian Reservation in Arizona under a license required by federal, and not state, statute. Petitioners Paul and Lorena Williams, husband and wife, were members of the Navajo Nation, and purchased goods from Lee on credit. When they refused to pay for the merchandise, Lee sued them in the Superior Court of Arizona. The Williamses asked for a dismissal of the charges, claiming that the action could only be settled by a tribal court. The Superior Court refused to dismiss, and, on appeal, the Arizona State Supreme Court affirmed, finding that no federal law existed prohibiting civil suits between Indians and non-Indians to be settled in state courts. Because, as Justice Hugo Black wrote, "this was a doubtful determination of the important question of state power over Indian Affairs, we granted certiorari." Arguments in the case were heard before the court on 20 November 1958, and it was Justice Black who delivered the unanimous opinion of the court on 12 January 1959. In reversing the Arizona Supreme Court's decision, the justices were declaring that it is a fundamental power of Indian nations, granted to them by Congress, to settle civil suits involving members of their respective nation, and not of state courts. Justice Black opined,

> Today the Navajo Courts of Indian Offenses exercise broad criminal and civil jurisdiction which covers suits by outsiders against Indian defendants. No Federal Act has given state courts jurisdiction over such controversies. In a general statute Congress did express its willingness to have any State assume jurisdiction over reservation Indians if the State Legislature or the people vote affirmatively to accept such responsibility. To date, Arizona has not accepted jurisdiction, possibly because the people of the State anticipate that the burdens accompanying such power might be considerable... There can be no doubt that to allow the exercise of state jurisdiction here would undermine the authority of the tribal courts over Reservation affairs and hence would infringe on the right of the Indians to govern themselves. It is immaterial that respondent is not an Indian. He was on the Reservation and the transaction with an Indian took place there....The cases in this Court have consistently guarded the authority of Indian governments over their reservations. Congress recognized this authority in the Navajos in the Treaty of 1868, and has done so ever since. If this power is to be taken away from them, it is for Congress to do it. Reversed.

Winnemucca, Sarah (Paiute) (c. 1844–1891)

Her Indian name was *Thocmetony* ("Shell Flower") or *Sonometa* ("White Shell"), but she is better known as Sarah Winnemucca, or Sarah Hopkins, her married name; she was, however, one of the earliest Native American woman writers to capture the flavor and characteristics of her Paiute culture. She was born about 1844 among the Paiute people (then spelled Piute) at Humboldt Sink in what is now Nevada. Her father, Winnemucca II, was chief of the tribe, and was the son of the man who John Charles Fremont named "Captain Truckee," a wise and knowing Paiute chieftain. Although she lived for a portion of her childhood in the San Joaquin Valley area of California, she returned to Nevada, where she moved into the home of a white family and was named Sarah Winnemucca. She had attended a convent school in California, and that seems to have been her only education. Starting in 1868, she served as an interpreter between her people on the Paiute reservation and the whites that surrounded it. In 1876, she taught at the Indian school on the Malheur Reservation in Oregon. She also served as the guide and interpreter to General Oliver Otis Howard during the Bannock War in Oregon during 1878. When the Paiutes were forcibly removed to the Yakima Indian reservation in what is now Washington State in 1879, she and her father traveled to Washington, D.C., to reverse the decision, but to no avail. She then began lecturing in San Francisco about the wrongs perpetrated against her people, and she became a leading spokesman of those who saw the government's policy towards the Indians as cruel and unjust.

A San Francisco reporter wrote of one of her lectures,

> San Francisco was treated to the most novel entertainment it has ever known, last evening, in the shape of an address by Sarah, daughter of Chief Winnecmucca....The Princess wore a short buckskin dress, the skirt bordered with fringe and embroidery....On her head she wore a proud head dress of eagle's feathers....The lecture was unlike anything ever before heard in the civilized world—eloquent, pathetic, tragical at times; at others her quaint anecdotes, sarcasms and wonderful mimicry surprised the audience again and again into bursts of laughter and rounds of applause. There was no set lecture from [a] written manuscript, but a spontaneous flow of eloquence. Nature's child spoke in natural, unconstrained language, accompanied by gestures that were scarcely ever surpassed by any actress on the stage...[T]he Indian girl walked upon the stage in an easy, unembarrassed manner, and entered at once upon the story of her race.

And although she met in 1880 with President Rutherford B. Hayes and Interior Secretary Carl Schurz (the latter who promised to help return her people to their reservation), nothing was done.

In 1881, she married Lieutenant L. H. Hopkins, a white army officer who sympathized with her plight. She conducted a rather extensive lecture tour of the East, and she was sponsored by women's suffrage advocates Elizabeth Peabody and Mary Tyler Peabody Mann. In 1883, as a result of the lectures on behalf of her people, she published *Life Among the Piutes: Their Wrongs and Claims*, which was edited for her by Mary Tyler Mann. Historian A. LaVonne Brown Ruoff, in commenting on Winnemucca's landmark work, observes

> *Life Among the Piutes* is among the most imaginative personal and tribal histories of the nineteenth century. Winnemucca uses the narrative technique of mixing personal experience and tribal ethnography and the authenticating device of including letters from well-known whites to document her moral character and achievements, both methods used by earlier Indian autobiographers. But whereas these writers made conversion to Christianity and the spiritual journey central to their narratives, Winnemucca never alludes to these. Her central theme is Indian-white relations, a secondary theme in the narratives of earlier writers.

Sarah Winnemucca lived only eight years after the publication of her famed work, and in that time she fought continuously to get the Paiute lands back for her people. General Howard, in his 1908 work *Famous Indian Chiefs I Have Known*, called her "sweet and handsome" and described her as "very quick and able." She died of consumption (tuberculosis) on her sister's ranch near Monida, Montana, on 16 October 1891 at the age of 50. She was known as "The Princess," but the Paiute people called her "Mother."

References Gehm, Katherine, *Sarah Winnemucca: Most Extraordinary Woman of the Paiute Nation* (1975); Ghent, W. J., "Winnemucca, Sarah." In Dumas Malone et al., eds., *Dictionary of American Biography* (1930–88); Morrison, Dorothy Nafus, *Chief Sarah: Sarah Winnemucca's Fight for Indian Rights* (1980); "Preliterate Traditions at Work." In David H. Brumble III, *American Indian Autobiography* (1988); Ruoff, A. LaVonne Brown, "Western American Writers, 1854–1960." In J. Golden Taylor, ed., *A Literary History of the American West* (1987); Sands, Kathleen M., "Hopkins, Sarah Winnemucca." In Gretchen M. Bataille, ed., *Native American Women: A Biographical Dictionary* (1993); Wilkins, Thurman, "Winnemucca, Sarah." In Edward T. James, ed., *Notable American Women, 1607–1950: A Biographical Dictionary* (1971).

Winters et al. v. United States (207 U.S. 564 [1908])

Decided by the Supreme Court on 6 January 1908, *Winters* involved the issue of whether water could be diverted from white settlements to irrigate Indian reservations. In 1900, plaintiffs Henry Winters, John W. Acker, Agnes Downs, and others, entered the area of the Milk River in Montana near the Fort Belknap Indian Reservation and attempted to build a dam to divert the navigable waters of the river, used to irrigate Indian lands on the reservation, for their own personal use. The United States government sued to stop construction of the dam on the grounds that although the act of Congress of 15 April 1874 granted the Indians of Montana reservations to be apart from the state of Montana (the Fort Belknap reservation was established in 1888), the reservations were for "the bare right of the use and occupation thereof at the will of and sufferance of the government of the United States." Winters sued in a Montana district court, but the court upheld the government's action enjoining construction of the dam. The Ninth Circuit Court of Appeals affirmed the lower court ruling, and Winters sued to the U.S. Supreme Court.

The Court ruled 8–1 (Justice David Josiah Brewer dissenting) that the Indians had no rights to land or waters outside of their reservations. Justice Joseph McKenna wrote the court's opinion, in which he stated that "the power of the government to reserve the waters and exempt them from appropriation under the state laws is not denied, and could not be." Professor Daniel McCool wrote in 1987 about the decision, "The Winters Doctrine of federal reserved water rights is one of the most important and controversial concepts in western water law. The landmark case of *Winters v. United States* established for the first time an explicit recognition of Indian (and hence federal) reserved water rights. Prior to *Winters*, these rights were implied, but never specifically recognized by either statute or case law. *Winters* and a series of subsequent cases have firmly established the legal principle of reserved Indian water rights as an implicit outgrowth of the federal policy of reserving lands for Indian tribes." These cases include *United States v. Powers, Federal Power Commission v. Oregon et al., United States v. District Court in and for Eagle County, U.S. District Court in and for Water Division No. 5, Cappaert v. United States, Colorado River Water Conservation District v. United States, United States v. New Mexico, Arizona v. California, Nevada et al. v. United States, Arizona et al. v. San Carlos Apache Tribe of Arizona, and Montana et al. v. Northern Cheyenne Tribe of the Northern Cheyenne Indian Reservation.*

See also *Colorado River Water Conservation District v. United States*; *Montana et al. Northern Cheyenne Tribe of the Northern Cheyenne Indian Reservation et al.*; *Nevada et al. v. United States et al.*

References Florio, Roger, "Water Rights: Enforcing the Federal-Indian Trust after *Nevada v. United States*." *American Indian Law Review*, 13 (1); McCool, Daniel, "Precedent for the Winters Doctrine: Seven Legal Principles." *Journal of the Southwest*, 29 (2).

Wise Statement (1925)

On 15 December 1925, Senator William C. Bruce of Maryland took to the floor of the U.S. Senate to introduce the statement of Jennings C. Wise, counsel for the Indian Board of Cooperation of California, entitled "A Plea for the Indian Citizens of the United States." The following is excerpted from Wise's report:

As counsel for the Indian Board of Cooperation of California, a philanthropic association for the special purposes of ameliorating the lot of the 18 tribes of California Indians; as counsel for the Yankton tribe of Sioux Indians, of South Dakota; and as associate counsel for the Six Nations of New York, I have the honor to present to you certain facts relating to the Indian citizens of the United States generally, and to request that I be afforded an opportunity to appear before your honorable committees and make to them the plea herein presented.

In 1823 the Supreme Court of the United States, speaking through Chief Justice Marshall, defined the political status of the tribal Indians. The tribes were then declared to be dependent communities and the tribal Indians the wards of the United States. (*Johnson v. McIntosh*, 8 Wheat. 543; *Cherokee Nation v. State of Georgia*, 5 Pet. 48; *Worcester v. State of Georgia*, 6 Pet. 515; *United States v. Kagama*, 118 U.S. 375; *Choctaw Nations v. United States*, 119 U.S. 1). Over the tribal relations of the Indians Congress has ever been held to possess plenary authority. (*Lone Wolf v. Hitchcock*, 187 U.S. 553, 565; The Question of Aborigines, Snow).

By the act of Congress approved June 2, 1924 [Indian Citizenship Act of 1924], however, every noncitizen Indian born within the territorial limits of the United States was declared to be a citizen of the United States. Thus, 148 years after the United States had assumed political jurisdiction over the Indians, they were elevated from the status of a dependent political wardship to that of full citizenship, and as citizens, with all the constitutional rights of such, assumed a definite place in the body politic of the Nation.

The effect of the transformation which they have undergone has not been fully recognized. Whatever the status of the United States with respect to the property of the political wards of the nation may have been prior to June 2, 1924, the enfranchising act of that date, it is submitted, definitely fixed its status as the trustee at law of so much of the property of the

Indians as remained in its hands. In the law of nations and the municipal law of the United States there is no sanction for any other relation between a sovereign state and its citizens of whose property it retains control.

The report of the commissioner of Indian Affairs for 1924 shows that there are still about 150,000 full-blooded tribal Indians who, with other legal Indians, hold in common tribal lands that have not yet been allotted in severalty. Under the existing law the unallotted tribal lands of these Indians necessarily remain under the control of the United States, and, though the tribal Indians, like all others, are citizens, it is clear that until they are prepared and elect to take their lands in severalty the Government is morally bound to continue in the relation of political guardian while discharging the trust with respect to their property imposed by the act of June 2, 1924.

Political history fails to disclose another instance of such a relation. It is a unique relation, even more peculiar than that existing with respect to the tribes between 1776 and 1924, and one that requires to be very carefully considered by Congress. Plainly, many of the laws and practices designed to meet the case of political dependents are no longer suited to the needs of citizens and are inconsistent with the legal relation existing between citizens and a sovereign trustee.

Reference Statement of Jennings C. Wise in *Congressional Record: Proceedings and Debates of the First Session of the Sixty-Ninth Congress, also the Special Session of the Senate of the United States of America* (1926).

Women's National Indian Association

The Women's National Indian Association (WNIA) was one of the largest Indian rights organizations to exist during the nineteenth century, and except for a few distant articles and a study by Helen Wanken, the WNIA remains virtually unknown in it work for Indian reform. The WNIA was essentially the creation of Mary Lucinda Bonney, an education reformist who started the Chestnut Street Female Seminary in Philadelphia and who desired to assist American Indians during her long life. Initially she was a founder and member of the Woman's Union Missionary Society of America for Heathen Lands, which sent female missionaries to the Orient, but in 1879, with the aid of Amelia Stone Quinton, a fellow reformer who aided debtors to avoid prison, she founded the group called the Committee of Ways and Means, which drafted a petition asking President Rutherford B. Hayes "to prevent the encroachment of white settlers upon Indian Territory, and to guard the Indians in the enjoyment of all the rights which have been guaranteed to them on the faith of the nation." After they delivered it, they saw that such reformers as Reverend Henry Benjamin Whipple and Thomas H. Tibbles were continuing in their work, and so they did as well. Reforming the group of "concerned Christian women," it was renamed the Central Indian Committee, the Indian Treaty-Keeping and Protective Association, and the National Indian Association. By 1883, it was finally called the Women's National Indian Association, and Bonney and Quinton served as president and vice president. The mission of the organization was: "1st. To aid by every means for securing all laws needed by the Indians of the United States. 2d. To send and support suitable missionaries and instructors to reside among Indians, to labor for their help industrially, politically, educationally, morally and religiously." A second petition was delivered to U.S. Senator Henry L. Dawes on 21 February 1882 and calling for citizenship for Indians and the allotment of their land in severalty, reads:

Again the women of a national Indian association beg leave to present to your honorable body the petition they have circulated and received again from the people of the United States. Their roll represents at a low estimate considerably more than a hundred thousand citizens—instead of thirteen thousand as did their first, three years ago—and is an earnest plea for a righteous, speedy, and permanent settlement of the Indian question.

Among the petitioners are many hundreds of churches which have adopted the petition by a unanimous rising vote, this often having been taken at a regular Sabbath service; various popular meetings have also here presented their plea similarly expressed; while the roll contains names of members of legislative bodies, of governors, judges, and lawyers; names of bishops and many hundreds of the clergy—among the latter the entire ministry of three denominations in the city of Philadelphia, numbering nearly three hundred; names of the professors and students of theological seminaries like those at Hartford, Cambridge, Rochester, and Upland; colleges and universities like Yale, Harvard, Brown, Cornell, Rochester, Washington, and Lee; names of editors of leading periodicals; the boards of hundreds of missionary and other benevolent societies, not a few of these being national ones, with names of art, literary, and social clubs. Besides all of these the roll contains the signatures of hundreds of business and manufacturing firms who control capital to the amount of many millions of dollars, and who employ many thousands of operatives—all showing that not only has there been a rapid growth of settlement among the religious and intellectual leaders of the community demanding legislation which shall end oppression of Indians and secure to them the full opportunity for industrial, mental, and religious development, but that the commercial interests of our land also are fast coming to demand a just and speedy settlement of the Indian question.

Permit an expression from the association presenting to-day to your honorable body their third annual petition—an association having sixteen State committees and one in each of the larger cities, with helpers in every State, all these committees being composed of patriotic Christian women—permit these to say that into their ears and hearts comes the cry of suffering, undefended, ever-endangered Indian women and children, and that this cry is our appeal to you to secure for them legal protection; that the plea of Indian women for the sacred shield of law is the plea of the sisters, wives, and mothers of this nation for them, the plea of all womanhood, indeed, on their behalf to you as legislators and as men. Permit us also to say that in laboring by every means in our power to fill our land with a knowledge of the present condition of the Indians, and of our national obligations to them, we most deeply feel that while justice demands the recognition of Indian personality before the law, thus most surely and simply, it seems to us, securing to Indians protection and fostering care, we yet feel that legislation securing this recognition will be an honor to the present Congress and to our beloved country. For this legislation we most earnestly and respectfully pray.

Through petitions to Congress and the conveyance of missionaries to the Indians to aid them in education, the WNIA (in 1901 the *Women's* was dropped from the title, allowing men to join the group), whose power began to wane in the Progressive era, fought against Victorian stereotypes and the image of women fighting for causes with zealousness and enthusiasm. The organization's official journal, the *Indian's Friend*, was published until 1951, when the last remnants of the organization, merely a few auxiliaries in distant states, met and dissolved the group.

See also Rambaut, Mary Lucinda Bonney; Quinton, Amelia Stone.

References "Proceedings on the Occasion of the Presentation of the Petition of the Women's National Indian Association, by Hon. H. L. Dawes, of Massachusetts, in the Senate of the United States, February 21, 1882" (1882); Wanken, Helen M., *'Women's Sphere' and Indian Reform: The Women's National Indian Association, 1879–1901* (Ph.D. dissertation, Marquette University, 1981); "Work of the Women's National Indian Association." *Indian's Friend* 5 (5).

Worcester, Samuel Austin (1798–1859)

He was the litigant in one of the most important Supreme Court cases in the history of the United States: *Worcester v. Georgia*, in which the court ruled that Indian reservations were "nations" subject only to the laws of the United States and not the states. Yet little is known of this missionary, a man who gave most of his life to the Cherokee Indians he loved so much. Born at Worcester, Massachusetts, on 19 January 1798, the son of Reverend Leonard Worcester and Elizabeth (née Hopkins) Worcester, he was a member of one of this nation's earliest and greatest families. Samuel Austin Worcester was descended from William Worcester, who emigrated from England to the Massachusetts Bay Colony before 1640 and whose descendants included Reverend Noah Worcester (1758–1837), known as "The Friend of Peace"; Reverend Samuel Worcester (1770–1821); Joseph Emerson Worcester (1784–1865), the historian and lexicographer whose *Dictionary of the English Language* is considered one of the greatest works of its kind. Samuel Austin Worcester was also related to Lucy Winthrop, sister of Massachusetts Governor John Winthrop, and Esther Edwards, sister of the firebrand preacher Jonathan Edwards, whose teachings were instrumental in the religious revival of the Great Awakening.

Samuel Worcester moved to Peacham, Vermont, at an early age and was educated by his father. He subsequently received his elementary school education at the Peacham Academy under the direction of Jeremiah Evarts, later a founder of the American Board of Commissioners of Foreign Missions, which Samuel Worcester would later join. In 1819 Worcester graduated from the University of Vermont, where his uncle, the Reverend Dr. Samuel Austin, was president, and from the Theological Seminary in Andover, Massachusetts, in 1823.

Over the next two years, while studying under Evarts, Worcester decided to become a missionary among the Cherokee Indians in Georgia. He was ordained as a minister at the Park Street Church in Boston on 25 August 1825. The previous month he had married Ann Orr of Bedford, New Hampshire, who was herself a member of an illustrious family. Following Worcester's ordination, he and his wife left for Brainerd, Tennessee, where they labored among the Cherokee for three years until moving to the Cherokee "capital" at New Echota, Georgia, where they worked to translate portions of the Bible into Cherokee, and, with the aid of such persons as Sequoyah (George Guess) and Elias Boudinot, helped start the *Cherokee Phoenix*, the first newspaper to be printed in the Cherokee language. Historian Henry Warner Bowden comments, "In 1825...Worcester joined other dedicated missionaries at Brainerd, pledging himself to enhance Cherokee spiritual and material well-being through education." It was at this same time that the issue of whether the Georgia state officials would get the Cherokees to live under state law or be forced out was coming to a head. White missionaries living among the Indians and giving them encouragement did not help the state's cause. On 16 May 1831, Governor George R. Gilmer of Georgia wrote to Worcester,

> Sir, it is...my official duty to cause all white persons residing within the territory of the state occupied by the Cherokees to be removed therefrom, who refuse to take the oath to support the constitution and laws of the state. Information has been received of continued resistance within that territory, without complying with the requisites of the law, and of your claim to be exempted from its operation, on account of your holding the office of postmaster of New Echota. You have no doubt been informed of your dismissal from that office....You are also informed that the government of the United States does not recognize as its agents the missionaries acting under the direction of the American Board of Foreign Missions....I am still desirous of giving you and all others similarly situated, an opportunity of avoiding the punishment which will certainly follow your further residence

within the state contrary to its laws. You are, therefore, advised to remove from the territory of Georgia occupied by the Cherokees. Col. Sanford, the Commander of the Guard, will be requested to have this letter delivered to you, and to delay your arrest until you have had the opportunity of leaving the state.

One of the most concise biographies of Worcester is Nevada Couch's *Pages from Cherokee Indian History* (1884), a publication of the Worcester Academy of Vinita, Indiana Territory. In it, Couch writes,

His work of translating, with the aid of an educated Cherokee [identified as Elias Boudinot], was soon interrupted by the unrighteous laws of Georgia; but the yearly almanac, and two or three important tracts, were scattered among the people, most of whom judged him a very learned man who could know so much about times, seasons, sun, moon and stars. Dr. Worcester entered most heartily into whatever served the best interests of the Cherokee Nation. When he saw new and unlawful encroachments made upon their lands, the sure precursors of a forced removal, with its attendant hardships and cruelties, his heart was touched with sympathy, and he spoke boldly and acted fearlessly in their defense. He, and the other missionaries who acted in concert with him, became marks for the special hostility of those who were determined to deprive the Indians of their country and their homes. Dr. Worcester regarded the course they were pursuing as both wicked and cruel, and the laws they were enacting, as unconstitutional.

Seized several times by authorities but released, Worcester was finally arrested and sentenced on 16 September 1831 to four years' imprisonment at hard labor. Several persons, including the famed abolitionist attorney William Wirt, interceded in the federal courts in an effort to secure Worcester's release. In the meantime, Worcester and his compatriots stayed in jail. His letters from prison are reminiscent of Martin Luther King's famous letter from Birmingham jail, written during the height of the civil rights movement. One such letter, reproduced in the *Cherokee Phoenix* on 30 July 1831, outlines the extraordinary efforts Worcester made to save the Cherokees from their removal west, which he knew would be disastrous. By 1833, however, Worcester saw that his time in prison was not helping the Cherokees in any appreciable way and he accepted Georgia's clemency at the same time that he told his beloved Cherokees that confrontation was useless and removal inevitable. After being released on 14 January 1833, he agreed to leave the Cherokee Nation and he embarked with his charges on the calamitous Trail of Tears. He set up his new mission at Park Hill, Indian Territory, and began again the printing of a translated Bible, hymn books, and the *Cherokee Almanac*, issued from 1838 until 1861. In 1841, he founded the Cherokee Bible Society, which helped to distribute his religious materials among the Cherokee people. It was in this mission that Worcester spent his last years. After the death of his first wife, Worcester remarried, but upon his death on 20 April 1859, he was buried next to his first wife in the Worcester Cemetery in Park Hill. Authors Jack Frederick Kilpatrick and Anna Gritts Kilpatrick write, "For thirty-four years Samuel Worcester...set the lamp of his life in the forests of Cherokeeia. From that day in October 1825, when he arrived at Brainerd Mission in Tennessee, until he was laid to rest in Cherokee soil at Park Hill in the West, he served his adopted people with all his might. He preached to them, he prayed over them; he taught their young and he healed their sick; and he cheerfully went to prison for the privilege of doing so. If during the period of Samuel Worcester's ministry the Cherokees came to know the full force of the hate of the white man, they also learned the lengths to which the love of a white man could go."

See also Robertson, Alice Mary; *Worcester v. Georgia.*

References Bass, Althea, *Cherokee Messenger* (1936); Bowden, Henry Warner, *American Indians and Christian Missions: Studies in Cultural Conflict* (1981); Couch, Nevada, *Pages from Cherokee History*, *as Identified with Samuel Austin Worcester, D.D., for 34 Years a Missionary of the American Board of Commissioners for Foreign Missions among the Cherokees* (1884); Dale, Edward E., "Worcester, Samuel Austin." In Dumas Malone et al., eds., *Dictionary of American Biography* (1930–88); Kilpatrick, Jack Frederick and Anna Gritts Kilpatrick, eds., *New Echota Letters: Contributions of Samuel A. Worcester to the* Cherokee Phoenix (1968); Spaulding, Joe Powell, *The Life of Alice Mary Robertson* (Ph.D. dissertation, University of Oklahoma, 1959).

Worcester v. Georgia (6 Peters [31 U.S.] 515 [1832])

The second of the two controversial *Cherokee Nation* cases, *Worcester* tried the patience of the Supreme Court and the might of the U.S. government. Prior to the Civil War, the case of *Samuel Worcester, Plaintiff in Error, v. the State of Georgia*, was perhaps the closest the United States had come to a clash between the federal government and states' rights. In the first case, *Cherokee Nation v. Georgia*, the Supreme Court found that Indian nations were "domestic dependent nations" but refused to accept jurisdiction after Georgia extended her state laws over the Cherokee Nation. After the *Cherokee Nation* decision, Georgia passed an all-encompassing statute forcing all white persons living on reservations to swear an oath of allegiance to the state and obtain a permit for being among the Indians. Reverend Samuel Austin Worcester, a missionary among the Cherokees, was arrested, along with fellow missionaries B. F. Thompson and Elizur Butler, by Georgia authorities because they refused to comply with the law. Worcester pleaded that he was a citizen of Vermont and was under the oath of the president of the United States to live among the Cherokees as a missionary. Worcester was convicted in the Superior Court of Gwinnett County and sentenced "to hard labor in the penitentiary for four years." The U.S. Supreme Court intervened, issuing a writ of error to the judges of the superior court to send the trial record and proceedings to the Supreme Court for a hearing into Worcester's case. The case was decided without dissent on 3 March 1832, Chief Justice John Marshall writing the court's opinion, which lasts 84 pages in the Lawyer's Edition of the case. In effect, he overturned the earlier decision in *Cherokee Nation*, decided the previous term, and held that since Indian nations were wards of the federal government, they were free from the imposition of state laws. The Chief Justice started by explaining, "The defendant is a State, a member of the Union, which has exercised the powers of government over a people who deny its jurisdiction, and are under the protection of the United States. The plaintiff is a citizen of the State of Vermont, condemned to hard labor for four years in the penitentiary of Georgia, under color of an act which he alleges to be repugnant to the Constitution, laws, and treaties of the United States." In a blow to states' rights, Marshall explained that the court considered Indian nations to be separate and autonomous territories under the protection of the United States government, thus enumerating what is considered the "trust responsibility" of the government.

The Indian nations had always been considered as distinct, independent political communities, retaining their original natural rights, as the undisputed possessors of the soil from time immemorial, with the single exception of that imposed by irresistible power, which excluded them from intercourse with any other European potentate than the first discoverer of the coast of the particular region claimed: and this was a restriction which those European potentates imposed on themselves, as well as on the Indians. The very term "nation," so generally applied to them, means "a people distinct from others." The Constitution, by declaring treaties already made, as well as those to be made, to be the supreme law of the land, has adopted and sanctioned the previous treaties with the Indian nations, and consequently admits their rank among those powers who are capable of making treaties. The words "treaty" and "nation" are words of our own language, selected in our diplomatic and legislative proceedings, by ourselves, having each a definite and well understood meaning. We have applied them to Indians, as we have applied them to the other nations of the earth. They are applied to all in the same sense [at 557–58].

Marshall also thundered against what he saw was an attempt to nullify federal laws with state action. "If the objection to the system of legislation, lately adopted by the legislature of Georgia, in relation to the Cherokee nation, was confined to its extra-territorial operation, the objection, though complete, so far as respected mere right, would give this court no power over the subject," he wrote.

But it goes much further. If the review which has been taken be correct, and we think it is, the acts of Georgia are repugnant to the Constitution, laws, and treaties of the United States. They interfere forcibly with the relations established between the United States and the Cherokee Nation, the regulation of which, according to the settled principles of our Constitution, are committed exclusively to the government of the Union. They are in direct hostility with treaties, repeated in a succession of years, which mark out the boundary that separates the Cherokee country from Georgia; guaranty to them all the land within their boundary; solemnly pledge the faith of the United States to restrain their citizens from trespassing on it; and recognize the pre-existing power of the nation to govern itself. They are in equal hostility with the acts of Congress for regulating this intercourse, and giving effect to the treaties. The forcible seizure and abduction of the plaintiff in error, who was residing in the nation with its permission, and by authority of the President of the United States, is also a violation of the acts which authorize the chief magistrate to exercise this authority. . . Will these powerful considerations avail the plaintiff in error? We think they will. He was seized and forcibly carried away while under guardianship of treaties guarantying the country in which he resided, and taking it under the protection of the United States. He was seized while performing, under the sanction of the Chief magistrate of the Union those duties which the humane policy adopted by Congress had recommended. He was apprehended, tried, and condemned, under color of a law which has been shown to be repugnant to the Constitution, laws, and treaties of the United States [at 558].

Before announcing the decision, Marshall wrote to Richard Peters, the official court reporter of the Supreme Court, "It was my intention to have concluded the argument in the missionary case [a reference to *Worcester*] with a statement that this point had been elaborately argued and after deliberate consideration decided in the case of *Cohens v. The Commonwealth of Virginia* [6 Wheaton 264 (1821)], a case involving the rights of individuals to run lotteries]; but in the hurry with which the argument was framed it slipped my memory. It is now too late to correct this confusion, but I wish a note of reference at the end of the last sentence of the argument, which is: 'He is not less entitled to the protection of the constitution, laws and treaties of his country' and place at the bottom of the page the case to which the reference is made—*Cohens v. Virginia* 6 Wh[eaton] 264." Legend has it that following the release of the court's opinion, President Andrew Jackson said, "John Marshall has made his decision. Now let him enforce it," challenging the chief justice to force Georgia to obey the federal law. Marshall, angered by the president's intransigence, wrote to Justice Joseph Story, "I yield slowly and reluctantly to the conviction that our Constitution cannot last. The Union has been prolonged thus far by miracles. I fear they cannot continue."

Worcester is landmark law and has formed the foundation of many cases, too numerous to name here, that the Supreme Court has decided in the more than 160 years since the ruling was handed down. Professor Carole E. Goldberg of the University of California, Los Angeles, wrote in 1975, "While early decisions of the U.S. Supreme Court intimated that reservations were wholly separate from the states and hence immune from state legislative and judicial intrusion, this principle has been undermined [but] no comparably clear-cut standard has emerged to replace it." The heart of *Worcester* has been nonetheless been upheld through such decisions as *Williams* and *McClanahan v. Arizona State Tax Commission*. The decision may even have had an influence on who succeeded Marshall as chief justice. Supreme Court historian G. Edward White explains, "When McLean supported Marshall's view in *Worcester* that states had no power to regulate the affairs of Indians within their territory, Jackson was reportedly upset, and Lewis Cass, Jackson's secretary of war, attacked the decision, including McLean's separate opinion, in the Washington *Globe*. McLean drafted a reply, writing as 'A Member of Congress,' but was unable to get it published. The episode may have cost McLean any possibility of succeeding Marshall as Chief Justice."

See also *McClanahan v. State Tax Commission of Arizona*; *United States v. McBratney*; *Williams v. Lee*; Worcester, Samuel Austin.

References Burke, Joseph C., "The Cherokee Cases: A Study in Law, Politics and Morality." *Stanford Law Review* 21 (2); Goldberg, Carole E., "Public Law 280: The Limits of State Jurisdiction over Reservation Indians." *UCLA Law Review* 22; Kittrie, Nicholas N. and Eldon D. Wedlock, Jr., eds., *The Tree of Liberty: A Documentary History of Rebellion and Political Crime in America* (1986); John Marshall to Joseph Story, quoted in Shnayerson, Robert, *An Illustrated History of the Supreme Court of the United States* (1986); John Marshall to Richard Peters, 23 March 1832, RG 267, MT 57, Roll 1, "Original Opinions of the Justices of the Supreme Court Delivered at the January Term 1832, and Opinions and Other Case Papers of Chief Justice Marshall, 1834 and 1835 Terms"; Strickland, Rennard, ed., *Felix Cohen's Handbook of Federal Indian Law* (1982); White, G. Edward, *The Marshall Court and Cultural Change, 1815–1835* (1991).

Wounded Knee (1890)

This assault on a group of mostly unarmed Sioux Indians by U.S. troops is among history's most infamous and appalling massacres of Native Americans. On 28 December 1890, soldiers of the U.S. Seventh Cavalry under the command of Major Samuel Whitside intercepted Big Foot's band of about 350 Minneconjous en route to Pine Ridge Agency, South Dakota. The troops, who had been sent into the region to quell unrest associated with the spread of the Ghost Dance and to arrest the critically ill Big Foot, moved the Indians to Wounded Knee Creek and assigned them a camping area overnight. The following day, when the soldiers, now under the command of Colonel James Forsyth, had assembled the Indians and were disarming them, a shot was fired, probably by a young Sioux man. Whether the shot was fired at random, in the air, or at the troops is uncertain, but the cavalry immediately opened fire on the Indians with their carbines and heavy Hotchkiss guns. When the firing finally ended, over 150 Sioux were dead; some estimates put the figure at nearly twice that number. Many of the casualties were women and children. Some 25 troopers were killed, as well, at least some of them by their own fire.

There are many misconceptions of the events leading up to and surrounding the massacre. On 11 February 1891, Commissioner of Indian Affairs Thomas Jefferson Morgan sat down with several Indian witnesses to the massacre, among them Turning Hawk, Captain Sword, Spotted Horse, and American Horse, and heard what may be the best recollections of the event.

Turning Hawk [speaking through an interpreter identified only as Mr. Cook]: Mr. Commissioner, my purpose today is to tell you what I know of the condition of affairs at the agency where I live. A certain falsehood [the Ghost Dance] came to our agency from the west which had the effect of a fire upon the Indians, and when this certain fire came upon our people those who had farsightedness and could see into the matter made up their minds to stand up against it and fight it. The reason we took this hostile attitude to this fire was because we believed that you yourself would not be in favor of this particular mischief-making thing; but just as we expected, the people in authority did not like this thing and we were quietly told that we must give up or have nothing to do with this certain movement. Though this is the advice from our good friends in the East, there were, of course, many silly young men who were longing to become identified with the movement, although they knew that there was nothing absolutely bad, nor did they know there was anything absolutely good, in connection with the movement.

In the course of time we heard that the soldiers were moving toward the scene of the trouble. After awhile some of the soldiers finally reached our place and we heard that a number of them also reached our friends at Rosebud. Of source, when a large body of soldiers is moving toward a certain direction they inspire a more or less amount of awe, and it is natural that the woman and children who see this large moving mass are made afraid of it and be put in a condition to make them run away. At first we thought that Pine Ridge and Rosebud were the only two agencies where soldiers were sent, but finally we heard that the other agencies fared likewise. We heard and saw that half our friends at Rosebud agency, from fear at seeing the soldiers, began the move of running away from their agency toward ours [Pine Ridge], and when they had gotten inside of our reservation they there learned that right ahead of them at our agency was another large crowd of soldiers, and while the soldiers were there, there was constantly a great deal of false rumor flying back and forth. The special rumor I have in mind is the threat that the soldiers had come there to disarm the Indians entirely and to take away all their horses from them. That was the oft-repeated story.

So constantly repeated was this story that our friends from Rosebud, instead of going to Pine Ridge, the place of their destination, veered off and went to some other direction toward the "Bad Lands." We did not know definitely how many, but understood there were 300 lodges of them, about 1,700 people. Eagle Pipe, Turning Bear, High Hawk, Short Bull, Lance, No Flesh, Pine Bird, Crow Dog, Two Strike, and White Horse were the leaders.

The people after veering off in this way, many of them who believe in peace and order at our agency, were very anxious that some influence should be brought upon these people. In addition to our love of peace we remembered that many of these people were related to us by blood. So we sent out peace commissioners to the people who were thus running away from their agency.

I understood at the time that they were simply going away from fear because of so many soldiers. So constant was the word of these good men from Pine Ridge agency that finally they succeeded in getting away half of the party from Rosebud, from the place where they took refuge, and finally were brought to the agency at Pine Ridge. Young-Man-Afraid-of-His-Horses, Little Wound, Fast Thunder, Louis Shangreau, John Grass, Jack Red Cloud, and myself were some of these peacemakers.

The remnant of the party from Rosebud not taken to the agency finally reached the wilds of the Bad Lands. Seeing that we had succeeded so well, once more we went to the same party in the Bad Lands and succeeded in bringing these very Indians out of the depths of the Bad Lands and were being brought toward the agency. When we were about a day's journey from our agency we heard that a certain band of Indians from the Cheyenne River agency was coming toward Pine Ridge in flight [these are considered to be from Big Foot's band].

Captain Sword: Those who actually went off of the Cheyenne River agency probably number 303, and there were [some] from the Standing Rock reserve with them, but as to their number I do not know. There were a number of Oglallas, old men and several school boys, coming back with that very same party, and one of the very seriously wounded boys was a member of the Oglalla boarding school at Pine Ridge agency. He was not on the warpath, but was simply returning to his agency and to his school after a summer visit to his relatives on the Cheyenne River.

Turning Hawk: When we heard that these people were coming toward our agency we also heard this. These people were coming toward Pine Ridge agency, and when they were almost on the agency they were met by the soldiers and surrounded and finally taken to the Wounded Knee creek, and there at a given time their guns were demanded. When they had delivered them up, the men were separated from their families, from their tipis, and taken to a certain spot. When the guns were thus taken and the men thus separated, there was a crazy man, a young man of very bad influence and in fact a nobody, among that bunch of Indians [who] fired his gun, and of course the firing of a gun must have been the breaking of a military rule of some sort, because immediately the soldiers returned fire and indiscriminate killing followed.

Spotted Horse: This man shot an officer in the army; the first killed this officer. I was a voluntary scout at that encounter and I saw exactly what was done, and that was what I noticed; that the first shot killed an officer. As soon as this shot was fired the Indians immediately began drawing their knives, and they were exhorted from all sides to desist, but this was not obeyed. Consequently the firing began immediately on the part of the soldiers.

Turning Hawk: All the men who were in a bunch were killed right there, and those who escaped that first fire got into the ravine, and as they went along up the ravine for a long distance they were pursued on both sides by the soldiers and shot down, as the dead bodies showed afterwards. The women were standing off at a different place from where the men were stationed, and when the firing began, those of the men who escaped the first onslaught went in one direction up the ravine, and then the women, who were bunched together at another place, went entirely in a different direction through an

Miniconjou Sioux chief Big Foot's frozen body lies at Wounded Knee in the Pine Ridge Agency of South Dakota after U.S. troops killed men, women, and children at an encampment on 28 December 1890; there were few survivors. Black Elk, an Oglala Sioux who saw the killing field, wrote, "A people's dream died there. It was a beautiful dream . . . "

open field, and the women faced the same fate as the men who went up the deep ravine.

American Horse: The men were separated, as has already been said, from the women, and they were surrounded by the soldiers also. When the firing began, of course the people who were standing immediately around the young man who fired the first shot were killed right together, and then they turned their guns, Hotchkiss guns, etc., upon the women who were in the lodges standing there under a flag of truce, and of course as soon as they were fired upon they fled, the men fleeing in one direction and the women running in two different directions. So that there were three general directions in which they took flight.

There was a woman with an infant in her arms who was killed as she almost touched the flag of truce, and the women and children of course were strewn all along the circular village until they were dispatched. Right near the flag of truce a mother was shot down with her infant; the child not knowing that its mother was dead was still nursing, and that especially was a very sad sight. The women as they were fleeing with their babies were killed together, shot right through, and the women who were very heavy with child were also killed. All the Indians fled in these three directions, and after most all of them had been killed a cry was made that all those who were not killed or wounded should come out of their places of refuge, and as soon as they came in sight a number of soldiers surrounded them and butchered them there.

Of course we all feel very sad about this affair. I stood very loyal to the government all through those troublesome days, and believing so much in the government and being so loyal to it, my disappointment was very strong, and I have come to Washington with a very great blame on my heart. Of course it would have been all right if only the men were killed; we would almost feel grateful for it. But the fact of the killing of the women, and more especially the killing of the young boys and girls who are to go to make up the future strength of the Indian people, is the saddest part of the whole affair and we feel it very sorely.

I was not there at the time before the burial of the bodies, but I did go there with some of the police and the Indian doctor and a great many people, men from the agency, and we went through the battlefield and saw where the bodies were from the track of the blood.

Turning Hawk: I had just reached the point where I said that the women were killed. We heard, besides the killing of the men, of the onslaught also made upon the women and children, and they were treated as roughly and indiscriminately as the men and boys were.

Of course this affair brought a great deal of distress upon all the people, but especially upon the minds of those who stood loyal to the government and who did all that they were able to do in the matter of bringing about peace. They especially have suffered much distress and are very much hurt at heart. These peacemakers continued on in their good work, but there were a great many fickle young men who were ready to be moved by the change in the events there, and consequently, in spite of the great fire that was brought upon all, they were ready to assume any hostile attitude. These young men got themselves in readiness and went in the direction of the scene of battle so they might be of service there. They got there and finally exchanged shots with the soldiers. This party of young men was made up from Rosebud, Oglalla (Pine Ridge), and members of any other agencies that happened to be there at the time. While this was going on in the neighborhood of Wounded Knee—the Indians and soldiers exchanging shots—the agency, our home, was also fired into by the Indians. Matters went on in this strain until the evening came on, and then the Indians went off down by White Clay creek. When the agency was fired upon by the Indians from the hillside, of course the shots were returned by the Indian police who were guarding the agency buildings.

Although fighting seemed to have been in the air, yet those who believed in peace were still constant in their work. Young-Man-Afraid-of-His-Horses, who had been on a visit to some other agency in the north or northwest, returned, and immediately went out to the people living about White Clay creek, on the border of the Bad Lands, and brought his people out. He succeeded in obtaining the consent of the people to come out of their place of refuge and return to the agency. Thus the remaining portion of the Indians who started from Rosebud were brought back into the agency. Mr. Commissioner, during the days of the great whirlwind out there, these good men tried to hold up a counteracting power, and that was "Peace." We have now come to realize that peace has prevailed and won the day. While we were engaged in bringing about peace our property was left behind, of course, and most of us lost everything, even down to the matter of guns with which to kill ducks, rabbits, etc., shotguns, and guns of that order. When Young-Man-Afraid brought the people in and their guns were asked for, both men who were called hostile and men who stood loyal to the government delivered up their guns.

In his third annual message to Congress in 1891, President Benjamin Harrison addressed the massacre at Wounded Knee:

The outbreak among the Sioux which occurred in December last is as to its causes and incidents fully reported upon by the War Department and the Department of the Interior. That these Indians had some just complaints, especially in the matter of the reduction of the appropriation for rations and in the delays attending the enactment of laws to enable the Department to perform the engagements entered with them, is probably true; but the Sioux tribes are naturally warlike and turbulent, and their warriors were excited by their medicine men and chiefs, who preached the coming of an Indian messiah who was to give them power to destroy their enemies. In view of the alarm that prevailed among the white settlers near the reservation and of the fatal consequences that would have resulted from an Indian incursion, I placed at the disposal of General Miles, commanding the Division of the Missouri, all such forces as were thought by him to be required. He is entitled to the credit of having given thorough protection to the settlers and of bringing the hostiles into subjection with the least possible loss of life....

Since March 4, 1889, about 23,000,000 acres have been separated from Indian reservations and added to the public domain for the use of those who desire to secure free homes under our beneficent laws. It is difficult to estimate the increase of wealth which will result from the conversion of these waste lands into farms, but it is more difficult to estimate the betterment which will result to the families that have found renewed hope and courage in the ownership of a home and the assurance of a comfortable subsistence under free and healthful conditions. It is also gratifying to be able to feel, as we may, that this work had proceeded along line of justice toward the Indian, and that he may now, if he will, secure to himself the good influences of a settled habitation, the fruits of industry, and the security of citizenship.

See also Ghost Dance; Wounded Knee (1973); Wovoka.

References Brown, Dee, *Bury My Heart at Wounded Knee* (1970); "[Harrison's] Third Annual Message." In Richardson, James, comp., *A Compilation of the Messages and Papers of the Presidents, 1789–1914* (1897–1917).

Wounded Knee (1973)

Three years after a small contingent of Indians occupied Alcatraz Island, the American Indian Movement (AIM) besieged the small town of Wounded Knee at the Pine Ridge Agency in South Dakota to protest the power of Oglala Sioux Nation President

Richard Wilson. In 1890, Wounded Knee had been the site of one of the worst massacres of Indians in American history. On 28 February 1973, several hundred Oglala Lakota people and their backers stormed a church on the Pine Ridge reservation and took hostages to call attention to the fight against Wilson and to put an end his corrupt tribal government. Upon these natives' request, militants from AIM joined them. The *New York Times* reported that "the embattled Indians relayed demands to Washington that the Senate Foreign Relations Committee hold hearings on treaties made with the Indians, that the Senate start a 'full-scale investigation' of Government treatment of the Indians, and that another inquiry be started into 'all Sioux reservations in South Dakota.'" Armed policeman, U.S. marshals, BIA and tribal police, and F.B.I. agents were already at Pine Ridge to investigate charges against Wilson leveled by the Oglala Civil Rights Organization. The two sides then settled down to a stalemate, which lasted for 71 days. In an editorial in the *Wall Street Journal*, writer Greg Conderacci wrote, "On a scrap of yellow paper pasted to the door of this town's trading post is the slogan of the uprising at Wounded Knee: 'It is better to die on your feet than to live on your knees.'"

Thirty-seven days after the siege began, AIM activist Russell Means and presidential assistant Leonard Garment agreed to suspend the confrontation while Means went to Washington to work out a deal with the government. Among the sections of the agreement were an investigation of the Oglala tribal government and a complete audit of the tribal council's finances. After Means went to Washington, the deal collapsed and the siege went on. During this period, two firefights occurred between federal agents and the Indians, leaving two AIM members, Frank Clearwater and Buddy Lamont, and a federal agent,

Armed members of the American Indian Movement stand ready at Wounded Knee in March 1973, when 11 hostages were taken. The initial objective was to remove Oglala Sioux Nation President Richard Wilson from office.

Lloyd Grimm, dead. It wasn't until 8 May when a final deal was reached, and those inside the church laid down their arms and surrendered.

In an interview with one of the Wounded Knee participants, Carter Camp, and an attorney for AIM, Mark Lane, Art Kunkin of the *Los Angeles Free Press* asked, "How do you see the Wounded Knee situation now that the American Indian Movement occupation has ended, in terms of your expectations from the beginning?" Camp answered, "At the beginning our expectations weren't as high as they were at the time our traditional chiefs and headmen came in and declared Wounded Knee an independent nation. When we initially went into Wounded Knee, we thought that we were simply going to dramatize the situation on the Pine Ridge Indian Reservation by showing the corruptness of that particular branch of the Bureau of Indian Affairs that was governing Indians lives there. We also thought there was about a ninety percent chance that, if we held that territory, the federal government would have no choice but to come in and rip us off completely. Even though we had proof that we were invited there by the Indian residents in Wounded Knee, it looked as though the government would have no choice but to do their law enforcement bit." He added, "After the initial stages, when we were fighting very hard every day without fortification, and we were able to hold our perimeters through the first two days, we knew that we could probably stay there for some time...until, at least, the government had time to marshall a large force to come against us. Our expectations began to rise until, at the very peak of the occupation, our expectation was that we would be there forever. Our expectation was that from there the war against this government by the Indian people would spread to every bit of Indian country in this United States. That was the high point of our expectations and then they ebbed."

See also American Indian Movement; Banks, Dennis J.; Means, Russell Charles; Wounded Knee (1890).

References "Armed Indians Seize Wounded Knee, Hold Hostages." *New York Times*, 1 March 1973, 1; Conderacci, Greg, "At Wounded Knee, Is It War or PR?" *Wall Street Journal*, 20 March 1973, 26; "Indians and U.S. Sign Agreement at Wounded Knee." *New York Times*, 6 April 1973, 1, 19; Kunkin, Art, "The Legal Case for Wounded Knee Occupiers." *Free Press* (Los Angeles), 15 June 1973, 6; "Occupation of Wounded Knee Is Ended." *New York Times*, 9 May 1973, 1, 37.

Wovoka (Numu or Northern Paiute) (1856?-1932)

His visions sparked the Ghost Dance, the most provocative revival movement to be embraced by Indians of the western United States in the late nineteenth century, but its impulse led to the massacre at Wounded Knee in 1890. Named Wovoka ("the Cutter") or Wanekia ("One Who Makes Life"), the prophet and medicine man known by the English name of Jack Wilson was born about 1856, according to biographer Keith A. Winsell, "in Smith Valley or Mason Valley, Nevada, as one of four sons of Tavid [or Tavibo, as other sources identify him], also known as Numo-tibo's, a well-known medicine man." When Wovoka was 14, he was sent to live with a Scotch-Irish family, the Wilsons, on their farm near present-day Yerrington, Nevada. Adopted by these people, he was named Jack Wilson, but went by the Indian name Wovoka.

Wovoka's life is not well documented until 1888, when he became sick with a fever and began having hallucinations. When he recovered, he told those around him that he had experienced a mystical vision. As Lester George Moses wrote in a biography of James Mooney, an ethnologist who later interviewed Wovoka, "A time would come, Wovoka told the faithful, when all Indians living and dead would be reunited in aboriginal splendor on a remade earth. Indians would be free forever from destitution, disease, death, and non-Indians. To hasten the transformation, Wovoka encouraged his followers to perform certain rituals, the most spectacular and pervasive of which was a circular dance, known by various names but renowned as the Ghost Dance. In their exhaustion from performing the dance and in their longing for validation of the prophet's vision, the ghost dancers would collapse and 'die.' After returning to consciousness, they would tell about their encounters with loved ones long dead, harbingers from a world to come."

The Ghost Dance called on Indians to shun European ways, such as schooling, Christianity, and particularly alcohol. Wovoka's vision was inherently revolutionary. Professor Sam Gill explains, "Many of these prophetic movements were millenarian in character and a great many of them arose in the northwestern United States during the nineteenth century.…[Wovoka's] message predicted that the degradations and changes of the world would be destroyed in a major cataclysmic event, but that the world would be restored to its pristine condition, with the European-Americans removed. The many native peoples who had died would be restored to life. The animals and the territories of the tribal people would be wholly restored; that is, restored for those who faithfully followed the mandates of the Ghost Dance prophecy." Ethnologist James Mooney attempted to investigate the Ghost Dance phenomenon and interviewed Wovoka just after the Wounded Knee massacre. Lester George Moses writes, "Mooney attempted to suggest that Wovoka's religion, described by the Commissioner of Indian Affairs as heathenish and barbarous, was no more fantastic in its precepts than were the more tradition-bound religions of the larger American society; that one's skepticism concerning prophets diminished in direct proportion to the number of years that separated the faithful from the revelation. To liken the Ghost Dance religion of Wovoka to that of Mohammad, Flagellants, Fifth Monarchy Men, or Millerites, was not to scoff at individual differences, but to stress that element common to the experience—a profound difference. Later anthropologists would label such phenomena 'crisis cults' or 'revitalization movements.'"

After the Ghost Dance precipitated events leading to the massacre of more than 150 Sioux Indians at Wounded Knee in 1890, Wovoka largely withdrew from the public eye; historian Carl Waldman attributes this withdrawal to Wovoka's shock at the bloodshed Wounded Knee. Wovoka thereafter advocated peaceful coexistence with whites and settled down with his wife and children on the Walker River Reservation near Schurz, Nevada, where he died, just a month after his wife of some 50 years, on 29 September 1932 from prostate cancer. His grave marker indicates that he was 74 years old.

See also Ghost Dance; Handsome Lake Movement; Wounded Knee (1890).

References Gill, Sam D., "Native American Religions." In Charles H. Lippy and Peter W. Williams, eds., *Encyclopedia of the American Religious Experience: Studies of Traditions and Movements* (1988); Moses, Lester George, *The Indian Man: A Biography of James Mooney* (1984); Moses, Lester George, "James Mooney and Wovoka: An Ethnologist's Visit with the Ghost Dance Prophet." *Nevada Historical Society Quarterly* 23 (2); Waldman, Carl, *Who Was Who in Native American History: Indians and Non-Indians From Early Contacts through 1900* (1990); Winsell, Keith A., "Wovoka." In Sharon Malinowski, ed., *Notable Native Americans* (1995).

Zimmerman, William, Jr.
See Brophy, William Aloysius.

Zitkala-Sa
See Bonnin, Gertrude Simmons (Yankton Lakota).

Chronology

1492 Ships under the command of Christopher Columbus land on Hispaniola in the Caribbean in search of a western route to the Orient.

1511 Antonio de Montesinos, a Catholic priest, denounces Spanish treatment of native populations in the New World. The movement started by Montesinos leads to Father Bartolomé de las Casas' 1542 work, *Destruction of the Indies*, which becomes the first book to expose the annihilation of native peoples.

1512 Under the leadership of Father de las Casas, the Spanish government enacts the *Laws of Burgos*, a series of edicts designed to end Indian slavery, call upon large land owners to improve their treatment of Indian laborers, and demand that Indians join the Catholic Church or be destroyed.

1532 Spanish scholar and writer Francisco de Victoria formulates his principles of the rights of natives of the New World, establishing the Indians' "right of possession" over these lands.

1537 In his papal bull entitled, *Sublimus Deus*, Pope Paul III lends support to Victoria's principles when he writes, "[N]otwithstanding whatever may have been or may be said to the contrary, the said Indians and all other people who may later be discovered by Christians, are by no means to be deprived of their liberty or the possession of their property, even though they be outside the faith of Jesus Christ; and that they may be and should, freely and legitimately, enjoy their liberty and the possession of their property; nor should they be in any way enslaved; should the contrary happen, it shall be null and of no effect."

1542 King Charles V of Spain advances Victoria's doctrine of 1532 in his "New Laws of the Indies." This edict includes such provisions as "Indians are free persons and vassals of the Crown," and "Nothing is to be taken from the Indians except in fair trade."

1630 The Dutch West India Company's policy entitled "New Project of Freedoms and Exemptions" obligates the officials of the company to bargain and procure land from the Indians of New Netherlands.

1633 The General Court of the Massachusetts Colony establishes the first land allotment policy for the Indians decreed by a non-Indian government.

1754 English colonists meet in congress at Albany, New York, to discuss a unified colonial Indian policy.

1763 King George III of England signs a proclamation setting aside "reserved lands" in the colonies for Indians and forbids the colonies from issuing patents or establishing surveys on Indian lands.

1772 Samson Occom's *A Sermon Preached at the Execution of Moses Paul* is published, the first printed work by a Native American.

1775 The Continental Congress names Indian commissioners for the north, middle, and southern "departments" of the colonies.

1778 An Indian treaty between the fledgling United States and the Delaware Indians is signed, the first time such a pact is reached.

1781 Article IX of the Articles of Confederation confers upon the Congress "the sole and exclusive rights and power of...regulating the trade and managing all affairs with the Indians, not members of any of the states, provided that the legislative right of any state within its own limits be not infringed or violated."

1784 The federal government signs a treaty with the Six Nations of the Iroquois; officials of New York state, disagreeing with the pact, later sign their own covenant with the Six Nations, which is at odds with the federal treaty in the area of boundaries.

1785 The U.S. government signs the Treaty of Hopewell with the Cherokee Indians.

1787 As embodied in the U.S. Constitution, in what is called the Indian Commerce Clause, the government is obligated "To regulate Commerce with foreign Nations, and among the several States, and with the Indian tribes."

Congress enacts the Northwest Ordinance, which proclaims that the "utmost good faith" be shown to the Indians in all dealings with them, and that their land and property "shall never be taken from them without their consent."

1789 In the first congressional action dealing directly with Native Americans, Congress establishes the Department of War; among the duties of the department are "such other matters...as the President of the United States shall assign to the said department...relative to Indian affairs."

In the third congressional action dealing with Indians, Congress appropriates $20,000 for "the expense of negotiating and treating with the Indian tribes," as well as providing for the assignment of commissioners.

1790 Congress enacts the Trade and Intercourse Act of 1790, which outlaws all "trade and intercourse" with the Indians without the express permission of the U.S. government.

1791 The Cherokees sign the Treaty of Holston with the U.S. government, in which the United States "solemnly guarantees to the Cherokee Nation, all their lands not hereby ceded," while the Cherokees situate themselves "under the protection of the said United States, and of no other sovereign whatsoever."

1794 The first treaty involving the education of Indians is signed with the Oneida, Stockbridge, and Tuscarora Indians.

1803 After negotiating with France for acquisition of the Louisiana Purchase, President Thomas Jefferson begins the first removal policy, directing the government to "remove" all eastern Indian tribes to the newly purchased lands.

1806 Congress establishes the "Office of the Superintendent of Indian Trade" within the War Department.

1819 Congress enacts the Civilization Fund Act, to make "provision for the civilization of the Indian tribes adjoining the frontier settlements and to establish a fund to "encourage the activities of benevolent societies in providing schools for the Indians."

1820 The Reverend Jedidiah Morse, after traveling among the Indians of the Mississippi Valley and the Great Lakes region, reports to Secretary of War John C. Calhoun, "They are certainly an intelligent and noble part of our race, and capable of high moral and intellectual improvement....They are a race, who on every correct principle ought to be saved from extinction, if it be possible to save them."

1821 Sequoyah invents an 86-letter alphabet in the Cherokee language.

1823 The U.S. Supreme Court, in the first case to come before the court dealing with Indian land rights, holds in *Johnson and Graham's Lessee v. McIntosh* that Indians cannot sell their land directly to anyone except the United States, and that all such sales are null and void.

1823 Under the leadership of Samuel Austin Worcester and Elias Boudinot (Cherokee), the first edition of the *Cherokee Phoenix* is issued, half in Cherokee and half in English.

The Georgia state legislature decrees that all Indians within the state's borders will come under the state's jurisdiction within six months.

1829 William Apes's *A Son of the Forest: The Experience of William Apes*, is the first substantial autobiography to be published by a Native American writer.

In his first annual message to Congress, President Andrew Jackson comments on the advantages of the removal of Native Americans from the eastern United States.

1830 Congress enacts the Indian Removal Act, which authorizes the forcible removal of American Indians from the eastern United States to western lands.

1832 In the landmark Supreme Court decision in *Worcester v. Georgia*, the court holds that state laws regulating commerce or any dealings with Indians are superseded by federal statutes.

1835 William Apes's *Indian Nullification of the Unconstitutional Laws of Massachusetts, relative to the Marshpee Tribe* is the first work of protest published by a Native American.

In his seventh annual message, President Andrew Jackson tells Congress, "The plan of removing the aboriginal people who yet remain within the settled portions of the United States to country west of the Mississippi River approaches its consummation." The infamous "Trail of Tears," in which thousands of Indians are forcibly relocated to Indian Territory, is the immediate result of Jackson's removal policy.

The Cherokee are forced to abandon their land when they endorse the Treaty of New Echota. The treaty is signed by General William Carroll and John F. Schermerhorn, representatives of the United States, and such Cherokee leaders as Elias Boudinot and Major Ridge.

1851 Congress enacts the Indian Appropriations Act of 1851, building on the ideas of Congressman Robert Ward Johnson, chairman of the House Committee on Indian Affairs, to enlarge the Bureau of Indian Affairs and fully establish the government's reservation policy.

1854 Congress amends the Trade and Intercourse Act of 1834 to allow for the prosecution in federal courts of an Indian who has already been tried in Indian tribal court.

1855 President Franklin Pierce establishes the practice of setting aside public lands as Indian reservations without prior congressional approval.

1857 The Supreme Court holds in *Fellows v. Blacksmith* that only the government, not individuals, can remove Indians from their ancestral lands.

1860 In *Doe ex dem. Mann v. Wilson*, the Supreme Court holds that Indians may convey their land to whites if the land has not been surveyed and a patent issued, if the Indian title to that land is about to be extinguished.

1862 Interior Secretary Caleb Blood Smith enunciates an alternative government Indian policy that recognizes the tribes as being under the authority of the United States. He calls for the idea of distinguishing the tribes as "quasi-independent nations" because "they have none of the elements of nationality; they are within the limits of the recognized authority of the United States and must be subject to its control."

The U.S. Supreme Court holds that Indians are competent to convey their land to others in *Crews et al. v. Burcham et al.*

1864 Troops under the command of Colonel John Chivington and Major Scott J. Anthony attack a peaceful settlement of Cheyenne and Arapaho Indians at Sand Creek, Colorado, murdering more than 100 people, mostly women and children.

1866 Captain William J. Fetterman and 80 men under his command are ambushed and killed by Sioux warriors under Red Cloud in the so-called Fetterman Massacre.

1867 The Supreme Court overturns state laws taxing Indians on reservations in the landmark cases decided under the umbrella name of *The New York Indians.*

With the end of the fight against slavery, former abolitionists and other reformers begin efforts to improve conditions for Native Americans. Such reformers as Lydia Maria Child, Peter Cooper, and John Beeson lead the way. A congressional committee investigating the plight of American Indians releases the Doolittle Commission report.

Congress establishes the Indian Peace Commission to confer with the Indian nations "waging war against the United States or committing depredations upon the people thereof" and to determine what can be done to end the warfare. The commission will present its report to President Johnson the following year.

1868 The United States signs a peace treaty with the Nez Percé, the last such covenant signed with an Indian nation before Congress outlaws treaty-making with Indians in 1871.

1869 President Ulysses S Grant appoints Seneca chief and brigadier general Ely Samuel Parker as commissioner of Indian affairs.

1870 Troops under the command of Major Edward Baker sweep down on a Piegan village on Montana's Marias River, killing 173 Indians, most of them suffering from smallpox.

1871 With the passage of the Indian Appropriations Act of 1871, Congress ends the government's policy of making treaties with the Indians. The act states, "hereafter no Indian nation or tribe within the territory of the United States shall be acknowledged or recognized as an independent nation, tribe, or power with whom the United States may contract by treaty."

In *207 Half Pound Papers of Smoking Tobacco v. United States*, also known as *Boudinot v. United States*, the Supreme Court holds that tobacco products grown and sold on Indian reservations are liable to federal taxation.

1873 In *Holden v. Joy*, the Supreme Court finds that Indian tribes are to be considered as states, but not foreign states and not with the power of states that have joined the Union, when the title to their land has been extinguished and its interest designated to the United States for settlement.

1877 In *Beecher v. Wetherby et al.*, the Supreme Court finds that the only right Indians have to their native lands is the right of occupancy and that the government has the right to sell those lands at any time.

The first issue of the *Council Fire*, published under the editorship of white reformer *Alfred Benjamin Meacham*, appears.

The Supreme Court holds in *Bates v. Clark* that the definition of "Indian country" must be strictly defined.

1879 In *Harness v. Hyde*, the Supreme Court holds that a summons cannot be served by a non-Indian court on a non-Indian residing on an Indian reservation.

1881 Helen Hunt Jackson's *A Century of Dishonor*, which excoriates the government for its treatment of American Indians, is published.

1882 The Indian Rights Association, destined to become the largest organization created to fight for the rights of Native Americans, is founded.

1883 Sarah Winnemucca's *Life among the Piutes: Their Wrongs and Claims*, one of the first books by a Native American woman, is published.

Secretary of the Interior Henry Moore Teller authorizes the establishment of tribal courts on reservations to try crimes that fall outside the jurisdiction of state courts.

The first Lake Mohonk Conference of Friends of the Indian is held in Lake Mohonk, New York. The series of conferences will continue until 1916.

In *Ex parte Crow Dog*, the Supreme Court holds that an Indian cannot be tried in state or federal courts, but only in tribal courts, for the crime of murder against another Indian.

1884 The Supreme Court holds in *Elk v. Wilkins* that because reservations are not considered as states, Indians on reservations are not citizens as defined by the Fourteenth Amendment. The decision effectively denies reservation Indians the right to vote.

1885 Reformer Thomas A. Bland founds the National Indian Defense Association.

In response to the 1883 Supreme Court decision in *Ex parte Crow Dog*, Congress makes it a federal crime for one Indian to murder another. This action is codified in the Indian Major Crimes Act.

1886 The Supreme Court holds in *Eastern Band of Cherokee Indians v. The United States and the Cherokee Nation* that members of the Cherokee Nation who stayed behind after the removal of the tribe in 1835 are not members of the established Cherokee Nation in Oklahoma

The Supreme Court awards the Choctaw Nation almost $3 million for lands taken from the Indians in 1855.

1887 Congress passes the *General Allotment Act*, which allots all Indian lands in severalty, excepting lands of the Five Civilized Tribes.

1890 In its decision in *Cherokee Nation v. Southern Kansas Railway Company*, the Supreme Court holds that the government can take Indian lands but, under the theory of *eminent domain*, must compensate the Indians appropriately.

Troops of the Seventh Cavalry led by Colonel James W. Forsyth massacre a group of mostly unarmed Sioux Indians at Wounded Knee in South Dakota.

1891 In striking down a congressional action that made adultery a federal crime in the Indian Major Crimes Act, the Supreme Court, in *Ex parte Mayfield*, holds that such matters are properly within the jurisdiction of tribal courts.

1893–1905 The Commission to the Five Civilized Tribes in the Indian Territory, also known as the Dawes Commission, dissolves the tribal governments of the Five Civilized Tribes of Oklahoma against their wishes and allots 20 million acres of land in severalty to 90,000 allottees.

1894 The Supreme Court holds in *United States v. Blackfeather* that when one tribe integrates another into its nation it must share the proceeds from land sales.

1895 The Supreme Court in *Maricopa & Phoenix Railroad v. Territory of Arizona* holds that when a railroad is granted a right-of-way through an Indian reservation but is not taxed by the federal government, a state or territorial government may tax the line.

In *Frost v. Wenie*, the Supreme Court holds that when the government has finished using Indian lands that it claimed for a specific purpose, it must return those lands to the Indians and cannot sell them as public land for settlement.

1896 In *Alberty v. United States*, the Supreme Court finds that the freed slave of an Indian cannot be considered an Indian even if tribal laws state otherwise.

In *Talton v. Mayes*, the Supreme Court finds that the Cherokee Nation has a right to execute an Indian who murdered another Indian in the Cherokee Nation.

1897 The Supreme Court holds in *Nofire et al. v. United States* that "the jurisdiction of the [tribal] courts of the Cherokee Nation over offenses committed by one Indian upon the person of another includes not only Indians by birth, but also citizens of the Nation by adoption."

1898 The tribal governments of the Five Civilized Tribes are broken up and the land of the nations allotted against their will with passage of the Curtis Act.

1899 In *Stephens v. Cherokee Nation*, the Supreme Court finds that Congress has "plenary power of legislation" in dealing with the affairs of Indians.

In *Jones v. Meehan*, the Supreme Court holds that even in the area of allotments, a responsibility of the federal government, a treaty that allowed an allotment to be passed from one Indian to his or her heirs must be honored.

1900 The U.S. Census counts 237,196 Indians living in the United States.

1901 *Old Indian Legends* by Indian activist Gertrude Simmons Bonnin is published.

In *Barker v. Harvey*, the Supreme Court holds unanimously that Mission Indians receiving land grants from Mexico have no right of title to their land under the laws of the United States.

1902 The autobiographical *Indian Boyhood* by *Dr. Charles Alexander Eastman* is published.

In *Cherokee Nation et al. v. Hitchcock*, the Supreme Court holds that the secretary of the interior has the power to issue mineral leases on Indian lands without the consent of the Indian nations.

1905 In the case of *In re Heff*, the Supreme Court holds that once Indians have received their allotments, making them U.S. citizens, the sale of alcohol to them is not against the law.

1906 The Supreme Court holds in *Oregon v. Hitchcock* that states and courts cannot intervene in the allotment process.

Congress passes the Burke Act, which withholds citizenship from Indians until the end of the trust period for their allotments, guaranteeing that they cannot sell their lands without the approval of the secretary of the interior.

The Supreme Court holds in *Naganab v. Hitchcock* that Congress has the plenary power over Indian affairs to authorize the secretary of the interior to dispose of surplus Indian woodlands as public lands.

In the Cherokee Intermarriage Cases, the Supreme Court holds that whites married to Cherokees cannot participate in the allotment of Cherokee lands.

The Supreme Court allows states to tax Indians only when the Indians have been allotted their lands and made full citizens of the United States in *Goudy v. Meath*.

1907 With passage of the Lacey Act, Congress allows Indians who have had lands allotted to them to also make use of tribal funds placed in the U.S. Treasury for their exclusive use.

The U.S. Supreme Court holds in *United States ex rel. West v. Hitchcock.* that the secretary of the interior can deny an allotment of Indian land to a white man married to an Indian.

Congress seeks to protect the control of the purchase of products of Indian industry with the passage of the Buy Indian Act.

The Supreme Court allows for the religious teaching of Indian children utilizing government appropriations set aside in a treaty-created fund in *Quick Bear v. Leupp et al.*

1909 Three weeks after hearing arguments in *Fleming et al. v. McCurtain et al.*, the Supreme Court finds that "persons of Choctaw and Chickasaw blood and descent" who have not been included on allotment rolls already drawn up cannot have the rolls reopened so as to share in allotments.

1910 In *Conley v. Ballinger et al.*, the Supreme Court finds that Indian tribes no longer in existence have no right to protect the cemeteries containing their dead.

1911 Indian activists Dr. Charles Alexander Eastman, Dr. Carlos Montezuma, attorney Thomas L. Sloan, Henry Standing Bear, Charles E. Dagenett, and Laura M. Cornelius join with non-Indian professor Fayette McKenzie to form the Society of American Indians.

The Supreme Court in *Tiger v. Western Investment Company* holds that Congress, within its plenary power over Indian affairs, has the right to decide the conditions under which Indians may sell their allotments.

1912 Dr. Carlos Montezuma founds *Wassaja*, the official journal of the Society of American Indians and the first militantly pro-Indian periodical.

The Supreme Court finds in *Heckman v. United States* that Congress has the right to extend restrictions on the alienation of Indian allotments and that the United States can sue in federal court to uphold those restrictions.

In *Deming Investment Company v. United States*, the U.S. Supreme Court holds that Seminoles who are not full-blood Indians but have attained the age of majority can, without the permission of the secretary of the interior, sell or convey their allotments.

In three important cases all decided on the same day, the Supreme Court holds that when allotments are held by the original allottee, by federal law they must remain untaxable for the entire period of alienation. The cases are *Choate v. Trapp*, *English v. Richardson*, and *Gleason et al. v. Wood et al.*

In two separate cases, the Supreme Court deals with the question of the introduction of spirits and liquors into "Indian country": In *Ex parte Webb*, the court upholds the right of Congress to ban intoxicating liquors from "Indian country" and to make the introduction of such liquors a violation of federal law. In *Clairmont v. United States*, the court finds that when an Indian nation cedes land to the government and that land is used for a railroad's right-of-way, persons carrying alcoholic beverages on the train are not considered to be carrying it into "Indian country."

1913 The Supreme Court holds in *Donnelly v. United States* that lands added to an Indian reservation by executive order, even if those lands are not native to that particular nation of Indians, must be considered as "Indian country" in matters of law.

1914 The Supreme Court decides that a federal statute prohibiting the introduction and sale of alcohol into Indian country is constitutional in *Pronovost v. United States.* On the same day, the court holds in *Perrin v. United States* that Congress has the final authority to determine whether former Indian lands are to be free from the sale of intoxicating liquors.

In *Bowling v. United States*, the Supreme Court holds that "[t]he guardianship of the Federal government over an Indian does not cease when an allotment is made and the allottee becomes a citizen of the United States."

In *Johnson v. Gearlds*, the Supreme Court finds that even though an Indian nation had ceded some land to the United States, that land must still be considered as "Indian country" in matters regarding the sale of alcohol.

In *Choctaw, Oklahoma, & Gulf Railway Company v. Harrison*, the Supreme Court holds that when the federal government allows a company to mine or unearth minerals from lands on an Indian reservation, a state may not tax that company because it is to be considered a federal instrumentality.

1916 In *Lane v. United States ex rel. Mickadiet*, the Supreme Court finds that an act of Congress does not prevent the secretary of the interior from reopening a heirship investigation into the division of allotments.

In *Levindale Lead & Zinc Mining Company v. Coleman*, the Supreme Court finds that whites who hold allotments on Indian reservations are not subject to Congress' restrictions placed on the alienation of allotments without the consent of the secretary of the interior.

The Supreme Court decides in *New York ex rel. Kennedy v. Becker* that a state's interest in conservation outweighs Indians' interest in fishing in waters that do not belong to an Indian reservation.

1917 Commissioner of Indian Affairs Cato Sells reports that more Indians are being born than are dying, reversing a centuries-long population decline.

In *Dickson v. Luck Land Company*, the Supreme Court finds that an Indian must attain the age of majority to be able to receive his patent for his allotment and thus to be able to convey it properly.

1918 The Native American Church is founded in Oklahoma.

In *Brader v. James*, the Supreme Court decides that the children of Indian allotees could not convey, or sell, their inherited allotments without the prior approval of the secretary of the interior. On the same day, in *Egan v. McDonald*, the Supreme Court holds that adult Indians heirs may convey the title to their lands without the prior approval of the Secretary of the Interior. Further, it also decided in *Lane et al. v. Morrison*, that monies held in trust by the U.S. government for Indians could be spent in ways that Indians did not want to improve their lives.

1919 (15 December) The Supreme Court, in *United States v. Board of County Commissioners of Osage County, Oklahoma*, holds that Indian allotments could not be subject to state taxation, and that the United States, as the holder in fee and "protector of the Indians," still had an interest in their protection even after the restrictions on alienation and taxation were lifted by Congress.

1920 The U.S. Census reports 244,437 Native Americans living in the United States.

The Supreme Court holds in *Nadeau et al. v. Union Pacific Railroad Company* that during the period between an Indian nation's cession of its lands to the government and the government's allotment of those lands, the lands may be considered as "public lands" and can be opened for development, sale, or lease as a right-of-way for railroads.

1921 Gertrude Simmons Bonnin's autobiographical *American Indian Stories* is published.

The Supreme Court holds in *La Motte et al. v. United States.* that the sale of allotted lands by Indians to non-Indians can legally be stopped by the secretary of the interior.

In *Blanset v. Cardin*, the Supreme Court upholds the right of the secretary of the interior to approve the will of an Indian even if that will conflicts with the laws in the state in which the Indian resides.

1922 The Association on American Indian Affairs, a Native American rights organization, is founded.

The Supreme Court decides in *Gillespie v. Oklahoma* that the income of a lessee from the lease of a restricted Indian allotment is exempt from all state taxes.

In a series of cases combined into *Ewert v. Bluejacket et al.*, the Supreme Court holds that government employees involved in any way with Indian affairs may not trade or buy allotments from Indians.

1924 The Committee of One Hundred, a national Indian rights group, urges changes in federal Indian policy in its report to President Calvin Coolidge.

With the passage of the *Indian Citizenship Act*, Congress extends the full privileges of U.S. citizenship to Native Americans.

1926 In response to the report of the Committee of One Hundred, Secretary of the Interior Hubert Work requests a two-year study of how to change Indian government policy.

The Supreme Court holds in *First Moon v. White Tail* that the secretary of the interior has the sole power to decide which Indians are to be the heirs to the allotments of deceased Indians.

The Supreme Court in *Childers v. Beaver et al.* holds that Indian allotments passed on as inheritances are not subject to state inheritance taxes.

In *Jaybird Mining Company v. Weir*, the Supreme Court holds that royalties paid to the secretary of the interior from proceeds of minerals extracted from Indian allotments are exempt from state taxes.

1927 The Supreme Court finds in *Jones v. Prairie Oil & Gas Company* that a federal law refusing the rights of minor Indian allottees to lease or sell their allotments is a violation of the Fifth Amendment to the Constitution.

1928 *The Problem of Indian Administration*, also known as *The Meriam Report*, edited by Louis Meriam of the University of Chicago, is published. The landmark report, which had been requested by the secretary of the interior in 1926, argues that the administration of Indian affairs, particularly the allotment policy, has failed dismally and must be replaced with a new policy.

1929 President Herbert Hoover appoints Charles James Rhoads as commissioner of Indian affairs and J. Henry Scattergood as assistant commissioner, ushering in an era of Indian policy reform.

1930 The *Preston-Engle Report* is released, a landmark study that investigates the condition of irrigation facilities on Indian reservations.

1931 In *Halbert et al. v. United States*, the Supreme Court holds that Indians of mixed-blood heritage must be included in land allotments.

1933 Indian activist John Collier is appointed commissioner of Indian affairs, a position he will hold until 1945.

1934 To increase the funding for the education of Indian children, Congress passes the *Johnson-O'Malley Act*.

With the support of Indian Commissioner John Collier, Congress enacts the *Indian Reorganization Act*, which ends the government's allotment policy, established in 1887, and returns the rights to Indian lands to the Indians themselves.

1935 Congress passes the *Indian Arts and Crafts Board Act*, which establishes a government commission within the Department of the Interior for the advancement and support of the Indian arts and crafts industry.

1936 Congress passes the Thomas-Rogers Act, also known as the *Oklahoma Indian Welfare Act of 1936*, which extends the provisions of the Indian Reorganization Act of 1934 to Indians in Oklahoma, who were initially exempted from the 1934 legislation.

In *British-American Oil Producing Company v. Board of Equalization of the State of Montana et al.*, the Supreme Court differentiates between reservations established by executive order and those created by Congress in considering whether Congress has the power to allow states to tax the production of mineral resources on reservations.

1939 The Supreme Court holds in *Minnesota v. United States* that the United States, as the holder of fee in severalty for Indian allotments, is an "indispensable party" to proceedings held to condemn those lands for compensated takings made by a state.

1942 In *Tulee v. Washington*, the Supreme Court holds that a state has the right to impose restrictions on the rights of Indians to fish for conservation purposes, but has no right to charge a fee for a fishing license.

1943 The Supreme Court holds in *Board of County Commissioners et al. v. Seber et al.* that lands bought with restricted funds received from the lease of oil and gas on Indian lands are immune from state taxation.

The Supreme Court holds in *Oklahoma Tax Commission v. United States* that Congress does not explicitly prohibit states from taxing Indian estates to collect inheritance and other taxes.

1943–1945 The work of the Navajo Code Talkers during World War II saves the lives of many U.S. soldiers and is credited with helping achieve the Allied victory on Iwo Jima.

1944 A House of Representatives select committee recommends "the final solution to the Indian problem" by withdrawing, or terminating, federal services to Indian reservations.

In *Arenas v. United States*, the Supreme Court holds that when Indians are promised allotment patents, the secretary of the interior, by law, must deliver them.

Delegates representing over 50 Indian tribes assemble in Denver, Colorado, and found the National Congress of American Indians. The preamble to the group's constitution declares that it is their intention "to enlighten the public, preserve Indian cultural values, seek an equitable adjustment of tribal affairs, and secure and preserve their rights under treaties."

1945 The Supreme Court holds in *Northwestern Bands of Shoshone Indians v. United States* that a treaty between the United States and an Indian tribe establishing a reservation does not create a title of occupancy for that tribe and that the tribe cannot be awarded damages by the government for the extinguishment of their control over the reservation lands.

1946 Congress creates the Indian Claims Commission, designed to handle Indian land claims; Indians are allowed five years to file such a claim. In those five years, the commission will receive a total of 852 claims in 370 petitions.

1947 In *Confederated Bands of Ute Indians v. United States*, the Supreme Court holds that Indian lands that are part of a reservation but were established by executive order and not by congressional action can be taken by the government without compensation.

1948 The Bureau of Indian Affairs secretly draws up lists of tribes for termination.

In a landmark case, the Arizona Supreme Court holds in *Harrison et al. v. Laveen* that it is a violation of the civil rights of American Indians to deny them the right to vote in state and local elections.

The Commission on Organization of the Executive Branch of the Government, the so-called Hoover Commission, releases its report calling for the rapid assimilation of Indians into American society.

1949 President Harry S Truman names Hoover Commission member John Ralph Nichols to be the commissioner of Indian affairs.

1950 The U.S. Census records 357,499 Indians in the United States.

President Truman signs the Navajo-Hopi Rehabilitation Act, which authorizes the expenditure of $88 million in a 10-year period to "promote the rehabilitation of the Navajo and Hopi Tribes of Indians and a better utilization of the resources of the Navajo and Hopi Indian Reservations."

1953 The House of Representatives enacts House Concurrent Resolution 108, a nonstatutory declaration of Congress' intent in the field of Indian affairs to terminate all federal supervision of the Indian nations.

Congress enacts Public Law 280, which terminates federal responsibility over Indian tribal affairs and transfers the obligations to the states.

1954 With passage of the Menominee Termination Act of 1954, Congress ends the federal relationship specifically with the Menominee Tribe of Wisconsin, but begins to advance the concept with other nations as well.

1955 The Supreme Court finds lands in *Tee-Hit-Ton Indians, an Identifiable Group of Alaska Indians, v. United States* that because Congress had not recognized an Indian tribe's assertions of ownership of certain lands that it claimed were part of its ancestral lands, the government is not responsible to compensate those Indians for the taking of timber from the disputed lands.

In order "to authorize the leasing of restricted Indian lands for public, religious, educational, recreational, residential, business, and other purposes requiring the grant of long term leases," Congress enacts the Indian Long Term Leasing Act of 1955.

1960 In a landmark ruling, the Supreme Court, in *Federal Power Commission v. Tuscarora Indian Nation*, allows the taking, with compensation, of Indian land to be used for water storage facilities under the Federal Power Act.

1961 The National Indian Youth Council, a youth-oriented Native American rights organization, is founded.

The American Indian Chicago Conference is held at the University of Chicago under the direction of Dr. Sol Tax; 460 Indians representing 90 tribes draft a "Declaration of Indian Progress." The results of the conference will be reported to President John F. Kennedy in 1962.

1962 The Supreme Court upholds the rights of Indian communities to fish beyond what are considered their "recognized rights" in the landmark decision in *Metlakatla Indian Community, Annette Islands Reserve, v. Egan*.

1964 Indian activists from the National Indian Youth Council begin to use the "fish-in" as a device to protest the refusal by the state of Washington to recognize fishing rights established under treaty.

The American Indian Capital Conference on Poverty meets in Washington, D.C.

1968 In a special message to Congress entitled "The Forgotten American," President Lyndon B. Johnson reports, "Political equality and compensation for [the Indians'] ancestral lands are not enough. The American Indian deserves a chance to develop his talents and share fully in the future of our Nation." On that same day, he signs Executive Order 11399, establishing the National Council on Indian Opportunity.

In *Peoria Tribe of Indians of Oklahoma et al. v. United States*, the Supreme Court holds that when the government violates a treaty involving Indian land claims and the sale of that land, the government must compensate the Indians.

As part of the Fair Housing Act of 1968, Congress enacts a "Bill of Rights" for American Indians in the so-called Indian Civil Rights Act of 1968.

In the first of three landmark decisions in the area of Indian fishing rights, the Supreme Court finds in *Puyallup Tribe, etc. v. The Department of Game of Washington et al.* that "treaty provisions did not preclude the state from regulating the manner of fishing and restricting commercial fishing in the interest of conservation, provided that such regulation was a reasonable and necessary exercise of the state's police power and did not discriminate against the Indians." On the same day, the court decides in *Menominee Tribe of Indians v. United States* that the Menominee Termination Act of 1954 did not end the Menominee tribe's fishing rights honored by a federal treaty.

1969 *Custer Died for Your Sins: An Indian Manifesto*, by Vine Deloria, Jr., is published.

In a report delivered to President Richard Nixon, Indian scholar Alvin M. Josephy, Jr., reports on possible areas of Indian reform to be addressed by the new administration.

Indian writer N. Scott Momaday wins the Pulitzer Prize for his *House Made of Dawn*.

Indians of All Tribes activists occupy Alcatraz Island in San Francisco Bay, California.

Indian activists meet to form the Concerned Indian American Coalition, the forerunner of the American Indian Movement.

1971 In, *Kennerly and Kennerly, Petitioners, v. District Court of the Ninth Judicial District of Montana, et al.*, the Supreme Court finds that tribal, not state, courts have jurisdiction over civil matters arising on a reservation.

The Office of Economic Opportunity announces that it has joined with the Departments of Labor, Urban Development, and Health, Education, and Welfare to establish the Model Urban Indian Center Program, designed to offer federal assistance to modernize and improve Indian communities in urban areas.

Congress enacts the *Alaska Native Claims Settlement Act*, which divides the state of Alaska into 12 regional "corporations," or entities, of Alaska Natives who share a "common heritage," extinguishes further Alaska Native title to lands in the state, orders an enrollment of all such Alaska Natives to be conducted within two years after the passage of the act, and establishes an "Alaska Native Fund" of some $462,500,000 to be appropriated to the Alaska Natives over a period of 11 fiscal years.

1972 Congress establishes a policy within the Interior Department to improve Indian education with passage of the Indian Education Act of 1972.

The Trail of Broken Treaties protest originates during the Rosebud, South Dakota, Tribal Fair. Three different elements of the protest will converge in St. Paul, Minnesota, before proceeding to their final destination, Washington, D.C.

Richard Oakes, a Mohawk activist involved in the occupation of Alcatraz Island in 1969 and 1970, is murdered in California.

1973 After the tribal authority of the Pine Ridge Reservation refuses to investigate the murder on the reservation of Raymond Yellow Thunder, American Indian Movement activists begin a 71-day siege of the village of Wounded Knee to protest the government's policies toward Indians and the tactics of tribal chairman Dick Wilson.

The Supreme Court holds in *McClanahan, etc. v. State Tax Commission of Arizona* that Indians on reservations are exempt from state income taxes unless there is specific congressional action subjecting them to such taxes. On the same day, the court finds that states are allowed to levy some taxes on companies doing business on reservations in *Mescalero Apache Tribe v. Franklin Jones, commissioner of the Bureau of Revenue of the State of New Mexico, et al.*

In *Keeble v. United States*, the Supreme Court finds that an Indian on trial has the right to have a jury consider a charge not listed in the Indian Major Crimes Act.

In *Puyallup Tribe v. The Department of Game of the State of Washington et al.*, the Supreme Court holds that while a state ban on nets used for fishing is discriminatory against Indians, the Indians do not have an absolute right to unlimited fishing.

President Nixon signs the *Menominee Restoration Act* into law, reestablishing that tribe under federal protection.

1973 Congress enacts the Headstart, Economic Opportunity, and Community Partnership Act of 1974, which is designed "to promote the goal of economic and social self-sufficiency for American Indians, Hawaiian Natives and Alaskan Natives."

The Supreme Court holds in *Morton, Secretary of the Interior, v. Ramon Ruiz et ux.* that Indians may be eligible for assistance benefits under the Snyder Act of 1921, even though they might live off the reservation, so long as they do not break their social and economic contacts with the reservation.

With the passage of the Indian Financing Act of 1974, Congress establishes a scheme to provide working capital "to develop and utilize Indian resources."

In *Morton, Secretary of the Interior, v. C. R. Mancari et al.* and *Amerind v. C. R. Mancari et al.*, the Supreme Court finds that the preferential hiring of American Indians for employment in the Bureau of Indian Affairs does not violate the Equal Employment Opportunities Act of 1972.

1975 In the lower court decision of *Joint Tribal Council of the Passamaquoddy Tribe et al. v. Morton*, the District Court of Maine finds that Indian tribes are under the protection of the Nonintercourse Act of 1790.

Congress passes the Indian Self-Determination and Education Assistance Act of 1975 "to provide maximum Indian participation in the Government of the Indian people; to provide for the full participation of Indian tribes in programs and services conducted by the Federal Government for Indians and to encourage the development of human resources of the Indian people; to establish a program of assistance to upgrade Indian education; [and] to support the right of Indian citizens to control their own educational activities."

The Supreme Court holds in *Antoine et ux. v. Washington* that "once Congress ratifies an agreement with a tribe of Indians, the provisions of that agreement, including hunting and fishing rights, must be protected for those Indians."

FBI agents Jack Coler and Ronald Williams enter the Pine Ridge Reservation in search of an young Indian man, Jimmy Eagle, to serve him with a robbery warrant. A firefight ensues, leaving Coler, Williams, and a Coeur d'Alene Indian, Joe (Killsright) Stuntz dead. Eagle, Leonard Peltier, and two other activists in the American Indian Movement are indicted in the deaths of Coler and Williams. Peltier flees to Canada but will be arrested, extradited to the United States, and eventually tried and convicted on murder charges.

1976 In *Fisher v. The District Court of the Sixteenth Judicial District of Montana, In and For the County of Rosebud (In the Matter of the Adoption of Ivan Firecrow, etc.)*, the Supreme Court holds that the rulings of Indian tribal courts as to the adoptions of Indian children are final and cannot be appealed to courts outside of the tribe.

In *Colorado River Water Conservation District v. United States*, the Supreme Court holds that the McCarran Amendment does not defer Indian water rights lawsuits from state to federal courts.

In *Moe, etc., et al. v. The Confederated Salish and Kootenai Tribes of the Flathead Reservation et al.*, the Supreme Court strikes down personal state fees imposed on Indians as invalid, but upholds the right of states to require Indians selling tobacco products on the reservation to non-Indians to tax those products as a "minimal burden" upon the Indians.

The Supreme Court strikes down personal property taxes against Indians without the prerequisite congressional intent in *Bryan v. Itasca County*.

The *Indian Health Care Improvement Act* is enacted to "implement the Federal responsibility for the care and education of the Indian people by improving the services and facilities of Federal Indian health programs and encouraging maximum participation of Indians in such programs."

1977 In *United States v. Antelope et al.*, the Supreme Court holds that Indians are "members of quasi-sovereign tribal entities," and as such are considered to be under federal, not state, jurisdiction.

In *Puyallup Tribe, Inc., and Ramona Bennett v. The Department of Game of the State of Washington et al.*, the third important Washington State fishing case, the Supreme Court holds that a lower court cannot regulate the taking of fish by individual tribal members and that Washington State can manage the fishing industry on the Puyallup reservation. The decision allows the state to place a fixed total on the number of fish caught by the tribe.

The Department of the Interior vests all power over Indian affairs in the new position of assistant secretary of the interior for Indian affairs, abolishing the office of the commissioner of Indian affairs.

1978 The Supreme Court holds in *Oliphant and Belgarde v. The Suquamish Indian Tribe et al.* that Indian tribal courts, because of the limited power given to reservations by Congress, do not have the jurisdiction to try non-Indians for offenses committed on Indian land.

Congress enacts the American Indian Religious Freedom Act to protect the traditional religious practices and religions of Native Americans.

Congress establishes regulations for Indian adoptions and foster care when it enacts the Indian Child Welfare Act.

1979 Congress enacts the Archaeological Resources Protection Act of 1979 "to secure, for the present and future benefit of the American people, the protection of archaeological resources and sites which are on public lands and Indian lands, and to foster increased cooperation and exchange of information between governmental authorities, the professional archaeological community, and private individuals having collections of archaeological resources and data which were obtained before the date of the enactment of this Act."

1980 The Census Bureau reports 1,366,676 Native Americans in the United States.

In *Andrus, Secretary of the Interior, et al. v. Glover Construction Company*, the Supreme Court requires that non-discriminatory bids must be entered into for work in Indian service contracts.

In *Central Machinery Company v. Arizona State Tax Commission*, the Supreme Court holds that federal law prevents the state of Arizona from taxing the sale of machinery on an Indian reservation.

1981 In *Montana v. United States*, the Supreme Court finds that an Indian tribe has no right to regulate fishing by non-Indians on non-Indian lands located within a reservation's boundaries when no important tribal interests are directly affected.

1982 In *Merrion et al. v. Jicarilla Apache Tribe*, the Supreme Court holds that Indian tribes, apart from states, have the power to tax companies doing work on the reservation and that this power does not violate the Commerce Clause of the U.S. Constitution.

1983 Congress provides for the consolidation of Indian heirship lands with the passage of the Indian Land Consolidation Act.

In *New Mexico v. Mescalero Apache Tribe*, the Supreme Court holds that federal law prohibits the application of state regulations regarding hunting and fishing on Indian reservations.

The Supreme Court holds that McCarran Amendment calls for state, not federal, court jurisdiction over water adjudications, even those involving Indian reservations, in *Montana et al. v. Northern Cheyenne Tribe of the Northern Cheyenne Indian Reservation et al.*, an umbrella case involving several Indian reservations.

1984 In the first of two cases called *Three Affiliated Tribes of the Fort Berthold Reservation v. Wold Engineering, P.C. et al.*, the Supreme Court finds that states may assume control over Indian civil and criminal matters only if the Indians themselves vote for such a change in jurisdiction.

1985 The Supreme Court holds in *Oregon Department of Fish and Wildlife, et al. v. Klamath Indian Tribe* that an Indian tribe's special and reserved right to hunt and fish on lands is abrogated when the tribe cedes that land to the government.

In its decision in *County of Oneida, New York, et al., v. Oneida Indian Nation of New York State, et al.*, the Supreme Court finds that counties that have taken land from Indian tribes are responsible for reimbursing those tribes for the land, while the counties cannot ask the state government to reimburse them for the cost.

The Supreme Court rules that Indian tribes and nations can impose taxes on companies doing business on reservations without the prior approval of the secretary of the interior in the landmark case of *Kerr-McGee Corporation v. Navajo Tribe of Indians, et al.*

The Supreme Court holds that Indians must collect sales taxes from non-Indians who purchase goods in stores on Indian reservations in *California State Board of Equalization et al. v. Chemehuevi Indian Tribe.*

1986 The use of social security numbers by the government is found by the Supreme Court not to violate an Indian's right to the free exercise of his or her religion in *Bowen et al. v. Roy et al.*

In the second case titled *Three Affiliated Tribes of the Fort Berthold Reservation v. Wold Engineering, P.C. et al.*, the Supreme Court holds that Public Law 280 does not allow a state to "disclaim" jurisdiction over Indian civil and criminal matters.

Congress passes the Indian Alcohol and Substance Abuse Prevention and Treatment Act of 1986, which authorizes the Indian Health Service to assume responsibility over the problem of alcohol and substance abuse among Indian people.

In an historic vote, Wilma Pearl Mankiller, deputy chief of the Cherokees, is elected principal chief of that nation, the first woman to head a major Indian tribe.

In *California et al. v. Cabazon Band of Mission Indians et al.*, the Supreme Court holds that state laws governing Indian gambling on reservations are null and void.

1988 Congress enacts the Alaska Native Claims Settlement Act Amendments of 1987 to allow shareholders of stock in each Alaska Native corporation to be permitted to decide "when restrictions on alienation of stock issued as part of the settlement should be terminated, and whether Natives born after December 18, 1971, should participate in the settlement."

The Supreme Court finds that the Free Exercise clause of the U.S. Constitution does not prohibit the government from building roads or harvesting timber on a piece of land held to be religiously sacred by Indian tribes in the area in *Lyng v. Northwest Indian Cemetery Protective Association.*

The Supreme Court holds that a state may refuse unemployment benefits to persons convicted of using peyote in the landmark cases *Oregon v. Smith* and *Oregon v. Black.*

Congress enacts the Tribally Controlled Schools Act authorizing the secretary of the interior to provide grants to Indian tribes and tribal organizations that operate tribally controlled schools.

In the *Indian Gaming Regulatory Act of 1988*, Congress establishes a system for the operation of casino gaming on Indian reservations.

1989 The Supreme Court finds in *Cotton Petroleum Corp. v. New Mexico* that because the Commerce clause of the Constitution does not recognize Indian nations as "states," without congressional intent a state can impose separate taxes, unlike those levied by the tribe, on a company doing business on a reservation.

In *Brendale v. Confederated Tribes and Bands of the Yakima Indian Nation et al.*, a divided Supreme Court holds that while Indian tribes may not exercise zoning control over privately held lands on a reservation, it may apply such restrictions on land considered "closed" by the tribe.

1990 The Supreme Court holds for the second time that a state may deny unemployment benefits to persons who have used peyote in *Oregon, et al. v. Smith, et al.*

Congress establishes the National Indian Policy Center as a government "think tank" on Indian issues.

The Supreme Court rules in *Duro v. Reina et al.* that Indians from one reservation cannot be tried by a tribal court for crimes committed on another reservation.

The Native American Languages Act, enacted by Congress, seeks to "preserve, protect, and promote the rights and freedom of Native Americans to use, practice, and develop Native American languages."

Congress enacts the Native American Graves Protection and Repatriation Act "to protect Native American burial sites and the removal of human remains, funerary objects, sacred objects, and objects of cultural patrimony on Federal, Indian and Native Hawaiian lands."

1990–1991 Approximately 450 Navajos serve in the U.S. military during the Persian Gulf War.

1991 A Navajo tribal court convicts Navajo Chairman Peter MacDonald of conspiracy, fraud, and ethics violations, and removes him from office.

The Supreme Court finds that although Indians are immune to state taxes on reservations, a state may force them to collect taxes on goods sold to non-Indians on reservations in *Oklahoma Tax Commission v. Citizen Band Potawatomi Indian Tribe of Oklahoma.*

The Census Bureau announces that the 1990 Census counts 1,878,285 Native Americans in the United States.

1992 Ben Nighthorse Campbell (Northern Cheyenne) is elected to the U.S. Senate, the second Native American to serve in that body.

1993 Ada Elizabeth Deer becomes the first Native American woman to head the Bureau of Indian Affairs.

The Supreme Court holds in *Oklahoma Tax Commission v. Sac and Fox Nation* that states are prohibited, minus explicit congressional intent, to tax the members of an Indian nation who live on the reservation, but may tax non-members.

1994 In *Department of Taxation and Finance of New York, et al. v. Milhelm Attea & Bros., Inc., etc., et al.*, the Supreme Court holds that a state tax scheme to collect taxes on cigarettes sold on Indian reservations is not a violation of the Indian Trader Statutes.

1995 The U.S. government announces that it will compensate four tribes in the Pacific Northwest for the government's flooding of ancient fishing grounds for construction of dams in the 1930s and 1940s.

1996 In *Seminole Tribe of Florida v. Florida et al.*, the Supreme Court finds that states may not be sued to allow Indian nations to open casinos on reservations.

Bibliography

Aaseng, Nathan, *Navajo Code Talkers* (New York: Walker, 1992).

Abbot, Austin, "Indians and the Law." *Harvard Law Review* 2 (4) (1888): 167–179.

Abel, Annie H., "Proposals for an Indian State, 1778–1878." *Annual Report of the American Historical Association for the Year 1907* (1908): 87–104.

Abourezk, James, "Special Introduction." *North Dakota Law Review* 49 (2) (1973): 235–236.

Adair, James, *The History of the American Indians, Particularly Those Nations Adjoining the Mississippi, East and West Florida, Georgia, South and North Carolina, and Virginia* (London: Edward and Charles Dilly, 1775).

Adams, David W., *The Federal Indian Boarding School: A Study of Environment and Response, 1879–1919* (Ph.D. dissertation, University of Indiana at Bloomington, 1975).

Adams, Evelyn C., *American Indian Education: Government Schools and Economic Progress* (New York: King's Crown, 1946).

Ahern, Wilbert H., "Assimilationist Racism: The Case of the 'Friends of the Indian.'" *Journal of Ethnic Studies* 4 (2) (1976): 23–32.

Alden, John R., "The Albany Congress and the Creation of the Indian Superintendencies." *Mississippi Valley Historical Review* 27 (2) (1940): 198–210.

Alexander, Hartley Burr, *The World's Rim: Great Mysteries of the North American Indians* (Lincoln: University of Nebraska Press, 1953).

Ambler, J. Richard; Alexander L. Lindsey, Jr.; and Mary Anne Stein, *Survey and Excavations on Cummings Mesa, Arizona and Utah, 1960–61* (Flagstaff: Northern Arizona Society of Science and Art, 1964).

American Friends Service Committee, *Uncommon Controversy: Fishing Rights of the Muckleshoot, Puyallup and Nisqually Indians* (Seattle: University of Washington Press, 1970).

American Indian Policy Review Commission, Final Report: Submitted to Congress May 17, 1977 (Washington, DC: Government Printing Office, 1977).

Anderson, Edward F., *Peyote: The Divine Cactus* (Tucson: University of Arizona Press, 1980).

Andrist, Ralph K., *The Long Death: The Last Days of the Plains Indians* (New York: Macmillan, 1964).

Annual Report of the Commissioner of Indian Affairs to the Secretary of the Interior for the Year 1880 (Washington, DC: Government Printing Office, 1880).

Annual Report of the Commissioner of Indian Affairs to the Secretary of the Interior for the Fiscal Year Ended June 30, 1921 (Washington, DC: Government Printing Office, 1921).

Annual Report of the Commissioner of Indian Affairs to the Secretary of the Interior for the Fiscal Year Ended June 30, 1923 (Washington, DC: Government Printing Office, 1923).

Annual Report of the Commissioner of Indian Affairs to the Secretary of the Interior for the Fiscal Year Ended June 30, 1925 (Washington, DC: Government Printing Office, 1925).

Annual Report of the Commissioner of Indian Affairs to the Secretary of the Interior for the Fiscal Year Ended June 30, 1926 (Washington, DC: Government Printing Office, 1926).

Annual Report of the Commissioner of Indian Affairs to the Secretary of the Interior for the Fiscal Year Ended June 30, 1931 (Washington, DC: Government Printing Office, 1931).

Annual Report of the Commissioner of Indian Affairs to the Secretary of the Interior for the Fiscal Year Ended June 30, 1931 (Washington, DC: Government Printing Office, 1932).

Annual Report of the Commissioner of Indian Affairs to the Secretary of the Interior for the Fiscal Year Ended June 30, 1932 (Washington, DC: Government Printing Office, 1932).

Annual Report of the Commissioner of Indian Affairs to the Secretary of the Interior for the Fiscal Year Ended June 30, 1934 (Washington, DC: Government Printing Office, 1934).

Apes, William, *The Experiences of Five Christian Indians of the Pequot Tribe* (Boston: James B. Dow, 1833).

———, *Indian Nullification of the Unconstitutional Laws of Massachusetts, Relative to the Marshpee Tribe; or, the Pretended Riot Explained* (Boston: Jonathan Howe, 1835).

Armstrong, William H., *A Friend to God's Poor: Edward Parmelee Smith* (Athens: University of Georgia Press, 1993).

———, *Warrior in Two Camps: Ely S. Parker, Union General and Seneca Chief* (Syracuse, NY: Syracuse University Press, 1978).

Augsburg, Paul D., *Bob and Alf Taylor: Their Lives & Lectures* (Morristown, TN: Morristown, 1925).

Bach, Arthur, *Administration of Indian Resources in the United States* (Ph.D. dissertation, University of Iowa, 1942).

Bagley, Annette Traversie, ed., *The Native American Image on Film: A Programmer's Guide for Organizations and Educators* (Washington, DC: American Film Institute, 1980).

Bailey, Paul, *Ghost Dance Messiah* (Tucson, AZ: Westernlore, 1986).

Ballantine, Betty, and Ian Ballantine, eds., *The Native Americans: An Illustrated History* (Atlanta, GA: Turner, 1993).

Bancroft, Frederic, ed., *The Speeches, Correspondence and Political Papers of Carl Schurz* (New York: Putnam's, 1913).

Bannon, Helen Marie, "The Idea of Civilization and American Indian Policy Reformers in the 1880s." *Journal of American Culture* 1 (4) (1978): 787–799.

———, *Reformers and the 'Indian Problem,' 1878–1887 and 1922–1934* (Ph.D. dissertation, Syracuse University, 1976).

Barker, Robert W., "The Indian Claims Commission: The Conscience of the Nation in Its Dealings with the Original Americans." *Federal Bar Journal* 20 (Summer 1960).

Barns, George C., *Denver, the Man: The Life, Letters and Public Papers of the Lawyer, Soldier, and Statesman* (Wilmington, OH: Shenandoah, 1949).

Barsh, Russel Lawrence, "Indigenous North America and International Law." *Oregon Law Review* 62 (1) (1983): 73–126.

———, "Issues in Federal, State, and Tribal Taxation of Reservation Wealth: A Survey and Economic Critique." *Washington Law Review* 54 (1978–79): 531–586.

———, "The Omen: Three Affiliated Tribes v. Moe and the Future of Tribal Self-Government." *American Indian Law Review* (1977).

Barsh, Russel Lawrence, and James Youngblood Henderson, *The Road: Indian*

Tribes and Political Liberty (Berkeley: University of California Press, 1980).

———, "Tribal Courts, the Model Code, and the Police Idea in American Indian Policy." *Law & Contemporary Problems* 40 (Winter 1976): 25–60.

Barsh, Russel Lawrence, and Ronald Trosper, "Title I of the Indian Self-Determination and Education Assistance Act of 1975." *American Indian Law Review* 361 (1975).

Bass, Althea, *Cherokee Messenger* (Norman: University of Oklahoma Press, 1936).

Bataille, Gretchen M., ed., *Native American Women: A Biographical Dictionary* (New York: Garland, 1993).

Bataille, Gretchen M., and Charles L. P. Silet, eds., *The Pretend Indians: Images of Native Americans in the Movies* (Ames: Iowa State University Press, 1980).

Bataille, Gretchen M., and Kathleen M. Sands, eds., *American Indian Women: A Guide to Research* (New York: Garland, 1991).

Bean, Jerry L., "The Limits of Indian Tribal Sovereignty: The Cornucopia of Inherent Powers." *North Dakota Law Review* 49 (2) (Winter 1973): 303–332.

Beauchamp, William M., *Aboriginal Occupation of New York* (New York State Museum, 1900).

Beaver, R. Pierce, *Church, State, and the American Indians: Two and a Half Centuries of Partnership in Missions between Protestant Churches and Government* (St. Louis: Concordia, 1966).

Beeson, John, *A Plea for the Indians; with Facts and Features of the Late War in Oregon* (New York: privately published, 1858).

Behrens, Jo Lea Wetherilt, "In Defense of 'Poor Lo': National Indian Defense Association and *Council Fire's* Advocacy for Sioux Land Rights." *South Dakota History* 24 (3–4) (Fall/Winter 1994): 153–173.

———, *In Defense of 'Poor Lo': The* Council Fire's *Advocacy of American Indian Civil Rights, 1878–1889* (Master's thesis, University of Nebraska at Omaha, 1992).

Bell, William Gardner, "A Dedication to the Memory of John Gregory Bourke, 1846–1896." *Arizona and the West* 13 (4) (Winter 1971): 318–322.

Bennett, Louis LaFollette, "Problems and Prospects in Developing Indian Communities." *Arizona Law Review* 10 (6) (Winter 1968): 649–660.

Berger, Edward B., "Indian Mineral Interest: A Potential for Economic Advancement." *Arizona Law Review* 10 (6) (Winter 1968): 675–690.

Berk, Robert, "Case Notes: Indian Law. State Preempted from Enforcing Its Hunting and Fishing Regulations against Non-Indians on the Reservation: *New Mexico v. Mescalero Apache Tribe*, 103 S.Ct. 2378 {1983}." *Arizona State Law Journal* 1984, 191–210.

Berkhofer, Robert F., Jr., *Salvation and the Savage: An Analysis of Protestant Missions and American Indian Response, 1787–1862* (Lexington: University of Kentucky Press, 1965).

———, *The White Man's Indian: Images of the American Indian from Columbus to the Present* (New York: Knopf, 1978).

Berman, Howard R., "The Concept of Aboriginal Rights in the Early Legal History of the United States." *Buffalo Law Review* 27 (1977–78): 637–667.

Bernstein, Barton J., and Allen J. Matusow, eds., *The Truman Administration: A Documentary History* (New York: Harper & Row, 1966).

Bieder, Robert Eugene, *Science Encounters the Indian, 1820–1880* (Norman: University of Oklahoma Press, 1986).

———, *The American Indian and the Development of Anthropological Thought in the United States, 1780–1851* (Ph.D. dissertation, University of Minnesota at Minneapolis, 1972).

Biographical Directory of the United States Congress, 1774–1989, Senate Document 100–34, 100th Congress, 2d Session (Washington, DC: Government Printing Office, 1989).

Biographical and Historical Index of American Indians and Persons Involved in Indian Affairs (Boston: G. K. Hall, 1966).

Black, Henry Campbell, *Black's Law Dictionary: Definitions of the Terms and Phrases of American and English Jurisprudence, Ancient and Modern* (St. Paul, MN: West, 1990).

Bland, Thomas Augustus, *A Brief History of the Late Military Invasion of the Home of the Sioux* (Washington, DC: The National Indian Defence Association, 1891).

———, *A History of the Sioux Agreement: Some Facts Which Should Not Be Forgotten* (Washington, DC: National Indian Defense Association, 1888).

———, *Pioneers of Progress* (Chicago: privately published, 1906).

Block, Maxine, ed., *Current Biography 1941* (New York: Wilson, 1941).

Blodgett, Harold, *Samson Occom* (Hanover, NH: Dartmouth College Press, 1935).

Blumm, Michael C., "Hydro-Power vs. Salmon: The Struggle of the Pacific Northwest's Anadromous Fish Resources for a Peaceful Co-Existence with the Federal Columbia Power System." *Environmental Law* 11 (1980–1981): 211–300.

Boender, Debra R., *Glenn Emmons of Gallup* (Master's thesis, University of New Mexico, 1976).

Bonnin, Gertrude Simmons, *American Indian Stories* (Glorieta, NM: Rio Grande, 1921).

———, *Old Indian Legends* (Boston: Ginn, 1901).

Bowden, Henry Warner, *American Indians and Christian Missions: Studies in Cultural Conflict* (Chicago: University of Chicago Press, 1981).

Bowser, Eileen, *The Transformation of Cinema, 1907–1915* (New York: Scribner's, 1990).

Boyer, Florence M., *The Life and Works of Helen Hunt Jackson* (Master's thesis, Columbia University, 1929).

Boyum, William, "Health Care: An Overview of the Indian Health Service." *American Indian Law Review* 14 (2) (1989): 241–268.

Brandes, Raymond Stewart, "A Dedication to the Memory of Frank Hamilton Cushing, 1857–1900." *Arizona and the West* 4 (3) (Autumn 1962): 197–200.

———, *Frank Hamilton Cushing: Pioneer Americanist* (Ph.D. dissertation, University of Arizona, 1965).

Brecher, Joseph R., "Federal Regulatory Status and Indian Self-Determination: Some Problems and Some Proposed Legislative Solutions." *Arizona Law Review* 19 (2) (1977): 285–312.

Bremer, Richard G., *Indian Agent and Wilderness Scholar: The Life of Henry Rowe Schoolcraft* (Mount Pleasant, MI: Clark Historical Society, 1987).

A Brief Statement of the Rights of the Indians of the Seneca Indians in the State of New York to Their Lands in That State (Philadelphia: W. H. Pile,1872).

Brophy, William A., and Sophie D. Aberle, *The Indian: America's Unfinished Business: Report of the Commission on the Rights, Liberties, and Responsibilities of the American Indian* (Norman: University of Oklahoma Press, 1966).

Brown, Ira V., *Lyman Abbott, Christian Evolutionist: A Study in Religious Liberalism* (Westport, CT: Greenwood, 1970).

Brumble, H. David, III, *American Indian Autobiography* (Berkeley: University of California Press, 1988).

Bryfonski, Dedria, and Phyllis Carmel Mendelson, eds., *Twentieth-Century Literary Criticism: Excerpts from Criticism of the Works of Novelists, Poets, Playwrights, Short Story Writers, and Other Creative Writers Who Lived between 1900 and 1960, from the First Published Critical Appraisals to Current Evaluations* (Detroit: Gale, 1978–95).

Buntin, Arthur A., *The Indian in American Literature, 1680–1760* (Ph.D. dissertation, University of Washington at Seattle, 1961).

Burgess, Larry E., *The Lake Mohonk Conferences on the Indian, 1883–1916* (Ph.D. dissertation, Claremont Graduate School, 1972).

———, "'We'll Discuss at Mohonk.'" *Quaker History* 60 (1) (1971): 14–28.

Burke, Joseph C., "The Cherokee Cases: A Study in Law, Politics and Morality."

Stanford Law Review 21 (2) (February 1969): 500–531.

Burnett, Donald L., Jr., "An Historical Analysis of the 1968 'Indian Civil Rights' Act." *Harvard Journal of Legislation* 9 (4) (1972): 557–626.

Burt, Larry, *Tribalism in Crisis: Federal Indian Policy, 1953–1961* (Albuquerque: University of New Mexico Press, 1982).

Cadwalader, Sandra L., and Vine Deloria, Jr., eds., *The Aggressions of Civilization: Federal Indian Policy since the 1880s* (Philadelphia: Temple University Press, 1984).

Calloway, Colin G., *New Directions in American Indian History* (Norman: University of Oklahoma Press, 1988).

Campbell, Gregory R., "The Changing Dimension of Native American Health: A Critical Understanding of Contemporary Native American Health Issues." *American Indian Culture and Research Journal* 13 (3–4) (1989): 1–20.

———, *Plains Indian Historical Demography and Health. The Political Economy of Ill Health: Changing Northern Cheyenne Health Patterns and Economic Underdevelopment* (Ph.D. dissertation, University of Michigan at Ann Arbor, 1987).

Canby, William C., Jr., *American Indian Law in a Nutshell* (St. Paul, MN: West, 1981).

Candee, Marjorie Dent, ed., *Current Biography 1954* (New York: Wilson, 1954).

Canfield, George F., "The Legal Position of the Indian." *American Law Review* 15 (January 1881): 21–37.

Carlson, Leonard A., *Indians, Bureaucrats, and Land: The Dawes Act and the Decline of Indian Farming* (Westport, CT: Greenwood, 1981).

Carly, Kenneth, *The Sioux Uprising of 1862* (St. Paul: Minnesota Historical Society, 1961).

Carmony, Donald F., ed., "William P. Dole: Wabash Valley Merchant and Flatboatman." *Indiana Magazine of History* 67 (4) (December 1971): 335–363.

Carter, Clarence E. and John P. Bloom, eds., *The Territorial Papers of the United States* (Washington, DC: Government Printing Office, 1944–1969).

The Case of the Seneca Indians in the State of New York. Illustrated by Facts. Printed for the Information of the Society of Friends [Hicksite], by Direction of the Joint Committee on Indian Affairs, of the Four Yearly Meetings of Friends of Genesee, New York, Philadelphia, and Baltimore (Philadelphia: Merrihew and Thompson, 1840).

Chalou, George Clifford, *The Red Pawns GoTo War: British-American Relations, 1810–1815* (Ph.D. dissertation, Indiana University at Bloomington, 1971).

Chambers, Reid Peyton, "Judicial Enforcement of the Federal Trust Responsibility to Indians." *Stanford Law Review* 27 (5) (May 1975): 1213–1248.

Champagne, Duane, ed., *Native America: Portrait of the Peoples* (Detroit: Visible Ink, 1994).

———, *The Native North American Almanac: A Reference Work on Native North Americans in the United States and Canada* (Detroit: Gale, 1994).

Chapman, Berlin B., "Charles Curtis and the Kaw Reservation." *Kansas Historical Quarterly* 15 (4) (November 1947): 337–351.

Chaput, Donald, "Generals, Indian Agents, Politicians: The Doolittle Survey of 1865." *Western Historical Quarterly* 3 (1972): 269–282.

Child, Lydia Maria, *An Appeal for the Indians* (New York: Tomlinson, 1868).

Chroust, Anton-Hermann, "Did President Jackson Actually Threaten the Supreme Court of the United States with Nonenforcement of Its Injunction against the State of Georgia?" *American Journal of Legal History* 4 (1) (January 1960): 76–78.

Churchill, Ward, and Jim Vander Wall, *Agents of Repression: The FBI's Secret Wars against the Black Panther Party and the American Indian Movement* (Boston, MA: South End, 1988).

Churchill, Ward; Norbert Hill; and Mary Ann Hill, "Media Stereotyping and Native Response: An Historical Overview." *Indian Historian* 11 (4) (1978): 45–56.

Cleary, Michael, "Finding the Center of the Earth: Satire, History, and Myth in *Little Big Man.*" *Western American Literature* 15 (3) (1980): 195–211.

Clifton, James A., ed., *Being and Becoming Indian: Biographical Studies of North American Frontiers* (Chicago: Dorsey, 1989).

Clinton, Robert N. et al., "Judicial Enforcement of the Federal Restraints on Alienation of Indian Land: The Origins of the Eastern Land Claims." *Maine Law Review* 17 (1979).

Clinton, Robert N., "Isolated in Their Own Country: A Defense of Federal Protection of Indian Autonomy and Self-Government." *Stanford Law Review* 33 (6) (1981): 979–1068.

Cocks, James F., III, *The Selfish Savage: Protestant Missionaries and Nez Percé and Cayuse Indians, 1835–1847* (Ph.D. dissertation, University of Michigan at Ann Arbor, 1975).

Coen, Rena Neumann, *The Indian as Noble Savage in 19th Century American Art* (Ph.D. dissertation, University of Minnesota at Minneapolis, 1969).

Cohen, Felix S., "The Erosion of Indian Rights, 1950–53: A Case Study in Bureaucracy." *Yale Law Journal* 62 (3) (February 1953): 348–390.

———, "Indian Rights and the Federal Courts." *Minnesota Law Review* 24 145 (1940).

———, "Original Indian Title." *Minnesota Law Review* 32 28 (1947).

———, *The Spanish Origin of Indian Rights in the Law of the United States.* 31 Georgetown Law Journal 1 (1942).

Colbert, Thomas Burnell, "Visionary or Rogue? The Life & Legacy of Elias Cornelius Boudinot." *Chronicles of Oklahoma* 65 (3) (Fall 1987): 268–281.

Colby, William Munn, *Routes to Rainey Mountain: A Biography of James Mooney, Ethnologist* (Ph.D. dissertation, University of Wisconsin at Madison, 1977).

Coleman, Michael Christopher, "Not Race, But Grace: Presbyterian Missionaries and American Indians, 1837–1893." *Journal of American History* 67 (1) (1980): 41–60.

———, *Presbyterian Missionaries and Their Attitudes to the American Indian, 1837–1893* (Ph.D. dissertation, University of Pennsylvania, 1977).

Collier, John, *On the Gleaming Way: Navajos, Eastern Pueblos, Zuñis, Hopis, Apaches, and Their Land; and Their Meanings to the World* (Denver: Sage, 1962).

Collins, Richard B., "Implied Limitations on the Jurisdiction over Indian Tribes." *Washington Law Review* 54 (1978–79): 479–525.

Condition of the Indian Tribes: Report of the Joint Special Committee, Appointed under Joint Resolution of March 3, 1865, with an Appendix (Washington, DC: Government Printing Office, 1867).

Converse, Harriet Maxwell, "The Seneca New-Year Ceremony and Other Customs." *Indian Notes* 7 (2) (1930).

Copway, George, *Organization of a New Indian Territory, East of the Missouri River.* (New York: S. W. Benedict, 1850).

Corkran, David H., *The Cherokee Frontier: Conflict and Survival, 1740–62* (Norman: University of Oklahoma Press, 1962).

Costner, Kevin et al. *Dances with Wolves: The Illustrated History of the Epic Film* (New York: Newmarket, 1990).

Cotterill, Robert S., *The Southern Indians: The Story of the Civilized Tribes Before Removal* (Norman: University of Oklahoma Press, 1954).

Couch, Nevada, *Pages from Cherokee History, as Identified with Samuel Austin Worcester, D.D., for 34 Years a Missionary of the American Board of Commissioners for Foreign Missions among the Cherokees* (St. Louis: Studley, 1884).

Council on Interracial Books for Children, eds., *Chronicles of American Indian Protest* (Greenwich, CT: Fawcett, 1971).

Covington, James Warren, *The Seminoles of Florida* (Gainesville: University Press of Florida, 1993).

Crane, Fred A., *The Noble Savage in America, 1815–1860: Concepts of the Indian with*

Special Reference to the Writers of the Northeast (Ph.D. dissertation, Yale University, 1952).

Cravens, Dollye Hefner, *Standard Bearer of the Cherokees: The Life of William Wirt Hastings* (Master's thesis, Oklahoma Agricultural and Mechanical College, 1942).

Cree, Linda, "The Extension of County Jurisdiction over Indian Reservations in California: Public Law 280 and the Ninth Circuit." *Hastings Law Journal* 25 (6) (1974): 1451–1506.

Critchlow, Donald T., "Lewis Meriam, Expertise, and Indian Reform." *Historian* 47 (1981): 325–344.

Crutchfield, James, *Timeless Tennessee* (Huntsville, AL: Strode, 1984).

Current, Richard N., ed., *Encyclopedia of the Confederacy* (New York: Simon & Schuster, 1993).

Curtis, Edward Sheriff, *The North American Indian: Being a Series of Volumes Picturing and Describing the Indians of the United States and Alaska* (New York: Johnson Reprints, 1970).

Cushing, Frank Hamilton, "Zuñi Fetiches." *Second Annual Report of the Bureau of Ethnology* (Washington, DC: Government Printing Office, 1883).

Dale, Edward Everett, *The Indians of the Southwest: A Century of Development under the United States* (Norman: University of Oklahoma Press, 1949).

Danforth, Sandra C., "Repaying Historical Debts: The Indian Claims Commission." *North Dakota Law Review* 49 (2) (Winter 1973): 359–404.

Danky, James P., ed., *Native American Periodicals and Newspapers, 1828–1982: Bibliography, Publishing Record, and Holdings* (Westport, CT: Greenwood, 1984).

Danziger, Edmund J., Jr., *Indians and Bureaucrats: Administering the Reservation Policy during the Civil War* (Urbana: University of Illinois Press, 1974).

Darnell, Regna Diebold, *The Development of American Anthropology, 1879–1920: From the Bureau of American Ethnology to Franz Boas* (Ph.D. dissertation, University of Pennsylvania at Philadelphia, 1969).

Debo, Angie, *A History of the Indians of the United States* (Norman: University of Oklahoma Press, 1970).

DeFrance, Charles Q., "Some Recollections of Thomas H. Tibbles." *Nebraska History Magazine* 13 (4) (October-December 1932): 238–247.

DeJong, David H., *Promises of the Past: A History of Indian Education in the United States* (Golden, CO: North American, 1993).

———, "'See the New Country': The Removal Controversy and Pima-Maricopa Water Rights, 1868–1879." *Journal of Arizona History* 33 (4) (Winter 1992): 367–398.

DeLeon, David, ed., *Leaders from the 1960s: A Biographical Sourcebook of American Activism* (Westport, CT: Greenwood, 1994).

Dellwo, Robert D., "Indian Water Rights: The Winters Doctrine Updated." *Gonzaga Law Review* 6 (Spring 1971): 215–240.

Deloria, Vine, Jr., *American Indian Policy in the Twentieth Century* (Norman: University of Oklahoma Press, 1985).

———, *Behind the Trail of Broken Treaties: an Indian Declaration of Independence* (New York: Delacorte, 1974).

———, *Custer Died for Your Sins: An Indian Manifesto* (Norman: University of Oklahoma Press, 1988).

———, "Indian Law and the Reach of History." *Journal of Contemporary Law* 4 (Winter 1977): 1–13.

———, *The Nations Within: The Past and Future of American Indian Sovereignty* (New York: Pantheon, 1984).

Deloria, Vine, Jr., and Clifford M. Lytle, *American Indians, American Justice* (Austin: University of Texas Press, 1983).

———, *The Nations Within: The Past and Future of American Indian Sovereignty* (New York: Pantheon, 1984).

Dennis, Henry C., ed., *The American Indian, 1492–1976: A Chronology and Fact Book* (Dobbs Ferry, NY: Oceana, 1977).

Department of the Interior, *Report of the Commissioner of Indian Affairs to the Secretary of the Interior, 1925* (Washington, DC: Government Printing Office, 1925).

———, *Report of the Commissioner of Indian Affairs to the Secretary of the Interior, 1926* (Washington, DC: Government Printing Office, 1926).

DeRosier, Arthur H., Jr., *The Removal of the Choctaw Indians* (Knoxville: University of Tennessee Press, 1970).

Dictionary of Wisconsin Biography (Madison: State Historical Society of Madison, 1960).

Dippie, Brian W., *Catlin and His Contemporaries: The Politics of Patronage* (Lincoln: University of Nebraska Press, 1990).

———, "Government Patronage: Catlin, Stanley, and Eastman." *Montana* 44 (4) (Autumn 1994): 40–53.

———, *The Vanishing American: Popular Attitudes and American Indian Policy in the Nineteenth Century* (Ph.D. dissertation, University of Texas at Austin, 1970).

———, *The Vanishing American: White Attitudes and U.S. Indian Policy* (Middletown, CT: Wesleyan University Press, 1982; paperback reprint, Lawrence: University Press of Kansas, 1991).

Dobyns, Henry F., *Native American Historical Demography: A Critical Bibliography* (Bloomington: Indiana University Press, 1976).

Dockstader, Frederick J., *Great North American Indians: Profiles in Life and Leadership* (New York: Van Nostrand Reinhold, 1977).

Dorcy, Michael Morgan, *Friends of the Indian, 1922–1934: Patterns of Patronage and Philanthropy* (Ph.D. dissertation, University of Pennsylvania, 1978).

Downes, Randolph C., *Council Fires on the Upper Ohio: A Narrative of Indian Affairs in the Upper Ohio Valley until 1795* (Pittsburgh: University of Pittsburgh Press, 1940).

———, "A Crusade for Indian Reform, 1922–1934." *Mississippi Valley Historical Review* 32 (2) (December 1945): 331–354.

Drake, Samuel G., *Indian Biography, Containing the Lives of More Than Two Hundred Indian Chiefs, etc.* (Boston: Josiah Drake, 1832).

———, *The Book of the Indians; or, Biography and History of the Indians of North America, from Its First Discovery to the Year 1841* (Boston: O. L. Perkins, 1841).

Drinnon, Richard, *Keeper of the Concentration Camps: Dillon S. Myer and American Racism* (Berkeley: University of California Press, 1987).

Driver, Harold E., *Indians of North America* (Chicago: University of Chicago Press, 1969).

DuMars, Charles T., "Indictment under the 'Major Crimes Act': An Exercise in Unfairness and Unconstitutionality." *Arizona Law Review* 10 (6) (Winter 1968): 691–705.

DuMars, Charles T.; Marilyn O'Leary; and Albert E. Utton, *Pueblo Indian Water Rights* (Tucson: University of Arizona Press, 1984).

Eastman, Charles Alexander, *Indian Boyhood* (Boston: Little, Brown, 1933).

Eastman, Charles Alexander, and Elaine Goodale Eastman, *Wigwam Evenings: Sioux Stories Retold* (Lincoln: University of Nebraska Press, 1990).

Ebert, Roger, *Roger Ebert's Video Companion: 1995 Edition* (Kansas City, MO: Andrews and McMeel, 1994).

Edmunds, R. David, ed., *American Indian Leaders: Studies in Diversity* (Lincoln: University of Nebraska Press, 1980).

Ehle, John, *Trail of Tears: The Rise and Fall of the Cherokee Nation* (New York: Anchor, 1988).

Elley, Derek, cons. ed., *Variety Movie Guide* (New York: Prentice-Hall, 1992).

Ellicott, Karen Sue, *The Portrayal of the American Indian Woman in a Select Group of American Novels* (Ph.D. dissertation, University of Minnesota, 1979).

Ellison, George, ed., *James Mooney's History, Myths, and Sacred Formulas of the Cherokees* (Asheville, NC: Bright Mountain, 1992).

Ericson, Jack T., *Indian Rights Association Papers: A Guide to the Microfilm Edition, 1864–1973* (Glen Rock, NJ: Microfilming Corporation of America, 1975).

Evarts, Jeremiah, *Essays on the Present Crisis in the Condition of the American Indians* (Boston: Perkins and Marvin, 1829).

Evarts, Jeremiah, ed., *Speeches on the Passage of the Bill for Removal of the Indians Delivered in the Congress of the United States, April and May 1830* (Boston: Perkins and Marvin, 1830).

Ewers, John C., "George Catlin, Painter of the Indians and the West." *Annual Report of the Smithsonian Institution for 1955* (1956): 483–506.

———, "Gustavus Schon's Portraits of Flathead and Pend d'Oreille Indians, 1854." *Smithsonian Miscellaneous Collections* 110 (7) (1948).

———, "Not Quite Redmen: The Plains Illustrations of Felix O. C. Darley." *American Art Journal* 3 (2) (1971): 88–98.

Ewy, Marvin, "Charles Curtis of Kansas: Vice President of the United States, 1929–1933." *Emporia State Research Studies* 10 (2) (December 1961).

Executive Orders Relating to Indian Reservations, 1855–1922 (Wilmington: Scholarly Resources, 1975).

Fannin, Paul J., "Indian Education: A Test Case for Democracy." *Arizona Law Review* 10 (6) (Winter 1968): 661–674.

Farb, Perter, *Man's Rise to Civilization: The Cultural Ascent of the Indians of North America* (New York: Dutton, 1978).

Faust, Richard H., "William Medill: Commissioner of Indian Affairs, 1845–1849." *Old Northwest* 1 (2) (June 1975): 129–140.

Federal Indian Policies: From the Colonial Period through the Early 1970s (Washington, DC: Bureau of Indian Affairs, 1975).

Fielder, Mildred, *Sioux Indian Leaders* (Seattle: Superior, 1975).

Fifty United States Civil Service Commissioners: Biographical Sketches, Biographical Sources, Writings (Washington, DC: U.S. Civil Service Commission, 1971).

Finn, Marie T., ed. *The American Bench: Judges of the Nation* (Sacramento: Forster-Long, 1993).

Fischer, LeRoy H., ed., *The Civil War Era in Indian Territory* (Los Angeles: Morrison, 1974).

Fisher, Alice Poindexter, *The Transformation of Tradition: A Study of Zitkala Sa and Mourning Dove, Two Traditional American Indian Writers* (Ph.D. dissertation, City University of New York, 1979).

Fixico, Donald L., *Termination and Relocation: Federal Indian Policy, 1945–1960* (Albuquerque: University of New Mexico Press, 1986).

Flake, David K., *A History of Mormon Missionary Work with the Hopi, Navaho, and Zuni* (Master's thesis, Brigham Young University, 1965).

Fletcher, Alice C., *Indian Education and Civilization: A Report Prepared in Answer to Senate Resolution of February 23, 1885*, A Report of the Bureau of Education, Senate Executive Document No. 95, 48th Congress, 2d Session.

Florio, Roger, "Water Rights: Enforcing the Federal-Indian Trust after *Nevada v. United States.*" *American Indian Law Review* 13 (1) (1987): 79–98.

Foley, Rudolf Xavier, *Origins of the Indian Reorganization Act of 1934* (Ph.D. dissertation, Fordham University, 1937).

Foreman, Grant, *The Five Civilized Tribes* (Norman: University of Oklahoma Press, 1934).

———, *Indian Removal: The Emigration of the Five Civilized Tribes of Indians* (Norman: University of Oklahoma Press, 1932).

Foy, Felician A., O.F.M., ed., *1995 Catholic Almanac* (Huntington, IN: Our Sunday Visitor, 1994).

Franks, Kenny A., *Stand Watie and the Agony of the Cherokee Nation* (Memphis, TN: Memphis State University Press, 1979).

Fredericks, John, III, "Indian Lands: Financing Indian Agriculture: Mortgaged Indian Lands and the Federal Trust Responsibility." *American Indian Law Review* 16 (1) (1989): 105–133.

Freeman, John Finley, *Henry Rowe Schoolcraft, 1793–1864* (Ph.D. dissertation, Harvard University, 1960).

Freeman, John Leiper, *The New Deal for the Indians: A Study in Bureau-Committee Relations in American Government* (Ph.D. dissertation, Princeton University, 1952).

Friar, Ralph E. and Natasha A. Friar, *The Only Good Indian—The Hollywood Gospel* (New York: Drama Book Specialists,1972).

Friend, Ruth Ellen, *Helen Hunt Jackson: A Critical Study* (Ph.D. dissertation, Kent State University, 1985).

Fritz, Henry E., *The Movement for Indian Assimilation, 1860–1890* (Philadelphia: University of Pennsylvania Press, 1963).

Fuller, Clarissa Parsons, *Frank Hamilton Cushing's Relations to Zuñi and the Hemenway Southwestern Expedition, 1879–1889* (Master's thesis, University of New Mexico, 1945).

Furtaw, Julia C., ed., *Native Americans Information Directory* (Detroit: Gale, 1993).

Gara, Larry, *The Presidency of Franklin Pierce* (Lawrence: University Press of Kansas, 1991).

Gasaway, Laura N.; James L. Hoover; and Dorothy M. Warden, *American Indian Legal Materials: A Union List* (Stanfordville, NY: Coleman, 1980).

Gehm, Katherine, *Sarah Winnemucca: Most Extraordinary Woman of the Paiute Nation* (Phoenix: O'Sullivan, Woodside, 1975).

Getches, David H.; Daniel M. Rosenfelt; and Charles F. Wilkinson, *Case and Materials on Federal Indian Law* (St. Paul, MN: West, 1979).

Gibson, Arrell Morgan, "The Centennial Legacy of the General Allotment Act." *Chronicles of Oklahoma* 65 (3) (Fall 1987): 228–251.

Gilbert, Bil, *God Gave Us This Country: Tekamthi and the First American Civil War* (New York: Atheneum, 1989).

Gilcreast, Everett Arthur, *Richard Henry Pratt and American Indian Policy, 1877–1906: A Study of the Assimilation Movement* (Ph.D. dissertation, Yale University, 1967).

Goldberg, Carole E., "A Dynamic View of Tribal Jurisdiction to Tax Non-Indians." *Law & Contemporary Problems* 40 (Winter 1976): 166–189.

———, "Public Law 280: The Limits of State Jurisdiction over Reservation Indians." *UCLA Law Review* 22 (1974–75): 535–594.

Graham, Judith, ed., *Current Biography 1992* (New York: Wilson, 1992).

———, *Current Biography Yearbook 1994* (New York: Wilson, 1994).

Graham, Otis L., Jr., and Meghan Robinson Wander, eds., *Franklin D. Roosevelt, His Life and Times: An Encyclopedic View* (Boston: G. K. Hall, 1985).

Grant, C. L., *Letters, Journals and Writings of Benjamin Hawkins* (Savannah, GA: Beehive, 1980).

Graybill, Florence Curtis, and Victor Boesen, *Edward Sheriff Curtis: Visions of a Vanishing Race* (New York: Crowell, 1976).

Green, Jesse D., "The Man Who Became an Indian," *New York Review of Books.* 22 (9) (29 May 1975): 31–33.

Green, Jesse D., ed., *Zuñi: Selected Writings of Frank Hamilton Cushing* (Lincoln: University of Nebraska Press, 1979).

Green, Michael D., *The Politics of Indian Removal: Creek Government and Society in Crisis* (Lincoln: University of Nebraska Press, 1982).

Green, Rayna D., *The Image of the Indian in the Popular Imagination: An Analysis of Oral, Visual, and Ideational Materials* (Ph.D. dissertation, Indian University at Bloomington, 1973).

Griffith, Benjamin W., Jr., *McIntosh and Weatherford, Creek Indian Leaders* (Tuscaloosa: University of Alabama Press, 1988).

Grinde, Donald A., Jr., *The Iroquois and the Founding of the American Nation* (San Francisco: Indian Historian, 1977).

Grinnell, George Bird, *The Fighting Cheyennes* (Norman, Oklahoma: University of Oklahoma Press, 1956).

Gross, Michael Paul, "Indian Control for Quality Indian Education." *North Dakota Law Review* 49 (2) (Winter 1973): 237–266.

Grossman, Mark, *The ABC-Clio Companion to the Environmental Movement* (Santa Barbara, California: ABC-Clio, 1994).

Groves, William Hinton, *The Evolution of American Indian Policy: From Colonial Times to the Florida Treaty (1819)* (Ph.D. dissertation, Florida State University, 1982).

Guttmann, Allen, *States' Rights and Indian Removal: The Cherokee Nation v. the State of Georgia* (Boston: Heath, 1965).

Hafford, William E., "The Navajo Code Talkers," *Arizona Highways*, 65 (2) (February 1989): 32–45.

Hagan, William T., *American Indians* (Chicago: University of Chicago Press, 1961).

———, "Civil Service Commissioner Theodore Roosevelt and the Indian Rights Association." *Pacific Historical Review* 44 (1975): 187–200.

———, *Indian Policy and Judges: Experiments in Acculturation and Control* (New Haven, CT: Yale University Press, 1966).

———, *The Indian Rights Association: The Herbert Welsh Years, 1882–1904* (Tucson: University of Arizona Press, 1985).

———, "Kiowas, Comanches and Cattlemen, 1867–1906: A Case Study of the Failure of U.S. Reservation Policy," *Pacific Historical Review* 40 (1971): 333–355.

Hall, Kermit L., ed., *The Oxford Companion to the Supreme Court of the United States* (New York: Oxford University Press, 1992).

Hardy, Gail J., *American Women Civil Rights Activists: Biobibliographies of 68 Leaders, 1825–1992* (Jefferson, NC: McFarland, 1993).

Harlan, Judith, *American Indians Today: Issues and Conflicts* (New York: Franklin Watts, 1987).

Harmon, George D., "Benjamin Hawkins and the Federal Factory System." *North Carolina Historical Review* 9 (2) (1932): 138–152.

———, *Sixty Years of Indian Affairs: Political, Economic and Diplomatic, 1789–1850* (Chapel Hill: University of North Carolina Press, 1941).

Harring, Sidney L., "Crow Dog's Case: A Chapter in the Legal History of Tribal Sovereignty." *American Indian Law Review* 14 (2) (1989): 191–239.

Harte, John Bret, *The San Carlos Indian Reservation, 1872–1886: An Administrative History* (Ph.D. dissertation, University of Arizona, 1972).

Hasse, Larry J., *Termination and Assimilation: Federal Indian Policy, 1943 to 1961* (Ph.D. dissertation, Washington State University, 1974).

Hatley, Marvin T., III, *The Dividing Path: The Direction of Cherokee Life in the Eighteenth Century* (Master's thesis, University of North Carolina at Chapel Hill, 1977).

Hauptman, Laurence M., "Senecas and Subdividers: Resistance to Allotment of Indian Lands in New York, 1875–1906." *Prologue* 5 (2) (Summer 1977): 105–116.

Hayden, Joseph R., *The Senate and Treaties, 1789–1817: The Development of the Treaty-Making Functions of the United States Senate during Their Formative Period* (New York: Macmillan, 1920).

Hecht, Robert A., "Oliver LaFarge, John Collier, and the Hopi Constitution of 1936." *Journal of Arizona History* 26 (2) (Summer 1985): 145–162.

———, *Oliver LaFarge and the American Indian: A Biography* (Metuchen, NJ: Scarecrow, 1991).

Heckewelder, John, *History, Manners, and Customs of the Indian Nations* (Philadelphia: Historical Society of Pennsylvania, 1876).

———, *A Narrative of the Mission of the United Brethren Among the Delaware and Mohegan Indians from Its Commencement in the Year 1740 to the Close of the Year 1820* (Philadelphia: M'Carty and Davis, 1820).

Hertzberg, Hazel W., *American Pan-Indianism: The Formative Years, 1900–1934* (Ph.D. dissertation, Columbia University, 1968).

———, *The Search for an American Indian Identity: Modern Pan-Indian Movements* (Syracuse, NY: Syracuse University Press, 1971).

Hilger, Michael, *The American Indian in Film* (Metuchen, NJ: Scarecrow, 1986).

Hill, Edward E., *The Office of Indian Affairs, 1824–1880: Historical Sketches* (New York: Clearwater, 1974).

Hinsley, Curtis M., Jr., *The Development of a Profession: Anthropology in Washington, DC, 1846–1903* (Ph.D. dissertation, University of Wisconsin, 1976).

———, *The Smithsonian and the American Indian: Making a Moral Anthropology in Victorian America* (Washington, DC: Smithsonian, 1981).

Hirschfelder, Arlene, *American Indian Authors* (New York: Association on American Indian Affairs, 1970).

Hirschfelder, Arlene, and Martha Kreipe de Montaño, *The Native American Almanac: A Portrait of Native America Today* (New York: Prentice-Hall, 1993).

History of Gallatin, Saline, Hamilton, Franklin and Williamson Counties, Illinois (Chicago: Goodspeed, 1887).

Hodge, Frederick Webb, ed., *Handbook of American Indians North of Mexico* (Washington, DC: Bureau of American Ethnology, 1907–10).

Hoig, Stan, *The Sand Creek Massacre* (Norman: University of Oklahoma Press, 1961).

Holford, David M., "The Subversion of the Indian Land Allotment System, 1887–1934." *Indian Historian* 8 (1) (Spring 1975): 11–21.

Holm, Bill, and George I. Quimby, *Edward S. Curtis in the Land of the War Canoes: A Pioneer Cinematographer in the Pacific Northwest* (Seattle: University of Washington Press, 1980).

Holm, Tom, *Indians and Progressives: From the Vanishing Policy to the Indian New Deal* (Ph.D. dissertation, University of Oklahoma, 1978).

Holt, H. Barry, and Gary Forrester, *Digest of American Indian Law: Cases and Chronology* (Littleton, CO: Rothman, 1990).

Horan, James D., *The McKenney-Hall Portrait Gallery of American Indians* (New York: Crown, 1972).

Horsman, Reginald, *Expansion and American Indian Policy, 1783–1812* (East Lansing: Michigan State University Press, 1967).

Hough, Walter, "Alice Cunningham Fletcher." *American Anthropologist* 25 (2) (1923): 254–258.

Hoxie, Frederick E., *Beyond Savagery: The Campaign to Assimilate the American Indians, 1880–1920* (Ph.D. dissertation, Brandeis University, 1977).

M., *A Final Promise: The Campaign to Assimilate the Indians, 1880–1920* (Lincoln: University of Nebraska Press, 1984).

———, "Redefining Indian Education: Thomas J. Morgan's Program in Disarray," *Arizona and the West* 24 (Spring 1982): 5–18.

Hoxie, Frederick E., ed., *Indians in American History: An Introduction* (Arlington Heights, IL: Harlan Davidson, 1988).

Hughes, Thomas, *Indian Chiefs of Southern Minnesota, Containing Sketches of the Prominent Chieftains of the Dakota and Winnebago Tribes from 1825 to 1865* (Minneapolis, MN: Ross & Haines,1969).

Hundley, Norris, "The Dark and Bloody Ground of Indian Water Rights: Confusion Elevated to Principle." *Western History Quarterly* 9 (4) (1978): 455–482.

———, "The 'Winters' Decision and Indian Water Rights: A Mystery Reexamined." *Western History Quarterly* 13 (January 1982).

Hunt, Gaillard, ed., *The Writings of James Madison* (New York: Putnam's, 1908).

Hurtado, Albert L., and Peter Iverson, eds., *Major Problems in American Indian History: Documents and Essays* (Lexington, MA: Heath, 1994).

Indian Affairs, 1964: A Progress Report from the Commissioner of Indian Affairs (Washington, DC: Government Printing Office, 1968).

Indian Affairs, 1966: A Progress Report from the Commissioner of Indian Affairs (Washington, DC: Government Printing Office, 1968).

Indian Affairs, 1968: A Progress Report from the Commissioner of Indian Affairs (Washington, DC: Government Printing Office, 1968).

"The Indian Battle for Self-Determination." *California Law Review* 58 (1970).

"Indian Law: The Pre-Emption Doctrine and Colonias De Sante Fe." *Natural Resources Law Journal* 13 (1973).

"Indian Taxation: Underlying Policies and Present Problems." *California Law Review* 59 (1971).

Investigation into Indian Affairs, before the Committee on Appropriations of the House of Representatives: Argument of N. P. Chipman, on Behalf of Hon. E. S. Parker, Commissioner of Indian Affairs (Washington, DC: Powell, Ginck, 1871).

Israel, Daniel H., "The Reemergence of Tribal Nationalism and Its Impact on Reservation Resource Development." *University of Colorado Law Review* 47 (1976).

Israel, Daniel H. and Thomas L. Smithson, "Indian Taxation, Tribal Sovereignty and Economic Development." *North Dakota Law Review* 49 (2) (Winter 1973): 267–302.

Iverson, Peter, *Carlos Montezuma and the Changing World of American Indians* (Albuquerque: University of New Mexico Press, 1982).

Jackson, Curtis E. and Marcia J. Galli, *A History of the Bureau of Indian Affairs and Its Activities among Indians* (San Francisco: R & E Research, 1977).

Jackson, Helen Hunt, *A Century of Dishonor: A Sketch of the United States Government's Dealings with Some of the Indian Tribes* (Boston: Roberts Brothers, 1887).

———, *Ramona* (Boston: Roberts Brothers, 1885).

Jackson, Helen Hunt, and Abbot, Kinney, *Report of Mrs. Helen Hunt Jackson and Abbot Kinney on the Mission Indians in 1883, Abbreviated* (Boston: Stanley and Usher, 1887).

Jaimes, M. Annette, ed., *The State of Native America: Genocide, Colonization, and Resistance* (Boston: South End Press, 1992).

James, Edward T., ed., *Notable American Women, 1607–1950: A Biographical Dictionary* (Cambridge, MA: Belknap, 1971).

James, Harry C., *Pages from Hopi History* (Tucson, AZ: University of Arizona Press, 1974).

Jennings, Francis, *The Invasion of America: Indians, Colonization, and the Cant of Conquest* (New York: Norton, 1976).

Johansen, Bruce E., *Forgotten Founders: Benjamin Franklin, the Iroquois, and the Rationale for the American Revolution* (Ipswich, MA: Gambit, 1982).

Johnson, Elias, *Legends, Traditions and Laws of the Iroquois, or Six Nations, and History of the Tuscarora Indians* (Lockport, NY: Union, 1881).

Johnson, Herbert A., et al., eds., *The Papers of John Marshall* (Chapel Hill: University of North Carolina Press, 1974–84).

Johnson, John W., ed., *Historic U.S. Court Cases, 1690–1990: An Encyclopedia* (New York: Garland, 1992).

Johnson, Ralph W., and E. Susan Crystal, "Indians and Equal Protection." *Washington Law Review* 54 (1978–1979): 587–631.

Jones, George E., Jr., *The American Indian in the American Novel (1875–1950)* (Ph.D. dissertation, New York University, 1958).

Josephy, Alvin M. Jr., *Now That the Buffalo's Gone: A Study of Today's American Indians* (New York: Knopf, 1989).

———, *Red Power: The American Indians' Fight for Freedom* (New York: American Heritage, 1971).

"A Jurisprudential Symposium in Memory of Felix S. Cohen." *Rutgers Law Review* 9 (2) (Winter 1954): 345–356.

Keller, Robert H., Jr., *American Protestantism and United States Indian Policy, 1869–82* (Lincoln: University of Nebraska Press, 1983).

Kelly, D. G., "Indian Title: The Rights of American Natives in Lands They Have

Occupied since Time Immemorial." *Columbia Law Review* 75 (1975): 655–686.

Kelly, Lawrence, *The Navajos and Federal Indian Policy, 1913–1934* (Ph.D. dissertation, University of New Mexico, 1961).

Kelly, William Henderson, "Indian Adjustment and the History of Indian Affairs." *Arizona Law Review* 10 (6) (Winter 1968): 559–578.

Kelly, William Henderson, ed., *Indian Affairs and the Indian Reorganization Act: The Twenty Year Record* (Tucson: University of Arizona Press, 1954).

Kelsey, Harry, "The Doolittle Report of 1867: Its Preparation and Shortcomings." *Arizona and the West* 17 (Summer 1975): 107–120.

Kickingbird, Kirk, and Karen Ducheneaux, *One Hundred Million Acres* (New York: Macmillan, 1973).

Kilpatrick, Jack Frederick, and Anna Gritts Kilpatrick, eds., *New Echota Letters: Contributions of Samuel A. Worcester to the Cherokee Phoenix* (Dallas: Southern Methodist University Press, 1968).

Kinney, J. P., *A Continent Lost—A Civilization Won: Indian Land Tenure in America* (Baltimore: Johns Hopkins Press, 1937).

Kinsman, Clare, ed., *Contemporary Authors: A Bio-Bibliographical Guide to Current Authors and Their Works* (Detroit: Gale, 1962–1995).

Kirkendall, Richard S., ed., *The Harry S. Truman Encyclopedia* (Boston: G. K. Hall, 1989).

Kirkpatrick, D. L., ed., *Reference Guide to American Literature* (Chicago: St. James, 1987).

Kittrie, Nicholas N., and Eldon D. Wedlock, Jr., eds., *The Tree of Liberty: A Documentary History of Rebellion and Political Crime in America* (Baltimore: Johns Hopkins University Press, 1986).

Koppes, Clayton R., "From New Deal to Termination: Liberalism and Indian Policy, 1933–1953." *Pacific Historical Review* 46 (1977): 543–566.

Krupat, Arnold, ed., *Native American Autobiography: An Anthology* (Madison: University of Wisconsin Press, 1994).

Kvasnicka, Robert M., and Herman J. Viola, eds., *The Commissioners of Indian Affairs, 1824–1977* (Lincoln: University of Nebraska Press, 1979).

LaBarre, Weston, *The Peyote Cult* (New York: Schocken, 1969).

Lambertson, G. M., "Indian Citizenship." *American Law Review* 20 (March-April 1886): 183–193.

"Land Claims Under the Indian Nonintercourse Act." *British Columbia Environmental Affairs Law Review* 7 (1978).

Lanman, Charles, *Biographical Annals of the Civil Government of the United States* (Washington, DC: Anglim, 1876).

LaPotin, Armand S., ed., *Native American Voluntary Organizations* (Westport, CT: Greenwood, 1987).

Laws of the Colonial and State Governments, Relating to Indians and Indian Affairs, from 1633 to 1831, Inclusive (Washington, DC: Thompson and Homans, 1832).

Lazarus, Edward, *Black Hills/White Justice: The Sioux Nation versus the United States, 1775 to the Present* (New York: HarperCollins, 1991).

Letter from the Secretary of War, Transmitting Copies of the Report and Proceedings of the Commissioners Appointed to Treat with the Creek Nation of Indians, for an Extinguishment of Their Claim to Land, Lying within the State of Georgia, Etc. (Washington, DC: Gales and Seaton, 1825).

Leupp, Francis Ellington, *In Red Man's Land: A Study of the American Indian* (New York: Revel, 1914).

———, *The Indian and His Problem* (New York: Scribner's, 1910).

———, *The Latest Phase of the Southern Ute Question: A Report* (Philadelphia: Indian Rights Association, 1895).

Linquist, Gustavus, *The Red Man in the United States: An Intimate Study of the Social, Economic, and Religious Life of the American Indians* (New York: Doran, 1923).

Lippy, Charles H., and Peter W. Williams, eds., *Encyclopedia of the American Religious Experience: Studies of Traditions and Movements* (New York: Scribner's, 1988).

Littlefield, Daniel F., Jr., and James W. Parins, *A Biobibliography of Native American Writers, 1772–1924* (Metuchen, NJ: Scarecrow, 1981).

Long, Anton V., *Senator Bursum and the Pueblo Indians Lands Act of 1924* (Master's thesis, University of New Mexico, 1949).

Lord, William B., and Mary G. Wallace, eds., *Proceedings of the Symposium on Indian Water Rights and Water Resources Management* (Bethesda, MD: American Water Resources Association, 1989).

Love, William Deloss, *Samson Occom and the Christian Indians of New England* (Boston: Pilgrim, 1899).

Lovett, Clara Maria, *Carl Schurz, 1829–1906: A Biographical Essay and a Selective List of Reading Materials in English* (Washington, DC: Library of Congress, 1983).

Lowrie, Walter, and Matthew St. Clair Clarke, eds., *American State Papers: Documents, Legislative and Executive, of the Congress of the United States, from the First Session of the First to the Third Session of the Thirteenth Congress, Inclusive: Commencing March 3, 1789, and Ending March 3, 1815* (Washington, DC: Gales and Seaton, 1832).

Lowrie, Walter, and Walter S. Franklin, eds., *American State Papers: Documents, Legislative and Executive, of the Congress of the United States* (Washington, DC: Gales and Seaton, 1834).

Lurie, Nancy Oestreich, "The Lady from Boston and the Omaha Indians." *American West* 3 (4) (Fall 1966): 31–33, 80–85.

———, "Menominee Termination." *Indian Historian* 4 (4) (Winter 1971): 31–45.

Mainero, Lina, ed., *American Women Writers: A Critical Reference Guide from Colonial Times to the Present* (New York: Ungar, 1993).

Malinowski, Sharon, ed., *Notable Native Americans* (Detroit: Gale, 1995).

Malone, Dumas et al., eds., *Dictionary of American Biography* (New York: Scribner's, 1930–88).

Maltin, Leonard, *Leonard Maltin's Movie and Video Guide: 1996 Edition* (New York: Signet, 1995).

Mankiller, Wilma, and Michael Wallis, *Mankiller: A Chief and Her People* (New York: St. Martin's, 1993).

Manypenny, George W., *Our Indian Wards* (Cincinnati: Robert Clarke, 1880).

Marden, David L., "Anthropologists and Federal Indian Policy Prior to 1940." *Indian Historian* 5 (4) (Winter 1972): 19–26.

Mardock, Robert Winston, *The Reformers and the American Indian* (St. Louis: University of Missouri Press, 1971).

Mark, Joan, *A Stranger in Her Native Land: Alice Fletcher and the American Indians* (Lincoln: University of Nebraska Press, 1988).

Martin, Minerva L., *Helen Hunt Jackson in Relation to Her Time* (Ph.D. dissertation, University of Louisiana, 1940).

Mason, W. Dale, "'You Can Only Kick So Long…': American Indian Movement Leadership in Nebraska." *Journal of the West* 23 (3) (July 1984): 21–31.

Mather, Cotton, *The Life and Death of the Renown'd Mr. John Eliot; Who Was the First Preacher of the Gospel to the Indians in America* (London: John Dunton, 1691).

Mather, Increase, *A Relation of the Troubles Which Have Hapned in New-England, By Reason of the Indians There. From the Year 1614, to the Year 1675.* (Boston: John Foster, 1677).

Mathes, Valerie Sherer, *Helen Hunt Jackson and Her Indian Reform Legacy* (Austin: University of Texas Press, 1990).

Matthiessen, Peter, *In the Spirit of Crazy Horse* (New York: Viking Penguin, 1991).

Mattingly, Arthur H., "The Great Plains Peace Commission of 1867." *Journal of the West* 15 (3) (July 1976): 23–37.

Maxfield, Peter C., "Tribal Control of Indian Mineral Development." *Oregon Law Review* 62 (1) (1983): 49–72.

May, Antoinette, *Helen Hunt Jackson: A Lonely Voice of Conscience* (San Francisco: Chronicle, 1987).

McCool, Daniel C., *Command of the Waters: Iron Triangles, Federal Water Development, and Indian Water* (Berkeley: University of California Press, 1987).

———, "Precedent for the Winters Doctrine: Seven Legal Principles." *Journal of the Southwest* 29 (2) (Summer 1987): 164–178.

McCoy, Isaac, *History of Baptist Indian Missions: Embracing Remarks on the Former and Present Conditions of the Aboriginal Tribes, Their Former Settlement within the Indian Territory, and Their Future Prospects* (Washington, DC: Morrison, 1840).

———, *Remarks on the Practicability of Indian Reform, Embracing Their Colonization* (Boston: Lincoln & Edmunds, 1827).

McCracken, Harold, *George Catlin and the Old Frontier* (New York: Dial, 1959).

McDonnell, Janet A., *The Dispossession of the American Indian, 1887–1934* (Bloomington: Indiana University Press, 1991).

McGuire, Thomas R., "Illusions of Choice in the Indian Irrigation Service: The Ak Chin Project and an Epilogue." *Journal of the Southwest* 30 (2) (Summer 1988): 200–221.

McHenry, Robert, ed., *Famous American Women: A Biographical Dictionary from Colonial Times to the Present* (New York: Dover, 1980).

McKenney, Thomas L., *Memoirs, Official and Personal; with Sketches of Travels among the Northern and Southern Indians; Embracing a War Excursion and Descriptions of Scenes along the Western Borders* (New York: Paine and Burgess, 1846).

McKenney, Thomas L., and James Hall, *History of the Indian Tribes of North America, with Biographical Sketches and Anecdotes of the Principal Chiefs. Embellished with One Hundred and Twenty Portraits, from the Indian Gallery in the Department of War, at Washington* (Philadelphia: Frederick W. Greenough, 1838).

McLaughlin, William G., *Cherokees and Missionaries, 1789–1839* (New Haven, CT: Yale University Press, 1984).

McLoone, John J., "Indian Hunting and Fishing Rights." *Arizona Law Review* 10 (6) (Winter 1968): 725–740.

McLoughlin, William G., *Cherokees and Missionaries, 1789–1839* (New Haven, CT: Yale University Press, 1984).

McMullin, Thomas A., and David Walker, *Biographical Directory of American Territorial Governors* (Westport, CT: Meckler, 1984).

McQuaid, Kim, "William Apes, Pequot: An Indian Reformer in the Jacksonian Era." *New England Quarterly* 50 (4) (1977): 605–625.

Means, Russell, *Where White Men Fear to Tread: The Autobiography of Russell Means* (New York: St. Martin's, 1995).

Meeds, Lloyd, "The Indian Policy Review Commission." *Law & Contemporary Problems* 40 (Winter 1976): 9–11.

Meriam, Lewis, ed., *The Problem of Indian Administration* (Baltimore: Johns Hopkins Press, 1928).

Miner, Craig, and William E. Unrau, *The End of Indian Kansas: A Study of Cultural Revolution, 1854–1871* (Lawrence: Regents Press of Kansas, 1978).

Mohr, Walter H., *Federal Indian Relations 1774–1788* (Philadelphia: University of Pennsylvania Press, 1933).

Momaday, Navarre Scott, *The Names* (New York: Harper Colophon Books, 1976).

Moody, Marshall Dwight, *A History of the Board of Indian Commissioners and Its Relationship to the Administration of Indian Affairs, 1869–1900* (Master's thesis, American University, 1951).

Mooney, James, *The Ghost Dance Religion and the Sioux Outbreak of 1890* (Washington, DC: Bureau of American Ethnology, 1896).

Moorehead, Warren K., *The American Indian in the United States: Period 1850–1914* (Andover, MA: Andover, 1914).

Moquin, Wayne, and Charles Van Doren, eds., *Great Documents in American Indian History* (New York: Praeger, 1973).

Moritz, Charles, ed., *Current Biography 1962* (New York: Wilson, 1962).

———, *Current Biography 1967* (New York: Wilson, 1967).

———, *Current Biography 1974* (New York: Wilson, 1974).

———, *Current Biography 1978* (New York: Wilson, 1978).

Morrison, Dorothy Nafus, *Chief Sarah: Sarah Winnemucca's Fight for Indian Rights* (New York: Atheneum, 1980).

Morse, Jedidiah, *A Report to the Secretary of War of the United States, on Indian Affairs, Comprising a Narrative of a Tour Performed in the Summer of 1820* (New Haven: Converse, 1822).

Moses, Lester George, *The Indian Man: A Biography of James Mooney* (Urbana: University of Illinois Press, 1984).

Moses, Lester George, "James Mooney and Wovoka: An Ethnologist's Visit with the Ghost Dance Prophet." *Nevada Historical Society Quarterly* 23 (2) (Summer 1980): 71–86.

Moses, Lester George, and Margaret Connell Szasz, "'My Father, Have Pity on Me!' Indian Revitalization Movements of the Late-Nineteenth Century." *Journal of the West* 23 (1) (January 1984): 5–15.

Moses, Lester George, and Raymond Wilson, eds., *Indian Lives: Essays on Nineteenth- and Twentieth-Century Native American Leaders* (Albuquerque: University of New Mexico Press, 1985).

Munroe, James Phinney, *A Life of Francis Amasa Walker* (New York: Holt, 1923).

Murchison, Kenneth S., *Digest of Decisions Relating to Indian Affairs* (Washington, DC: Government Printing Office, 1901).

Myer, Dillon S., *Uprooted Americans* (Tucson: University of Arizona Press, 1971).

Nabokov, Peter, ed., *Native American Testimony: A Chronicle of Indian-White Relations from Prophecy to the Present, 1492–1992* (New York: Viking, 1991).

Nammack, Georgiana C., *Fraud, Politics, and the Dispossession of the Indians: The Iroquois Land Frontier in the Colonial Period* (Norman: University of Oklahoma Press, 1969).

Nash, Philleo, *The Place of Religious Revivalism in the Formation of the Intercultural Community on Klamath Reservation* (Ph.D. dissertation, University of Chicago, 1937).

———, "Science, Politics, and Human Values: A Memoir." *Human Organization* 45 (3) (Fall 1986): 189–201.

National Cyclopedia of American Biography (New York: James T. White, 1898–1977).

National Indian Defense Association, *The Sioux Nation and the United States: A Brief History of the Treaties of 1868, 1876, and 1889, between that Nation and the United States* (Washington, DC: National Indian Defense Association, 1891).

"The New York Indians' Right to Self-Determination." *Buffalo Law Review* 22 (1973).

Newton, Bernard, *The Economics of Francis Amasa Walker: American Economics in Transition* (New York: Kelley, 1968).

Nickeson, Steve, "The Structure of the Bureau of Indian Affairs." *Law & Contemporary Problems* 40 (Winter 1976): 61–76.

Nys, Ernest, ed, *Victoria, Francisco de, 'De Indis et de Ivre Belli: Relectiones'* (Washington, DC: Carnegie Institution, 1917).

O'Brien, Sharon, *American Indian Tribal Governments* (Norman: University of Oklahoma Press, 1989).

O'Callaghan, Edmund Bailey, ed., *Documents Relative to the Colonial History of the State of New York* (Albany: State Historical Society of New York, 1856).

Occom, Samson, *A Sermon Preached at the Execution of Moses Paul, an Indian Who was Executed at New Haven on the 2nd of September 1772 for the Murder of Mr. Moses Cook, Late of Waterbury, on the 7th of December 1771. Preached at the Desire of Said Paul by Samson Occim, Minister of the Gospel and Missionary to the Indians, New Haven, 1772* (New Haven, CT: Thomas and Samuel Green 1772).

O'Connell, Barry, ed., *On Our Own Ground: The Complete Writings of William Apess, a Pequot* (Amherst: University of Massachusetts Press, 1992).

Olson, James C., *Red Cloud and the Sioux Problem* (Lincoln: University of Nebraska Press, 1965).

Olson, James S., and Raymond Wilson, *Native Americans in the Twentieth Century* (Urbana: University of Illinois Press, 1984).

Osborne, William S., *Lydia Maria Child* (Boston: Twayne, 1980).

Osgood, Phillips Endicott, *Straight Tongue: A Story of Henry Benjamin Whipple, First Episcopal Bishop of Minnesota* (Minneapolis, MN: Denison, 1958).

Otis, Delos Sackett, *The Dawes Act and the Allotment of Indian Lands* (Norman: University of Oklahoma Press, 1973).

Painter, Charles Cornelius Coffin, *The Condition of Affairs in Indian Territory and California: A Report by Prof. C. C. Painter, Agent of the Indian Rights Association* (Philadelphia: Indian Rights Association, 1888).

Papers Relating to Talks and Councils Held with the Indians in Dakota and Montana Territories in the Years 1866–1869 (Washington, DC: Government Printing Office, 1910).

Parker, Arthur C., *The Life of General Ely S. Parker, Last Grand Sachem of the Iroquois and General Grant's Military Secretary* (Buffalo, NY: Buffalo Historical Society, 1919).

Parman, Donald L., *The Indian Civilian Conservation Corps* (Ph.D. dissertation, University of Oklahoma, 1967).

Parman, Donald L., ed., "Lewis Meriam's Letters during the Survey of Indian Affairs, 1926–1927." *Arizona and the West* 24 (Autumn 1982): 253–280; 24 (Winter 1982): 341–370.

Parsley, Jon Keith, "Regulation of Counterfeit Indian Arts and Crafts: An Analysis of the Indian Arts and Crafts Act of 1990." *American Indian Law Review* 18 (2) (1990): 487–537.

Patterson, Andrew M., and Maureen Brodoff, eds., *The John Collier Papers, 1922–1968: A Guide to the Microfilm Edition* (Sanford, NC: Microfilming Corporation of America, 1980).

Patterson, Lotsee, and Mary Ellen Snodgrass, *Indian Terms of the Americas* (Englewood, CO: Libraries Unlimited, 1994).

Paul, Doris A., *The Navajo Code Talkers* (Philadelphia: Dorrance, 1973).

Pearce, Roy Harvey, *The Savages of America: A Study of the Indian and the Idea of Civilization* (Baltimore: Johns Hopkins University Press, 1953).

Pelcyger, Robert S., *Indian Water Rights: Some Emerging Frontiers* (Rocky Mountain Mineral Law Institute, 1976).

———, "Justices and Indians: Back to Basics." *Oregon Law Review* 62 (1) (1983): 29–48.

———, "The Winters Doctrine and the Greening of the Reservations." *Journal of Contemporary Law* 4 (Winter 1977): 19–37.

Peroff, Nicholas C., *Menominee DRUMS: Tribal Termination and Restoration, 1954–1974* (Norman: University of Oklahoma Press, 1982).

Peters, Richard, *The Case of the Cherokee Nation against the State of Georgia: Argued and Determined at the Supreme Court of the United States, January Term 1831, with an Appendix Containing the Opinion of Chancellor Kent on the Case; the Treaties between the United States and the Cherokee Indians; the Act of Congress of 1802* (Philadelphia: Grigg, 1831).

Petty, Kenneth E., "Accomodation of Indian Treaty Rights in an International Fishery: An International Problem Begging for an International Solution." *Washington Law Review* 54 (1978–1979): 403–458.

Phillips, Ulrich Bonnell, *Georgia and States' Rights: A Study of the Political History of Georgia from the Revolution to the Civil War, with Particular Regard to Federal Relations* (Washington, DC: Government Printing Office, 1908).

Philp, Kenneth R., "Albert B. Fall and the Protest from the Pueblos, 1921–23." *Arizona and the West* 12 (3) (Autumn 1970): 237–254.

———, *John Collier's Crusade for Indian Reform, 1920–1954* (Tucson: University of Arizona Press, 1977).

Philp, Kenneth R., ed., *Indian Self-Rule: First-Hand Accounts of Indian-White Relations from Roosevelt to Reagan* (Salt Lake City: Howe, 1986).

Phinney, Edward Sterl, *Alfred B. Meacham: Promoter of Indian Reform* (Ph.D. dissertation, University of Oregon at Salem, 1963).

Pisani, Donald, "Irrigation, Water Rights, and the Betrayal of Indian Allotment." *Environmental Review* 10 (Fall 1986): 157–176.

Pound, Merritt B., *Benjamin Hawkins: Indian Agent* (Athens: University of Georgia Press, 1951).

Priest, Loring Benson, *Uncle Sam's Stepchildren: The Reformation of United States Indian Policy, 1865–1887* (New Brunswick, NJ: Rutgers University Press, 1942).

Proceedings of the Great Peace Commission of 1867–1868 (Washington, DC: Institute for the Development of Indian Law, 1975).

Prucha, Francis Paul, *American Indian Policy in the Formative Years: The Indian Trade and Intercourse Acts, 1790–1834* (Lincoln: University of Nebraska Press, 1970).

———, "Andrew Jackson's Indian Policy: A Reassessment." *Journal of American History* 56 (December 1969): 527–539.

———, *A Bibliographical Guide to the History of Indian-White Relations in the United States* (Chicago: University of Chicago Press, 1977).

———, *The Great Father: The United States Government and the American Indians* (Lincoln: University of Nebraska Press, 1984).

———, *Indian-White Relations in the United States: A Bibliography of Works Published, 1975–1980* (Lincoln: University of Nebraska Press, 1982).

———, *The Indians in American Society: From the Revolutionary War to the Present* (Berkeley: University of California Press, 1985).

———, *United States Indian Policy: A Critical Bibliography* (Bloomington: Indiana University Press, 1977).

Prucha, Francis Paul, ed., *Americanizing the American Indians: Writings by the 'Friends of the Indian,' 1880–1890* (Cambridge, MA: Harvard University Press, 1973).

———, *Documents of United States Indian Policy* (Lincoln: University of Nebraska Press, 1990).

———, *United States Indian Policy: A Critical Bibliography* (Bloomington: Indiana University Press, 1977).

Public Papers of the Presidents of the United States: Herbert Hoover, Containing the Public Messages, Speeches, and Statements of the President, March 4 to December 31, 1929 (Washington, DC: Government Printing Office, 1974).

Public Papers of the Presidents of the United States: Lyndon B. Johnson, Containing the Public Messages, Speeches, and Statements of the President, January 1 to June 30, 1968 (Washington, DC: Government Printing Office, 1970).

Public Papers of the Presidents of the United States: Richard Nixon, Containing the Public Messages, Speeches, and Statements of the President, 1970 (Washington, DC: Government Printing Office, 1971).

Putney, Diane T., *Fighting the Scourge: American Indian Morbidity and Federal Policy, 1897–1928* (Ph.D. dissertation, Marquette University, 1980).

Radke, August C., Jr., *John Tyler Morgan, an Expansionist Senator, 1877–1907* (Ph.D. dissertation, University of Washington at Seattle, 1953).

Ranquist, Harold A., "The *Winters* Doctrine and How It Grew: Federal Reservation of Rights of the Use of Water." *Brigham Young University Law Review* 4 (1975): 639–734.

Rathbone, Perry T., *Charles Wimar, 1828–1862: Painter of the Indian Frontier* (St. Louis, MO: City Art Museum of St. Louis, 1946).

Reiblich, G. Kenneth, "Indian Rights under the Civil Rights Act of 1968." *Arizona Law Review* 10 (6) (Winter 1968): 617–648.

Report on Indian Health—Task Force Six: Indian Health, Final Report to the American Indian Policy Review Commission, 1976.

Richardson, James, comp., *A Compilation of the Messages and Papers of the Presidents, 1789–1914* (New York: Bureau of National Literature, 1897–1917).

Robinson, Doane, *A History of the Dakota or Sioux Indians from Their Earliest Traditions and First Contact with White Men to the Final Settlement of the Last of Them upon Reservations and the Subsequent Abandonment of the Old Tribal Life* (Minneapolis, MN: State Historical Society, 1904).

Robinson, Edgar Eugene, and Paul Carroll Edwards, eds., *The Memoirs of Ray Lyman Wilbur, 1875–1949* (Stanford, CA: Stanford University Press, 1960).

Ross, Norman A., ed., *Index to the Decisions of the Indian Claims Commission* (New York: Clearwater, 1973).

Rostow, Eugene V., "Felix Cohen." *Yale Law Journal* 63 (2) (December 1953): 141–143.

Rothe, Anne, ed., *Current Biography 1947* (New York: Wilson, 1947).

———, *Current Biography 1950* (New York: Wilson, 1950).

Royce, Charles C., comp., *Indian Land Cessions in the United States* (Washington, DC: Government Printing Office, 1900).

Ruoff, A. LaVonne Brown, *American Indian Literatures: An Introduction, Bibliographic Review, and Selected Bibliography* (New York: Modern Language Association of America, 1990).

Ryan, Carmelita S., *The Carlisle Indian Industrial School* (Ph.D. dissertation, Georgetown University, 1962).

Sabatini, Joseph D., comp., *American Indian Law: A Bibliography of Books, Law Review Articles and Indian Periodicals* (Albuquerque: American Indian Law Center, School of Law, University of New Mexico, 1973).

Salabiye, Velma S., and James R. Young, "American Indian Leaders and Leadership of the Twentieth Century: A Bibliographical Essay." *Journal of the West* 23 (3) (July 1984): 70–76.

Salisbury, Neal E., *Conquest of the 'Savage': Puritans, Puritan Missionaries, and Indians, 1620–1680* (Ph.D. dissertation, University of California at Los Angeles, 1972).

Salzman, M., Jr., "Geronimo: The Napoleon of Indians," *Journal of Arizona History* 8 (4) (Winter 1967): 215–247.

The Sand Creek Massacre: A Documentary History (New York: Sol Lewis, 1973).

Satz, Ronald N., *American Indian Policy in the Jacksonian Era* (Lincoln: University of Nebraska Press, 1975).

Schaaf, Gregory, *Wampum Belts and Peace Trees: George Morgan, Native Americans and Revolutionary Diplomacy* (Golden, CO: Fulcrum, 1990).

Schimmel, Julie, *John Mix Stanley and Imagery of the West in Nineteenth Century Art* (Ph.D. dissertation, New York University, 1983).

Schmeckebier, Laurence F., *The Office of Indian Affairs: Its History, Activities and Organization* (Baltimore: Johns Hopkins University Press, 1927).

Schoenebaum, Eleanora W., ed., *Political Profiles: The Nixon/Ford Years* (New York: Facts on File, 1979).

Schoolcraft, Henry Rowe, *Algic Researches, Comprising Inquiries Respecting the Mental Characteristics of the North American Indian: First Series, Indian Tales and Legends* (New York: Harper, 1839).

———, *Historical and Statistical Information Respecting the History, Condition and Prospects of the Indian Tribes of the United States: Collected and Prepared under the Direction of the Bureau of Indian Affairs, Per Act of Congress of March 3d, 1847* (Philadelphia: Lippincott, Grambo, 1851–1857).

Schrader, Robert Fay, *The Indian Arts & Crafts Board: An Aspect of New Deal Indian Policy* (Albuquerque: University of New Mexico Press, 1983).

Schurz, Carl, "Present Aspects of the Indian Problem." *North American Review* 133 (7) (July 1881): 1–24.

Schusky, Ernest L., *Political Organization of Native North Americans* (Washington, DC: University Press of America, 1981).

Seagle, William, "The Murder of Spotted Tail." *Indian Historian* 3 (4) (Fall 1970): 10–22.

Second Annual Report of the Executive Committee of the Indian Rights Association (Philadelphia: Indian Rights Association, 1885).

Seitz, Don Carlos, *From Kaw Teepee to Capitol: The Life Story of Charles Curtis, Indian, Who Has Risen to High Estate* (New York: Stokes, 1928).

Sennett, Ted, *Great Hollywood Movies* (New York: Abrams, 1983).

Shadburn, Don L., "Cherokee Statesmen: The John Rogers Family of Chattahoochee." *Chronicles of Oklahoma* 50 (1) (Spring 1972): 12–40.

Shames, Priscilla, *The Long Hope: A Study of American Indian Stereotypes in American Popular Fiction, 1890–1950* (Ph.D. dissertation, University of California at Los Angeles, 1969).

Sheehan, Bernard W., *Seeds of Extinction: Jeffersonian Philanthropy and the American Indians* (Chapel Hill: University of North Carolina Press, 1973).

Sifakis, Stewart, *Who Was Who in the Civil War* (New York: Facts on File, 1988).

Silsbee, Marianne C. D., *A Half Century in Salem* (Boston: Houghton Mifflin, 1887).

Simmons, Clyde R., "The Indian Wars and U.S. Military Thought, 1865–1890." *Parameters* 22 (1) (Spring 1992): 60–72.

Skyes, Merlyn C., *A History of the Attempts of the United States Government to Re-establish Self-Government among the Indian Tribes, 1934–1949* (Master's thesis, Bowling Green State University, 1950).

Slotkin, James Sydney, *The Peyote Religion: A Study in Indian-White Relations* (Glencoe, IL: Free Press, 1956).

Smith, Jane F., and Robert M. Kvasnicka, ed., *Indian-White Relations: A Persistent Paradox* (Washington, DC: Howard University Press, 1976).

Snider, John Michael, *The Treatment of American Indians in Selected American Literature: A Radical Critique* (Ph.D. dissertation, University of Illinois at Urbana-Champaign, 1983).

Snodgrass, Jeanne O., comp., *American Indian Painters: A Biographical Directory* (New York: Museum of the American Indian, Heye Foundation, 1968).

Snow, Dean R., *The Archaeology of North America: American Indians and Their Origins* (New York: Thames and Hudson, 1980).

Snow, Jerry Whistler, *Sac and Fox Tribal Government from 1885 through Reorganization under the Oklahoma Indian Welfare Act in 1937* (Master's thesis, University of Oklahoma, 1970).

Sparks, Joe P., "The Indian Stronghold and the Spread of Urban America." *Arizona Law Review* 10 (6) (Winter 1968): 706–724.

Spaulding, Joe Powell, *The Life of Alice Mary Robertson* (Ph.D. dissertation, University of Oklahoma, 1959).

Speeches on the Passage of the Bill for the Removal of the Indians, Delivered in the Congress of the United States, April and May, 1830 (Boston: Perkins and Marvin, 1830).

Spicer, Edward H., *A Short History of the Indians of the United States* (New York: Van Nostrand Reinhold, 1969).

Springer, James Warren, "American Indians and the Law of Real Property in Colonial New England." *American Journal of Legal History* 30 (1) (January 1986): 25–58.

Stefon, Frederick J., "Significance of the Meriam Report of 1928." *Indian Historian* 8 (3) (Summer 1975): 2–8.

Stevens, Walter B., *St. Louis: History of the Fourth City, 1763–1909* (Chicago and St. Louis: Clarke, 1909).

Stewart, Omer C., *Peyote Religion: A History* (Norman: University of Oklahoma Press, 1987).

Strickland, Rennard, "The Puppet Princess: The Case for a Policy-Oriented Framework for Understanding and Shaping American Indian Law." *Oregon Law Review* 62 (1) (1983): 11–28.

Strickland, Rennard, ed., *Felix S. Cohen's Handbook of Federal Indian Law* (Charlottesville, VA: Michie, 1982).

Stuart, Paul, *The Indian Office: Growth and Development of an American Institution, 1865–1900* (Ann Arbor, MI: UMI, 1979).

Sturtevant, William C., series ed., *Handbook of North American Indians* (Washington, DC: Smithsonian, 1983).

Sutton, Imre, ed., *Irredeemable America: The Indians' Estate and Land Claims* (Albuquerque: University of New Mexico Press, 1985).

Svaldi, David, *Sand Creek and the Rhetoric of Extermination: A Case-Study in Indian-White Relations* (Lanham, MD: University Press of America, 1989).

Swindler, William F., "Politics as Law: The Cherokee Cases." *American Indian Law Review* 3 (1) (1975): 7–20.

Szasz, Margaret, *Education and the American Indian: The Road to Self-Determination since 1928* (Albuquerque: University of New Mexico Press, 1977).

Tatum, Lawrie, *Our Red Brothers and the Peace Policy of President Ulysses S. Grant* (Lincoln: University of Nebraska Press, 1970).

Taylor, Benjamin J., "Indian Manpower Resources: The Experiences of Five Southwestern Reservations." *Arizona Law Review* 10 (6) (Winter 1968): 579–596.

Taylor, Graham D., *The New Deal and American Indian Tribalism: The Administration of the Indian Reorganization Act, 1934–45* (Lincoln: University of Nebraska Press, 1980).

Taylor, J. Golden, ed., *A Literary History of the American West* (Fort Worth: Texas Christian University Press, 1987).

Taylor, James P., *Life and Career of Sen. Robert Love Taylor* (Nashville, TN: Bob Taylor, 1913).

Taylor, Lloyd C., Jr., *To Make Men Free: An Interpretive Study of Lydia Maria Child* (Ph.D. dissertation, Lehigh University, 1956).

Taylor, Theodore W., *American Indian Policy* (Mt. Airy, MD: Lomond, 1983).

———, *The Bureau of Indian Affairs* (Boulder, CO: Westview, 1984).

Taylor, William B., "Land and Water Rights in the Viceroyalty of New Spain." *New Mexico Historical Review* 50 (3) (July 1975): 189–212.

Tennessee: The Volunteer State, 1769–1923 (Nashville, TN: Clarke, 1923).

Thelen, David Paul, *The New Citizenship: Origins of Progressivism in Wisconsin, 1885–1900* (St. Louis: University of Missouri Press, 1972).

Thompson, Gregory Coyne, *The Origin and Implementation of the American Indian Reform Movement, 1867–1912* (Ph.D. dissertation, University of Utah, 1981).

Thrapp, Dan L., *Encyclopedia of Frontier Biography* (Spokane, WA: Clarke, 1990).

Toqueville, Alexis De, *Democracy in America* (Garden City, NY: Doubleday, 1969).

Townsend, Maurice Karlen, *The Rehabilitation of the American Indians under the Indian Reorganization Act* (Master's thesis, University of Chicago, 1950).

Trail of Broken Treaties: B.I.A., I'm Not Your Indian Anymore (Rooseveltown, NY: Akwesasne Notes, 1976).

Trennert, Robert A., Jr., *Alternative to Extinction: Federal Indian Policy and the Beginnings of the Reservation System, 1846–1851* (Philadelphia: Temple University Press, 1975).

———, "Indian Sore Eyes: The Federal Campaign to Control Trachoma in the Southwest, 1910–40." *Journal of the Southwest* 32 (2) (Summer 1990): 121–144.

———, "Peaceably If They Will, Forceably If They Must: The Phoenix Indian School, 1890–1901." *Journal of Arizona History* 20 (3) (1979): 297–322.

———, "William Medill's War with the Indian Traders, 1847." *Ohio History* 82 (1) (Winter 1973): 46–62.

"Tribal Property Interests in Executive-Order Reservations: A Compensable Indian Right." *Yale Law Journal* 69 (1960).

Troccoli, Joan Carpenter, *First Artist in the West: George Catlin Paintings and Watercolors from the Collection of Gilcrease Museum* (Tulsa, OK: Gilcrease Museum, 1993).

Truettner, William H., *The Natural Man Observed: A Study of Catlin's Indian Gallery* (Washington, DC: Smithsonian, 1979).

Tyler, S. Lyman, *A History of Indian Policy* (Washington, DC: Government Printing Office, 1973).

Udall, Stewart L., "The State of the Indian Nation: An Introduction." *Arizona Law Review* 10 (6) (Winter 1968): 553–558.

United States Code Congressional and Administrative News, 100th Congress, 1st Session (1987).

United States Code Congressional and Administrative News, 100th Congress, 2d Session (1988).

United States Code Congressional and Administrative News, 83d Congress, 1st Session (1953).

United States Code Congressional and Administrative News, 90th Congress, 2d Session (1968).

United States Code Congressional and Administrative News, 92d Congress, 1st Session (1971).

United States Code Congressional and Administrative News, 92d Congress, 2d Session (1972).

United States Code Congressional and Administrative News, 95th Congress, 2d Session (1978).

U.S. Congress. House of Representatives, *Annual Report of the Commissioner of Indian Affairs for the Year 1831*, House Executive Document No. 2, 22d Congress, 1st Session (serial 216).

———, *Annual Report of the Commissioner of Indian Affairs for the Year 1832*, House Executive Document No. 2, 22d Congress, 2d Session (serial 233).

———, *Annual Report of the Commissioner of Indian Affairs for the Year 1835*, House Executive Document No. 2, 24th Congress, 1st Session (serial 286).

———, *Annual Report of the Commissioner of Indian Affairs for the Year 1848*, House Executive Document No. 1, 30th Congress, 2d Session (serial 537).

———, *Annual Report of the Commissioner of Indian Affairs for the Year 1849*, House Executive Document No. 5, 31st Congress, 1st Session (serial 550).

———, *Annual Report of the Commissioner of Indian Affairs for the Year 1850*, House Executive Document No. 1, 31st Congress, 2d Session (serial 595).

———, *Annual Report of the Commissioner of Indian Affairs for the Year 1851*, House Executive Document No. 2, 32d Congress, 1st Session (serial 636).

———, *Annual Report of the Commissioner of Indian Affairs for the Year 1856*, House Executive Document No. 1, 34th Congress, 3d Session (serial 893).

———, *Annual Report of the Commissioner of Indian Affairs for the Year 1858*, House Executive Document No. 2, 35th Congress, 2d Session (serial 997).

———, *Annual Report of the Commissioner of Indian Affairs for the Year 1862*, House Executive Document No. 1, 37th Congress, 3d Session (serial 1157).

———, *Annual Report of the Commissioner of Indian Affairs for the Year 1863*, House Executive Document No. 1, 38th Congress, 1st Session (serial 1182).

———, *Annual Report of the Commissioner of Indian Affairs for the Year 1866*, House Executive Document No. 1, 39th Congress, 1st Session (serial 1284).

———, *Annual Report of the Commissioner of Indian Affairs for the Year 1868*, House Executive Document No. 1, 40th Congress, 3d Session (serial 1366).

———, *Annual Report of the Commissioner of Indian Affairs for the Year 1869*, House Executive Document No. 1, 41st Congress, 2d Session (serial 1414).

———, *Annual Report of the Commissioner of Indian Affairs for the Year 1871*, House Executive Document No. 1, 42d Congress, 2d Session (serial 1505).

———, *Annual Report of the Commissioner of Indian Affairs for the Year 1872*, House Executive Document No. 1, 42d Congress, 3d Session (serial 1560).

———, *Annual Report of the Commissioner of Indian Affairs for the Year 1874*, House Executive Document No. 1, 43d Congress, 2d Session (serial 1639).

———, *Annual Report of the Commissioner of Indian Affairs for the Year 1876*, House Executive Document No. 1, 44th Congress, 2d Session (serial 1749).

———, *Annual Report of the Commissioner of Indian Affairs for the Year 1878*, House Executive Document No. 1, 45th Congress, 3d Session (serial 1850).

———, *Annual Report of the Commissioner of Indian Affairs for the Year 1881*, House Executive Document No. 1, 47th Congress, 1st Session (serial 2018).

———, *Annual Report of the Commissioner of Indian Affairs for the Year 1882*, House Executive Document No. 1, 47th Congress, 2d Session (serial 2100).

———, *Annual Report of the Commissioner of Indian Affairs for the Year 1886*, House Executive Document No. 1, 49th Congress, 1st Session (serial 2467).

———, *Annual Report of the Commissioner of Indian Affairs for the Year 1887*, House Executive Document No. 1, 50th Congress, 1st Session (serial 2542).

———, *Annual Report of the Commissioner of Indian Affairs for the Year 1888*, House Executive Document No. 1, 50th Congress, 2d Session (serial 2637).

———, *Annual Report of the Commissioner of Indian Affairs for the Year 1889*, House Executive Document No. 1, 51st Congress, 1st Session (serial 2725).

———, *Annual Report of the Commissioner of Indian Affairs for the Year 1890*, House Executive Document No. 1, 51st Congress, 2d Session (serial 2841).

———, *Annual Report of the Commissioner of Indian Affairs for the Year 1891*, House Executive Document No. 1, 52d Congress, 1st Session (serial 2934).

———, *Annual Report of the Commissioner of Indian Affairs for the Year 1893*, House Executive Document No. 1, 53d Congress, 2d Session (serial 3210).

———, *Annual Report of the Commissioner of Indian Affairs for the Year 1894*, House Executive Document No. 1, 53d Congress, 3d Session (serial 3306).

———, *Annual Report of the Commissioner of Indian Affairs for the Year 1896*, House Document No. 5, 54th Congress, 2d Session (serial 3489).

———, *Annual Report of the Commissioner of Indian Affairs for the Year 1900*, House Document No. 5, 56th Congress, 2d Session (serials 4101 and 4102): 1900.

———, *Annual Report of the Commissioner of Indian Affairs for the Year 1903* House Document No. 5, 58th Congress, 2d Session (serials 4645 and 4646).

———, *Annual Report of the Commissioner of Indian Affairs for the Year 1904*, House Document No. 5, 58th Congress, 3d Session (serials 4798 and 4799).

———, *Annual Report of the Commissioner of Indian Affairs for the Year 1905*, House Document No. 5, 59th Congress, 1st Session (serials 4959 and 4960).

———, *Annual Report of the Commissioner of Indian Affairs for the Year 1908*, House Document No. 1046, 60th Congress, 2d Session (serial 5453).

———, *Annual Report of the Commissioner of Indian Affairs for the Year 1909*, House Document No. 107, 61st Congress, 2d Session (serial 5747).

———, *Annual Report of the Commissioner of Indian Affairs for the Year 1910*, House Document No. 1006, 61st Congress, 3d Session (serial 5976).

———, *Annual Report of the Commissioner of Indian Affairs for the Year 1911*, House Document No. 120, 62d Congress, 2d Session (serial 6223).

———, *Annual Report of the Commissioner of Indian Affairs for the Year 1918*, House Document No. 1455, 65th Congress, 3d Session (serial 7498).

U.S. Congress. House of Representatives. *Department of the Interior and Related Agencies Appropriations for 1982*, Hearings before the Subcommittee on the Department of the Interior and Related Agencies, a Subcommittee of the Committee on Appropriations, 97th Congress, 1st Session, 1981.

———. *Destitution of Sioux Indians: Letter from the Secretary of the Interior [Orville H. Browning],*

Transmitting a Copy of a Communication from the Acting Commissioner of Indian Affairs Relative to the Great Destitution of the Sioux Indians, near Devil's Lake, Dakota Territory, House Executive Document No. 76, 40th Congress.

———. *Documents Submitted by the Chairman on Indians Affairs, Accompanied by a Bill for the Establishment of a General Superintendency of Indian Affairs in the Department of War*, House Document No, 146, 19th Congress, 1st Session (serial 138).

———. *Hostilities with the Creek Indians: Message from the President of the United States Transmitting the Information Required by a Resolution of the House of Representatives, of the 1st of July Last, in Relation to the Hostilities Then Existing with the Creek Indians*, House Executive Document No. 154, 24th Congress, 2d Session.

———. *Investigation of Indian Frauds: Report of the Committee on Indian Affairs, Concerning Frauds and Wrongs Committed against the Indians, with Many Statistics of Value in the Management of Indian Affairs*, House Report No. 98, 42d Congress, 3d Session.

———. *Lands To Indians in Severalty*, House Report No. 165, 45th Congress, 3d Session (serial 1866).

———. *Letter from the Secretary of War, Transmitting the Information Required by a Resolution of the House of Representative of the 15th Ultimo, in Relation to our Indian Affairs Generally*, House Document No. 117, 20th Congress, 2d Session (serial 186).

———. *Message from the President of the United States, Transmitting Sundry Documents in Relation to the Various Tribes of Indians within the United States, and Recommending a Plan for Their Future Location and Government*, House Document No. 64, 18th Congress, 2d Session (serial 116).

———. *Rations to Emigrating Indians*, House Report No. 502, 22d Congress, 1st Session (serial 228).

———. *Reorganization of the Indian Department: Letter from the Secretary of War, Transmitting a Plan for the Reorganization of the Indian Department, in Compliance with the Resolution of the House of Representatives of the 2d of March Last*, House Document No. 103, 26th Congress, 1st Session.

———. *Report of the Committee on Indian Affairs, in Relation to the Execution of the Act of Last Session, Abolishing the Indian Trading Establishments*, House Report No. 104, 17th Congress, 2d Session (serial 87).

———. *Report of the Indian Peace Commission*, House Executive Document No. 97, 40th Congress, 2d Session (serial 1337).

———. *Report of the Secretary of War, of a System, Providing for the Abolition of the Existing Indian Trade Establishments of the United States, and Providing for the Opening of the Trade with the Indians to Individuals, under Suitable Conditions*, House Document No. 25, 15th Congress, 2d Session (serial 17).

———. *Standing and Select Committees of the House of Representatives of the United States, Fiftieth Congress, First Session, Commencing Monday, December 5, 1887*, House Miscellaneous Document No. 2, 50th Congress, 1st Session.

———. *Testimony in Relation to the Ute Indian Outbreak Taken by the Committee on Indian Affairs in the House of Representatives*, House Miscellaneous Document No. 38, 46th Congress, 2d Session (serial 1931).

———. *The Indian Problem: Resolution of the Committee of One Hundred appointed by the Secretary of the Interior and a Review of the Indian Problem*, House Document No. 149, 68th Congress, 1st Session (serial 8273): 1924.

———. *Transfer of Indian Bureau*, House Report No. 240, 44th Congress, 1st Session.

U.S. Congress. Senate. *Annual Report from the Office of Indian Affairs for the Year 1824*, Senate Document No. 1, 18th Congress, 2d Session (serial 108).

———, *Annual Report from the Office of Indian Affairs for the Year 1826*, Senate Document No. 1, 19th Congress, 2d Session (serial 144).

———, *Annual Report from the Office of Indian Affairs for the Year 1827*, Senate Document No. 1, 20th Congress, 1st Session (serial 163).

———, *Annual Report from the Superintendent of Indian Affairs for the Year 1830*, Senate Document No. 1, 21st Congress, 2d session (serial 203).

———, *Annual Report of the Commissioner of Indian Affairs for the Year 1837*, Senate Document No. 1, 25th Congress, 2d Session (serial 314).

———, *Annual Report of the Commissioner of Indian Affairs for the Year 1847*, Senate Executive Document No. 1, 30th Congress, 1st session (serial 503).

———, *Annual Report of the Commissioner of Indian Affairs for the Year 1859*, Senate Executive Document No. 2, 36th Congress, 1st Session (serial 1023).

———, *Annual Report of the Commissioner of Indian Affairs for the Year 1860* Senate Executive Document No. 1, 36th Congress, 2d Session (serial 1078).

———, *Communication from Thomas L. McKenney, Superintendent of Indian Trade, to the Chairman of the Committee on Indian Affairs*, Senate Document No. 10, 17th Congress, 1st Session (serial 59).

———, *Documents Relative to Indian Trade. Submitted to the Senate by the Committee on Indian Affairs*, Senate Document No. 60, 17th Congress, 1st Session (serial 59).

———, *Kiowa, Comanche, and Apache Indian Reservation: Letter from the Secretary of the Interior in Response to Resolution of the Senate of January 13, 1899, Relative to Condition and Character of the Kiowa, Comanche, and Apache Indian Reservation, and the Assent of the Indians to the Agreement for the Allotment of Lands and the Ceding of Unallotted Lands*, Senate Document No. 77, 55th Congress, 3d Session (serial 3731).

———, *Letter of the Secretary of the Interior, Communicating, in Compliance with a Resolution of the Senate of the 8th Instant, Information Touching the Origins and Progress of Indian Hostilities on the Frontier*, Senate Executive Document No. 13, 40th Congress, 1st Session.

———, *Letter from the Secretary of the Interior Transmitting...Report to the President by the Indian Peace Commission, January 7, 1868*, Senate Executive Document No. 10, 44th Congress, 2d Session.

———, *Letter from the Superintendent of Indian Trade [Thomas L. McKenney], to the Chairman on Indian Affairs, Communicating a Report in Relation to Indian Trade*, Senate Document No. 19, 16th Congress, 2d Session (serial 42).

———, *Message of the President of the United States, Communicating, in Answer to a Senate Resolution of January 30, 1878, information in relation to a survey of lands in the Indian Territory*, Senate Executive Document No. 32, 45th Congress, 2d Session.

———, *Message of the President of the United States, Communicating, in Answer to a Senate Resolution of May 7, 1879, Information in Relation to an Alleged Occupation of a Portion of the Indian Territory by White Settlers*, Senate Executive Document No. 20, 46th Congress, 1st Session.

———, *Message of the President of the United States, Communicating the Report and Journal of Proceedings of the Commission Appointed to Obtain Certain Concessions from the Sioux Indians*, Senate Executive Document No. 9, 44th Congress, 2d Session.

———, *Survey of Conditions of Indians of the United States*, Senate Report 1490, 70th Congress, 2d Session.

———, *Survey of the Conditions of the Indians in the United States*, Hearings before a Subcommittee of the Committee on Indian Affairs, U.S. Senate, 71st Session, 2d Session.

———, *Survey of Conditions of the Indians in the United States: Hearing before a Subcommittee of the Committee on Indian Affairs Pursuant to S. Res. 341, a Resolution Providing for a General Survey of the Conditions of the Indians in the United States, and for Other Purposes* (Washington, DC: Government Printing Office, 1927).

———, Committee on the Judiciary. Subcommittee to Investigate the Administration of the Internal Security Act and Other Internal Security Laws, *Revolutionary Activities within the United States: The American Indian Movement*, 94th Congress, 2d Session.

———, Select Committee on Indian Affairs. *Federal Programs of Assistance to American Indians: A Report Prepared for the Senate*

Select Committee on Indian Affairs of the United States Senate by Richard S. Jones, Specialist in American National Government, 97th Congress, 2d Session.

U.S. Department of the Interior. Information Service, *Address by Glenn L. Emmons, Commissioner of Indian Affairs, before the Governors' Interstate Indian Council, Sheridan, Wyoming, 6 August 1956.*

———, *American Indians and American Society: Remarks by Commissioner of Indian Affairs Philleo Nash, before the Institute on Human Relations, Fisk University, Nashville, Tennessee, 29 June 1965.*

The United States Government Manual, 1994/1995 (Washington, DC: Government Printing Office, 1994).

The United States Indian Service (Washington, DC: Department of the Interior, Bureau of Indian Affairs, 1962).

Unrau, William E., *Mixed-Bloods and Tribal Dissolution: Charles Curtis and the Quest for Indian Identity* (Lawrence: University Press of Kansas, 1989).

Utley, Robert M., *Frontier Regulars: The United States Army and the Indian, 1866–1891* (Lincoln: University of Nebraska Press, 1973).

———, *The Indian Frontier of the American West, 1846–1890* (Albuquerque: University of New Mexico Press, 1984).

Utley, Robert M., and Wilcomb E. Washburn, *Indian Wars* (Boston: Houghton Mifflin, 1977).

Utter, Jack, *American Indians: Answers to Today's Questions* (Lake Ann, MI: National Woodlands, 1993).

Vance, John T., "The Congressional Mandate and the Indian Claims Commission." *North Dakota Law Review* 45 (Spring 1969).

Vaughn, Alden T., ed., *Early American Indian Documents: Treaties and Laws, 1607–1789* (Washington, DC: University Press of America, 1979).

Vecsey, Christopher, *Traditional Ojibwa Religion and Its Historical Changes* (Ph.D. dissertation, Northwestern University, 1977).

Vecsey, Christopher, and Robert W. Venables, eds., *American Indian Environments: Ecological Issues in Native American History* (Syracuse, NY: Syracuse University Press, 1980).

Veeder, William H., "Indian Water Rights in the Upper Missouri River Basin." *North Dakota Law Review* 59 (Fall 1974): 617–637.

Viola, Herman J., *Ben Nighthorse Campbell: An American Warrior* (New York: Orion Books, 1993).

———, *The Indian Legacy of Charles Bird King* (Washington, DC: Smithsonian, 1976).

———, *Thomas L. McKenney, Architect of America's Early Indian Policy: 1816–1830* (Chicago: Sage, 1974).

———, *Thomas L. McKenney and the Administration of Indian Affairs 1824–1830* (Ph.D. dissertation, Indiana University, 1970).

Vlasich, James A., *Pueblo Indian Agriculture, Irrigation and Water Rights* (Ph.D. dissertation, University of Utah, 1980).

Vogel, Virgil J., *This Country Was Ours: A Documentary History of the American Indian* (New York: Harper & Row, 1972).

Waldecker, Alice Virginia, *Administration and Legislative Reforms in American Indian Relations, 1928–1934* (Master's thesis, Smith College, 1945).

Waldman, Carl, *Who Was Who in Native American History: Indians and Non-Indians from Early Contacts through 1900* (New York: Facts on File, 1990).

Waldman, Henry, et al., eds., *Dictionary of Indians of North America* (St. Clair Shores, MI: Scholarly, 1978).

Walker, Francis A., *The Indian Question.* (Boston: Osgood, 1874).

Wallace, Anthony F. C., *The Long, Bitter Trail: Andrew Jackson and the Indians* (New York: Hill and Wang, 1993).

Walters, Williams, "Review Essay: Preemption, Tribal Sovereignty, and Worcester v. Georgia." *Oregon Law Review* (1983): 127–144.

Waltmann, Henry G., "Circumstantial Reformer: President Grant & the Indian

Problem." *Arizona and the West* 13 (4) (Winter 1971): 323–342.

———, *The Interior Department, War Department, and Indian Policy, 1865–1887* (Ph.D. dissertation, University of Nebraska at Lincoln, 1962).

Wanken, Helen M., *'Women's Sphere' and Indian Reform: The Women's National Indian Association, 1879–1901* (Ph.D. dissertation, Marquette University, 1981).

Warrior, Robert Allen, *Tribal Secrets: Recovering American Indian Intellectual Traditions* (Minneapolis: University of Minnesota Press, 1995).

Washburn, Wilcomb E., *The Assault on Indian Tribalism: The General Allotment Law (Dawes Act) of 1887* (Malabar, FL: Krieger, 1986).

———,"The Historical Context of American Indian Legal Problems." *Law & Contemporary Problems* 40 (Winter 1976): 12–24.

———, *Red Man's Land/White Man's Law: A Study of the Past and Present Status of the American Indian* (New York: Scribner's, 1971).

———,"The Society of American Indians." *Indian Historian* 3 (1) (Winter 1970): 21–23.

Washburn, Wilcomb E., comp., *The American Indian and the United States: A Documentary History* (Westport, CT: Greenwood, 1979).

Washburn, Wilcomb E., ed., *The Indian and the White Man* (Garden City, New York: Anchor, 1964).

Wasserman, Maurice M., *The American Indian as Seen by the Seventeenth Century Chroniclers* (Ph.D. dissertation, University of Pennsylvania at Philadelphia, 1954).

Weinberger, Caspar, Jr., "Classic Images of Dying Nations Enjoy a Rebirth." *Smithsonian* 6 (1) (April 1975): 82–89.

Welch, Deborah Sue, *Zitkala-Sa: An American Indian Leader, 1876–1938* (Ph.D. dissertation, University of Wyoming, 1985).

Welch, Rebecca Hancock, *Alice Cunningham Fletcher, Anthropologist and Indian Rights Reformer* (Ph.D. dissertation, George Washington University, 1980).

Wellman, Paul I., Jr., *Death in the Desert: The Fifty Years' War for the Great Southwest* (Lincoln: University of Nebraska Press, 1987).

Welsh, Michael, "Community, the West, and the American Indian." *Journal of the Southwest* 31 (2) (Summer 1989): 141–158.

———, "Origin of Western Film Companies, 1887–1920." *Journal of the West* 22 (4) (October 1983): 5–16.

West, Terry, *Centennial Mini-Histories of the Forest Service* (Washington, DC: U.S. Department of Agriculture, 1992).

Weyler, Rex, *Blood of the Land: The Government and Corporate War against the American Indian Movement* (New York: Everest House, 1982).

Whipple, Henry Benjamin, *Lights and Shadows of a Long Episcopate, Being Reminiscences and Recollections of the Right Reverend Henry Benjamin Whipple, D.D., LL.D., Bishop of Minnesota* (London and New York: Macmillan, 1899).

White, G. Edward, *The Marshall Court & Cultural Change, 1815–1835* (New York: Oxford University Press, 1991).

White, Richard, *Roots of Dependency: Subsistence, Environment, and Social Change among the Choctaws, Pawnees, and Navajos* (Lincoln: University of Nebraska Press, 1983).

Whitford, William Clarke, *Colorado Volunteers in the Civil War: The New Mexico Campaign in 1862* (Denver: State Historical and Natural History Society, 1906).

Whitman, Alden, ed., *American Reformers: An H. W. Wilson Biographical Dictionary* (New York: Wilson, 1985).

Whitner, Robert Lee, *The Methodist Episcopal Church and Grant's Peace Policy: A Study of the Methodist Agencies, 1870–1882* (Ph.D. dissertation, University of Minnesota, 1959).

Who Was Who in America, 1897–1942 (Chicago: Marquis Who's Who, 1981).

Wiget, Andrew, *Critical Essays on Native American Literature* (Boston: G. K. Hall, 1985).

Wilkins, David E., "Johnson v. M'Intosh Revisited: Through the Eyes of Mitchel v. United States." *American Indian Law Review* 19 (1) (1991): 159–181.

Wilkins, Thurman, *Cherokee Tragedy: The Story of the Ridge Family and the Decimation of a People* (New York: Macmillan, 1970).

Wilkinson, Charles F., *American Indians, Time, and the Law: Native Societies in a Modern Constitutional Democracy* (New Haven, CT: Yale University Press, 1987).

———,"Cross-Jurisdictional Conflicts: State Authority on Federal and Indian Lands." *UCLA Journal of Environmental Law & Policy* 135 (1982).

Wilkinson, Charles F., and Eric R. Biggs, "The Evolution of the Termination Policy." *American Indian Law Review* 2 (1977).

Wilkinson, Charles F., and John M. Volkman, "Judicial Review of Indian Treaty Abrogation: 'As Long as the Water Flows and the Grass Grows upon the Earth': How Long a Time Is That?" *California Law Review* 63 (1975).

Willard, Frances E., and Mary Livermore, eds., *A Woman of the Century: Fourteen Hundred Seventy Biographical Sketches accompanied by Portraits of Leading American Women in All Walks of Life* (Buffalo, NY: Moulton, 1893).

Williams, Robert A., Jr., *The American Indian in Western Legal Thought: The Discourses of Conquest* (London/New York: Oxford University Press, 1990).

———, "The Medieval and Renaissance Origins of the Status of the American Indian in Western Legal Thought." *Southern California Law Review* 57 (1) (1983): 1–99.

———, "Small Steps on the Long Road to Self-Sufficiency for Indian Nations: The Indian Tribal Governmental Tax Status Act of 1982." *Harvard Journal on Legislation* 22 (1985).

Williams, Walter L., "Twentieth-Century Indian Leaders: Brokers and Providers." *Journal of the West* 23 (3) (July 1984): 3–6.

Wilson, Dorothy Clarke, *Bright Eyes: The Story of Susette LaFlesche, an Omaha Indian* (New York: McGraw-Hill, 1974).

Wilson, James Grant, and John Fiske, eds., *Appletons' Cyclopædia of American Biography* (New York: Appleton, 1888–1900).

Wilson, Raymond, "Dr. Charles A. Eastman, Early Twentieth-Century Reformer." *Journal of the West* 23 (3) (July 1984): 7–12.

———, *Dr. Charles Alexander Eastman (Ohiyesa): Santee Sioux* (Ph.D. dissertation, University of New Mexico at Albuquerque, 1977).

Wolf, Roger C., "Needed: A System of Income Maintenance for Indians." *Arizona Law Review* 10 (6) (Winter 1968): 597–616.

Wolfley, Jeannette, "Jim Crow, Indian Style: The Disenfranchisement of Native Americans." *American Indian Law Review* 16 (1) (1991): 167–202.

Wright, Peter M., "John Collier and the Oklahoma Indian Welfare Act of 1936." *Chronicles of Oklahoma* 50 (3) (Autumn 1972): 347–371.

Wunder, John R., *'Retained by the People': A History of American Indians and the Bill of Rights* (New York: Oxford University Press, 1994).

Wunder, John R., ed., *Working the Range: Essays on the History of Western Land Management and the Environment* (Westport, CT: Greenwood, 1985).

Wyatt, Kathryn C., "The Supreme Court, *Lyng*, and the *Lone Wolf* Principle." *Chicago-Kent Law Review* 65 (2) (1989): 623–655.

Zarbin, Earl, *All the Time a Newspaper: The First 100 Years of the Arizona Republic* (Phoenix, AZ: Phoenix Newspapers, 1990).

Ziontz, Alvin J., "After Martinez: Civil Rights under Tribal Government." *University of California at Davis Law Review* 12 (1) (March 1979): 1–35.

Zylyff (Thomas Henry Tibbles): *The Ponca Chiefs: An Indian's Attempt to Appeal from the Tomahawk to the Courts* (Boston: Lockwood, Brooks, 1880).

Illustration Credits

ii UPI/Corbis-Bettmann.
5 J. H. Bratley Collection, BR61-325, Denver Museum of Natural History.
7 UPI/Corbis-Bettmann.
14 UPI/Corbis-Bettmann.
28 UPI/Corbis-Bettmann.
37 UPI/Corbis-Bettmann.
48 Courtesy Bureau of Indian Affairs, U.S. Department of the Interior.
57 UPI/Corbis-Bettmann.
58 Corbis-Bettmann.
76 UPI/Corbis-Bettmann.
95 Photofest.
98 Courtesy Bureau of Indian Affairs.
101 Courtesy Office of Public Relations, University of Colorado, Boulder.
103 F-798, Colorado Historical Society, Denver.
115 1355-WPA, Colorado Historical Society, Denver.
130 UPI/Corbis-Bettmann.
132 National Anthroplogical Archives 4473, Smithsonian Institution.
140 Corbis-Bettmann.
142 Corbis-Bettmann.
164 UPI/Corbis-Bettmann.
170 American Antiquarian Society, Worcester, Massachusetts.
175 Woolaroc Museum, Bartlesville, Oklahoma.
186 Corbis-Bettmann.
213 Photofest.
217 UPI/Corbis/Bettmann.
219 UPI/Corbis-Bettmann.
222 F44,177, Colorado Historical Society.
232 UPI/Corbis-Bettmann.
246 National Anthropological Archives 55,530, Smithsonian Institution.
248 National Anthropological Archives P-4-B, Smithsonian Institution.
259 UPI/Corbis-Bettmann.
267 Courtesy Native American Rights Fund, Boulder, Colorado.
268 UPI/Corbis-Bettmann.
287 National Anthropological Archives 906-B, Smithsonian Institution.
294 UPI/Corbis-Bettmann.
321 UPI/Corbis-Bettmann.
325 F-42,630, Colorado Historical Society, Denver, Colorado.
334 F-7100, Colorado Historical Society, Denver, Colorado
339 Corbis-Bettmann.
351 UPI/Corbis-Bettmann.
354 F-6013, Colorado Historical Society, Denver, Colorado.
369 UPI/Corbis-Bettmann.
428 Corbis-Bettmann.
431 UPI/Corbis-Bettmann.

Index